o/p ⊑ 12-75

D1029853

WHO'S WHO
ON THE SCREEN

COMPILED BY **JOHN WALTER SKINNER**

Madeleine Productions   Worthing, England.

For all film buffs, everywhere...

First edition
Copyright © 1983 by John Walter Skinner
All Rights Reserved

Concept, research, design, layout, publishing and distribution
by *JOHN WALTER SKINNER* for
Madeleine Productions,
15 Wallace Avenue, Worthing BN11 5RA, W. Sussex

Typeset in Times Roman 7 & 8pt.
by Pat Reader Typesetting, Alresford, Essex
Headlines by Steyning Graphics Limited, Steyning, Sussex

Printed in Great Britain by
The Apollo Press, Worthing, Sussex
Production consultant: Peter Owen
Bound by R.J. Acford, Chichester, Sussex

Research: please credit *'Skinner's WHO'S WHO ON THE SCREEN (1983)'*

ISBN 0 905380 02 9

INTRODUCTION

The prolonged production schedule of this book became the subject of a running joke among my friends. During this three year period the editor was invariably greeted with 'How's the book coming on?', and, 'You're not still working on that book, are you?', or, more pointedly, 'Haven't you finished that book yet?'. Well, I can assure you that there were times when I honestly wondered whether it would ever be completed! Being very much a 'maverick' in the film book publishing world, not only have I been responsible for researching all the facts and selecting all the photographs for *WHO'S WHO ON THE SCREEN*, but also the additional graft of design, layout, paste-up, publishing and distribution.

However, enough self-adulation, now a brief introduction. With such a current deluge, even plethora, of motion-picture books, you may well ask, 'Why another reference book?'. In compiling this work my goal has been to record a cross-section of leading and supporting players (the latter category so often neglected, in my opinion) active in today's movies. At a price the average filmgoer can afford, I have attempted to 'bridge the gap' between the expensive reference book and the annual volume which offers the reader information that he or she does not require (production personnel, etc.). Not since the days of *PICTURE SHOW'S WHO'S WHO ON THE SCREEN* has there been a fully-illustrated reference book with each artiste represented by a biography and photograph.

I have selected, hopefully without bias, those artistes working in British and American pictures. Although the filmographies are incomplete (this task would have been absolutely impossible for me to undertake single-handed, bearing in mind there are 800-plus celebrities to research), the reader will benefit from such additional facts as family details (often with exact dates — something of an obsession to the author!), important stage productions, T.V. series, etc., and, as an added bonus, a list of book titles, should the researcher wish to examine individual careers more fully (in most cases I have quoted *British* publishers).

The task of selecting entries has been somewhat agonising in as much as deciding who to include and who to leave out — the somewhat precarious state of our industry today contributes to this — some leading players star in a couple of movies, but then return to the stage for a few years before stepping in front of the cameras again. As production on *WHO'S WHO* progressed, my obsession to include more and more celebrities increased, and for technical reasons it became necessary to include an Addenda (see pages 123-126).

WHO'S WHO ON THE SCREEN is by no means a critical analysis, a practice, in my opinion, that has often marred similar works. The careers of major stars are essayed more fully, but less text coverage does not reflect his or her ability!

Finally, in many ways, *WHO'S WHO ON THE SCREEN* is intended to be like a good movie — well-produced, informative, entertaining, and with a distinguished cast — with the latter category the reader should have no complaints!

JOHN WALTER SKINNER
Worthing, August, 1983

ABBREVIATIONS

A.Aw. *Academy Award*

Am.A.D.A. *American Academy of Dramatic Art*

A.S.M. *Assistant Stage Manager — generally regarded as one of the first jobs an aspiring artiste secures in the theatre, helping with every aspect of a play backstage, occasionally performing a role.*

Actors' Studio *founded in New York in 1947 by Elia Kazan, which adopted the 'Method' approach to acting.*

appd. *appeared*

Aw. *Award*

B. *place and date of birth is given. Where data is unavailable or research details have conflicted a question mark appears.*

B.A. *Best Actor/Actress (following education details: a Bachelor of Arts degree).*

B.A.F.T.A. *British Academy of Film & T.V. Arts (formerly the British Film Academy and the Society of Film & T.V. Arts).*

B.F.A.Aw. *British Film Academy Award.*

B.S.A. *Best Supporting Actor/Actress*

B'casts *Broadcasts*

B'way *Broadway — in New York, the symbol for the commercial theatre in the United States.*

c. *circa (about).*

C.B.E. *Commander of Order of the British Empire.*

C.F.F. *Children's Film Foundation.*

Co. *County/Company.*

d. *daughter.*

dec. *deceased.*

dir. *directed.*

div. *divorced.*

ed. *where educated.*

esp. *especially.*

gt. *great.*

H.S. *High School.*

H'wood *Hollywood.*

inclu. *including.*

intn'l *international.*

L.A. *Los Angeles.*

L.A.M.D.A. *London Academy of Music & Dramatic Art.*

Litt.D. *Doctor of Literature.*

m. *mother.*

M.C. *Military Cross.*

md. *married.*

mini-ser. *mini-series — see 'T.V. movie'.*

N.T. *The National Theatre — Britain's State-supported theatre, operating from 1963 for several years from the Old Vic, London, now at it's permanent base on the South Bank of the Thames.*

Nat.Serv. *National Service.*

N.Y. *New York.*

nom. *nomination.*

O.B.E. *Officer of British Empire Order.*

off B'way *off Broadway — productions regarded experimental and non-commercial.*

p/b *paperback edition.*

P'house *Playhouse.*

pro. *professional.*

prod. *production.*

? *uncertainty regarding place/date of birth, marriage details, spelling of name, etc. owing to conflicting details in various reference sources.*

q.v. *quod vide (which see — refer to separate entry for this artiste).*

R.A.D.A. *The Royal Academy of Dramatic Art — founded in London in 1904 by Beerbohm Tree and regarded as one of the best dramatic schools in Great Britain.*

R.S.Co. *The Royal Shakespeare Company — founded at Stratford-Upon-Avon in 1864 as the Shakespeare Memorial Theatre, renamed the R.S.C. in 1960. It's London base is now at the Barbican Centre in the City.*

rep *repertory — a repertory company, a professional regional theatre group, specialising in the presenting of plays weekly, fortnightly, etc.. The U.S. equivalent is a stock company.*

retd. *returned.*

rev. *revised edition.*

S'peare *Shakespeare.*

s/play *screenplay.*

s'ship *scholarship.*

sch. *school.*

sep. *separated.*

ser. *series — see 'T.V. movie'.*

sev. *several.*

S.W.E.T. *Society of West End Theatres.*

T.V. movie *a Television movie — a movie made-for-television, of feature-film length, a formula originating in the U.S.A.. Very often a T.V. movie is 'released' in cinemas in the States, but in G.B. only given a T.V. showing. Also, a movie intended for cinema release, but considered un-commercial, is eventually screened on T.V.! A T.V. movie is often a 'pilot' film for a proposed T.V. series. A T.V. movie of several episodes is categorised as a 'Mini-series', sometimes under the 'Best Sellers' banner.*

U.C.L.A. *University of California, Los Angeles.*

u/study *an understudy — an important job, especially in the West End (q.v.) for an actor/actress, who attends every performance, having studied a role to be a replacement, often at very short notice. In a musical production, an understudy is usually given a supporting role.*

Univ. *University.*

Var. Club *Variety Club of Great Britain.*

w. *wife.*

W.End *the West End — of London, the symbol of the commercial theatre in Great Britain.*

W.W.II *World War II.*

JOSS ACKLAND

B. N. Kensington, London, 29.2.28; father Norman Ackland, journalist; Ed: Dame Alice Owen's Sch.; worked in a brewery, then dairy farm; studied at Central Sch. of Speech & Drama, professional debut 1945; md: actress Rosemary Kirkcaldy (seven children — son Paul died tragically in Oct. 1982); in '55 family moved to Africa, Mr Ackland working as tea planter, later returned to stage there as actor, disc-jockey and script-writer; returned to U.K. in 1957, later becoming well-known, esp. in T.V. and theatre (Old Vic, R.S.C., etc.); films, mainly support: SEVEN DAYS TO NOON (50, uncredited); CRESCENDO (69); THE HOUSE THAT DRIPPED BLOOD (70); VILLAIN (71); ENGLAND MADE ME (73); THREE MUSKETEERS (73); S*P*Y*S, PENNY GOLD, OPERATION DAYBREAK, GREAT EXPECTATIONS (T.V. movie), THE BLACK WINDMILL (all 1974); ROYAL FLASH (75); SAINT JACK, THE BIGGEST BANK ROBBERY (T.V. movie), STAR ROCK (all 1979); DANGEROUS DAVIES-THE LAST DETECTIVE (80, T.V. movie); 1982 stage triumph as Falstaff in 'Henry IV', Parts I & II (R.S.C.).

BROOKE ADAMS

B. New York City, 1949. Ed. Dalton; High School of Performing Arts; Inst. of American Ballet; Lee Strasberg. Professional debut age 6 in 'Finian's Rainbow'; T.V. series 1965 'O.K. Crackerby'. During teens worked in repertory and television. T.V. includes: 'James Dean—Portrait of a Friend', 'The Last of the Belles', 'Flatbush/ Avenue J', 'The Tony Randall Show', 'The Bob Newhart Show', 'Police Woman'. Movies: CAR WASH (76), DAYS OF HEAVEN (78), INVASION OF THE BODYSNATCHERS (78), CUBA (79), A MAN, A WOMAN AND A BANK (79), TELL ME A RIDDLE (81), UTILITIES (81).

EDIE ADAMS

B. Kingston, Pennsylvania, U.S.A., 16.4.31(?). Real name Elizabeth Edith Enke. Grew up in Tenafly, N. Jersey. Ed. Columbia Univ. and Juilliard School (studying opera), N.Y. Won beauty competitions ('Miss U.S. Television'), appd. on Broadway from Feb. 1953 in 'Wonderful Town', other shows since. Also studied at Traphagen School of Fashion in 1956. T.V. includes: 'Ernie Kovacs Show' (1953 & 1956); 'Edie Adams Show' (1963). She wed Ernie Kovacs 1954 (he died 1962); Marty Mills, wed 16.8.64 (div.); trumpeter Peter Candoli 1972 (former husband of Betty Hutton). Movies: THE APARTMENT (60), LOVER COME BACK (62), CALL ME BWANA (63), LOVE WITH A PROPER STRANGER (64), THE BEST MAN (64), THE HONEY POT (67), UP IN SMOKE (78), THE HAPPY HOOKER (80).

MAUD ADAMS

B. Lulea, Sweden. Real name Maud Wikstrom. At 18 she won a modelling contest run by major Swedish magazine and given year's contract; became full-time model when she went to Paris 1965-67; in the U.S. appeared in adverts and T.V. commercials; in 1970 was coached in drama by Warren Robertson, making screen debut in THE CHRISTIAN LIQUORICE STORE (70), then 2 Canadian films, U-TURN and MAHONEY'S ESTATE; Andrea in THE MAN WITH THE GOLDEN GUN (74), ROLLERBALL (74), THE DIAMOND MERCENARIES (75), LAURA (79), HOSTAGE TOWER (79) PLAYING FOR TIME (T.V. movie), TATTOO (both 1980); Md: Don Adams, British businessman (div.); recent: 'Chicago Story' (T.V. ser.), LAURA, TARGET EAGLE (all 1982), OCTOPUSSY (83).

JENNY AGUTTER

B. Taunton, Somerset 20.12.52. Father, Derek Agutter, head of Combined Services Entertainment, parents met in Forces in Egypt. Ed. Elmhurst Ballet School; aged 11, chosen for Disney movie, THE BALLERINA (64). Motion pictures: EAST OF SUDAN (64); STAR! (67); GATES OF PARADISE (68); THE RAILWAY CHILDREN (70, Var. Cl. 'Most Promising Artiste' Award); I START COUNTING (70); WALKABOUT (70); LOGAN'S RUN (76); EAGLE HAS LANDED (76); EQUUS (76); MAN IN THE IRON MASK (77, T.V. movie); DOMINIQUE (77); RIDDLE OF THE SANDS (78); SWEET WILLIAM (78). She has appeared on T.V. on many occasions; recent stage: lead as 'Hedda', The Round House, London; recent movies: MISS RIGHT (80); AMY ON HER LIPS (80, T.V. movie) and BEULAH LAND (T.V. movie, 1980); 1982: acting with R.S.Co.

CLAUDE AKINS

B. Nelson, Georgia 25.5.18. Ed. Northwestern Univ.; was salesman in Indiana; appeared in rep. at Barter Theatre, first Broadway role in 'The Rose Tattoo' (51), then toured. Came to the screen in FROM HERE TO ETERNITY (54), previously did T.V. bits ('Superman' etc.) Movies include: CAINE MUTINY (54), THE DEFIANT ONES (59), RIO BRAVO (59), INHERIT THE WIND (60), THE KILLERS (64), RETURN OF THE 7 (66), DEVIL'S BRIGADE (68), and BATTLE FOR THE PLANET OF THE APES (73). Mr Akins is married, has appeared regularly on T.V. for 30 years, recently in IN TANDEM (74,T.V. movie); THE BROKEN BRIDGE (77, T.V. movie) and series: 'Laredo' (66); 'Movin' On' (74) and 'The Misadventures of Sheriff Lobo' (79).

EDDIE ALBERT

B. Rock Island, Illinois, U.S.A. 22.4.08. Real name Edward Albert Heimberger. Ed. Univ. of Minnesota. Pro. debut as singer 1933; on N.B.C. radio in trio called 'Threesome'; Broadway debut 1935 in 'O Evening Star'; came to screen 1938 in BROTHER RAT (same play Broadway 1937). Over 60 movies include FOUR WIVES (39); SMASH UP (47); CARRIE (52), ROMAN HOLIDAY (53), OKLAHOMA! (55), ROOTS OF HEAVEN (58), CAPT. NEWMAN, M.D. (63). Married actress Margo in 1945; 1 daughter Maria, 1 son, Edward (q.v.). Mr Albert has appeared regularly in U.S. stage and T.V. Recent movies and T.V.: ESCAPE TO WITCH MOUNTAIN (75), BIRCH INTERVAL (76), CRASH (78, T.V. movie), WHEN TIME RAN OUT (79), AIRPORT '80: THE CONCORDE (79), TROUBLE IN THE HIGH WATER (T.V. movie & short-lived ser.), PETER & PAUL (mini-ser., both 1980), TAKE THIS JOB & SHOVE IT (81), GOLIATH AWAITS (mini-ser., 1982), DREAMSCAPE (83).

EDWARD ALBERT

B. Los Angeles, Calif., U.S.A. 20.2.51. Son of Eddie Albert. Ed. U.C.L.A.; special merit scholarship to Oxford Univ., England. Has played on U.S. stage in 'Hamlet' and 'The Glass Menagerie' in L.A.; 'Our Town' (Long Beach, replacing his father). Entered movies as Production Assistant on PATTON (69) in Spain. Since coming to the screen in 1972 in BUTTERFLIES ARE FREE (winning 1973 Golden Globe Award), has been seen in FORTY CARATS (74), MIDWAY (75), THE DOMINO PRINCIPLE (76) and THE GREEK TYCOON (78). Mr Albert is an expert musician (played as studio musician in L.A. and London), an accomplished photographer and has also helped to develop a cultural and education centre for Mexican-Americans in L.A. His most recent screen work includes WHEN TIME RAN OUT (80), GALAXY OF TERROR (81), BUTTERFLY (82), THE COURAGEOUS (83).

JACK ALBERTSON

B. Malden, Ma., . .10. Commenced career as straight man in burlesque; New York stage includes 'Meet the People' (1940), 'A Lady Says Yes' (1945), 'Top Banana' (1951) and 'The Subject Was Roses' (1964, won Oscar — BSA — 1968 — when filmed); much T.V. includes regular in 'Jack Carter & Co.' (1949), Walter Burton in 'Room For One More' (1962), Lt. Cdr. Virgil Stoner in 'Ensign O'Toole' (1962/63), Dr Andrew Sellers in 'Dr Simon Locke' (1971); many movies include MIRACLE ON 34TH STREET (47), TOP BANANA (54); EDDY DUCHIN STORY (56); MAN OF A THOUSAND FACES (57); TEACHER'S PET (58); THE SHAGGY DOG STORY (59); THE GEORGE RAFT STORY (61); LOVER COME BACK (62); THE PATSY (64); CHANGES (69); JUSTINE (69); THE MONK (69, T.V. movie); RABBIT RUN (70); CLEAR AND PRESENT DANGER (70, T.V. movie); WILLY WONKA & THE CHOCOLATE FACTORY (71); POSEIDON ADVENTURE (72); DEAD & BURIED (80); *Mr Albertson died of terminal cancer in L.A., November 1981.*

5

ALAN ALDA

A household name with his performance in TV's MASH series, Alan Alda is the son of actor Robert Alda. New York City born, on 28.1.36, Alda attended Fordham University, appeared in repertory, studied improvisation under Paul Sills and had further studies in Europe with his father, acting in Rome in 1955. His Broadway debut came in 1959 in 'Only in America' and he won acclaim there with his work in 'Purlie Victorious' (61). Alan Alda came to the screen in 1963 in GONE ARE THE DAYS! and has been seen also in PAPER LION (68), THE EXTRAORDINARY SEAMAN (69), MOONSHINE WAR (70), JENNY (70), THE MEPHISTO WALTZ (71), TO KILL A CLOWN (72), CALIFORNIA SUITE (78), THE SEDUCTION OF JOE TYNAN (78, also wrote) and SAME TIME, NEXT YEAR (79). An only child, Mr Alda suffered polio when aged 7, but was cured. He is married to Arlene Weiss, a clarinettist with the Houston Symphony Orchestra and they have three daughters. In 1972 he commenced the highly successful MASH T.V. series, portraying Hawkeye Pierce, the series winning him two Emmy Awards, one for Best Actor, the other for his direction of several episodes. The series ended in February, 1983. T.V. movies include THE GLASS HOUSE, PLAYMATES (both 1972), ISN'T IT SHOCKING (73), KILL ME IF YOU CAN (77), and in 1975 he wrote a short-lived T.V. series, 'We'll Get By'. In 1981 he directed, scripted and acted in THE FOUR SEASONS.
ALAN ALDA: AN UNAUTHORISED BIOGRAPHY by Jason Bonderoff; New American Library; p/b, 1982.

JOHN ALDERTON

B. Gainsborough, Lincs. 27.11.40. Ed. Kingston High School, Hull. Considered career as architect, did several jobs, then studied R.A.D.A.; York Rep. 1961; discovered there and won role of Dr Richard Moone in ATV's 'Emergency Ward 10', great success in role 1963-65. Md. actress Jill Browne 1964 (div.); came to screen uncredited in OPERATION CROSSBOW (64). Films: THE SYSTEM (64); DUFFY (68); HANNIBAL BROOKS (68); YOU CAN'T WIN 'EM ALL (70); PLEASE, SIR (71); ZARDOZ (73) and IT SHOULDN'T HAPPEN TO A VET (76). West End stage since 1965, also R.S.Co. 1969. Best known on British T.V. for numerous series: 'Please, Sir' (70-71); 'Upstairs, Downstairs' (73); 'My Wife Next Door' (73); 'Wodehouse Playhouse' (75), others. 2nd wife is actress Pauline Collins (md. May 1970) and they have 3 children, sons Nicholas & Richard and daughter Catherine Bridie. John and his wife recently appeared successfully on West End stage in 'Rattle of a 'Simple Man' (80/81); T.V. ser. 1983: 'Father's Day'.

JANE ALEXANDER

B. Boston, Mass., USA, 28.10.39; Real name Jane Quigley; Ed: Beaver County Day School, Sarah Lawrence Coll., and the Univ. of Edinburgh; stage débût as child in 'Treasure Island', Boston; first stage success B'way, 1968, as Eleanor Bachman in 'The Great White Hope' (won 'Tony' Aw.), repeated this role for screen débût, 1970 (Oscar nom., BSA); others: A GUNFIGHT (71); NEW CENTURIONS (72); ALL THE PRESIDENT'S MEN (76); THE BETSY (78); KRAMER VS. KRAMER (79); BRUBAKER (80); NIGHT CROSSING (81); Jane's many T.V. movies include WELCOME HOME JOHNNY BRISTOL (72); MIRACLE ON 34TH. STREET (73); THIS WAS THE WEST THAT WAS, DEATH BE NOT PROUD (both 1974); ELEANOR & FRANKLIN: THE WHITE HOUSE YEARS (as Eleanor Roosevelt), A CIRCLE OF CHILDREN (both 1977); LOVEY: A CIRCLE OF CHILDREN, PART II, A QUESTION OF LOVE (both 1978); PLAY FOR TIME (81, 'Emmy' Aw., BSA).

MUHAMMAD ALI

B. Louisville, Kentucky, 17.2.42. Real name Cassius Marcellus Clay; boxing from the age of 12, Ali subsequently won 108 bouts as an amateur; turned pro. after winning Olympic Gold Medal as light-heavyweight in 1960; joined U.S. Black Muslim movement, adopting name of Muhammad Ali; World Heavyweight Champion 1964, 1974, 1978; movies: BLOOD MONEY (62, cameo); THE GREATEST (77); FREEDOM ROAD (78); BODY & SOUL (81). Md. Veronica, his 4th wife.
MUHAMMAD ALI by Richard Durham; Granada: London 1976.

KAREN ALLEN

B.   ; stage career began in 'Saint', church-sponsored play in Washington, D.C., also touring England and Scotland; Washington Theatre Project and Washington Theatre Lab., 1982 stage: 'Monday After the Miracle'; films: NATIONAL LAMPOON'S ANIMAL HOUSE (78); CRUISING, THE WANDERERS, MANHATTAN (all 1979); A SMALL CIRCLE OF FRIENDS (80); EAST OF EDEN (T.V. movie), RAIDERS OF THE LOST ARK (both 1981); SPLIT IMAGE (82).

NANCY ALLEN

B. New York City, 1950. The youngest of 3 children, her father being a policeman, Nancy took dancing lessons from the age of 5, later enrolling at New York's High School of Performing Arts as a dance major; from the age of 15 she was appearing in T.V. commercials and commenced studies at the Lee Strasberg Theatre Institute; having appeared in over 100 T.V. commercials she came to the big screen with a small role in THE LAST DETAIL (73); she is wed to Brian de Palma, who has directed several of her movies; films: CARRIE (76); I WANNA HOLD YOUR HAND (78); HOME MOVIES (79); 1941 (79); DRESSED TO KILL (80); BLOW OUT (81); STRANGE INVADERS, THE BUDDY SYSTEM (both 1982).

PATRICK ALLEN

B. Nyasaland 17.3.27. Came to U.K. as a child during WWII, evacuated to Canada. Ed. McGill Univ., Montreal; did radio work; returned to U.K. 1953: West End; R.S.Co.; Movies include: DIAL M FOR MURDER (54); 1984 (55); HIGH TIDE AT NOON (57); I WAS MONTY'S DOUBLE (58); CAPTAIN CLEGG (62); NIGHT OF THE BIG HEAT (67); PERSECUTION (74); WILD GEESE (77), many others. Much T.V. includes 'Crane' and 'Brett' series. Md. actress Sarah Lawson, 2 sons Stephen, Stuart. Mr Allen runs his own T.V. commercial studios and his voice is heard over many commercials. Recent T.V.: Gen. Auchinleck in 'Churchill & the Generals' (79); 'Trial of Lady Chatterley' (80); MURDER IS EASY (T.V. movie, 81); 'East Lynne' (82).

WOODY ALLEN

The son of Martin and Nettie Konigsberg, Allen Stewart Konigsberg, to give his full real name, was born in Brooklyn, New York on 1.12.35. Educated at the City College of N.Y. and N.Y. University, Woody Allen began his career as a stand-up comic, commencing script-writing at 17 and 'contributing 50 gags a day for famous comedians'. His first wife was Harlene Rosen, a teacher, whom he married when he was 21, but they divorced in 1959. His Broadway plays include 'From A-to-Z' (60), 'Don't Drink the Water' (66), which he scripted, and 'Play it Again, Sam' (69) in which he also appeared as Allen Felix. Woody's highly successful film career commenced with WHAT'S NEW, PUSSYCAT (65, actor/script) and the following: CASINO ROYALE (actor/co-wrote); WHAT'S UP, TIGER LILY (67, narrated/acted); TAKE THE MONEY & RUN (69, co-script, acted, directed); DON'T DRINK THE WATER (69, wrote only); BANANAS (71, directed/scripted/acted); EVERYTHING YOU ALWAYS WANTED TO KNOW ABOUT SEX, BUT WERE AFRAID TO ASK (72, directed/scripted/acted); screen version PLAY IT AGAIN, SAM (72, directed/scripted/acted); SLEEPER (73, directed/scripted/acted); LOVE & DEATH (75, script/acted); THE FRONT (76, acted); INTERIORS (78, directed/scripted); MANHATTAN (79, co-script/directed/acted). A second marriage, to actress Louise Lasser, in 1965, ended in divorce. ANNIE HALL (in which he acted and co-scripted) won him an Oscar as director of 1977. He is also an accomplished jazz musician. His most recent films are STARDUST MEMORIES (80, acted/dir./scripted), A MIDSUMMER NIGHT'S SEX COMEDY (82, acted/dir./scripted) and BROADWAY DANNY ROSE (83, acted/dir./scripted).
WOODY ALLEN & HIS COMEDY by Eric Lax; Elm Tree Books: London, 1976; *LOSER TAKES ALL: THE COMIC ART OF WOODY ALLEN* by Maurice Yacowar; Frederick Ungar Publishing Co.: N.Y., 1979; *WOODY ALLEN: AN ILLUSTRATED BIOGRAPHY* by Myles Palmer; Proteus: London, 1980; *THE MAGIC OF WOODY ALLEN* by Diane Jacobs; Robson Books: London, 1982; *WOODY ALLEN: JOKING ASIDE* by Gerald McKnight; W.H. Allen: London, 1982.

MELODY ANDERSON

B. Alberta, Canada, . .55. Melody, now a U.S. citizen, studied at Carlton University, and holds an Honors Degree in journalism; she was a model, and, aged 20, she tried to get work as a T.V. journalist in Canada, but failed owing to her female status; she travelled to Auckland, New Zealand, and worked there for 5 months; her work then took her to Mascot Airport, Sydney, Australia, as reporter/interviewer, and later to Singapore and Hong Kong; destined to become an actress, she returned to the States and studied with Michael V. Gazzo, appearing in commercials and T.V. movies such as ELVIS (79); Melody co-starred with Sam Jones (qv) in FLASH GORDON (79) and her other movies have included PLEASURE COVE (78), DEAD AND BURIED (80).

RICHARD ANDERSON

B. Long Branch, New Jersey, U.S.A. 8.8.26. Was office boy at M-G-M; U.S. Army WWII; stage debut summer stock in Santa Barbara and Laguna Playhouse; given a 6 yr. contract by M-G-M when introduced by Cary Grant to executives who had heard Anderson in radio broadcast. Many movies include 12 O'CLOCK HIGH (50); ACROSS THE WIDE MISSOURI (51); STUDENT PRINCE (54); PATHS OF GLORY (57); COMPULSION (59); 7 DAYS IN MAY (64); DOCTORS' WIVES (71). Mr Anderson was md. to Katherine Thalberg (d. of Norma Shearer); 3 children: Ashley, Brooke, Deva. His T.V. series: 'Bus Stop' (1961/62) 'Perry Mason' (1965/66); 'Dan August' (1970 75); 'Bionic Woman' (1976-78) and '$6M. MAN (1974-78). Recent T.V. Movie: MURDER BY NATURAL CAUSES (79).

BIBI ANDERSSON

B. Stockholm, Sweden, 11.11.35. Parents: Josef and Karin Andersson; ed. Royal Dramatic School, Sweden; Bibi became star of Swedish films, later internationally; md. Kjell Grede (writer/director) 1960 (div. 1973), 1 daughter Jenny (born 1973); many films include SMILES OF A SUMMER NIGHT (53); THE SEVENTH SEAL (56); WILD STRAWBERRIES (57); THE FACE (58); BRINK OF LIFE (58); THE DEVIL'S EYE (60); SQUARE OF VIOLENCE (63); NOW ABOUT THESE WOMEN (64); MY SISTER, MY LOVE (66); DUEL AT DIABLO (66); PERSONA (66); LE VIOL (67); THE STORY OF A WOMAN (69); THE KREMLIN LETTER (69); A PASSION (69); THE TOUCH (71); MY HUSBAND, MY MISTRESS AND I (76); AN ENEMY OF THE PEOPLE (77); I NEVER PROMISED YOU A ROSE GARDEN (77); QUINTET (78); AIRPORT '80—THE CONCORDE (79); THE MARMALADE REVOLUTION (79); I WANT TO BE A WOMAN (80); TWICE A WOMAN (81).

URSULA ANDRESS

B. Berne, Switzerland, 19.3.36. German parents, Anna & Rolf (a diplomat) Andress. Ursula has 4 sisters and 1 brother. Was at a Rome party when she received film offers; made 3 movies in Rome, including THE LOVES OF CASANOVA, when she was 18; went to Hollywood, md. actor/director John Derek 1957 (div. 1966); international star as Honey in DR. NO (61). Motion pictures include: FOUR FOR TEXAS (63); FUN IN ACAPULCO (64); SHE (64); WHAT'S NEW, PUSSYCAT? (65); THE 10TH VICTIM (65); BLUE MAX (66); PERFECT FRIDAY (70); 5 AGAINST CAPRICORN (72); DOPPIO DELITTO (78); PRISONER OF THE CANNIBAL GOD (79); FOUR TIGERS IN LIPSTICK (79); SAFARI EXPRESS (80); 1 son, Dmitri Alexandre Hamlin, born 19.5.80, father actor Harry Hamlin, her CLASH OF THE TITANS (81) co-star; MEXICO IN FLAMES, TEN DAYS THAT SHOOK THE WORLD (both 1982).

ANTHONY ANDREWS

B. London, 12.1.47. Ed. Royal Masonic School. Father was musical arranger/conductor during 1940s with Jack Payne etc., mother was a dancer. Took catering course; worked briefly for farmer selling chickens and cream; stage debut Chichester as A.S.M.; Guildford Rep. and tour of north; much T.V. ('Dixon of Dock Green', 'The Fortunes of Nigel'); Movies: A WAR OF CHILDREN (73, T.V. movie); TAKE ME HIGH (74); QBVII (74, T.V. movie); OPERATION DAYBREAK (74); PERCY'S PROGRESS (75); THE ADOLESCENTS (77); Md. heiress Georgina Simpson (father, endocrinologist Dr L. Simpson); 1 son Joshua, 1 daughter Jessica; Mr Andrews' stage co. Andsomest Prods. presented 'Great American Backstage Musical' 1978. Recent T.V. roles in 'Danger U.X.B.' (78, ser.); Sebastian in 'Brideshead Revisited' (81, Golden Globe Aw. T.V., B.A.); 'La Ronde' (82); voted 'Best Dressed Man' by Menswear Assoc.; Co-partner Stage-screen Prods.; THE NIGHT PARADISE (81); as IVANHOE, as THE SCARLET PIMPERNEL, THE DARK SECRET OF THE BLACK BAYOU (all T.V. movies, 1982).

DANA ANDREWS

B. Collins, Mississippi, 1.1.12; real name Carver Dana Andrews. Ed. Sam Houston Coll.; wanted to be playwrite, but 1930-31 was accountant; singer, advised to try acting and played Pasadena Playhouse 3 yrs. from 1937. Came to screen 1940 in THE WESTERNER. Over 65 movies include KIT CARSON (40); OXBOW INCIDENT (43); LAURA (44); A WALK IN THE SUN (45); BEST YEARS OF OUR LIVES (46); MY FOOLISH HEART (50); COMMANCHE (56); NIGHT OF THE DEMON (57). Md. 1. Janet Murray 1932 (dec. 1935), 1 son David (dec. 1964); 2. actress Mary Todd 1939, 2 daughters Kathryn, Susan, 1 son stephen. Dana's father was a clergyman, his brother is Steve Forrest, actor. Broadway: 'The Captains & the Kings' (62). T.V. series 1969-72 'Bright Promise'. Recent motion pictures: AIRPORT 75 (75); LAST TYCOON (76); IKE: THE WAR YEARS (78, T.V. movie, as Gen. George Marshall) and THE PILOT (78).

HARRY ANDREWS

In show-business for 48 years, in which he has given solid performances on stage as well as motion pictures, Harry Andrews was born in Tonbridge, Kent on 10.11.11 and educated at Wrekin College. His father was a doctor and he was the youngest of 5 children. Intending a career in the police, a colleague introduced him to the Liverpool Rep., where he made his professional debut in 1933. His stage career has been almost entirely distinguished in Shakespearean roles on the British and Broadway stage. During WWII he served with distinction with the Police Reserves; London Scottish Regiment; 1940, commissioned as 2nd Lieutenant, seeing action with Monty's 11th Armoured Brigade in Europe. Mr Andrews came to the screen in 1952 in the appropriate role as the R.S.M. in THE RED BERET. In over 60 films his best work includes A HILL IN KOREA (56), ICE COLD IN ALEX (58), THE HILL (64) and THE DEADLY AFFAIR (66). In 1966 he was awarded a Commander Order of the British Empire. His most recent TV appearances were as Tolstoy in 'A Question of Faith' (1979); 'A Question of Guilt' (1980); 'The Seven Dials Mystery' (1981) and as the Headmaster in 'A.J. Wentworth, B.A.' (series, 1982). In August, 1982, he played in 'Uncle Vanya' at London's Haymarket Theatre. Mr Andrews' most recent movies include PRINCE & THE PAUPER, EQUUS (both 76), SUPERMAN, THE FOUR FEATHERS, WATERSHIP DOWN (voice only), DEATH ON THE NILE, THE MEDUSA TOUCH, THE BIG SLEEP (all 77) and S.S. TITANIC (80).

JULIE ANDREWS

Star of one of the all-time box-office successes, THE SOUND OF MUSIC, Julie Andrews was born in Walton-on-Thames, Surrey on October 1st 1935. Her real name is Julia Wells; her father, Edward Wells, was a teacher, her mother, Barbara, a pianist. Her parents divorced when she was very young, and her mother married Ted Andrews, and as a trio, they toured in variety, pantomime, revue, and appeared on radio and T.V. Miss Andrews was taught music by her step-father and studied voice with the famous opera singer Madame Stiles-Allen. She made her London stage debut in 1947 at the London Hippodrome in Val Parnell's 'Starlight Roof', bringing the house down when she sang an operatic aria. In 1954 she embarked on her highly successful musical shows, commencing with Polly Brown in 'The Boyfriend', Eliza in 'My Fair Lady' (56, London and Broadway) and Queen Guenevere in 'Camelot', Broadway 1960. She wed set designer Tony Walton in 1959. Julie came to the screen in MARY POPPINS in 1964, a sensational musical success, followed by THE AMERICANISATION OF EMILY (64), THE SOUND OF MUSIC (65), TORN CURTAIN (66), HAWAII (66), THOROUGHLY MODERN MILLIE (67), STAR! (68), DARLING LILI (69), TAMARIND SEED (73), 10 (79), LITTLE MISS MARKER (79). Divorcing Mr Walton in 1968, she wed film director Blake Edwards on 12.11.69. She has a daughter, Emma Kate, from her first marriage and the Edwards' adopted a Vietnamese orphan, Amy Leigh. The couple work closely for Operation California, visiting orphanages, schools and hospitals in Vietnam and Cambodia. Julie won an Oscar in 1964 for her MARY POPPINS role. Recent films include S.O.B. (81), VICTOR/VICTORIA (82, Oscar nom., BA; Golden Globe Aw.), THE MAN WHO LOVED WOMEN (83, all directed by her husband). *JULIE ANDREWS: THE STORY OF A STAR* by John Cottrell; A. Barker: London, 1968; p/b: 1969; *JULIE ANDREWS* by Robert Windeler; W.H. Allen: London, 1970; rev. 1982.

FRANCESCA ANNIS

B. London, 14.5.45; mother Brazilian, former actress Mariquita Annis. Studied at Corona Academy, originally intended to be a ballerina. Came to screen 1958 in children's film THE CAT GANG. Movies include: CLEOPATRA (63); EYES OF ANNIE JONES (63); FLIPPER & THE PIRATES (64); PLEASURE GIRLS (65); much T.V. and Broadway 1969 in 'Hamlet'; she has 2 daughters, Charlotte Emily (b. Feb. 1979, the other born 16.7.80), father is photographer Mr Patrick Wiseman. Miss Annis became well-known on T.V. playing Lillie Langtry in 'Lillie' (ITV 1978) winning T.V. Times Actress Aw.; 'Why Didn't They Ask Evans?' (79); 'The Secret Adversary' (82, ser.); other films: MACBETH (71); PENNY GOLD (74); COMING OUT OF THE ICE (T.V. movie, 82); KRULL (83).

SUSAN ANTON

B. California. 5'11½" tall. Won 'Miss California' award aged 17, commenced career as singer in night clubs. Md. Jack —, her manager (div.). Stars as Goldine Serafin, in GOLDEN GIRL (78); stage 1982: 'They're Playing Our Song' (USA); SPRING FEVER (83).

MICHAEL ANSARA

B. Lowell, Massachusetts, 15.4.22. Studied stage at Pasadena Playhouse; served in U.S. Army; repertory and tours, came to screen in ACTION IN ARABIA (44). Many films include: ONLY THE VALIANT (51); THE ROBE (53); LONE RANGER (56); TEXAS ACROSS THE RIVER (66); STAND UP AND BE COUNTED (72). Md. Barbara Eden, actress (div.), 1 son Matthew. Guested on T.V. ('Star Trek' etc.) many times, own series: 'Law of the Plainsman' (1959-62) and 'Broken Arrow' (1956-60) as Cochise; he has played Red Indians in numerous movies. Recent big screen: MOHAMMAD, MESSENGER OF GOD (77); THE MANITOU (78); GUNS & THE FURY (82).

SUSAN ANSPACH

B. N.Y. City, .44 (39?); of German/French/Spanish extraction; Ed: Catholic Univ., Actors' Studio; B'way: 'Hair'; md: ?, 2 children (div.); movies inclu. FIVE EASY PIECES, THE LANDLORD (both '70); PLAY IT AGAIN, SAM (72); BLUME IN LOVE (73); NASHVILLE (75); THE BIG FIX (78); RUNNING (79); THE DEVIL & MAX DEVLIN (80); GAS, MONTENEGRO (both 81); PIGS OR PEOPLE, DEADLY ENCOUNTER (both 82).

ANN-MARGRET

Of Swedish parentage, Ann-Margret was born Ann-Margret Olsson in Valsobyn, Jamtland, Sweden on April 28th 1941. At the age of 5 she moved with her family to the United States, living in Fox Lake, Winnetka and Wilmette, Illinois. After a year at Northwestern University, aged 20 she joined a night-club act, singing and dancing with a small combo. Comedian George Burns (q.v.) invited her to appear with him at 'The Sahara', Las Vegas and subsequently Jack Benny guested her on his TV show. Since coming to the screen in POCKETFUL OF MIRACLES (61), Ann has been seen in STATE FAIR (62), BYE-BYE-BIRDIE (62), VIVA LAS VEGAS (64), KITTEN WITH A WHIP (65), BUS RILEY'S BACK IN TOWN (65), THE PLEASURE SEEKERS (65), ONCE A THIEF (65), THE CINCINNATI KID (65), MADE IN PARIS (66), THE SWINGER (66), STAGECOACH (66), MURDERER'S ROW (66), THE TIGER & THE PUSSYCAT (67), MR KINKY (68), C.C. & CO. (70), R.P.M. (71), CARNAL KNOWLEDGE (71), THE TRAIN ROBBERS (72), THE OUTSIDE MAN (73), TOMMY (74). On 28.5.67 she wed actor/personal manager Mr Roger Smith, he has 3 children from a previous marriage. On 10.9.72 during a cabaret at Sahara Hotel, Lake Tahoe, Nevada, Ann fell 22 feet onto a stage, but courageously survived the ordeal, suffering much injury. Latest movies: LAST RE-MAKE OF BEAU GESTE, JOSEPH ANDREWS, CHEAP DETECTIVE (all 77), CACTUS JACK (78), MIDDLE-AGE CRAZY, MAGIC (both 79), LOOKIN' TO GET OUT (80), I OUGHT TO BE IN PICTURES, RETURN OF THE SOLDIER (both 82). Oscar-nominated for TOMMY, she toured the U.S. successfully in cabaret in 1982. *ANN-MARGRET: A PHOTO EXTRAVAGANZA & MEMOIR* by Neal Peters & David Smith; a Delilah Book: N.Y., 1981; Large p/b.

ANNE ARCHER

B. Los Angeles, . . . Parents theatrical; ed. Claremont College (Degree: Theatre Arts), appeared in summer stock, 1st major role in 'Glad Tidings'; md.1. business William L. Davis (div.). 1 son Tommy; Broadway includes: 'A Couple of White Chicks Sitting Around Talking'; many T.V. movies and series including Carol in 'Bob & Carol & Ted & Alice' (1973); movies: THE HONKERS (72); CANCEL MY RESERVATION (72); ALL-AMERICAN BOY (73); GOOD GUYS WEAR BLACK (78); PARADISE ALLEY (78); HERO AT LARGE (80); RAISE THE TITANIC (80); GREEN ICE (81); WALTZ ACROSS TEXAS (82); md. 2. actor/writer Terry Jastrow, forming Astor Films; T.V. series 1982: 'The Second Family Tree'.

ALAN ARKIN

Before coming to the screen in 1966, Alan Arkin was a distinguished stage artiste in other capacities apart from acting. He was born in New York City on 26 March 1934. After attending Los Angeles City College, L.A. State College and Bennington College, Vermont, where he majored in drama, Arkin made his professional début with the Compass Players at the Crystal Palace, St. Louis in 1959. He had always wanted to be an actor since his father took him to the cinema as a child. His New York debut came in 1961 in the revue 'From the Second City' and he won acclaim on Broadway two years later in 'Enter Laughing', winning Tony and Variety Awards. Coming to the screen in 1966 in THE RUSSIANS ARE COMING, THE RUSSIANS ARE COMING, Mr Arkin has been seen in WOMAN TIMES SEVEN (67); WAIT UNTIL DARK (67); INSPECTOR CLOUSEAU (68); THE HEART IS A LONELY HUNTER (68); POPI (69); THE MONITORS (69); CATCH 22 (70); LITTLE MURDERS (71, also directed); DEADHEAD MILES (72); LAST OF THE RED HOT LOVERS (72); FREEBIE AND THE BEAN (74); RAFFERTY AND THE GOLD DUST TWINS (75); HEARTS OF THE WEST (75); THE 7½% SOLUTION (76). He has made short movies, directed and composed for Broadway stage, written a book on photography and recorded folk-music LP's for children. Divorced from his first wife, whom he wed during college in 1955 (two sons, Adam and Matthew), he wed Barbara Dana in 1964 (one son, Anthony). Recent movies: THE OTHER SIDE OF HELL, THE DEFECTION OF SIMAS KUDIRKA (both T.V. movies, 1978); THE MAGICIAN OF LUBLIN, THE IN-LAWS (both 1979); SIMON (80; IMPROPER CHANNELS, CHU CHU & THE PHILLY FLASH (both 81) and THE RETURN OF CAPTAIN INVINCIBLE (82).

ELIZABETH ASHLEY

B. Ocala, Florida, 30.8.39; real name Elizabeth Cole. Ed. Louisiana State Univ.; ballet dancer; fashion model/T.V. commercials; studied for stage Neighborhood Playhouse 1959 ('Camino Real', 'Crucible') and under Philip Burton; stock companies, understudying; great success on Broadway in 'Take Her, She's Mine' (1961—Tony Award) and 'Barefoot in the Park' (1963). Movies: THE CARPETBAGGERS (64); SHIP OF FOOLS (65); THE THIRD DAY (65); MARRIAGE OF A YOUNG STOCKBROKER(71); WHEN MICHAEL CALLS (71, T.V. movie); FACE OF FEAR(71, T.V. movie); SECOND CHANCE 71, T.V. movie); PAPERBACK HERO (73); GOLDEN NEEDLES (74); ONE OF MY WIVES IS MISSING(75, T.V. movie); RANCHO DELUXE (75); 92 IN THE SHADE (75); GREAT SCOUT & CATHOUSE THURSDAY 76); COMA (77). Md. 1. Richard Mathews (div.), 2. 1962 James Farentino (div.), 3. George Peppard 18.4.66, 1 son Christopher 1968 (div.), 4. James McCarthy 1975. Recent movies: CORKY 79); PATERNITY (81); SVENGALI, SPLIT IMAGE (both 1982).

ROBIN ASKWITH

B. Southport, Lancs, 12.10.50. Small roles in IF (68); BARTLEBY (70); NICHOLAS & ALEXANDRA (72), others before starring as Timothy Lea in CONFESSIONS OF A WINDOW CLEANER (74) .... OF A POP PERFORMER(75) .... OF A DRIVING INSTRUCTOR (76); also QUEEN KONG, LET'S GET LAID, STAND UP, VIRGIN SOLDIERS (all 77); BRITANNIA HOSPITAL (82).

WILLIAM ATHERTON

B. Orange, Connecticut, 30.7.47. Ed. High School; scholarship to Pasadena Playhouse; Carnegie Technical College of Drama 1965; tours, incl. Europe; N.Y.: 'Little Murders' 1969. Movies: THE NEW CENTURIONS (72); CLASS OF '44 (73); SUGARLAND EXPRESS (74); DAY OF THE LOCUST (76). Sang 'What'll I Do' behind credits of THE GREAT GATSBY (74); also in LOOKING FOR MR GOODBAR (77); CENTENNIAL (mini-ser. 78); TOMORROW'S CHILD (T.V. movie, 1981).

FRED ASTAIRE

A great Hollywood star in the true sense of the word, bringing sheer joy to millions all over the world, Fred Astaire was born Frederick Austerlitz in Omaha, Nebraska 10.5.1899. Named after his father, who was a salesman, young Fred went just as a partner for his sister Adele to a dancing class, but the couple had a natural ability which soon attracted professional attention. In1906 they commenced their careers in vaudeville, touring the States. Aged 11 he made his 1st N.Y. appearance; in 1917 they were on Broadway and here they appeared also in 'The Love Letter' (21); 'The Bunch & Judy' (22); 'Flirting' (23) and came to London with success in 'Stop Flirting' in May 1923. In the early 30's Hollywood beckoned and he came to the screen in 1933 in DANCING LADY (Adele married and retired from show-biz a year earlier). Teaming with Ginger Rogers in 1933 for FLYING DOWN TO RIO their memorable movies together were ROBERTA (35), TOP HAT (35), FOLLOW THE FLEET, SWINGTIME (both 36), SHALL WE DANCE (37), CAREFREE (38), THE STORY OF VERNON & IRENE CASTLE (39) and THE BARKLEYS OF BROADWAY (48). Mr Astaire wed Phyllis Livingston-Potter in 1933 and they had 2 children, son Fred, Jr. (1941) and Ava (1942). Other splendid movies included HOLIDAY INN (42), ZIEGFELD FOLLIS (46), EASTER PARADE (48) and THE BAND WAGON (53). Widowed in 1954, he recently wed a jockey, Robyn Smith, in L.A. 27.6.80. His sister Adele passed away January 25th 1981. Mr Astaire made several T.V. appearances including the series 'It Takes a Thief' (1968-70). In 1949 the Academy of Motion Picture Arts & Sciences awarded him a special Oscar for his 'unique artistry and his contributions to the technique of musical pictures'. Recent movies: TOWERING INFERNO (74), THAT'S ENTERTAINMENT (74 and sequel, 76, joint-guest/Narrator), PURPLE TAXI (78), THE MAN IN THE SANTA CLAUS SUIT (T.V. movie, 1978), GHOST STORY (81). Recipient of American Film Institute Life Achievement Award in 1981.
STEPS IN TIME (autobio.); Heinemann: London, 1960; p/b: Da Capo Press: N.Y., 1981; *FRED ASTAIRE & HIS WORK* by Alfonse Hackl; L.S.P.: Vienna, 1970: *FRED ASTAIRE: A PICTORIAL TREASURY OF HIS FILMS* by Howard Thompson; Falcon Enterprises: N.Y., 1970; *FRED ASTAIRE & GINGER ROGERS BOOK* by Arlene Crose; W.H. Allen: London, 1972; *STARRING FRED ASTAIRE* by Stanley Green & Burt Goldblatt; W.H. Allen: London, 1974; *FRED ASTAIRE STORY*; Radio Times Special (mag.); B.B.C.; Oxley Press, 1975; *FRED ASTAIRE* by Benny Green; Hamlyn: London, 1979.

RICHARD ATTENBOROUGH

Recently fulfilling a personal ambition by filming the life of GANDHI, Richard Attenborough is the son of Frederick L. Attenborough, who was Principal of Leicester Univ. College. He was born Richard Samuel Attenborough in Cambridge on 29 August 1923, and attended Wyggeston Grammar School, Leicester. Awarded the Leverhulme Scholarship to study in London at R.A.D.A., he made his first stage appearance in 'Ah, Wilderness!', at the Intimate Theatre, Palmer's Green. Emerging from R.A.D.A. in 1942 with the Bancroft Medal, it was that year that the young actor came to the screen as the young stoker who deserted his post at the height of battle in IN WHICH WE SERVE. His stage and screen career was interrupted in 1943 with service in the R.A.F. as an air gunner-cameraman. As an actor his best films have been BRIGHTON ROCK (47, great success, also on the stage); THE GUINEA PIG (49); THE BOYS IN BROWN (50); PRIVATE'S PROGRESS (55); THE MAN UPSTAIRS (58); THE ANGRY SILENCE (59); GUNS AT BATASI (64) and LOOT (71). In all these roles he showed great versatility. Turning point in career came in 1959 when he formed Beaver Films with Bryan Forbes, co-producing ANGRY SILENCE, LEAGUE OF GENTLEMEN (59, also acted), WHISTLE DOWN THE WIND (61) and SEANCE ON A WET AFTERNOON (64, also acted). His son, Michael, and daughters, Jane and Charlotte, from his successful marriage to former actress Sheila Sim, are all following careers in the Arts. Knighted for his service to the British film industry in particular, Sir Richard has directed the memorable anti-war movie OH, WHAT A LOVELY WAR! (68) and also YOUNG WINSTON (71); A BRIDGE TOO FAR (76); MAGIC (78). He serves on the board of numerous organisations, including Pro-Chancellor of Sussex Univ., Chairman R.A.D.A., Governor of National Film School, Director of the Young Vic, Director of Chelsea F.C. and Deputy Chairman of Channel 4. GANDHI (82) awards have included the Martin Luther King Jr. Non-violent Peace Prize, Hollywood Oscars for Best Director and Film, citations as Best Director from the Hollywood Foreign Press Association, the Directors' Guild of America, BAFTA and India's Locus Decoration and Padma Bhushan awards. In March, 1983, BAFTA also honoured him with a Fellowship.
IN SEARCH OF GANDHI (semi-autobio.); The Bodley Head: London, 1982.

JEAN-PIERRE AUMONT

B. Paris, 5.1.13(?); real name Jean-Pierre Salomons. Studied at Paris Conservatoire of Drama; French stage from age 16, then French films, including JEAN DE LA LUNE (32); HOTEL DU NORD (38); French army 1940 (Croix de Guerre); to Canada, U.S., Broadway & 1st Hollywood movie CROSS OF LORRAINE 43). Md. Maria Montez 1943 (dec. 1951); Free French Army; Paris stage; retd. Hollywood 1946. 2nd marriage: Marisa Pavan, March 1956 (div. 1965, but re-md. 1969); 2 sons, Jean-Claude, Patrick. Best movies: ASSIGNMENT IN BRITANY (43); FIRST GENTLEMAN (G.B. 48); LILI (53); FIVE MILES TO MIDNIGHT (63); daughter from 1st marriage, Maria. Recent movies: DAY FOR NIGHT (73); CATHERINE & CO (76); SOMETHING SHORT OF PARADISE (79); BEGGARMAN, THIEF (79, T.V. movie); much B'way; BLACKOUT (81); NANA 82); guest: 'Hart to Hart' (82, T.V.).

CHARLES AZNAVOUR

B. Paris, 22.5.24.; real name Varenagh Aznourian. Parents Armenian, father Misha, ex-baritone, chef/owner of restaurant on the Rue de la Huchette. Left school, appeared on stage as actor, during war became songwriter, composing his 1st tune 'Il y a deux hiboux dans le beffroi' in 1942; attended Paris's famous School of the Music Hall; formed writing partnership with Pierre Roche, writing material for M. Chevalier; later becoming solo international cabaret star. Came to screen in 1958 in LA TETE CONTRE LES MURS. Md. Ulla Thorssell, a Swede 1967; 3 children. Movies include: TIREZ SUR LE PIANISTE (60); CANDY (68); ADVENTURERS (70); GAMES (70); AND THEN THERE WERE NONE (75); TIN DRUM (79); sang 'We Had It All' in THE GOLDEN LADY (79). Broadway includes own production 'World of Charles Aznavour', 1965; AN EVENING WITH CHARLES AZNAVOUR (video, 1982).
YESTERDAY WHEN I WAS YOUNG by Charles Aznavour; W.H. Allen: London, 1979.

LAUREN BACALL

B. New York City, 16.9.24; real name Betty Joan Perske. Ed. Highland Manor, N.Y.; Julia Richmond High School, N.Y. City; fashion model; American Academy of Dramatic Arts; N.Y. début 1942 walking on in 'Johnny 2x4'; to Hollywood and became big star of 40s: TO HAVE AND HAVE NOT (44); THE BIG SLEEP (46); KEY LARGO (48); YOUNG MAN WITH A HORN (50). Md. Humphrey Bogart 1945 (dec. 1957), 1 son, Stephen 1948, 1 daughter, Leslie 1952; after 10 movies in 1950s, retd. to Broadway 1959 and became star, esp. in 'Applause' (1970—'Tony Award'), also London. Md. Jason Robards Jr. 1961, but div. 1969, 1 son, Sam, b. 16.12.61. Recent movies: MURDER ON THE ORIENT EXPRESS (74); THE SHOOTIST (76); guest in 'Rockford Files' (T.V. 1979); THE FAN, HEALTH (both 1980); N.Y. stage 1981: 'Woman of the Year'.
Autobiography: *LAUREN BACALL BY MYSELF*. Jonathan Cape: London 1979; paperback Coronet 1979.

BARBARA BACH

B. —.48. Mother Irish Roman Catholic, fathe Austrian. Md. at 18 to Italian film produce Augusto Gregorini (div.); 2 children, Francesc and Gian Andrea. Was model, commenced fil career in Italy in THE ODYSSEY; 8 films o continent, last being THE SEA WOLF, wit Mr Franco Nero (q.v.); became star as Maje Anya Amasova in Bond movie SPY WHO LOVEI ME (77). Other movies THE TARANTULA THE BLACK STOMACH: THE HUMANOIL FORCE 10 FROM NAVARONE (78); JAGUA LIVES (78); BIG ALLIGATOR RIVER (79 THE BRAVE YOUNG MEN OF WEINBERC (79); CAVE MAN (80, wed co-star Ringo Stai (qv) in London, 27.4.81); THE COOLER (82 short); GIVE MY REGARDS TO BROAI STREET (83).

CATHERINE BACH

B. Warren, Ohio, 1.3.54 (?); Mexican/Germa parentage; grew up in Faith, S. Dakota; aged saw uncle in play and wanted to be an actress; scl plays, summer stock; waitress, secretary befoi small TV/movie parts; screen debut: TH WIDOW, then in MIDNIGHT MAN, THUN DERBOLT & LIGHTFOOT (both 74); HUSTL (75); md: David Shaw (div.); Catherine is a accomplished ballet/jazz dancer; success fror 1979 as Daisy Duke in TV series 'The Dukes Hazzard'; WHITE WATER (82, T.V. movie

JIM BACKUS

B. Cleveland, Ohio, 25.2.13. Ed. University School, Cleveland; Am. A.D.A.; repertory and vaudeville; radio announcer/actor. Md. actress Henriette Kaye 1943. Came to the screen in 1942. Movies include THE GREAT LOVER (49), PAT & MIKE (52); REBEL WITHOUT A CAUSE (55); MAN OF A 1000 FACES (57); IT'S A MAD, MAD, MAD, MAD WORLD (63). Broadway includes 'Hitch Your Wagon!' (1937); T.V.: 'I Married Joan' (1952-55); 'The Jim Backus Show' (1960); 'Blondie' (1968), others. Mr Backus provided the voice of cartoon character 'Mr Magoo', series won Oscar in 1950s. Recent movies: NOW YOU SEE HIM, NOW YOU DON'T (72), PETE'S DRAGON (77); GOOD GUYS WEAR BLACK (78); THERE GOES THE BRIDE (79); London stage 1979 'Hello Dolly', Drury Lane; ANGELS BRIGADE (80).

HERMIONE BADDELEY

B. Broseley, Shropshire, 13.11.06. Privately tutored; Margaret Morris's School of Dancing; toured 3 yrs., London début 1918. Became very successful stage artiste, especially in revue, making occasional movies since 1928, including: KIPPS (41); BRIGHTON ROCK (47—repeating stage role); PICKWICK PAPERS (52); ROOM AT THE TOP (59 A A Nom.); MARY POPPINS (64); UP THE FRONT (72); THERE GOES THE BRIDE (79). Md. 1. Hon. David Tennant (div.); 2. Capt. J.H. Willis, M.C.; much T.V. and work in the U.S.A., including 'Maude' series 1974-77; SECRET OF NIMH (82, voice only).

ALAN BADEL

Alan Badel was born in Rusholme, a district of Manchester, on 11 September 1923, and educated at Burnage Higl School in his home town and trained for the stage at R.A.D.A. 1939-1941, winning a Gold Medal. He made his firs professional appearance on the stage at Oxford in 1940, but the war interrupted his career and he served 1942-194 with the Parachute Regiment 6th Airborne Division. Returning to the stage in 1947 Mr Badel became one of our mos distinguished stage actors, especially in Shakespearean roles at Birmingham, Stratford-Upon-Avon and the Old Vic. H came to the screen in 1941 uncredited in THE YOUNG MR PITT. His numerous appearances include THE STRANGER LEFT NO CARD (53); SALOME (53, as John the Baptist); MAGIC FIRE (56, as Richard Wagner) THIS SPORTING LIFE (63); CHILDREN OF THE DAMNED (64) and in more recent years his movies includ ARABESQUE (66); WHERE'S JACK? (68); OTLEY (69); THE ADVENTURERS (70); THE DAY OF THE JACKAL (72); FORCE TEN FROM NAVARONE (77); TELEFON (77); THE MEDUSA TOUCH (77) AGATHA (78); RIDDLE OF THE SANDS (78); NIJINSKY (79) and SHOGUN (80). Wed for many years t actress Yvonne Owen, their daughter Sarah is a successful actress. Of French parentage, Alan Badel will be fondl remembered for his work on T.V. as Edmund Dantes in 'The Count of Monte Cristo' (1965). Most recent T.V. worl includes 'The Woman in White' and as Sir Fretful Plagiary in 'The Critic' (both 1982).
Mr Badel died of a heart attack on March 19, 1982.

CARROLL BAKER

B. Johnstown, Pennsylvania, 28.5.31. Ed. Greensburg High School; St. Petersburg Jr. Coll., Florida. Studied dancing from age 11; commenced pro. career as night club dancer touring south U.S.; went to N.Y. studied Actors' Studio. Md. Lew Ritter (div.). Broadway 1953 'Escapade', success in 'All Summer Long' (1954) lead to Hollywood debut in EASY TO LOVE. Other movies include GIANT (56); BABY DOLL (56 A A Nom.); THE BIG COUNTRY (58); BUT NOT FOR ME (59); BRIDGE TO THE SUN (61); THE CARPETBAGGERS (64); HARLOW (65); THE SWEET BODY OF DEBORAH (68). Md. Jack Garfein, director, 3.4.55, 2 children Blanche (1956), Herschel (1958). Carroll has in recent years made movies in Europe. Latest work: Andy Warhol's BAD (77); THE WORLD IS FULL OF MARRIED MEN (79) and A WATCHER IN THE WOODS (79). Daughter Blanche is an actress and won 'Emmy' T.V. Aw. for 'Holocaust' (78). Carroll's latest: STAR 80, RED MONARCH (both 1982).

GEORGE BAKER

B. Vatna, Bulgaria, 1.5.31. Ed. Lancing Coll., Sussex, but joined Deal Rep. Co. aged 15; 7 years rep., West End début Aug. 1953; that year came to the screen in small role in THE INTRUDER; much work on stage in 1950s and 1960s ('Old Vic' etc.) and 1955 onwards was star Associated British Pictures: DAMBUSTERS (55); THE SHIP THAT DIED OF SHAME (55); THE MOONRAKER (57); A HILL IN KOREA (57); NO TIME FOR TEARS (59). Father was a diplomat. In more recent years has concentrated on stage, also as artistic director. Recent T.V. 'I, Claudius' (BBC 1976); guest in 'Minder' (ITV 1980); 'Lady Killers' (ITV 1980). Movies: SPY WHO LOVED ME (77); 39 STEPS (78), HOPSCOTCH (79). Wrote play 'The Fatal Spring' (BBC 1980) to acclaim. Md. Julia Squire, 2 daughters. Recent T.V.: 'Triangle' (82); 'The Secret Adversary' (82).

JOE DON BAKER

B. Groesbeck, Texas, c. 1937. Was studying business administration when talked into taking part in play at College; 2 yrs. U.S. Army; Actors' Studio; success on Broadway in 'Marathon 33' (1963) and 'Blues for Mr Charlie' (1964). Movies include: COOL HAND LUKE (67—dèbut); GUNS OF THE MAGNIFICENT 7 (69); ADAM AT 6 A.M. (70); WILD ROVERS(71); WELCOME HOME, SOLDIER BOYS (72); JUNIOR BONNER(72); CHARLEY VARRICK (73); WALKING TALL (73); THE OUTFIT (74); GOLDEN NEEDLES (74); FRAMED (75); MITCHELL (75); CHECKERED FLAG OR CRASH (77); SPEED TRAP (77). T.V. includes: 'Streets of Fear' (78, T.V. movie); 'The Force' (79, T.V. movie); 'Chief of Detectives' (in U.S.: 'Eischied'), pilot & series 1979; 'Power' (mini-ser. 1980); JOY STICKS (82).

MICHAEL BALFOUR

B. Detroit(?), U.S.A., 1918. U.S. stage, circus, burlesque, rep., came to England and since 1944 in JUST WILLIAM'S LUCK has played in countless British movies and T.V. programmes, often as heavy. Movies include: MOULIN ROUGE (53); THE SEA SHALL NOT HAVE THEM (54); FIEND WITHOUT A FACE (58); THE PRIVATE LIFE OF SHERLOCK HOLMES (69); THE CANTERBURY TALES (72); THE PRISONER OF ZENDA (78). Recent T.V.: 'Angels' (79); 'Turning Point' (guest, 82).

MARTIN BALSAM

B. New York City, 4.11.19; full name Martin Henry Balsam. Ed. DeWitt Clinton High School, Bronx, N.Y.; New School for Social Research. 1 stage appearance as teenager in N.Y.; worked as shipping clerk, mechanic, salesman, radio operator, waiter, usher; pro. dèbut at Red Barn, N.Y. 1941, then U.S. Army WWII combat engineers and air force 1941-45; retd. to stage 1947, becoming distinguished actor in this medium, that year selected by Lee Strasberg and Elia Kazan for famed Actors' Studio. Came to the screen 1954 in ON THE WATERFRONT. Movies include: 12 ANGRY MEN; TIME LIMIT (57); AL CAPONE (59); PSYCHO (60); THE CARPET-BAGGERS(64); 7 DAYS IN MAY (64); GOOD GUYS & THE BAD GUYS (69). Md. 1. 1952: Pearl L. Somner (div. 1954); 2. 1957: Joyce Van Patten (div. 1962), 1 daughter Talia; 3. 1963: Irene Miller, 1 son Adam, 1 daughter Zoe. Oscar, BSA 1965, for A 1000 CLOWNS; more recently: THERE GOES THE BRIDE, CUBA, HOUSE ON GARIBALDI STREET (all 79); THE SALAMANDER (both 80); LITTLE GLORIA, HAPPY AT LAST (mini-ser. 82).

RONNIE BARKER

B. Bedford, 25.9.29. Ed. City of Oxford High School. Worked as a bank clerk, but did amateur theatricals with Oxford Theatre Players 1946; pro. dèbut with Aylesbury Rep. Co. in 1948; after rep., including Manchester and Oxford, made West End dèbut in 1955; worked continually in radio, theatre and T.V. as an actor, making movie dèbut in WONDERFUL THINGS (58) in small role. Other work in this genre include THE CRACKSMAN (62); DOCTOR IN DISTRESS (63); THE BARGEE (64) and A HOME OF YOUR OWN (64). Very popular on T.V. from late 60s in 'The Frost Report', 'Frost on Sunday', his own series 'Hark at Barker' and in 70s immensely successful partnering Ronnie Corbett in BBC's 'The Two Ronnies'. Md. Joy Tubb, 1 daughter Charlotte, 2 sons Larry, Adam. Awarded O.B.E. 1978. Other movies: FUTTOCK'S END (70, also wrote); ROBIN & MARIAN (76, as Friar Tuck) and PORRIDGE (79, also T.V. series); Variety Club of G.B. winner (with Mr Corbett); Personalities of the Year 1980 for 'The Two Ronnies' (also stage-show); recent T.V.: 'Open All Hours' (83).

TOM BAKER

B. Liverpool, 20.1.36(?). Mother a devout Roman Catholic, father away at sea. Brought up in the tough Scotland Rd. area of Liverpool. At school enjoyed acting, was offered job aged 15 at Abbey Theat., Dublin, but mother declined; at that age went to a monastery in Jersey, later at Shropshire as a noviciate. Aged 21 left and did Nat. Service in merchant navy and did troop shows; studied Rose Bruford drama school; repertory, incl. late night revue in York playing a 'dog' when talent scout from Nat. Theatre saw him, interview with Olivier followed and Tom joined famed Nat. Theatre— dèbuting as a horse! Good work at National and Bristol Old Vic lead to 1st film role as Rasputin in NICHOLAS & ALEXANDRA (72). Md. 1. Anne (daughter of famous rosegrower Alfred Wheatcroft) 1960, 2 sons: Daniel (c. 1961) and Piers (c. 1966), (div.). Other films: THE CAN-TERBURY TALES(72); LUTHER; SINBAD'S GOLDEN VOYAGE; VAULT OF HORROR (all 1973); THE MUTATIONS (74). Working on a building site, auditioned and obtained role of 'Dr. Who' on BBC T.V. The role won Tom admirers young and old, the series viewed in 37 countries, watched by 100 million (in U.S.A. shown on 130 stations alone), played role 1974-80. Mr Baker wed, on 13.12.80, Lalla Ward, his 'Doctor Who' co-star; recent stage: 'Hedda Gabler' and T.V.: 'Hound of the Baskervilles' (as Holmes, both 1982).

IAN BANNEN

B. Airdrie, Scotland, 29.6.28. Brought up in Coatbridge, nr Glasgow. Ed. Ratcliffe Coll., Leics.; in 1947, holidaying in Eire, offered and spent weeks at Gate Theatre, Dublin; Nat. Service; considered journalism, got bit part in movie POOL OF LONDON and then spent 4 yrs. at Stratford-on-Avon, with Shakespeare Memorial Theatre Co. Films include, after giving noticeable performances on T.V., PRIVATE'S PROGRESS (55); THE LONG ARM (56); CARLTON BROWNE OF THE F.O. (58); THE FRENCH MISTRESS (60); THE HILL (65); Oscar nomi-nation for FLIGHT OF THE PHOENIX (65). Mr Bannen has played on B'way and T.V. includes 'Tinker, Tailor, Soldier, Spy' (79); 'Cousin Phillis' (ser., 82); 'The Hard Word' (ser., 83); Md: Marilyn Salisbury, 1978; other movies inclu. THE INGLORIOUS BASTARDS (78); A WATCHER IN THE WOODS (79); EYE OF THE NEEDLE (80).

GENE BARRY

B. N.Y. City, 14.6.21; real name Eugene Klass. Ed. New Utrecht High School, Brooklyn; as a youngster excelled at football, played violin and sang well at school; awarded scholarship to Chatham Sq. School of Music; local radio singing lead to job as vocalist with Teddy Powell band; impressed producer Max Rheinhardt, cast on Broadway in 'Rosalinda' (1942). Other Broadway: 'New Moon', 'Die Fledermaus' (1942); 'Merry Widow' (1943); 'Catherine Was Great' (1944, with Mae West). Md. Betty Kalb (stage name Julie Carson) 22.10.44, 2 sons Michael (1946), Frederic (1953), adopted daughter Liza. Mr Barry won 'Critics' Award' 1949 in off-Broadway play 'Idiot's Delight'; gained Paramount contract 1951, came to screen in THE ATOMIC CITY (52). Others: WAR OF THE WORLDS (53); ALASKA SEAS (54); RED GARTERS (54); NAKED ALIBI (54); BACK FROM ETER-NITY (56); THUNDER ROAD(58); SUBTER-FUGE (69). Very popular on T.V.: series: 'Bat Masterson' (1959-61); Amos Burke in 'Burke's Law' (1963-66), a great hit; 'The Name of the Game' (1968-71) and 'The Adventurer' (1972). He has also appeared successfully in cabaret. Mr Barry's films of the 70s include: DO YOU TAKE THIS STRANGER? (70, T.V. movie); THE DEVIL & MISS SARAH (71, T.V. movie); THE SECOND COMING OF SUZANNE (73, T.V. movie); GUYANA, CRIME OF THE CENTURY (80, Spain).

ANNE BANCROFT

Deservedly winning an Academy Award for her performance in THE MIRACLE WORKER in 1962, Anne Bancroft was born Anna Maria Italiano on 17 September 1931 in the Bronx, New York City. She was keen on acting at school and appeared with local dramatic societies — she applied and was accepted to study at the American Academy of Dramatic Art for two years. Appearing at the Neighborhood Playhouse in New York, she was spotted by a T.V. producer and given a leading role, working for a while under the name of Anna Marno. Playing in more than fifty T.V. shows in two years, she was soon called to Hollywood, coming to the screen in DON'T BOTHER TO KNOCK, in 1952. After roles in such movies as TREASURE OF THE GOLDEN CONDOR (53); DEMETRIUS AND THE GLADIATORS (54); GORILLA AT LARGE (54); NEW YORK CONFIDENTIAL (55); NIGHTFALL (56); and THE GIRL IN SILK STOCKINGS (57) Miss Bancroft returned, disillusioned by her roles, to Broadway — met producer Fred Coe through actor Richard Basehart, and won a role and critical (Tony Award) accolades for TWO FOR THE SEESAW (58), followed a year later by THE MIRACLE WORKER (repeated for the screen). Her first husband was Marty May, actor (1954-1957); she wed actor/director Mr Mel Brooks (qv) on 5.8.64 (he has three children from previous marriage) and they have a son, Maximilian. Other movies include: THE PUMPKIN EATER (64, A.A.Nom.); THE SLENDER THREAD (65); THE GRADUATE (68, A.A. Nom.); YOUNG WINSTON (71); PRISONER OF SECOND AVENUE (75); LIPSTICK (76); SILENT MOVIE (76); THE TURNING POINT, (77, A.A.Nom.); JESUS OF NAZARETH (77, T.V. movie, as Mary Magdalene); FATSO (79 also directed); THE ELEPHANT MAN (79) and TO BE OR NOT TO BE (83, produced and co-starring her husband).

RICHARD BASEHART

B. Zanesville, Ohio, U.S.A., 31.8.14. Ed. local schools. Father Harry T. Basehart, editor of 'Zanesville, Ohio, Times-Signal'. 1st job as reporter, but sacked for 'impulsive behaviour'; surveying crew radio announcer, other jobs; stage début 1932 local Co.; 5 yrs. with Hedgerow Theatre, Moylan; Broadway 1943 N.Y. Critics' 'Variety' Award 1945 for 'The Hasty Heart'. Md. 1. Stephan Klein 1940 (dec. 1950). Came to screen 1947 in CRY WOLF, other pics. incl. HE WALKED BY NIGHT (48), THE BLACK BOOK (49), FOURTEEN HOURS (51), TITANIC (53), MOBY DICK (56), TIME LIMIT (57); THE BROTHERS KARAMAZOV (58), as HITLER (63); THE SATAN BUG (65). Md: 2. Valentina Cortesa, actress (in movie HOUSE ON TELEGRAPH HILL (51) together), 1 son John 1951, 2 daughters Jenna & Gayla 1952 & 1953, (div.). Has continued to act on U.S. stage with success, esp. in Shakespeare. Popular on T.V. esp. 'Voyage to the Bottom of the Sea' 1964-68 as Admiral Nelson. Md. 3. Diana Lottery, c. 1967. Recent T.V.: 1 episode 'Greatest Heroes of the Bible'. Latest movies: TERROR OF DR. CHANEY (77); ISLAND OF DR. MOREAU (77); BEING THERE (79); MARILYN: THE UNTOLD STORY (80); KNIGHT RIDER (T.V. movie, 1981).

NED BEATTY

B. Kentucky . . . .; Seven years experience in numerous productions with Barter Theatre, Virginia appeared on Broadway in 'The Devils' (1963) 'The Lonesome Train' (1965); 'Hard Travelin' (1965); 'The Great White Hope' (1967); 'The Iceman Cometh' (1968); 'The Night Threat Spent in Jail' (1970). Cast by John Boorman in DELIVERANCE (72), screen début in this production. Other movies: THE THIEF WHO CAME TO DINNER (72), NASHVILLE (75) W.W. & THE DIXIE DANCE KINGS (75) ALL THE PRESIDENT'S MEN (76), SILVER STREAK (76), EXORCIST II: THE HERETIC (77); NETWORK (77); GRAY LADY DOWN (77); SUPERMAN: THE MOVIE (78, as Otis). 1941 (79); WISEBLOOD (79); INCREDIBLE SHRINKING WOMAN (79); HOPSCOTCH (79). Starred in U.S. T.V. series 'Szysznyk' (77) as Nick Szysznyk. Recent movies: THE AMERICAN SUCCESS COMPANY (80); ANSWERS (T.V. movie, 1 segment), SOME SUNNY DAY (both 1982); STAND ON IT (83).

ALAN BATES

Alan Bates has still remained one of Britain's top film actors, celebrating twenty years in that medium, owing to his adroit selection of roles. Allestree, Derbyshire born, on 17.2.34, he is the son of Harold and Florence Bates and attended the Herbert Strutt Grammar School, Belper in Derbyshire. As a youngster aged 11 he portrayed his first stage role as Prince Arthur in a school production of 'King John'. Upon leaving school he went to R.A.D.A., did two years National Service in the RAF 1954-1955, first appearing professionally with the Midland Theatre Co., Coventry, in 1955. A year later he commenced his highly successful career on the London Stage, especially at the Royal Court Theatre, including Cliff in 'Look Back in Anger'. Alan Bates came to the screen in 1960 in THE ENTERTAINER and has been seen in WHISTLE DOWN THE WIND (61); A KIND OF LOVING (62); THE CARETAKER (63); THE RUNNING MAN (63); NOTHING BUT THE BEST (64); ZORBA THE GREEK (65); GEORGY GIRL (66); KING OF HEARTS (67); FAR FROM THE MADDING CROWD (67); THE FIXER (68); WOMEN IN LOVE (69); THREE SISTERS (70); THE GO-BETWEEN (70); A DAY IN THE DEATH OF JOE EGG (71); THE IMPOSSIBLE OBJECT (73); BUTLEY (73); ROYAL FLASH (75). He has continued to appear regularly on the stage ('The Caretaker', 'Butley', winning 'Evening Standard' Best Actor Award 1975 for 'Otherwise Engaged') in the West End and Broadway. Married to Victoria Ward, they have twin sons. Recent stage: 'Stage Struck', Vaudeville Theatre. Recent movies: AN UNMARRIED WOMAN (77); THE SHOUT (78); THE ROSE (79); NIJINSKY (79); VERY LIKE A WHALE (79, T.V. movie); THE TRESPASSER (80, T.V. movie); QUARTET (80) and THE WICKED LADY (83). Recent T.V. credits include 'Voyage Round My Father' (82), 'An Englishman Abroad' (83) and on stage in 'A Patriot For Me' (83).

WARREN BEATTY

Continual involvement in the production of his own motion pictures has sustained the success for Warren Beatty in movies for twenty-one years. His elder sister Shirley MacLaine (qv) is a successful actress and Warren was born 30 March 1937 in Richmond, Virginia. His mother, Kathlyn, was a dancer, and after graduating from Northwestern University the young actor ventured to New York, played piano at a 58th Street lounge, and sometimes worked as a labourer in order to pay for acting lessons. Learning his craft in small roles on T.V., the North Jersey Playhouse and summer stock, it was while doing a stint in the latter in 1959 that Beatty was picked by playwright William Inge for a role in his Broadway play 'A Loss of Roses'. Although the play ran for a few weeks only, Beatty was a success in his role and he went to Hollywood, having also had a role in a situation-comedy series 'The Many Loves of Dobie Gillis'. He came to the screen in 1961 in SPLENDOUR IN THE GRASS and has been seen in THE ROMAN SPRING OF MRS STONE (62); ALL FALL DOWN (62); LILITH (65); MICKEY ONE (65); PROMISE HER ANYTHING (66); KALEIDOSCOPE (66); a tremendous success with cult film BONNIE AND CLYDE (67, which he also produced, A.A. Nom.); THE ONLY GAME IN TOWN (69); McCABE AND MRS MILLER (71); DOLLARS (72); THE PARALLAX VIEW (74); SHAMPOO (75, also produced, co-wrote); THE FORTUNE (75); HEAVEN CAN WAIT (78, produced, co-directed, co-wrote and acted) and REDS (81, acted, directed, produced, co-wrote), the latter winning Warren an Oscar and Golden Globe Award as Best Director.
THE FILMS OF WARREN BEATTY by Lawrence J. Quirk. Citadel: Secaucus, N.J., USA 1979.
WARREN BEATTY by Suzanne Munshower; W.H. Allen: London, 1983.

BONNIE BEDELIA

B. New York City, 25.3.48; Ed: Hunter College; Broadway: 'Isle of Children' (1962); 'The Playroom' (1965); 'My Sweet Charlie' (1966). T.V. includes 'Love of Life' (series); 'Love Story: Love Came Laughing' (1973); series: 'The New Land' (1974). Movies include: THE GYPSY MOTHS (69), THEY SHOOT HORSES, DON'T THEY (70, success as the pathetic pregnant contestant), THEN CAME BRONSON (70), LOVERS & OTHER STRANGERS (70), THE STRANGE VENGEANCE OF ROSALIE (72), HAWKINS ON MURDER (73, T.V. movie), THE BIG FIX (78), SALEM'S LOT (T.V. movie, 1979), HEART LIKE A WHEEL (82).

MICHAEL BECK

B. Horseshoe Lake, Arkansas, . .48; brought up on farm on banks of Mississippi river. Attended college on football scholarship; came to London to study at Central School of Music & Drama, later appearing in repertory and BBC productions. In U.S. series of distinction: 'Holocaust' (1977). Big screen work includes: MADMAN (77); Swan in THE WARRIORS (78); stars opposite Olivia Newton-John in XANADU (80); others: ALCATRAZ: THE WHOLE SHOCKING STORY (T.V. movie, 1980); BATTLETRUCK, MEGAFORCE (both 1982); TRIUMPHS OF A MAN CALLED HORSE (83).

JOHN BECK

B. Chicago . . . . Has appeared in repertory and many T.V. series including 'Bonanza', 'Hawaii Five-O' and regular in short-lived 1971 series 'Nichols'. Md. Tina, 3 children. Films include: MRS POLLIFAX, SPY (71); LAWMAN (71); PAT GARRETT & BILLY THE KIND (73); SLEEPER (73); ROLLERBALL (75); THE BIG BUS (76); AUDREY ROSE (77); THE OTHER SIDE OF MIDNIGHT (77); T.V. ser. '83: Mark Graison in 'Dallas'.

NOAH BEERY JR.

B. N.Y. City, 10.8.13. Father Noah Beery, screen actor, who was brother of Wallace Beery. Ed. Urban & Harvard Military Acad., N. Hollywood High School. Entered films 1920 as child in Fairbanks' MARK OF ZORRO. Became a familiar and much-loved character player of movies, esp. T.V. which includes: 'Circus Boy' (1956-58); 'Doc Elliot' (1974) and recently Joseph 'Rocky' Rockford in 'The Rockford Files' (1974-80). Md: Maxine Jones, 3 children (div.)

TOM BELL

B. Liverpool.... 34(?). Son of a local tradesman, one of 7 children; Mr Bell's mother encouraged her son to go into rep. aged 15; studied Bradford Civic Theatre School; discharged from Nat. Serv. after 3 months, then 8 years of rep. including Swansea, York, Cheltenham and the Shannon Players, Ireland, during lean times worked as deckchair attendant, street photographer; success at Royal Court Theatre, 'Progress to the Park'—play moved to West End. Came to the screen in 1961 in THE KITCHEN and has been seen in PAYROLL (61); H.M.S. DEFIANT (62); L-SHAPED ROOM (62, a great success), A PRIZE OF ARMS (63); BALLAD IN BLUE (65); HE WHO RIDES A TIGER (66); THE LONG DAY'S DYING (68); IN ENEMY COUNTRY (68); LOCK UP YOUR DAUGHTERS (69); ALL THE RIGHT NOISES (69). Md. Lois Daine (div.), 1 son Aran. Much T.V. incl. 'The Sailor's Return' (77, T.V. movie); series: 'Out' (1978), 'Holocaust' (U.S. 1978, as Eichmann), 'Sweet Nothings' (BBC 1980) and acclaimed series 'Sons and Lovers' (BBC 1981) Mr Bell also had success at the Criterion Theatre in 1979 in the play 'Bent'. 82: 'Hedda Gabler' (stage), 'King's Royal' (T.V. ser.)

JEAN-PAUL BELMONDO

B. Neuilly-sur-Seine, France, 9.4.33. Tutored for the stage by Raymond Girard and studied at the Paris Conservatoire d'Art Dramatique (equivalent of England's R.A.D.A.). His father, named Jean-Paul Belmondo, was a sculptor, his mother a painter. Their son, after studies, did Nat. Serv. in Algeria, retd. to stage in France and formed a theatrical company with Annie Girardot and Guy Bedos, playing mainly in comedy. Started in small screen roles (e.g. SOIS BELLE ET TAIS-TOI; DRÔLE DE DIMANCHE (late '50s)), starred in LES COPAINS DU DIMANCHE, movie was never shown theatrically, but director Claude Chabrol saw it and cast Belmondo in A DOUBLE TOUR (59). Became a super-star of French cinema after his role in Jean-Luc Godard's BREATHLESS (60). Movies include LA VIACCIA (60); TWO WOMEN (61); UNSINGE EN HIVER (62); THAT MAN FROM RIO (64); IS PARIS BURNING? (66); LE VOLEUR (67); THE BRAIN (68); A MAN I LIKE (69); STAVISKY (74). Md: Elodie, a ballerina, 1953, 1 son Paul (c. 1963), 2 daughters (c. 1959 & 1965); more recent movies: LE GUIGNOLA (80); THE PROFESSIONAL, L'AS DES AS (both 1982).

JOHN BELUSHI

Became well-known on American T.V. show 'Saturday Night Live' from 1975. Movies include: NATIONAL LAMPOON'S ANIMAL HOUSE ('78); GOIN' SOUTH (78); OLD BOYFRIENDS (79); THE BLUES BROTHERS (79); JUNGLE BURGER (79); CONTINENTAL DIVIDE (80). Md. Judy Jacklin; NEIGHBOURS (81). *Mr Belushi died in Hollywood, 5.3.82.*

RICHARD BENJAMIN

B. New York, 22.5.38. Ed. N.Y. High School of Performing Arts; Northwestern Univ., where he met wife, actress Paula Prentiss (wed. 26.10.61). Won Best Actor award; during univ. made pro. début in summer stock; much stage, incl. N.Y. Shakespeare Festival (1963), tours 'Tchin, Tchin', 'Barefoot in the Park' (also directed London prod.), 'The Odd Couple'. Broadway début 1966 in 'Star-Spangled Girl'. Came to the screen 1953 in teenage role in THUNDER OVER THE PLAINS, and has been seen in GOODBYE COLUMBUS (69); CATCH 22 (70); DIARY OF A MAD HOUSEWIFE (70); MARRIAGE OF A YOUNG STOCKBROKER (71); THE STEAGLE (71); PORTNOY'S COMPLAINT (72); THE LAST OF SHEILA (73); WEST-WORLD (73); THE SUNSHINE BOYS (75). Mr Benjamin co-starred with wife Paula in comedy series, 'He and She' 1967-68. They have a son, Ross Thomas, born 1974. Recent movies: LOVE AT FIRST BITE (78); LAST MARRIED COUPLE IN AMERICA (79), FIRST FAMILY (80), SATURDAY THE 14th (81), MY FAVOURITE YEAR (81, directed only). 'Quirk' was a short-lived series of 1978.

HYWEL BENNETT

B. Garnant, S. Wales, 8.4.44; full name Hywel Thomas Bennett. Father was a policeman; family moved to London when Hywel was 5, education Clapham Grammar School. Joined Nat. Youth Theatre, London, when 14, spending 5 yrs. with co., winning scholarship to R.A.D.A. Md. disc jockey Cathy McGowan (div.), 1 daughter Emma (b. circa 1971). Repertory includes Leatherhead, Salisbury and appeared in Edinburgh Festival and West End. Came to the screen opp. Hayley Mills in THE FAMILY WAY (66) and has been seen in TWISTED NERVE (68), THE VIRGIN SOLDIERS (69); THE BUTTERCUP CHAIN (70); LOOT (71); PERCY (71); ENDLESS NIGHT (72); IT'S A 2'6" ABOVE THE GROUND WORLD (72); and ALICE'S ADVENTURES IN WONDERLAND (72). More recently has won acclaim for his T.V. roles in 'Pennies from Heaven' (BBC 1977), 'Malice Aforethought' (BBC 1978), 'Tinker, Tailor, Soldier, Spy' (BBC 1978) and his own series, playing the title role of 'Shelley' (1980/82); 'The Critic' (82, as Mr Puff).

JILL BENNETT

B. Penang, Fed. Malay States, 24.12.30. Father a rubber planter. Ed. Godalming; Amersham Rep.; then studied R.A.D.A. Became very distinguished stage actress (Shakespeare Memorial Theatre, Royal Court, Old Vic, etc.) who makes occasional movie appearances: MOULIN ROUGE (52); HELL BELOW ZERO (54); LUST FOR LIFE (56); THE CRIMINAL (60); THE SKULL, THE NANNY (both 65); CHARGE OF THE LIGHT BRIGADE (68); INADMISSABLE EVIDENCE (68); MISTER QUILP (75); FULL CIRCLE (77); FOR YOUR EYES ONLY (81); others. Md. 1. Willis Hall (div.), 2. John Osborne. recent T.V.: 'Country' (81), 'The Aerodrome' (83); BRITANNIA HOSPITAL (82).

TOM BERENGER

B. Chicago, Illinois, ... Ed. Univ. of Missouri. Appeared in repertory and New York productions, incl. 'The Rose Tattoo', 'Electra', 'A Streetcar Named Desire' and a T.V. series, 'One Life to Live'. Movies include: THE SENTINEL (76); LOOKING FOR MR. GOODBAR (77); IN PRAISE OF OLDER WOMEN (78); BUTCH & SUNDANCE: THE EARLY YEARS (78); THE DOGS OF WAR (80); BEYOND THE DOOR (82); THE BIG CHILL (83); FEAR CITY (83).

ROBBY BENSON

B. Dallas, Texas, 21.1.56. Parents both in profession; father writer, mother actress. Appeared on Broadway as child in 'King and I', and has done much stage and T.V. work, incl. series 'Search for Tomorrow'. Movies: JEREMY (73); JORY (73); THE GODFATHER—PART II (74); DEATH BE NOT PROUD (75, T.V. movie); LUCKY LADY (75); ODE TO BILLY JOE (76); THE DEATH OF RITCHIE (77, T.V. movie); ONE ON ONE (77, co-wrote screenplay with father); ICE CASTLES (78); THE END (78); WALK PROUD (78); TRIBUTE (80); THE CHOSEN (82); HARRY & SON (83).

MARISA BERENSON

B. New York City, 15.2.48; Her grandmother is fashion designer Elsa Schiaparelli, her father Robert Berenson, American foreign service official and shipping magnate, and her great uncle was art historian and collector Bernard Berenson. Miss Berenson was a top fashion model before making her screen début in Visconti's DEATH IN VENICE (71). Her movies include: THE GARDEN OF THE FINZI-CONTINIS (72); CABARET (72); BARRY LYNDON (75); THE RISE & RISE OF CASANOVA (77); KILLERFISH (78); PLAYING FOR TIME (80, T.V. movie); S.O.B. (80); and TOURIST (80, U.S. T.V. series). Her sister Berry is married to actor Anthony Perkins (q.v.).

HELMUT BERGER

B. Saltzburg, Austria, ...45. Ed. Feldkirk College and the Univ. of Perugia. Came to the screen in 1966 in THE WITCHES for Visconti and has been seen in THE YOUNG TIGERS (67); THE DAMNED (68); DO YOU KNOW WHAT STALIN DID TO WOMEN (70); DORIAN GRAY (70); THE GARDEN OF THE FINZI-CONTINIS (72); CABARET (72); LUDWIG (73); ASH WEDNESDAY (73); CONVERSATION PIECE (75); THE ROMANTIC ENGLISHWOMAN (75); VICTORY AT ENTEBBE (76); SALON KITTY (77); HEROIN (80); THE COURAGEOUS (83).

CANDICE BERGEN

One of the most attractive actresses to emerge from Hollywood in recent years must be Candice Bergen, who is the daughter of famous ventriloquist/comedian Edgar Bergen. She was born in Beverly Hills, California on 9 May 1946, and her mother was actress Frances Weston. Educated in California, Washington, Switzerland and the Univ. of Pennsylvania, it was at the latter that she made a name for herself in acting, writing and photography. A top model, she made her screen debut in 1966 in THE GROUP and has since been seen in THE SAND PEBBLES (66); THE DAY THE FISH CAME OUT (67); VIVRE POUR VIVRE (67); THE MAGUS (68); THE ADVENTURERS (69); SOLDIER BLUE (69); GETTING STRAIGHT (70); CARNAL KNOWLEDGE (71); THE HUNTING PARTY (71); T.R. BASKIN (72); 11 HARROW HOUSE (74); BITE THE BULLET (75); THE WIND AND THE LION (76). Candice's work as a photo-journalist includes assignments in China with ex-President Nixon, the Masai people of Kenya, an ex-President Ford article at the White House and a profile on Haile Selassie in Ethiopia. Recent movies: A NIGHT FULL OF RAIN (77); THE DOMINO PRINCIPLE (77); OLIVER'S STORY (78); RICH AND FAMOUS (80) and GANDHI (82). Miss Bergen wed French film director Mr Louis Malle at Lugagnac, Southern France, 27.9.80. Her talent as an actress was recognised with an Academy Award nomination for her performance in Alan Pakula's STARTING OVER in 1979. In GANDHI she portrays 'Life' photographer Margaret Bourke White.

INGRID BERGMAN

It is hard to believe that in 1978 Ingrid Bergman was celebrating her 42nd year in the motion-picture industry, having come to the screen in 1936 in her native Sweden, where she was born in Stockholm on 29 August 1915. Her father, Justus Bergman, was Swedish, and her mother, Friedel, German-born. Sadly Miss Bergman's parents died when she was young and she was cared for by an uncle and aunt. Educated at Lyceum, Flickor, it was there that she wrote, directed and appeared in a school play in 1932, and later enrolled at the Royal Dramatic Theatre School, Stockholm. Before the end of her first term, she was selected by Svensk Films for a small role in MUNKBROGREVEN (34). Within 2 years she had appeared in 11 films, starring in 9. Her work in INTERMEZZO (36) brought her to the attention of David O. Selznick who invited her to star in the Hollywood version in 1939. Her radiant performance opposite Leslie Howard made her a world star, and she went on to appear in such movies as RAGE IN HEAVEN, ADAM HAD 4 SONS, DR JEKYLL AND MR HYDE (all 41); ONLY ONE NIGHT (42, Sweden); CASABLANCA, FOR WHOM THE BELL TOLLS (43); GASLIGHT (44); THE BELLS OF ST. MARY'S, SPELLBOUND, SARATOGA TRUNK (45); NOTORIOUS (46); ARCH OF TRIUMPH, JOAN OF ARC (48); UNDER CAPRICORN (49); STROMBOLI (50); EUROPA 51 (51); WE THE WOMEN (53); JOURNEY TO ITALY, JOAN AT THE STAKE, FEAR (54); ANASTASIA (56); PARIS DOES STRANGE THINGS (57); INDISCREET, THE INN OF THE 6TH HAPPINESS (58); GOODBYE AGAIN (61); THE VISIT, THE YELLOW ROLLS-ROYCE (64); FUGITIVE IN VIENNA (67); CACTUS FLOWER (69); A WALK IN THE SPRING RAIN (70); FROM THE MIXED UP FILES OF MRS BASIL E. FRANKWEILER, MURDER ON THE ORIENT EXPRESS (74); A MATTER OF TIME (76). Miss Bergman has wed 3 times: to dentist Dr Petter Lindstrom (md. 1937-50, 1 daughter Pia (born 1938); to film director Roberto Rossellini (1950 — annulled 1957, 1 son Roberto Jr, 1950, and twins, 1952, Isabella, Ingrid, former married to director Martin Scorsese) and to impresario Lars Schmidt 1958 (divorced). She has won Oscars for her work in GASLIGHT (44), ANASTASIA (56) and MURDER ON THE ORIENT EXPRESS (74) and appeared successfully on the Broadway and London stage. Her most recent movies are Ingmar Bergman's AUTUMN SONATA (78) and a T.V. movie, A WOMAN CALLED GOLDA (82), as Golda Meir, winning her an Emmy award.
Miss Bergman died in London on the Sunday evening of August 29, 1982, after a long fight against cancer.
INGRID BERGMAN—AN INTIMATE PORTRAIT by Joseph Henry Steele. W.H. Allen: London, 1960
INGRID BERGMAN—MY STORY by I.B. (with Alan Burgess); Michael Joseph: London; p/b: Sphere, 1981.

RODNEY BEWES

B. Bingley, Yorks, 27.11.37. Was child actor for the BBC, entered R.A.D.A., but called up for Nat. Service in R.A.F., retd. to R.A.D.A., but dismissed after 1 term; went into rep. for 3 yrs. incl. Stockton-on-Tees, Hull, York; London début 1961 at the Comedy in 'A Night Out'. Became very popular on T.V. with his series 'The Likely Lads' (1966-68); 'Dear Mother, Love Albert' (1970-72, also co-wrote, produced) and 'Whatever Happened to the Likely Lads?' (1973). Many films include: BILLY LIAR (63); DECLINE & FALL (68); SPRING & PORT WINE (70); ALICE'S ADVENTURES IN WONDERLAND (72); THE THREE MUSKETEERS (73); THE SPACEMAN & KING ARTHUR (78); SAINT JACK (79); WILDCATS OF ST. TRINIANS (79); Mr Bewes is married to fashion designer Daphne Black; they have 3 sons (triplets) Joe, Tom & Billy and 1 daughter Daisy.

BILL BIXBY

B. San Francisco, 22.1.34. Ed. San Francisco City Coll., Univ. of Calif., Berkeley. A 4th generation San Franciscan, moved to L.A. after college and tour of duty in army. While a lifeguard, an ad. agency executive spotted him and sent Bixby to Detroit where he posed for mags and worked in auto commercials. Studied acting at actors' workshop, an agent got him small roles in movies LONELY ARE THE BRAVE (62); IRMA LA DOUCE (63). Went to Broadway, played in 'Under the Yum Yum Tree' (64) and also film version. Co-starred in popular T.V. series 'My Favourite Martian' (1963-66) and 'The Courtship of Eddie's Father' (1967-72). Movies: RIDE BEYOND VENGEANCE (66); SPINOUT (67); DOCTOR, YOU'VE GOT TO BE KIDDING (67); SPEEDWAY (68); CLAMBAKE (68). Md. Brenda Benet 1971, 1 son Christopher Sean, b. 23.9.74. Other T.V. work includes: 'Congratulations It's A Boy' (1971, T.V. movie), 'The Couple Takes a Wife' (1972, T.V. movie), 'The Invasion of Johnson County' (1976, T.V. movie), 'Rich Man, Poor Man, Book I' (1976, mini-series) and lead in 'The Magician' (1973-74, series). Recent movie: THE APPLE DUMPLING GANG (75). Recent hit series: Dr David Barber in 'The Incredible Hulk' (1978) and films INCREDIBLE HULK — THE MOVIE (79); MURDER IS EASY (T.V. movie, 1982).

JACQUELINE BISSET

Stunningly attractive Jacqueline Bisset has emerged in recent years an international star, appearing in movies in such diverse locales as Paris, Bermuda, Greece, Germany and Korea. Weybridge, Surrey-born, on 13 September 1944, her father, Dr Max Fraser Bisset, a Scotsman, is general practitioner in Reading, while her mother, Arlette, who is French, was a lawyer who escaped the Germans in 1940 by cycling from Paris to the coast and managed to get aboard a British trooper. Young Jackie (who has a brother) studied ballet from the age of 3-16 at a school in Berkshire, completed her education at the French Lycee School in London and at 18 began modelling, working as a waitress to pay her way. She came to the screen in 1964 with small roles in THE KNACK, CUL-DE-SAC (65); CASINO ROYALE (66) and in TWO FOR THE ROAD (67) one critic noted: 'For the 10 minutes she was on the screen nobody noticed the star'. She went to the States and continued her career from there — THE SWEET RIDE, THE DETECTIVE (67); BULLITT, THE FIRST TIME, CAPE TOWN AFFAIR (S. Africa) (68); AIRPORT, L'ECHELLE BLANCHE (69); THE GRASSHOPPER (70); THE MEPHISTO WALTZ, BELIEVE IN ME, SECRETS (71); JUDGE ROY BEAN, STAND UP AND BE COUNTED (72); DAY FOR NIGHT, THE THIEF WHO CAME TO DINNER (73); THE SPIRAL STAIRCASE (74); MURDER ON THE ORIENT EXPRESS (75); ST. IVES, THE SUNDAY WOMAN (76); THE DEEP, THE GREEK TYCOON, TOO MANY CHEFS (77); I LOVE YOU, I LOVE YOU (78); WHEN TIME RAN OUT, INCHON! (79); RICH AND FAMOUS (81); CLASS (82).

KAREN BLACK

One of the top stars to emerge from Hollywood in the 70's is undoubtedly Karen Black and her performance opposite Jack Nicholson in FIVE EASY PIECES in 1969 won her an Oscar nomination. Born Karen Blanche Ziegler in Park Ridge, Illinois on 1 July 1942, her father, Norman, was an engineering sales director, and her mother, Elsie Reif, is author of a number of prize-winning children's books. From an early age she acted in school plays, taking lessons in piano, ballet and singing: at fourteen she was already working in summer stock. Karen majored in drama at Northwestern Univ., joined Hecscher House in New York, appearing in Shakespeare. From 1962 (in 'We're Civilised?') she was on Broadway and in 1965 she won acting nomination in 'The Playroom'. In 1960 she wed Charles Black. She came to the screen in 1967 in YOU'RE A BIG BOY NOW and has been seen in HARD CONTRACT (68); EASY RIDER (69); FIVE EASY PIECES (69, Golden Glove Award); A GUNFIGHT, DRIVE HE SAID, CISCO PIKE, BORN TO WIN (all 71); PORTNOY'S COMPLAINT, THE PYX (72); RHINOCEROS (73); THE OUTFIT, LAW AND DISORDER, THE GREAT GATSBY (74, Golden Globe Award); DAY OF THE LOCUST, NASHVILLE, AIRPORT 75 (75); FAMILY PLOT, CRIME AND PASSION (76); BURNT OFFERINGS, THE STRANGE POSSESSION OF MRS OLIVER (T.V. movie), CAPRICORN ONE (77); THE LAST WORD, IN PRAISE OF OLDER WOMEN, KILLERFISH (78); VALENTINE (79); THE OTHER SIDE OF FEAR (79, T.V. movie) and 'Power' (80, U.S. mini-series). Divorced from her first husband, Miss Black had a short-lived marriage to actor Skip Burton in 1973. She wed Mr Kit Carson, a writer on 4.7.75 and a son, Hunter, was born that year. She has an elder sister who appears in 'Another World' (U.S. T.V. series). Karen's most recent movies are CHANEL SOLITAIRE (80, France); MISS RIGHT (80, Rome) and THE GRASS IS SINGING (81, a Swedish/Zambian co-production); SEPARATE WAYS (81) and BREATHLESS (83).

LINDA BLAIR

B. Westport, Connecticut, Jan. 1959. Came to the screen in 1974 as the devil-possessed Regan in THE EXORCIST (Oscar nom.) and film work has included BORN INNOCENT (74, T.V. movie), AIRPORT 75 (75); SARAH T: PORTRAIT OF A TEENAGE ALCOHOLIC (75, T.V. movie); VICTORY AT ENTEBBE (76); EXORCIST: THE HERETIC (77); ROLLER BOOGIE (79); WILD HORSE HAND (79); HELL NIGHT (81); RUCKUS (81); CHAINED HEAT (83).

ROBERT BLAKE – *see page 123*

COLIN BLAKELEY

B. Bangor, Co. Down, N. Ireland, 23.9.30. Ed. Sedbergh School, Yorks. Worked in father's sports retail business, appd. with Bangor Operatic Soc.; prof. début 1958 with Ulster Group, Belfast; 1st London appearance 1959 at Royal Court and became distinguished stage actor (esp. with Old Vic, R.S.C.) also on Broadway. Came to the screen in SATURDAY NIGHT & SUNDAY MORNING (60) and his many films include: THIS SPORTING LIFE (63); A MAN FOR ALL SEASONS (66); DECLINE & FALL OF A BIRD WATCHER (68); ALFRED THE GREAT (68); THE PRIVATE LIFE OF SHERLOCK HOLMES (69, as Dr Watson); YOUNG WINSTON (71); NATIONAL HEALTH (73); MURDER ON THE ORIENT EXPRESS (74); IT SHOULDN'T HAPPEN TO A VET (76); EQUUS (76, also stage). Md. actress Margaret Whiting, 3 sons (incl. twins). Many T.V. appearances incl. 'Donkey's Years' (1979). Recent movies: THE BIG SLEEP (77); NIJINSKY (79); THE DAY CHRIST DIED (T.V. movie), THE DOGS OF WAR, LITTLE LORD FAUNTLEROY (all 80); 'Red Monarch' (T.V. 83), 'King Lear' (T.V. 83, as Kent).

BRIAN BLESSED

B. Mexborough, Yorks., 9.10.37. Father a miner. Several jobs, incl. steeplejack, Nat. Serv. RAF Parachute Reg.; studied Bristol Old Vic, 4 yrs. rep.; big break in 'Z Cars' 1961 T.V. Much theatre and T.V. Films: COUNTRY DANCE (69); A LAST VALLEY (69); THE TROJAN WOMEN (71); HENRY VIII & HIS 6 WIVES (73); MAN OF LAMANCHA (73). Md. 1. Anne Bomann (div.), 1 daughter Catherine, 2. Hildegard Neil, 1 daughter Rosalind. Mr Blessed appeared in show, 'Cats' (81-83); other movies: FLASH GORDON (79); HIGH ROAD TO CHINA, HOUND OF THE BASKERVILLES
(both 83).

CLAIRE BLOOM

B. London, 15.2.31. Ed. Badminton School, Bristol; Fern Hill Manor, New Milton; studied at Guildhall School with Eileen Thorndike, Central School. Aged 15 joined Oxford Rep., 2 yrs. later was at Stratford-on-Avon playing Ophelia opp. Paul Scofield in 'Hamlet'. Claire came to the screen in 1948 and has been seen in THE BLIND GODDESS (48); LIMELIGHT (52); INNOENTS IN PARIS (52); THE MAN BETWEEN (53); RICHARD III (56); ALEXANDER THE GREAT (56); BROTHERS OF KARAMAZOV (58); LOOK BACK IN ANGER (59); THE BUCCANEER (59); THE CHAPMAN REPORT (61); THE WONDERFUL WORLD OF THE BROTHERS GRIMM (63); 80,000 SUSPECTS (63); THE HAUNTING (63); THE OUTRAGE (64); HIGH INFIDELITY (65); THE SPY WHO CAME IN FROM THE COLD (66); CHARLY (68); 3 INTO 2 WON'T GO (69); THE ILLUSTRATED MAN (69); A SEVERED HEAD (69); RED SKY AT MORNING (71); A DOLL'S HOUSE (73). Md. 1. Rod Steiger 1959 (div.), 1 daughter Anna Justine (b. 1960), 2. Hilliard Elkins 1969 (div.). Miss Bloom has appeared on Broadway and T.V. with equal success. More recent work: ISLANDS IN THE STREAM (75); 'Brideshead Revisited' (T.V. ser., 82); 'These Are Women' (82, stage).

LIMELIGHT & AFTER: THE EDUCATION OF AN ACTRESS (autobio.); Weidenfeld & Nicholson: London, 1982.

DIRK BOGARDE

Although still involved as an actor in European films Dirk Bogarde has emerged as a major literary talent in recent years, penning two highly entertaining autobiographies and a first novel. He comes from an artistic family — his father, Ulrich, was art editor of the London Times, his mother Margaret a former actress. He was born Derek Van Den Bogaerde at Hampstead, N. London on 28 March 1921, and educated at the Allen Glens College, Glasgow, Univ. College, London and Chelsea Polytechnic, studying commercial art and scenic design. In 1939 he worked backstage at London's Embassy Theatre and later the 'Q' Theatre, earning 7/6d a week as teamaker/carpenter. An actor fell ill and young Bogarde replaced him. He then worked as an actor with the Amersham Rep. for a season. After serving his country with distinction in the Army during World War II, the actor managed to get a good role in the play 'Power Without Glory' at Notting Hill's Lindsay Theatre, was duly signed to a Rank Organisation movie contract and for the next 20 years remained one of Britain's most popular film actors. His movies include: ESTHER WATERS (47, début); QUARTET (48); SO LONG AT THE FAIR (49); DOCTOR IN THE HOUSE (53, a great success); SIMBA (54); THE SLEEPING TIGER (54); CAST A DARK SHADOW (55); THE SPANISH GARDENER (56); A TALE OF TWO CITIES (58); SONG WITHOUT END (60, as Lizst); VICTIM (61); I COULD GO ON SINGING (63); THE SERVANT (63); KING AND COUNTRY (64); DARLING (65); ACCIDENT (67) and OUR MOTHER'S HOUSE (67). In 1969 Mr Bogarde went to reside in France and had success in two pictures directed by Visconti: THE DAMNED (69) and DEATH IN VENICE (70). During the war he was involved with the Royal Corps of Signals, was Brigade Intelligence Officer at 2nd Army HQ as Air Photographic Interpreter working on D-Day strategy and later served in Malaya and Java. He won Best Actor awards for his work in the films THE SERVANT and DARLING from the British Film Academy. Dirk Bogarde's most recent films are PROVIDENCE (76); A BRIDGE TOO FAR (77); DESPAIR (78) and THE PATRICIA NEAL STORY (81, T.V. movie).

THE FILMS OF DIRK BOGARDE by Margaret Hinxman and Susan D'Arcy. LSP Books: London, 1974.
A POSTILLION STRUCK BY LIGHTNING by Dirk Bogarde. Chatto and Windus: London, 1977; pb: Triad/Panther 1978.
SNAKES AND LADDERS by Dirk Bogarde. Chatto and Windus: London, 1978; pb: Triad/Granada, 1979.
A GENTLE OCCUPATION — A novel by Dirk Bogarde. Chatto and Windus: London, 1980.
VOICES IN THE GARDEN (novel); Chatto and Windus: London, 1981. p/b: Granada, 1983.
AN ORDERLY MAN (autobio.); Chatto & Windus Ltd., The Hogarth Press: London, 1983.

FLORINDA BOLKAN

B. Ceara, Brazil, 15.2.41(?); real name Florinda Soares Bulcao; of Portuguese, French, Italian and Brazilian Indian extraction. Her father was a poet who died when she was young. Florinda worked in public relations for an airline in Brazil, a plane crash she nearly caught made her leave, she went to Paris and studied at Sorbonne and Ecole des Arts. By chance on the Isle of Ischia she was discovered by Luchino Visconti who gave her a screen test. Films include: CANDY (68); ONE NIGHT AT DINNER (68); THE LAST VALLEY (69); THE DAMNED (70); THE ANONYMOUS VENETIAN (71); ROMANCE (71); A MAN TO RESPECT (72); ROYAL FLASH (75); A BRIEF VACATION (75); FLAVIA (77); THE WORD (79, U.S. T.V. mini-series).

JAMES BOOTH

B. Croydon, Surrey, 19.12.33; real name James Geeves-Booth. Ed. Southend Grammar School. Father was a probation officer. 4 yrs. with firm selling min. ore; s'ship to R.A.D.A. Wife Paula Delaney gave him 1st pro. job at New Lindsay Theatre, Notting Hill 1950; Old Vic, West End, Joan Littlewood's Theatre Workshop ('Fings Ain't Wot They Used t'Be' esp.). Movies include: IN THE NICK (59); TRIALS OF OSCAR WILDE (60); THE HELLIONS (61); IN THE DOG HOUSE (62); SPARROWS CAN'T SING (63); ZULU (64); SECRET OF MY SUCCESS (65); ROBBERY (67); MAN WHO HAD POWER OVER WOMEN (70); MACHO CALLAHAN (71); THAT'LL BE THE DAY (74); moved to U.S. mid-1970s: MURDER IN PEYTON PLACE (T.V. movie), AIRPORT 77 (77); WHEELS, EVENING IN BYZANTIUM (both mini-ser., 1978); ZORRO — THE GAY BLADE (81).

ERNEST BORGNINE

B. Hamden, Connecticut, 24.1.17. Mother, Anna, an aristocratic Italian (grandfather was advisor to King Victor Emmanuel), father, Charles, metallurgist. Ed. New Haven, appd. school plays. Truck driver; in U.S. Navy 1935-45, during WWII as C.P.O. Gunners Mate; under the G.I. Bill studied to be actor at the Randall School of D.A., Hartford; did stock, joined Barter Theatre in Virginia, spotted in 'Harvey' play by Brock Pemberton and did the play on Broadway, plus 'Hamlet', 'Mrs McThing' (1952, with Helen Hayes); Md: 1. Rhoda Kemins, a nurse, 1949-58, 1 daughter Nancy b. 1953. Mr Borgnine came to the screen 1951 in WHISTLE AT ETON FALLS. Other movies include: REMEMBER THAT FACE (51); FROM HERE TO ETERNITY (53); THE BOUNTY HUNTER (54); BAD DAY AT BLACK ROCK (54); MARTY (55, Academy Award Best Actor); JUBAL (56); THE BEST THINGS IN LIFE ARE FREE (56); THE VIKINGS (58); TORPEDO RUN (58); PAY OR DIE (60); SUMMER OF THE SEVENTEENTH DOLL (61); THE DIRTY DOZEN (67); ICE STATION ZEBRA (68); HANNIE CAULDER (71). Md. 2. Katy Jurado, actress, 31.12.59-June 1963, 3. Ethel Merman, June 1964, but div. after 5 months, 4. Donna Rancourt (1966-72), 1 son Christopher 1966, 1 daughter Sharon 1967. Mr Borgnine had his own T.V. series 'McHale's Navy' from 1962-66. 5th wife is Norwegian, Toke, wed Nov. 1972. Recent movies: CONVOY (77); THE DOUBLE McGUFFIN (78); WHEN TIME RAN OUT (79); BLACK HOLE (79); ALL QUIET ON THE WESTERN FRONT (79); SUPER FUZZ (79); ESCAPE FROM NEW YORK, HIGH RISK, DEADLY BLESSING (all 1981); THE GRADUATES OF MALIBU HIGH (82).

DAVID BOWIE

B. London, 8.1.47; real name David Jones. Started his musical career playing tenor sax in school band aged 15. A year later he joined progressive blues group 'The Lower Third', then went solo with acoustic guitar. For 2 yrs. he was involved with Buddhism, also wrote and performed in a mime company. In 1969 started an arts lab. in Beckenham and album 'Space Oddity' was an international hit; further hit albums include: 'The Man Who Sold the World (1970); 'Hunky Dory' (1971); 'The Rise & Fall of Ziggy Stardust and the Spiders from Mars' (1972) and 'Aladdin Sane' ('73). He came to the screen in 1969 in VIRGIN SOLDIERS and has been seen in THE MAN WHO FELL TO EARTH (75); JUST A GIGOLO (78); THE HUNGER, 'Baal' (T.V., both 1982); MERRY CHRISTMAS, MR LAWRENCE (83); stage '80: 'Elephant Man' (U.S.).
DAVID BOWIE: IN HIS OWN WORDS; Omnibus Press: London, 1980; Large p/b; *DAVID BOWIE BLACK BOOK* by Barry Miles; Omnibus Press: London, 1980; Large p/b; *BOWIE AN ILLUSTRATED RECORD* by Roy Carr & Charles Shaar Murray; Eel Pie Publishers: N.Y., 1981.

RICHARD BOONE

B. Los Angeles, Calif. 18.6.17. Ed. Stanford Univ. 1934, in boxing team 1936-37, expelled after rag-day joke!. Worked S. Calif. oilfields unsuccessful painter (Md. 1. Jane Hopper (div.) and short story writer; WWII naval crackshot won competitions, 4 yrs. aerial gunner in South Pacific; through G.I. Bill after war studied at Actors' Studio, joined Neighbourhood Playhouse and appeared Broadway in 'Medea' (1947) (u/stud. Gielgud); 'The Man', 'The Hasty Heart', 'Macbeth'; Md. 2. singer Mimi Kelly (1949-51). Came to screen in 1951 in HALLS OF MONTEZUMA Movies include: THE DESERT FOX (51). RED SKIES OF MONTANA (52); VICKI (53); THE ROBE (53); DRAGNET (54); MAN WITHOUT A STAR (54); AWAY ALL BOATS (56); LIZZIE (57); THE ALAMO (60); RIO CONCHOS (64); THE WAR LORD (66); THE ARRANGEMENT (69); THE KREMLIN LETTER (70). Mr Boone became well-known on T.V. for the series: 'Medic' (1954-56); 'Have Gun, Will Travel' (1957-63) and 'Hec Ramsey' (1972-74). In recent years he had been cultural ambassador of Florida. He had retired to the State to return to his first artistic interest—painting. *Mr Boone, 5 times Oscar-nominated, died of throat cancer on January 11, 1981, at St. Augustine, Florida. He leaves a widow, Claire, whom he wed in 1951, and their son, Peter, born 1953.*

TIMOTHY BOTTOMS

B. Santa Barbara, Calif., 30.8.51; Father, James 'Bud' Bottoms, taught art at Santa Barbara High School, where Timothy and younger brothers Joseph, Sam and Ben were educated. Tim as a youngster was interested in acting—in 1967 toured Europe with the Santa Barbara Madrigal Soc. and played in local productions of 'West Side Story' and 'Romeo and Juliet'. In the latter, discovered by talent scout and came to the screen 1970 in JOHNNY GOT HIS GUN and has since been seen in THE LAST PICTURE SHOW (71); LOVE, PAIN & THE WHOLE DAMN THING (72); THE PAPER CHASE (73); OPERATION DAYBREAK (74); THE WHITE DAWN (74); THE CRAZY WORLD OF JULIUS VROODER (74); MONEY CHANGERS (76, T.V. movie); A SMALL TOWN IN TEXAS (76); ROLLER-COASTER (77); THE OTHER SIDE OF THE MOUNTAIN: PART II, HURRICANE (both 78); FIRST HELLO (79); Md: Alicia Cory, 1 son Bartholomew (b. 77); HIGH COUNTRY, EAST OF EDEN (mini-ser, both 81); TIN MAN (83).

Brother Joseph (b. 22.4.54) has been in such movies as THE DOVE (74); HOLOCAUST (mini-ser., 1977); HIGH ROLLING, THE BLACK HOLE, CLOUD DANCER (both 1979); KING OF THE MOUNTAIN (81).

JUDI BOWKER

B. Shawford, Hampshire, 6.4.54. At the age of 15, while at ballet school, a photo of her appeared in 'The Daily Telegraph Magazine', which was shown by a theatrical agent to Mr Franco Zeffirelli, the director, who subsequently gave her the role of Sister Clare in his movie BROTHER SUN, SISTER MOON (69); T.V. includes 'Black Beauty' (regular, as Vicky), 'South Riding', 'The Glittering Prizes', more recently Eileen in 'Wilfred and Eileen' (81) and 'Little Miss Perkins' (82); Judi also played with National Theatre, in the movie EAST OF ELEPHANT ROCK (76) and co-starred as Andromeda in CLASH OF THE TITANS (81).

PETER BOWLES

B. London, 16.10.36. Brought up in Nottingham, father a Rolls Royce engineer. Ed. Nottingham High Pavement Grammar School. Has always wanted to act, at school excelled at verse speaking and plays. Won scholarship to R.A.D.A. at 16, an actor at 18 with Old Vic, then rep. and 1959 joined Bristol Old Vic Co., particular success in 'Happy Haven' which came to London. For several years a familiar face on T.V., made motion picture début in 1963 in small role in LIVE NOW, PAY LATER. Md. Susan Bennett (met her at R.A.D.A.), 1 daughter Sacha, 2 sons Guy & Adam. Movies include: THE YELLOW ROLLS-ROYCE (63); INFORMERS (64); BLOW-UP (66), CHARGE OF THE LIGHT BRIGADE (68); LAUGHTER IN THE DARK (69); EYE WITNESS (70); ENDLESS NIGHT (71); A DAY IN THE DEATH OF JOE EGG (72); THE OFFENCE (72); FOR THE LOVE OF BENJI (75); THE DISAPPEARANCE (77). Much T.V. includes 'The Crezz', 'Rumpole of the Bailey', 'Only When I Laugh' and opposite Penelope Keith in the highly popular 'To the Manor Born' (BBC 1979 & 1980) as Richard de Vere; recently in 'Vice Versa' (81); 'The Bounder' (82); 'The Irish R.M.' (83).

PETER BOYLE

B. Philadelphia, Pa. . . . 37. After receiving his education at La Salle College, he joined the Christian Brothers order as a monk but renounced in the early 60s and went to N.Y. Acted on Broadway in 'The Thick Ear' (1964), in off-Broadway prods. and joined The Second City in Chicago. In 1970 appeared on CBS T.V. in 'Comedy Tonight' and came to the screen in JOE. Movies: T.R. BASKIN (72); THE CANDI-DATE (73); STEELYARD BLUES (73); SLITHER (73); THE FRIENDS OF EDDIE COYLE (73); KID BLUE (73); CRAZY JOE (74); YOUNG FRANKENSTEIN (74, as the monster); THE SWASHBUCKLER (75); TAIL GUNNER JOE (76, T.V. movie, as Joseph McCarthy), TAXI DRIVER(76), F.I.S.T. (77), THE BRINK'S JOB (78), BEYOND THE POSEIDON ADVENTURE, IN GOD WE TRUST, WHERE THE BUFFALO ROAM (all 79); OUTLAND (81); HAMMETT (82); YELLOWBEARD (83).

NEVILLE BRAND

B. Kewanee, Ill., 13.8.21. The fourth most deco-rated U.S. serviceman in WWII. Ed. High School, Kewanee; went straight into the U.S. army, serving from 1936-46. Upon discharge decided to become an actor and studied in New York. Came to the screen in D.O.A. (Dead on Arrival) in 1949. He has played in many movies, mostly in formidable roles: HALLS OF MONTEZUMA (51); STALAG 17 (53); RIOT IN CELL BLOCK 11 (54); MOHAWK (55); LOVE ME TENDER (56); THE TIN STAR (57); CRY TERROR (58); THE SCARFACE MOB (59, as Al Capone); THE BIRDMAN OF ALCA-TRAZ (62, as the warder); THAT DARN CAT (65); THE TRAIN ROBBERS (73); SCALA-WAG (74); PSYCHIC THRILLER (75). Is married; appd. on Broadway 1962 in 'Night Life' and a familiar face on T.V. as guest star in such series as 'General Electric Theatre', 'The Un-touchables' (1959-64 often, as Al Capone) and his own Western series 'Laredo', as Reese Bennett (1962-65). Recent movies: EATEN ALIVE (77); HI-RIDERS (78); THE NINTH CON-FIGURATION, WITHOUT WARNING, ANGELS BRIGADE (all 1980).

WILFRED BRAMBELL

B. Dublin, 22.3.12. Ed. Kingstown Grammar School. Reporter with Irish Times 9 yrs. As a child entertained war wounded, joined famed Dublin Gate & Abbey Theatres. Has appd. extensively in rep., West End, tours, radio & T.V.; became household name in T.V. series 'Steptoe & Son' (1964) and 2 film spin-offs. Usually plays cameos in films. Movies include: ANOTHER SHORE (48); DRY ROT (56); SERIOUS CHARGE (58); WHAT A WHOP-PER(61); IN SEARCH OF THE CASTAWAYS (62); THREE LIVES OF THOMASINA (63), A HARD DAY'S NIGHT (64); CROOKS IN CLOISTER (64); WHERE THE BULLETS FLY (66); WITCHFINDER GENERAL (68); CASANOVA (70); STEPTOE & SON (72); STEPTOE & SON RIDE AGAIN (74); HIGH RISE DONKEY (79). Has played on Broadway in 'Kelly' (1965) and 'The Canterbury Tales (68). T.V. '82: 'Island of Adventure'.
ALL ABOVE BOARD by Wilfred Brambell. W.H. Allen: London, 1976.

BERNARD BRESSLAW

B. London, 25.2.34. The son of an East London tailor's presser, Mr Bresslaw studied for the stage at R.A.D.A.; Nat. Serv. clerk and driver in R.A.S.C.; got his break after working in the theatre, including West End début in 'The McRoary Whirl', in the 50s, becoming well-known on T.V. as the dopey private Popplewell in 'The Army Game' series, in 1957-58. Came to the screen in 1954 in MEN OF SHERWOOD FOREST and the 6'6" tall actor has been seen in dozens of movies including UP IN THE WORLD (56); I ONLY ARSKED (59, film version of his 'Army Game' T.V. success); TOO MANY CROOKS(58); THE UGLY DUCKLING (59); CARRY ON COWBOY (66); CARRY ON SCREAMING (66); MOON ZERO TWO (69); UP POMPEII (70); VAMPIRA (74); ONE OF OUR DINOSAURS IS MISSING (74). Mr Bresslaw is married with 3 sons. He had his own show on T.V. and recently appeared in the movies HAWK THE SLAYER (80); KRULL (83).

MARLON BRANDO

Now in his 31st year as a motion-picture actor, this highly controversial, enigmatic and oft-mimmicked actor has remained at the top of his professsion through selecting roles in such landmark movies as LAST TANGO IN PARIS, THE GODFATHER and APOCALYPSE NOW. His stage and film performances of the 1940's and 1950's are much-remembered by his fellow-performers, critics and public, acknowledged to be the best of their kind. Born Marlon 'Bud' Brando at Omaha, Nebraska on 3 April 1924, the son of Marlon Brando Sr. and wife Dorothy, the family moved to Evanston, and a little later to Libertyville, Illinois. Young Marlon entered Shattuck Military Academy at Faribault, Minnesota, but left at 18 because he didn't like the discipline. Employed as a mason for 2 months, he decided to become an actor and went to New York, living with sister Frances (an artist) in Greenwich Village. A year's study with Dramatic Workshop followed by a season of stock at Sayville, Long Island lead to him being discovered by an agent and cast in I REMEMBER MAMA on Broadway in 1944. There he played in 'Candida', 'A Flag is Born' and 'Truckline Cafe' (a great success in latter — all 1946), opposite Tallulah Bankhead in 'The Eagle has Two Heads' (1947) and was selected by Elia Kazan to appear in 'A Streetcar Named Desire' (1947). His motion pictures: THE MEN (50, debut); A STREETCAR NAMED DESIRE (51); VIVA ZAPATA (52); JULIUS CAESAR (53, as Mark Antony); THE WILD ONE (53); ON THE WATERFRONT (54, Academy Award — Best Actor); DESIREE (54, as Napoleon); GUYS AND DOLLS (55); THE TEAHOUSE OF THE AUGUST MOON (56); SAYONARA (57); THE YOUNG LIONS (58); THE FUGITIVE KIND (60); ONE-EYED JACKS (60, also directed); MUTINY ON THE BOUNTY (62); THE UGLY AMERICAN (63); BEDTIME STORY (64); THE SABOTEUR (65); THE CHASE (66); THE APPALOOSA (66); A COUNTESS FROM HONG KONG (67); REFLECTIONS IN A GOLDEN EYE (67); CANDY (68); THE NIGHT OF THE FOLLOWING DAY (68); QUEIMADA (70); THE NIGHTCOMERS (71); THE GODFATHER (72, Academy Award); THE LAST TANGO IN PARIS (73); THE MISSOURI BREAKS (76); SUPERMAN (as Jor-El, Superman's father), APOCALYPSE NOW (77); THE FORMULA (80). Mr. Brando has been wed three times, to: Anna Kashfi (1957-1960, 1 son Christian); Movita Castaneda, actress (1960-1962, 1 son Miko, 1960, 1 daughter Rebecca, 1961, 1 son Tehoto, 1961); Tarita (1962, 1 daughter, Cheyenne, 1970, div. 1972). As well as winning Oscars, he has been nominated on five other occasions. BRANDO by Chas. Hamblett; p/b; 1962; BRANDO by Joe Morella & Edw. Z. Epstein; Thomas Nelson, 1973; BRANDO by Bob Thomas; W.H. Allen, 1973; BRANDO by Rene Jordan; p/b; Pyramid/W.H. Allen, 1973; BRANDO by Ron Offer; Henry Regnery (Chicago), 1973; FILMS OF MARLON BRANDO by Tony Thomas; Citadel (U.S.A), 1974; BRANDO by David Shipman; MacMillan, 1975; THE BRANDO I KNEW by Carlo Fiore; Granada, 1976; MARLON BRANDO by Alan Frank; Galley Press, 1982.

BEAU BRIDGES

B. Hollywood, Calif., 9.12.41. Eldest of Lloyd Bridges' two sons; real name Lloyd Vernet Bridges. Ed. U.C.L.A.; Univ. of Hawaii. Came to the screen as child actor in FORCE OF EVIL (48); RED PONY (48); and ZAMBA THE GORILLA (49); then university and many T.V. roles ('Ben Casey' etc.) and regular in series 'Ensign O'Toole' (1962-63). Returned to screen in THE INCI-DENT (67) and his many movies include: FOR LOVE OF IVY (68); GAILY, GAILY (69); THE CHRISTIAN LICORICE STORE (71); CHILD'S PLAY (72); HAMMERSMITH IS OUT (72); YOUR 3 MINUTES ARE UP(73); LOVING MOLLY (73); THE OTHER SIDE OF THE MOUNTAIN (75); DRAGONFLY (76); SWASHBUCKLER(76); TWO-MINUTE WARNING (76); GREASED LIGHTNING (77); SHIMMERING LIGHT (78); THE RUNNER STUMBLES (78); THE FIFTH MUSKETEER (78); NORMA RAE (79); HONKY TONK FREEWAY (80); NIGHT CROSSING (81). Beau has played in 'All My Sons' on stage; opposite his father on Broadway in 'Where's Daddy?' (1966). Further T.V. work includes a series, 'Married' (79); THE CHILD STEALER (T.V. movie, 1977); recent movies: HEART LIKE A WHEEL, WITNESS FOR THE PROSECUTION (T.V. movie, both 1982).

JEFF BRIDGES

B. Los Angeles, Calif., 4.12.49. Youngest of Lloyd Bridges' sons. When a youngster appeared in his father's T.V. series on several occasions, also, aged 14, toured with him in 'Anniversary Waltz'. Coached in drama by Uta Hagen in New York, coming to the screen in 1970 in HALLS OF ANGER, he has since been seen in THE LAST PICTURE SHOW (71, Oscar nom.); FAT CITY (71); BAD COMPANY (72); THE LOLLY-MADONNA WAR (73); THE LAST AMERICAN HERO (73); THE ICEMAN COMETH (73); THUNDERBOLT & LIGHT-FOOT (74, Oscar nom.); RANCHO DELUXE, HEARTS OF THE WEST (both 1975); KING KONG, STAY HUNGRY (both 1976); HUR-RICANE, SOMEBODY KILLED HER HUSBAND (both 1978); WINTER KILLS (79); AMERICAN SUCCESS COMPANY (80); HEAVEN'S GATE, TRON, CUTTER'S WAY (all 1981); KISS ME GOODBYE (82). Jeff's a song-writer, is wed to Susan (1 daughter, Belle).

EILEEN BRENNAN – *see page 123*

LLOYD BRIDGES

B. San Leandro, Calif., 15.1.13. Ed. U.C.L.A. Original intention to become lawyer, but got interested in drama at univ. Appeared in summer stock and Broadway, latter included 'Othello', 'Good and Evil' (both 1937), 'Audition of the Apprentice Theatre' (1939), 'Susannah & the Elders (1940). Played opp. actress Dorothy Simpson and they wed 1938. Seen by a Columbia talent scout and from 1941 he appeared until 1944 in 28 movies at that studio continuously including HERE COMES MR JORDAN (41); STAND BY ALL NETWORKS (42); THE HEAT'S ON (43); LOUISIANA HAYRIDE (44). Other movies include: CANYON PASSAGE (46); SECRET SERVICE INVESTIGATOR (48); MOONRISE (49); HOME OF THE BRAVE (49); LITTLE BIG HORN (51); HIGH NOON (52); PLYMOUTH ADVENTURE (52); THE TALL TEXAN (53); APACHE WOMAN (55); WETBACKS (56); THE RAINMAKER (56); THE GODDESS (58); AROUND THE WORLD UNDER THE SEA (66); ATTACK ON THE IRON COAST (68); THE LOVE WAR (70, T.V. movie); TO FIND A MAN (72); HAUNTS OF THE VERY RICH (72, T.V. movie); RUNNING WILD (73). A very popular actor on American T.V. Mr Bridges' work in this medium includes guesting in 'The Bigelow Theatre' (1950); 'Footlights Theatre' (1952); 'Kraft Suspense Theatre' (1964); Wild Bill Hickok in 'Wild Bill Hickok—the Legend & The Man' (1964); 'Roots' (1977) and his own series: 155 episodes as Mike Nelson in 'Sea Hunt' (1958); 'The Lloyd Bridges Show' (1962-63); 'The Loner' (1965); 'San Francisco International Airport' (1970-71) and 'Joe Forrester' (1975). His successful marriage has produced 2 sons, Beau & Jeff (q.v.)—both actors, and a daughter, Lucinda (b. 1953). Recent movies: STOWAWAY TO THE MOON (77, T.V. movie); SHIMMERING LIGHT (78); DISASTER ON THE COASTLINER (79, T.V. movie); BEAR ISLAND (79); MISSION GALACTICA: THE CYCLON ATTACK (79); AIRPLANE! (80); MOVIOLA: THIS YEAR'S BLONDE (80, T.V. movie); EAST OF EDEN (81, mini-ser.); AIRPLANE II: THE SEQUEL (82); THE GRACE KELLY STORY (83, T.V. movie).

JAMES BROLIN

B. Los Angeles, Calif., 18.7.40.; real name James Bruderlin. Father, Henry Bruderlin, was a building contractor. Aged 15, did studio tour and wanted to be in films. In acting class at High School and U.C.L.A., did plays in evenings, took part-time jobs to pay for acting tuition, including work at dad's construction firm. 1st acting job on T.V.'s 'Bus Stop', started in small roles in movies such as GIDGET (59); TAKE HER, SHE'S MINE (63); GOODBYE CHARLIE (64); JOHN GOLDFARB, PLEASE COME HOME (65); VON RYAN'S EXPRESS (65); FANTASTIC VOYAGE (66); contracted to Fox, then Universal. Md. Jane Agee 1966, who was casting director at Fox for 'Batman' series, in which James appeared: 2 sons, Joss & Jess, born 1968 & 1972. Other movies: CAPETOWN AFFAIR (68, S. Africa); THE BOSTON STRANGLER (68); SKYJACKED (72); WESTWORLD (73); GABLE & LOMBARD (75, as Gable); THE CAR (77); CAPRICORN ONE (77); STEEL COWBOY (78, T.V. movie); NIGHT OF THE JUGGLER (78); THE AMITYVILLE HORROR (79); HIGH RISK (80). Mr Brolin won a U.S. T.V. Emmy award for 'Outstanding performance by an actor in a supporting role in drama' in 1970 for his portrayal of Dr Kiley in 'Marcus Welby, M.D.'; WHITE WATER (T.V. movie, 1982).

JIM BROWN

B. St. Simons Island, New York, 17.2.36. Ed. Manhasset High School; Syracuse University. For 9 yrs. played American football with the Cleveland Browns and in 1964 was voted Professional Athlete of the Year, that year coming to the screen in RIO CONCHOS. Has been seen in THE DIRTY DOZEN (67); ICE STATION ZEBRA (68); 100 RIFLES (69); TICK, TICK, TICK (70); THE GRASSHOPPER (70); EL CONDOR (70); KENNER (71); SLAUGHTER (72); BLACK GUN (72); SLAUGHTER'S BIG RIP-OFF (73); I ESCAPED FROM DEVIL'S ISLAND (73); THE SLAMS (74); THREE THE HARD WAY (74); TAKE A HARD RIDE (75). Mr Brown founded the Black Economic Union, has several business interests. KID VENGEANCE, FINGERS (both 1977); ONE DOWN, TWO TO GO (82).

CHARLES BRONSON

For Charles Bronson the road to movie stardom has been long, but no one deserves success more than the granit featured actor, one of the few male super-stars to emerge from Hollywood in the 1970s. He was born Charles Denr Bunchinsky on 3 November 1921 in the small mining community of Ehrenfield, Pennsylvania. His family was very poo his father, Walter, a Lithuanian of Russian descent. Charles, the fifth son of a large family, was educated in the loc school and South Fork High School. He took a succession of jobs — miner, then drafted into the U.S. Army in 1943 tail-gunner on a B-29 seeing action on 25 missions, in 1946 discharged and went to New York, then Philadelphia a under the G.I. Bill of Rights studied at the Hussain Art School, there he got his first taste of theatre working backsta and playing walk-on roles. During the summer months he worked in several jobs in Atlantic City, working as deck-ch attendant and barker. In September 1948 he went to New York with a struggling actor, Jack Klugman, they worked postmen and in small roles on the stage. On 30 September 1949 Bronson wed Harriet Tendler, moved to California a studied at the Pasadena Playhouse, making one of his earliest screen appearances YOU'RE IN THE NAVY NO' (51, billed as Charles Buchinski). Throughout the 1950s he was in dozens of T.V. programmes and movies supporting roles, from 1954 in DRUM BEAT onwards he was billed as Bronson. In 1958/1959 he starred in his ov T.V. series, 'Man With a Camera' and from 1961 in THE MAGNIFICENT SEVEN, giving a typically rugged y likeable performance, his movie success was assured. His many films include: THE GREAT ESCAPE (63); TH SANDPIPER (65); THE DIRTY DOZEN (67); TWINKY (69); RED SUN (71); THE MECHANIC (7 VALACHI PAPERS (72); MR MAJESTYK (73); DEATH WISH (74); THE STREETFIGHTER (75 BREAKHEART PASS (76); RAID ON ENTEBBE (77); WHITE BUFFALO (77); TELEFON (77). From h first marriage, he has 2 children: Suzanne Frances (born 27.2.55) and Anthony Charles (born 19.2.61). On 5.10.68 wed British actress Jill Ireland and a daughter, Zuleika Jill, was born 4.8.71. Other films: CABO BLANC(BORDERLINE (both 79); DEATH HUNT (80); DEATH WISH II (82); 10 TO MIDNIGHT (83). CHARLE BRONSON: SUPERSTAR by Stephen Whitney; Robert Hale: London, 1978; p/b: Dell: N.Y., 1975; Corone London, 1980; BRONSON! by W.A. Harbinson; W.H. Allen: London, 1976; THE FILMS OF CHARLE BRONSON by Jerry Vermilye; Citadel; Secaucus: N.J., 1980; BRONSON by David Downing; W.H. Allen: Londo

198

MEL BROOKS

B. Brooklyn, N.Y., 28.6.26; real name Melvin Kaminsky. As a youngster did impersonations, was pianist and drummer. Made a name as writer, especially on Broadway: 'New Faces of '52' (1952, also acted); 'Once Over Lightly' (1952); 'Shinbone Alley' (1957); 'All American' (1962). Md. 1. Florence Baum 1950, 1 daughter Stephanie, b. 1951, 2 sons Nicholas b. 1952, Edward b. 1953. Other work as writer includes Sid Caesar's 'Broadway Review' and 'Your Show of Shows' (latter great success of early 1950s T.V., contributing with Neil Simon, Woody Allen & others) and (with Buck Henry) the 007 spoof series 'Get Smart' (1965-70). Md. 2. actress Anne Bancroft (q.v.) 1964, 1 son Maximilian b. 1972. Mr Brooks 1st movie was NEW FACES (54) which he wrote. In the 60s & 70s made several spoof successes: THE PRODUCERS (67, wrote-produced-directed); THE 12 CHAIRS (70, wrote-directed); BLAZING SADDLES (74, acted-directed-co-scripted); YOUNG FRANKEN-STEIN (75, directed-co-scripted); SILENT MOVIE (76, starred-directed-co-wrote-produced); HIGH ANXIETY (77, starred-produced-directed-co-wrote-composed/sung title song). Recent: MUPPET MOVIE (guest, 79); HISTORY OF THE WORLD: PART 1 (81, star/dir.); TO BE OR NOT TO BE (83, star/prod.). COMIC ART OF MEL BROOKS by Maurice Yacowar; W.H. Allen: London, 1982.

CORAL BROWNE

B. Melbourne, Australia, 23.7.13. Ed. Melbourne. Stage début Australia 1931; London 1934 became very distinguished stage actress, West End, Shakespearean roles, tours, Broadway. Md. 1. Philip Pearman (dec.). Occasional movies: THE AMATEUR GENTLEMAN (36); BLACK LIMELIGHT (38); LET GEORGE DO IT (40); PICCADILLY INCIDENT (46); AUNTIE MAME (58); ROMAN SPRING OF MRS STONE (61); DR. CRIPPEN (63); NIGHT OF THE GENERALS (66); KILLING OF SISTER GEORGE (68); THE RULING CLASS (71); THEATRE OF BLOOD (73); DROWNING POOL (75). Md. 2. Mr Vincent Price (q.v.) 1974, with whom she appd. in T.V. series 'Time Express' in 1979; 'An Englishman Abroad' (B.B.C. 1983).

YUL BRYNNER

Although affectionately recognised by millions universally for his King of Siam role, essayed so magnificently on screen and (since 1951) on stage, the career and work of Yul Brynner has revealed many talents in various categories of show-business. He was born on Sakhalin Island (north of Japan, now in the USSR) on 11 July 1915. Biographical sources state his father was a Manchurian mining engineer, his mother a Romany gypsy. 'Youl' is Mongolian for 'Over the horizon'. It appears that in his early teens he went to Paris and sang in night clubs with gypsy groups, later becoming a trapeze artist in the Cirque D'Hiver but he sustained a shoulder injury. Remaining in Paris, he joined the Theatre des Maturins, run by Georges and Ludmilla Piteoff, learning every job. He also studied at the Sorbonne, graduating with a degree in Philosophy. In 1941 he was touring the States, that year appearing on Broadway in 'Twelfth Night' and 'The Tidings Brought to Mary' (1942). During the war he was announcer/commentator, in French, for the U.S. Governments O.W.I. In 1946 he appeared on Broadway and London in 'Lute Song' and moved into US T.V. as a distinguished director, including 'Studio One', 'The Actors' Studio' and the 'Danger' series. In 1944 Mr Brynner had wed former actress Virginia Gilmore; a son, Rocky, was born in 1945. Broadway in 1951 had seen his first performance in 'The King and I', the role winning him Tony and numerous other awards — when filmed in 1956 he deservedly won an Academy Award. His films include: PORT OF NEW YORK (49); THE TEN COMMANDMENTS (56); ANASTASIA (56); THE BUCCANEER (58); SOLOMON AND SHEBA (59); THE MAGNIFICENT 7 (60); ESCAPE FROM ZAHRAIN (62); TARAS BULBA (63); INVITATION TO A GUNFIGHTER (64); RETURN OF THE 7 (66); THE DOUBLE MAN (67); THE MADWOMAN OF CHAILLOT (69); THE LIGHT AT THE EDGE OF THE WORLD (71); CATLOW (72); THE SERPENT (72); WESTWORLD (73); THE ULTIMATE WARRIOR (75, T.V. movie); FUTURE WORLD (76). His second wife was Doris Kleiner (wed 1960) and they had a daughter Victoria, in 1962. On September 22 1971 he wed Jacqueline de Croisset, they have two Vietnamese orphans, Melody and Mia. In 1979/1980 he played opposite Virginia McKenna in 'The King and I' at the London Palladium, another outstanding success. Now divorced from his third wife, he wed Cathy Lee in San Francisco on 5.4.83, where he has yet again been performing as the King of Siam.

HORST BUCHHOLZ

B. Berlin, 4.12.33; real name Horst Werner Buchholz. Father a shoe maker. Aged 14 escaped from a children's camp in Czechoslovakia, fired on while swimming the Elbe. Studied at Ludwig Drama School; started stage career in 'walk-on' roles in Berlin at 5/- a night; graduated to better roles in 'Richard III', 'Peter Pan' and leads in 'Himmel Ohne Stern' (1955) and 'Die Halbstarken' (1956). Came to screen 1957 in CONFESSIONS OF FELIX KROLL. Others include ENDSTATION LIEBE (58); MONTIPI (58); SKY WITHOUT STARS (58); TIGER BAY (59, G.B.); RESURRECTION (59); DAS TOTENSCHIFF (60); THE MAGNIFICENT 7 (61, U.S.A.); FANNY (61); ONE, TWO, THREE (61); NINE HOURS TO RAMA (62); MARCO POLO (64); THAT MAN IN ISTANBUL (66); CERVANTES (66); THE GREAT WALTZ (72). Md. actress Myrium Bru, 1 son Christopher b. 1962, 1 daughter Beatrice b. 1963. Horst appd. Broadway Oct. 1959 in 'Cheri'; 1963 in 'Andorra'. Recent movies: SAVAGE BEES (77); THE AMAZING CAPTAIN NEMO, AVALANCHE EXPRESS, FROM HELL TO VICTORY, THE PILOT (all 1978); BERLIN TUNNEL 21 (T.V. movie, 1981); SAHARA (83).

PETER BULL

B. London, 9.15p.m., 21.3.12. Ed. Winchester College; Tours Univ., France; father was M.P.; 1st stage appearance London, 1933; rep., own company; entered movies 1934; WWII in Royal Navy, awarded D.S.C.; familiar face on stage, T.V. and the films, latter include THE AFRICAN QUEEN (51); (not in BEN-HUR (59)); TOM JONES (62); DR STRANGELOVE (63); Bull LOCK UP YOUR DAUGHTERS (69); UP THE FRONT (72); JOSEPH ANDREWS (76); THE BRUTE (77); THE TEMPEST (79); not THE MIRROR CRACK'D (81); teddy bear consultant 'Brideshead Revisited' (1981, T.V.) — my client Aloysius is open to offers; author of several humorous autobiographies, plus 'Peter Bull's Book of Teddy Bears' (1977), 'Bully Bear Goes Punk' (1981), 'Bully Bear Goes to Hollywood' (1982); recent film: DEAD ON TIME (83, short).
I KNOW THE FACE, BUT ... Peter Davies Ltd.: London, 1959.

ALFRED BURKE

B. Peckham, London, 28.2.18. Ed: Walworth Central. Trained at R.A.D.A.; stage début: Shere, Surrey 1939; several years rep., Old Vic 1952, West End; well-known on T.V. for his series 'The Public Eye' as Frank Marker and Richter in 'Enemy at the Door'. Movies: TOUCH AND GO (56); THE MAN UPSTAIRS (58); THE ANGRY SILENCE (59); BITTER VICTORY (59); MOMENT OF DANGER (60); TRIALS OF OSCAR WILDE (60); CHILDREN OF THE DAMNED (64); THE NANNY (65); A DAY IN THE LIFE OF IVAN DENISOVICH (70). Md. Barbara, 2 sets of twin sons. Recent movie: HOUSE ON GARIBALDI STREET (79, as Eichmann); T.V.: 'Number 10' (1983).

GENEVIEVE BUJOLD

B. Montreal, Canada, 1.7.42. Ed. Convent; 3 yrs. Montreal Conservatory of Drama. Md. 1. — — (biology student, 18 months marriage). Played leads for both Montreal's Fr. language Co.'s; in 1965 won Best Comedienne Award; starred in film about a girl called Genevieve; toured Russia & France with Montreal Rep. Co. — seen by Alain Resnais and cast in his LA GUERRE EST FINIE (63). In 1965 she wed film director Paul Almond who directed her in ISABEL (67) and T.V. plays (1 son Matthew b. 1968). Other films incl. KING OF HEARTS (67); AN ACT OF THE HEART (70) before Hal Wallis selected her for his ANNE OF THE 1000 DAYS (70, A Aw. Nom. B.A.). Divorced from Mr Almond in 1973, her other films are THE TROJAN WOMEN (71); EARTHQUAKE (74); OBSESSION (76); THE SCARLET BUCCANEER (76); LOVE AND OTHER CRIMES (76); COMA (77); ANOTHER MAN, ANOTHER CHANCE (77); HANOVER STREET (78); SHERLOCK HOLMES—MURDER BY DECREE (78), LAST FLIGHT OF NOAH'S ARK (79); THE FINAL ASSIGNMENT (80); MISTRESS IN PARADISE (T.V. movie), MONSIGNORE (both 1982).

GEORGE BURNS

B. New York City, 20.1.1896; real name Nathan Birnbaum. Started on stage aged 12, eldest of 4 boy singers called 'The Peewee Quartet'; then roller-skater; in 100s of vaudeville acts—including 'Burns & Lorraine', but dissolved p/ship with Miss Lorraine when he met Gracie Allen and 'Burns & Allen' act commenced in 1925. They married a year later. (Mr Burns had been previously married to Hannah Siegel, a vaudeville partner.) Burns and Allen appeared on Broadway with great success in 'Vaudeville' (1926; 1930; 1931; 1949) and 'Friars Club Frolic' in 1933; on radio and their 'George Burns and Gracie Allen Show' was one of the highspots of 50s T.V. comedy, running from 1950 to Miss Allen's retirement in 1958 (she died 28.8.64). Mr Burns appeared on his own show in 1958. His movies (*with Gracie): *THE BIG BROADCAST (32), *INTERNATIONAL HOUSE (33); *COLLEGE HUMOUR (33); *SIX OF A KIND (34); WE'RE NOT DRESSING (34); *MANY HAPPY RETURNS (34); *LOVE IN BLOOM (35); *HERE COMES COOKIE (35); *THE BIG BROADCAST OF 1936/and 1937 (36); *COLLEGE HOLIDAY (36); *A DAMSEL IN DISTRESS (37); *COLLEGE SWING (38); *HONOLULU (39); *TWO GIRLS AND A SAILOR (44); THE SUNSHINE BOYS (75, Best Supporting Actor Oscar); SGT. PEPPER'S LONELY HEARTS CLUB BAND (78); OH GOD (78); JUST YOU AND ME, KID (79); GOING IN STYLE (79); OH, GOD! BOOK II (80); 'George Burns & Other Sex Symbols' (T.V., 1982). Mr Burns and Gracie adopted 2 children: Sandra Jean and Ronald Jon.
I LOVE HER, THAT'S WHY by George Burns. W.H. Allen: London, 1956.
LIVING IT UP by George Burns. W.H. Allen: London, 1977.
THE THIRD TIME ROUND by George Burns. W.H. Allen: London, 1980.

RICHARD BURTON

It may be true to state that Richard Burton's much publicised association with Liz Taylor (qv) contributed to hi reaching the big time as a top name in the movies, but before CLEOPATRA he was already a stage and a film actor c distinction. He was born Richard Walter Jenkins at Pontrhyd-y-fen, Glamorgan in Wales on 10 November 1925. Hi father was a coal miner and young Richard was educated at Port Talbot Secondary School and Exeter College, Oxfor Univ. One of 13 children, while still in his teens he was discovered by Emlyn Williams and made his stage debut at th Royal Court Theatre, Liverpool in 'Druid's Rest' in 1943, playing the same role in London in January 1944. At Oxfor he appeared with the Dramatic Society, followed by a 3 year stint in the RAF 1944-1947. After further stage work h came to the screen in THE LAST DAYS OF DOLWYN in 1949 and that year he wed Sybil Williams (5.2.49). In th early 50s he played in the great Shakespearean roles with the Old Vic Company as well as appearing in numerous films mostly for Fox including WATERFRONT (50); GREEN GROW THE RUSHES (51); MY COUSIN RACHAE (52, Oscar Nom.); THE ROBE (53, Oscar Nom.); THE DESERT RATS (53); THE PRINCE OF PLAYERS (54 THE RAINS OF RANCHIPUR (55); ALEXANDER THE GREAT (55); SEA WIFE (57); LOOK BACK L ANGER (59); THE LONGEST DAY (62); CLEOPATRA (63). Divorced from his first wife in 1963, Mr Burton we Liz Taylor the following year. Their films together include: THE V.I.P.'s (63); THE SANDPIPER (65); WHO' AFRAID OF VIRGINIA WOOLF? (66); THE TAMING OF THE SHREW (67); THE COMEDIANS (67 BOOM (68); UNDER MILK WOOD (71); HAMMERSMITH IS OUT (72). Divorcing in 1974, they re-married i 1975, but divorced a year later. Scoring a success in 'Camelot' on Broadway in 1960, he recently repeated his Kin Arthur role. Further Oscar nominations were for his work in BECKET (64); THE SPY WHO CAME IN FROM TH COLD (65); VIRGINIA WOOLF (66); ANNE OF THE 1,000 DAYS (69); and EQUUS (77). He had 2 daughter from his first marriage, Jessica in 1950, and Kate in 1951. The latter is an actress, making a success in 1980 with th American Theatre Co. in New England (in 'The Front Page'). His third wife, Susan Hunt, whom he wed in 1974 divorced him in 1982. In more recent years his films have included THE MEDUSA TOUCH, THE WILD GEESI (both 1977); ABSOLUTION, BREAKTHROUGH (both 1978); CIRCLE OF TWO (79) and as WAGNER (83) In April 1973, he played in the U.S.A. in 'Private Lives', and wed Sally Hay in Las Vegas, 3.7.83.
RICHARD BURTON by Ruth Waterbury (p/b); Mayflower Books: London, 1965.
BURTON — A CLOSE-UP by John Cottrell and Fergus Cashin; Prentice/Hall: London, 1971; p/b: 1974.
RICHARD BURTON by Paul Ferris; Weidenfeld & Nicholson; London, 1982; p/b: N.E.L.:1983.
RICHARD BURTON by Fergus Cashin; W.H. Allen: London, 1982.

MARK BURNS

B. Worcestershire, 30.3.36. Played supporting roles in such movies as TUNES OF GLORY (60); QUEEN'S GUARDS (61); PRIZE OF ARMS (62); LIFE AT THE TOP (65); THE JOKERS (66); I'LL NEVER FORGET WHAT'S 'IS NAME (67) before playing Capt. Morris in THE CHARGE OF THE LIGHT BRIGADE (68). His other movies include: THE ADVENTURES OF GERARD (70); A DAY ON THE BEACH (70); DEATH IN VENICE (70); A TIME FOR LOVING (72); JUGGERNAUT (74); HOUSE OF THE LIVING DEAD (74, won acting award); THE LONG RETURN (75). T.V. includes 'Dracula' (1979) as Dr Seward. Recent movies: THE STUD (78); HOME BEFORE MIDNIGHT (78); THE BITCH (79); CHAMPIONS (83); 'Bergerac' (T.V., 1983). Md: actress Jane How, 1977, 1 son Jack, born July, 1981.

ELLEN BURSTYN

B. Detroit, Michigan, 7.12.32; real name Edna Rae Gilhooly(ley?). Majored at Art; aged 18 fashion model in Texas and md. 1. William Alexander, salesman (div.); for a short while danced in Montreal; went to N.Y. and did T.V. commercials, spent 1 year on the Jackie Gleason Show; early in career used professional names: Kerri Flynn, Erica Dean, Edna Rae and Ellen McRae—as the latter appeared on Broadway 1957 in 'Fair Game', T.V.'s 'The Doctors' (1963), 'Iron Horse' (1966-67) and early movies GOODBYE CHARLIE and FOR THOSE WHO THINK YOUNG (both 64). Md. 2. Paul Roberts, director, 1957 (div.); 3. Neil Burstyn, 1961 (div. 1970). Studied stage-craft at Actors' Studio, N.Y. Movies: TROPIC OF CANCER (69); PIT STOP (69); ALEX IN WONDERLAND (70); LAST PICTURE SHOW (72, N.Y. Critics' Award; Oscar nom.); KING OF MARVIN GARDENS (72); THE EXORCIST (73, Oscar nom. BSA); THURSDAY'S GAME (74, T.V. movie); HARRY AND TONTO (74); ALICE DOESN'T LIVE HERE ANYMORE (75, Academy Award); PROVIDENCE (77); SAME TIME, NEXT YEAR (78, had also played this role Broadway 1975, gaining award); A DREAM OF PASSION (78); SILENCE OF THE NORTH (79); RESURRECTION (80). Ellen Burstyn has a son, Jefferson, born in 1962.

GARY BUSEY

B. Tulsa, Oklahoma, 1944. Ed. at the College of Kansas. First acting job on T.V. was in 'High Chaparral' episode in 1970. Other T.V. included 'Gunsmoke'—'I was the last actor to die in that series,' he says; 'The Texas Wheelers' (1974) with Mark Hamill (q.v.), a short-lived series, and THE EXECUTION OF PRIVATE SLOVIK, a T.V. movie. Feature films include roles in YOU AND ME (72); ANGELS HARD AS THEY COME (72); LAST AMERICAN HERO (72); DIRTY LITTLE BILLY (73); THUNDERBOLT & LIGHTFOOT (74); HEX (74); GUMBALL RALLY (76); A STAR IS BORN (76); STRAIGHT TIME (77); BIG WEDNESDAY (77) and gained an Oscar nomination for his roles as Buddy Holly in THE BUDDY HOLLY STORY (78). Gary is singer with rock group 'Teddy Jack Eddy Rendezvous'. Recent movies: CARNY (79); BARBAROSA (80); CAPITOL CAB (83).

RAYMOND BURR

B. New Westminster, Brit. Columbia, Canada, 21.5.17; full name Raymond William Stanley Burr. Father: hardware dealer, mother: concert pianist. Ed. Stanford Univ., Univ. California, Columbia Univ., Univ. of Chungking (another source of reference states: '...left school at 13, became sheep-herder, travelling salesman, stock clerk, store manager and forest ranger in Oregon'); Toronto summer theatre aged 19; cafe singer in Paris; taught acting at Columbia Univ.; stage in London; 1943 directed at Pasadena Playhouse; 1944 Broadway in 'The Duke in Darkness'; WWII in Marines, spent much time entertaining servicemen with Broadcasts for Armed Forces Radio. Md. 1. Annette Sutherland 1939 (died 1943 in same plane crash as Mr Leslie Howard, actor). Mr Burr came to the screen in 1946 in SANQUENTIN and for 10 years he played in 90 movies, mainly in 'heavy' roles (including the classic REAR WINDOW in 1954) before his tremendous success as 'Perry Mason' in the T.V. series 1957-66 which won him Emmy awards. His son by his first wife, Michael, died of Leukaemia, his 2nd marriage to Isabella Ward ended in divorce, and Mr Burr's third wife, Laura Andrina Morgan, whom he wed in 1950, died five years later of cancer. Other T.V. includes the series 'Ironside' (1967-74) and 'Kingston: Confidential' (1977). Through the Foster Parents' Plan Mr Burr adopted 25 destitute youngsters; he owns an island in the South Pacific and the Swarthe-Burr art gallery. Recent work: 'Centennial' (mini-series 1978), DISASTER ON THE COASTLINER (79, T.V. movie); THE CURSE OF KING TUTANKHAMEN'S TOMB, OUT OF THE BLUE (both 1980); PETER & PAUL (mini-ser., 1981); THE RETURN (81); stage 1983: 'Underground' (U.K.).

RED BUTTONS

B. Bronx, N.Y. City, 5.2.19; real name Aaron Schwatt/Chwatt(?). At 13 was singing bellhop at Dinty Moore's City Island Tavern (earning his nickname); worked on burlesque circuit of N.Y.'s 'Borscht Belt'; comedian at Catskill's Mountain resort; appeared on Broadway in 'Vickie' (1942), Moss Hart's 'Winged Victory' (also tour) (1943), 'Barefoot Boy With Cheek' (1947) and a great success in 'Hold It' (1948). Came to screen in movie version of 'Winged Victory' as Corporal Red Buttons (he served in Air Corps). Md. 1. Roxanne, Burlesque performer, 1947 (div. 1951); 2. Helayne McNorton 1951 (div. 1963). Movies: SAYONARA (57, Oscar—Best Supporting Actor), IMITATION GENERAL (58); THE BIG CIRCUS (59); HATARI (62); FIVE WEEKS IN A BALLOON (62); THE LONGEST DAY (62); A TICKLISH AFFAIR (63); YOUR CHEATING HEART (65); UP FROM THE BEACH (65); HARLOW (65); STAGECOACH (66); THEY SHOOT HORSES, DON'T THEY (69); WHO KILLED MARY WHAT'S HER NAME? (71); POSEIDON ADVENTURE (72); GABLE & LOMBARD (75); VIVA KNIEVAL! (77); THE USERS (78, T.V. movie). Much T.V. incl. versions of stage hits, his own series 'The Red Buttons Show' (1952-55), 'The Double Life of Henry Phyfe' (1966). Night-club work; Royal Variety Perf., London 1979. Md. 3. Alicia Pratt 1964, 1 daughter Amy (b. 1966). Red's recent movies: C.H.O.M.P.S. (79); MOVIE, MOVIE (79); THAT'S LIFE (79); WHEN TIME RAN OUT (79); LEAVE 'EM LAUGHING (81, T.V. movie).

JAMES CAAN

James Caan hit the big time in 1972 after his work as Sonny Corleone in THE GODFATHER, a performance which won him an Oscar nomination, and he recently turned to direction. The son of Arthur Caan and his wife Sophie, James was born 26 March 1939 in the Bronx, New York City. Dad was in the wholesale meat business and he is the eldest of 3 children (brother Ronnie, sister Barbara). At Rhodes High School, Manhattan he was Class President and excelled at sports including basketball. At 16 he graduated to Michigan State Univ., played freshman football and made swimming team, but, missing his friends, was transferred to Hofstra College on Long Island for 2nd year, majoring in pre-law, economics, business management and history. None of these subjects sustained his interest, so he decided to be an actor, training with Sanford Meisner at Neighbourhood Playhouse and 2 years with Wynn Handman. Début: off-Broadway in 'La Ronde' (60) for 9 months; bits in T.V. series ('Naked City', etc.) and Broadway: 'Mandingo' (1961); 'Blood, Sweat and Stanley Poole' (1961) and more T.V. Md: 1. Dee Jay Mattis 1961 (a dancer, div. 1966). Mr Caan came to the screen in 1963 uncredited in IRMA LA DOUCE and his motion-pictures include: LADY IN A CAGE (64); RED LINE 7000 (65); EL DORADO (67); COUNTDOWN (67); SUBMARINE X-1 (68); THE RAIN PEOPLE (69); RABBIT RUN (70); T.R. BASKIN (71); BRIAN'S SONG (71, T.V. movie) THE GODFATHER (72); SLITHER (73); CINDERELLA LIBERTY (75); FREEBIE AND THE BEAN (75); THE GAMBLER (75); FUNNY LADY (75); ROLLERBALL (75); KILLER ELITE (76); A BRIDGE TOO FAR (76). He has a daughter, Tara, born 1964 from his first marriage — he wed model Sheila Ryan in 1976 and a son, Scott Andrew, was born that year. James's brother Ronnie is executive vice-president and co-partner of their Tara Films production company. Mr Caan's recent movies: COMES A HORSEMAN (77); CHAPTER TWO (79); HIDE IN PLAIN SIGHT (79, starred/directed); VIOLENT STREETS (80); KISS ME GOODBYE (82).

SID CAESAR

B. Yonkers, N.Y., 8.9.22. Ed. Yonkers High School. Father Max Caesar, restaurant owner. At 14 was bouncer at dad's restaurant; studied saxophone at Juilliard School of Music; played with 3 dance bands; 1942 joined U.S. Coast Guard, playing in their orchestra, writing revue sketches; 1944 starred in N.Y. in revue 'Tars and Spars', coming to the screen in this production in 1945; other film: THE GUILT OF JANET AMES (47). In 1943 Mr Caesar had wed Florence Levy. After Broadway's 'Make Mine Manhattan' (1948) moved into T.V., partnering Imogen Coca in 'Admiral Broadway Revue' (1949) which lead to the couple's highly successful 'Your Show of Shows', running 1950-54 and one of the highlights of 50s U.S. T.V. His other T.V. successes include: 'Caesar's Hour' (1954-57); 'Caesar Presents' (1955); 'The Hollywood Palace' (frequent guest 1960s) and 'Sid Caesar Invites You' (1958). He has won frequent awards for his T.V. work, including 5 'Emmies'; Broadway 1962: 'Little Me'; movies: IT'S A MAD, MAD, MAD, MAD WORLD (63); THE SPIRIT IS WILLING (67); A GUIDE FOR THE MARRIED MAN (67); THE BUSY BODY (67); TEN FROM YOUR SHOW OF SHOWS (74, T.V. shows of 50s—10 amalgamated); AIRPORT 75, SILENT MOVIE (76); GREASE, CHEAP DETECTIVE, BARNABY & ME (all 77); FIENDISH PLOT OF DR. FU MANCHU (80); HISTORY OF WORLD: PT. 1 (81); ALBY'S SPECIAL (83); autobio: *WHERE HAVE I BEEN?*

DYAN CANNON

B. Tacoma, Washington, U.S.A., 4.1.37(?); real name Samille Diane Friesen. Ed. Univ. of Washington; model, did promotional work for 1957 film LES GIRLS. Studied acting with Sanford Meisner, acted in small roles in movies RISE & FALL OF LEGS DIAMOND (59); THIS REBEL BREED (60); co-starred in TV serial 'Full Circle' (1960-61); on Broadway in 'The Fun Couple' (1962); 'The 90 Day Mistress' (1967) and toured in 'How to Succeed in Business Without Really Trying'. Wed Mr Cary Grant 1965 (1 daughter Jennifer b. 1966) div. 1968. Movies: BOB & TED & CAROL & ALICE (69, Oscar nom.); DOCTORS' WIVES (70); ANDERSON TAPES (71); LOVE MACHINE (71); SHAMUS (72); SUCH GOOD FRIENDS (72); THE BURGLARS (72); LAST OF SHEILA (73); CHILD UNDER A LEAF (74); THE VIRGINIA HILL STORY (74, T.V. movie); HEAVEN CAN WAIT (76); LADY OF THE HOUSE (77, T.V. movie); REVENGE OF THE PINK PANTHER (77); NUMBER-ONE (Dyan directed/produced/wrote/edited/scored—47 min. feature); HONEYSUCKLE ROSE (79); COAST TO COAST (80); DEATH TRAP, AUTHOR! AUTHOR! (both 1982).

CHERYL CAMPBELL

Ed. St. Albans Grammar School. Father a B.O.A.C. pilot. Started career at A.S.M. Palace Theatre, Watford; 3 yrs. study London Academy of Music & Drama emerging as 'Student of the Year'; rep. Birmingham, Glasgow's Citizen's Theatre; 1st T.V. role 'Z Cars'; first lead as 'Emma' (1974). 1975: National Theatre: 'John Gabriel Borkman'. Miss Campbell has given brilliant performances on T.V., especially in 'Pennies from Heaven' (BBC 1978); 'Duke of Wellington', 'Malice Aforethought' and her work as Vera Brittain in 'Testament of Youth' (BBC 1979) was acclaimed, winning her 'Best T.V. Actress of '79' awards as voted by T.V. & Journalists Guild, and the British Film and T.V. Academy. films: MCVICAR (79); HAWK THE SLAYER (80); CHARIOTS OF FIRE (81); GREYSTOKE, THE LEGEND OF TARZAN, LORD OF THE APES (83); stage 1983: 'Miss Julie'.

CAPUCINE

B. Toulon, France, 6.1.35; real name Germaine Lefebvre. Her father: a French industrialist. Capucine studied at Saumur, France, receiving B.A. Degree. She became a top fashion model in Paris, went to N.Y. where she was discovered by agent/producer Charles Feldman and came to the screen opposite Dirk Bogarde in SONG WITHOUT END (60). Her other movies: NORTH TO ALASKA (61); WALK ON THE WILD SIDE (62); THE LION (62); THE PINK PANTHER (63); THE 7TH DAWN (64); WHAT'S NEW, PUSSYCAT? (66); THE HONEY POT (67); TALE OF THE FOX (68); THE QUEENS (68); FRAULEIN DOKTOR (69); SATYRICON (70); THE EXQUISITE CADAVER (70); RED SUN (72); ARABIAN ADVENTURE (78); FROM HELL TO VICTORY (78); JAGUAR LIVES (78); THE CON ARTISTS (81); TRAIL OF THE PINK PANTHER (82).

MICHAEL CAINE

One of the most successful screen actors to emerge from Britain in the mid-60s; it took Michael Caine many years of hard work to achieve his deserved success in movies. Born Maurice Joseph Micklewhite in Bermondsey, East London on 14 March 1933, his father (also called Maurice) was a Billingsgate fishporter, his mother, Ellen, an office cleaner. At the age of 6 he was evacuated with his brother Stanley to Wargrave, Berks and later to Norfolk. Young Maurice was educated at Wilson's Grammar School, Peckham, leaving at 16½ to work at the offices of Jay Lewis, film producer and then to despatch clerk with Peak Films, Wardour Street; operated a pneumatic drill as road labourer; got a job in a tea warehouse near Tower Bridge, then worked a cement mixer on construction sites; two years National Service as infantryman, 2nd year in Korea seeing action with Royal Fusiliers; demobbed, aged 20, worked Smithfield Market. Through 'Stage' paper got a job as A.S.M. at Horsham Rep. Co. Sussex 1953, £2 a week; graduated to leads roles; 2 months in hospital with malaria; joined Lowestoft Rep. Co., met first wife Patricia Haines, married 1955, daughter Dominique born 1956; joined Joan Littlewood's Theatre Workshop Co.; 1st T.V. role 'The Lark', when working in a laundry got first screen role in A HILL IN KOREA (56); did walk-on roles on T.V.: good theatre including tour of 'Long, Short and the Tall'; Royal Court, March 1960: 'The Room' and 'The Dumb Waiter'; 'Next Time I'll Sing To You', Criterion Theatre and T.V. play 'The Compartment', a success. Uncredited film roles in such pictures as BULLDOG BREED, DAY THE EARTH CAUGHT FIRE and then Sir Stanley Baker and Cy Endfield cast him in ZULU (63) which was the turning point in his career; THE IPCRESS FILE (65) and ALFIE (66) consolidated it. Best films: HURRY SUNDOWN (67); PLAY DIRTY (68); THE ITALIAN JOB (69); TOO LATE THE HERO (70); THE LAST VALLEY (70); GET CARTER (71); SLEUTH (73); BLACK WINDMILL (74); THE MARSEILLES CONTRACT (74); THE MAN WHO WOULD BE KING (75). The name 'Caine' was chosen by the actor after the CAINE MUTINY movie. Divorced from his first wife (who died of lung cancer in 1978), he wed former Guyanan model/beauty queen Shakira Baksh in 1973 and they have a young daughter, Natasha. Michael's latest films: ASHANTI (78); CALIFORNIA SUITE (78); BEYOND THE POSEIDON ADVENTURE (78); DRESSED TO KILL (79); THE HAND (80); ESCAPE TO VICTORY (81); THE JIGSAW MAN, EDUCATING RITA, THE HONORARY CONSUL (all 1983).
RAISING CAINE by William Hall; Sidgwick & Jackson: London, 1981; p/b: Arrow, 1982.

CLAUDIA CARDINALE

B. Tunis, N. Africa, 15.4.39. French mother, Italian father, Sicilian ancestry. Ed. College Paul Cambon. Studying in Tunis to become teacher; won title 'Most Beautiful Girl in Tunis' and trip to Venice, where she was discovered by Franco Cristaldi, producer of Vides Co. She returned to Tunis, but decided to take up offer of movies and appeared in 20, mainly Italian, incl. I SOLITI IGNOTI (58); LA RAGAZZA CON LA VILIGIA (61). First starred: IL BELL' ANTONIO (59); ROCCO & HIS BROTHERS (60). Intn'l. movies include: UPSTAIRS & DOWNSTAIRS (58, G.B.); THE LEOPARD (62); THE PINK PANTHER (63, G.B.); CIRCUS WORLD (64, Spain); BLINDFOLD (65, U.S.); LOST COMMAND (66, Fr.-U.S.); PROFESSIONALS (66, U.S.); THE RED RENT (69, co-production), many others. In 1980 disclosed Claudia has son, Patrick Cristoldi, born in U.K. when she was 18, he is working as assistant director, she is also a grandmother. A daughter, Claudia, was born in 1979 (father: director, Pasquale Squitieri). Miss Cardinale's recent movies: ESCAPE TO ATHENA (78); CORLEONE (79, Italy); THE SALAMANDER, THE SKIN (both 80); FITZCARRALDO (81); THE GIFT (82).

ART CARNEY

B. Mount Vernon, N.Y., 4.11.18. Ed. A.B. Davis High School, Mt. Vernon. Commenced career on radio doing impersonations of Roosevelt, Eisenhower, etc. Screen début 1941 in POT O' GOLD; U.S. Army 1944-45. Md. 1. Jean Myers 1940 (div.), 1 daughter Eileen, 2 sons Brian (b. 1942), Paul (b. 1952). Entered U.S. T.V. in 1948, becoming major star of that medium in 50s incl.: 'Cavalcade of Stars' (1950-52); 'Henry Morgan's Great Talent Hunt' (1951); regular in 'The Honeymooners' since 1955; 'Jackie Gleason Show' (1952-57 & 1966-70), and won numerous Emmy awards; much Broadway incl. 'Rope Dancers' (1957); 'Take Her, She's Mine' (1961) and 'The Odd Couple' (1965). Movies: YELLOW ROLLS-ROYCE (64); GUIDE FOR THE MARRIED MAN (67); HARRY AND TONTO (74, Academy Award) W.W. & THE DIXIE DANCE KINGS (75); WON TON TON (76); LANIGAN'S RABBI (76, T.V. movie); THE LATE SHOW (77); STEEL (78); GOING IN STYLE (79); ROADIE (79); ALCATRAZ: THE WHOLE SHOCKING STORY (as Robert Stroud, T.V. movie, 1980); ST. HELEN'S, TAKE THIS JOB & SHOVE IT (both 1981); MENAGE A TROIS (82); Md: 2. Barbara Isaac, Dec. 1966).

DAVID CARRADINE

B. Hollywood, California, 8.10(?).40. Father John Carradine (q.v.). Ed. San Francisco State; repertory experience; early T.V.: 'Armstrong Circle Theatre', 'East Side, West Side'; came to screen in TAGGERT (65); Broadway 1965: 'Royal Hunt of the Sun'. T.V. series 1966 'Shane'; movies: BUS RILEY'S BACK IN TOWN (65); TOO MANY THIEVES (65, T.V. movie, G.B.); THE VIOLENT ONES (69); HEAVEN WITH A GUN (69); YOUNG BILLY YOUNG (69); THE GOOD GUYS AND THE BAD GUYS (69); GALLERY OF HORRORS (70); THE McMASTERS (70); MACHO CALLAHAN (70); BOXCAR BERTHA (72). T.V. series: 'Kung Fu' (1972-75). 1 son Seagull, b. 1972 (md. actress Barbara Hershey (q.v.). YOU & ME (73, also directed); DEATH RACE 2000 (75); CANNONBALL (76); BOUND FOR GLORY (76, as folk-singer Woody Guthrie); GRAY LADY DOWN (77); THE SERPENT'S EGG (78); CLOUD DANCER (79); DEATH SPORT (79); THE LONG RIDERS (79); GAUGIN THE SAVAGE (79, T.V. movie); RALLY, HIGH NOON: PT. II—RETURN OF WILL KANE (80); AMERICANA (81, stars, directs, co-produces, co-scored); Q — THE WINGED SERPENT (82); LONE WOLF McQUADE (83).

KEITH CARRADINE

B. San Mateo, Calif., 8.8.51(?). Father John Carradine (q.v.). Ed. Colorado State Univ., majoring in Drama; then '3 months cooking Kentucky Fried Chicken'; big break on Broadway in 'Hair' for 1 year, playing Claude for 6 months; came to the screen in A GUNFIGHT (70); played in 'Tobacco Road' with father, Florida. Movies: McCABE & MRS MILLER (71); IDAHO TRANSFER (72); EMPEROR OF THE NORTH (73); THIEVES LIKE US (74); HEX (74); NASHVILLE (75); THE DUELLISTS (76); LUMIERE (76); WELCOME TO L.A. (77); PRETTY BABY (77); OLD BOYFRIENDS (79); AN ALMOST PERFECT AFFAIR (79); THE LONGRIDERS (79); A RUMOUR OF WAR (80); SOUTHERN COMFORT (81). Keith won Oscar for his song 'I'm Easy' in NASHVILLE (writing 3 songs for movie). Other brother, Robert, has appeared in COMING HOME (77); THE BIG RED ONE (78); LONG RIDERS (79); BLACKOUT, HEARTACHES (both 81); TAG, JOY RIDE (both 82); Christopher is not in show-biz.

IAN CARMICHAEL

B. Kingston-upon-Hull, Yorks, 18.6.20. Father optician with family jewellery/silversmiths in Hull. Ed. Prep. School Scarborough; Bromsgrove, Worcs. As youngster wanted to run dance-band; R.A.D.A., but WWII intervened—Sandhurst; Officer 22nd Dragoons, posted to Regt. in Whitby, met wife Pym—md. 1943—Staff Officer with 30th Armoured Brig., D-Day; demobbed 1947 as Major; 2 daughters born, Lee & Sally; entered show-biz doing song & dance, revue, acting, directed concert parties etc. Mr Carmichael came to screen as extra, can be glimpsed in BOND STREET (48); TROTTIE TRUE, DEAN MR PROHACK (49). Early 50s much T.V., West End, support in films: COLDITZ STORY (54); STORM OVER THE NILE (55) emerging as star in SIMON & LAURA (55, also stage); PRIVATE'S PROGRESS (55); LUCKY JIM (57); portraying the genial, upper-class type, most of his film successes being produced by the Boulting Brothers. In the 60s popular in West End comedies, tours and especially as Bertie Wooster in BBC's 'World of Wooster' series (1964-65) and 'Bachelor Father' and 'Lord Peter Wimsey'. Other films include: I'M ALRIGHT, JACK (59); THE AMOROUS PRAWN (62); SMASHING TIME (67); FROM BEYOND THE GRAVE (73) and recently THE LADY VANISHES (78).
WILL THE REAL IAN CARMICHAEL... MacMillan: London, 1979. p/b: Futura, 1980

LESLIE CARON

B. Paris, 1.7.31(?); full name Leslie Claire Margaret Caron. Mother Margaret, U.S. born, father Claude, chemist. Ed. convent of the Assumption; after allied invasion WWII, she and brother Aimery went to Cannes; after war studied ballet at Nat. Conservatoire du Paris; aged 15 danced solo for Petit's Ballet des Champs-Élysees; lead in 'La Rencontre', became star, toured Europe & Asia, seen by Gene Kelly in this role and came to the screen in his AN AMERICAN IN PARIS (51). Md. 1. George Hormel 1951-54. Miss Caron delighted in movies of 50s, especially musicals: STORY OF 3 LOVES (53); LILI (53); THE GLASS SLIPPER (54); DADDY LONG-LEGS (55); GIGI (58). Md. 2. Mr Peter Hall, theatre director, 1956-66 (1 son Christopher 1957, 1 daughter Jennifer 1958). Other movies include: THE MAN WHO UNDERSTOOD WOMEN (59); FANNY (61); THE L-SHAPED ROOM (62, British Film Award); FATHER GOOSE (64); A VERY SPECIAL FAVOUR (65); PROMISE HER ANYTHING, IS PARIS BURNING? (66). Md. 3. Michael Laughton, producer (div.); other movies: QVII (T.V. movie, 1974); VALENTINO (76); THE MAN WHO LOVED REDHEADS (77); GOLDEN GIRL (78); THE CONTRACT (81); THE UNAPPROACHABLE (82).

JOHN CARRADINE

B. Greenwich Village, N.Y., 5.2.06; real name Richmond Reed Carradine. Ed. Episcopal Acad. & Graphic Art School in Philadelphia, Pa.; N.Y. Art School. Father a journalist, mother a doctor. Aged 19 in 'Camille' at St. Charles Theatre, N. Orleans; marine artist/portrait painter to Hollywood and artist for DeMille; in 'Little Group Theatre' prods. and came to screen using name of 'John Peter Richmond' in TOL'ABLE (30). First billed as John Carradine in BRIDE OF FRANKENSTEIN (35). Since then has appeared in over 130 movies including the classics: CAPTAINS COURAGEOUS (37); ALEXANDER'S RAGTIME BAND (38); STAGECOACH (39); GRAPES OF WRATH (40); THE BLACK SWAN (42). Md. 1. Ardanelle Cosner (1935, 2 sons David (q.v.) 1940, Bruce John 1941, div. 1944). During 40s played on Broadway, toured reciting Shakespeare, but continued in movies esp. as 'Dracula' in 2. Md. 2. Sonia Sorel (1945, 4 sons: John Arthur Jr. 1946, Christopher John 1947, Keith Ian (q.v.) 1949(?), Robert Reed 1953) (div. 1955). Md: 3. Doris Rich (1956, dec. 1971). Broadway 1962: 'A Funny Thing Happened on the Way to the Forum'. Md. 4. Emily Cisneros. Recent movies: THE SENTINEL (76); DEATH AT LOVE HOUSE (76, T.V. Movie), GOLDEN RENDEZVOUS (77); WHITE BUFFALO (77); SUNSET COVE (78, guest); CARRADINES IN CONCERT (79, documentary with 3 sons); THE MONSTER CLUB (80); THE HOWLING, THE BOGEYMAN, DEATH HOUSE, DARK EYES, THE NESTING (all 1981); THE SECRET OF NIMH (animation-voice only), GOLIATH AWAITS (mini-ser.), THE HOUSE OF LONG SHADOWS (all 1982).

BARBARA CARRERA

B. Nicaragua, 31.12.51; seen in New York by designer Lily Dache which lead to contract to the Eileen Ford Agency. As a top New York model, Barbara made the covers of top magazines and film producers brought her to the screen in 1971 in BILLY JACK, she returned to modelling and the same producers cast her in THE MASTER GUNFIGHTER (75) and she gave up modelling. Other movies: EMBRYO (76); THE ISLAND OF DR. MOREAU (77); the mini-series 'Centennial' (1978); WHEN TIME RAN OUT (79) CONDORMAN (80); I, THE JURY, MATT HOUSTON (T.V. movie, both 82); LONE WOLF McQUADE, NEVER SAY NEVER AGAIN (both 1983).

VERONICA CARTWRIGHT

B. Bristol, England, 20.4.49. Aged 4, family moved to Toronto, Canada, settling in L.A. 2 years later. Began career aged 6 as child model in T.V. commercials, and won fame as the 'Kellogg's Girl' in ads.; aged 11 co-starred as Rosalie in movie THE LOUDEST WHISPER (61); then IN LOVE AND WAR (62); won Emmy Award, aged 14, in U.S. film 'Tell Me Not in Mournful Numbers'. Films: SPENCER'S MOUNTAIN (64); THE BIRDS (64); T.V. series 1964-66: 'Daniel Boone'. More recent movies: INSERTS (75); INVASION OF THE BODYSNATCHERS (77); ALIEN (78); BEYOND THE POSEIDON ADVENTURE (79); THE RIGHT STUFF (82). Younger sister, Angela (b.9.9.52), appd. in T.V. ser. 'Lost in Space' (65-68).

JEAN-PIERRE CASSEL

B. Paris, 27.10.32; originally a dancer, appeared on the stage in France before becoming major actor in French films, later in international movies. Broadway 1960: 'L'Idiote'. Films include: GAMES OF LOVE (60); THE GAY DECEIVER (60); FIVE DAY LOVER (61); THE VANISHING CORPORAL (62); LA RONDE (64); THOSE MAGNIFICENT MEN IN THEIR FLYING MACHINES (65); IS PARIS BURNING? (66); JEU DE MASSACRE (67); OH! WHAT A LOVELY WAR (68); THE BEAR AND THE DOLL (69); BAXTER (71); THE DISCREET CHARM OF THE BOURGEOISIE (72); THE THREE MUSKETEERS (73); MURDER ON THE ORIENT EXPRESS (75); THAT LUCKY TOUCH (75); FROM HELL TO VICTORY (78); TOO MANY CHEFS (80); ALICE (81, Poland); THE GRAZIOSI CASE (81, T.V. movie).

JOHN CASTLE

B. Croydon, Surrey, 14.1.40. Ed. Brighton Coll., Trinity Coll., Dublin. Studied for the stage at R.A.D.A.; stage début 1964, Regents Park, in 'Henry V'. Has since played a variety of roles including Shakespeare—'Hamlet', Malcolm in 'Macbeth'; title role of 'Luther', in 'Under Milk Wood', 'A Month in the Country', many others. Came to the screen in BLOW UP (66) and has been seen in THE LION IN WINTER (68); THE PROMISE (69); ANTHONY & CLEOPATRA (71); MAN OF LA MANCHA (72); MADE (72); THE INCREDIBLE SARAH (75); ELIZA FRASER (76, Australia); EAGLE'S WING (77); NIGHTSHIFT (79); SECOND TO THE RIGHT AND ON TILL MORNING (79). Md. Maggie. Mr Castle has made many appearances on T.V., including '3 Hostages', 'I Claudius', 'Penmaric' and more recently in 'Strangers' (82).

GEORGE CHAKIRIS

B. Norwood, Ohio, U.S.A., 16.9.34. Went to Hollywood and got dance job in movie WHITE CHRISTMAS and Paramount contract, but inactive at studio, got dancing work in movies MEET ME IN LAS VEGAS, THERE'S NO BUSINESS LIKE SHOW BUSINESS and BRIGADOON in mid-50s. After further study secured role of Riff in London prod. of 'West Side Story', played Bernardo in movie version, winning Oscar for Best Supporting Actor 1961. Other movies: TWO AND TWO MAKE SIX (60); DIAMOND HEAD (63); FLIGHT FROM ASHIYA (63); KINGS OF THE SUN (63); 633 SQUADRON (64); THE HIGH BRIGHT SUN (65); IS PARIS BURNING? (66); THE YOUNG GIRLS OF ROCHEFORT (67); THE BIG CUBE (69). Recent work: Dracula in 'Passion of Dracula' (London stage—1978); movie: WHY NOT STAY FOR BREAKFAST? (78).

LYNDA CARTER

B. Phoenix, Arizona, 24.7.52. Ed. Arizona State Univ. Became professional song-writer and singer at 15, earning $25 a weekend at the Pizza Inn; toured for 4 yrs. with rock 'n' roll band; won several beauty contests in Arizona, qualified for Miss World 1972 finals, won Miss World/U.S.A. 1973; studied dramatics with Stella Adler and Charles Conrad; appeared in small T.V. roles/ commercials before winning title role of 'Wonder Woman' in the T.V. series 1977-78-79. Md. Ron Samuels 28.5.77, her agent. Other T.V.: 'The Lynda Carter Special' (1979); guest in 'The Muppet Show' (1979); 'The Last Song (1980, T.V. movie, also sang title song); 'Babies for Sale' (1981, T.V. movie). Lynda has appeared in cabaret at Caesar's Palace, Las Vegas; in 1980 toured Europe in concert, incl. London Palladium; she has won 'the Most Beautiful Woman in the World' honour, voted by the Intn'l. Acad. of Beauty , London; 'one of the Ten Best Dressed/ Tressed Women in U.S.' and 'One of the Most Exciting Women in the World' as voted by the Intn'l. Bachelors' Assoc.; beauty and fashion director of Maybelline Cosmetics; title role: RITA HAYWORTH: THE LOVE GODDESS (T.V. movie, 1983).

JOHN CASSAVETES

B. New York, 9.12.29. Ed. Colgate Univ.; Am.A.D.A.; of Greek descent; director Gregory Ratoff gave him first break on N.Y. stage; came to screen in N.Y. in TAXI (54) and was seen also in THE NIGHT HOLDS TERROR (55); CRIME IN THE STREETS (56); A MAN IS TEN FEET TALL (57); AFFAIR IN HAVANA (57); SADDLE THE WIND (58); VIRGIN ISLAND (58). Much T.V. included: guest actor in 'Omnibus' (1954), 'Elgin T.V. Hour' (1955), 'Alcoa Theatre' (1958), 'Chrysler Theatre' (1963) and own series 1959: 'Johnny Staccato'. Md. actress Gena Rowlands, 2 daughters Alexandra (b. 1965), Zoe (b. 1970) and 1 son Nicholas (b. 1967). In 60s and 70s emerged as talented writer/director also. Other movies include: THE WEBSTER BOY (61); SHADOWS (61, 16mm dir. only); TOO LATE BLUES (62, directed); A CHILD IS WAITING (62, directed); THE KILLERS (64, T.V. movie); THE DIRTY DOZEN (67); THE DEVIL'S ANGELS (67); ROSEMARY'S BABY (68); FACES (68, screenplay/directed); HUSBANDS (70, acted/screenplay/directed); MACHINE GUN McCAIN (70); MINNIE & MOSKOWITZ (71, directed/screenplay); A WOMAN UNDER THE INFLUENCE (74, (directed/screenplay); KILLING OF A CHINESE BOOKIE (76, directed/screenplay); TWO MINUTE WARNING (76); OPENING NIGHT (77); THE FURY (78); BRASS TARGET (78). His wife has appeared in several of his movies, including the award-winning GLORIA (80, directed). Recent films as actor: INCUBUS, TEMPEST, WHOSE LIFE IS IT, ANYWAY? (all 1981).

ADOLFO CELI

B. Messina, Sicily, 27.2.22. Ed. Rome Academy. For 14 years was director at the Brazilian Theatre in San Paulo, also directing films and T.V. plays in that country. Md. in Jan. 1966. Movies include: THAT MAN FROM RIO (64); EL GRECO (64); VON RYAN'S EXPRESS (64); AGONY & THE ECSTASY (65); THUNDERBALL (65); GRAND PRIX (67); THE HONEY POT (67); THE BOBO (67); GRAND SLAM (68); DANGER-DIABOLIK (68); THE DIRTY HEROES (69); FRAGMENT OF FEAR (70); MURDERS IN THE RUE MORGUE (71); HITLER—THE LAST 10 DAYS (73); AND THEN THERE WERE NONE (75); HOLOCAUST 2000 (77); CAFE EXPRESS (81); MONSIGNORE (82); is divorced. 1 son and 1 daughter; B.B.C. T.V. 1982: 'The Borgias' (ser.).

STOCKARD CHANNING

B. New York City . . .44; real name Susan Williams Antonia Stockard. Ed. Radcliffe Coll. (Honours). The youngest of 2 daughters of shipping magnate, brought up in Park Avenue. On Broadway 1970 in 'Arsenic & Old Lace', in 1972 joined chorus as dancer/singer in N.Y. prod. of 'Two Gentlemen of Verona', understudying lead, eventually played lead in L.A. Came to the screen 1972 in bit part as nurse in THE HOSPITAL, then played good role in T.V. drama 'The Girl Most Likely' which lead to co-starring in THE FORTUNE (76) opp. Warren Beatty & Jack Nicholson. Md. 1. Walter Channing, Harvard businessman (div.); 2. Paul Schmidt, Professor of Slavic Languages, Univ. of Texas (div.). Movies: THE BIG BUS (76); GREASE (77); THE CHEAP DETECTIVE (77); SWEET REVENGE (77); THE FISH THAT SAVED PITTSBURGH (77); SILENT VICTORY (78); RALLY (80); WITHOUT A TRACE (83).

RICHARD CHAMBERLAIN

Richard Chamberlain, with careful choice of roles in the three main fields of acting, has remained a successful artiste for 20 years. Born George Richard Chamberlain in Beverly Hills on 31 March 1935, his father was a manufacturer, his mother a singer. He studied at the Vista Grammar and High School, Beverly Hills and Pamara College where he majored in art. During the last term appeared in play 'Arms and the Man' and chose acting as a career, but had to serve 2 years in the U.S. Army, winning his sergeant's stripes in Korea. After this he got an agent to represent him and soon won roles on T.V. shows such as 'Thriller', 'Gunsmoke', 'The Deputy', before being selected to play the title role of 'Dr. Kildare', in which he had a great personal success, the series running for 5 years from 1961. He had come to the screen in 1960 in THE SECRET OF THE PURPLE REEF, and his 60s films were A THUNDER OF DRUMS (62); TWILIGHT OF HONOR (63); JOY IN THE MORNING (65); PETULIA (68); THE MADWOMAN OF CHAILLOT (69). Richard played on Broadway in the musical version of 'Breakfast at Tiffany's' in 1966, and essayed 'Hamlet' there in 1969, playing the role also on US T.V. and coming to Britain to play the Danish prince with the Birmingham Rep. (the first American actor since Barrymore in 1929). Here he played in 'Portrait of a Lady' on BBC, filmed JULIUS CAESAR (70); THE MUSIC LOVERS (70, as Peter Tchaikovsky); LADY CAROLINE LAMB (72, as Lord Byron) and went to Spain to portray Aramis in the two MUSKETEER films, THE THREE/FOUR MUSKETEERS, in 1973. His movies since: THE TOWERING INFERNO (75); THE SLIPPER AND THE ROSE, THE COUNT OF MONTE CRISTO (T.V. movie, both 1976); THE LAST WAVE (Australia), THE MAN IN THE IRON MASK (T.V. movie), THE SWARM (all 1977); SHOGUN (mini-series, 1980); BELLS (81) and he has more recently appeared on stage in 'Arms & the Man' at the Summer Festival, Williamstown, New England.

GERALDINE CHAPLIN

B. Santa Monica, California, 31.7.44. Father, the late Sir Charles Chaplin, comic genius of the screen; mother, Oona (daughter of playwright Eugene O'Neill). Ed. Royal Ballet School. She has 4 sisters, 3 brothers. Movies: DR ZHIVAGO (66); STRANGER IN THE HOUSE (67); I KILLED RASPUTIN (68); LA MADRIGUERA (69); THE HAWAIIANS (70); ZERO POPULATION GROWTH (72); INNOCENT BYSTANDERS (72); THE HOUSE WITHOUT FRONTIERS (72); THE 3 MUSKETEERS (73); NASHVILLE (75); CRIA CUERVOS (75); BUFFALO BILL & THE INDIANS (76); ROSELAND (77); WELCOME TO L.A. (77); A WEDDING (78); THE MASKED EDGE (78); REMEMBER MY NAME (79); MAMA TURNS A HUNDRED (79); THE MIRROR CRACK'D (81). Broadway 1966: 'The Little Foxes'. 1 son, Shane, born 1974, father is Carlos Saura, who has directed several of her pictures. VOYAGE EN DOUCE (81); 'My Cousin Rachel' (B.B.C. 1983).

CYD CHARISSE

B. Amarillo, Texas, 8.3.22; R.N.: Tula Ellice Finklea. Father Ernest, jeweller, who loved ballet; ballet lessons aged 8; aged 12 to Hollywood Professional School, studying ballet; joined Col. de Basil of 'Ballet Russe', toured U.S. 1 year; father died; toured with 'Russe' co. Europe. Md. 1. Nico Charisse 1939, instructor, returned to Hollywood; 1 son,, Nicky, b. 1940. Came to screen in 1943 in SOMETHING TO SHOUT ABOUT, then in MISSION TO MOSCOW (43); in ballet sequence of ZIEGFELD FOLLIES (45), made a great impression. Miss Charisse delighted millions with her dancing in MGM classics of the 40s & 50s; best work included THE UNFINISHED DANCE (47); SINGIN' IN THE RAIN (53); THE BAND WAGON (53); BRIGADOON (54); IT'S ALWAYS FAIR WEATHER (55) and INVITATION TO THE DANCE (57). Divorced in 1947, wed Tony Martin, 9.5.48, actor/singer; 1 son, Tony Jr. (b. 1950). Other movies include: TWO WEEKS IN ANOTHER TOWN (62); MAROC 7 (67); and 7 CITIES TO ATLANTIS (77).
THE TWO OF US by Tony Martin & C.C. (as told to Dick Kleiner). Mason/Charter: New York, 1976.

IAN CHARLESON

B. Edinburgh, Scotland, . .49. The son of an Edinburgh printer, as a child Ian played the piano well, had a high tenor voice and sang in the church choir. He won a scholarship to the Royal High School, Edinburgh, and got his first taste of acting in a play, 'Kith & Kin'. At Edinburgh University he studied architecture, gaining his M.A. in Fine Arts, but was active in the dramatic society, his roles included Malvolio. Switching to an acting career, he trained at the London Academy of Music & Drama and has worked steadily since 1972. He played in the movie JUBILEE (78) and co-starred as Eric Liddell in the highly successful, Oscar-winning movie CHARIOTS OF FIRE (81), Ian receiving a Variety Club award. His T.V. work has included 'Ladykillers' (1981), series 'The Search for Alexander the Great', 'Something's Got to Give' (1982) — recent stage hit: 'Guys and Dolls' (N.T. 1982, as Sky Masterson); GANDHI (82) ; ASCENDANCY (83); LOUISIANA (83).

CHEVY CHASE

B. New York City, 8.10.43. Ed. Bard Coll. When at school wrote scripts with Kenny Shapiro which became underground T.V., off Broadway show and 1974 film called GROOVE TUBE; became popular 1975/76 in T.V. show 'Saturday Night Live' winning 2 Emmy Awards as actor/writer. Movies: FOUL PLAY (78); SEEMS LIKE OLD TIMES (79); UNDER THE RAINBOW (81); MODERN PROBLEMS (81); NATIONAL LAMPOON'S VACATION (82); DEAL OF THE CENTURY (83).

LOIS CHILES

B. Texas. A former model, appeared in THE WAY WE WERE (75) and THE GREAT GATSBY (75). Went to New York and studied acting, returning to the screen in DEATH ON THE NILE (77); COMA (77); and as C.I.A. heroine Holly Goodhead in MOONRAKER (79); regular as Holly in 'Dallas' (U.S. T.V. 1983).

JULIE CHRISTIE

Although her films have been infrequent, Miss Christie, since gaining an Oscar in the mid-60s, has shrewdly selected her roles in always better-than-average movies in the capable hands of the most talented directors. She was born in Chukua, Assam, India on 14 April 1941, her father being a tea planter. Aged 8 she came to England, educated at boarding schools and spending a year in France to learn the language. After a spell at Brighton Technical College, she studied acting at London's Central School, making her début during summer months at Frinton Repertory. Appearing in the drama school production of 'Diary of Anne Frank', she won the lead role in BBC T.V.'s 'A For Andromeda' serial, and on the strength of this came to the screen in the comedies CROOKS ANONYMOUS (62) and THE FAST LADY (63). John Schlesinger, remembering her work at drama school, gave her an important role, although only 8 minutes on the screen, in BILLY LIAR (63), winning her praise. Julie then did a season to gain solid acting experience with Birmingham Rep., then toured with the R.S. Co., in E. Europe, Moscow, USA (including Broadway in 'The Comedy of Errors' (64)). She returned to the screen in YOUNG CASSIDY and DOCTOR ZHIVAGO (both '65), and, as Diana in DARLING she won an Oscar in 1965. Her other movies are FAHRENHEIT 451 (66); FAR FROM THE MADDING CROWD (67); PETULIA (68); IN SEARCH OF GREGORY (69); THE GO-BETWEEN (71); McCABE & MRS MILLER (71, Oscar Nom.); DON'T LOOK NOW (73); SHAMPOO (75); THE DEMON SEED, HEAVEN CAN WAIT (both 77); THE ROARING FORTIES (81); MEMOIRS OF A SURVIVOR, RETURN OF THE SOLDIER, 'The Animals Film' (T.V., narrator, all 1982) and HEAT & DUST (83).

CANDY CLARK

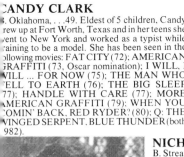

B. Oklahoma, . . .49. Eldest of 5 children, Candy grew up at Fort Worth, Texas and in her teens she went to New York and worked as a typist while training to be a model. She has been seen in the following movies: FAT CITY (72); AMERICAN GRAFFITI (73, Oscar nomination); I WILL, I WILL ... FOR NOW (75); THE MAN WHO FELL TO EARTH (76); THE BIG SLEEP (77); HANDLE WITH CARE (77); MORE AMERICAN GRAFFITI (79); WHEN YOU COMIN' BACK, RED RYDER? (80); Q: THE WINGED SERPENT, BLUE THUNDER (both 1982).

NICHOLAS CLAY

B. Streatham, London, 18.9.46. Father in regular army; ed. Scotland, Vienna, Cairo, Suez; trained at RADA; repertory (Nottingham, etc.), N.T. player; T.V. includes 'Suspicion', 'Love Story', 'Play of the Week'; movies include THE NIGHT DIGGER (71); THE DARWIN ADVENTURE (72), ZULU DAWN (78); md. Lorna; recently co-starred in international movies such as EX-CALIBUR (81, as Sir Lancelot); LADY CHATTERLEY (81, as Mellors); EVIL UNDER THE SUN (82); HOUND OF THE BASKER-VILLES (83); T.V. 1982: 'In a Glass Darkly', 'Russian Night 1941'.

JILL CLAYBURGH

B. New York City, 30.4.44. Father, company vice-president; mother at one time worked for theatre producer David Merrick; grandmother, Alma, was famous opera singer. Ed. Sarah Lawrence; studied philosophy and drama; joined Boston Theatre Co.; played on Broadway in 'The Sudden & Accidental Re-Education of Horse Johnson' (1968); 'Calling in Crazy' (1969); 'The Nest' (1970); 'The Rothschilds' (1970); others. Came to screen in THE WEDDING PARTY (70) and has been seen in PORTNOY'S COMPLAINT (72); THE THIEF WHO CAME TO DINNER (72); TERMINAL MAN (74); Carole Lombard in GABLE & LOMBARD (75); SIL-VER STREAK (77); SEMI-TOUGH (77); AN UNMARRIED WOMAN (77, Oscar nom.); STARTING OVER (78, Oscar nom.); LA LUNA (79); IT'S MY TURN (79). Md. David Rabe (playwright) 1979. Jill has given good performances on T.V., including T.V. movie 'Hustling' in 1975; THE FIRST MONDAY IN OCTOBER (81); I'M DANCING AS FAST AS I CAN (82).

SUSAN CLARK

B. Sarnid, Ontario, Canada, 8.3.40(?). Stage debut: Flint, Michigan, aged 17; came to G.B., studied at R.A.D.A.; theatre at York, 6 yrs. in rep., T.V. in G.B. Md. — — (writer—div.) Ret'd. to Canada in 1965, starred for CBS in 6 prods., landing Universal contract. Movies: BANNING (67); MADIGAN (68); COOGAN'S BLUFF (68); COLOSSUS (69); TELL THEM WILLIE BOY IS HERE (69); SKULLDUGGERY (69); VALDEZ IS COMING (70); THE SKIN GAME (71); SHOWDOWN (73); TRAPPED (73, T.V. movie); THE MIDNIGHT MAN (74); AIRPORT 75 (75); THE APPLE-DUMPLING GANG (75); AMELIA EAR-HART (76, T.V. movie); CITY OF FIRE (78); SHERLOCK HOLMES—MURDER BY DECREE (78); NORTH AVENUE IRREGU-LARS (79). Won Emmy Award for portrayal of world's greatest female athlete Babe Didrikson Zacharias in BABE (75, T.V. movie) and appd. in 3 episodes of 'McNaughton's Daughter' (1976 T.V.); Md: 2. Alex Karras, footballer-turned-actor, her NOBODY'S PERFEKT (81) and PORKY'S (82) co-star.

JOHN CLEESE

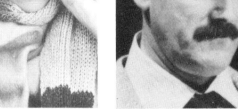

B. Weston-super-Mare, Somerset, 27.10.39. Ed. Clifton College, Cambridge Univ., gaining success in 'Cambridge Footlights Revue' and 'The New Cambridge Circus' which played in London's West End, toured. Cleese appearing in both shows Broadway in 1964 & 65; remaining there for 'Half a Sixpence'. Gained tremendous success on T.V. as satirist, esp. with David Frost in 'The Frost Report'. Md. 1. U.S. actress Connie Booth (1 daughter Cynthia) div.. International star in BBC's 'Monty Python's Flying Circus' series. Movies include: INTERLUDE (68); THE BEST HOUSE IN LONDON (68); THE MAGIC CHRISTIAN (69); THE RISE & RISE OF MICHAEL RIMMER (70. co-scripted); AND NOW FOR SOMETHING COMPLETELY DIFFERENT (71); THE LOVE BAN (72); MONTY PYTHON AND THE HOLY GRAIL (74); THE LIFE OF BRIAN (79); THE SEC-RET POLICEMAN'S BALL (79); THE GREAT MUPPET CAPER (80, guest); THE TIME BANDITS (81); SECRET POLICE-MAN'S OTHER BALL. MONTY PYTHON'S MEANING OF LIFE (both 82); PRIVATES ON PARADE. YELLOWBEARD (both 83); Md: 2. U.S. actress Barbara Trentham. 17.2.81.

JAMES COBURN

Never quite attaining the rank of Super star, James Coburn has remained one of Hollywood's busiest actors for the last two decades, a popular actor whose lithe frame and broad grin is equally at home in actioners or comedy. The son of James Coburn Sr., he was born on 31 August 1928 at Laurel, Nebraska. At the age of 5, after the family business went broke, the Coburns moved to Los Angeles, and James studied acting eventually at Los Angeles City College. After being drafted into the US Army he went to New York in search of acting 'with $23 in my pocket'. Living at a friend's flat he was lucky in his first week, when through a girlfriend, he phoned a casting director which eventually landed him a T.V. commercial advertising a new rubber golf ball. Soon after he got a commercial, advertising an electric razor, which for 2½ years helped pay for 'acting classes and 3 square meals a day'. After this, with fellow actors, he ran a theatre off-Broadway which went bankrupt, but he managed to gain a few T.V. roles, and he next appeared in rep. at Detroit. Returning to Los Angeles he got an agent, and came to the screen in RIDE LONESOME (58), then he was seen in FACE OF A FUGITIVE (59). On 11 November 1959 he wed Beverly Kelly and a son James Jr. was born 22 May 1961. In 1960/61 he was a regular as Jeff Durain in the 'Klondike' series, but 1960 marked his break in movies as 'Texas', the knife-fighter, as one of THE MAGNIFICENT SEVEN. Since then his moves have included: HELL IS FOR HEROES (62); THE GREAT ESCAPE (63); CHARADE (63); THE MAN FROM GALVESTON (64); THE MAERICANIZATION OF EMILY (64); MAJOR DUNDEE (65); A HIGH WIND IN JAMAICA (65); THE LOVED ONE (65); WHAT DID YOU DO IN THE WAR, DADDY? (66); DEAD HEAT ON A MERRY-GO-ROUND (66); OUR MAN FLINT (66); WATERHOLE 3 (67); IN LIKE FLINT (67); THE PRESIDENT'S ANALYST (67); DUFFY (68); HARD CONTRACT (68); CANDY (68); BLOOD KIN (69); A FISTFUL OF DYNAMITE (71); THE CAREY TREATMENT (72); THE HONKERS (72); A REASON TO LIVE, A REASON TO DIE (72); PAT GARRETT AND BILLY THE KID (73); LAST OF SHEILA (73); HARRY IN YOUR POCKET (73); THE INTERNECINE PROJECT (74); BITE THE BULLET (75); HARD TIMES (76); SKY RIDERS (76); THE LAST HARD MEN (76); MIDWAY (77); CROSS OF IRON (77); FIREPOWER (78); THE MUPPET MOVIE (78, guest); LOVING COUPLES (78); MIDNIGHT MATINEE (80); BALTIMORE BULLET (80); HIGH RISK, LOOKER (both 1981) and VALLEY OF THE DOLLS (81, T.V. movie).

JAMES COCO

B. New York City, 21.3.29. Ed. Evander Child's High School. Entered theatre in teens, stage-managing tour. Worked in 100s of jobs including kitchen-hand, toy salesman, waiter. Studied dramatic art under Uta Hagen at the Berghof Studio; appeared extensively in repertory and became distinguished character actor on Broadway in such prods. as 'Salome', 'Hotel Paradise', 'A Passage to India', 'The Devils', 'Fragments', 'Last of Red Hot Lovers'. Movies include: ENSIGN PULVER (64); STRAWBERRY STATEMENT (69); A NEW LEAF (70); TELL ME THAT YOU LOVE ME, JUNIE MOON (70); SUCH GOOD FRIENDS (71); MAN OF LA MANCHA (72, also stage); THE WILD PARTY (74); MURDER BY DEATH (76); THE CHEAP DETECTIVE (77); WHOLLY MOSES (79); THE FRENCH-ATLANTIC AFFAIR (79, T.V. movie); ONLY WHEN I LAUGH (81, Oscar nom. BSA); THE CURIOUS CASE OF SANTA CLAUS (T.V. movie 1982). Mr Coco has guested many times on T.V. and had 2 series: 'Calucci's Apartment' (73) and 'The Dumplings' (76).

GEORGE COLE

B. London, 22.4.25. Ed. Morden Council School. Aged 14, appeared in 'White Horse Inn' show, Blackpool, Sept. 1939, followed by playing Ronald in 'Cottage to Let', 1940, London and tour and making his screen debut in this role in 1941. Since then has become well-known face in movies, theatre and especially T.V. Md. Penny Morrell, 1 daughter Tara, 1 son Toby. Films include HENRY V (44); QUARTET (48, segment: The Kite); SCROOGE (51); TOP SECRET (51); OUR GIRL FRIDAY (53); A PRIZE OF GOLD (55); THE BELLES OF ST. TRINIAN'S (55, as 'Flash Harry' and in 3 sequels); THE GREEN MAN (57); CLEOPATRA (62); ONE-WAY PENDULUM (64); THE VAMPIRE LOVERS (70); FRIGHT (71); TAKE ME HIGH (73); THE BLUEBIRD (76), others. Radio includes 15 yrs. in 'Life of Bliss'. Recent T.V.: stars opp. Dennis Waterman (q.v.) in 'Minder' series; stage 1982: 'The Pirates of Penzance'; T.V. series 1982: Trevor in 'The Bounder'.

JOAN COLLINS

Although may of her movies have been unremarkable, it should be pointed out that Joan Collins is one of the very few, if not the only, remaining British star actress from the early 1950's to be still taking lead roles in films. It was inevitable that Joan (born London 23 May 1933) should want to become an actress since her father, Will Collins, ran a theatrical agency in the 30s with Lew Grade. Educated at 13 schools, due to war, including Francis Holland School, Joan studied at R.A.D.A., in her spare time modelling for ladies' magazines. She was discovered by agent Bill Watts, and, still in her teens, Joan came to the screen uncredited in LADY GODIVA RIDES AGAIN (51) as a beauty contestant and started in small roles in THE WOMAN'S ANGLE and I BELIEVE IN YOU (both 52). She wed actor Maxwell Reed in 1952, did stage roles and continued to make films such as COSH BOY (53), TURN THE KEY SOFTLY (53) and OUR GIRL FRIDAY (54). In 1954 she appeared in the epic LAND OF THE PHARAOHS which brought her to Hollywood and landed a Fox contract, appearing in such pictures as VIRGIN QUEEN (55); THE GIRL IN THE RED VELVET SWING (55); SEA WIFE (56); ISLAND IN THE SUN (56); THE BRAVADOS (58) and SEVEN THIEVES (59). After teaming with Crosby and Hope in THE ROAD TO HONG KONG (62) she wed singer/actor Anthony Newley in 1963 (divorcing Reed in 1957) and they had three children, Tara Cynara (born 12.10.63), Alexander Anthony (born 8.9.65) and Sacha (born circa 1966). Her other 60s movies included: LA CONGUINTURA (64); WARNING SHOT (68); SUBTERFUGE (68); HIERONYMUS MERKIN (68, with Newley) and THE EXECUTIONER (69). Divorcing Newley in 1971, she wed music and film producer Ron Kass in Jamaica in 1972 and their daughter Katyana was born 20.6.72. Continuing her film career in the 70s she appeared in QUEST FOR LOVE (70); FEAR IN THE NIGHT (71); TALES FROM THE CRYPT (72); ALFIE DARLING (74); THE MONEYCHANGERS (76, T.V. movie); EMPIRE OF THE ANTS (Sci-Fi Aw.), THE BIG SLEEP (both 1977); SUNBURN (78); GAMES FOR VULTURES and THE BITCH (both 1979). Her husband, from whom she is now separated, produced her hit movie, THE STUD (77), and also her return to the stage, 'The Last of Mrs Cheyney' (80/81). Following two movies in 1982, HOMEWORK and NUTCRACKER, Joan achieved a vast following on T.V. internationally in the role of Alexis Carrington in 'Dynasty' (82-   , winning her a Golden Globe Award), and, in December, 1982, she was voted 'Female Star of 1982' by the Hollywood Women's Press Club. *PAST IMPERFECT* by Joan Collins (autobio.); W.H. Allen, 1978; p/b: Coronet, 1979; *JOAN COLLINS' BEAUTY BOOK*; MacMillan: London, 1980; *KATY: A FIGHT FOR LIFE* (account of her daughter's recovery from a coma); Victor Gollancz: London, 1982.

SEAN CONNERY

Amazingly, it has been 20 years since Connery deservedly won fame in the first Bond film, DR NO, and since then thi solid Scot has given consistently good performances in his movies in roles completely diverse from the 007 character The eldest son of Joseph Connery and his wife Effie, he was born Thomas Connery on 25 August 1930 i Fountainbridge, a district of Edinburgh, Scotland. Educated at Darroch, he commenced earning a wage as part-tim milk deliveryman (his father was a furniture removal van driver) at the age of 13, and, leaving school, worked at it full time. A succession of jobs followed: joined navy as armourer, but left owing to duodenal ulcer; coalman; Frencl polisher; steelworker; road labourer; did weight-training and modelled at Edinburgh College of Art; came to London fo 'Mr Universe', winning Bronze medal; he was an excellent footballer; cleaned printing presses; dance-hall bouncer an summer of 1950 worked as life-guard. Connery had at this time done 5 weeks work in the touring production of 'Th Glorious Days' (with Anna Neagle) when it played in Edinburgh, and while in London as 'Mr Universe' contestant had heard that jobs were being auditioned for in the tour of 'South Pacific'. He applied and got a chorus job, toured the U.K. later given a supporting role, and he decided to train seriously as an actor. He came to London, studied acting with Ya Malmgren and played in rep. at Kew and at Oxford. He came to the screen in 1955 in NO ROAD BACK and afte further small roles in TIME LOCK (56), HELL DRIVERS (57) and ACTION OF THE TIGER (57) it was hi performance in 'Requiem for a Heavyweight' (replacing Jack Palance) that won him a Fox contract, playing opposite Lana Turner in ANOTHER TIME, ANOTHER PLACE (58). He did further good work on T.V. at this time in 'Anna Christie', 'The Crucible', 'Macbeth' and 'Anna Karenina' and more movies such as DARBY O'GILL AND THE LITTLE PEOPLE (59); THE FRIGHTENED CITY (60) and ON THE FIDDLE (60). In 1961 he was cast as James Bond in DR NO and the rest is history and he appeared as 007 in FROM RUSSIA WITH LOVE (63); GOLDFINGER (64); THUNDERBALL (66); YOU ONLY LIVE TWICE (67) and DIAMONDS ARE FOREVER (72). He wed actress Diane Cilento in late November 1962, and their son, Jason, was born in 1963. His many other movies include MARNIE (65); THE HILL (65); A FINE MADNESS (66); THE MOLLY MAGUIRES (69); THE RED TENT (69); THE ANDERSON TAPES (71); THE OFFENCE (72); ZARDOZ (74); THE MAN WHO WOULD BE KING (76); THE NEXT MAN (76). Divorced from Miss Cilento in 1974, the following year he wed Micheline Roquebrune, an artist. Mr Connery has several business interests, including a stake in several banks in U.S. and a 600 acre pig and cattle farm in Iowa. An accomplished golfer, his most recent films are FIRST GREAT TRAIN ROBBERY (78); METEOR (78); CUBA (79); THE TIME BANDITS (80); OUTLAND (81); THE MAN WITH THE DEADLY LENS, 5 DAYS ONE SUMMER (both 1982); SWORD OF THE VALIANT (83) and he returns as 007 in NEVER SAY NEVER AGAIN (83).
SEAN CONNERY — GILT EDGED BOND by Richard Gant. pb: Mayflower/Dell, 1967
SEAN CONNERY: A BIOGRAPHY by Kenneth Passingham; Sidgwick & Jackson: London, 1983.
SEAN CONNERY: HIS LIFE & FILMS by Michael Feeley Callan; W.H. Allen: London, 1983.

LEWIS COLLINS

B. Birkenhead, Cheshire, 26.5.46. Ed. Bidston Primary & Grange School, B'head. Hairdresser; numerous other jobs; bass guitarist with 'The Mojos' and other groups; studied with L.A.M.D.A.; rep., much theatre incl. Prospect Theatre Co., West End, tours. T.V. includes 'Z Cars' (début), 'Rooms', 'The New Avengers', 'The Cuckoo Waltz' and became well-known on British T.V. with his performance as Bodie in 'The Professionals', opposite Martin Shaw (q.v.). Mr Collins who is an expert rifle and pistol shot, has appeared in CONFESSIONS OF A DRIVING INSTRUCTOR (76, uncredited), starred in WHO DARES WINS (82); 'A Night on the Town' (B.B.C./Video, 1983).

KENNETH CONNOR

B. Portsmouth, Hants, 1918. Studied for the stage at the Central School of Speech & Drama, winning gold medal; much stage includes Bristol Old Vic, the Old Vic and revue—'One Over the Eight'; many radio and T.V. performances. Movies include: THERE WAS A YOUNG LADY (53); THE BLACK RIDER (55); THE LADY-KILLERS (55); DAVY (57). From 1958 commenced highly successful comedy appearances in the 'CARRY ON . . .' series, with CARRY ON SERGEANT, specialising 'up-tight' roles; DENTIST IN THE CHAIR (60); GONKS GO BEAT (65). Md. Mickie, 1 son. Recent movie: CARRY ON EMMANUELLE (78); stage 1982: 'Getting Married', T.V. 1982: 'East Lynne'.

CHUCK CONNORS

B. New York City, 10.4.21. Ed. Seton Hall Coll. E. Orange, N.J. Father was in police; Connors who is 6'5½" tall, became baseball & basketbal star, playing for Brooklyn Dodgers, the Chicago Cubs and L.A. Angels, interrupted by spell in U.S. Army instructing cadets in tank warfare a West Point; a baseball star in L.A., he was advised to try acting, did T.V. parts and came to the screen in PAT AND MIKE (52) and his many movies include SOUTH SEA WOMAN (53); NAKED ALIBI (54); TARGET ZERO (55); DESIGNING WOMAN (57); THE BIG COUNTRY (58); as GERONIMO (62); MOVE OVER, DARLING (63); RIDE BEYOND VENGEANCE (66); CAPT. NEMO & THE FLOATING CITY (69). Md. 1. model Elizabeth Jane Riddle 1942, 4 sons Michael (b. 1943), Jeffrey (b. 1944), Steven (b. 1945), Kevin (b. 1946). Very popular on T.V. in his series 'Rifleman' (1958-63); 'Arrest & Trial' (1963); 'Branded' (1965); and 'Cowboy in Africa' (1967). Md. 2. Indian actress Kamala Devi 1963. Recent T.V./ movies: EMBASSY (72); PANCHO VILLA (72); SOYLENT GREEN (72); PROUD & THE DAMNED (73, T.V. movie); THE NIGHT THEY TOOK MISS BEAUTIFUL (77, T.V. movie); ROOTS (77, T.V.); TOURIST TRAP (78); VIRUS (80); DAY OF THE ASSASSIN (80); LA MUJERES DE JERENIAS (80); AIRPLANE II: THE SEQUEL (82).

MIKE CONNORS

B. Fresno, Calif., 15.8.25; real name — —(?) Ohanian. Ed. U.C.L.A. Father, an American lawyer; 3 yrs. U.S. Air Force WWII; won athletic ship to univ. (B.A.) then law school but became actor after 1st pro. job as lawyer. Came to screen 1952 in SUDDEN FEAR; others include TEN COMMANDMENTS (56); WHERE LOVE HAS GONE (64); GOOD NEIGHBOUR SAM (64); HARLOW (65); STAGECOACH (66); KISS THE GIRLS AND MAKE THEM DIE (67). Md. Mary Lou Wiley 1950, 1 son Matthew, daughter Dana. Popular on U.S. T.V. in series: 'Tightrope' (1959-60) and 'Mannix' (1967-75, Golden Globe Award). Recent movies: AVALANCHE EXPRESS (78); THE ROCKET (79); S.S. CASINO, HIGH MIDNIGHT (both T.V. movies, 79); DEATH OF OCEAN VIEW PARK (T.V. movie, 80); THE DOORMAN (83); T.V. ser. 82/83: 'Today's F.B.I.'.

ROBERT CONRAD

B. Chicago, Ill., 1.3.35; real name Conrad Robert Falk. Studied drama at Northwestern Univ; show-biz début as a nightclub singer, also worked for dairy and on a ship; got small roles on T.V. ('Lawman') and movies (THUNDERING JETS (58)) before becoming popular on T.V. as regular actor in 'Hawaiin Eye' (1959-63) and 'Wild Wild West' (1965-69) series. Md. Joan, 2 daughters Joan and Nancy. Movies include: PALM SPRINGS WEEKEND (63); YOUNG DILLINGER (65); MURPH THE SURF (75); SUDDEN DEATH (77); THE LADY IN RED (79). Mr Conrad has a nightclub act and is seriously interested in Spanish dancing, speaks Spanish fluently. Recent T.V.: series 'Centennial' (78); 'The Duke' (78); THE WILD, WILD, WEST REVISITED (T.V. movie, 79); series 'Nero Wolfe' (81); THE MAN WITH THE DEADLY LENS (82).

WILLIAM CONRAD

B. Louisville, Kentucky, 27.9.20. Ed. Fullerton Coll. Worked in many capacities for radio station KMPC in L.A., announcer/writer/director; WWII fighter pilot; became Matt Dillon on radio in 'Gunsmoke'. Came to the screen as one of THE KILLERS (46). Other movies: ARCH OF TRIUMPH (48); ONE-WAY STREET (50); CRY DANGER (51); LONE STAR (52); THE NAKED JUNGLE (54); DESERT SONG (54); JOHNNY CONCHO (56); THE RIDE BACK (57); others. Became T.V. director ('True', 'Klon-dike' series), co-producer ('77 Sunset Strip') and narrator ('The Fugitive') and motion picture producer/director of TWO ON A GUILLOTINE (64); BRAINSTORM (65); others. Produced CHAMBER OF HORRORS (66); AN AMERICAN DREAM (67); COUNTDOWN (68); a popular T.V. actor as 'Cannon' (ser. 1971-75). Recent: RETURN OF FRANK CANNON (T.V. movie, 80); SCHOCKTRAUMA, THE MIKADO (both T.V. movies, 82).

TOM CONTI

B. Glasgow, Scotland, 1942. Of Scottish/Italian parentage; studied stagecraft at Glasgow Coll. of Drama and appeared in rep. at Glasgow Citizen's Theatre and Edinburgh. Stage plays include: 'Savages', 'Let's Murder Vivaldi', 'Don Juan', 'Whose Life Is It Anyway?' (winning Tony Award—Broadway). Directed 'Lastlicks' on Broadway and 'Before the Party' (West End 1980). Md. actress Kara Wilson 1967, 1 daughter Nina. Mr Conti's movies: THE LIFE OF GALILEO (74); FLAME (74); ECLIPSE (75); THE DUELLISTS (76); FULL CIRCLE (76); THE WALL (80, T.V. movie); BLADE ON THE FEATHER (80, T.V. movie). Recent theatre: 'They're Playing Our Song' (London 1980/81). Won acclaim in 1976 for his performance on BBC T.V. in 'The Glittering Prizes' (76); recent stage: directed 'The Housekeeper' (82); starred in 'Romantic Comedy' (83); MERRY CHRISTMAS, MR LAWRENCE, REUBEN, REUBEN (both 83).

PETER COOK

B. Torquay, Devonshire, 13.11.37. Father was Colonial Office official in Nigeria. Ed. Radley College & Cambridge Univ.; at the latter wrote successful revues 'Pieces of Eight' and 'One Over the Eight', staged successfully in London in 1959 and 1961 respectively; with Jonathan Miller, Alan Bennett and Dudley Moore (q.v.) appeared in 'Beyond the Fringe' at Edinburgh, London and Broadway (1962). Md. 1. Wendy Snowden (div.). Very successful on T.V., work includes: 'On the Braden Beat' (creating character' Spotty Muldoon'), 'Not Only...But Also' (with Dudley Moore) and guesting on chat shows. Films: THE WRONG BOX (66); BEDAZZLED (67); A DANDY IN ASPIC (68); THE BED-SITTING ROOM (69); MONTE CARLO OR BUST (69); THE RISE & RISE OF MICHAEL RIMMER (69). Md. 2. actress Judy Huxtable; co-founder 'Private Eye', satirical mag.; 'The Two of Us' (U.S. T.V. ser. 1981); recent films: HOUND OF THE BASKER-VILLES (77); SECRET POLICEMAN'S BALL (80); DEREK & CLIVE (82, video); YELLOW-BEARD (83, also co-wrote); SUPERGIRL (84).

ALEX CORD

B. Floral Park, New York, 3.8.31; real name Alexander Viespi. Aged 12, contracted polio in left leg, contrived own exercises and recovered. N.Y. Univ. Aged 16 riding, roping, and steer wrestling throughout U.S.A. for 5 yrs. Interest in Shakespeare and acting after seeing movie RICHARD III (56); enrolled S'peare Acad., Connecticut, played in classics; Actors' Studio, N.Y.; 2 seasons summer stock; Stratford S'peare tour 1961; London Stage: 'Play With a Tiger' (1962), 'The Umbrella', 'The Rose Tattoo' (1963); BBC T.V. 'The Joker'. Had come to screen uncredited in THE CHAPMAN REPORT (62); small roles on T.V. ('Route 66'); from 1964 starred on big screen in SYNANON (G.B.: GET OFF MY BACK); STAGECOACH (65, in original John Wayne role); THE BROTHER-HOOD (68); DEAD OR ALIVE (69); STILETTO (69); THE LAST GRENADE (69); THE DEAD ARE ALIVE (72); CHOSEN SURVIVORS (74); GENESIS (73, T.V. movie—1st of 3 'pilot' films); FIRE (76); SIDEWINDER ONE (77); GRAYEAGLE (77); Md. actress Joanna Pettet 1968 (1 son Damion b. 1968). T.V. includes: Best Sellers: 'Beggarman, Thief' (1979); ser. 'W.E.B.' (78); GOLIATH AWAITS (82, mini-ser.)

BILL COSBY

B. North Philadelphia, 12.7.37(?). Father, a navy steward. Ed. Germantown High School; Temple Univ., Philadelphia. Excelled at football at Univ.; while there worked in bar and owing to his ability to make people laugh was advised to become comedian. In 1962 went to N.Y. and landed $60-a-week job at Gaslight Coffee House, Greenwich Vill.; soon offered nightclub/T.V. work, appd. 20 times with Johnny Carson, 7 with Jack Paar; serious actor début as Alexander Scott in T.V. series 'I Spy', winning several Emmy Awards (1965-68). Md. Camille Hanks 1964, 4 daughters: Erika (b. 1965), Erinn (b. 1966), Ensa (b. 1973), Evin (b. 1976), 1 son Ennis (b. 1970). Movies: HICKEY & BOGGS (72); UPTOWN SATUR-DAY NIGHT (74); LET'S DO IT AGAIN (76); MOTHER JUGS AND SPEED (76); A PIECE OF THE ACTION (77); CALIFORNIA SUITE (78). Mr Cosby's other T.V. shows: 'The Bill Cosby Show' (1969-71), 'Fat Albert & the Cosby Kids' (1972, animated cartoon-host/voice) and 'Cos' (1976); he has recorded many comedy and singing albums. Recent movie: THE DEVIL & MAX DEVLIN (80).

JAMES COSSINS

B. Beckenham, Kent, 4.12.33. Mr Cossins has appeared extensively in repertory, West End, Broadway ('Portrait of a Queen' 1968), television, including 'The Beggar's Opera', 'Special Branch' (1970), 'Mad Jack', 'Rainbird', 'The Breaking of Colonel Keyser', 'The Pallisers'. His many movies include HOW I WON THE WAR (67); THE ANNIVERSARY (68); OTLEY (69); THE RISE & RISE OF MICHAEL RIMMER (70); WUTHERING HEIGHTS (70); VILLAIN (71); S.W.A.L.K. (71); THE MAN WITH THE GOLDEN GUN (74). Recent T.V.: 'Don't Forget to Write' (1977); 'Just William' (1977); 'Prince Regent' (1979); 'It Shouldn't Happen to a Vet' (1979); 'Jukes of Piccadilly' (1980); 'Why Didn't They Ask Evans?' (80); 'Confessions of Felix Krull — Confidence Man' (82); 'Number 10' (83); Geoffrey in 'Goodnight & God Bless' (83, ser.); recent films: SPHINX, LOOPHOLE (both 1981); GANDHI (82).

JOSEPH COTTEN

B. Petersburg, Virginia, 15.5.05. Father, Post Office Superintendant. On leaving school at 17, worked at all jobs in a little theatre group, and studied stagecraft at the Hickman School of Expression, Washington, D.C.; A.S.M./under-study Belasco Theatre 1930; stock Boston 1931-32; in 30s on Broadway, incl. 'Jezebel', 'Postman Always Ring Twice', 'Philadelphia Story' (& tour). Joined Orson Welles' famous Mercury Players, coming to the screen in the former's CITIZEN KANE (40). Md. Lenore Kipp 1931 (dec. 1960). His best films included THE MAGNIFICENT AMBERSONS (42); JOUR-NEY INTO FEAR (42); SHADOW OF A DOUBT (43); GASLIGHT (44); I'LL BE SEEING YOU (45); PORTRAIT OF JENNIE (48); THE THIRD MAN (49); HALF ANGEL (51); NIAGARA (52); many others. Md. 2. Patricia Medina 1960, appd. on stage together, tour 1964; narrator: 'Hollywood & the Stars' 1963-64. Recent movies: THE HEARSE (79); HEAVEN'S GATE (80); THE SURVIVOR (80); GUYANA—CRIME OF THE CENTURY (80); SCREAMERS, DELUSION (both 1981).

TOM COURTENAY

One of several brilliant young stage and screen actors to emerge from Britain in the early 60s, Tom Courtenay ha: always remained popular with film and theatregoers. The son of Thomas (a painter and cleaner of fishing trawlers) an Annie Courtenay, he was born in Hull on 25 February 1937. Brought up in the Hessle Road district of Hull's docklanc Mr Courtenay first showed an interest in acting after the reading of the lessons at prayers at Kingston High School, Hul At University College, London, he read English, but failed his degree and switched his studies, training for the stage a R.A.D.A. In 1960 he immediately joined the Old Vic Co., debuting as Konstantin Treplyef in 'The Seagull' a Edinburgh and after appearing with this Co. in Shakespearean roles in 1961, that year he took over from Albert Finne (qv) the role of Billy Fisher in 'Billy Liar' at the Cambridge Theatre. A year later Tony Richardson selected him for hi screen debut as the borstal boy in THE LONELINESS OF THE LONG DISTANCE RUNNER, to much acclaim and his film appearances have been: PRIVATE POTTER (62); BILLY LIAR (63); KING AND COUNTRY (64) OPERATION CROSSBOW (65); KING RAT (65); DOCTOR ZHIVAGO (66, Academy Award Nom., BSA THE NIGHT OF THE GENERALS (66); THE DAY THE FISH CAME OUT (67); A DANDY IN ASPIC (68 OTLEY (69); ONE DAY IN THE LIFE OF IVAN DENISOVICH (71); CATCH ME A SPY (71). Tom Courtena: has continued to win acclaim for his many roles on the stage including Andri in 'Andorra' (1964); Trofimov in 'Th Cherry Orchard' (1966); 'Hamlet' (1968); Young Marlow in 'She Stoops to Conquer' (1969); Capt. Bluntschli i 'Arms and the Man' (1973) and Norman in 'The Norman Conquests' (1974). He is separated from actress Chery Kennedy, whom he wed in 1973. 1981 was a good year for the actor — at the Queen's Theatre, London, his work in 'Th Dresser' won him the 'Drama' magazine and 'Standard' Awards as Best Actor, and he played in 'The Misanthrope' a the Round House. 1982 saw him at the Aldwych Theatre in the title role of the musical version of 'Andy Capp', and h filmed THE DRESSER in 1983.

MICHAEL CRAIG

B. Poona, India, 27.1.29(?); real name Michael Gregson; Ed: Upper Canada Coll., Toronto; Father a soldier. Aged 3, came to England; at 10, went to Canada; 1944-49 served in Merchant Navy, travelling the world; 1949 joined Farnham Rep., appd. in 'Merchant of Venice'; rep. at York, Windsor, Oxford; at latter seen in 'A Man About the House' and given film contract—commencing with PASSAGE HOME (55). Before this had worked in movies as an extra and had minor roles in MALTA STORY (53) and THE LOVE LOTTERY (54); his many other movies include: CAMPBELL'S KINGDOM (58); THE SILENT ENEMY (58); SEA OF SAND (59); SAPPHIRE (59); THE ANGRY SILENCE (59, story Mr Craig's idea); MYSTERIOUS ISLAND (61); PAYROLL (61); LIFE FOR RUTH (62); STOLEN HOURS (63); LIFE AT THE TOP (65); STAR! (68); TWINKY (69); VAULT OF HORROR (73). Md. Susan —, 1 daughter Jessica, 2 sons, Stephen & Michael. Mr Craig has continued his stage career, incl. R.S. Co., West End, Broadway and Australia, in latter 1977 made movie THE IRISHMAN, appd. in 'The Tempest' (Sydney Opera House). Recent movie: THE TIMELESS LAND (79). T.V.: guest in 'The Professionals', 'Shoestring' (1980); stars in BBC 1 series, 'Triangle' (1981-83); recent film: TURKEY SHOOT (82, Australia).

GEMMA CRAVEN

B. Dublin, 1.6.50. Ed. Loretta Coll., Dublin and St. Bernard's Convent, Westcliff-on-Sea. Aged 3, won singing competition; aged 4, stage debut in school prod.; piano lessons from age 5. During teens family moved to Westcliff-on-Sea, Gemma made pro. debut 1968 as the maid in 'Let's Get a Divorce', after studying at Bush Davies School, Romford; summer season Blackpool; panto. Watford; 1970 West End debut Anya in 'Fiddler on the Roof'; continued and various roles in rep., West End incl.: Sabrina in 'Sabrina Fair', Leatherhead 1972: Rose Trelawny in 'Trelawny', West End 1972; Chichester Festival seasons 1973 & 74, coming to the screen in Bryan Forbes' THE SLIPPER AND THE ROSE as Cinderella, winning Evening News Film Award for Most Promising Actress' and 'Variety Club Award for Film Actress' of 1976. Much T.V. incl. 'Harry Secombe Show', 'Emily', Amalia in musical 'She Loves Me', numerous chat shows, panel games, acclaimed BBC T.V. series 'Pennies from Heaven' (1978); stage tour 'Side by Side by Sondheim' (1978), West End 1979: 'Songbook'; 80/81: 'They're Playing Our Song'—'Best Actress in a Musical' (Soc. of W. End Theatre); 82/83: 'Song and Dance'. Wed actor Fraser Hines 20.12.81. Film 1978: WHY NOT STAY FOR BREAK-FAST? Recent T.V.: 'East Lynne' (82); 'Wagner' (mini-ser., 1983).

MICHAEL CRAWFORD

B. Salisbury, Wiltshire, 19.1.42. Ed. St. Michae Coll., Bexley; Oakfield School, Dulwich; choi boy at St. Paul's Cathedral. Left school aged 1 and came to the screen 1958 in 2 children's film SOAP BOX DERBY and BLOW YOUR OW. TRUMPET. As boy soprano appd. in stag prods. 'Let's Make an Opera' and 'Noyes Fludde over 600 broadcasts on radio; 1960s theatr 'Come Blow Your Horn' (1962); 'Travellin Light' (1965); 'The Anniversary' (1966). Movie TWO LIVING, ONE DEAD (62); THE WA LOVER (62); TWO LEFT FEET (63); TH KNACK (64); A FUNNY THING HAPPENE ON THE WAY TO THE FORUM (66); TH JOKERS (66); HOW I WON THE WAR (67 HELLO DOLLY (69); THE GAMES (69 HELLO GOODBYE (70); ALICE'S ADVEN TURES IN WONDERLAND (72). Divorce from wife Gabrielle in Sept. 1975, he has daughters, Lucy & Emma. Very popular on T.V creating character Frank Spencer in 'Som Mothers Do 'Ave 'Em'. Other stage: 'No Se Please, We're British' (1971); 'Billy' (1974/75 'Flowers for Algernon' (79); appd. Broadwa 1967. Recent stage: 'Barnum' (81/82, London film: CONDORMAN (80).

BRODERICK CRAWFORD

B. Philadelphia, 9.12.11. Mother, Helen Broderick, actress; father, Lester Pendergast, actor; grand-parents opera singers. As a youngster toured in vaudeville with parents; tried boxing and worked as seaman, urged by parents to train as engineer, but chose show-biz career: radio; 13 weeks stooge for the Marx Bros; stock; Broadway: 'Point Valaine', 'Sweet Mystery of Life' (both 1935); created with acclaim role of Lennie in 'Of Mice & Men', Broadway 1937, and came to screen 1937 in WOMAN CHASES MAN, SUBMARINE D-1. Md. Kay Griffith, singer 1940, 3 sons: Kim (adopted), Chris (b. 1948), Kelly (b. 1951), div. 1961. Early films: AMBUSH (39); BEAU GESTE (39); ISLAND OF LOST MEN (39); WHEN THE DALTONS RODE (40); TEXAS RANGERS RIDE AGAIN (40); THE BLACK CAT (41); TIGHT SHOES (41); BROADWAY (42); MEN OF TEXAS (42). Served as Sergeant U.S.A. AF 1942-45. More movies: THE RUN-AROUND (46); BLACK ANGEL (46); SLAVE GIRL (47); THE FLAME (47); won Oscar 1949 as Willie Stark in ALL THE KING'S MEN. In 1950s made 17 films including BORN YESTERDAY (51), but well-known on T.V. as Dan Matthews in 'Highway Patrol' for 156 episodes from 1956. Md. 2. Joan Tabor, actress 1962 (div. 1967). Other T.V.: 'King of Diamonds' (1961) and 'The Interns (1970/71). Md. 3. Mary Alice Mitchell 1973. Recent movies: PRIVATE FILES OF J. EDGAR HOOVER (78); A LITTLE ROMANCE (79); THERE GOES THE BRIDE (79); HARLEQUIN (79).

RICHARD CRENNA

B. Los Angeles, 30.11.26(?). Ed. Belmont High School and Univ. of S. Calif., but commenced career on radio series 'Boy Scout Jamboree' aged 11, which ran for 11 years. Md. Penni Smith 1950, 2 daughters (Seana b. 1952, Maria b. 1965), 1 son (Richard Jr. b. 1959). T.V. series 1952-56: 'Our Miss Brooks' (also radio). Came to screen 1952 in PRIDE OF ST. LOUIS, IT GROWS ON TREES, RED SKIES OF MON-TANA; OVER EXPOSED (56). T.V. series 1957-63: 'The Real McCoys'. More movies: JOHN GOLDFARB, PLEASE COME HOME (65); MADE IN PARIS (65); SAND PEBBLES (66); WAIT UNTIL DARK (67); STAR (68); MAROONED (69); THE DESER-TER (70); THIEF (71, T.V. movie); DOCTORS' WIVES (71); RED SKY AT MORNING (71). T.V. series 1964-65: 'Slattery's People' and 1976-77: 'All's Fair'; has also directed on T.V. recent films: WILD HORSE HANK, DEATH SHIP, HOUND OF HELL (T.V. movie, all 1979); STONE COLD DEAD (80); BODY HEAT (81); FIRST BLOOD (82); TABLE FOR FIVE (83).

BERNARD CRIBBINS

B. Oldham, Lancs, 29.12.28. Ed. St. Anne's Elementary School, Oldham. Stage début: Oldham Rep., aged 14, becoming pro. there in 1943. National Service as paratrooper. Rep.: Piccolo Players, Manchester, Queen's Players, Hornchurch. Md. Gillian McBarnet. West End début 1956 in musical version of 'Comedy of Errors', many others. Movies from 1960 incl. TOMMY THE TOREADOR, TWO-WAY STRETCH (both 1960); THE GIRL ON THE BOAT (62); THE WRONG ARM OF THE LAW (63); CARRY ON JACK (63); CROOKS IN CLOISTERS (64); SHE (65); DALEKS-INVASION EARTH 2150 (66); DON'T RAISE THE BRIDGE, LOWER THE RIVER (68). Much T.V. including 'Cribbins', 'Jackanory', 'The Country Wife', 'Val Doonican' (series); T.V. commercials (voice of 'Buzby'); stage: 'Not Now, Darling' (London and tour 1973), 'There Goes the Bride' (1974). Hit singles include 'Right, Said Fred'. Recent movies: THE WATER BABIES (78); DANGEROUS DAVIES—THE LAST DETECTIVE (T.V. movie, 1980); series 1983: as 'Cuffy'.

GRAHAM CROWDEN

B. Edinburgh, Scotland, 30.11.22. Ed. Edinburgh Academy. Md. Phyllida Hewat. Stage début student ASM Stratford 1944; rep.: Dundee, Stratford E., Nottingham, Bristol Old Vic, Citizen's Theatre, Glasgow. Mr Crowden has given distinguished performances with Royal Court Theatre, the Old Vic Co. (and tours) over the years. Entered films 1958 and his work in this medium includes: IF... (68); LEO THE LAST (70); CLOCKWORK ORANGE (71); PERCY (71); THE RULING CLASS (72); O LUCKY MAN (73); THE FINAL PROGRAMME (73). Recent T.V. (all BBC): 'The Camerons', 'Dr. Who', 'The Sun Trap', 'King's Royal'; films: BRITANNIA HOSPITAL (82); THE MISSIONARY (83).

ROBERT CULP

B. Berkeley, Calif., 16.8.30. Father, a lawyer. Ed. Stockton Coll. of the Pacific; Washington Univ.; San Francisco State. Once a champion pole-vaulter, studied acting with Herbert Berghof. Broadway début 1953 in 'The Prescott Proposals'—in off Broadway prods.: 'He Who Gets Slapped', 'Diary of a Scoundrel' (both 1956), 'A Clearing in the Woods (1957). Md. 1. Nancy Wilner, 3 sons, Joshua (b. 1961), Jason (b. 1962), Joseph (b. 1963), 1 daughter, Rachel (b. 1964), div. 1967. Came to screen 1962 in PT 109, having previously starred as Texas Ranger Hoby Gilman in series 'Trackdown', 1957-59, and guested in several series. Other movies: SAMMY, THE WAY-OUT SEAL (62); THE RAIDERS (63); SUNDAY IN NEW YORK (64); RHINO! (64); BOB & CAROL & TED & ALICE (69); HANNIE CAULDER (71); HICKEY & BOGGS (72, and directed). Md. 2. actress France Nuyen, div. 1969; 3. Sheila Sullivan 1971. Kelly Robinson in T.V. series 'I Spy' 1965-68, directing and wrote several episodes. T.V. movies: SEE THE MAN RUN (72); A CRY FOR HELP (75) and other features include: SKY RIDERS (76); THE GREAT SCOUT AND CATHOUSE THURSDAY (76); GOLDEN GIRL (78); A CRY FOR JUSTICE (T.V. movie, 1978); HOT ROD (T.V. movie, 1980); KILLJOY (T.V. movie, 1981).

HUME CRONYN

B. London, Ontario, Canada, 18.7.11. Ed. Ridley Coll.; McGill Univ.; travelled Europe, E. Indies; studied at American Acad. of D.A. 1932-34, also teaching drama; since 1931, when he appeared with Nat. Stock Co., Washington D.C., he has become one of the most distinguished actors in the American theatre, where he has also directed. Wed actress Jessica Tandy 1942, 1 son Christopher (b. 1943), 1 daughter Tandy (b. 1945). Came to screen 1943 in SHADOW OF A DOUBT and his films have included CROSS OF LORRAINE (43); THE SEVENTH CROSS (44, Oscar nom.); LIFEBOAT (44); THE POSTMAN ALWAYS RINGS TWICE (46); BRUTE FORCE (47); TOP O' THE MORNING (4' '); CROWDED PARADISE (56); SUNRISE A CAMPOBELLO (60); CLEOPATRA (63 HAMLET (64); GAILY, GAILY (69); THE ARRANGEMENT (70); THERE WAS A CROOKED MAN (70); THE PARALL VIEW (74). Recent theatre: 'The Gin Game' (London, 1979, also T.V. movie, 1982); recent movies: ROLLOVER, HONKY TONK FREEWAY (both 1981); THE WORLD ACCORDING TO GARP (82).

ROLAND CULVER

B. Highgate, N. London, 31.8.1900. Ed. Highgate Coll. World War 1 fighter pilot Royal Flying Corps 1918. Studied optics, art, engineering before training for the stage at R.A.D.A. Stage début 1925 at Hull; that year also commenced his long and distinguished career on the London stage, his plays included '77 Park Lane' (1928), 3 years in 'French Without Tears'. Came to screen in 77 PARK LANE (32); others include NELL GWYNN (34); PARADISE FOR TWO (37); FRENCH WITHOUT TEARS (39); QUIET WEDDING (40). Md. 1. Daphne Rye (div.). Stage 1944, Viscount Goring in 'An Ideal Husband', his favourite role; 'first British actor to go to Hollywood after WWII', to play in TO EACH HIS OWN (46). Other movies include: DEAD OF NIGHT (45, The Linking Story); DOWN TO EARTH (47, U.S.A.); THE EMPEROR WALTZ (48, U.S.A.); TRIO (50, as W. Somerset Maugham); THE HOLLY AND THE IVY (54); THE MAN WHO LOVED REDHEADS (55); BONJOUR TRISTESSE (58); THE YELLOW ROLLS ROYCE (63). Mr Culver has appeared several times on Broadway and with England's Old Vic. Md. 2. Nan Hopkins. Recent T.V. 'Saint Joan' as the Inquisitor (BBC 1979) and The Judge in 'A Question of Guilt' (BBC 1980). Awarded O.B.E. 1980. Recent films: NO LONGER ALONE (77); THE MISSIONARY (83).

NOT QUITE A GENTLEMAN. William Kimber. 1979.

JAMIE LEE CURTIS

The daughter of Tony Curtis and Janet Leigh, she was born in November 1958, educated at Beverly Hills High School and Westlake School for Girls. She appeared on T.V. in such series as 'Charlie's Angels' and 'Operation Petticoat' (1977/78 as Lt. Barbara Duran). Her movies have included HALLOWEEN (78); PROM NIGHT (79); THE FOG, TERROR TRAIN, ROAD GAMES (all 1980); HALLOWEEN II (81); THE DOROTHY STRATTON STORY (T.V. movie, 1982); TRADING PLACES (83).

TONY CURTIS

Although in recent years his name perhaps holds less prestige than it did in the 50s and 60s, Tony Curtis still remains an actor of immense appeal, witness his work in recent T.V. movies. The son of Mono Schwartz, who had been a well-known actor in Hungary, Tony Curtis was born Bernard Schwartz in New York on 3 June 1925. His Hungarian immigrant parents found the new language difficult to master, so his father became a tailor. Brought up in the tough Bronx area of New York, he was in gang skirmishes as a youngster; when 12 he joined a Boy Scout and credits a man named Paul Schwartz (no relation) for straightening him out and giving him self-respect. Educated at the Jones memorial Settlement House and Seward Park High School, New York; during World War II he joined the navy, serving aboard U.S.S. Dragonette, a submarine, but injured a leg when loading a torpedo. After medical treatment he completed his education, joined a dramatic workshop and acted with Empire Players, Newark; Cherry Lane Theatre and while appearing in Greenwich Village production 'Golden Boy' in title role was discovered by Universal-International scout, Robert Goldstein, and sent to the Hollywood studio, where he was given vigorous training in film technique. Given very small roles to start with in such movies as CITY ACROSS THE RIVER, JOHNNY STOOL PIDGEON, FRANCIS (all 49), he was seen dancing with Yvonne DeCarlo in CRISS CROSS, the public remembered him and the studio gave him leading roles in such pictures as THE PRINCE WHO WAS A THIEF (51); THE SON OF ALI BABA (52); HOUDINI (53) and BLACK SHIELD OF FALWORTH (54). Tony wed actress Janet Leigh (qv) on 4 June 1951 and they had 2 daughters, Kelly Lee (born 17.6.56) and Jamie Lee (qv) (born November 1958). In the late 50s Curtis progressed to more intelligent roles in such movies as TRAPEZE (56); MISTER CORY (57); SWEET SMELL OF SUCCESS (57); THE DEFIANT ONES (58, for which he was Oscar nominated) and SOME LIKE IT HOT (59). Divorced from Miss Leigh in 1963, he wed Christine Kaufmann, his TARAS BULBA (62) co-star in 1964 and two daughters, Alexandra and Allegra, were born in 1964 and 1966. Other 60s movies included: THE OUTSIDER (61); CAPT. NEWMAN M.D. (63); GOODBYE CHARLIE (64); THE GREAT RACE (65); DROP DEAD DARLING (67) and THE BOSTON STRANGLER (68). In 1970/1971 he co-starred with Roger Moore (qv) in T.V. series 'The Persuaders' and had wed in 1968 Leslie Allen. His other movies include: YOU CAN'T WIN 'EM ALL (70); SUPPOSE THEY GAVE A WAR AND NOBODY CAME (71); LEPKE (75); THE LAST TYCOON (76); THE MANITOU (78); THE USERS (78, T.V. movie); LITTLE MISS MARKER (79); THE TITLE SHOT (79); THE MIRROR CRACK'D, MOVIOLA: THE SCARLETT O'HARA YEARS (T.V. movie, all 1980) and BRAINWAVES (82). His third marriage has ended in divorce and in 1980 he was on stage in Los Angeles in 'I Ought To Be In Pictures'.

PETER CUSHING

Peter Cushing, one of Britain's best-loved actors, and for over 40 years a movie actor, is still remembered for his work in definitive T.V. productions of the 50s and for the Hammer horror cycle when he reached the pinnacle of his career. The son of George, a quantity surveyor, and Nellie Cushing, he was born in Kenley, Surrey on 26 May 1913. Educated at Purley Secondary School, he idolised Tom Mix as a youngster and thus made an acting career his goal, although he worked for 3 years in his father's office upon leaving school, but in his spare time he appeared in amateur theatricals and studied voice production under Cairns James at the Guildhall School. Bill Fraser, who then ran the Connaught Theatre, Worthing, gave young Cushing his first job there at the age of 22, paying him 75p a week, and debuting in the play 'The Middle Watch'. After four years of rep. including a spell at Southampton, he went to Hollywood, having saved some money, his father also paying his fare 'one-way'. The actor managed to obtain work at Edward Small Studios, doubling Louis Hayward in the 'split screen' work on MAN IN THE IRON MASK (39), playing roles in the films VIGIL IN THE NIGHT, CHUMPS AT OXFORD (both 1939); LADDIE (40); THEY DARE NOT LOVE (41); and spent 2 weeks on Broadway in 'The Seventh Trumpet' (1941). Returning to Britain and owing to sustained ear trouble he was turned down by the forces, instead toured with E.N.S.A., where he met his wife, actress Helen Beck. From 1943 he appeared frequently in the West End, toured with Olivier's Old Vic Co. in 1948, making his British screen début in HAMLET that year, as Osric. But it was in T.V. he gained his reputation as an actor with a wider following winning Best Actor laurels in 1954 and 1955, the latter for '1984', this performance being responsible for landing the role of Victor Frankenstein in Hammer's CURSE OF FRANKENSTEIN in 1957. Since then he has played over 60 movies of that genre, the best of which he co-starred with Christopher Lee (qv), including DRACULA (58); THE MUMMY (58) and HOUND OF THE BASKERVILLES (59); in the latter as Sherlock Holmes, a role he has deftly played in a T.V. series. Widowed in 1971, Mr Cushing continues to immerse himself in film work, his most recent being: HITLER'S SON (77); THE BATTLE FLAG (78); A TOUCH OF THE SUN (78); ARABIAN ADVENTURE (78); HOUDINI (78); A TALE OF TWO CITIES (81, T.V. movie); HOUSE OF THE LONG SHADOWS, HELEN & THE TEACHER (T.V. movie) and SWORD OF THE VALIANT (all 1983).

JIM DALE

B. Rothwell, Northants, 15.8.35; real name James Smith. Ed. Kettering & District Grammar School. Father was a steel-worker; encouraged his son in stage career; stage début 1951 in Kettering, toured Halls for 3 yrs.; Nat. Serv. in RAF; a discovery of Carol Levis, in 1958 Jim compered T.V. show '6-5 Special', became a pop singer, also coming to the screen in spin-off of this show. Other films include: THE IRON MAIDEN (62); CARRY ON JACK (64, and 5 more in series); LOCK UP YOUR DAUGHTERS (69); THE NATIONAL HEALTH (73, also stage); DIGBY—THE BIGGEST DOG IN THE WORLD (73). Also distinguished song writer ('The Winter's Tale', 'Shalako', 'Georgy Girl' (Oscar nom.)) and stage actor—National Theatre, Edinburgh Festival, West End, Broadway (on latter won awards in 1974/75 for 'Scapino' & 1980 'Tony' award for portrayal of showman P.T. Barnum in 'Barnum'). Md. Patricia Gardiner (Sep. 1980), 1 daughter: Belinda, 3 sons: Murray, Adam, Toby. Recent movies: PETE'S DRAGON (77); THE SPACEMAN & KING ARTHUR (78); SCANDALOUS (83). Md. 2: Julie Schaefer, boutique owner.

ROGER DALTREY

B. Hammersmith, London, 3.1.44. Was an apprentice sheet-metal worker for 5 yrs., then attained popularity in the mid-1960s as vocalist with 'The Who' group (Pete Townshend, John Entwistle and the late Keith Moon), formerly known as 'The Detours' and 'High Numbers'. Their first hit was 'I Can't Explain' in 1964. Mr Daltrey and 'The Who' performed in the movie WOODSTOCK (70), but his first major role in a movie was the lead in TOMMY (74), based on Pete Townshend's rock-opera, first performed in 1968 and in the States in 1970. He has a son from his first marriage (born c. 1964) and another was born c. 1967, in Sweden, named Mateus. Mr Daltrey's most recent movies are THE KIDS ARE ALRIGHT (a 'Who' compilation film, 1978) and John McVicar in McVICAR (80). He and his wife Heather have two daughters, Rosie and Willow. Winner 'Best Actor', Festival International du Film Musical (Paris), for McVICAR. *THE WHO: MAXIMUM R & B* by Richard Barnes; Eel Pie Publishing: London, 1982.

PHIL DANIELS

B. King's Cross, London, 25.10.58. Father a caretaker. Ed. local schools and from 1972, the Anna Scher Theatre; acting début, aged 13, in T.V.'s 'Falstaff'. Other T.V. incl. 'The Molly Wopsies', 'The Destructors', 'Scum', 'Four Idle Hands', 'Nelson'. Theatre incl.: 'Line 'em', 'American Days', 'Class Enemy', 'Penny Whistle', 'Julius Caesar'; has his own band, 'Phil Daniels & the Cross', sings and plays guitar. Came to the screen in BUGSY MALONE (76). Others: Boy Pullen in ZULU DAWN (78); Jimmy the Mod in QUODROPHENIA (79); Slasher Richards in SCUM (80) and Danny in BREAKING GLASS (80); recent T.V.: 'A Midsummer Night's Dream' (as Puck, 1981); 'I Remember Nelson' (82); 'Smoke' (83).

TIMOTHY DALTON

B. Colwyn Bay, N. Wales, . . .44(?). Father, advertising executive; his grandparents were noted music-hall performers. Mr Dalton decided to become actor after seeing 'Macbeth' at Old Vic. 1964 joined Nat. Youth Theatre; 2 yrs. at R.A.D.A.; re-joined NYT; Prospect Theatre Co. tour of U.K. and Australia; Birmingham Rep.; a T.V. role in 'Saturday While Sunday' led to screen début 1968 as King Philip of France in LION IN WINTER (68); ret'd. to B'ham: 'Saint Joan' and others; movie: CROMWELL (70) as Prince Rupert; tour of 'Henry V' as Chorus. Other movies include THE VOYEUR (71); WUTHERING HEIGHTS (71, as Heathcliffe); MARY, QUEEN OF SCOTS (71); then to U.S.A.; SEXTETTE (77); AGATHA (77, G.B.); FLASH GORDON (79); CHANEL SOLITAIRE (81, France).

BEVERLY D'ANGELO

B. Columbus, Ohio, . . . Following visual arts studies and work in Italy, Beverly returned to U.S.A. and became a cartoonist for the Hanna-Barbera Studios in Hollywood. Her next venture took her to Canada as a coffeehouse singer and also performed with a rock band called Elephant. Following work with the Charlotte Town Festival Co., she debuted on Broadway in 'Rock-a-bye Hamlet' and one of her first screen roles was in 1976 in the mini-series, 'Captains & the Kings'; she came to the big screen in THE SENTINEL (77) and has been seen in FIRST LOVE (77); EVERY WHICH WAY BUT LOOSE (78); HAIR (79); HIGH POINT (79); THE COALMINER'S DAUGHTER (80); HONKY TONK FREEWAY (81); PATERNITY (81); NATIONAL LAMPOON'S VACATION (82).

SUZANNE DANIELLE

B. Putney, London, 14.1.57; trained Bush Davies Stage Sch., has appeared in such shows as 'The Morecambe & Wise T.V. Special' and 'The Mike Yarwood Show' (in the latter impersonating the Princess of Wales) and episodes of 'Tales of the Unexpected', 'Hammer House of Horror'; her many movies include GOLDEN LADY (78); ARABIAN ADVENTURE (78); CARRY ON EMMANUELLE (79); SIR HENRY AT RAWLINSON'S END (80); FLASH GORDON (81); T.V. ser. 'Jane' (82); 'Strangers' (82); THE BOYS IN BLUE (83).

BLYTHE DANNER

B. Philadelphia, . . Ed. Bard. College; Blythe played in stock and then many N.Y. plays including 'The Infantry' (1966), 'Up Eden' (1968), 'Summertree' (1968), 'The Miser' (1969, winner—Theatre World Award, B.A.), 'Butterflies are Free' (1969); md. writer/producer Bruce Paltrow; early movies: 1776 (72); TO KILL A CLOWN (72); LOVIN' MOLLY (74); HEARTS OF THE WEST (75); FUTUREWORLD (76); she is very well-known on T.V., including the series 'Adam's Rib' as Amanda Bonner (1973) and many T.V. movies such as DR COOK'S GARDEN (71); SIDEKICKS (74); ARE YOU IN THE HOUSE ALONE? (78); TOO FAR TO GO (79); more recent work includes movies THE GREAT SANTINI (79); MAN, WOMAN, AND CHILD (82); INSIDE THE THIRD REICH (mini-ser. 1982); HELEN & THE TEACHER (T.V. movie, 1983).

SYBIL DANNING

B. Austria, . . ; dental assistant in Salzburg, moved to Germany, becoming model; supporting roles to recent leads; many films inclu. METEOR (77); BATTLE BEYOND THE STARS, MAN WITH BOGART'S FACE, THE SWAP (all 1980); SWEET DIRTY TONY, SEPARATE WAYS (both 1981); JULIE DARLING, HERCULES, THE 7 MAGNIFICENT GLADIATORS, SAS-MALKO (all 1982); CHAINED HEAT (83).

NIGEL DAVENPORT

B. Shelford, Cambridge, 23.5.28. Ed. St. Peter's, Seaford; Cheltenham Coll.; Trinity Coll., Oxford. Formerly a member of Oxford Univ. Dramatic Society, made pro. début Savoy Theatre, London 1952 and this distinguished British actor's stage work includes seasons: Stratford 1953, Chesterfield 1954-55; 1st season English Stage Co. 1956, created role of Peter in 'A Taste of Honey', Stratford E. and West End 1959, Broadway and L.A. 1960. Came to screen 1958 in LOOK BACK IN ANGER. Many others include: PEEPING TOM (59); IN THE COOL OF THE DAY (63); A HIGH WIND IN JAMAICA (65); WHERE THE SPIES ARE (66); A MAN FOR ALL SEASONS (66, as the Duke of Norfolk); SINFUL DAVY (67); PLAY DIRTY (68); ROYAL HUNT OF THE SUN (69); A LAST VALLEY (70); VILLAIN (70); LIVING FREE (71); MARY, QUEEN OF SCOTS (72). Md. 1. Helena White, 1 daughter Laura; 2. Maria Aitken 1972, 1 son Jack (b. 1973) (div. 18.11.80). Very well known on T.V., recently played in 'Prince Regent' (79); 'Don't Rock the Boat' (82); recent movies: ZULU DAWN, THE LONDON CONNECTION (both 1978); NIGHT HAWKS (80); CHARIOTS OF FIRE (81); STRATA (82); GREYSTOKE (83).

KIM DARBY

B. N. Hollywood, Calif., 8.7.48; real name Deborah Zerby. Ed. Swanson's Ranch School, Van Nuys High School. Her parents, who later divorced, were dancing team known as 'The Zerbys'. Known as Derby Zerby, she changed her name to Kim 'after the loveliest girl in High School'. As youngster, spent most of her time with grandparents, although performed in musical shows with parents. Failed to get into High School plays, but managed to get place with Desilu Workshop, making pro. début aged 16 in 'Mr Novak' T.V. series. Stage début, aged 18, in 'The Porcelain Years'. Came to screen in 1965 in BUS RILEY'S BACK IN TOWN and has been seen in THE RESTLESS ONES (65); THE KARATE KILLERS (67); Mattie Ross in TRUE GRIT (69); A TIME FOR GIVING (69); THE STRAWBERRY STATEMENT (70); NORWOOD (70); RED SKY AT MORNING (70); THE GRISSOM GANG (70). Md. 1. actor James Stacy 1967, 1 daughter Heather (b. 1968) (div.); 2. James Westmoreland 1970 (div.). Other work: 'Rich Man, Poor Man' (1976, T.V. series), THE ONE AND ONLY (78); GIRLS OF THE ROAD (79, T.V. movie).

BRAD DAVIS

B. Tallahassee, Florida, . .50. Real name Robert Davis; as youngster appeared in summer stock in Atlanta, Georgia, including 'The Fantastics', '110 in the Shade'; to N.Y. and Am.A.D.A.; N.Y. debut in 'Crystal and Fox 6' and in California worked on 'Stop Thief' and 'Song of Myself'; screen work includes SYBIL (76, T.V. movie); THE SECRET LIFE OF JOHN CHAPMAN (76, T.V. movie); ROOTS (77, mini-series) and big screen role of Billy Hayes in MIDNIGHT EXPRESS (77) earned him acclaim and Golden Globe Aw.; md. Susan; other stage includes 'The Elusive Angel' and movies A SMALL CIRCLE OF FRIENDS (80); RUMOUR OF WAR (80); CHARIOTS OF FIRE (81); T.V. 1981 (GB); 'Mrs Reinhardt'; QUERELLE (82, Germany).

BETTE DAVIS

With no fewer than two Oscars and ten Academy Award nominations for her acting in motion-pictures, Bette Davis remains undoubtedly one of the most distinguished American ladies of the screen. The daughter of Harlow Davis, a lawyer, and his wife Ruth, she was born Ruth Elizabeth Davis at Lowell, Massachusetts on 5 April 1908. After attending High Schools in New York and Newton, Mass. and the Cushing Academy, also studying dancing with the Mariarden School, she studied acting with the John Murray Anderson School. She made her stage début with the George Cukor Stock Co. in Chicago in 1928, later appearing on Broadway in 'The Earth Between' in 1929 and several other productions which landed her a minor contract to Universal Studios, arriving in Los Angeles on 23 December 1930. She came to the screen in BAD SISTER (31), but after four more movies she became disillusioned and her contract was dropped. Preparing a return to New York, actor George Arliss insisted she appear with him in his movie THE MAN WHO PLAYED GOD (32). This resulted in a Warner Brothers contract and in the next eight years she made 34 movies, including CABIN IN THE COTTON (32); OF HUMAN BONDAGE (34, on loan to RKO, which made her a star); FRONT PAGE WOMAN (35); DANGEROUS (35, Academy Award); PETRIFIED FOREST (36); JEZEBEL (38, Academy Award); THE OLD MAID (39); DARK VICTORY (39, Oscar nom.); THE PRIVATE LIVES OF ELIZABETH & ESSEX (39) and THE LETTER (40, Oscar nom.). From 1932-38 she had been married to Harmon O. Nelson Jr. and in 1940 she wed Arthur Farnsworth, but she was widowed in 1943. Her third husband was William Grant Sherry, and their daughter, Barbara, was born in 1946. Her 1940s films included: THE LITTLE FOXES (41, Oscar nom.); THE MAN WHO CAME TO DINNER (41); NOW, VOYAGER (42, Oscar nom.); MR SKEFFINGTON (44, Oscar nom.); THE CORN IS GREEN (45) and DECEPTION (46). Divorcing Mr Sherry in 1949, the following year she wed her ALL ABOUT EVE co-star Gary Merrill, adopting 2 children, Margot and Michael. They divorced in 1960. She made few films in the 1950s, appeared on Broadway in 1952 in the revue 'Two's Company', got a further Oscar nom. for THE STAR (52) and toured in 'The World of Carl Sandburg' 1959/60). Her come-back picture, WHATEVER HAPPENED TO BABY JANE? (62) won her further acclaim and she has worked steadily in movies, television and appeared on stage in 'An Informal Evening with Bette Davis' since 1974. She received the American Film Institute Life Achievement Award in 1977. Recent screen work: HARVEST HOME, DEATH ON THE NILE (77); RETURN TO WITCH MOUNTAIN (78); WATCHER IN THE WOODS (79); STRANGERS — THE STORY OF MOTHER AND DAUGHTER (Emmy Aw., 79, T.V. movie); FAMILY REUNION (81, mini-ser.); A PIANO FOR MRS CIMINO, LITTLE GLORIA, HAPPY AT LAST (mini-ser.) and RIGHT OF WAY (all T.V., 1982). *BETTE DAVIS* by Peter Noble; Skelton-Robinson; London, 1948; *THE LONELY LIFE* (autobio.); MacDonald: London, 1962; *THE FILMS OF BETTE DAVIS* by Gene Ringgold; Citadel: Secaucus, N.J., 1966; *BETTE DAVIS* by Jerry Vermilye: Pyramid: N.Y., 1973; p/b: Star Books: London, 1974; *MOTHER GODDAM: THE STORY & CAREER OF BETTE DAVIS* by Whitney Stine; W.H. Allen: London, 1975; p/b: Berkeley Medallion: U.S.A., 1974; *BETTE: A BIOGRAPHY OF BETTE DAVIS* by Charles Higham; N.E.L.: London, 1981; *BETTE DAVIS: HER FILM & STAGE CAREER* by Jeffrey Robinson; Proteus Publ. Co. Inc.: N.Y. & London, 1982; Large p/b.

JIM DAVIS

B. Dearborn, Missouri, 26.8.15; real name Marlin Davis. Went to Hollywood as salesman for an oil company and entered movies, having had dramatic training. Scores of films include: STRANGE CARGO (42); GALLANT BESS (46); THE FABULOUS TEXAN (47); WINTER MEETING (48, starred opp. Bette Davis); CAVALRY SCOUT (52); THE FIGHTING 7th (52); THE LAST COMMAND (54); THE MAVERICK QUEEN (56); ALIAS JESSE JAMES (59); FORT UTAH (66); RIO LOBO (70); BIG JAKE (71); BAD COMPANY (72); THE PARALLAX VIEW (74). Md. Blanche, former professional swimmer, 1949. 1 daughter Tara. T.V. includes guest in several series such as 'Streets of San Francisco', 'Caribe' and his own series 'The Cowboys' (1974) as U.S. Marshall Bill Winter, and the tremendously successful 'Dallas' (from 1978), his role of John 'Jock' Ewing making him a household name. Recent movie: THE DAY TIME ENDED (79).
Mr Davis died in his sleep in Los Angeles on 27.4.81 following surgery for a perforated ulcer.

OSSIE DAVIS

B. Cogdell, Georgia, 18.12.17; Ed: Howard Univ.; actor/playwright/director/teacher; much NY stage from '46; movies: NO WAY OUT (50); FOURTEEN HOURS (51); THE JOE LOUIS STORY (53); THE CARDINAL, GONE ARE THE DAYS (both 1963, latter screen version of his play, 'Purlie Victorious'); SHOCK TREATMENT (64); THE HILL (65); A MAN CALLED ADAM (66); THE SCALPHUNTERS (67); THE OUTSIDER (67, T.V. movie); NIGHT GALLERY (T.V. movie), SAM WHISKY, SLAVES (all 1969); COTTON COMES TO HARLEM (70, directed); THE SHERIFF (T.V. movie); KONGI'S HARVEST (directed, both 1971); BLACK GIRL (directed); MALCOLM X (both 1972); GORDON'S WAR (73); LET'S DO IT AGAIN (75); COUNTDOWN AT KUSINI (76); BILLY: PORTRAIT OF A STREET KID (77, T.V. movie); HOT STUFF (78); KING (78, mini-ser., as Martin Luther King, Sr); ROOTS: THE NEXT GENERATION (79, mini-ser.); Md: actress Ruby Dee; ALL GOD'S CHILDREN (T.V. movie, 1980).

JUDY DAVIS – see page 123 31

ISABEL DEAN

B. Aldridge, Staffordshire, 29.5.18; real name Isabel Hodgkinson. Ed. Edgbaston High School, Birmingham & Wendover. Father, a solicitor. Isabel studied painting at Birmingham School of Art, joined Cheltenham Rep. as scenic artist 1937, played small roles and decided on acting career instead. Rep.: Brighton, Norwich, West End and became distinguished player in variety of roles including Shakespearean (Juliet, Hermia, Ophelia) and a well-known face on T.V. Md. writer/director William Fairchild, 2 daughters: Caroline and Angela; div. 1972. movies include: THE PASSIONATE FRIENDS (47); THE LAST PAGE (52); THE WOMAN'S ANGLE (52); 24 HOURS OF A WOMAN'S LIFE (52); THE STORY OF GILBERT & SULLIVAN (53); OUT OF THE CLOUDS (55); VIRGIN ISLAND (58); THE LIGHT IN THE PIAZZA (62); A HIGH WIND IN JAMAICA (64); INADMISSABLE EVIDENCE (68); CATCH ME A SPY (71); RANSOM (76); ROUGH-CUT (79); FIVE DAYS ONE SUMMER (82); recent T.V.: 'The Bad Sister' (82).

OLIVIA DE HAVILLAND

B. Tokyo, Japan, 1.7.16. Father: attorney — mother: actress; ed. California schools, Notre Dame Convent, Belmont; school play won her introduction to Max Reinhardt and role in play and later film debut in A MIDSUMMER NIGHT'S DREAM (35); awarded Warner Bros. contract, includes playing in 8 movies with Errol Flynn including CAPTAIN BLOOD (35), ADVENTURES OF ROBIN HOOD (38); distinguished film career includes role of Melanie in GONE WITH THE WIND (39, Oscar nom. BSA); HOLD BACK THE DAWN (41, Oscar nom. B.A.); TO EACH HIS OWN (46, Oscar, B.A.); THE SNAKE PIT (48, Oscar nom. B.A.); THE HEIRESS (49, Oscar, B.A.); many other awards; md: 1. Marcus Goodrich (1946-52), 1 son Benjamin (born 1949); 2. Pierre Galante (1955), 1 daughter Giselle (born 1956); also Broadway actress; more recent screen work includes POPE JOAN (72); AIRPORT '77; THE SWARM (77); ROOTS: THE NEXT GENERATIONS (79, mini-series); MURDER IS EASY (81, T.V. movie).
book (NOT autobio.): EVERY FRENCHMAN HAS ONE; Random House, N.Y., 1961.

ALAIN DELON

Although he cannot be regarded as a major international star, particularly in the States (very few French actors can, or have been), Alain Delon has undoubtedly been one of the most successful screen actors to emerge from France. Born in Sceaux, in the Paris suburbs on 8 November 1935, he was brought up by foster parents, as his mother and father divorced early in his life. Upon leaving school, several of which he was expelled from owing to bad behaviour, he took a course in cooked meats, with the intention of going into the delicatessen trade, receiving his diploma. At 17, however, he enlisted in the armed forces as a rifleman in Indo-China during the Vietnamese campaign, seeing much action, including hand-to-hand fighting. Upon his release in 1955, he returned to Paris, £30 in debt. He worked as an office boy and later as an unloader at the Halles (the equivalent of London's Covent Garden). It was there he was noticed by actress Brigitte Auber, who took him to the 1957 Cannes Film Festival where a meeting with an agent landed him a Selznick contract in Hollywood. However, Alain cancelled this contract after being 'discovered' again in a Paris street by a talent scout who introduced him to director Yves Allegret who cast the youngster in his first movie, QUAND LA FEMME S'EN MELE, in 1957. It was the start of a highly successful film career, his movies have included PLEIN SOLEIL (59); ROCCO AND HIS BROTHERS (60); THE ECLIPSE (61); THE LEOPARD (62); THE BIG SNATCH (63); THE BLACK TULIP (64); THE YELLOW ROLLS-ROYCE (64); ONCE A THIEF (65); LOST COMMAND (66); IS PARIS BURNING? (66); TEXAS ACROSS THE RIVER (66); LES AVENTURIERS (66); HISTOIRES EXTRAORDINAIRES (67); DIABOLICALLY YOURS (67); GIRL ON A MOTORCYCLE (67); LA PISANE (67); JEFF (68); BORSALINO (70, also produced); THE SICILIAN CLAN (70); RED SUN (71); THE ASSASSINATION OF TROTSKY (72); SCORPIO (72); BORSALINO & CO. (73); SHOCK (74); ZORRO (74); FLIC STORY (75); MR KLEIN (76); DEATH OF A CORRUPT MAN (77); THE CHILDREN ARE WATCHING (77); AIRPORT '79—THE CONCORDE (79); TEHERAN 43 (80). Mr Delon has appeared on the stage with Romy Schneider in "'Tis a Pity She's a Whore'. He wed Francine Conovas on 13.8.64 and a son, Tony, was born 30.9.64. He is divorced from his second wife, actress Nathalie Delon.

DOM DELUISE

B. Brooklyn, 1.8.33. Ed. Tufts Coll. After spending two seasons with Cleveland Playhouse, has had successful career on Broadway, T.V. and motion pictures; made impression in T.V.'s 'The Garry Moore Show' in early 1960s as 'Dominick the Great'. Broadway includes: 'The Jackass' (1960), 'Another Evening with Harry Stoomes' (1961), 'All in Love' (1961), 'Half-Past Wednesday' (1962), 'Around the World in 80 Days' (1963/64), 'The Student Gypsy' (1963), 'Too Much Johnson' (1964). T.V. includes: 'The Dom DeLuise Show' (1968), 'The Golddiggers' (1971, guest) and many other shows, 'Roman Holidays' (1972, cartoon-voice only). Movies: FAIL SAFE (64); THE BUSYBODY (67); THE GLASS-BOTTOM BOAT (67); THE 12 CHAIRS (70); WHO IS HARRY KELLERMAN? (71); EVERY LITTLE CROOK & NANNY (72); THE ADVENTURES OF SHERLOCK HOLMES' SMARTER BROTHER (75); SILENT MOVIE (76); THE WORLD'S GREATEST LOVER (77); CHEAP DETECTIVE (77); THE END (79); FATSO (79); THE LAST MARRIED COUPLE IN AMERICA (79); HOT STUFF (80, also directed); WHOLLY MOSES! (80); HISTORY OF THE WORLD: PART I, THE CANNONBALL RUN (both 1981); THE SECRET OF NIMH (82, animation-voice only).

CATHERINE DENEUVE

B. Paris, France, 22.10.43; real name Catherine Dorleac. Father Maurice Dorleac, actor. Catherine started acting aged 15 with her sister Francoise (who was tragically killed in a car accident in 1968 after appearing in several movies). Her movies include LES PORTES CLAQUET (60); VICE & VIRTUE (62); THE UMBRELLAS OF CHERBOURG (64, making her a star & winning French film award); REPULSION (65); WHO WANTS TO SLEEP? (65); LES CREATURES (66); THE YOUNG GIRLS OF ROCHEFORT (67); BELLE DE JOUR (67); BENJAMIN (68); MANON 70 (68); MAYERLING (68); THE APRIL FOOLS (69); THE MISSISSIPPI MERMAID (69); TRISTANA (70); IT ONLY HAPPENS TO OTHERS (71); DIRTY MONEY (72); HUSTLE (76); MARCH OR DIE (77); A NOUS DEUX (79). Miss Deneuve has also modelled for 'Chanel' in the States. She has a son, Christian, born in 1963, the father being director Roger Vadim. She wed photographer David Bailey 18.8.65, but they div in 1970. Her daughter, Chiara-Charlotte, was born in 1972, the father—actor Marcello Mastroianni (q.v.). Recent movies: LE DERNIER METRO (Cesar Aw., Best Actress), JE VOUS AIME (both 1980); HOTEL OF THE AMERICAS, THE HUNGER (both 1982).

MAURICE DENHAM

B. Beckenham, Kent, 23.12.09; Ed: Tonbridge School. Formerly an engineer, made rep. debut Hull 1934, West End debut 1936, becoming distinguished actor of stage, screen and radio. Stage includes: 'Fallen Angels' (1949), 'Who's Your Father?' (1958), Old Vic—'Macbeth' (1961), others. Radio: 'ITMA', 'Much Binding in the Marsh'. 5 years in army WWII. Movies (debut 1946) include: BLANCHE FURY (48); IT'S NOT CRICKET (48); THE MILLION POUND NOTE (54); SIMON & LAURA (55); SINK THE BISMARK (60); THE SEVENTH DAWN (64); THE ALPHABET MURDERS (65); THE MIDAS RUN (69); VIRGIN & THE GYPSY (70); NICHOLAS & ALEXANDRA (71); SHOUT AT THE DEVIL (76); many, many others. Md. Margaret Dunn, 3 children. Scores of T.V. plays & series, recently 'Schalcken the Painter' (79); 'The Potting Shed' (81); 'The Agatha Christie Hour' (82).

BO DEREK

B. . . . .; worked as a fashion model under her real name, Mary Cathleen Collins. She was spotted by an agent who introduced her to film director, photographer and former film star John Derek who directed her in movie ONCE UPON A LOVE (73). Wed to Mr Derek, Bo had a supporting role in the movie ORCA—THE KILLER WHALE (77), produced a film for her husband, LOVE YOU (77), described as a 'soft porn classy love story' and became a star with her performance in 10 (79) and has since been seen in A CHANGE OF SEASONS (80); Jane in TARZAN THE APEMAN (81); BOLERO (83).

ROBERT DENIRO

Robert DeNiro was born in the E. Side of N.Y. on August 17, 1943. His parents were artists and students of famous painter Hans Hoffman. At the age of 2, they separated and the youngster lived with his mother. Father, Robert DeNiro Sr., became a gifted abstract impressionist. Young Robert developed an interest in acting and studied with Stella Adler and Lee Strasberg, appeared in off-Broadway prods., workshop theatre & college years in the classics. His films have been THE WEDDING PARTY (69); HI, MOM (70); BLOODY MAMA (70); BORN TO WIN (71); THE GANG THAT COULDN'T SHOOT STRAIGHT (71); JENNIFER ON MY MIND (?); BANG THE DRUM SLOWLY (73); MEAN STREETS (73); THE GODFATHER—PART II (74, Oscar winner, Best Supporting actor); TAXI DRIVER (76, Oscar nom.); THE LAST TYCOON (77); 1900 (77); THE DEER HUNTER (77); THE RAGING BULL (79, as Jake La Motta, 1948 middleweight boxing champion—Best Dramatic Actor Award (Golden Globe); Academy Award winner); THE SWAP (?). Mr DeNiro wed Diahanne Abbot, actress, 1976. They have a son, Rafael, and a daughter, Nina, from Miss Abbott's previous marriage. His most recent movies are TRUE CONFESSIONS (81); THE KING OF COMEDY, ONCE UPON A TIME IN AMERICA (both 1982).

WILLIAM DEVANE

B. Albany, N.Y., ...; won scholarship to study at the American Academy of Dramatic Art and appeared on Broadway in many prods., such as 'Othello' (1964), 'Tragic History of Dr. Faustus' (1964), 'Coriolanus' (1965), 'MacBird' (1967), 'Ceremony of Innocence' (1968), 'Hamlet' (1968), 'Romeo & Juliet' (1968). Mr Devane was four years with Joe Papp's New York Shakespearean Company. He also won acclaim in N.Y. and San Francisco in the production of 'One Flew Over the Cuckoo's Nest'. His film appearances have included THE PURSUIT OF HAPPINESS (71); McCABE AND MRS MILLER (71); MY OLD MAN'S PLACE (73); FAMILY PLOT (75); THE BAD NEWS BEARS IN BREAKING TRAINING (77); YANKS (78). He has appeared on numerous occasions on television and these programmes include T.V. movies MISSILES IN OCTOBER, as President Kennedy; FROM HERE TO ETERNITY (and the subsequent series—Sergeant Wilt Warden). His most recent films are ROLLING THUNDER (80); HONKY TONK FREEWAY, RED FLAG — THE ULTIMATE GAME (T.V. movie, both 1981); JANE DOE (T.V. movie, 83).

ANTON DIFFRING

B. Koblenz, Germany, 20.10.18(?). After receiving his training for the stage in Vienna and the academy of Drama in Berlin, he appeared extensively on the stage, making his first English-speaking debut in Canada, performing in Toronto in a production of 'Richard III'. Mr Diffring played on Broadway in 'Winners and Losers', 'The Deputy of Paris' and 'Faust' in 1947 and came to Britain in 1950 to play in the movie STATE SECRET. He has since then been seen in scores of films, often seen as German officers in war pictures, he had a brief spell in horror movies, and has worked successfully in French and German films. Films include: STATE SECRET (50); THE WOMAN'S ANGLE (52); ALBERT R.N. (?); THE RED BERET (53); THE SEA SHALL NOT HAVE THEM (54); THE COLDITZ STORY (55); I AM A CAMERA (56); THE BLACK TENT (56); THE MAN WHO COULD CHEAT DEATH (59); CIRCUS OF HORRORS (60); INCIDENT AT MIDNIGHT (?); THE HEROES OF TELEMARK (65); THE BLUE MAX (65); FAHRENHEIT 451 (?); THE DOUBLE MAN (67); COUNTER-POINT (67); WHERE EAGLES DARE (?); ZEPPELIN (71); THE SWISS CONSPIRACY (?); OPERATION DAYBREAK (74, as Reinhard Heydrich); VALENTINO (76). Mr Diffring also appeared on T.V. on numerous occasions broadcast on radio. Recent films: VICTORY (?); SAS-MALKO (82).

MELINDA DILLON

B. Hope, Arkansas, 13.10.39. Won acting scholarship to Goodman Theatre School; progressed to N.Y. stage, work included 'Caucasian Chalk Circle' (1961), 'Burning of the Lepers' (1962), 'Who's Afraid of Virginia Woolf?' (1962, Tony nom.), 'You Know I Can't Hear You When the Water's Running' (67); md. actor Richard Libertini (div.), 1 son Ritchie; was member of Paul Sills Rep. Co.; screen debut in THE APRIL FOOLS (69) and she has been seen in BOUND FOR GLORY (77); SLAP SHOT (77); CLOSE ENCOUNTERS OF THE THIRD KIND (77); F.I.S.T. (78); THE CRITICAL LIST (78, T.V. movie); TRANSPLANT (79, T.V. movie); ABSENCE OF MALICE (Oscar nom. BSA), SAVAGE HARVEST, HELLINGER'S LAW, THE SHADOW BOX (last 2 T.V. movies, all 81); A CHRISTMAS STORY (83).

BRUCE DERN

B. Chicago, Ill., 4.6.36. Ed. Univ. of Pennsylvania. Grandfather was governor of state of Utah; appeared on Broadway 1958 in 'Shadow of a Gunman' and studied at Actors' Studio, N.Y., with Gordon Phillips and Elia Kazan; bartender in 'Sweet Bird of Youth' (Broadway 1959). Came to screen in small film roles—WILD RIVER (60); THE CRIMEBUSTERS (62); MARNIE (64); many others. Appeared in off-Broadway prods.: 'Waiting for Godot', 'Orpheus Descending'. Regular featured player in T.V. series 1962/63 'Stoney Burke'. Other movies include: HUSH, HUSH, SWEET CHARLOTTE (64); ST. VALENTINE'S DAY MASSACRE (67); WAR WAGON (67); HANG 'EM HIGH (69); THEY SHOOT HORSES, DON'T THEY (69); BLOODY MAMA (70); recognition in THE COWBOYS (71); 1st starring role in SILENT RUNNING (72); KING OF THE MARVIN GARDENS (72); THE LAUGHING POLICEMAN (73); THE GREAT GATSBY (74); SMILE (75); POSSEE (75); FAMILY PLOT (75); WON TON TON, THE DOG WHO SAVED HOLLYWOOD (75); THE TWIST (76); BLACK SUNDAY (76); THE DRIVER (77); COMING HOME (77). Md. 1. Diane Ladd 1965, 1 daughter Laura (div.); 2. Andrea Beckett 1969. Recent movies: MIDDLE-AGE CRAZY (79) and TATTOO (80). Daughter Laura has appeared in movies FOXES and ALL NIGHT LONG. Mr Dern's latest films: HARRY TRACY — DESPERADO, THAT CHAMPIONSHIP SEASON (both 1982).

ANGIE DICKINSON

B. Kulm, N. Dakota, 30.9.31(?). Angie, whose real name is Angeline Brown, is the daughter of parents who were journalists and owned the local newspaper. The family moved to Glendale, Calif. when she was 10 and she received her education at Parochia Schools, Heart Coll. & Glendale Coll. in L.A. Taking a secretarial course, she won a beauty competition organised by a local radio station, took an interest in acting and studied hard at Batami Schneider's Acting Workshop. In 1954 she came to the screen in LUCKY ME, saying one line of dialogue; also appeared in T.V. programmes ('4 Star Playhouse', 'Meet Willie', 'Line-Up', 'Chrysler Theatre' etc.) and after supporting roles in 11 further movies T.V. director Chris Nyby urged Mr Howard Hawks to test her for RIO BRAVO (59), and, also impressing 'Duke' Wayne, Angie landed the role of Feathers and attained movie stardom. Her movies include: BRAMBLE BUSH (60); THE SINS OF RACHEL CADE (61); JESSICA (62); CAPT. NEWMAN, M.D. (63); THE KILLERS (64, T.V. movie); THE CHASE (66); CAST A GIANT SHADOW (66); POINT BLANK (66); SAM WHISKEY (68); PRETTY MAIDS ALL IN A ROW (70); THIEF (71, T.V. movie); BIG BAD MAMA (74). She wed Gene Dickinson in 1952, but they divorced. A familiar face on T.V. as Sgt. Suzanne 'Pepper' Martin ('Police Woman' (1974-79) series), she wed composer Burt Bacharach in 1965, their daughter Lea 'Nikki' was born a year later. Recent movies: KLONDIKE (79); DRESSED TO KILL (79, Angie named 'Female Star of the Year' by U.S. Theatre Owners); PEARL (79, 3-part T.V. movie); DEATH HUNT (80); CHARLIE CHAN & THE CURSE OF THE DRAGON QUEEN (80); JIGSAW (80).

BRADFORD DILLMAN

B. San Francisco, Calif., 14.4.30. The son of wealthy socialites, Dean and Josephine Dillman, he was educated at Yale Univ., graduated in 1951, worked in stock and studied at the Actors' Studio. His Broadway debut was in June 1953 in 'The Scarecrow', other work in N.Y. included 'Third Person' (1955, winning him the 'Daniel Blum Theatre Award') and particularly as Edmund Tyrone in 'Long Day's Journey Into Night' (1956/57), winning him a Fox contract and he came to the screen in A CERTAIN SMILE in 1958. Divorced from Frieda Harding, actress, in 1962 (they wed 1956), they had 2 children: Jeffrey—born 1958, and Pamela, born 1959. Mr Dillman wed model Suzy Parker in 1963. His movies include: COMPULSION (59); CIRCLE OF DECEPTION (61); FRANCIS OF ASSISI (61); A RAGE TO LIVE (65); THE HELICOPTER SPIES (67); THE BRIDGE AT REMAGEN (69); SUPPOSE THEY GAVE A WAR AND NOBODY CAME (71); BROTHER JOHN (71); THE WAY WE WERE (73); THE RESURRECTION OF ZACHARY WHEELER (71, T.V. movie); DELIVER US FROM EVIL (74, T.V. movie); ADVENTURES OF THE QUEEN (75, T.V. movie). He appeared as Capt. David Young in the British T.V. series 'Court Martial' (1965). From his marriage to Miss Parker he has 2 children, Dinah (b. 1965) and Christopher (b. 1969). His recent movies: LOVE & BULLETS (77); THE SWARM (78); PIRANHA (78); TOURIST (series 1980); GUYANA—CRIME OF THE CENTURY (80).

DIANA DORS

B. Swindon, Wiltshire, 23.10.31; real name Diana Mary Fluck. Ed. Colville House, Swindon. Aged 13, Diana won a beauty contest at Weston-Super-Mare, came to the screen 2 years later in THE SHOP AT SLY CORNER, went to R.A.D.A., won medals for her acting, and, groomed for stardom by the Rank School, appeared immediately in the movies HOLIDAY CAMP (47); OLIVER TWIST (48); GOOD TIME GIRL (48); THE CALENDAR (49); HERE COME THE HUGGETTS (49); DANCE HALL (50); LADY GODIVA RIDES AGAIN (51); THE WEAK AND THE WICKED (52); IS YOUR HONEY-MOON REALLY NECESSARY? (52); IT'S A GRAND LIFE (53), becoming the 'blonde bomb-shell' of British movies. Her first husband was the late Dennis Hamilton and her other movies of the 1950s include: A KID FOR TWO FARTHINGS (55); MISS TULIP STAYS THE NIGHT (55); AS LONG AS THEY'RE HAPPY (55); YIELD TO THE NIGHT (56, her best role, as condemned murderess); I MARRIED A WOMAN, THE UNHOLY WIFE (56, both U.S.A.); THE LONG HAUL (57); TREAD SOFTLY, STRANGER (58); PASSPORT TO SHAME (59). Her 2nd husband was actor/comedian Richard Dawson, they had 2 children, Mark in 1960 and Gary in 1962. In the 60s she made occasional movies and acted on T.V. and on the stage, married actor Alan Lake (q.v.) in 1968 and had a son, Jason, in 1969. Miss Dors' further work includes movies WEST 11 (63); BABY LOVE (69); DEEP END (71); THE AMAZING MR BLUNDEN (72); NOTHING BUT THE NIGHT (72) and recent T.V.: 'Just William' series (1976/77), the play 'Dr Jekyll & Mr Hyde' (1980) and her own chat show, 'Diana Dors Show', in 1981.
Autobiographies: SWINGIN' DORS. Paperback: World Distributors: London, 1960. FOR ADULTS ONLY. W.H. Allen: London, 1978. Paperback: Star, 1978. BEHIND CLOSED DORS. W.H. Allen: London, 1979; DORS BY DIANA; Mac-Donald/Futura: London, 1981; p/b: MacD./F., 1981.

KAREN DOTRICE

B. Guernsey, Channel Islands, 9.11.55. F father is actor Roy Dotrice. She entered movies a child actress appearing in Disney's THE THRI LIVES OF THOMASINA (63); MARY PO PINS (64) and THE GNOME-MOBILE (6 having previously appeared on the stage aged 5 'The Caucasian Chalk Circle' at the Aldwy with her father. Her T.V. work includes: 'Dicke of London' (76), 'She Fell Among Thieves' (7 and Karen won the 'Variety Club Award' 1980 Best Actress for her performance in Don Shar THE 39 STEPS. Her sister Michele is als popular stage/TV actress.

ROY DOTRICE

B. Guernsey, Channel Islands, 26.5.23. E Dayton Academy. In his late teens was ir prisoner-of-war camp in Germany and beca interested in the theatre, entertaining with fell troops in revue 'Back Home' in 1945. Worl extensively in repertory, including Liverp Manchester, Oldham, for 10 years. He is wed actress Kay Newman and they have 3 daughte Michele, Karen and Yvette. In 1955 he founc the Guernsey Rep. Co., staying there for 2 y acting and directing. In July 1958 he joined Royal Shakespeare Co. and has since becom distinguished actor, working mainly on the st and in T.V. In 1967 he won acclaim for his o man show, 'Brief Lives' at Hampstead, sub quently appearing in this on Broadway, T (winning award) and in 1969 at The Criter Theatre, giving a record 213 performances. E movies include: THE HEROES OF TEl MARK (65); A TWIST OF SAND (68); LOC UP YOUR DAUGHTERS (68); BUTTERC CHAIN (69); TOOMORROW (69); ONE C THOSE THINGS (70, Denmark); NICHOL & ALEXANDRA (71); TALES FROM Tl CRYPT (72); THE LAST OF LINDA CLE] (81, short); other stage includes 'The Passion Dracula' (78), Fagin in 'Oliver!' (79), 'Murde Mind' (82), US tour, 'Churchill' (one-man shc 82).

KIRK DOUGLAS

Kirk Douglas has remained at the top of his profession since he came to the screen in 1946, owing to his careful selection of screen roles, working with the world's greatest directors and making the shrewd move in the 1950s by venturing into his own productions. He was born Issur Danielovitch in Amsterdam, N.Y., on 9 December 1916, his parents being Russian immigrants from the south of Moscow. They were very poor and from an early age he had to earn money to support the family (which included 6 sisters). He recalls he had over 40 jobs before becoming an actor. He attended Wilbur Lynch High School becoming interested in dramatics, and from 1935-39 St. Lawrence University, graduating with a B.A. degree. He was also an excellent sportsman, excelling at wrestling. After attending the Am.A.D.A., when he first appeared professionally in summer stock and changed his name to Kirk Douglas, he did two tiny roles on Broadway and was called up for WWII service. From 1942-44 he served in the US Navy, discharged medically after an accident involving a depth charge. Douglas had wed Bermuda-born actress Diana Dill on 2.11.43 and sons Michael (qv) and Joel were born 25.9.44 and 23.1.47 respectively. After further roles on radio, Broadway, in particular the play 'The Wind is Ninety' (1945), and due to the encouragement of former fellow drama student Lauren Bacall (qv), Douglas was given a role for producer Hal Wallis in the movie THE STRANGE LOVE OF MARTHA IVERS (46). His performance was received well, and after one more role on Broadway in 'Woman Bites Dog', he decided upon a career in movies. After six more pictures, including MOURNING BECOMES ELECTRA (47) and A LETTER TO THREE WIVES (48) he became a top star with *CHAMPION (49) as a ruthless boxer. The 1950s proved to be his most successful years with such pictures as THE GLASS MENAGERIE (50); ACE IN THE HOLE (51); DETECTIVE STORY (51, Picturegoer Award, Best Actor); *THE BAD & THE BEAUTIFUL (52); THE JUGGLER (53); ACT OF LOVE (53); 20,000 LEAGUES UNDER THE SEA (54); MAN WITHOUT A STAR (55); INDIAN FIGHTER (55, his first production for his own company, Bryna (named after his mother)); *LUST FOR LIFE (56, as artist Van Gogh); GUNFIGHT AT O.K. CORRAL (57, as Doc Holliday); PATHS OF GLORY (57); THE VIKINGS (58, Bryna Prod.); LAST TRAIN FROM GUN HILL (59). Divorcing his 1st wife in 1951, Douglas wed Belgian-born Anne Buydens in 1954. They are happily married and have 2 sons, Peter (born 23.11.55) and Eric (born 21.6.58). He was Executive Producer of SPARTACUS (59/60), playing the title role, the picture emerging as one of the best of the 'epic' cycle. His 31 pictures since then have included LONELY ARE THE BRAVE (62); THE LIST OF ADRIAN MESSENGER (63); SEVEN DAYS IN MAY (64); CAST A GIANT SHADOW (66); THE BROTHERHOOD (68); THERE WAS A CROOKED MAN (70); SCALAWAG (73, directed); POSSEE (75, directed); and most recently THE FURY (77); CACTUS JACK (78); SATURN 3 (79); THE FINAL COUNTDOWN (79, produced by son Peter); HOME MOVIES (79); THE MAN FROM SNOWY RIVER (81, Australia); EDDIE MACON'S RUN and REMEMBRANCE OF LOVE (both 1982). (*indicates Academy Award nomination).
THE FILMS OF KIRK DOUGLAS by Tony Thomas: Citadel: Secaucus, New Jersey, 1972.

MELVYN DOUGLAS

B. Macon, Georgia, 5.4.01; real name Melvyn Edouard Hesselberg. Educated at St. Laurence & Nebraska Universities. His father was a concert pianist, and Melvyn studied for a while at the Toronto Conservatory of Music. Still in his teens he played in Shakespearean productions (incl. 'Merchant of Venice' as Bassanio), having previously considered a career as a writer, and worked as lift operator, farm operator, newspaper reporter and salesman. Founded own stock co. at Madison, Wisconsin and made Broadway debut Jan. 1928 in 'A Free Soul', coming to the screen in 1931 in TONIGHT OR NEVER, repeating stage role. Became polished screen star in such movies as THE OLD DARK HOUSE (32); DANGEROUS CORNER (34); THE LONE WOLF RETURNS (35); CAPTAINS COURAGEOUS (37), I MET HIM IN PARIS (37); THAT CERTAIN AGE (38); NINOTCHKA (39). Md. 1. — —, 2 sons: Gregory (b. 1920), Melvyn Jr. (b. 1921); 2. Helen Gahagan 1931 (actress/congresswoman), 1 son Pierre (b. 1933),

1 daughter Mary (b. 1935). During WWII 1941-42 served in civilian defence service, Washington; 1942-45 served in U.S. Army in Far East, demobilized with rank of major. continued to work with distinction in many theatre and movie prods., including, stage: '2 Blind Mice' (1949 & tour), 'Time Out For Ginger' (1952 & tour U.S.A. & Australia), 'The Best Man' (1960 & tour, Emmy Award); movies: MR BLANDINGS BUILDS HIS DREAM HOUSE (48); THE GREAT SINNER (49); BILLY BUDD (62); HUD (63, Oscar, Best Supporting Actor); I NEVER SANG FOR MY FATHER (70, Oscar nom.); THE SEDUCTION OF JOE TYNAN (78); BEING THERE (79, Academy Award, Best Supporting Actor) and THE CHANGE-LING (79). Much T.V. work includes 'The Statesman' as Benjamin Franklin. Recent movies: GHOST STORY (81); HOT TOUCH (81); TELL ME A RIDDLE (81).
Mr Douglas died on August 4, 1981.

MICHAEL DOUGLAS

B. New Brunswick, N. Jersey, 25.9.44. Father, actor/producer/director Kirk Douglas (q.v.). Ed. Black Fox Military Acad., Choate; Univ. of Calif. (studying drama). Michael worked on his father's picture LONELY ARE THE BRAVE (62), but went through a spell living on a 'commune'. Decided to become actor after work on HEROES OF TELEMARK (65); entered T.V. in 'The Experiment', and did theatre work before appearing in the movies HAIL HERO (70); ADAM AT 6 A.M. (70); SUMMERTIME (71); NAPOLEON AND SAMANTHA (72); WHEN MICHAEL CALLS (72, T.V. movie) and as Insp. Steve Keller in 'Streets of San Francisco' (1972-76, T.V. series). He co-produced the film ONE FLEW OVER THE CUCKOO'S NEST IN 1975 (winning 5 Oscars, including Best Picture) and his more recent films are COMA (77); THE CHINA SYNDROME (78) and IT'S MY TURN (79). His production co. is named Bigstick Productions and in 1977 he wed Diandra Murrell Luker. RUNNING (81, Canada); STAR CHAMBER (82).

SARAH DOUGLAS

B. Stratford-on-Avon, 12.12.52; trained to teach English and Drama; Sarah worked in a factory, in a sterilising dept. of a hospital and spent a while in France; at 20 she entered the TV and film industry — she is now a familiar face on the small screen, working in such series as 'Esther Waters', 'Warship', 'Return of the Saint', 'Bergerac', the movies THE FINAL PROGRAMME (73); THE BRUTE (76); PEOPLE THAT TIME FORGOT (77) and especially as Ursu in SUPERMAN (78) and SUPERMAN II (81).

BRAD DOURIF

B. Huntington, W. Virginia, 18.3.50. Ed. prep schools in Aiken, S. Carolina & Colorado Springs; Marshall Univ.; from age of 16-19 played various roles with Greenbrier Rep. Theatre, W. Virginia; went to N.Y. and joined the Circle Repertory Co. and moved into T.V.; distinguished film debut as mental patient Billy Bibitt in ONE FLEW OVER THE CUCKOO'S NEST (75, Oscar nom. BSA, BAFTA Award); played off-Broadway in 'When You Comin' Back, Red Ryder?'; Mr Dourif's other movies include SERGEANT MATLO-VICH VS. THE U.S. AIRFORCE (78, T.V. movie); EYES OF LAURA MARS (78); STUDS LONIGAN (79, mini-series); WISE BLOOD (79); HEAVEN'S GATE (80); RAGTIME (81).

:SLEY-ANN DOWN

Clapham, London, 17.3.54. The eldest of the 2 ghters of James Down (caretaker of the Terri-al Army Centre, Putney) and his wife, Isabella. mmenced career aged 10 as child model. vies: THE SMASHING BIRD I USED TO OW (uncredited 1969); ALL THE RIGHT ISES (69); WITHOUT A GOODBYE (70); SAULT (70); COUNTESS DRACULA (71); ALAWAG (71); POPE JOAN (71); A TLE NIGHT MUSIC (76, unreleased); ANNIGAN (76); THE PINK PANTHER RIKES AGAIN (77); THE BETSY (77, lywood); HANOVER STREET (78); THE ST GREAT TRAIN ROBBERY (78); UGHCUT (79); SPHINX (81). T.V. includes: blic Eye', 'Hark at Barker', very popular as ly Georgina in 'Upstairs, Downstairs' series 74/75), 'The One & Only Phyllis Dixey' (78). the age of 15 she won title 'Britain's Most utiful Teenager'. Her sister Angela is a model. ley-Ann wed Argentine-born assistant film ctor Mr Henri Gabriel in February 1980. ent T.V.: 'Unity (BBC 1981) and stage: Eliza olittle in 'Pygmalion' (Young Vic, London, . 1981); div. March 1982; Md: 2. director liam Friedkin, 1982, 1 son, Jake (b. 6.12.82); JRDER IS EASY (T.V. movie, 1981).

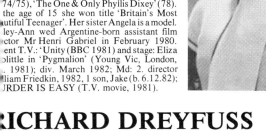

DENNIS DUGAN

B. Wheaton, Illinois, ... Dennis started training for acting while at Junior High School and joined Goodman's Theatre in Chicago, attending workshops and appearing in summer stock. He went to N.Y., worked as a clerk for a market research firm, played roles in Broadway and off-Broadway prods., including 'Tom Paine' and 'The House of Blue Leaves' (1971, lead). Moved into T.V., including roles in 'The Waltons', 'Rockford Files', 'Police Story', 'M.A.S.H.', 'Cannon', 'Love, American Style', 'Rich Man, Poor Man' and the lead in series 'Richie Brockelman, Private Eye' (1978). His motion picture appearances include HARRY & WALTER GO TO NEW YORK (76); THE SPACEMAN AND KING ARTHUR (78) and THE HOWLING (80).

ICHARD DREYFUSS

th appearances in two of the most successful pictures of all time, JAWS and CLOSE ENCOUNTERS OF THE IRD KIND and winning the 1977 Academy Award for Best Actor in THE GOODBYE GIRL, Richard Dreyfuss emerged as one of the most successful of Hollywood's younger actors. Born in Brooklyn, N.Y. on 29 October 47(?) he is the son of Richard Dreyfuss Sr., a lawyer/restaurateur, and his wife Gerry. He grew up in Los Angeles, ended Beverly Hills High School and had always wanted to act, making his pro. début in 'In Mama's House' at the llery Theatre, L.A. From the mid-1960s he worked regularly on the stage, including 'Journey to the Day', 'Incident Vichy', 'People Need People', 'But Seriously' (1969), on and off-Broadway, in T.V. shows, including 'The Big lley', 'Mod Squad', 'The Bold Ones' and his movies have included roles in VALLEY OF THE DOLLS (67); THE RADUATE (67); HELLO DOWN THERE (68); THE YOUNG RUNAWAYS (69); Baby Face Nelson in LLINGER (73); AMERICAN GRAFFITI (73); THE APPRENTICESHIP OF DUDDY KRAVITZ (74); SERTS (75); JAWS (76); VICTORY AT ENTEBBE (76); CLOSE ENCOUNTERS OF THE THIRD KIND); THE GOODBYE GIRL (77, Academy Award; Golden Globe Award; British Academy Award); THE BIG X (78); THE COMPETITION (80) and WHOSE LIFE IS IT ANYWAY? (80). In 1972 he appeared on the stage h Henry Fonda (qv) in 'Time Of Your Life', and, in March, 1983, he wed T.V. writer/producer Jeramie Rain. His est movie is THE BUDDY SYSTEM (83).

NDREW DUGGAN

, 28.12.23. Broadway debut 1942 inter-ed by war service in U.S. Army; played in . in such plays as 'The Innocents' (1950), nt Your Wagon' (1951), 'Rose Tattoo' (1951), gile Fox' (1954); md. Betty, children: Dick, cy; became well-known character actor in s and esp. T.V.; movies include PATTERNS ; 3 BRAVE MEN (57); THE BRAVADOS ; WESTBOUND (59); MERRILL'S MA-UDERS (62); CHAPMAN REPORT (62); E GLORY GUYS (65); IN LIKE FLINT ; IT'S ALIVE! (74); PRIVATE FILES OF DGAR HOOVER (78, as Lyndon Johnson); includes series: Cal Calhoun in 'Bourbon et Beat' (59/60), George Rose in 'Room For More' (1962) and Murdoch Lancer in 'Lancer' 58-70); T.V. movies: FORGOTTEN MAN ; FIREHOUSE (73); PANIC ON THE (74); RICH MAN, POOR MAN (76, mini-es); OVERBOARD (78); BACKSTAIRS THE WHITE HOUSE (79, mini-series, as ght Eisenhower); THE INCREDIBLE JRNEY OF DR MEG LAUREL (79).

KEIR DULLEA

B. Cleveland, Ohio, 30.5.36. Ed. San Francisco State Coll. Trained for the stage at the Sanford Meisner Neighbourhood Playhouse. His family moved to N.Y. when he was three and he was raised in N.Y.'s Bohemian Greenwich Village appeared in stock with the John Drew Theatre, Totem Pole Playhouse and Berkshire Playhouse and was on Broadway 1959 in 'Season of Choice'. Came to the screen in 1961 in THE HOODLUM PRIEST and has been seen in DAVID & LISA (62); THE THIN RED LINE (64); MAIL ORDER BRIDE (64); BUNNY LAKE IS MISSING (65); MADAME X (66); THE FOX (68); DE SADE (68); 2001: A SPACE ODYSSEY (68); POPE JOAN (72); PAUL & MICHELLE (73); THE PAPERBACK HERO (73); BLACK CHRISTMAS (75); LEOPARD IN THE SNOW (76); LAW AND ORDER (76, T.V. movie); FULL CIRCLE (77); THE HOS-TAGE TOWER (79); BRAVE NEW WORLD (80, 2-part T.V. movie). He is divorced from actress Margot Bennett. He has frequently re-turned to the stage in such roles as Dr Tennyson in 'Dr Cook's Garden' (1967), Don Baker in 'Butter-flies Are Free' (1969) and Brick in 'Cat on a Hot Tin Roof' (1974). Recent movies: NO PLACE TO HIDE (T.V. movie, 1981); THE NEXT ONE, BRAINWAVES (both 1982).

FAYE DUNAWAY

Miss Dunaway won a deserved Oscar in 1976 in recognition for her fine performance in NETWORK, celebratin decade as a movie actress, her portrayal of Bonnie Parker in BONNIE AND CLYDE bringing her into the big-tir Her full name is Dorothy Faye Dunaway and she was born in Bascom, Florida on 14 January 1941, the daughter John Dunaway, U.S. Army sergeant, and his wife Grace. She was educated at Leon High School, Tallahasee, Flori at Arkansas, Utah, Germany (where her father was serving), the University of Florida (where she played 'Medea' i play) and appeared in summer stock in small roles before being awarded a scholarship to attend the Boston Univers School of Fine and Applied Arts, studying acting with Ted Kazanoff, in order to get her B.A. After she graduated, Llo Richards, who had directed her in 'The Crucible', introduced her to Elia Kazan and she joined the Lincoln Rep. Co. H New York début was in 1962 when she took over the role of Margaret More in 'A Man For All Seasons'. Otl productions included 'After the Fall' (1964), 'But For Whom Charlie' (1964) and in 'Hogan's Goat' (1965) she v discovered by Sam Spiegel and came to the screen in THE HAPPENING (66). A year later she made BONNIE AT CLYDE and in this stylishly violent gangster movie her performance received an Oscar nomination. Her other mov have included HURRY SUNDOWN (67); THE THOMAS CROWN AFFAIR (68); THE EXTRAORDINAI SEAMAN (69); A PLACE FOR LOVERS (69); THE ARRANGEMENT (69); PUZZLE OF A DOWNFA CHILD (70); LITTLE BIG MAN (70); DOC (71); THE DEADLY TRAP (71); OKLAHOMA CRUDE (7 THREE MUSKETEERS/FOUR MUSKETEERS (73/74); THE TOWERING INFERNO (74); CHINATOV (74, Oscar nom.); THREE DAYS OF THE CONDOR (75); NETWORK (76, winning Oscar, Best Actress); TI VOYAGE OF THE DAMNED (77); THE EYES OF LAURA MARS (77) and THE CHAMP (7 Miss Dunaway returned to the stage in 1972 to play in 'Old Times' and Blanche du Bois in 'A Streetcar Named Desi in 1973, both in L.A. More recent movies are THE FIRST DEADLY SIN (80); MOMMIE DEAREST (81, as Jc Crawford); as EVA PERON (82, T.V. movie); THE WICKED LADY (83) and SUPERGIRL (84). She wed Pe Wolfe of the J. Geils Rock Band in 1974, but they are divorced. She has a son, Liam, the father being Terry O'Neill, photographer.

CHARLES DURNING

B. Highland Falls, N.Y., 28.2.33. Mr Durning is a distinguished Broadway actor whose work includes 'In April Once' (1955), 'The Hour Glass' (1955) and Shakespearean prods., such as 'Julius Caesar' (1962), 'The Tempest' (1962), 'Twelfth Night' (1963) and 'Henry V' (1965). Coming to the screen in 1965, his movies include HARVEY MIDDLEMAN, FIREMAN (65); I WALK THE LINE (70); THE PURSUIT OF HAPPINESS (71); THE CONNECTION (73, T.V. movie); THE STING (73); THE FRONT PAGE (74); DOG DAY AFTERNOON (75); THE HINDENBERG (75); BREAKHEART PASS (75); HARRY & WALTER GO TO NEW YORK (76); THE CHOIRBOYS (77); TWILIGHT'S LAST GLEANING (77). He has appeared on T.V. in his own series, 'The Cop & the Kid' (1975/76) and the 'Best Sellers'— 'Captains and Kings' (1976) and 'Studs Lonigan' (1980). Recent work: 'Mass Appeal' (stage 1982); movies: STARTING OVER (79); WHEN A STRANGER CALLS, ATTICA: STORY OF A PRISON RIOT (T.V. movie, both 1980); TRUE CONFESSIONS, SHARKEY'S MACHINE (both 1981); THE BEST LITTLE WHOREHOUSE IN TEXAS (Oscar nom., BSA), TOOTSIE (both 1982).

SHELLEY DUVALL

B. Houston, Texas, . .50. Shelley, who has three younger brothers, was brought up on her lawyer father's 450-acre cattle ranch near Houston. At school she had no interest in acting but studied hard, becoming a top student, later studying nutritiion, macrobiotics and diet therapy. At a Houston party she met director Mr Robert Altman who advised her to try acting and she came to the screen in his BREWSTER McCLOUD (70). She has since played in McCABE & MRS MILLER (71); THIEVES LIKE US (74); won the Best Actress Award at Cannes for THREE WOMEN (77); played on T.V. in 'Bernice Bobs Her Hair' (1977) and more recent movies for her are THE SHINING (80), POPEYE (80, as Olive Oyl), TIME BANDITS (81).

ROBERT DUVALL

A solid supporting actor in movies from 1963, it was not until 1972 that Robert Duvall's acting was recognised by Academy with a nomination for his work in THE GODFATHER and since then he has steadily worked his way to top of his profession in a variety of roles. Born in San Diego, California in 1930, he is the son of a former U.S. N admiral. At school he showed no interest in acting until his teens, when his mother, an amateur actress, persuaded him become one. At Principia College, Illinois he gained his degree in drama, having shown previous interest in a career an athlete. After two years in the U.S. army, he studied acting with Sandy Meisner at the Neighborhood Playhous New York, while working as a dishwasher, postal clerk and truck driver, amongst others. He appeared in 75 sto productions and Broadway included 'Mrs Warren's Profession' (1958), 'Call Me By My Rightful Name' (1961) and such Hollywood T.V. series as 'Route 66', 'Naked City', 'The Defenders', 'Outer Limits' and 'Great Ghost Tal Discovered for the screen by director Robert Mulligan, his first movie was TO KILL A MOCKINGBIRD, in 196 His others have included CAPTAIN NEWMAN, M.D. (64); NIGHTMARE IN THE SUN (65); THE CHA (66); COUNTDOWN, THE DETECTIVE, BULLITT (all 68); TRUE GRIT, THE RAIN PEOPLE (6 M.A.S.H., THE REVOLUTIONARY (70); THX 1138, LAWMAN (71); TOMORROW, THE GODFATHE THE GREAT NORTHFIELD-MINNESOTA RAID (as Jesse James); JOE KIDD (72); BADGE 373, LAI ICE, THE OUTFIT (73); THE CONVERSATION, THE GODFATHER: PART II, WE'RE NOT THE JETS (74, directed); BREAKOUT, KILLER ELITE, THE 7% SOLUTION (75, as Dr Watson); THE EAGLE H. LANDED, NETWORK (76); APOCALYPSE NOW (77, British Film Award, Best Supporting Actor); TI GREATEST, THE BETSY (77). Mr Duvall is divorced from his wife, Barbara, and has occasionally returned Broadway. He played Gen. Eisenhower in IKE: THE WAR YEARS (78, T.V. movie) and more recently starre THE GREAT SANTINI (79); PURSUIT (80); TRUE CONFESSIONS (81); TENDER MERCIES (82) ; ANGELO, MY LOVE (83, also directed). His second wife is Gail Young, actress, and producer of the last-nan movie.

PETER EGAN

B. London, 29.9.46. Ed. St. George's Secondary Modern School, Maida Vale. Wanted to become artist, but studied for stage at R.A.D.A. Stage: seasons—Chichester, Royal Shakespeare Co., Nat. Theatre, Pitlochry Festival. Md. Actress Myra Frances, 1 daughter Rebecca. Many T.V. roles including Oscar Wilde in series 'Lillie' and as the 'Prince Regent' (BBC 1979). Movies include ONE BRIEF SUMMER (69); THE HIRELING (73, BAFTA Award, Most Promising Newcomer); CALLAN (74); HENNESSY (75). Recent T.V.: 'Dear Brutus' (BBC 1981) and produced West End/tour of play 'Rattle of a Simple Man' (1981). Movie: CHARIOTS OF FIRE (81). Recent stage: 'Arms and the Man' (1981/82); T.V.: 'Reilly' (82); 'Strangers' (83).

LISA EICHHORN

B. New York, ... Brought up in Reading, Pennsylvania, Miss Eichhorn won a scholarship from Rotary International to study English at Oxford and appeared with the Oxford Univ. Dramatic Society. After attending R.A.D.A., she was selected by director John Schlesinger for the movie YANKS (78) and has since been seen in THE EUROPEANS (79); CUTTER AND BONE (79); WHY SHOULD I LIE? (80); THE WALL (T.V. movie, 1980); 'East Lynne' (T.V., 1982); Md: actor Treat Williams (qv).

CLINT EASTWOOD

For thirteen consecutive years Clint Eastwood has appeared in the Top Ten of the American exhibitors poll, adequate proof of this actor's extraordinary box-office appeal — he is one of the very few remaining truly international stars whose name alone will guarantee a movie's success. San Francisco born, on 31 May 1930 he is the son of Clinton Eastwood Snr. and his wife Ruth. Owing to the Depression, Eastwood Snr. lost his job as a cost accountant and worked at several jobs, including gas station attendant, his son attending 10 schools. The family (Clint has a sister, Jeanne) settled in Oakland, California, and father worked for the Container Corporation of America. Clint attended Oakland Technical High School, L.A. from 1946-48 and then took a succession of jobs: a lumberjack with the Weyerhauser Lumber Co., Springfield, Oregon; stoker at Bethlehem Steel Plant, Seattle; moved to Renton, nr. Seattle — there worked as lifeguard and in parts dept. at Boeing Aircraft Plant. Following 2 years in the U.S. Army as a swimming instructor, an acquaintance, who knew a movie director, urged the 6'4" Eastwood to go to Hollywood and get a screen test. He did this, but the director had left the studio so he instead enrolled at L.A. City College, having wed Maggie Johnson on December 19, 1953. Months passed, but his time was encouraged by a photographer to screen test which proved successful, landing a contract with Universal Studios. For 4 years he played tiny roles in such pictures as REVENGE OF THE CREATURE (55), but the turning point came in 1958 when he was cast as Rowdy Yates in 'Rawhide', a T.V. series which ran for 7 years, gaining him recognition. In 1964 he had filmed in Spain a western, A FISTFUL OF DOLLARS, and, after two more similar formula 'spaghetti westerns', the movies had earned Eastwood enormous popularity in Europe and the actor, returning to America, was very soon elevated to super-stardom in such movies as HANG 'EM HIGH (68); COOGAN'S BLUFF (68); WHERE EAGLES DARE (69); PAINT YOUR WAGON (69, a musical); KELLYS HEROES (70) and TWO MULES FOR SISTER SARA (70). Eastwood has two children, Kyle, born in 1968, and Alison, born in 1972. In 1969 he set up his own production company, Malpaso Productions. His many other movies have included THE BEGUILED (71); PLAY MISTY FOR ME* (71); DIRTY HARRY (71); JOE KIDD (72); BREEZY (73, * only), HIGH PLAINS DRIFTER* (73); MAGNUM FORCE (73); THUNDERBOLT & LIGHTFOOT (74); THE EIGER SANCTION* (75); THE OUTLAW, JOSEY WALES* (76); THE GAUNTLET* (77); EVERY WHICH WAY BUT LOOSE (78); ESCAPE FROM ALCATRAZ (79); BRONCO BILLY* (80); ANY WHICH WAY YOU CAN (80); FIREFOX* (82); HONKYTONK MAN* (83, co-starring son Kyle) and SUDDEN IMPACT* (84). (*Denotes Mr Eastwood also directed).

MOVIN' ON by Peter Douglas; pb: Starbook, 1974;
CLINT EASTWOOD: THE MAN BEHIND THE MYTH by Patrick Agan; Robert Hale: London, 1977
CLINT EASTWOOD: ALL AMERICAN ANTI-HERO by David Downing & Gary Herman; large pb: Omnibus Press: New York and G.B., 1977.
THE MAN WITH NO NAME by Iain Johnstone; Plexus Publishing Ltd.: London, 1981; large pb.
THE FILMS OF CLINT EASTWOOD by Boris Zmijewsky and Lee Pfeiffer: Citadel: Secaucus, N.J., 1982.

SAMANTHA EGGAR

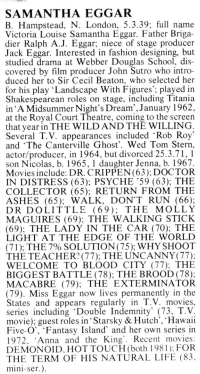

B. Hampstead, N. London, 5.3.39; full name Victoria Louise Samantha Eggar. Father Brigadier Ralph A.J. Eggar; niece of stage producer Jack Eggar. Interested in fashion designing, but studied drama at Webber Douglas School, discovered by film producer John Sutro who introduced her to Sir Cecil Beaton, who selected her for his play 'Landscape With Figures'; played in Shakespearean roles on stage, including Titania in 'A Midsummer Night's Dream', January 1962, at the Royal Court Theatre, coming to the screen that year in THE WILD AND THE WILLING. Several T.V. appearances included 'Rob Roy' and 'The Canterville Ghost'. Wed Tom Stern, actor/producer, in 1964, but divorced 25.3.71, 1 son Nicolas, b. 1965, 1 daughter Jenna, b. 1967. Movies include: DR. CRIPPEN (63); DOCTOR IN DISTRESS (63); PSYCHE '59 (63); THE COLLECTOR (65); RETURN FROM THE ASHES (65); WALK, DON'T RUN (66); DR DOLITTLE (69); THE MOLLY MAGUIRES (69); THE WALKING STICK (69); THE LADY IN THE CAR (70); THE LIGHT AT THE EDGE OF THE WORLD (71); THE 7% SOLUTION (75); WHY SHOOT THE TEACHER? (77); THE UNCANNY (77); WELCOME TO BLOOD CITY (77); THE BIGGEST BATTLE (78); THE BROOD (78); MACABRE (79); THE EXTERMINATOR (79). Miss Eggar now lives permanently in the States and appears regularly in T.V. movies, series including 'Double Indemnity' (73, T.V. movie); guest roles in 'Starsky & Hutch', 'Hawaii Five-O', 'Fantasy Island' and her own series in 1972, 'Anna and the King'. Recent movies: DEMONOID, HOT TOUCH (both 1981); FOR THE TERM OF HIS NATURAL LIFE (83, mini-ser.).

JACK ELAM

B.   , Arizona,   .16(?). Aged 5 gleaned cotton from stripped pods; sightless left eye owing to childhood fight; various jobs, including manager of Hollywood Boulevard Theatre and a Bel-Air hotel; in 1936 was accountant for Standard Oil, ended up in Hollywood working with Sam Goldwyn and eventually got film work as character heavy; scores of films include THE SUNDOWNERS (50); RAWHIDE (51); RANCHO NOTORIOUS (52); CATTLE QUEEN OF MONTANA (54); KISS ME, DEADLY (55); MAN FROM LARAMIE (55); THE COMANCHEROS (62); THE WAY WEST (66); RIO LOBO (70); SUPPORT YOUR LOCAL GUNFIGHTER (71). Jack is very well-known on T.V. in such series as 'The Dakotas' (1963, as Deputy J.D. Smith); as George Taggart in 'Temple Houston' (1963/64) and as Zack Wheeler in 'The Texas Wheelers' (1974/75); more recent work: THE NORSEMAN (78); LACY & THE MISSISSIPPI QUEEN (78, T.V. movie); 'Struck By Lightning' (1979, series); THE SACKETTS (79, T.V. movie); THE CANNONBALL RUN (81); 'Father Murphy' (series 1982/83).

BRITT EKLAND

B. Stockholm, Sweden, 6.10.42. Aged 15, starred in a toothpaste commercial, went to a Stockholm drama school, played small roles on T.V. and toured with Swedish Theatre Co. Came to screen 1963 with small role in movie TO BED OR NOT TO BED (in Italy). Md. Peter Sellers, actor. 19.2.64, 1 daughter Victoria b. 20.1.65. (div. 1969). Movies include: AFTER THE FOX (66); THE BOBO (67); THE DOUBLE MAN (68); THE NIGHT THEY RAIDED MINSKY'S (68); AT ANY PRICE (69); STILETTO (69); TINTOMARA (70); THE CANNIBALS (70); CARTER (70); A TIME FOR LOVING (70); NIGHT HAIR CHILD (71); BAXTER (71); ENDLESS NIGHT (72); ASYLUM (72); THE WICKER MAN (72); ULTIMATE THRILL (73); THE MAN WITH THE GOLDEN GUN (74); ROYAL FLASH, HIGH VELOCITY (75); CASANOVA (76); SLAVERY (76); KING SOLOMON'S TREASURES (76); directed movie THE BOY in 1972. G.B. stage debut 'Mate', Comedy Theatre, 1978, London. Has son, Nicholai; father is Lou Adler, film/record producer. Britt released disco-single 'Do It To Me' in 1980. Recent movies: HOSTAGE TOWER (79); THE MONSTER CLUB (80); DARK EYES (81); VALLEY OF THE DOLLS (Mini-ser. 1981).
Autobiography: *TRUE BRITT*. pb: Sphere: London, 1980.

DENHOLM ELLIOTT

B. London, 31.5.22. Ed. Malvern Coll. Trained for stage at R.A.D.A. WWII in Bomber Command but captured and served 1942-45 in German prison camp. Stage debut 1945: Amersham, Bucks; London debut: Criterion Theatre in 'The Guinea Pig' 1946 and has since become one of Britain's most accomplished actors, winning several awards in G.B. and on Broadway. Came to screen in 1949 in DEAR MR PROHACK. Other movies include: THE SOUND BARRIER (52); THE CRUEL SEA (53); THE NIGHT MY NUMBER CAME UP (55); PACIFIC DESTINY (56); NOTHING BUT THE BEST (64). Md. 1. actress Virginia McKenna (q.v.—div.); 2. Susan Robinson, 1 daughter Jennifer, 1 son Mark. Further films: KING RAT (65); HERE WE GO ROUND THE MULBERRY BUSH (67); TOO LATE THE HERO (69). One of Britain's busiest film/T.V. actors. Recent stage: 'The Paranormalist' (82); T.V.: 'School Play' (79), 'Blade on the Feather' (80, BAFTA Aw. BA); movies: ZULU DAWN, GAMES FOR VULTURES (both 1978); CUBA, BAD TIMING, SAINT JACK (all 1979); RISING DAMP (Ev. Standard Aw., BA, 1980); SUNDAY LOVERS ('An Englishman's Home'), RAIDERS OF THE LOST ARK, 'Marco Polo' (ser. all 1981); BRIMSTONE & TREACLE (82); THE MISSIONARY, THE WICKED LADY, HOUND OF THE BASKERVILLES (all 1983).

SAM ELLIOTT

B. Sacramento, Calif., 9.8.44; R.N.: Samuel Pack Elliott. An only child, his father was official for the Fish & Wild Life Service; mother is retired physical training instructor. At Univ. Sam studied psychology and English Lit.,; was also water safety instructor, but still wanted to be actor, when, at 10, saw troupe performing at State Fair. After compulsory spell in American Reserves for military service, he worked his way to Hollywood, worked for construction firm, which paid for acting classes, eventually signed by 20th Cent. Fox. Movies include: BUTCH CASSIDY & THE SUNDANCE KID (69); GAMES (69); FROGS (72); THE BLUE KNIGHT (73); LIFEGUARD (76); THE LEGACY (78). Well-known on T.V. in 'Molly & Lawless John' (72, T.V. movie), 'Evel Knievel' (75, T.V. movie), 'The Aspen Murder' (78, T.V. movie) and Best Sellers: Sam Damon in 'Once an Eagle' (76); 'The Sacketts' (79, T.V. movie); 'Murder in Texas' (81, T.V. movie); 'Shadow Riders' (82, T.V. movie).

LINDA EVANS

B. Hartford, Conn., ... At the age of 2 months, she moved with family to Los Angeles and took dramatic lessons while at High School. Appearances in T.V. commercials, including advertising soft drinks, led to to T.V. roles. She came to the screen in 1963 in TWILIGHT OF HONOR and then made THOSE CALLOWAYS (64) and COCK-A-DOODLE-DO (65) before appearing in the long-running western T.V. series 'The Big Valley' as Audra from 1965-66. Miss Evans was married to actor/photographer John Derek from 1969-74. Her other T.V. series include 'Hunter' as Marty Shaw in 1977 and the current 'Dynasty'. Other movies: THE KLANS-MAN (74) and the recent TOM HORN (79) opp. the late Steve McQueen. Her role as Krystle in 'Dynasty' T.V. ser. won Linda a Golden Globe Aw. in 1982.

PETER FALK

B. N.Y. City, 16.9.27. Ed. Ossining H.S. (grad. 1945); Hamilton Coll. Served as cook in Merchant Marine visiting Europe & S. America; ret'd. to Hamilton Coll. 1946-48; New School for Social Research (B.A. in political science); Maxwell School of Syracuse Univ., gaining M.A. in public administration, then taking a post as efficiency expert for the Budget Bureau, Hartford, Conn. Always, since aged 16, interested in acting and took a course, with Eva Le Gallienne at Westport in 1955, year later Broadway roles in 'The Feast With the Statue', 'Saint Joan', 'Death of a Scoun-drel'; 1957 studied Meisner Workshop and 'Lady's Not For Burning', Broadway. Came to screen 1958 in WIND ACROSS THE EVERGLADES. others: MURDER INC. (60); POCKETFUL OF MIRACLES (61) (both Oscar nom. BSA's); THE BALCONY (63); ROBIN & THE 7 HOODS (64); THE GREAT RACE (65); HUSBANDS (70). Md. 1. Alyce Mayo, 2 daughters Katherine (b. 1961), Jacqueline (b. 1962) div. 1977; 2. Shera Lynn Danese 1977, 2 daughters Kackie, Cath. Became star with series as Lt. 'Columbo' (1971-77); previous series: 'The Trials of O'Brien' (1965). Mr Falk, who, at the age of 3 had his right eye removed owing to a tumour, has won several 'Emmy' Awards. Recent movies: MURDER BY DEATH (77); TODAY IS FOREVER (77); CHEAP DETECTIVE (77); THE BRINK'S JOB (78); THE IN-LAWS (79); . . . ALL THE MARBLES, THE GREAT MUPPET CAPER (guest, both 1981); stage 1981: 'Knives' (L.A.).

MIA FARROW

B. Los Angeles, California, 9.2.45.(?) Ed. Mary-mount, L.A. & Cygnet House, London. Daughter of film director John Farrow and actress Maureen O'Sullivan. Stage début: Madison Avenue Playhouse, New York in 'The Importance of Being Earnest' 1963; world recognition as Allison Mac-kenzie in 'Peyton Place' T.V. series 1964-66. Md. 1. Frank Sinatra 1966 (div. 1968); 2. Andre Previn, composer/conductor, 1970 (div.) 1 son Kym (b. 1974), twins—Matthew & Sacha. Movies: FUNS AT BATASI (65); A DANDY IN ASPIC (68); ROSEMARY'S BABY (68); SECRET CEREMONY (68); JOHN AND MARY (69); BLIND TERROR (71); FOLLOW ME (72); SCOUNDREL IN WHITE (72); THE GREAT GATSBY (73); SCOUNDREL IN FRANCE (74). London stage début 1972 playing title role of 'Mary Rose'; acted with Royal Shakespeare Co. in 1975. Recent movies: A WEDDING (77); FULL CIRCLE (77); DEATH ON THE NILE (77); HURRICANE (78); AVALANCHE (79); A MIDSUMMER NIGHT'S SEX COMEDY, SARAH (both 1982); BROADWAY DANNY ROSE (83).

DAVID ESSEX

B. East London, 23.7.47; real name David Cook. The son of an East End docker, as a youngster David Essex played for West Ham United Boys' soccer team, was a barrow boy, worked on the dodgems and later performed in a blues band as singer and drummer. Interested in acting, he worked in rep., understudied Tommy Steele in 'Dick Whittington' at the London Palladium and his big show-biz break came when he played Jesus in the rock musical 'Godspell' for two years. In the 70s he became a rock star with hit singles including 'Rock On' (1973), 'Lamplight' (1973), 'Gonna Make You A Star' (1974) and 'Stardust' (1975), which he also composed. He came to the screen in 1973 as Jim Mclain in THAT'LL BE THE DAY and has been seen in STARDUST (75) and SILVER DREAM RACER (79), again writing the score. He has a son, Sonny, and a daughter, Verity, from his marriage to Maureen —. Other stage roles include Guevara in 'Evita' (78/79), Lord Byron in 'Child Byron' (81).

DAVID ESSEX STORY by George Tremlett; p/b: Futura: London, 1974.

ADAM FAITH

B.W. London, 23.6.40. Father, W. London coach-driver; mother, charlady, both dec.; latter great influence on his life and made him work hard. Adam, whose real name is Terence Nelhams, left school and worked for 35/- as silk-screen printer. He saw James Dean in EAST OF EDEN and wanted to be in movies. Through mother, who worked at Rank's as cleaner, he got job as office boy, becoming assistant film editor. Had in the meantime formed skiffle-group, 'The Worried Men', getting club work in the West End and was discovered for T.V. by Jack Good. Eventually had No.1 song hit 'What Do You Want?' and went immediately into movies: BEAT GIRL (59); WHAT A WHOPPER! (61); NEVER LET GO (61); and MIX ME A PERSON (63). Decided to study his craft seriously and went into rep., appearing from Glasgow to Bromley, from Shakespeare to 'Billy Liar'. he is married to Jackie, former Lionel Blair dancer and they have a daughter, Katya. Mr Faith had a T.V. series 'Budgie' in 1972 and has since appeared in the movies STARDUST (75); YESTERDAY'S HERO (79) and McVICAR (79). Early autobiography: *DEAR ME*. pb. 1961.

JAMES FARENTINO

B. Brooklyn, N.Y., 24.2.38. Studied Am.A.D.A.; off-Broadway and on Broadway in 'Night of the Iguana' (1961) and 'In the Summer House' (1964); appeared on 'daytime T.V.' and early Hollywood 60s series incl. 'Ben Casey', '12 O'Clock High', 'Laredo', 'The Bold Ones'. Md. 1. Elizabeth Ashley (q.v.) 1962 (div.); 2. Michelle Lee, 1 son David (b. 1969); movies include: ENSIGN PULVER (64); PSYCHOMANIA (64); THE WAR LORD (66); THE RIDE TO HANGMAN'S TREE (66); THE PAD (& HOW TO USE IT) (66, Gold Globe Award); BANNING (67); ROSIE! (68); ME, NATALIE (69); THE STORY OF A WOMAN (70); THE FAMILY RICO (72, T.V. movie). T.V. series: 'The Lawyers' (1969-72) and Jefferson Keyes in 'Cool Million' (1972/73). Stage 1973 Broadway: A Streetcar Named Desire'. Recent movies: JESUS OF NAZARETH (mini-ser, 1977); FINAL COUNTDOWN (79); DEAD & BURIED (81); SOMETHING SO RIGHT, EVITA PERON (both T.V. movies, 82); ser. 'Dynasty' (82/83).

FARRAH FAWCETT

B. Corpus Christi, Texas, 2.2.48; real name Mary Farrah Leni Fawcett. The youngest daughter of James and Pauline Fawcett, her father was a pipeline contractor for the oilfields. Farrah attended the W.B. Ray High School, Corpus Christi and the Univ. of Texas, at Austin, where she studied art. It was there she was voted 'one of the most beautiful Coeds', the university mailing photos of Farrah to Hollywood agents. Although she wanted to continue with her studies, she eventually agreed to meet publicist David Mirisch, who handled the early years of her career. Coming to the screen in 1970 with small roles in LOVE IS A FUNNY THING and MYRA BRECKINRIDGE, she also appeared in over 100 T.V. commercials, including 'Ultra-Brite' toothpaste and T.V. movies such as MURDER ON FLIGHT 502 and THE GREAT AMERICAN BEAUTY CONTEST. She wed actor Lee Majors (q.v.) on 28.7.73, and after appearing in such series as '$6m Man', 'Harry O', 'Owen Marshall' and the movie LOGAN'S RUN (75) she starred in her own series as Jill Munroe, one of 'Charlie's Angels' (1976-77) which achieved much popularity for her. Farrah's other movies: SOMEBODY KILLED HER HUSBAND (78); SUNBURN (78); SATURN 3 (79); THE CANNONBALL RUN, MURDER IN TEXAS (T.V. movie, both 1981); 'Butterflies Are Free' (stage 1981). Biographies in paperback: *FARRAH* by Patricia Burstein. Signet: U.S.A., 1977. *FARRAH AND LEE* by Connie Berman. Tempo Books: N.Y., 1977.

MARTY FELDMAN

B. East Ham, London, . . .34(?); Kiev ancestry. Mr Feldman was for 15 years a T.V. scriptwriter, including the 'Bootsie & Snudge' series, becoming a performer in 1967 in 'At Last the 1948 Show', followed by his own show, 'Marty' (68/69). Md. Lauretta Sullivan. Has been seen in the following movies: EVERY HOME SHOULD HAVE ONE (69); THE BED-SITTING ROOM (69); YOUNG FRANKENSTEIN (74, as Igor); THE ADVENTURES OF SHERLOCK HOLMES' SMARTER BROTHER (75); SILENT MOVIE (76); THE LAST RE-MAKE OF BEAU GESTE (76, directed, acted, co-wrote); SEX WITH A SMILE (77, Italy—2nd story); IN GOD WE TRUST (80, directed, acted, co-wrote). U.S. T.V. includes 'Dean Martin Presents' (70) and 'The Marty Feldman Comedy Machine' (72).
Mr Feldman died of a heart attack in Mexico City on December 12, 1982 after completing the movie, YELLOWBEARD.

MEL FERRER

B. Elberon, N.J., 25.8.17; real name Melchior Gaston Ferrer. Ed. Princeton Univ. During summer appd. in stock at Cape Cod Playhouse, Dennis, Mass.; contd. to do summer seasons there while, upon leaving Univ., worked in Mexico as writer, penning children's book 'Tito's Hats', and was publisher in Vermont. Appd. on Broadway in 'Importance of Being Earnest' (1937) and others including 'Kind Lady' (1940); then served as disc-jockey on local radio stations, later becoming NBC producer/director. In 1945 entered films as dialogue director and also was a success on Broadway in 'Strange Fruit'. Md. 1. Barbara C. Tripps 1940, 2 daughters: Mela (b. 1940), Pepa (b. 1941), 1 son: Chris (b. 1941); 2. Frances Pilchard 1942, 1 son Mark (b. 1944), div. 1953. Films include LOST BOUNDARIES (49); THE SECRET FURY (50, directed only); VENDETTA (50, directed only); THE BRAVE BULLS (51); SCARAMOUCHE (52); KNIGHTS OF THE ROUND TABLE (54, as King Arthur); WAR AND PEACE (56); THE SUN ALSO RISES (57); GREEN MANSIONS (59, directed only); FALL OF THE ROMAN EMPIRE (64); SEX AND THE SINGLE GIRL (64). Md. 3. Audrey Hepburn (q.v.) 1954, 1 son Sean (b. 1960); 4. Elizabeth Soukotine, 18.2.71. Mr Ferrer is founder of the La Jolla Playhouse Theatre, California and has produced several movies. His recent film appearances include: THE NORSEMAN (78); AMAZING CAPT. NEMO (78); TOP OF THE HILL (78, T.V. movie); BIG ALLIGATOR RIVER (79); NIGHTMARE CITY (80); LILI MARLEEN, SCREAMERS (both 1981); MILLE MILLIARDS DE DOLLARS (82); T.V. ser.: 'Falcon Crest' (82).

JOSE FERRER

B. Santurce, Puerto Rico, 8.1.09/or 12(?) Parents: Maria and Rafael Ferrer; Ed: New York and Princeton Univ., originally studied architecture, but turned to the stage, debuting on a showboat on Long Island 1934. After stock at Suffern, N.Y. 1935, tour (and ASM) in 'A Slight Case of Murder', he first played on Broadway in latter prod. in 1935 which marked the beginning of a highly successful stage career as actor and producer, including S'pearean prods. Md. 1. Uta Hagen 1938, 1 daughter Leticia (b. 1940), div. 1948; 2. Phyllis Hill 1948, div. 1953. Came to screen in 1948 in JOAN OF ARC (BSA, Oscar nom.). others incl.: WHIRLPOOL (49); CYRANO DE BERGERAC (50, Oscar, also played role on stage 1947); MOULIN ROUGE (52, Oscar nom., as Toulouse Lautrec); MISS SADIE THOMPSON (53); CAINE MUTINY (54); COCKLESHELL HEROES (55, also directed); THE GREAT MAN (56, wrote, directed); I ACCUSE (58, directed). Mr Ferrer has also appeared in musicals and worked on the stage in G.B. Md. 3. Rosemary Clooney 1953, 2 sons: Miguel (b. 1954), Raphael (b. 1955), 3 daughters: Maria (b. 1956), Gabriel (b. 1957), Monsita (b. 1958), div. 1968. Recent movies: FEDORA, VOYAGE TO ATLANTIS (77); PRIVATE FILES OF J. EDGAR HOOVER (78); THE SWARM (78); AMAZING CAPT. NEMO (78); FIFTH MUSKETEER (78); THE FRENCH ATLANTIC AFFAIR (79); BLOODY BIRTHDAY (guest), BATTLECREEK BRAWL, THE RED TIDE (all 1980) GIDEON'S TRUMPET, PETER & PAUL (mini-ser., both T.V., 1980); EASTER SUNDAY, BERLIN TUNNEL 21 (T.V. movie, both 1981); AND THEY'RE OFF, A MIDSUMMER NIGHT'S SEX COMEDY (both 1982); TO BE OR NOT TO BE (83).

JON FINCH

B. Caterham, Surrey, 2.3.42. Father a merchant banker. At school was involved in school plays; entered profession on the stage management side, working in rep., incl. the Ashcroft Theatre, Croydon; first T.V. role in 'Z Cars' (1967). Between acting jobs worked as car mechanic, night-club bouncer. Other T.V. incl. 'Mary, Queen of Scots', 'Steve', 'Counterstrike', lead in 'Ben Hall' series (Australia 1976), guest 'The New Avengers'. Movies: THE VAMPIRE LOVERS (70); THE HORROR OF FRANKENSTEIN (70); FRENZY, MACBETH (71); SUNDAY, BLOODY SUNDAY (72); LADY CAROLINE LAMB (72); UN FLIC (72, A Cop); THE FINAL PROGRAMME (73); DIAGNOSIS MURDER (74); BATTLEFLAG (76); THE MAN WITH THE GREEN CROSS (77); UNE FEMME INFIDELE (77); DEATH ON THE NILE (77). Recent T.V.: title role 'Henry IV' (Part 1), 'The Martian Chronicles'; latest movies: LA SABINA (79); BREAKING GLASS (79); PETER & PAUL (mini-ser., 1980); THE THREAT (81); GIRO CITY (82).

SALLY FIELD

Winning an Oscar recently for her performance in NORMA RAE, Sally Field, although one of Hollywood's brightest and younger stars, is by no means a newcomer to her profession. Her mother is Margaret 'Maggie' Field, an actress, and her step-father is Jock Mahoney, the ace stuntman-turned-actor. Sally was born on 6 November 1946 in Pasadena, California and attended Birmingham High in the San Fernando Valley and after graduating she enrolled at Valley State College, and, having 'always wanted to act' she also took a course at Columbia Studios workshop during the summer. It was while there she was spotted by a casting director, screen tested, and given the lead in the comedy series 'Gidget', which made her name in 1965-66, embarking on a highly successful T.V. career. Her T.V. movies in 1972 were HOME FOR THE HOLIDAYS, MAYBE I'LL COME HOME IN THE SPRING and MARRIAGE YEAR ONE and her popular T.V. series, apart from 'Gidget', were 'Flying Nun' (1967-70) and 'The Girl With Something Extra' (1973-74). Sally also appeared occasionally as Clementine Hale in 'Alias Smith & Jones' (1971-72). She is divorced from her high school sweetheart, Steve Craig, whom she wed in 1968, having two children, Peter (in 1969), and Eli (in 1972). Her motion-picture appearances have been in THE WAY WEST (66); STAY HUNGRY (76); SMOKEY & THE BANDIT (77); HEROES (77); THE END (77); HOOPER (78); BEYOND THE POSEIDON ADVENTURE (79); NORMA RAE (79, Oscar, BA); SYBIL (79); SMOKEY & THE BANDIT II (80); BACK ROADS (81) and KISS ME GOODBYE (82).

FRANK FINLAY

B. Farnworth, Lancs., 6.8.26. Left school at 14, for 10 years worked in shops (including butcher's assistant) and factories, while attending night schools, studying English & Art; won Sir James Knott's ship to study at R.A.D.A.; stage debut: Guildford 1957, becoming very distinguished actor in stage prods., playing with Royal Court Co. on Broadway, Chichester Festival, National Theatre Co. on Broadway, Chichester Festival, National Theatre Co. and the West End. Md. Doreen Shepherd (former actress and journalist), 1 daughter: Cathy, 2 sons: Stephen, Daniel. Well-known on T.V., including appearances in 'Casanova', 'Hitler', 'Don Quixote', 'Voltaire', 'Count Dracula', 'Dear Brutus'. Many movies incl. LIFE FOR RUTH (62); OTHELLO (65, as Iago, filmed stage perf.); ROBBERY (67); CROMWELL (69); ASSAULT (71); SITTING TARGET (72); THE THREE MUSKETEERS (74, as Porthos); WILD GEESE (77); SHERLOCK HOLMES—MURDER BY DECREE (78); THE ENIGMA (81); stage 1981: 'Amadeus' (N.T.).

PETER FIRTH

B. Bradford, Yorkshire, 27.10.53. The son of a publican, Mr Firth was educated at Hanson Boys School and while in his teens, through a girlfriend, was introduced to a drama school, got a scholarship and studied there. Appeared with local company at Bradford Civic Playhouse (incl. show 'Camelot') and while appearing in local T.V. show for children was given role in T.V. series 'The Flaxton Boys' (1969). Appd. in several T.V. plays and series such as 'Here Comes the Double Deckers', 'Home and Away' and 'Country Matters', coming to the screen in 1973 in BROTHER SUN, SISTER MOON as St. Francis's youngest disciple. His other movies are DANIEL AND MARIA (73); DIAMONDS ON WHEELS (73); ACES HIGH (76, BAFTA Award—Most Promising Newcomer); EQUUS (76, also on U.S. stage and won Hollywood Golden Globe Award—Best Supporting Actor); JOSEPH ANDREWS (76); TESS (78); WHEN YOU COMIN' BACK, RED RYDER (80). Mr Firth is married, with a son, and recently won acclaim for his work on BBC T.V. in the play 'The Flipside of Dominick Hide' (1980); guest: TRISTAN AND ISOLDE (81, Germany); 'Aerodrome' (T.V. 1983).

ALBERT FINNEY

By successfully alternating his stage and screen roles, Albert Finney has remained one of Britain's major acting talents and in the motion-picture medium proves (with one film) to be a talented director, and, in the 70s, also emerges as a fine character actor. The son of Albert Finney, Snr., a bookmaker, and his wife Alice, he was born in Salford, Lancashire on 9 May 1936. At Salford Grammar School he gave good performances in plays and the young Finney was advised to try the stage as a career. He did, and learned his craft at R.A.D.A. for three years. In April 1956 he joined the Birmingham Repertory Company, staying with them for nearly 2 years and making his London début with the same company in 'Caesar and Cleopatra'. On the London stage he played with distinction in 'The Lilywhite Boys', 'Luther' and 'Billy Liar'. Having come to the screen in a small role in THE ENTERTAINER in 1959, he made a great impact as Arthur Seaton in SATURDAY NIGHT AND SUNDAY MORNING (1960), the first and best of the 'socially realistic' British movies of the 60s. The actor had wed Jane Wenham in 1957, the couple had a son, Simon, in 1958, but divorced in 1961. Continuing to appear regularly on the stage, including a tour of Mexico and S. America in 1961/62, Finney has made the occasional film appearance in the following: TOM JONES (63), playing the title role, based on the Henry Fielding novel, gaining an Oscar nomination; THE VICTORS (63); NIGHT MUST FALL (64, also co-produced); TWO FOR THE ROAD (67); CHARLIE BUBBLES (68, also directing, for his Company, Memorial Enterprises Ltd. (partner: Michael Medwin)); THE PICASSO SUMMER (69); SCROOGE (70, playing title role); GUMSHOE (72, also co-produced); ALPHA BETA (73, also stage) and MURDER ON THE ORIENT EXPRESS (74, as Hercule Poirot, Oscar nom.). In 1975 he played Hamlet with the Old Vic Company, he has also appeared on T.V. on several occasions. On 23 November 1978 he divorced his second wife, actress Anouk Aimee, whom he wed in 1970. In 1976 he appeared in the film THE DUELLISTS and more recently he has been very busy with films, appearing in WOLFEN, LOOPHOLE, LOOKER (all 1980); SHOOT THE MOON (81) and THE DRESSER (83). In 1982 he became a director of British Artists.

CARRIE FISHER

B. Los Angeles, Calif., 21.10.56; parents: Debbie Reynolds and Eddie Fisher. First appd. on stage with her mother, aged 13; left Beverly Hills H.S. at 15, joined chorus of N.Y. show 'Irene' and came to London to study at Central School of Speech & Drama. Carrie has appeared in the 1975 movie SHAMPOO, voted 'Newcomer of the Year' by Photoplay Mag. and she is best-known for her role of Princess Leia Organa in STAR WARS (76) and THE EMPIRE STRIKES BACK (79). She appd. at the London Palladium in 1974 with her mother, also on Broadway in 'The Ill-Fated Censored Scenes From Hong Kong'. T.V. includes: 'Come Back, Little Sheba' (ITV 1977) and her other movies are MONDO VIDEO (78); THE BLUES BROTHERS (79) UNDER THE RAINBOW (81); RETURN OF THE JEDI (83). Wed Paul Simon, 16.8.83.

ROBERT FLEMYNG

B. Liverpool, 3.1.12. Ed. Haileybury; awarded M.C. and Military O.B.E. during WWII; formerly a medical student, stage debut 1931 commencing long and distinguished theatrical career; md. Carmen Sugars, 1 daughter; film debut 1937 in HEAD OVER HEELS; many others include THE GUINEA PIG (49); THE MAN WHO NEVER WAS (55); WINDOM'S WAY (57); DEADLY AFFAIR (66); BATTLE OF BRITAIN (69); YOUNG WINSTON (71); TRAVELS WITH MY AUNT (73); GOLDEN RENDEZ-VOUS (77); MEDUSA TOUCH (78); 39 STEPS (78); much T.V. includes 'A Cotswold Death' (1982, BBC).

PETER FONDA

B. New York City, 23.2.39. Father Henry Fonda (qv); Ed. Univ. of Omaha; wrote and directed first play, aged 13, 'Stalag 17½'; studied acting at Univ. Mr Fonda starred in his first role on Broadway in 'Blood, Sweat & Stanley Poole', winning him numerous awards, including New York Critics' Most Promising Actor; has acted with Omaha P'House and in T.V.; came to the screen 1963 in TAMMY AND THE DOCTOR; md. Susan Brewer (daughter of an industrialist) 1961, div. 1974: 1 daughter Bridget, 1 son Justin; movies: THE VICTORS (63), LILITH (64), THE YOUNG LOVERS (64), THE WILD ANGELS (66), THE TRIP (67), SPIRITS OF THE DEAD (69), EASY RIDER (69, starred, produced, part-wrote), THE LAST MOVIE (71), THE HIRED HAND (71, and directed), TWO PEOPLE (73), DIRTY MARY, CRAZY LARRY (74), OPEN SEASON (74), RACE WITH THE DEVIL (75), 92 IN THE SHADE (75), KILLER FORCE (75), FUTUREWORLD (76), OUTLAW BLUES (76), WANDA NEVADA (78, also dir.), HIGH BALLIN'! (79), CANNON-BALL RUN (81), SPLIT IMAGE, DANCE OF THE DWARFS (both 1982), SPASMS (83).

LOUISE FLETCHER

B. Birmingham, Alabama, .7.34. Went to Los Angeles in early 20s and studied drama with Jeff Corey and did T.V. roles. Married producer and former agent Jerry Bick, 2 sons John and Andrew, (born in early 60s) and retired from acting for 10 years, but returned to play in movies THIEVES LIKE US (74); RUSSIAN ROULETTE (75); ONE FLEW OVER THE CUCKOO'S NEST (75, Oscar, Best Actress); EXORCIST II — THE HERETIC (77); CHEAP DETECTIVE (77); THE MAGICIAN (78); THE LADY IN RED (79); THE LUCKY STAR (79); MAMA DRACULA (80); STRANGE BEHAVIOR (81); BRAINSTORM, ONCE UPON A TIME IN AMERICA (both 1982).

HENRY FONDA

At the 1980 Oscar ceremony Henry Fonda received a special honorary award for his work as a screen actor, a career which has now covered 45 years and which he can look back on with much pride and satisfaction. The son of Wm. Brace Fonda and his wife Herberta, he was born Henry Jaynes Fonda on 16 May 1905 at Grand Island, Nebraska. Educated at Dundee Grade School, Central High School and the University of Minnesota (where he worked his way through by doing many jobs, including ice cream delivery man, petrol pump attendant and insurance salesman), intending to become a journalist, but he became interested in drama and joined the Omaha Community Playhouse for his first performance in 1925. After a season of stock at W. Falmouth, Cape Cod in 1928, he first appeared in New York, walking-on in 'The Game of Life and Death' (1929), followed by four more rep. seasons. After several Broadway roles he won acclaim in 1934 playing Dan Harrow in 'The Farmer Takes a Wife' and was signed for his screen début a year later in the same production, having been discovered by Walter Wanger. Fonda had been married from 1931-33 to Margaret Sullavan and wed Frances Brokaw in 1936, having a son, Peter (qv), and a daughter, Jane (qv). His 1930s films included THE TRAIL OF THE LONESOME PINE (36); THE MOON'S OUR HOME (36); YOU ONLY LIVE ONCE (37); JEZEBEL (38); SPAWN OF THE NORTH (38); JESSE JAMES (39); YOUNG MR LINCOLN (39, title role). For THE GRAPES OF WRATH (40) he received an Oscar nomination and during WWII he served with distinction in the U.S. Navy, earning a Bronze Star and Presidential Citation. Following such pictures as MY DARLING CLEMENTINE (46, as Wyatt Earp) and FORT APACHE (48) he returned to Broadway, achieving much success in 'Mister Roberts' for two years 1948-50, winning a Tony Award. In 1950 his 2nd wife died and he wed Susan Blanchard, adopting a daughter, Amy. His 50s films included the excellent MISTER ROBERTS (55); THE WRONG MAN (57); WAR AND PEACE (56); 12 ANGRY MEN (57); STAGE STRUCK (57) and THE TIN STAR (57). He had also ventured into T.V., working in such programmes as 'Producer's Showcase', 'Medalion Theatre', 'Showtime, USA' and his own western series 'The Deputy' (1959-61), as Simon Fry. He wed Alfreda Franchetti from 1957-62 and his fifth marriage took place on 3 December 1965, to Shirlee Mae Adams. In the last two decades he has appeared on the stage quite frequently, but made a number of movies including THE BEST MAN (64); FAIL SAFE (64); THE BATTLE OF THE BULGE (65); FIRECREEK (67); THE BOSTON STRANGLER (68); THE RED PONY (72, T.V. movie); ASH WEDNESDAY (73); MIDWAY (76); HOME TO STAY (77, T.V. movie); SWARM (77); METEOR (77); FEDORA (77); THE GREAT SMOKEY ROADBLOCK (78); CITY OF FIRE (78) and ON GOLDEN POND (80). Mr Fonda also played in a further T.V. series, 'The Smith Family' as Det. Sgt. Chad Smith, in 1971/72, and he filmed a T.V. movie, SUMMER SOLSTICE, in 1982. His work in ON GOLDEN POND won him Golden Globe and Academy Awards as Best Actor in 1981. Also a recipient of the American Film Institute's Life Achievement Award, Mr Fonda had a heart pace-maker implanted in 1974, and underwent heart surgery in May 1981. *Mr Fonda passed away in Los Angeles on Thursday, August 12, 1982.*
THE FABULOUS FONDAS by James Brough; W.H. Allen: London, 1973; pb: Star, 1975.
FONDA, MY LIFE (as told to Howard Teichmann); W. H. Allen: London, 1982.
HENRY FONDA: HIS LIFE & WORK by Norm Goldstein; Michael Joseph: London, 1982; Large p/b.

JANE FONDA

Being the daughter of a major acting talent undoubtedly helped the career of Jane Fonda in her early years, but there can be no doubt she is a fine actress, several of her recent movies gaining her deserved awards and international acclaim. The daughter of Henry Fonda from his 2nd marriage to Frances Brokaw, she was born Jayne Seymour Fonda on 21 December 1937 in New York City; she attended the Emma Willard School, Troy, New York and Vassar, where she was active in dramatics. Upon leaving college she went to Paris, studying painting and languages, returned to the States and did 3 summer stock plays, including 'The Country Girl' with her father at Omaha, Nebraska. Jane joined the Arts Student League in New York, appeared in 'The Male Animal' at Dennis, Mass. and then became one of the most popular models in New York, appearing on the cover of 4 leading magazines. Encouraged in her acting by Lee Strasberg, she was auditioned by Joshua Logan, appeared in a play for him 'There Was a Little Girl', and although it flopped she won Drama Critics' Award 1960, coming to the screen in Logan's TALL STORY (60). She returned to New York, playing in 'Invitation to a March' (1960), made the movies WALK ON THE WILD SIDE (61), THE CHAPMAN REPORT (62), PERIOD OF ADJUSTMENT (62), returned to Broadway again for 'The Fun Couple' (1962) and 'Strange Interlude' (63). Since then her films have included SUNDAY IN NEW YORK (63); THE LOVE CAGE (64); LA RONDE (64); CAT BALLOU (65); THE CHASE (66); ANY WEDNESDAY (66); HURRY SUNDOWN (67); BAREFOOT IN THE PARK (67); HISTOIRES EXTRAORDINAIRES (67); BARBARELLA (68) and THEY SHOOT HORSES, DON'T THEY (69, Oscar nom.). She wed French director Roger Vadim in 1965 and their daughter, Vanessa (named after Jane's friend, Vanessa Redgrave (qv)), was born in 1968. In the 1970s Jane filmed KLUTE (71, winning an Academy Award), STEELYARD BLUES (72); A DOLL'S HOUSE (74); FUN WITH DICK AND JANE (76); JULIA (77, Oscar nom.); COMING HOME (77, won Oscar); COMES A HORSEMAN (77); CALIFORNIA SUITE (78); CHINA SYNDROME (78, B.A.F.T.A. Award); ELECTRIC HORSEMAN (79) and NINE TO FIVE (80). Divorced from Vadim, Jane wed Tom Hayden in 1973, a political affairs writer and former activist. Their son, Troy (named after a Vietnamese resistance leader) was born that year. She had been a vigorous campaigner for various pressure groups, including American troop withdrawal in the Vietnamese war and her film company, I.P.C. (Indo-China Peace Campaign) produced COMING HOME. Her most recent films: ON GOLDEN POND (Oscar nom., BSA) and ROLL OVER (both 1981).

JANE FONDA by Thomas Kiernan; Talmy Franklin: London, 1973 & Putnam: New York, 1973; rev. 1982.
JANE FONDA: ALL AMERICAN ANTI-HEROINE by Gary Herman and David Downing; Omnibus Press: London, 1980.
THE FILMS OF JANE FONDA by George Haddad-Garcia; Citadel: Secaucus, N.J., 1981.
JANE FONDA by Fred Lawrence Guiles; Michael Joseph Ltd.: London, 1981.
JANE FONDA'S WORKOUT BOOK; Allen Lane: London, 1982.

BRYAN FORBES

, Stratford-atte-Bow, London, 22.7.26. Real ame John Theobald Clarke. Ed. Godwin Rd. lementary School; studied for the stage RADA; p: Rugby, Worthing, tours; Nat. Service; West nd—'Gathering Storm'; came to screen 1948 in HE SMALL BACK ROOM; more rep. including 'The Guinea Pig'; films: ALL OVER THE OWN (48), DEAR MR PROHACK (49); play eptember Tide' (9 months); films: THE OODEN HORSE (50), GREEN GROW HE RUSHES (51), APPOINTMENT IN ONDON (52); 1st literary success 'Truth Lies leeping' (short stories, 1951); md. 1. actress onstance Smith, Feb. 1951 (div.); films: SEA EVILS (53), WHEEL OF FATE (53), THE ILLION POUND NOTE (54), THE IN-PECTOR CALLS (54), others; also as 'John eton' wrote few articles for 'Picturegoer' paper, rly 50s; md. 2. actress Nanette Newman (qv) 127.8.56: daughters, Sarah (b. 21.5.59), Emma . 14.5.65); continued acting in movies in 50s, t also emerged as script-writer completing

BLACK KNIGHT (54), writing COCKLE-SHELL HEROES (56), BABY & THE BAT-TLESHIP (56), I WAS MONTY'S DOUBLE (58), others; with Richard Attenborough (qv) formed Beaver Films, 1958, making such quality films as THE ANGRY SILENCE (59), LEAGUE OF GENTLEMEN (60) (Forbes wrote both, acted latter), directed WHISTLE DOWN THE WIND (61), wrote/directed THE L-SHAPED ROOM (62); emerged as talented writer/director of productions in 60s and 70s, including: SEANCE ON A WET AFTERNOON (64, wd), KING RAT (65, wd), THE WHISPERERS (67, wd), RAGING MOON (70, wd), SLIPPER & THE ROSE (76, wd), INTERNATIONAL VELVET (78, wd); Prod. Chief—E.M.I., Elstree Studios, 1969-71; London 1980, directed 'Macbeth' (stage) and dir./wr. T.V. play 'Jessie' (80); President: Nat. Youth Theatre; stage 1982: acted/dir. 'Star Quality' (one-day gala perf.); also novelist/theatrical biographer.
Autobiography: *NOTES FOR A LIFE*; Collins: London, 1974; pb.

GLENN FORD

1980 Glenn Ford celebrated his 41st year as a motion-picture actor, remaining a popular screen performer who is still ery much in demand internationally. The amiable actor was born Gwyllyn Samuel Newton Ford on 1 May 1916 in uebec, Canada. His father was Newton Ford, a French-Canadian railroad executive and mill owner, and his mother, annah, was from Lancashire, England. Glenn's uncle was Sir John MacDonald, Prime Minister of Canada and a escendent of Martin Van Buren, eighth U.S. President. Young Ford, an only child, moved with his parents to Santa onica, California, when he was 7 and received his education at Santa Monica High School, where he was school ommissioner of entertainment, class officer and a varsity athlete in football, athletics and lacrosse. He graduated in 934 and chose a stage career, having, since the age of 4 (when he converted the family barn into a theatre), been terested in acting. He worked in stage management/understudying, his first job being with Herman Schumlin; he ayed the grocery boy in 'Children's Hour' (1935), was several years with The Players, a Santa Monica group, ppeared in 'Golden Boy' and 'Judgement Day' and was on Broadway in 1938 in 'Soliloquy'. Eventually he won a ontract with Columbia Pictures, signing on 1.10.39, changing his name to Glenn Ford after his father's manufacturing wn, Glenford, in Canada. Although his first picture, HEAVEN WITH A BARBED WIRE FENCE, was made at ox, most of his best pictures were with Columbia, including MY SON IS GUILTY (40); BABIES FOR SALE (40); EXAS (41); FLIGHT LIEUTENANT (42); GILDA (46); FRAMED (47); THE LOVES OF CARMEN (48); nd LUST FOR GOLD (49). Ford had wed Eleanor Powell on 23.10.43 and they had one child, Peter, born 5.2.45. uring the Second World War, he served in Europe and Asia, was decorated 12 times and shot down twice in helicopter orties in Vietnam, where he served as a reserve officer. Other pictures included FOLLOW THE SUN (51, as golfer en Hogan); THE BIG HEAT (53); THE BLACKBOARD JUNGLE (55); THE FASTEST GUN ALIVE (56); 10 TO YUMA (57) and THE SHEEPMAN (58). Divorced from Miss Powell in 1960, he wed Kathryn Hays in 966, but this marriage ended two years later. In the 1960s and 70s he continued in movies, but also moved into V with 2 series, as Sam Cade in 'Cade's County' (1971/72) and Rev. Tom Holvak in 'The Family Holvak' (1975/76). e wed Cynthia Howard on 10.9.77 and his most recent work includes 'Best Sellers: Once an Eagle' (76, T.V. movie), nathan Kent in SUPERMAN (76); 'An Evening in Byzantium' (78, T.V. movie); VIRUS (80), 'Best Sellers: eggarman, Thief' (79, T.V. movie) and 'The Sacketts' (80, T.V. movie); DAY OF THE ASSASSINS (80) and APPY BIRTHDAY TO ME (81) and THE DAY BREAKERS (82).

HARRISON FORD

B. Chicago, Illinois, 13.7.42. Mr Ford acted while attending Ripon Coll., Wisconsin and appd. in summer stock at Williams Bay, Wisconsin. In 1963 he went to Hollywood with his wife in a 'battered Volkswagen' and worked in a paint store, awaiting acting jobs. He appeared in a local production of 'John Brown's Body' and was later given a Columbia contract, 'delivering a telegram to James Coburn (qv) in DEAD HEAT ON A MERRY-GO-ROUND (66)', his first film, and small roles followed in LUV (67), JOURNEY TO SHILOH (68), GETTING STRAIGHT (70) and ZABRISKIE POINT (70) and he worked steadily in such T.V. shows as 'Gunsmoke', 'The Virginian' and 'Ironside'. In 1970 Harrison left the profession for three years to start his own business as a carpenter/building contractor and employed others. He returned to movies in AMERICAN GRAFFITI (73) and has since been seen in THE CONVERSATION (74), APOCALYPSE NOW (77), HEROES (77), as Solo in STAR WARS (77), THE EMPIRE STRIKES BACK (79) and RETURN OF THE JEDI (83); FRISCO KID, FORCE TEN FROM NAVARONE, HANOVER STREET (all 1978); RAIDERS OF THE LOST ARK (81); BLADE RUNNER (82); INDIANA JONES & THE TEMPLE OF DOOM (84); Md: 2. Melissa Mathison, March 1983.

STEVE FORREST

B. Huntsville, Texas, 29.9.   ; father a Baptist clergyman; brother is Dana Andrews (qv), celebrated actor; real name William Forrest Andrews; sch. plays; H.S., then joined U.S. Army, Europe; at U.C.L.A. majored in Psychology; stage/radio/TV brought movie contract; md: Christine, 3 sons; many movies inclu. SO BIG (54); LIVING IDOL (57); FLAMING STAR (60; YELLOW CANARY (63); RASCAL (69); WILD COUNTRY, THE LATE LIZ (both 1971); NORTH DALLAS FORTY (79); MOMMIE DEAREST (81); SAHARA (83); Steve's written for TV, also acted in 'The Baron' (GB, 1965/66 series), 'S.W.A.T.' (US, 1975/76, series), 'Manions of America' (mini-ser., 1981), others.

JOHN FORSYTHE

B. Penn's Grove, N. Jersey, 29.1.18. Real name John Lincoln Freund; originally a radio actor and baseball commentator,stage début 1939 in children's theatre, Broadway: 1942 in 'Vickie', 'Yankie Point' (42), 'Winged Victory' (43) for US Army Air Force; md. 1. Parker McCormick (div.), 2. Julie Warren (c. 1943), 2 daughters: Dall (b. 1954), Brooke (b. 1955) and 1 son: Page (b. 1956); came to screen in 1943 in DESTINATION TOKYO; Mr Forsythe has directed on stage and played in 'Mr Roberts' and is well-known on U.S. T.V., including Starlight Theatre', 'Studio One', 'Elgin T.V. Hour' (55), 'Lux Playhouse' (1959) and his movies included CAPTIVE CITY (52), ESCAPE FROM FORT BRAVO(53), THE TROUBLE WITH HARRY (56) and THE AMBASSADOR'S DAUGHTER (56). He returned to Broadway for 'Teahouse of the August Moon' (53/54) and 'Weekend' (68) and had his own T.V. series as Bentley Gregg in 'Bachelor Father' (57-62), 'The John Forsythe Show' (65/66) and as Michael Endicott in 'To Rome With Love' (69-71). SEE HOW THEY RUN was the first movie made for T.V., in 1964, and his other movies have included KITTEN WITH A WHIP (65), MADAME X (66), IN COLD BLOOD (67), TOPAZ (69), THE HAPPY ENDING (69), CRY PANIC (74, T.V. movie), THE HEALERS (75, T.V. movie), TAIL GUN JOE (76, T.V. movie), EMILY, EMILY (77, T.V. movie), THE USERS (78, T.V. movie), AND JUSTICE FOR ALL (79) 'Charlie's Angels' (ser. 1976-81, voice only); Blake Carrington in 'Dynasty' (ser. 1981-   ), Golden Globe Aw., BA.

FREDERIC FORREST

B. Waxahachie, Texas,   .   ; began career i stock, with La Mama Troupe, under the directic of Tom O'Horgan; went to L.A. in 1970 and cam to the screen in 1972 in WHEN THE LEGEND DIE and has been seen in THE DON IS DEAI (73), THE GRAVY TRAIN (74), THE CON VERSATION (74), PERMISSION TO KIL (76), THE MISSOURI BREAKS (76), APC CALYPSE NOW (77), FOUR DAYS II DALLAS (78, T.V. movie, as Lee Harve Oswald), THE ROSE (79), HAMMETT, ON FROM THE HEART (both 81), VALLE GIRL, SAIGON (both 83); Md: Marilou Henne

ROBERT FORSTER

B. Rochester, N.Y., 13.7.41 (42?); Ed: Heidelberg Coll., Alfred Univ., Rochester Univ.; stage N.Y., tours etc.; movies include. REFLECTIONS IN A GOLDEN EYE (67); THE STALKING MOON (68); MEDIUM COOL, JUSTINE (both 1969); PIECES OF DREAMS (70); BANYON (71, T.V. movie); JOURNEY THROUGH ROSEBUD, COVER ME BABE (both 1972); THE DON IS DEAD (73); DEATH SQUAD, NAKIA (both 1974 T.V. movies); THE CITY (77, T.V. movie); AVALANCHE (78); STANDING TALL (78, T.V. movie); BLACK HOLE (79); THE DARKER SIDE OF TERROR (79, T.V movie); ALLIGATOR (80); GOLIATH AWAITS (82, T.V. movie). VIGILANTE (82).

BARRY FOSTER

B. Beeston, Notts., 21.8.   ; Ed. Southall Count Grammar School; studied stagecraft at Centra School of Speech & Drama; formerly a plastic chemist; stage début: Co. Cork, Ireland 1952 i 'Merchant of Venice', becoming distinguishe actor of stage (West End, Broadway, Roy. Court, Nottingham P'House, etc.) and T.\ ('Hamlet', 'Mogul', 'Three Hostages', 'Van de Valk' (series), 'Fall of Eagles' (series), man others); md. singer Judith Shergold, 2 daughter. Joanna, Miranda; movies include: SEA OF SANI (56), YESTERDAY'S ENEMY (59), KING (COUNTRY (64), THE FAMILY WAY (66 ROBBERY (67), INSPECTOR CLOUSEA (67), BATTLE OF BRITAIN (69), RYAN' DAUGHTER (70), FRENZY (71), SWEENEY (76), others; recent stage: 'Born in the Garden (Bristol/London, 79/80); T.V.: 'Rear Colum' (80); 'How Many Miles to Babylon?' (82); 'Dea of an Expert Witness' (83); movies: WIL GEESE (77); HEAT & DUST (83).

JODIE FOSTER

B. Los Angeles, California 19.11.62. Mother, Evelyn Foster, a divorcee from Illinois and former Hollywood publicist; Jodie has 2 sisters, Lucinda and Constance, brother Buddy; aged 2½ she attended commercial audition with brother and got job; managed by her mother, Jodie worked steadily in T.V. commercials, made acting debut in T.V. series 'Mayberry, RFD' and was regular in others such as 'Bob & Ted & Carol & Alice' as Elizabeth Henderson (73) and Addie Pray in 'Paper Moon' (74); movies: NAPOLEON & SAMANTHA (72), MENACE OF THE MOUNTAIN (72), KANSAS CITY BOMBER (72), TOM SAWYER (73), ONE LITTLE INDIAN (73), ALICE DOESN'T LIVE HERE ANYMORE (75), TAXI DRIVER (76, Oscar nom. BSA), BUGSY MALONE (76, BAFTA award), LITTLE GIRL WHO LIVES DOWN THE LANE (76), ECHOES OF SUMMER (76), CANDLESHOE (77), FREAKY FRIDAY (77), MOI-FLEUR BLEUE (77), CARNY (79), LADIES OF THE VALLEY (79), FOXES (80). Jodie Foster was educated at the French Lycee, L.A. and Yale; SVENGALI, O'HARA'S WIFE (both 1982).

EDWARD FOX

Following his role of Edward the Eighth, performed with great dignity in the T.V. series, Edward Fox is now one of Britain's busiest and most popular actors. The son of the late Robin Fox, a well-known theatrical agent, he was born in London on 13 April 1937. His mother was a former actress and his first taste of filmdom was when, very young, he was up for a role in THE MINIVER STORY, but his timidity let him down (brother James was a child actor who has had later success in movies also). Edward Fox was educated at Harrow, then worked as a porter for Marks & Spencers, but was dismissed 'because he dressed too loud'. He then did National Service, gaining a commission in the North Lancashire Regiment. Deciding upon a theatrical career, he studied at RADA and worked for several years in rep. He entered movies in small roles in such prods. as THE MIND BENDERS (62), THE LONG DUEL (65), THE NAKED RUNNER (66), THE JOKERS (67), gaining larger parts in BATTLE OF BRITAIN (68), OH! WHAT A LOVELY WAR! (68) and THE BREAKING OF BUMBO (69). He had wed actress/model Tracy Reed when he was 21, but they are now divorced and have a daughter, Lucy, now in her 20s. Appearing regularly in television, Fox's film career was boosted when he won a BAFTA award for his work in THE GO-BETWEEN (71) and he has since been seen in DAY OF THE JACKAL (72); A DOLL'S HOUSE (73); GALILEO (74); THE DUELLISTS (76); THE SQUEEZE (76); A BRIDGE TOO FAR (76, as Lieutenant-General Brian Horrocks); THE BIG SLEEP (77); THE CAT & THE CANARY (77); FORCE TEN FROM NAVARONE (77); SOLDIER OF ORANGE (77) and THE MIRROR CRACK'D (80). He won a BAFTA award and T.V. Times readers award as Best Actor for his role as Edward, Duke of Windsor in the Thames T.V. series of 1978. In 1979 he appeared opposite Joanna David in the play 'Family Reunion' at the Vaudeville Theatre, London, more recently in 'Quartermaine's Terms' (81) and, in the title role of 'Hamlet' (Young Vic, 1982). His most recent movies are GANDHI (82), THE DRESSER (83) and THE SAGA OF H.M.S. BOUNTY (84).

ANTHONY FRANCIOSA

Winning acclaim on Broadway and an Oscar nomination for his work in A HATFUL OF RAIN, Anthony Franciosa was born in New York City on October 25, 1928, the son of Anthony and Jean Papaleo (Franciosa is his mother's maiden name), Italian immigrants. His father was a contractor and young Tony was brought up in the Italian district of N.Y., educated at the Benjamin Franklin High School. At the age of 17 he went with a pal who was auditioning with the N.Y. Y.M.C.A. dramatic group and Tony won a role instead! He was awarded a 4 year scholarship with the Dramatic Workshop and managed to appear on Broadway in such productions as 'Hamlet' (1948), 'City of Kings' (1949) and 'Yes Is For a Very Young Man' (1949) (although some reference books quote his Broadway début not until 1955). At this time he worked at an open-air theatre at Lake Tahoe, but the venture closed owing to lack of funds and he returned to New York, appearing in children's theatre. Between acting jobs Tony worked as a messenger boy, dishwasher, awning installer, in a printing works, as a welder and for a while went to sea as a steward, making trips to the Orient and Hong Kong. Returning to New York, he studied acting privately with Joseph Geiger, while working as a waiter. He had wed Beatrice Bakalyar in 1952 and eventually appeared on Broadway again in 'End as a Man', 'The Wedding Breakfast' (both 1953), and won acclaim in 1955 in 'A Hatful of Rain', having previously appeared in stock in Chicago and Boston. Hollywood beckoned in 1957; he made A FACE IN THE CROWD, THIS COULD BE THE NIGHT and repeated his HATFUL OF RAIN role. That year he also wed his Broadway 'Hatful...' co-star, Shelley Winters (qv). His movies have included: WILD IS THE WIND (58); THE LONG HOT SUMMER (58); THE NAKED MAJA (59, as artist Goya); CAREER (59); THE STORY ON PAGE ONE (59); GO NAKED IN THE WORLD (60); PERIOD OF ADJUSTMENT (62); RIO CONCHOS (64); THE PLEASURE SEEKERS (65); A MAN COULD GET KILLED (65). The 60s and 70s were busy years for the actor in T.V., his series being 'Valentine's Day' (1964/65) as Valentine Farrow, Jeff Dillon in 'The Name of the Game' (1968-71), Nick Bianco in 'Search' (1972/73) and the title role of 'Matt Helm' (1975). Divorcing Miss Winters in 1960, he wed Judy Balaban Kanter in 1962, daughter Nina born in 1964. Other movies include THE SWINGER (66); FATHOM (67); IN ENEMY COUNTRY (68); ACROSS 110TH STREET (72); LA CICALA (80, Italy); TEXAS LEGEND (80); HELP ME TO DREAM (81, Italy); KISS MY GRITS (82) and JULIE DARLING (82). Mr Franciosa has a son, born 4.6.71, the mother being Rita Thiel, and in 1981 he filmed an episode of 'Tales of the Unexpected' in Great Britain.

JAMES FRANCISCUS

B. Clayton, Missouri 31.1.34. Ed. Connecticut's Taft Prep. School and Yale Univ.; at univ. excelled at sport (star athlete-football, track and tennis), but turned to acting while recuperating from knee injury and had several plays produced at college, graduating in 1957 with degree in English; came to screen 1956 in FOUR BOYS AND A GUN, filmed in New York; md. Kathleen Wellman (daughter of director Wm. Wellman) on 28.5.60, 4 daughters: Jamie (1961), Jolie (1965), Kellie (1973) and Korie (1975); movies include THE OUTSIDER (61); YOUNGBLOOD HAWKE (64), MAROONED (69) and BENEATH PLANET OF THE APES, but equally well-known on T.V. in such series as 'Naked City' (58/59), John Novak in 'Mr Novak' (63-65), 'The Investigators' (61), 'Longstreet' (71/72), Dr Benjamin Elliott in 'Doc Elliott' (74) and 'Hunter' (77); several T.V. movies; recent films: THE GREEK TYCOON (77); CITY OF FIRE, KILLER FISH (both 78); WHEN TIME RAN OUT (79); NIGHT KILL, BUTTERFLY, JACQUELINE BOUVIER KENNEDY (T.V. movie, all 1982); THE COURAGEOUS (83).

LYNNE FREDERICK

B. Hillingdon, Middlesex 26.7.54. Ed. Notting Hill & Ealing High School for Girls, London; her father is American, mother—casting director Iris Frederick; Miss Frederick left school before she was 16 to appear in movie NO BLADE OF GRASS (69); much T.V., including 'Summer & Smoke', 'Follyfoot', 'The Lady from the Sea', 'The Pallisers'; her movies include: NICHOLAS & ALEXANDRA (71), VAMPIRE CIRCUS (71), Catherine Howard in HENRY VIII & HIS SIX WIVES (71), AMAZING MR BLUNDEN (72), THE LONG RETURN (74), VOYAGE OF THE DAMNED (76), THE PRISONER OF ZENDA (79), voted 'Face of 1971' by a British national newspaper; md. 1. Peter Sellers 1977 (dec. 1980); 2. David Frost, 25.1.81, div. June 1982; 3. Barry Unger, heart specialist, Dec. 1982.

FIONA FULLERTON

B. Kaduna, Nigeria, W. Africa 10.10.56. Parents: Brig. Bernard Fullerton (of the R.A.P.C.) and his wife Pamela. Ed. Elmshurst Ballet School, Surrey; lived abroad with parents in Nigeria, Singapore before settling in U.K., seen in school production and aged 11, cast as Diana in movie RUN WILD, RUN FREE (68), then appd. as Anastasia in NICHOLAS & ALEXANDRA (70); her photo appearing on cover of 'Sunday Times' magazine lead to title role in 1972 movie ALICE'S ADVENTURES IN WONDERLAND; T.V. includes: sang in 'Music of John Barry' and 'Nana Mouskouri Special' (73), 'A Friend Indeed' (73), 8 months as Nurse Rutherford in 'Angels' (BBC. 75/76), 'Dick Barton, Special Agent' (77) and 'Gaugin—The Savage' (79, T.V. movie—CBS); md: Simon MacCorkindale, 10.7.76 (div.1982); much stage work includes: 'Pinocchio' (74), title role 'Cinderella' (76/77, London Palladium); musicals: 'Something's Afoot' (78, Hong Kong), Sally in 'I am a Camera' (79, Plymouth), 'Bardado' (80, London); 'The Beggar's Opera' (80, London); movie 1979: THE HUMAN FACTOR; div. 1982; Max Factor advertising contract; recent stage: 'Gypsy' (81); Polly in 'The Boyfriend' (81); Guenevere in 'Camelot' (London 82/83).

RONALD FRASER

B. Bonnybridge, Scotland 11.4.30; Scottish parents—father was accomplished interior decorator; Mr Fraser trained as a chemist, after being brought up in London and Scotland; Nat. Service as A.D.C. to Governor of Cyprus, disc-jockeying at army broadcasting station, decided to become actor and trained RADA; dresser to Donald Wolfitt; small parts rep; u/studied Harold Pinter; acted at Glasgow Citizen's Theatre, Coventry Rep., 2 years with Queen's Players, Hornchurch; London début: 'The Good Sailor'; Old Vic 1954, toured Canada; West End success in 'Long, Short & the Tall' as Corp. McLeish; md. actress Elizabeth Howe, 2 daughters: Fiona, Alison (div. 1963); movies include THE SUNDOWNERS (60), THE LONG, THE SHORT & THE TALL (61), THE POT CARRIERS (62), THE PUNCH & JUDY MAN (63), CROOKS IN CLOISTERS (64), BEAUTY JUNGLE (64), THE WHISPERERS (67), SINFUL DAVEY (69), TOO LATE THE HERO (69), RENTADICK (72), PAPER TIGER (75), WILD GEESE (77), TRAIL OF THE PINK PANTHER (83); TV inclu. 'The Misfit', 'Spooner's Patch', 'Brideshead Revisited', 'Pygmalion' (as Col. Pickering), 'Pirates of Penzance' (83).

GERT FROBE

B. Zwickau, Germany, 5.2.12. Mr Frobe was a child violin protegy and began his stage career in 1935 in Germany. During WWII was a medic; on one occasion 'when German army took Munich worked between German and American lines'. After war was 'street musician' and appd. in German movie 'Berliner Ballade' (48) and became a leading box-office draw in German films. Md. Karen ———, 1 daughter: Beate; over 100 movies include: THE HEROES ARE TIRED (55), HE WHO MUST DIE (56), THE TESTAMENT OF DR MABUSE (64), as Auric GOLDFINGER (64, international fame), THOSE MAGNIFICENT MEN IN THEIR FLYING MACHINES (65), IS PARIS BURNING? (66), ROCKET TO THE MOON (67), MONTE CARLO OR BUST (69), DOLLARS (71), AND THEN THERE WERE NONE (75), THE SERPENT'S EGG (78), BLOODLINE (79).

CHRISTOPHER GABLE

B. London 13.3.40. Ed. Royal Ballet Schools; 10 years an international ballet dancer, including the Royal Ballet Co. at Covent Garden (he was one of their highest paid artistes) before switching to an acting career, starting in rep. at Watford; Mr Gable has appeared with companies at Oxford, Manchester, London and 1 year with R.S. Co.; first success on T.V. as Eric Fenby in 'Song of Summer' (68, BBC) and came to the screen in 1969 in WOMEN IN LOVE and has since filmed THE MUSIC LOVERS (70), Tony Brockhurst in THE BOYFRIEND (72) and THE SLIPPER & THE ROSE (76); md. Carole Needham, 1 daughter: Emma, 1 son: Tomas; T.V. includes: 'The Cherry Orchard', 'The Merchant of Venice', 'High Summer', 'Willy'. 'The Devil's Crown', 'The Hunchback of Notre dame' and recently portrayed Jack Buchanan in 'The Jack Buchanan Story'; stage 1981: 'The Misanthrope'; film 1983: ORPHEUS IN THE UNDERWORLD (T.V. movie).

AVA GARDNER

Ava Gardner, one of the last stars to be groomed as a glamour star by M-G-M, is still very active in movies, having recently completed THE KIDNAPPING OF THE PRESIDENT and THE PRIEST OF LOVE. The youngest of six children born to Jonas B. Gardner, a farmer, and his wife, Mary, she was born at Smithfield, N. Carolina on 24th December 1922. After attending high school in her home town and taking a secretarial course at Wilson, she saved some money and ventured to New York, visiting her sister Beatrice. The latter's father-in-law, being struck by Ava's beauty, took several photos and displayed them in a window of his photographic store on Fifth Avenue. These were seen by a clerk in M-G-M's New York office who sent the stills to studio top brass and Ava was soon on her way to California, signing a $50-a-week contract. Groomed by the studio, she appeared in small roles in such movies as WE WERE DANCING (42); KID GLOVE KILLER (42); HITLER'S MADMAN (43) and she was first billed in THREE MEN IN WHITE (44). She wed Mickey Rooney in 1942, but divorced a year later. In October 1945 she wed band-leader Artie Shaw and that year attained third billing in SHE WENT TO THE RACES, THE KILLERS (46) and THE HUCKSTERS (47) were star vehicles for her and in the fifties her best pictures were PANDORA & THE FLYING DUTCHMAN (51); SHOW BOAT (51, as Julie); SNOWS OF KILLIMANJARO (52) and in MOGAMBO (53) she received an Oscar nomination. On 7 November 1951 she had wed Frank Sinatra but the couple divorced in 1954. Further movies included LONE STAR (52); RIDE, VAQUERO! (53); THE BAREFOOT CONTESSA (54); BHOWANI JUNCTION (56); THE LITTLE HUT (57); THE SUN ALSO RISES (57); THE NAKED MAJA (59); ON THE BEACH (59); THE ANGEL WORE RED (60); 55 DAYS AT PEKING (63); SEVEN DAYS IN MAY (64); NIGHT OF THE IGUANA (64); THE BIBLE (66, as Sarah); MAYERLING (68); THE LIFE & TIMES OF JUDGE ROY BEAN (72); EARTHQUAKE (74); THE SENTINEL (76); CITY OF FIRE (78) and REGINA (82). In recent years she has made her home in London.
AVA: PORTRAIT OF A STAR by David Hanna; Anthony Gibbs & Phillips: London, 1961; pb: Panther, 1962.
AVA by Charles Higham; W.H. Allen: London, 1975.
AVA GARDNER by John Daniell; W.H. Allen: London, 1982.
AVA: A BIOGRAPHY by Roland Flamini; U.S.A., 1982.

JAMES GARNER

Amiable James Garner has never quite made super-star status but he has sustained his career for over 20 years in motion pictures, as well as being a popular face on T.V. from his early 'Maverick' days to his present 'Rockford Files' series. His real name is James Scott Baumgarner, the son of Weldon Baumgarner and his wife Mildred, and he was born in Norman, Oklahoma on 7 April 1928. His father ran an upholstery and carpentry business and James received his education at Norman High School. Upon leaving he worked in the Texas oilfields, spent a year in the Merchant Marine, working aboard a sea-going tug which operated from N. Orleans. The family (he has 2 brothers) moved to L.A. and he enrolled at Hollywood High School, also modelling part-time for a swimsuit company and worked at a gas station, but he returned later to Norman to complete his studies. In 1950 while working in the carpet trade he was called up and served with distinction as a sergeant in Korea, being awarded a Purple Heart, and was discharged in 1952. He studied business at UCLA, but gave up the course and decided upon an acting career. In New York he studied at the Berghof School and through a friend, Paul Gregory (now a producer, and whom he had previously known in Hollywood), won a role on Broadway in 'Caine Mutiny Court-Martial', toured with this production and went to Hollywood. Mr Garner wed Lois Clarke in Auguat 1956, after 2 weeks courtship. Their daughter Greta Scott was born 4 January 1958 (his wife has a daughter, Kimberly, from a previous marriage). In 1956 he had landed a contract with Warner Bros., coming to the screen in TOWARD THE UNKNOWN. After supporting roles in SHOOT-OUT AT MEDICINE BEND (57) and in T.V. series such as 'Cheyenne' he was given his own series, 'Maverick' and cast as Bret Maverick from 1957-60, which made him a T.V. star. However, the actor had a dispute over his contract and left the studio, having also starred in feature movies such as DARBY'S RANGERS (58); UP PERISCOPE (59) and CASH McCALL (59) at Warner's. It proved to be a wise move for Garner — he subsequently had better roles in such pictures as THE CHILDREN'S HOUR (62); THE GREAT ESCAPE (63); THE THRILL OF IT ALL (63); MOVE OVER, DARLING (63); THE AMERCANIZATION OF EMILY (64); 36 HOURS (64); MISTER BUDDWING (66); GRAND PRIX (66); HOUR OF THE GUN (67, as Wyatt Earp); SUPPORT YOUR LOCAL SHERIFF (69); THE SKIN GAME (71) and OUR LITTLE INDIAN (73). He moved back into T.V. in 1971/72 with 'Nichols', a short-lived series, but as Jim Rockford in 'The Rockford Files' (1974-80) he had considerable success, and, as 'Maverick', he was back in the saddle for a revival series in 1981. His most recent movies are HEALTH (79); THE LONG SUMMER OF GEORGE ADAMS (T.V. movie), THE FAN (both 1981); VICTOR/VICTORIA (82) and TANK (83).

ART GARFUNKEL

B. Queen's, New York 5.11.42(?). Ed. Columbia Univ. Mr Garfunkel grew up in New York with Paul Simon and at the age of 15 they became a harmony group, 'Tom & Jerry', performing a minor hit, 'Schoolgirl'. In 1966 they recorded No.1 hit 'The Sounds of Silence', others included 'Homeward Bound', 'I am a Rock' and their albums 'Bookends' and, in particular, their music and accompaniments to the movie THE GRADUATE (68), were best-sellers. In 1969 Garfunkel turned to acting, appearing in the movies CATCH 22 and CARNAL KNOWLEDGE (71). He returned to music for eight years, had wed Linda Grossman in October 1972 (now div.), but has recently returned to the big screen in Nicolas Roeg's acclaimed BAD TIMING (79).

TERI GARR

B. Lakewood, Ohio, . .52. Teri has played extensively on T.V. in such shows as 'The K Berry "Wow" Show' (1972), 'The Burns Schreiber Comedy Hour' (1973), 'The Sonny Cher Comedy Hour (1973/74), 'The Son Comedy Revue' (1974), 'Cher' (1975) and such motion-pictures as THE CONVERSATIO (74); YOUNG FRANKENSTEIN (74); LA & ORDER (76, T.V. movie); OH, GOD! (77 CLOSE ENCOUNTERS OF THE THIR KIND (77); HONKY TONK FREEWAY (81 STING II (82); TOOTSIE (82, Oscar nom BSA); THE BLACK STALLION RETURN MR MOM (both 1983).

BEN GAZZARA

B. New York City 28.8.30. Ed. City Coll., New York; brought up in Italian territories of New York, parents Sicilian immigrants; acted in Boys' Club productions, and trained in acting at Erwin Piscator's Dramatic Workshop and the Actors' Studio; stage début: 1952; N.Y. début in 1953 as Jocko De Paris in 'End as a Man', gaining New York Drama Critics' Award as 'Most Promising Actor', coming to the screen in 1957 in movie version; md. 1. Louise Erikson, 1 daughter: Elizabeth (div.), 2. Janice Rule, November 1961; Mr Gazzara has since won acclaim for many stage performances and played in 2 T.V. series: as Det. Sergeant Nick Anderson in 'Arrest & Trial' (63/64) and as Paul Bryan in 'Run For Your Life' (65-68); movies include: ANATOMY OF A MURDER (59), A RAGE TO LIVE (65), BRIDGE AT REMAGEN (69), CAPONE (75) and, more recently, BLOODLINE (79), SAINT JACK (79), INCHON, THEY ALL LAUGHED, A QUESTION OF HONOUR (T.V. movie, all 1981), TALES OF ORDINARY MADNESS (82).

JUDY GEESON

B. Arundel, Sussex 10.9.48. Began as a child actress, studying with the Corona Stage School and making acting début on T.V. in 1960 in 'Dixon of Dock Green'; numerous T.V. plays/series include 'The Newcomers', 'Lady Windermere's Fan', 'Poldark', 'Danger U.X.B.', 'Tales of the Unexpected'; motion-picture début 1963 in CFF film WINGS OF MYSTERY, many others include TO SIR WITH LOVE (66), HERE WE GO ROUND THE MULBERRY BUSH (66), BERSERK (67), PRUDENCE & THE PILL (69), THREE INTO TWO WON'T GO (69), 10 RILLINGTON PLACE (71), DOOMWATCH (72), FEAR IN THE NIGHT (72), BRANNIGAN (74), CARRY ON ENGLAND (76), THE EAGLE HAS LANDED (76), DOMINIQUE (77); Miss Geeson has appeared on stage at the Open Space Theatre, toured and played with the Young Vic and R.S. Co.; recent stage: 'Getting Married' (82); T.V.: 'Inseminoid' (ser. 81); movies: THE PLAGUE DOGS (82, voice), SHORT ENDS (short, 83).

CHRISTOPHER GEORGE

B. Royal Oak, Michigan, 25.2.29(?). Son of Greek immigrant parents, spoke Greek before English; at 6 helped his father, a travelling salesman, on the road; at H.S. drove trucks in Miami, where family settled; Marines; grad. from Miami Univ. in 1958 with B.A. in finance; at Stockton, Calif. ran cocktail lounge; returned to Miami, teamed up with friend, operated 110ft. boat transporting cargo in Caribbean; went to New York, studied acting with Wyn Handman; appd. little theatre productions; did T.V. roles ('Naked City', 'Bewitched', etc.), small movie roles and graduated to leads in such pics as EL DORADO (67), THE 1000 PLANE RAID (69), ESCAPE (69, T.V. movie), THE IMMORTAL (69, T.V. movie), THE DELTA FACTOR (70), TIGER BY THE TAIL (70), THE TRAIN ROBBERS (73), GRIZZLY (76); md. 1. (?), 2. Lynda Day 1970, children: Nicky, Casey (Mrs George is popular U.S. actress—they appd. together in GENTLE RAIN (66); Christopher has appd. in 2 T.V. series: Sgt. Sam Troy in 'Rat Patrol' (66-68) and 'The Immortal' (70) as Ben Richards; recently: WHISKY MOUNTAIN (77), DAY OF THE ANIMALS (78), EXTERMINATOR (79), GRADUATION DAY, CITY OF THE LIVING DEAD (both 1981), MORTUARY (83).

SUSAN GEORGE

B.   , 26.7.50. Mother musical comedy actress/ dancer 'Bubbles Percival'; father dance-band leader/saxophonist who once ran group 'Norman George & His Music'; pro. début aged 4, studied Corona Stage School; appd. in T.V. commercials, serials, etc.; 1962 played juvenile lead in West End's 'Sound of Music'; Children's films: CUP FEVER (65), DAVEY JONES' LOCKER (66); 1st feature THE SORCERERS (67), small roles in UP THE JUNCTION (67), BILLION DOLLAR BRAIN (67), 1st starring role: THE STRANGE AFFAIR (68), LOOKING GLASS WAR (69), ALL NEAT IN BLACK STOCKINGS (69), TWINKY (69), SPRING AND PORT WINE (70), EYEWITNESS (70), DIE SCREAMING MARIANNE (70), STRAW DOGS (72), DR JEKYLL & MR HYDE (73, T.V. movie), DIRTY MARY, CRAZY LARRY (73), SONNY & JED (74), MANDINGO (74), OUT OF SEASON (75), A SMALL TOWN IN TEXAS (76), TINTOREA (77), THE FINAL EYE (77, T.V. movie), TOMORROW NEVER COMES (77), VENOM, TEXAS LEGEND (both 1980), ENTER THE NINJA (81), THE HOUSE WHERE EVIL LIES, KISS MY GRITS (both 1982), THE JIGSAW MAN (83); engagement: actor Simon MacCorkindale, April, 1983 .

GIL GERARD

B. Little Rock, Arkansas,   .40. At university in Arkansas was singer with trio; upon leaving univ. became industrial chemist, advisor to Gov. Winthrop Rockefeller of State of Arkansas; went to New York, studied acting by day, worked as cabbie at night; was 'extra' in movie LOVE STORY (71); took leads in several musical road co. productions; also, 'in 400 T.V. commercials'; 2 years in T.V. 'soap opera' 'The Doctors' as Dr Alan Stewart; appd. as Lee Grant's youthful lover in AIRPORT '77, he had acted, co-directed, wrote and produced movie HOOCH (76); T.V. includes 'Baretta' and starred opp. Yvette Mimieux (qv) in T.V. movie KILLING STONE; 1979 lead role in movie and T.V. series BUCK ROGERS IN THE 25TH CENTURY for Universal; Mr Gerard wed actress Connie Sellecca in 1979, his 3rd marriage (first 2 wives have also been named 'Connie'), 1 son Gib (b. 1981); NOT JUST ANOTHER AFFAIR (T.V. movie, 1981), HEAR NO EVIL (T.V. movie, 1982).

RICHARD GERE

B. Syracuse, New York,   .49. One of a family of five, Richard Gere grew up in New York State and attended the University of Massachusetts where he majored in philosophy and took part in plays in college. Upon graduating he joined Provincetown Playhouse and then Seattle Repertory Theatre, where he also composed music for various productions. Reaching Broadway he played in 'Grease', 'Soon' and 'Habeas Corpus' and also came to London, playing in 'Grease' (1974) and as Christopher Sly in 'Taming of the Shrew' for the Young Vic. On T.V. he has played in 'Kojak', the T.V. movie 'Strike' and his feature film appearances have been REPORT TO THE COMMISSIONER (75), BABY BLUE MARINE (75), LOOKING FOR MR GOODBAR (77), DAYS OF HEAVEN (78), YANKS (78), BLOODBROTHERS (79) and AMERICAN GIGOLO (79); won acclaim B'way in 'Bent' (80); recent movies: AN OFFICER & A GENTLEMAN, BREATHLESS (both 1982), THE HONORARY CONSUL (83).

JOHN GIELGUD

Sir John Gielgud has been acclaimed as one of the greatest Shakespearean actors of all time and much of his masterly acting has fortunately been recorded for the screen, although he has made relatively few movies in his long career, spanning sixty years. Born in London, on 14 April 1904, he is the son of Frank Gielgud and his wife Kate, the latter related to the famous acting family of Terry. He was educated at Westminster School and studied for the stage, gaining scholarships to Lady Benson's School and R.A.D.A., making his professional début at the Old Vic, London on 7 November 1921, and thus began his highly distinguished career. His work on the stage has included: Charles Wykeham in 'Charley's Aunt' (1923), Romeo in 'Romeo and Juliet' (London, 1924), Ferdinand in 'The Tempest' (London, 1926), 1927 tour 'Constant Nymph', 1st New York appearance: 1928 in 'The Patriot', joined Old Vic Company September 1929: played Romeo again, Antonio in 'Merchant of Venice', Marc Antony in 'Julius Caesar', leads — 'Hamlet', 'Macbeth', 1932: Richard II in 'Richard of Bordeaux' (over 1 year's run, also directed), London 1934: played and directed 'Hamlet', London 1939: directed, played John Worthing in 'The Importance of Being Earnest'. Sir John had come to the screen in 1924 as Daniel in WHO IS THE MAN? and has been seen in THE CLUE OF THE NEW PIN (29); INSULT (32); as Inigo Jollifant in THE GOOD COMPANIONS (32, repeating his 1931 stage success); THE SECRET AGENT (36) and THE PRIME MINISTER (40, as Disraeli). In 1940 he played 'King Lear' at the Old Vic and Prospero in 'The Tempest' and during the War toured for ENSA in Army and RAF Garrison theatres, entertaining the troops in such locations as Malta, Gibraltar and Burma. He has continued to work ceaselessly in the theatre as actor and distinguished director in London, Stratford-on-Avon, New York, Rhodesia (1953), Paris, Antwerp, Brussels, Australia, N.Z., U.S.S.R., all Western European countries. His other films have included JULIUS CAESAR (53); RICHARD III (56); SAINT JOAN (57); BECKET (64, Oscar nom., BSA); CHARGE OF THE LIGHT BRIGADE (68); OH! WHAT A LOVELY WAR! (69); MURDER ON THE ORIENT EXPRESS (74, BAFTA Aw., BSA); PROVIDENCE (77); THE HUMAN FACTOR, ELEPHANT MAN (both 1979); THE SPHINX, THE FORMULA (both 1980); PRIEST OF LOVE, THE FIRST DEADLY SIN, ARTHUR (BSA Aw.: Oscar, Golden Globe) and CHARIOTS OF FIRE (all 1981). Knighted in 1953, other honours include a Chevalier of the Legion d'Honneur, Degree of Doctor of Laws (St. Andrews Univ.) and Hon. D. Litt., Oxford Univ. Sir John's most recent movies: INSIDE THE THIRD REICH (mini-ser.), HUNCHBACK OF NOTRE DAME (T.V. movie, both 1982); WAGNER, INVITATION TO THE WEDDING, THE SCARLET & THE BLACK (T.V. movie), THE WICKED LADY, SCANDALOUS and THE FAR PAVILIONS (all 1983). EARLY STAGES (autobiography); revised ed. (from 1939 work); Heinemann: London, 1974.   JOHN GIELGUD: AN ACTOR'S BIOGRAPHY IN PICTURES by Hallam Fordham; John Lehman, London, 1952.   JOHN GIELGUD by Ronald Hayman; H.E.B. Ltd.: London, 1971.   JOHN GIELGUD: AN ACTOR & HIS TIMES (with John Miller & John Powell); Sidgwick & Jackson: London, 1979.

PETER GILMORE

B. Leipzig 25.8.31. Father, businessman who travelled extensively; aged 6, came to G.B., grew up with relatives in Nunthorpe, Yorks; aged 14 came to London, made coffee percolators in garages; RADA; Nat. Serv. in army; took up singing, 20 years singer with 'Black & White Minstrels', also stooge to H. Secombe and Al Read; stage shows include: 'Grab Me a Gondola', 'Valmouth', 'Lock Up Your Daughters'; md. 1. Una Stubbs, 1 son: Jason (div.), 2. Jan Waters (div.); films: ('borrowed £2,000 from bank and went to Rome to get small part in epic(?)') I'VE GOTTA HORSE (65), GT. ST. TRINIAN'S TRAIN ROBBERY (66), 17 'CARRY ON ...' movies, 7 CITIES TO ATLANTIS (77), A MAN CALLED INTREPID (78, T.V. movie); very popular on T.V. in 'The Onedin Line'; MANSIONS OF AMERICA (mini-ser. 1982), 'You'll Never See Me Again' (T.V. 83).

PAUL MICHAEL GLASER

B. Cambridge, Mass. 25.3.43. Father architect, mother owns hospital, Boston; has 2 sisters; ed. Boston/Harvard Univ., grad. with Master's degree in acting/directing; 5 seasons stock; came U.K. 1964, RADA & Stratford; returned to U.S.A., stage success as Raskolnikov in 'Crime & Punishment' & New York in rock version of 'Hamlet': 'Man in the Glass Booth'; guest in many T.V. series ('Kojak' etc.), regular in 'Love is a Many Splendored Thing' (1973), 'Love is Life': movies: FIDDLER ON THE ROOF (71), BUTTERFLIES ARE FREE (72, also stage); tremendous popularity/success as Det. Dave Starsky in 'Starsky & Hutch'; md. c. August 1980, L.A. school teacher Elizabeth Meyers; LIGHT ON SYNANON, WAIT TILL YOUR MOTHER GETS HOME (both T.V. movies, 1982).

JULIAN GLOVER

B. St. John's Wood, London 27.3.35. Ed. St. Paul's School, Hammersmith and Alleyn's, Dulwich; acted at latter as Marc Antony in 'Julius Caesar'; pro. début: 1953 in panto., Bromley; studied RADA; became distinguished stage actor, playing at Royal Court Theatre, tours, West End, Edinburgh Fest., Prospect Theatre Co., Bristol, Old Vic etc.; Md: actress Isla Blair, 1 son; many T.V. appearances; movies: TOM JONES (63), GIRL WITH GREEN EYES (64), I WAS HAPPY HERE (65), THE MAGUS (68), ALFRED THE GREAT (69), THE LAST GRENADE (69), THE ADDING MACHINE (69), RISE & RISE OF MICHAEL RIMMER (70), WUTHERING HEIGHTS (70), NICHOLAS & ALEXANDRA (72), ANTHONY & CLEOPATRA (72), HITLER: THE LAST 10 DAYS (73), LUTHER (74), DEAD CERT (74), JUGGERNAUT (74), THE BRUTE (76), EMPIRE STRIKES BACK (80), FOR YOUR EYES ONLY (81); recent T.V.: 'Invasion' (80), 'Henry V' (79, as Constable of France); Q.E.D. (81); 'Nancy Astor' (ser., 1982); IVANHOE (T.V. movie, 1982, as King Richard); 'Dombey & Son' (83, ser.).

JEFF GOLDBLUM

B. Pittsburgh, 22.10.52; Mr Goldblum, who is 6'4" tall, has been seen in the following movies: DEATH WISH (74), NASHVILLE (75), ANNIE HALL (77), INVASION OF THE BODY-SNATCHERS (77), THANK GOD IT'S FRIDAY (78), REMEMBER MY NAME (79) and the T.V. series 'Tenspeed and Brown Shoe'. THE BIG CHILL (83).

RUTH GORDON

B. Wollaston, nr. Boston, Mass. 30.10.1896. Ed. Quincy High School, Mass.; studied for the stage at the Am.A.D.A.; first stage appearance New York 1915 as Nibbs in 'Peter Pan'; long and distinguished career on the American stage, including own stock co., Indianapolis 1922, 'The First Year' (New York 1922, and tour), 'The Fall of Eve', Booth 1925, 'The Wiser They Are' (1931), 'Three Cornered Moon' (1934), 'The Country Wife' (1935), 'Capt. Brassbound's Conversion' (1935); Miss Gordon has played in the United Kingdom & Europe and authored several plays; md. 1. Gregory Kelly 1918 (dec. 1927), 1 son Jones, 2. Garson Kanin 1942; her film work has included: CAMILLE (15), THE WHEEL OF LIFE (16), ABE LINCOLN IN ILLINOIS (40), DR EHRLICH'S MAGIC BULLET (40), TWO FACED WOMAN (41), EDGE OF DARKNESS (43), ACTION IN THE NORTH ATLANTIC (43), OVER 21 (author, acted in stage vers., 45), A DOUBLE LIFE (48, co-wrote with husband), ADAM'S RIB (49, co-wrote), THE MARRYING KIND (52, co-wrote), PAT AND MIKE (52, co-wrote), THE ACTRESS (53, author), ROSIE (58, author), INSIDE DAISY CLOVER (66), LORD LOVE A DUCK (66), ROSEMARY'S BABY (68, Oscar), WHATEVER HAPPENED TO AUNT ALICE? (69), WHERE'S POPPA? (70), HAROLD & MAUDE (72), THE BIG BUS (76).
Autobiographies: *MYSELF AMONG OTHERS* (1971) and *MY SIDE* (1976).

WALTER GOTELL

B. , 15.3.24. Ed. Seaford Coll., Leighton Park; father an architect; has appeared on stage in rep. at Liverpool, Sheffield, Colchester and other companies; on T.V. in 'Softly, Softly', 'The Main Chance', etc.; md. Yvonne Hills, 1 daughter Carol; many movies include: small roles in WE DIVE AT DAWN (43), WOODEN HORSE (50), ALBERT R.N. (53), AFRICAN QUEEN (52), I WAS MONTY'S DOUBLE (58), THE GUNS OF NAVARONE (61), SINK THE BISMARK (61), often seen as German officers; Mr Gotell has business interests, including engineering; other movies include FROM RUSSIA WITH LOVE (63), ENDLESS NIGHT (71), SPY WHO LOVED ME (77), THE STUD (77), LONDON CONNECTION (78), THE BOYS FROM BRAZIL (78), FOR YOUR EYES ONLY (81); recent T.V.: 'Barriers' (81, ITV), 'Airline' (82), 'County Hall' (82); films: MEMED (83), OCTOPUSSY (83).

MICHAEL GOUGH

B. Kuala Lumpur, Malaya 23.11.17. Ed. Rose Hill School, Tunbridge Wells, Durham School and Wye Agricultural Coll.; after studying for the stage at the Old Vic School in 1936, Mr Gough became a distinguished actor with appearances on Broadway, West End, Liverpool, Oxford, Drury Lane, Royal Court and S. American tour as well as appearing on many occasions on T.V.; his many films include BLANCHE FURY (47), ANNA KARENINA (48), THE SMALL BACK ROOM (49), BLACKMAILED (50), NIGHT WAS OUR FRIEND (51), THE SWORD AND THE ROSE (53), ROB ROY (53), RICHARD III (55), REACH FOR THE SKY (56), HORROR OF DRACULA (58, as Holmwood), HORRORS OF THE BLACK MUSEUM (59), MR TOPAZE (61), PHANTOM OF THE OPERA (62), DR TERROR'S HOUSE OF HORROR (64), THE SKULL (65), CURSE OF THE CRIMSON ALTAR (68), THE GO-BETWEEN (70), HENRY VIII & HIS 6 WIVES (72, as Duke of Norfolk), SAVAGE MESSIAH (72), LEGEND OF HELL HOUSE (73), GALILEO (74), SATAN'S SLAVE (76); md. 1. Diana Graves (div.), 2. Anne Leon (div.), 3. Anneke Wills; recent T.V.: 'Suez' (79), 'Smiley's People' (82), 'Strangers' (82); film: MEMED (83).

MICHAEL GOTHARD

B. London, .42. Mr Gothard has appeared on T.V. on numerous occasions, including 'Arthur of the Britons', 'The Machine Stops' and his many motion-picture appearances include his first, which was made in Paris with the 'underground movement', his British film début was in HEROSTRATUS (67) and has since been seen in UP THE JUNCTION (67), MICHAEL KOHLAAS (69), SCREAM AND SCREAM AGAIN (69), THE LAST VALLEY (70), THE DEVILS (71), WHO SLEW AUNTIE ROO? (71), THE VALLEY OBSCURED BY CLOUDS (72), THE THREE MUSKETEERS (73), 7 CITIES TO ATLANTIS (77) and FOR YOUR EYES ONLY (81). His recent T.V. includes: 'The Professionals', 'Tale of 2 Cities' and 'Shoestring'. IVANHOE (T.V. movie, 1982).

ELLIOTT GOULD

Elliott Gould, one of the few big names to emerge from Hollywood in the 70s, after his great success with BOB & CAROL & TED & ALICE and M*A*S*H, was born in Brooklyn, New York, on 29 August 1938, the son of Bernard Goldstein and his wife, Lucille. An only child, Elliott attended Profesional Children's School and Columbia University, but got his first taste of show-biz as a youngster aged 8, attending the Charlie Lowe Broadway Show-Business School for Children. On leaving University he studied acting with Vladimir Protevich, voice with Jerome Swinford and dance with Sonya Box and Bill Quinn. At the age of 19, he got a role in the chorus of 'Rumple' (Alvin Theatre, New York, 1957) after phoning the producer, impersonating an agent and singing the praises of a young actor named Elliott Gould! Other stage roles included: 3 'walk-on' parts, then taking over role of Polyte-le-Mou in 'Irma La Douce' (1960), 'Hit the Deck', Harry Bogen in 'I Can Get It For You Wholesale' (1962) and in this production he met an immensely talented, vibrant young girl — Barbra Streisand, and the couple wed in 1963. Their son, Jason, was born in 1966. Mr Gould came to London in May 1963 to play Ozzie in 'On the Town' and returned to the States for 'Drat! The Cat!' (1965), 'The Little Murders' (1967), tour of 'Luv' (1968) and 'A Way of Life' (1969). After appearing in a small role in THE NIGHT THEY RAIDED MINSKY'S (68), he has starred in the following movies: BOB & CAROL & TED & ALICE (69, Oscar nom.); M*A*S*H (70); GETTING STRAIGHT (70); MOVE (70); I LOVE MY WIFE (70); THE TOUCH (70, Sweden); LITTLE MURDERS (71, also prod.); THE LONG GOODBYE (72); BUSTING (73); S*P*Y*S (74); CALIFORNIA SPLIT (74); WHO? (74); NASHVILLE (74, guest); WHIFFS (76); I WILL...I WILL...FOR NOW (76); HARRY & WALTER GO TO N.Y. (76); A BRIDGE TOO FAR (76); THE SILENT PARTNER (77); CAPRICORN ONE (77); ESCAPE TO ATHENA (78); MATILDA (78); THE LADY VANISHES (78); THE MUPPET MOVIE (79, guest); DIRTY TRICKS (79); FALLING IN LOVE AGAIN (79); THE LAST FLIGHT OF NOAH'S ARK (79) and THE DEVIL & MAX DEVLIN (80). Elliott divorced Miss Streisand (qv) in 1971, wed Jennifer Bogart from 1973-75, but they re-married in Las Vegas on 10 June 1978. They have 2 children, Molly (born 1971) and Sam (born 1973). His T.V. appearances include 'Once Upon a Mattress' (64) and guesting in 'Saturday Night Live'. His current movie is ALBY'S SPECIAL (83).

STEWART GRANGER

B. Epsom, Surrey 6.5.13. Parents: Major James Stewart and his wife, Frederica. Real name James Lablanche Stewart. Ed. Epsom Coll.; early ambition: to become nerve specialist; attended medical school, but advised, due to his good looks, to try acting; film extra (EVERGREEN (34), others); studied stage-craft at Webber-Douglas School; rep.: Hull, Birmingham 1934-36; from 1937 London stage: 'Serena Blandish', 'Autumn', 'The House in the Square'; first movie credit as Laurence in SO THIS IS LONDON (39); after small role in CONVOY (40), joined British Army, but invalided out in 1942; movies include: THE MAN IN GREY (43), THURSDAY'S CHILD (43), FANNY BY GASLIGHT (43); md. 1. Elspeth March, 1 son James, 1 daughter Lindsay (div.); became very popular star of British movies, 2nd in Motion-Picture Herald poll of top box-office stars 1945; WATERLOO ROAD (44), CAESAR & CLEOPATRA (44), MAGIC BOW (46), CAPTAIN BOYCOTT (47), SARABAND FOR DEAD LOVERS (48), others; md. 2. Jean Simmons (qv) 1950-60, 1 daughter Tracy, b. 1956; went to U.S.A., MGM contract: KING SOLOMON'S MINES (51), SCARAMOUCHE (52), THE PRISONER OF ZENDA (52), YOUNG BESS (53), SALOME (53), BEAU BRUMMELL (54), MOONFLEET (55), BHOWANI JUNCTION (56), THE LITTLE HUT (57), NORTH TO ALASKA (60), Lot in SODOM & GOMORRAH (62), several others; md. 3. Caroline Lecerf (div.); SWORDSMAN OF SIENA (63), then various 'westerns' in Germany; HOUND OF THE BASKERVILLES (71, T.V. movie, as Holmes); Col. Alan MacKenzie in 'The Virginian' (U.S. T.V. series 70/71); business interests: Spain and Arizona; latest film: THE WILD GEESE (77).
SPARKS FLY UPWARDS; Granada Publishing: London, 1981. p/b: Granada, 1982.

PETER GRAVES

B. Minneapolis, Minnesota, 18.3.25. Real name Peter Arness; brother: actor Jim Arness; of German lineage; ed. Univ. of Minnesota; played clarinet and saxophone with local dance bands and at 16 became radio announcer; left H.S., joined U.S. Air Force for 2 years; boxer; studied drama at univ.; md. Joan Endress, college sweetheart, 3 daughters: Kelly (b. 19.10.51), Claudia (b. 1.11.54), Amanda (b. 21.5.58); summer stock; came to screen 1950 in ROGUE RIVER, numerous movies include: FORT DEFIANCE (52), RED PLANET MARS (52), STALAG 17 (53), WAR PAINT (53), BENEATH THE 12 MILE REEF (53), THE LONG GRAY LINE (54), BLACK TUESDAY (55), IT CONQUERED THE WORLD (56), WOLF LARSEN (59), A RAGE TO LIVE (65), BALLAD OF JOSIE (67), 5 MAN ARMY (68), CALL TO DANGER (73, T.V. movie); Mr Graves is best known as T.V. actor as has been seen in 'Your Play Time' (54), 'Studio 57' (55), 'T.V. Reader's Digest' (56) and his own series: as Jim Newton in 'Fury' (55-59), Chris Cobb in 'Whiplash' (61), Major Frank Whittaker in 'Court-Martial' (66) and James Phelps in 'Mission: Impossible' (67-73); recent movies: SPREE (78), THE CLONUS HORROR (79), AIRPLANE! (80), DISASTER IN THE SKY (T.V. movie, 1981), AIRPLANE II: THE SEQUEL (82), GUNS & THE FURY (82), 'The Winds of War' (mini-ser., 1983).

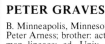

LORNE GREENE

B. Ottawa, Canada 12.2.15. Son of shoemaker, Daniel Greene, and wife, Dora; intended to become engineer, but at Queen's Univ., Kingston Ont., acted and directed plays for Drama Guild, becoming top radio announcer in Canada for Canadian Broadcasting Corp., 1939-43; after WWII returned to radio and founded rep. theatre in Toronto, appd. in S'peare at Stratford, Ont., was seen by talent scout and went to New York, gaining scholarship to P'house Theatre; md. 1. Rita Hands 1940, twins: Belinda and Charles (b. 1941), div. 1960; New York: 125 performances in 'The Prescott Proposals', appd. on T.V. and eventually discovered by Fletcher Markle, coming to screen in 1954 in THE SILVER CHALICE; others: TIGHT SPOT (55), AUTUMN LEAVES (56), PEYTON PLACE (57), BUCCANEER (58) and THE TRAP (58); became very well known on T.V.; in April 56 came to U.K. to film series 'Sailor of Fortune' as Grant Mitchell; back in the States from 1959-72 appeared as Ben Cartwright in the highly successful 'Bonanza'; others: Wade Griffin in 'Griff' (1973), guest: 'The Accused' (58), 'Moneychangers' (76), 'Roots' (77), many others; movies include: EARTHQUAKE (74), TIDAL WAVE (75), BATTLESTAR GALACTICA (78), JACK LONDON'S KLONDIKE FEVER (80), DISASTER IN THE SKY (1981, T.V. movie), 'Strike Force' (ser., 1981), HEIDI'S SONG (82, voice); Md: 2. Nancy Ann Deal, 1 daughter Gillian Donna (b. 9.1.68); 'New Wilderness' (ser., 1983).

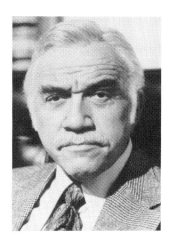

LEE GRANT

B.   31.10.30(?). Real name Lyova Rosenthal. Ed. Juilliard School, studying voice, violin and dance; aged 4 with Metropolitan Opera Co.; at 11, with American Ballet Co.; stage début: 1948 as Mildred in 'Joy to the World', becoming distinguished stage actress, including 'Lo and Behold', 'Wedding Breakfast', 'A Hole in the Head', 'Electra'; much T.V. including 'Plymouth Playhouse (1953), guest in many series, Stella Chernak in 'Peyton Place' (65/66), Fay Stewart in 'Fay' (75/76); came to screen 1951 in DETECTIVE STORY* as shop-lifter (in stage role, for which she won Critics' Circle Award), others include STORM FEAR (55), MIDDLE OF THE NIGHT (59), THE BALCONY (63), TERROR IN THE CITY (67), DIVORCE — AMERICAN STYLE (67), IN THE HEAT OF THE NIGHT (67), MAROONED (69), THE LANDLORD (70), PLAZA SUITE (71), PORTNOY'S COMPLAINT (72), THE INTERNECINE PROJECT (74), SHAMPOO (75), THE STRONGER (76, directed-short), VOYAGE OF THE DAMNED (77), AIRPORT 77, DAMIEN — OMEN II (77), THE SWARM (78), LITTLE MISS MARKER (79); Md: 1. Arnold Manoff (div.), 1 daughter Dinah; 2. Joseph Feury, 1962, 1 daughter: WHEN YOU COMIN' BACK, RED RYDER?, TELL ME A RIDDLE (directed only, both 1980), CHARLIE CHAN & THE CURSE OF THE DRAGON QUEEN (81), THE WILMAR EIGHT (T.V., directed), WILL THERE REALLY BE A MORNING? (T.V. movie), VISITING HOURS (all 1982); (*Oscar nom.).

CHARLES GRAY

B. Bournemouth, Dorset 29.8.28. Was engaged in estate agent's office before making stage debut at Regent's Park Open Air Theatre in 1952 in 'As You Like It'; 1953 played with Stratford Memorial Theatre; 1954-58, played many roles with Old Vic Co., including MacDuff in 'Macbeth' and toured U.S.A. and Canada; New York debut 1956; other stage includes Capt. Mavors in 'Expresso Bongo' (West End) and Maxime in 'Poor Bitos' (London & New York), winning Clarence Derwent Award; much T.V. from 1957, including 'The Captain of Koepenick', 'Hay Fever', 'Ross', 'Merchant of Venice', 'Upper Crusts' (series) and 'Hazell'; many films including: FOLLOW A STAR (60), THE ENTERTAINER (60), THE MAN IN THE MOON (61), MASQUERADE (65), NIGHT OF THE GENERALS (66), YOU ONLY LIVE TWICE (66), THE SECRET WAR OF HARRY FRIGG (67), DEVIL RIDES OUT (68), FILE OF THE GOLDEN GOOSE (69), EXECUTIONER (70), CROMWELL (70), DIAMONDS ARE FOREVER (72, as Blofeld), THE BEAST MUST DIE (74), 7 NIGHTS IN JAPAN (76), THE 7% SOLUTION (76), THE SILVER BEARS (77), THE LEGACY (78), IKE: THE WAR YEARS (T.V. movie, 78), SHOCK TREATMENT (82), JIGSAW MAN (83).

JOAN GREENWOOD

B. Chelsea, London, 4.3.21. Ed. St. Catherine's, Bramley, Surrey and R.A.D.A.; distinguished lady of stage and screen; stage debut 1938 in 'The Robust Invalid'; md. Andre Morell (c. 1959 (dec. 1978), 1 son, Jason; came to the screen in 1940 in JOHN SMITH WAKES UP (40); her many movies have included THE GENTLE SEX (42); THEY KNEW MR KNIGHT (44); LATIN QUARTER (44); A GIRL IN A MILLION (45); THE OCTOBER MAN (47); THE WHITE UNICORN (47); SARABAND FOR DEAD LOVERS (48); WHISKY GALORE (49); KIND HEARTS AND CORONETS (49); FLESH AND BLOOD (50); THE MAN IN THE WHITE SUIT (50); THE IMPORTANCE OF BEING EARNEST (52, as Gwendolen Fairfax); FATHER BROWN (54); MYSTERIOUS ISLAND (62); TOM JONES (63); THE MOONSPINNERS (64); GIRL STROKE BOY (71); THE UNCANNY (77); HOUND OF THE BASKERVILLES (77); THE WATER BABIES (78); Miss Greenwood's recent T.V. includes Play For Today: 'Country' (1981), 'Triangle' (1982, series, BBC, as Judith Harper).

HELMUT GRIEM

B. Hamburg, Germany,   .40. Educated at the Univ. of Hamburg, intending to become journalist, studied philosophy and literature, became involved in acting, won roles on German T.V., discovered by Visconti, coming to screen in his THE DAMNED (68); others include: THE McKENZIE BREAK (70), CABARET (72), LUDWIG (73), BREAKTHROUGH (78), THE GLASS CELL, MALOU (both 1981).

CHARLES GRODIN

B. Pittsburgh, Pa., 21.4.35. Ed. Univ. of Miami; studied stagecraft with Uta Hagen and Lee Strasberg; on Broadway in 'Tchin-Tchin' (62) and 'Absence of a Cello' (64); has also directed in New York and is noted T.V. script-writer; movies include: ROSEMARY'S BABY (68), HEARTBREAK KID (74), 11 HARROW HOUSE (74), KING KONG (76), THIEVES (77), SUNBURN (78), HEAVEN CAN WAIT (78), REAL LIFE (78), SEEMS LIKE OLD TIMES (79), INCREDIBLE SHRINKING WOMAN (79), IT'S MY TURN (80), THE GREAT MUPPET CAPER (81), THE LONELY GUY (83).

CLU GULAGER

B. . . .35. Mr Gulager played on Broadway in 'The Long Gallery' (1958) and is now a very familiar face on T.V. and the movies. His T.V. includes: occasionally seen as Baby Faced Mad Dog Coll in 'The Untouchables' (early 60s), as Billy the Kid in 'The Tall Man' (1960-62) and as Emmett Ryker in 'The Virginian' (1964-68). Other T.V.: 'The Survivors' (69/70), 'Once an Eagle' (76) and 'Wonderland Cove' (78). His many movies include: THE KILLERS (64), AND NOW, MIGUEL (66), WINNING (69), LAST PICTURE SHOW (71), McQ (74), THE MAN WHO LOVED CAT DANCING (74), THE OTHER SIDE OF MIDNIGHT (77) and TOUCHED BY LOVE (80). He is married to actress Miriam Byrd Nethery and sons John and Tom are rock composer and ballet dancer respectively.

DOMINIC GUARD

B. Hammersmith, London, 18.6.56. Cousin Pippa Guard is actress, his brother Christopher is also actor; Dominic has played in such movies as THE GO-BETWEEN (71); BEQUEST TO THE NATION (72); THE HANDS OF CORMAC JOYCE (74); PICNIC AT HANGING ROCK (75); ABSOLUTION (78); AN UNSUITABLE JOB FOR A WOMAN (81); GANDHI (82); recent stage: 'The Jeweller's Shop'; T.V.: 'Cousin Phillis' (82).

HARRY GUARDINO

B. Brooklyn, New York 23.12.25. Father, a bandleader; ed. Haaren H.S.; 3 years U.S. Navy; studied New York Dramatic Workshop; Broadway success, replacing Tony Franciosa (qv) in 'A Hatful of Rain' (55); others: 'One More River' (60), 'Natural Affection' (63), 'Anyone Can Whistle' (64), 'Rose Tattoo' (66); md. 1. Ann 1958, 1 daughter Michelle (b. 1959), 1 son Michael (b. 1962), div. 1969; films include: HOLD BACK TOMORROW (55), HOUSEBOAT (58), PORK CHOP HILL (58), THE 5 PENNIES (59), KING OF KINGS (61, as Barabbas), HELL IS FOR HEROES (62), RHINO! (64), MADIGAN (68), LOVERS AND OTHER STRANGERS (69), THE LONELY PROFESSION (69, T.V. movie), DIRTY HARRY (71), CAPONE (75), ST. IVES (76), THE ENFORCER (76), ROLLERCOASTER (77); md. 2. Jennifer Revson (73-74); Mr Guardino has guested on several occasions in T.V., appd. regularly as 'Monty Nash' (71) and as Hamilton Burger in 'Perry Mason' (73-74); recent movies include PLEASURE COVE (78), MATILDA (78) and ANY WHICH WAY YOU CAN (80).

ALEC GUINNESS

There can be surely few distinguished stage actors who can also look back on their film career with equal pride and pleasure as Sir Alec Guinness. He was born in London on 2 April 1914, the son of a banker. An only child, his parents separated, and he did not see his father after the age of eight. Receiving his education at Pembroke Lodge, Southbourne and Rodborough, Eastbourne, it was at the latter town that he started going to the theatre and decided upon acting as a career. However, upon leaving school he worked for a few months with an advertising agency while studying drama at the Fay Compton School and was encouraged by John Gielgud. Guinness made his stage début on 2 April 1934 with a walk-on role in 'Libel!' at the Playhouse Theatre and later that year played in Gielgud's production of 'Hamlet' and thus began his distinguished career in the British theatre, being particularly remembered for his work with the Old Vic (including world tours). In 1938 he wed actress Merula Salaman and they have one son, Matthew, who is a successful stage actor. During the war he served in the Royal Navy, eventually given a commission, a ship, a crew of 20 and saw action in the Mediterranean. After the war his stage career continued to go from strength to strength and he acted in his first movie, GREAT EXPECTATIONS (46), as Herbert Pocket (a reference source credits EVENSONG (33) as his first film, he probably appeared as an extra), and other successes immediately followed — OLIVER TWIST (48, as Fagin); KIND HEARTS AND CORONETS (49, playing eight roles); A RUN FOR YOUR MONEY (49); LAST HOLIDAY (50); THE MUDLARK (50, as Disraeli); THE LAVENDER HILL MOB (51, Oscar nom.); THE MAN IN THE WHITE SUIT (51); THE CARD (52); THE CAPTAIN'S PARADISE (52); THE MALTA STORY (53); FATHER BROWN (54); TO PARIS WITH LOVE (54); THE PRISONER (55); THE LADYKILLERS (55); THE SWAN (56) and BARNACLE BILL (57). Many of his best-remembered roles were in Ealing comedies, in retrospect some of the best produced in Britain. In 1957 Guinness deservedly won an Oscar for essaying the role of Col. Nicholson in THE BRIDGE OVER THE RIVER KWAI and in 1959 he received a Knighthood for his services to the acting profession. Theatre awards continued in 1960 for his work in 'Ross' in London and for 'Dylan' on Broadway in 1964. Further films included THE HORSES MOUTH (58), TUNES OF GLORY (60); LAWRENCE OF ARABIA (62); DOCTOR ZHIVAGO (66); CROMWELL (69, as Charles I); HITLER: THE LAST 10 DAYS (73, title role) and the fabulously successful STAR WARS (76). He was back in the West End in 1978 for 'The Old Country' and two years later, in Hollywood, received a Lifetime Achievement Oscar 'for advancing the art of screen acting'. He was back on the big screen in LOVESICK (83), and a poll conducted by Britain's 'Sunday Telegraph Magazine' voted him 'Most Liked Actor', obviously due to his work in the B.B.C. T.V. series, 'Tinker, Tailor, Soldier, Spy' (80, BA: T.V. Critics', BAFTA Awards) and 'Smiley's People' (82, BA: BAFTA Award).
ALEC GUINNESS by Kenneth Tynan; Rockliff: London, 1953.
ALEC GUINNESS ON THE SCREEN by Allan Hunter; Polygon Books: Edinburgh, 1982.

GENE HACKMAN

A dynamic and versatile actor of the 1970s, culminating in his Oscar-winning performance for THE FRENCH CONNECTION, Gene Hackman has had a long and hard struggle to reach the top of his profession. He was born in San Bernardino, California on 1 January 1931, the son of Eugene Ezra Hackman and his wife, Lydia. When he was 13 his parents separated, and his father, a newspaper reporter, returned the family to Danville, Illinois, where young Eugene Alden Hackman, to give his full name, remained with his mother. At the age of 16 he lied about his age, joined the Marines and went to Tsingtu, China, where he worked as a disc-jockey at his unit's radio station. Upon leaving the forces he worked for a number of radio and T.V. stations 'in the boondocks', then moved to New York to study acting. Struggling to get his first break in the theatre, he took a number of jobs including a Howard Johnson doorman in Times Square and furniture removal man. In 1956 he wed a bank secretary, Fay Maltese, and they have three children — Christopher, Elizabeth and Leslie. Gene eventually won roles on Broadway in 'Chaparral' (1958), 'The Saintliness of Margery Kempe' (1959), 'A Rainy Day in Newark' (1963) and small roles in T.V.: 'Brenner', 'The Naked City', 'Defenders', etc. but his role in Irwin Shaw's 'Children From Their Games' on Broadway in 1963 won him a Clarence Derwent award (although it folded after 1 performance) and was seen by director Robert Bresson who gave him his first movie role in LILITH (64). He was a great success on Broadway in the leading role as Cass Henderson in 'Any Wednesday' (1964) and after 'The National Look' and 'The Basement' (both 1967) he has concentrated on such movies as HAWAII (66); A COVENANT WITH DEATH (67); BANNING (67); BONNIE & CLYDE (67, Oscar nom. BSA); THE GYPSY MOTHS (68); MAROONED (69); DOWNHILL RACER (69); DOCTORS' WIVES (71); PRIME CUT (72); won an Oscar as 'Popeye' Doyle in THE FRENCH CONNECTION (72); THE POSEIDON ADVENTURE (73); SCARECROW (74); BITE THE BULLET (74); YOUNG FRANKENSTEIN (75); FRENCH CONNECTION II (75); LUCKY LADY (75); NIGHT MOVES (76); A BRIDGE TOO FAR (76); DOMINO PRINCIPLE (77) and MARCH OR DIE (77). He gained a further Oscar nomination for his work in I NEVER SANG FOR MY FATHER (71) and his own production company is known as Chelly Ltd. Mr Hackman's most recent movies are SUPERMAN (78); NIGHT PEOPLE (80); SUPERMAN II, REDS (both 81); UNDER FIRE, MISUNDERSTOOD (both 82) and EUREKA (83).

JULIE HAGERTY – *see page 123*

LARRY HAGMAN

B. Weatherford, Texas 21.9.31. Parents Ben Hagman, lawyer, and Mary Martin, musical stage star; ed.: 16 schools, including military school and Bard Coll., where he studied drama; stage début: Margo Jones Theatre, Dallas, winter 1949; summer season, Woodstock; 2 seasons with John Terrell Music Circus; London, mother's show 'South Pacific', in chorus 1951; Nat. Serv.—U.S. Air Force, based in G.B.—sent to France, Italy, N. Germany; in 50s appd. in several Broadway productions; md. Maj Lansing, former designer (Swedish) 1954, 1 daughter Heidi, 1 son Preston; several T.V. series: 'I Dream of Jeannie' (65-70), 'The Good Life' (71/72), 'Here We Go Again' (73) and from 1978 has played 'J.R. Ewing' in the highly successful 'Dallas' series, making him a household name; support in numerous films, including: FAIL SAFE (64), THE CAVERN (65), THE GROUP (66), STARDUST (74), HARRY & TONTO (74), THE EAGLE HAS LANDED (76); directed/acted SON OF BLOB (72); many T.V. movies; recent movies: S.O.B. (81); DEADLY ENCOUNTER (82).

KENNETH HAIGH

B. Mexborough, Yorkshire 25.3.31. Ed. Gunnersbury Grammar School, London; studied for the stage at Central School; had previously done National Service and worked as builder's labourer; stage début in 'Othello', Drogheda, Eire, 1952; rep. London, Regent's Park; tremendous success 1956/57 season at Royal Court Theatre, esp. as Jimmy Porter in 'Look Back in Anger', also played New York and toured in this production; Mr Haigh has appeared mainly on stage and T.V., making few films, these have included MY TEENAGE DAUGHTER (56), HIGH FLIGHT (56), SAINT JOAN (57, as Brother Martin), CLEOPATRA (63, as Brutus), A HARD DAY'S NIGHT (64), THE DEADLY AFFAIR (66), A LOVELY WAY TO GO (68), EAGLE IN A CAGE (71), MAN AT THE TOP (73, spin-off of his highly successful T.V. series), WALKING IN THE SUN (78, Sweden) and THE BITCH (79); md. model Myrna Stephens; recently acted with success on Broadway and Canada; Mr Haigh lectures on drama at Yale Univ., U.S., where he is an honorary professor; recent T.V.: 'Feelifax' (80, BBC); George Joseph Smith in 'Ladykillers' (81); 'Troilus & Cressida' (81); stage: title role, 'Othello' (82).

GEORGINA HALE

B. Ilford, Essex 4.8.43. Miss Hale has played such stage roles as Eliza in 'Pygmalion' (Thorndyke Theatre, Leatherhead), Nina in 'The Seagull' (at Derby) and Melanie in 'Boo Hoo' (Open Space Theatre). A popular T.V. actress, her appearances include Jean in 'Budgie' (71), as Solange in 'George Sand' (series), several 'Plays For Today' (BBC), 'Jubilee: Street Party' (BBC) and 'Crown Court'. She came to the screen as Phillipe in THE DEVILS in 1971 and has been seen in THE BOYFRIEND (71), BUTLEY (73), MAHLER (74, Most Promising Newcomer aw., BAFTA), IT'S A TWO FEET SIX INCHES ABOVE THE GROUND WORLD (74), VALENTINO (76), SWEENEY 2 (77), THE WORLD IS FULL OF MARRIED MEN (79), McVICAR (80), A WATCHER IN THE WOODS (80), THE WAITING ROOM (81). More recent T.V. has included 'Lady Killers' (as Ruth Ellis), 'Hammer's House of Horrors' (both 1980), 'Eden End' (81) and stage: 'Steaming' (1981/82, London, S.W.E.T. nom.: Best Comedy Actress), 'Summit Conference' (82).

MARK HAMILL

B. Oakland, California 25.9.52. One of seven children, Mark's father was a U.S. Navy Captain; ed. San Diego and San Jose, Calif.; Annandale and Williamsburg, Virg., New York City and H.S. Yokosuke & Yokohama, Japan; when in the 7th grade, appd. in school play and decided to become an actor, studied to be a theatre arts major at K.A. City Coll.; 1st T.V. appearnce: 'Bill Bosby Show' (70) and has since appeared in approx. 148 U.S. T.V. shows, including 9 months in ABC's 'General Hospital', as Doobie Wheeler in 'The Texas Wheelers' (74), 'The FBI', 'Owen Marshall', several T.V. movies including 'Sarah T—Confessions of a Teenage Alcoholic', 'Mallory', 'Delancy Street' and 'Eric'; provided voices for T.V. cartoon series 'Jeannie'; became overnight star in movie STAR WARS (76) as Luke Skywalker; md. Marilou York, a dental hygienist, 1 son: Nathan; movies: STINGRAY (77), CORVETTE SUMMER (78), THE BIG RED ONE (78), THE EMPIRE STRIKES BACK (79) and THE NIGHT THE LIGHTS WENT OUT IN GEORGIA (81); stage 1983: 'Amadeus'; RETURN OF THE JEDI (83).

GEORGE HAMILTON

B. Memphis, Tennessee 12.8.39(?). Parents: George William Hamilton (former composer of Broadway musicals), and his wife, Anne, a society lady; real name: George Stevens Hamilton; ed. at 25 schools including: Hawthorne, Calif., Military School, Gulfport, Miss., N.Y. Hackley Prep School and Palm Beach H.S., Florida. At latter George won Best Actor Award for State of Florida; through Mae Murray, friend of family, met top executive at MGM, New York, tested for movie AUNTIE MAME, made T.V. debut in small role in 'Rin Tin Tin' epis. and others, came to screen in 1958 in independent movie, CRIME & PUNISHMENT, USA, resulting in MGM contract; movies include: HOME FROM THE HILL (60), WHERE THE BOYS ARE (60), A THUNDER OF DRUMS (61), LIGHT IN THE PIAZZA (61), THE VICTORS (63), ACT ONE (63), VIVA MARIA (65), LONG RIDE HOME (67), THE POWER (68); md. Alana Collins 1972, 1 son Ashley Steven (b. 1974), div. 1976; Mr Hamilton has business interests in South, including 400 acre plantation; EVEL KNIEVEL (72), THE MAN WHO LOVED CAT DANCING (73), ONCE IS NOT ENOUGH (75), LOVE AT FIRST BITE (78, also co-prod.), FROM HELL TO VICTORY (78), THE USERS (78, T.V. movie), ZORRO—THE GAY BLADE (80); T.V. series including Duncan Carlyle in 'The Survivors' (69), Jack Brennan in 'Paris 7000' (70) and 'Roots' (77).

HARRY HAMLIN

B. Pasadena, California, . .52. Ed. private schools, L.A. and Pennsylvania; majored in theatre at Univ. of California, Berkeley and grad. from Yale 1974, with Degrees in Psychology and Theatre; 2 years American Conservatory Theatre, San Francisco, then acting début with them in 'Equus', others; came to screen in MOVIE, MOVIE (78); played in mini-series, 'Studs Lonigan' (1978); one son, Dmitri Alexandre, born 19.5.80, mother actress Ursula Andress (qv); other movies: CLASH OF THE TITANS (81); KING OF THE MOUNTAIN (81); MAKING LOVE (81); BLUE SKIES AGAIN (82).

SUSAN HAMPSHIRE

B. London 12.5.41(?). Originally trained in classical ballet at her mother's 'Hampshire School', Knightsbridge, but had made her screen debut as a girl in the WOMAN IN THE HALL (47) after being 'discovered' on London tube with her mother by a casting director; joined Festival Ballet at 15, danced Paris and N.Y.; worked West End store; 1957 A.S.M. at Bognor Regis Roof Garden Theatre; West End debut 1958 in 'Expresso Bongo' and has since played in many notable stage productions; movies include: UPSTAIRS & DOWNSTAIRS (59), DURING ONE NIGHT (60), LONG SHADOW (61), 3 LIVES OF THOMASINA (63), NIGHT MUST FALL (64), FIGHTING PRINCE OF DONEGAL (66), TRYGON FACTOR (67), MONTE CARLO OR BUST (69), DAVID COPPERFIELD (69), LIVING FREE (71), BAFFLED (72); md. 1. Pierre Granier-Deferre (film director) 1966, 1 son Christopher (b. 10.8.70), div. 12.9.74; 2. Eddie Kulukundis (Greek shipping owner/impresario) 5.4.81; Miss Hampshire delighted millions on T.V. with her acting as Fleur in 'The Forsyte Saga' (67, winning her U.S. Emmy aw.), 'First Churchills' (70, Emmy aw.) and 'Vanity Fair' (73, Emmy aw.); recent stage: 'Crucifer of Blood', 'Night & Day' (both West End 1979). 'The Barchester Chronicles' (T.V. ser., 1982). *SUSAN'S STORY* (autobio.); Sidgwick & Jackson: London, 1981.

IRENE HANDL

B. London 27.12.01. Father a banker; ed. Maida Vale H.S. for Girls; studied stagecraft for 1 year at Embassy School of Acting; stage début 1937 and that year had 2 years success as Beer in play 'George & Margaret' in West End; Miss Handl became well-known and much-loved character player of British films, T.V. and stage, having also toured abroad in the latter; many movies include: GIRL IN THE NEWS (41), TEMPTATION HARBOUR (46), SILENT DUST (48), ADAM & EVELYNE (50), ONE WILD OAT (51), THE BELLES OF ST. TRINIANS (54), A KID FOR TWO FARTHINGS (56), BROTHERS IN LAW (57), I'M ALRIGHT JACK (59), MAKE MINE MINK (60), THE REBEL (61), HEAVENS ABOVE (63), SMASHING TIME (67), ON A CLEAR DAY YOU CAN SEE FOREVER (70), PRIVATE LIFE OF SHERLOCK HOLMES (70), FOR THE LOVE OF ADA (72, spin-off of her T.V. series), ADVENTURES OF A PRIVATE EYE (76), THE HOUND OF THE BASKERVILLES (77), RIDING HIGH (81). IT'S YOUR MOVE (T.V. movie, 1982). IT'S YOUR MOVE (T.V. movie, 1982); Miss Handl has acted with the Nat. Theatre and as a writer works include 'The Sioux'; recent stage: 'Hedda Gabler' (82); in 1983 she received a special Variety Club Award for her contribution to British show-business'.

49

GERALD HARPER

B. London 15.2.29. Ed. Haileybury; original intention to become doctor; Nat. Service; R.A.D.A. 1949-51; much theatre, including debut 1951 in 'How He Lied to Her Husband', Liverpool Rep., tours, Old Vic, New York, Bristol Old Vic etc.; small roles in films ADMIRABLE CRICHTON (57), A NIGHT TO REMEMBER (58), LEAGUE OF GENTLEMEN (59), TUNES OF GLORY (60), PUNCH & JUDY MAN (63), WONDERFUL LIFE (65); md. 1. actress Jane Downs, 1 daughter Sarah Jane (div.), 2. Carla ———, 1 son Jamie; very popular on T.V. in such series as 'Skyport' (60), 'Adam Adamant' (66), 'Gazette' (68) and esp. 'Hadleigh' (sev. series 1969); has own prog. on 'Capital Radio'; recent T.V.: 'The Flockton Flyer' (78), 'Crown Court' (79); stage: 'Crucifer of Blood' (79/80), 'A Personal Affair' (82); movie: THE LADY VANISHES (78).

JULIUS W. HARRIS

A Broadway actor, he has appd. in 'The Amen Corner' (65), 'Bohikee Creek' (66), 'God Is a (Guess What?)' (68), 'String' (69), others and the movies NOTHING BUT A MAN (65), LIVE & LET DIE (72), SUPERFLY (72), TROUBLE MAN (72), SHAFT'S BIG SCORE (72), BLACK CAESAR (73), THE TAKING OF PELHAM 123 (74), VICTORY AT ENTEBBE (76, as Idi Amin), ISLANDS IN THE STREAM (77) and LOOKING FOR MR GOODBAR (77). Mr Harris appeared in the T.V. series 'Salty' in 1974, has guested in 'Cagney & Lacey' (83), etc.; several T.V. movies.

JESSICA HARPER – *see page 123*

VALERIE HARPER – *see page 123*

BARBARA HARRIS

B. Evanston, Illinois, . .37. Real name Sandra Markowitz; ed. Wright Junior Coll., Chicago, Goodman School of Theatre and the Univ. of Chicago; acted with several companies including: 'The Compass', Playwrights Theatre (Chicago 1959), Second City (Chicago 1960); New York début 1961 in 'From the Second City', becoming well-known for her stage roles, winning several awards, including her role as Rosalie in 'Oh, Dad, Poor Dad, Mama's Hung You in the Closet and I'm Feeling So Sad' (Obie aw.; movie version in 1966) and 4 roles in 'The Apple Tree' (Tony aw. 1966); Miss Harris came to the screen in 1965 in A THOUSAND CLOWNS and has been seen in WHO IS HARRY KELLERMAN AND WHY IS HE SAYING THOSE TERRIBLE THINGS ABOUT ME? (71, Oscar nom., BSA), PLAZA SUITE (71), THE WAR BETWEEN MEN AND WOMEN (72), MIXED COMPANY (74), NASHVILLE (75), FAMILY PLOT (76), MOVIE, MOVIE (78), SECONDHAND HEARTS (78), HILL'S ANGELS (79); other stage work includes 'Dynamie Tonight' (64), 'On a Clear Day You Can See Forever' (65) and 'Mahogonny' (70).

RICHARD HARRIS

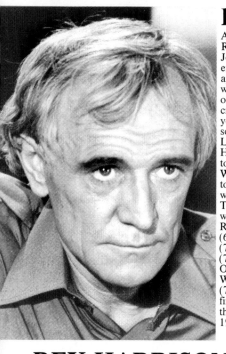

Although his recent screen roles have lacked the acclaim which brought him rapidly to the top in the early 60s, rugged Richard Harris has remained a popular screen actor, working internationally in a wide range of parts. Born Richard St. John Harris at Limerick, Ireland on 1 (31?) October 1933, he is the son of Ivan and Mildred Harris and at school he excelled at all sports, especially rugby, and his brother, Dermot, recalled that Richard 'was a mild, agreeable boy, and apart from sport, was only interested in movies'. In 1956 he won a place at London's Academy of Music and Drama, but within a year he was anxious to make headway in the profession, and, placing most of his savings in his own production of Clifford Odet's 'Country Girl' (performed under the title 'Winter Journey') it was staged at the Irving Theatre to critical acclaim, but flopped, and the actor was forced to 'sleep in a coal cellar for a while'. In the cast of his play was a young actress and deb., Elizabeth Rees-Williams (the daughter of Lord Ogmore), the couple wed in 1957 and had three sons — Damien (in 1958), Jared (in 1961) and Jamie (in 1964). Harris's career got under way when he joined Joan Littlewood's Theatre Workshop, playing in 'The Quare Fellow' and gaining a lead role in a T.V. play, 'The Iron Harp'. His effective performance was seen by a casting director for Associated-British and he landed a movie contract, coming to the screen in ALIVE & KICKING (58). He played minor roles in SHAKE HANDS WITH THE DEVIL (59), WRECK OF THE MARY DEARE (59), went to New York to appear in a T.V. play 'The Hasty Heart' and continued to work on the stage in 'A View From the Bridge', 'Man, Beast and Virtue' and 'Macbeth', touring Russia and E. Europe with the Old Vic Co. Following better film roles in THE LONG, THE SHORT & THE TALL (61), MUTINY ON THE BOUNTY (62), he was cast by Lindsay Anderson in THIS SPORTING LIFE (63) as a rugby player; the role won him acclaim and an Oscar nomination. His many movies since then have included THE BIBLE (65, as Cain); RED DESERT (65); MAJOR DUNDEE (65); HEROES OF TELEMARK (65); CAPRICE (66); CAMELOT (67, as King Arthur); THE MOLLY MAGUIRES (69); CROMWELL (70, title role); A MAN CALLED HORSE (70); BLOOMFIELD (71, also directed); THE SNOW GOOSE (71, T.V. movie); THE DEADLY TRACKERS (73); JUGGERNAUT (75); ROBIN AND MARIAN (75, as King Richard); GULLIVER'S TRAVELS (76); ORCA—THE KILLER WHALE (77); THE WILD GEESE (77); GOLDEN RENDEZVOUS (77); THE LAST WORD (78); HIGH POINT (79); YOUR TICKET IS NO LONGER VALID (79); GAMES FOR VULTURES (79); TARZAN THE APE MAN (81) and TRIUMPHS OF A MAN CALLED HORSE (82). Divorced from his first wife in July, 1969, Mr Harris wed model/actress Ann Turkel in 1974 but this marriage ended in 1981. Recently, in the States, he replaced Richard Burton as King Arthur in a stage revival of 'Camelot', in which he also played in London, 1982/83.

REX HARRISON

Rex Harrison is well admired and respected for his sophisticated playing in the movies and on the stage, culminating in his unique portrayal of Professor Higgins in 'My Fair Lady', a role he has recently returned to, in his 73rd year. The son of William Harrison and his wife, Edith, he was born in Huyton, Lancashire on 5 March 1908. Educated at Liverpool College, he joined the Liverpool Repertory Company at the age of 16, remaining there for three years, engaged as a student and doing walk-on roles. He then toured for three years (including 'Charley's Aunt') and in 1930 he first appeared in the West End and also came to the screen in THE GREAT GAME and THE SCHOOL FOR SCANDAL. In the 1930s he developed into a popular stage actor in London and New York, including over a year's run in FRENCH WITHOUT TEARS, married model Collette Thomas in 1934 (son Noel being born in 1935), and playing in such movies as GET YOUR MAN (34), STORM IN A TEACUP (37), THE CITADEL (38), NIGHT TRAIN TO MUNICH (40) and MAJOR BARBARA (40). During the war he served in the R.A.F.V.R., divorced his first wife in 1942, wed actress Lilli Palmer a year later and their son, Carey, was born in 1944. In 1945 he made the movies BLITHE SPIRIT and I LIVE IN GROSVENOR SQUARE and after THE RAKE'S PROGRESS (46) he went to the States to embark on a highly successful career there in such stage productions as Henry VIII in 'Anne of the 1000 Days' (1948/49, winning Tony Award), 'Bell, Book & Candle' (1950) and 'The Love of Four Colonels' (1953, also directing) and movies ANNA AND THE KING OF SIAM (46), THE GHOST AND MRS MUIR (47) and UNFAITHFULLY YOURS (48). In the 1950s his films included THE FOURPOSTER (52), KING RICHARD & THE CRUSADERS (54, as Saladin), THE CONSTANT HUSBAND (55) and THE RELUCTANT DEBUTANTE (58, opp. his 3rd wife, Kay Kendall, whom he wed in 1957 — she died tragically of leukaemia in 1959). On the stage he directed 'Nina' in London in 1955, directed/appeared in 'Bell, Book and Candle', London, for over 1 year and in March 1956 appeared in 'My Fair Lady' as Professor Higgins, the musical running on Broadway for 2 years, staying with the show in London for several months (winning an Academy Award in 1964 when the production was filmed). Oscar nominated for his Julius Caesar in the movie CLEOPATRA (63), he wed Rachel Roberts (qv) in Genoa on 21 March 1962. They divorced in 1971; that year he wed Elizabeth Harris on 26 August, but this marriage was ended on 16 December 1975. He has continued his stage career with great success, winning several awards, and his other movies have included THE YELLOW ROLLS-ROYCE (64); AGONY AND THE ECSTASY (65); DOCTOR DOLITTLE (67); STAIRCASE (69); DON QUIXOTE (72, T.V. movie); PRINCE AND THE PAUPER (76); SHALIMAR (77); ASHANTI (78); THE FIFTH MUSKETEER (78). Mr Harrison wed Swiss-born Mercia Tinker in December, 1978, and he recently played on T.V. in 'The Kingfisher' (82) and a tour/London production of 'Heartbreak House' (83).
REX (autobiography); MacMillan: London, 1974.

LISA HARROW

B. Auckland, New Zealand, . .43. Trained R.A.D.A. 1966-68; BBC radio rep., then joined R.S. Co. in February 1969, playing many roles for them, including Portia, and lectured in the U.S.A.; Lisa's films include THE TEMPTER (73); ALL CREATURES GREAT AND SMALL (74); IT SHOULDN'T HAPPEN TO A VET (75); THE FINAL CONFLICT (81); A MAN FROM A FAR COUNTRY (80); her T.V. includes 'The Expert', 'Miss Julie', 'Space 1990', 'The Professionals', 'Dr Jekyl and Mr Hyde', title role of 'Nancy Astor' (1982), 'Under Capricorn' (82, series); stage 1982: 'Man & Superman'.

GOLDIE HAWN

B. Washington D.C. 21.11.45; Full name: Goldie Jean Hawn; daughter of Edward Rutledge Hawn, musician, and his wife, Laura; aged 3, tap/ballet lessons, adding modern jazz to her repertoire at 11; at 18 operated successful dancing school with 150 pupils; studied drama in evenings; joined chorus of group at New York World's Fair; toured in 'Guys & Dolls', 'Kiss Me Kate', others; appeared as dancer on 'Andy Griffith Uptown-Downtown Show', discovered by agent Art Simon, given role of Sandy in short-lived series 'Good Morning, World' (67/68), then fabulous success 1968-70 as dumb blondie character on 'Rowan & Martin's Laugh-in', U.S. T.V.; md. 1. writer/ director/producer Gus Trikonis in May 1969 (div. 1973), 2. Bill Hudson 1976, 1 son Oliver (b. 1976), 1 daughter Kate (b. 1979); movies: THE ONE AND ONLY GENUINE ORIGINAL FAMILY BAND (68), CACTUS FLOWER (69, Oscar, BSA), THERE'S A GIRL IN MY SOUP (70), BUTTERFLIES ARE FREE (72), DOLLARS (72), SUGARLAND EXPRESS (73), THE GIRL FROM PETROVKA (74), SHAMPOO (75), THE DUCHESS AND THE DIRTWATER FOX (76), FOUL PLAY (77), SEEMS LIKE OLD TIMES (80) and PRIVATE BENJAMIN (80), on which Miss Hawn was executive producer and received an Oscar nomination. Voted 'Film Star of the Year 1982' by U.S. Nat. Assoc. of Theatre Owners. Recent movies: JUST FRIENDS (82); SWING SHIFT (83).

HELEN HAYES

B. Washington, D.C., 10.10.1900(?). Real name Helen Brown; ed. Sacred Heart Convent, Washington; began career as child, 1905, becoming one of America's most distinguished actresses; md. 1. Charles MacArthur, writer, 1928 (dec. 1956), 1 daughter Mary (1930-49), 1 adopted son James, successful actor; Miss Hayes came to the screen in 1917 in THE WEAVERS OF LIFE and has been seen in BABS (20); THE SIN OF MADELON CLAUDET (31, Oscar B.A.); ARROWSMITH (31); A FAREWELL TO ARMS (32); THE SON DAUGHTER (33); THE WHITE SISTER (33); ANOTHER LANGUAGE (33); NIGHT FLIGHT (33); WHAT EVERY WOMEN KNOWS (34); VANESSA (35); STAGE DOOR CANTEEN (43); MY SON JOHN (51); MAIN STREET TO BROADWAY (53); ANASTASIA (56); AIRPORT (70, Oscar BSA); DO NOT FOLD, SPINDLE OR MUTILATE (71, T.V. movie); HERBIE RIDES AGAIN (73); THE SNOOP SISTERS (73, T.V. movie and series (1973/74)); ONE OF OUR DINOSAURS IS MISSING (75); THE MONEY CHANGERS (76, mini-series); VICTORY AT ENTEBBE (76, T.V. movie); CANDLESHOE (77); A FAMILY UPSIDE DOWN (78, T.V. movie); MURDER IS EASY (81, T.V. movie); she has acted on the stage internationally and numerous honours include Doctor of Fine Arts from Princeton Univ., 1956. *ON REFLECTION* (autobio.); W.H. Allen: London, 1969.

DAVID HEDISON

B. Providence, Rhode Island 20.5.28. Real name Ara Heditsian; father a jeweller; when a youngster, saw a Ty Power movie 4 times, decided to become actor, but at 17 enlisted in U.S. Navy, on discharge attended Browne Univ., Providence, was door-to-door brush salesman to finance acting lessons; career commenced with New York Neighborhood School and debut off-Broadway in 'A Phoenix Too Frequent'; was radio announcer and on Broadway in 'Much Ado About Nothing' (52), eventually winning Most Promising Newcomer award for 'A Month in the Country' (56); movies THE ENEMY BELOW, THE FLY (58), SON OF ROBIN HOOD (59); up to this time known as 'Al' Hedison; T.V. includes: Victor Sebastian in 'Five Fingers' (59) and well-known as Capt. Lee Crane in 'Voyage to the Bottom of the Sea' (64-68); other movies include: LOST WORLD (60), MARINE'S LET GO (61), THE GREATEST STORY EVER TOLD (65, as Philip, the Apostle), KEMEK (69), LIVE & LET DIE (72), ADVENTURES OF THE QUEEN (75, T.V. movie), POWER WITHIN (79, T.V. movie), NORTH SEA HIJACK (79); frequent guest star U.S. & British T.V. series.

NIGEL HAVERS

B.   , 6.11.50. Nigel's father is Attorney General Sir Michael Havers, Q.C.; trained at the Arts Educational Trust; stage includes Prospect Theatre Co., Bristol Old Vic, R.S. Co.; much T.V. includes 'Edward II', 'Upstairs, Downstairs', 'The Glittering Prizes', 'A Horseman Riding By', 'After the Party', Randolph Churchill in 'Winston Churchill: The Wilderness Years' (1981) and acclaim as the son in 'Nancy Astor' (1982, series); film work includes POPE JOAN (72); FULL CIRCLE (78); TOO MANY CHEFS (78); BIRTH OF THE BEATLES (79); Lord Andrew Lindsey in CHARIOTS OF FIRE (81). Md: Carolyn, 1 daughter; recent stage: 'Importance of Being Ernest' (82).

STERLING HAYDEN

B. Montclair, New Jersey 26.3.16. Real name John Hamilton; ed. Browne & Nichols School, Cambridge, Mass; of Dutch-English descent, Mr Hayden's education was cut short at the age of 15 by finance, so he went to sea for 9 years: sailed U.S. Atlantic coast aboard schooner for 25 cents a month, subsequently sailing the 7 seas in 2/3 masted sailing ships (enduring 5 hurricanes), navigated U.S.'s fastest racing schooner and dug for buried treasure in the Galapagos Islands; lost all his money as part-owner of a ship and accepted a movie contract after friend had sent his photos to agent; md. 1. actress Madeleine Carroll, 1937-46; came to screen in VIRGINIA (40). After BAHAMA PASSAGE (41) returned to sea and during WWII served in U.S. Marine Corps; md. 2. Betty Ann de Noon 1947-55(?), 1 son Christian, 2 daughters Dana, Gretchen; many films include: EL PASO (49), ASPHALT JUNGLE (50), DENVER & THE RIO GRANDE (52), SO BIG (53), PRINCE VALIANT (54), JOHNNY GUITAR (54), THE LAST COMMAND (55, as Jim Bowie), THE KILLING (56), ZERO HOUR (57), DR STRANGELOVE (63), THE GODFATHER (72); md. 3. Catherine McConnell 1960, 1 son Matthew (b. 1961); recent movies: 1900 (77), WINTER KILLS (79), KING OF THE GYPSIES (79), THE OUTSIDER (79), THE FORMULA (80), VENOM (81), GAS (81).
THE WANDERER (autobiography); Longmans: London, 1964.

ROBERT HAYS

B. San Diego, California, . .48. Ed. San Diego State College; Mr Hays began his stage career with the Globe Theatre, San Diego, appearing for eight seasons; his T.V. movies include YOUNG PIONEERS, YOUNG PIONEERS' CHRISTMAS (both 76); DELTA COUNTY, USA (77); THE INITIATION OF SARAH (78) and he has played in such movies as AIRPLANE! (80); UTILITIES (81); TAKE THIS JOB AND SHOVE IT (81); SOME SUNNY DAY (82); TRENCHCOAT (82); AIRPLANE II: THE SEQUEL (82); in 1981 he formed his own production company. NOEE: SCANDALOUS (83).

DAVID HEMMINGS

B. Guildford, Surrey 18.11.41. Only son of sales manager for stationery firm; won cups for singing at school — aged 12 boy soprano in 'The Turn of the Screw', Venice, appd. with English Opera group; had wanted to be a scientist, but left school at 13; radio plays, came to screen as youngster in children's films: THE HEART WITHIN, 5 CLUES TO FORTUNE (57, both); repertory including Leicester; md. 1. actress Jenny Lewes (Mr Hemmings wed when he was 18), 1 daughter Deborah (she already had son, Dominic); stage includes Dylan Thomas in 'Adventures in the Skin Trade'; many movies include: SOME PEOPLE (60), 2 LEFT FEET (63), THE SYSTEM (64), EYE OF THE DEVIL (65); big break and super-stardom in BLOW-UP (66), CAMELOT (67, as Mordred), CHARGE OF THE LIGHT BRIGADE (68), A LONG DAY'S DYING (68); md. 2. actress Gayle Hunnicutt (qv) 1968, 1 son Nolan. div. 1974: ALFRED THE GREAT (69), THE WALKING STICK (69), UNMAN, WITTERING & ZIGO (70), others; formed company Hemdale: directed only: RUNNING SCARED (72), THE 14 (73), THE SURVIVOR (80), RACE FOR THE YANKEE ZEPHYR (81): acted: JUGGERNAUT (74), QUILP (74), THE SQUEEZE (77), COUP D'ETAT (77), DISAPPEARANCE (77), THIRST (77), JUST A GIGOLO (78), MURDER BY DECREE (78), CHARLIE MUFFIN (79, T.V. movie), HARLEQUIN (79); recent T.V.: lead as 'Dr Jekyll & Mr Hyde' (80); Mr Hemmings wed 19 March 1976 Pru de Casembroot, his former secretary: PRISONERS (82, N.Z., also co-produced); MAN, WOMAN & CHILD (83).

IAN HENDRY

B. Ipswich, Suffolk, 13.1.31. Ed. Culford Coll., Suffolk; father a provender miller; good sportsman, ran motor-cycle stunt team, considered auctioneering, but commenced career as stooge to Coco the Clown; Nat. Serv.; Central School Speech & Drama; Rep. including Hornchurch, Worthing, etc. stage success: 'Dinner With the Family'; came to screen uncredited ROOM AT THE TOP (57); md. 1. Joanna (div.); star of T.V.: 'The Avengers' (1st series), 'The Informer', etc.; many movies: IN THE NICK (61), became a star with LIVE NOW, PAY LATER (63), CHILDREN OF THE DAMNED (63), BEAUTY JUNGLE (64), THE HILL (65), others; md. 2. actress Janet Munro (dec.), 2 daughters: Sally, Alexandra; T.V. series: 'The Lotus Eaters'; many movies include: DOPPEL-GANGER (69), CARTER (70), TALES FROM THE CRYPT (72), THEATRE OF BLOOD (73), ASSASSIN (73), THE BITCH (79); Mr Hendry's 3rd wife is former nanny, Sandy, and they have a daughter, Emma Claire.

NICKY HENSON

B. London 12.5.45. 2nd son of British stage actor/comedian, the late Leslie Henson; ed: St. Bede's, Eastbourne & Charterhouse; studied stage management at RADA, but made state début as guitarist in 1961; well-known on British stage, work includes: London début 1963 'All Square', Mordred in musical 'Camelot' (64), 'Passion Flower Hotel' (65), Edinburgh Festival, tours, founder-member Young Vic Co. (appd. in 'Waiting for Godot', 'Romeo & Juliet' etc.), Broadway, Hong Kong Festival, R.S.C.; md. Una Stubbs, actress/dancer, 2 sons: Christian, Joe (div.); Mr Henson has appd. many times on T.V.; movies include: WITCHFINDER GENERAL (67), MOSQUITO SQUADRON (70), THERE'S A GIRL IN MY SOUP (70), THE LOVE BAN (72), VAMPIRA (74), ADVENTURES OF TOM JONES (75), NO.1 OF THE SECRET SERVICE (77); recent T.V.: 'Seagull Island' (79), guest 'Fawlty Towers' (79, BBC), ITV play 'Double Dealer' (80); recent stage: London: 'Rookery Nook' (79), Frederick Treves in 'The Elephant Man' (81, Lyttleton Theatre), 'Noises Off' (82, Savoy).

AUDREY HEPBURN

Audrey Hepburn, an actress with a natural refreshing beauty, has been in motion-pictures for thirty years, making comparatively few movies, but her roles have been selected wisely, being recognised by the Academy on four occasions. She was born Audrey Hepburn-Ruston on an estate near Brussels in Belgium on 4 May 1929, her parents being Joseph Anthony Hepburn-Ruston, a businessman of English-Irish ancestry, and Ella van Heemstra, a Dutch baroness. Her grandfather was Baron Arnond van Heemstra, at one time Governor of Surinam in Dutch Guiana. Miss Hepburn's parents divorced when she was 10, she was sent to boarding school in England, but when the war broke out returned to live with her mother in Holland, attended school under a Dutch name when the Germans invaded, and studied ballet in Arnhem. Behind locked doors she performed concerts to raise money for the Resistance and witnessed much tragedy under occupation. When the war ceased she continued her ballet studies in Amsterdam and later came to London in 1948 to study at the Marie Lambert Ballet School, making her professional début in the chorus of 'High Button Shoes'. She then had a small part and solo dance in Cecil Landeau's 'Sauce Tartare' and 'Sauce Piquante' respectively, scoring a success in the latter and was discovered for the big screen by Mario Zampi, débuting with small roles in LAUGHTER IN PARADISE (51), THE LAVENDER HILL MOB (51) and YOUNG WIVES' TALE (51). Coached in drama by actor Felix Aylmer, she gained her first lead role in Thorold Dickinson's THE SECRET PEOPLE (52) and while filming MONTE CARLO BABY (52) in France she was selected by Colette to play 'Gigi' on Broadway and when the play opened on 24 November 1951, it was an instant success. William Wyler tested her and gave her the role of the touring European princess who temporarily flees from stuffy palace duties for a ROMAN HOLIDAY (52), and for her performance Miss Hepburn won an Academy Award in 1953. Her other films included SABRINA FAIR* (54); WAR AND PEACE (56); FUNNY FACE (57); LOVE IN THE AFTERNOON (57); THE NUN'S STORY* (59); GREEN MANSIONS (59); THE UNFORGIVEN (60); BREAKFAST AT TIFFANY'S* (61); THE CHILDREN'S HOUR (62); CHARADE (63); PARIS WHEN IT SIZZLES (64); MY FAIR LADY (65, as Eliza); HOW TO STEAL A MILLION (66); TWO FOR THE ROAD (67); WAIT UNTIL DARK* (67) and ROBIN AND MARIAN (75). She had played on Broadway in 1954 in 'Ondine', winning a 'Tony' award, wed actor/producer Mel Ferrer (qv) in Switzerland on 25 September 1954, and their son, Sean, was born in 1960. Miss Hepburn's most recent pictures are BLOODLINE (79) and THEY ALL LAUGHED (81). Divorcing Mr Ferrer in 1968, she wed Italian psychiatrist Dr Andrea Dotti in 1969, and their son, Luca, was born the following year. (* denotes Oscar nomination.)

KATHARINE HEPBURN

Now entering her fiftieth year of screen acting, Katharine Hepburn can be described as America's first ambassadress to filmdom, being honored by the Academy on no fewer than 11 occasions (four times winner) and is perhaps best remembered for her 9 films opposite the late Spencer Tracy. She was one of five children, born to Dr Thomas Norval Hepburn, a surgeon, and his wife, Katharine, on 8(9?) November 1909 at Hartford, Connecticut. Attending Hartford High School, she displayed early interests in the stage and her father had a miniature theatre built at home where she acted and wrote plays. She also excelled at all sports and went on to attend Bryn Mawr College. Her parents were against a stage career but young Katharine managed to obtain her first job in Baltimore, joining Edwin Knopf's Repertory Company. Appearing in 'The Czarina', she was advised to go to New York by Kenneth McKenna and study voice. This she did and also had tuition from Mordkin of the Russian ballet, and understudied Hope Williams and Ulla Nazimova. Although she didn't get the chance to play their roles, in 1929 she toured for 5 weeks in 'Death Takes a Holiday', played in 1930 in 'A Month in the Country' and on Broadway in 1931 had success in 'Art and Mrs Bottle', then did stock at Ivoryton. She had wed Ludlow Ogden Smith in 1928, but the marriage lasted only six years. On Broadway in 'The Warrior's Husband' (1932), as Antiope, she scored a great success and a 5 year contract with R.K.O. Studios, coming to the screen that year in BILL OF DIVORCEMENT. After CHRISTOPHER STRONG (33) Miss Hepburn won her first Oscar for MORNING GLORY (33), which had a theatrical background, and she went on to appear in such fine movies as (* denotes Oscar nom.) LITTLE WOMEN (33, as Jo); ALICE ADAMS* (35); SYLVIA SCARLETT (35); MARY OF SCOTLAND (36, title role); STAGE DOOR (37); BRINGING UP BABY (38); HOLIDAY (38); THE PHILADELPHIA STORY* (40, repeating her 1939 stage role, as Tracey Lord); DRAGON SEED (44); THE AFRICAN QUEEN* (51); SUMMERTIME* (55); THE IRON PETTICOAT (56); THE RAINMAKER* (56); SUDDENLY LAST SUMMER* (59) and LONG DAY'S JOURNEY INTO NIGHT* (62). Miss Hepburn has appeared on T.V. and made frequent excursions back to Broadway, including 'Jane Eyre' (1936/37), Rosalind in 'As You Like It' (1950) and 'The Millionairess' (London & New York 1952). Her popular movies with Spencer Tracy were WOMAN OF THE YEAR* (42); KEEPER OF THE FLAME (43); WITHOUT LOVE (45); SEA OF GRASS (47); STATE OF THE UNION (48); ADAM'S RIB (49); PAT AND MIKE (52); THE DESK SET (57) and GUESS WHO'S COMING TO DINNER? (67, for which she won an Oscar). THE LION IN WINTER (68) brought her her third Oscar and her most recent work has been TROJAN WOMEN (71); A DELICATE BALANCE (73); ROOSTER COGBURN (75); THE CORN IS GREEN (78, T.V. movie); OLLY OLLY OXEN FREE (78) and ON GOLDEN POND (81, Oscar, BA).

THE FILMS OF KATHARINE HEPBURN by Homer Dickens; Citadel: Secaucus, N.J., USA; 1971, pb.
TRACY & HEPBURN by Garson Kanin; Angus & Robertson: London, 1972.
KATE by Charles Higham; W.H. Allen: London, 1976.
KATHERINE HEPBURN by Caroline Latham; Proteus Publishing Co. Inc.: N.Y. 1982.

CHARLTON HESTON

Charlton Heston, a super-star for over thirty years, is much admired and respected by his fellow performers as well as internationally by millions of filmgoers. He is perhaps best remembered as 'King of the Epics', culminating in 1959 with his Oscar for BEN HUR. He was born Charlton Carter at Evanston, Illinois on 4 October 1924, the son of Russell Whitford Carter and his wife, Lilla. When still a youngster (with a brother and sister) his parents divorced and his mother (whose maiden name was Charlton) married Mr Chester Heston, a timber mill operator. He attended New Trier High School, Winnetka, and at an early age took a keen interest in school plays in which he performed and later won a scholarship to Northwestern University, where he concentrated on dramatic arts and appeared in a student movie, PEER GYNT (42). He wed college sweetheart, actress Lydia Clarke, in 1944 at Greensboro, N.C., and immediately served for 18 months during WWII in the U.S. Air Force as a radio operator on a B-29 stationed in the Aleutions. Resuming his acting career, it took him four years only to reach the big-time — with his wife he co-founded the Thomas Wolfe Memorial Theatre, North Carolina, appearing in such productions as 'Glass Menagerie', 'State of the Union' and 'Kiss & Tell', secured his first role on Broadway as Proculeius in 'Anthony & Cleopatra' (running from 26.11.47 to 13.3.48), played a 13 week season at Summer Theatre, Mt. Gretna, Pa., then returned to Broadway for 'Leaf & Bough', 'Cock-a-Doodle-Doo' (1949), played Marc Antony in a 16mm production of JULIUS CAESAR, and finally became a star of early T.V. drama in such 'Studio One' plays as 'Of Human Bondage', 'Jane Eyre', 'Taming of the Shrew' and 'Wuthering Heights'. Movie producer Hal Wallis offered him a flexible contract to do films, but to be free to return to the stage and T.V. and Mr. Heston duly came to the big screen in DARK CITY (50). His next picture, as the circus boss, in THE GREATEST SHOW ON EARTH (52), made him a star and his many films since have included THE SAVAGE (52); RUBY GENTRY (52); THE PRESIDENT'S LADY (52, as Andrew Jackson); PONY EXPRESS (53, as Wild Bill Hickock); ARROWHEAD (53); BAD FOR EACH OTHER (53); THE NAKED JUNGLE (54); SECRET OF THE INCAS (54); PRIVATE WAR OF MAJOR BENSON (55); LUCY GALLANT (55); THE TEN COMMANDMENTS (56, as Moses); 3 VIOLENT PEOPLE (56); TOUCH OF EVIL (58); THE BIG COUNTRY (58); THE BUCCANEER (58) and BEN HUR (59), for which he won an Oscar. He had returned to the stage in 1956, touring in 'Detective Story' (opposite his wife) and playing New York in 'Mister Roberts'. Heston's son, Fraser, was born on 12 February 1955 and appeared, aged 3 months, as the infant Moses in TEN COMMANDMENTS. They adopted a daughter, Holly Ann, in August 1961. Further films have included EL CID (61); THE PIDGEON THAT TOOK ROME (62); DIAMOND HEAD (62); 55 DAYS AT PEKING (63); THE GREATEST STORY EVER TOLD (65, as John the Baptist); MAJOR DUNDEE (65); THE AGONY & THE ECSTASY (65, as Michelangelo); THE WAR LORD (65); KHARTOUM (66, as Gen. Gordon); PLANET OF THE APES (67); WILL PENNY (68); JULIUS CAESAR (70, as Marc Antony); THE OMEGA MAN (71); ANTONY & CLEOPATRA (71, also directed); SKYJACKED (72); THE THREE MUSKETEERS (73, as Cardinal Richelieu); THE LAST HARD MEN (76); TWO-MINUTE WARNING (76); GRAY LADY DOWN (77); THE MOUNTAIN MEN (79, (scripted by his son); THE AWAKENING (79) and MOTHER LODE (82, director/star (produced/written by his son)). in 1977 Charlton Heston received the Jean Hersholt Humanitarian Award from the Academy of Motion Picture Arts & Sciences.
CHARLTON HESTON by Michael Druxman; Pyramid: N.Y., 1976.
THE FILMS OF CHARLTON HESTON by Jeff Rovin; Citadel: Secaucus, N.J., 1977; pb.
THE ACTOR'S LIFE: JOURNALS 1956-1976 (edited by Hollis Alpert); Allen Lane: London, 1979; pb: Penguin, 1980.

BARBARA HERSHEY

B. Hollywood, California, .48. Ed: Hollywood High School; real name Barbara Hertzstein; 'While I was in school an agent asked the drama department to send down anybody they thought had the ability to handle the business at that age. They sent me. I got the agent and a T.V. series'; Kathy Monroe in 'The Monroes' (66/67, T.V.); came to screen in 1968 in WITH SIX YOU GET EGG ROLL; others: HEAVEN WITH A GUN (69), LAST SUMMER (69), THE PURSUIT OF HAPPINESS (69), LIBERATION OF L.B. JONES (70), THE BABY MAKER (71), BOXCAR BERTHA (72), THE LAST HARD MEN (76), THE STUNTMAN (77), YOU AND ME (78), A MAN CALLED INTREPID (78) and JUST A LITTLE INCONVENIENCE (80); guest in many T.V. series, starred in 'From Here to Eternity' (80); md. David Carradine (qv), 1 son Free (Calista?/Seagull) 1972; recent movies: ANGEL ON MY SHOULDER (80, T.V. movie), TAKE THIS JOB & SHOVE IT (80), AMERICANA (81) and THE ENTITY (81).

ARTHUR HILL

B. Melfort, Saskatchewan, Canada 1.8.22. Ed. Melford Schools, King Edward H.S., Vancouver & Univ. of British Columbia; father a lawyer; acted as boy in Seattle and summer theatre at Univ.; made pro. debut in England, at Wimbledon in 1948, a year later coming to British screen in MISS PILGRIM'S PROGRESS; continued to act on British stage, other films: THE BODY SAID NO! (50), SALUTE TO THE TOFF (52), LIFE WITH THE LYONS (54), others: New York debut 1955: 'The Matchmaker'; md. Peggy Hassard; many U.S. movies include UGLY AMERICAN (62), IN THE COOL OF THE DAY (63), HARPER (66), PETULIA (68), THE OTHER MAN (70, T.V. movie), RABBIT RUN (71), ANDROMEDA STRAIN (71); Broadway 1962: 'Who's Afraid of Virginia Woolf?' (Tony Aw.); T.V. series: as 'Owen Marshall—Counsellor at Law' (71-74), guest in other shows; recent work: FUTURE WORLD (76), TELL ME MY NAME (77, T.V. movie), DEATH BE NOT PROUD (75, T.V. movie), Pres. Roosevelt in 'Churchill & the Generals' (79, BBC), A LITTLE ROMANCE (79), RETURN OF FRANK CANNON (T.V. movie, 1980), REVENGE OF THE STEPFORD WIVES, TOMORROW'S CHILD (both T.V. movies), DIRTY TRICKS (all 1981), THE AMATEUR (82).

TERENCE HILL

B. Venice, Italy 29.3.40(?). Real name Mario Girotti; ed. Univ. of Rome; father a chemist, from Umbria, Italy, mother born in Dresden, Germany; in 1943 family (Mario also has 2 brothers) moved to Dresden, surviving bombing; aged 11, he went to Rome, later winning bronze medal in Italian national championships; came to the screen in HOLIDAY FOR GANGSTERS, after being discovered by the director, working in his first films under his real name: THE LEOPARD (63), 7 SEAS TO CALAIS (63) and then a long spell (1964-67) in 'spaghetti westerns', the first of which was GOD FORGIVES, I DON'T, his 1st English-speaking role; md. Lori, 2 children: Jess, Ross (latter adoped); changed screen name to 'Terence Hill'; BLOOD RIVER (67), BOOT HILL (69), ACE HIGH (69), BARBAGIA (70), THEY CALL ME TRINITY (70), MAN OF THE EAST (72), MY NAME IS NOBODY (73), WATCH OUT, WE'RE MAD (74), MR BILLION (76), CRIME BUSTERS (76), MARCH OR DIE (77), SUPER FUZZ (80), WHO FINDS A FRIEND FINDS A TREASURE (81).

PAT HINGLE

B. Denver, Colorado 19.7.23. Ed. Univ. of Texas; laborer, waiter and construction worker, stagecraft tuition at the Theatre Wing, Berghof Studio and Actors' Studio; stage debut N.Y. 1950 in 'Johnny Belinda', becoming distinguished actor in this medium, playing a wide variety of roles from Shakespeare to Tennessee Williams; T.V. debut: 1951 including 'Theatre 1960: An Early Winter' and occasionally seen as Dr John Chapman in 'Gunsmoke' series; many movies include: ON THE WATERFRONT (54), THE STRANGE ONE (57), NO DOWN PAYMENT (57), SPLENDOR IN THE GRASS (61), THE UGLY AMERICAN (63), NEVADA SMITH (66), SOL MADRID (68), HANG 'EM HIGH (68), JIGSAW (68), BLOODY MAMA (69), NORWOOD (69), W.U.S.A. (70), THE CAREY TREATMENT (72), ONE LITTLE INDIAN (73), RUN WILD (73), THE SUPER COPS (74), THE GAUNTLET (77), ELVIS—THE MOVIE (78, as Col. Tom Parker), NORMA RAE (79), DISASTER ON THE COASTLINER (79, T.V. movie), WHEN YOU COMIN' BACK, RED RYDER? (79).

DUSTIN HOFFMAN

Before winning his deserved Oscar in 1980, Dustin Hoffman had proved to be a fine actor in a wide range of roles, emerging as a major screen talent in the late 1960s. He is the son of Harry Hoffman, a furniture designer, and his wife, Lillian, and was born in Los Angeles, California, on 8 August 1937. He had originally intended to become a classical and jazz pianist and studied at the Los Angeles Conservatory and Santa Monica City College, where he majored in music, but he decided to become an actor (his first stage performance was in a school production of 'A Christmas Carol' at the John Burroughs Jun. H.S., Los Angeles, as Tiny Tim) and enrolled at the famous Pasadena Community Playhouse and studied with Barney Brown, Lonny Chapman and Lee Strasberg. Studying with the latter in New York, he remembered the city as being 'cold, lonely and terrifying', and the breaks were hard to find. Young Hoffman, during these lean times, worked as an attendant at a psychiatric institution, a waiter, coat-checker and soft-drink dispenser, toy demonstrator at Macy's and drama coach at an E. Harlem Boys' Club. Gradually he began to make a reputation on the stage — his début came in New York in 1960 in 'Yes Is For a Very Young Man' and roles followed in such plays as 'A Cook For Mr General' (1961), Dunlavin in 'The Quare Fellow', Ben in 'The Dumbwaiter', Pozzo in 'Waiting For Godot', Peter in 'The Cocktail Party' (last 4 parts at Theatre Company of Boston, 1964), 'Three Men on a Horse' (1964), Immanuel, a hunchbacked, Nazi homosexual in 'Harry, Noon & Night' (1965) and 'Journey of the Fifth Horse' as Zoditch, his performance winning an 'Obie' Award in 1966. Dustin's first movie was called MADIGAN'S MILLIONS in 1966 and this was followed by UN DOLLARO PER SETTE VIGLIACCHI (67) and THE TIGER MAKES OUT (67). After further stage roles in 'The Old Jew', 'Reverberations', 'Fragments' and 'Eh?' (all 1966) the London 'Times' hailed him as the 'finest new U.S. actor', the last play winning him 2 awards. Nervous during his screen-test, Mike Nichols, the director, cast him as THE GRADUATE (67), which proved to be the turning point in his screen career and his performance as Benjamin won him an Oscar nomination. Hoffman's other movies have been MIDNIGHT COWBOY (69, Oscar nom.); JOHN AND MARY (69); LITTLE BIG MAN (70); WHO IS HARRY KELLERMAN...? (72); ALFREDO ALFREDO (72); STRAW DOGS (72); PAPILLON (73); LENNY (75, Oscar nom.); MARATHON MAN (76); STRAIGHT TIME (77) and AGATHA (77). He wed former ballet dancer Anne Byrne on May 3, 1969. Their daughter, Jennifer Celia, was born in 1970 (his wife having a daughter, Karina, from a previous marriage). This marriage ended in divorce and early in 1981 he wed actress Lisa Gottesgen. Mr Hoffman has appeared on T.V. and directed on the stage. KRAMER VS. KRAMER won him an Oscar as Best Actor in 1979, and his recent hit, TOOTSIE (82), won him a Golden Globe Award and Oscar nomination.

JUDD HIRSCH

B. New York City, 15.3.35. Ed. City College of New York, Am. Acad. D.A.; stage début 1962, Colorado, then much New York theatre; popular on T.V.: 'Medical Story', 'Delvecchio' (1976/77 series, as Sgt. Dominick Delvecchio), 'Taxi' (1978 series — as Alex Rieger); movies include THE LAW (74, T.V. movie); SERPICO (74); FEAR ON TRIAL (75, T.V. movie); KING OF THE GYPSIES (78); ORDINARY PEOPLE (81); WITHOUT A TRACE (82).

EARL HOLLIMAN

B. Tennasas Swamp, nr. Delhi, Louisiana, U.S.A. 11.9.28. When his parents died he was adopted by the Holliman family — foster father died and Earl left school and waited at tables aged 14 for $5 a week. He then, at 15, hitchhiked his way to Hollywood to try his luck but was unsuccessful and joined U.S. Navy. Discharged when found to be too young, he studied at Louisiana State University, U.C.L.A. and joined the Pasadena Playhouse; small film roles from 1953: DESTI-NATION GOBI (53), BROKEN LANCE (54), BRIDGES AT TOKO-RI (54), THE BIG COMBO (55), GUNFIGHT AT O.K. CORRAL (57), THE RAINMAKER (57), LAST TRAIN FROM GUNHILL (57), many others; well-known on T.V. in series: Sundance in 'Hotel de Paree' (59/60), Mitch Guthrie in 'Wide Country' (62), occasionally as 'Wheat' in 'Alias Smith & Jones' (71/73) and more recently as Sgt. William Crowley in 'Police Woman' (74-78); other movies include SUMMER & SMOKE (61), THE SONS OF KATIE ELDER (65), BATTLE FOR ANZIO (68), A COVENANT WITH DEATH (68), TRAPPED (73, T.V. movie), SHARKEY'S MACHINE (81).

HAL HOLBROOK

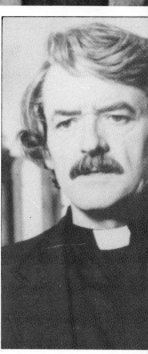

B. Cleveland, Ohio 27.2.25; Real name: Harold Rowe Holbrook Jr.; aged 2, his mother, Aileen Davenport, left home to become a showgirl with Ziegfeld Follies, so Hal was brought up by grandparents (uncle: George H. Rowe—actor/director); educated at Culver City Military Acad., graduating in 1942; WWII service; decided to be actor, studied Denison Univ., majoring in drama; stage début 1942, Cleveland, in 'The Man Who Came to Dinner'; became distinguished U.S. stage actor in variety of roles — Shakespearean etc. and is well-known for one-man show 'Mark Twain Tonight!' (from 1955, also world tour); md. 1. Ruby Elaine Johnston, actress, 1945, 1 daughter Victoria (born 1952), 1 son David (born 1955) div. 1964; T.V. included regular in 'The Brighter Day', from 1954, and as Senator Hays Stowe in 'The Bold Ones' (series 70/71, in which he won an Emmy Award); many movies include THE GROUP (66); WILD IN THE STREETS (68); THE PEOPLE NEXT DOOR (70); GREAT WHITE HOPE (70); SUDDENLY SINGLE (71, T.V. movie); MAGNUM FORCE (73); THE GIRL FROM PETROVKA (74); ALL THE PRESIDENT'S MEN (76); MID-WAY (76); JULIA (77); CAPRICORN ONE (77); md. 2. Carol Rossen, actress, 1 daughter Eve (born 1970); recent movies: THE KID-NAPPING OF THE PRESIDENT, THE FOG (both 80); CREEPSHOW, STAR CHAMBER (both 82).

WILLIAM HOLDEN

Mr Holden died at his home in Santa Monica, California in November, 1981.

Recently very active in movies, despite his numerous business interests, William Holden has been a popular star in every one of his films since first coming to the screen in 1938. Born William Franklin Beedle (Jr.) in O'Fallon, Illinois on 17 April 1918, his father was a successful chemist manufacturer and when a child, young William moved with his parents to Pasadena, near Los Angeles. Studying at Pasadena Junior College, he appeared in amateur theatricals, although at the time his ambition was to become a bacteriologist. In his late teens he appeared in a production at the Pasadena Playhouse, was discovered by a studio talent scout, appeared in a screen-test which initially was for an actress but Beedle was noticed by director Rouben Mamoulian and cast in his production of GOLDEN BOY in 1938. He chose the screen name of Holden when, in a studio publicity office, the publicist received a call from William Holden, assistant managing director of the 'Los Angeles Times', so he selected that name. His early films included OUR TOWN (40), THOSE WERE THE DAYS (40), ARIZONA (40), I WANTED WINGS (41), TEXAS (41), THE REMARK-ABLE ANDREW (42), YOUNG AND WILLING (43) and he wed the actress Brenda Marshall on 13 July 1941. They had two sons — Peter Westfield (born 17 November 1943) and Scott Porter (born 2 May 1946). She had a daughter, Virginia, from a previous marriage. Holden served for 4 years in the Forces, entering as a Private, but came out a First Lieutenant in the Air Corps. Back in pictures he made BLAZE OF NOON (47); DEAR RUTH (47); VARIETY GIRL (47); RACHEL AND THE STRANGER (48); APARTMENT FOR PEGGY (48); THE MAN FROM COLORADO (48); THE DARK PAST (49); STREETS OF LAREDO (49); MISS GRANT TAKES RICHMOND (49); DEAR WIFE (49); FATHER IS A BACHELOR (50) and his better roles followed in SUNSET BOULEVARD (50, Oscar nom.); UNION STATION (50); BORN YESTERDAY (50); FORCE OF ARMS (51); SUBMARINE COMMAND (51); BOOTS MALONE (52); THE TURNING POINT (52); STALAG 17 (53, for which he won an Oscar); THE MOON IS BLUE (53); FOREVER FEMALE (53); ESCAPE FROM FORT BRAVO (53); EXECUTIVE SUITE (54); SABRINA (54); THE COUNTRY GIRL (54); THE BRIDGES AT TOKO-RI (54); LOVE IS A MANY SPLENDORED THING (55); PICNIC (55); PROUD AND THE PROFANE (56); BRIDGE ON THE RIVER KWAI (57); THE KEY (58) and THE HORSE SOLDIERS (59). In more recent years Mr Holden has developed several business interests, including a game preserve for endangered species in Kenya, radio, electronic and racetrack investments and partnership of a Hong Kong Hotel. Divorced from Miss Marshall in 1971, his other movies have included THE COUNTERFEIT TRAITOR (62); THE LION (62); THE 7TH DAWN (64); CASINO ROYALE (67); DEVIL'S BRIGADE (68); THE WILD BUNCH (69); WILD ROVERS (71); BREEZY (73); OPEN SEASON (74); NETWORK (76, Oscar nom.); DAMIEN: OMEN II (77); FEDORA (77); ASHANTI (78); THE EARTHLING (79) and S.O.B. (80).
THE FILMS OF WILLIAM HOLDEN by Lawrence J. Quirk; Citadel: Secaucus, N.J.
GOLDEN BOY: THE UNTOLD STORY OF WILLIAM HOLDEN by Bob Thomas; Weidenfeld & Nicolson: London, 1983.

ANTHONY HOPKINS

One of Britain's most successful screen actors to emerge as a major international name during the last decade is Welsh-born Anthony Hopkins, his recent performance in THE ELEPHANT MAN contributing greatly to his popularity. An only child, he is the son of Richard Hopkins, a baker, and his wife, Muriel, and was born in Port Talbot on 31 December 1937. He had early inspirations to become a pianist and at school (Cowbridge Grammar, Glamorgan) he did not appear in plays, but he managed to obtain a scholarship to study at the Cardiff School of Music and Drama. After 2 years in the Royal Artillery, he worked briefly at Manchester's Library Theatre in 1960 as A.S.M., making his professional début in 'The Quare Fellow', and then went on to study at RADA, in London, from 1961-63. Following repertory at Leicester, Liverpool and Hornchurch, he made his London début in 1964 at the Royal Court and joined the National Theatre 2 years later where he played with distinction in such plays as 'A Flea in Her Ear'. He had also wed Petronella Barker, daughter of actor/comedian Eric Barker. Mr Hopkins came to the big screen in 1967 in THE WHITE BUS and has been seen in THE LION IN WINTER (68, as Richard the Lionheart); HAMLET (69, as Claudius); THE LOOKING GLASS WAR (70); WHEN 8 BELLS TOLL (70); YOUNG WINSTON (71, as Lloyd George, also played this role in 'The Edwardians' on T.V. (1972)); A DOLL'S HOUSE (73); THE GIRL FROM PETROVKA (73); JUGGERNAUT (74); ALL CREATURES GREAT AND SMALL (75); VICTORY AT ENTEBBE (76, as Prime Minister Rabin); A BRIDGE TOO FAR (77); INTERNATIONAL VELVET (77); AUDREY ROSE (77); MAGIC (78); THE ELEPHANT MAN (79) and he has played in several T.V. movies: QBVII (73); DARK VICTORY (76); LINDBERG KIDNAPPING CASE (76) and also acted on Broadway, including 'Equus' in 1974. His second wife is Jennifer Lynton, who was production secretary on his movie WHEN 8 BELLS TOLL. British T.V. plays include 'War and Peace' (73); 'Othello' (81) and 'A Married Man' (83, ser.). Recent films: MAYFLOWER: THE PILGRIMS' ADVENTURE (79); PETER & PAUL (mini-ser.), THE BUNKER (T.V. movie), A CHANGE OF SEASONS (all 1980); HUNCHBACK OF NOTRE DAME (82, T.V. movie) and THE SAGA OF H.M.S. BOUNTY (84).

IAN HOLM

B. Goodmayes, Essex 12.9.31. Real name Ian Holm Cuthbert; father a distinguished doctor specialising in mental health; ed. Chigwell Grammar School and studied for the stage at RADA; pro. stage début Stratford Memorial Theatre 1954 as spear carrier in 'Othello' and became very distinguished British stage actor, especially in Shakespearean roles, including 'Richard III' for the R.S. Co.; md. 1. Lynn Mary Shaw (div.); 2. Bridgit (met her at Stratford); films: THE BOFORS GUN (68, BFA Aw.), A MIDSUMMER NIGHT'S DREAM (68), O! WHAT A LOVELY WAR! (69), THE FIXER (69), A SEVERED HEAD (70), NICHOLAS & ALEXANDRA (71), MARY, QUEEN OF SCOTS (71, as Riccio), YOUNG WINSTON (72), THE HOMECOMING (73), JUGGERNAUT (74), MARCH OR DIE (76), SHOUT AT THE DEVIL (76), MAN IN THE IRON MASK (77), LES MISERABLES (78), ALIEN (78), S.O.S. TITANIC (79), ALL QUIET ON THE WESTERN FRONT (79), CHARIOTS OF FIRE (81, BAFTA Aw. BSA, Oscar nom., BSA); B'way 1967 'Tony' Aw.: 'The Homecoming'; much TV recent: 'After the Party' (82); recent movies: TIME BANDITS (81), RETURN OF THE SOLDIER, INSIDE THE THIRD REICH (mini-ser., both 1982), GREYSTOKE (83).

[BO] HOPKINS

[..], Greenwood, S.C., U.S.A. . . . Studied [d]rama with Uta Hagen in New York and Desilu [P]layhouse in Hollywood; came to the screen in [T]HE WILD BUNCH (69) and has been seen in [T]HE 1000 PLANE RAID (69), MONTE [W]ALSH (70), THE MOONSHINE WAR (70), [T]HE CULPEPPER CATTLE CO. (72), THE [G]ETAWAY (72), AMERICAN GRAFFITI [('7]3), WHITE LIGHTNING (73), THE MAN [W]HO LOVED CAT DANCING (73), THE [D]AY OF THE LOCUST (75), POSSE (75), [T]HE NICKEL RIDE (75), KILLER ELITE [('7]5), A SMALL TOWN IN TEXAS (76), [T]ENTACLES (77), THE MIDNIGHT EX-[P]RESS (78) and MORE AMERICAN GRAF-[F]ITI (79); Mr Hopkins has appeared on T.V. on [se]veral occasions including 'Aspen' (Mini-series [19]77) and the series 'Doc Elliot' (74, as Eldred [M]cCoy), 'The Rockford Files' (78, as John [C]ooper), 'Dynasty' (81/82, as Matthew); recent [m]ovies: THE PLUTONIUM INCIDENT (T.V. [m]ovie, 1980), SWEET SIXTEEN (82).

MICHAEL HORDERN

B. Berkhampsted 3.10.11. Ed. Brighton Coll.; was schoolmaster, then sold school textbooks, did amateur stage with St. Pancras People's Theatre; pro. début 1937 in 'Othello', London, becoming one of Britain's most distinguished stage actors, including notable Shakespearean roles; md. former actress Eve Mortimer, 1 daughter Joanna; came to the screen in 1939 in GIRL IN THE NEWS, his many movies include SCHOOL FOR SECRETS (46), PASSPORT TO PIMLICO (48), THE HEART OF THE MATTER (53), BABY & THE BATTLESHIP (55), THE SPANISH GARDENER (56), ALEXANDER THE GREAT (56), SINK THE BISMARK! (60), EL CID (61), DR SYN (63), KHARTOUM (66), A FUNNY THING HAPPENED ON THE WAY TO THE FORUM (66), THE BED-SITTING ROOM (69), ENGLAND MADE ME (72) and MR QUILP (74); Mr Hordern served during WWII in the Royal Navy, and he has played with all major stage companies, inclu. R.S.Co.; recent T.V.: as 'King Lear' (82); Knighthood: New Year's Honours, 1983; recent movies: WATERSHIP DOWN (voice), MEDUSA TOUCH (both 1977), THE MISSIONARY, YELLOWBEARD (both 1983).

BOB HOSKINS

B. Bury St. Edmunds, Suffolk 26.10.42. Ed. Stroud Green School, Finsbury Park, London; 3 years a trainee accountant, Bob Hoskins, at the age of 25, went to the Unity Theatre, St. Pancras 'for a drink' and was offered, and took, a role in the play 'The Feather Pluckers'; pro. début 1969 at Stoke-on-Trent in 'Romeo & Juliet' and he has played many roles, including Pinchwife in 'The Country Wife', title roles: 'Richard III', 'Lear', Pompey in 'Antony & Cleopatra', Doolittle in 'Pygmalion' and Bernie the Volt in 'Veterans'; many T.V. roles from 1972 including 'Villains', 'Softly, Softly', 'As Thick as Thieves', 'On the Move' and 'Three Piece Suite' before his dynamic performance as Arthur Parker, the sheet-music salesman in 'Pennies From Heaven' (78, BBC series) made him a star; md. Jane Livesey (div.) 2 children: Alexander, Sarah; other T.V. includes 'Sheppey' (79) and Arnie Cole in 'Flickers' (80); his films have been INSERTS (74), NATIONAL HEALTH (74), ROYAL FLASH (75) and more recently ZULU DAWN (78), THE LONG GOOD FRIDAY (80, 'Standard' Film Aw., BA), THE HONORARY CONSUL (83); Md: 2. teacher Linda Banwell, 12.6.82; recent stage: 'Duchess of Malfi' (81), 'Guys & Dolls' (82, Nat. Theatre, as Nathan Detroit).

DENNIS HOPPER

B. Dodge City, Kansas 17.5.36. Brought up on his grandparents' wheat farm. Later, family went to California and he attended H.S. there, appearing in productions with the San Diego Community Players, including 'Macbeth', 'Othello'. While working backstage at La Jolla Playhouse, California, encouraged in acting career by Dorothy McGuire, and went to Hollywood where he got T.V. work and on the strength of his performance in a show, landed a Warners' contract, and came to the screen in 1955 in I DIED A 1000 TIMES; many films include GIANT (55), GUNFIGHT AT OK CORRAL (57), KEY WITNESS (60), SONS OF KATIE ELDER (64), COOL HAND LUKE (67), HANG 'EM HIGH (68), TRUE GRIT (69), EASY RIDER (69, also directed), THE LAST MOVIE (71, also wrote/directed), KID BLUE (72); md. 1. Brooke Hayward 1961 (div. 1967), 1 daughter Marin; 2. Michelle Phillips (qv) 1970 (div.); 3. Darlene Halpin 1973; latest films: APOCALYPSE NOW (77), AMERICAN FRIEND (77), L'ORDRE ET LA SECURITE DU MONDE (78), FLESH COLOUR (78), OUT OF THE BLUE (also directed, 80), KING OF THE MOUNTAIN (81), WHITE STAR, RUMBLE FISH (both 1982), THE OSTERMAN WEEKEND (83).

JOHN HOUSEMAN

B. Bucharest, Rumania 22.9.02. Real name John Haussmann; ed. Clifton Coll., England; went to Argentina 1923 to conduct wheat export business, later moving to Canada & USA; became a distinguished stage producer from 1934 and co-founded the Mercury Theatre in 1937 with Orson Welles; md. Joan Courtney; during WWII was Chief of Overseas Radio Program Bureau; between stage prods., worked in Hollywood as Producer, esp. for MGM, working on THE BLUE DAHLIA (46), THE BAD & THE BEAUTIFUL (52), JULIUS CAESAR (53), LUST FOR LIFE (56), THIS PROPERTY IS CONDEMNED (66) and others; in 1973 Mr Houseman turned to film acting and won an Oscar as Best Supporting Actor for his performance in THE PAPER CHASE (as prof. Charles W. Kingsfield Jr., later making a T.V. series in this role, 1978) and has been seen in 3 DAYS OF THE CONDOR (75), ROLLERBALL (75), MEETING AT POTSDAM (76, T.V. movie, as Churchill), FEAR ON TRIAL (76, T.V. movie), THE CHEAP DETECTIVE (77), OLD BOYFRIENDS (79), WHOLLY MOSES!, THE FOG, MY BODYGUARD, GIDEON'S TRUMPET (T.V. movie, all 1980), GHOST STORY, BELLS (both 81); autobio: *RUNTHROUGH*: Simon & Schuster: N.Y., 1972.

RON HOWARD

B. Duncan, Oklahoma 1.3.54. Parents on stage: Rance and Jean Howard; aged 2, Ron acted with them in 'Seven Year Itch' at Baltimore's Hilltop Theatre; brother Clint is also actor; ed. Univ. S. California; came to the screen 1958 in THE JOURNEY and his films include THE MUSIC MAN (62), THE COURTSHIP OF EDDIE'S FATHER (63), SMOKE (69), THE WILD COUNTRY (71), AMERICAN GRAFFITI (73), HAPPY MOTHER'S DAY......LOVE GEORGE (73), THE SPIKE'S GANG (74) and THE SHOOTIST (76); md. Cheryl Alley 1975; Mr Howard has guested on T.V. on several occasions, including 'The Waltons', 'Happy Days' and appeared regularly in the series: 'The Andy Griffith Show' (1960-68, as Opie Taylor) and in 'The Smith Family' (1971-72). He directed/ starred in GRAND THEFT AUTO (77); directed NIGHT SHIFT (82); produced LEO AND LOREE (80).

FRANKIE HOWERD

B. York 6.3.22. Ed. Eltham, and Shooter's Hill Grammar School, London; father a professional soldier; real name Francis Alex Howard; hearing concerts in dad's Mess made him choose stage career; serving in Royal Artillery, wrote, produced and acted in shows; London début 1946 in 'Stage Door Canteen'; became well-known and loved comedian on radio, T.V. and eventually movies: RUNAWAY BUS (54), THE LADY-KILLERS (55), JUMPING FOR JOY (55), THE REVOLVING DOOR (56), A TOUCH OF THE SUN (56), FURTHER UP THE CREEK (59), THE COOL MIKADO (63), THE GT. ST. TRINIAN'S TRAIN ROBBERY (66), CARRY ON DOCTOR (68), UP POMPEII (70, and BBC T.V. series), UP THE CHASTITY BELT (71), UP THE FRONT (72), THE HOUSE IN NIGHTMARE PARK (73) and SGT. PEPPER'S LONELY HEARTS CLUB BAND (77); Mr Howerd has acted at London Palladium, West End and Broadway, the Old Vic and especially in T.V. and radio series. recent films: PIRATES OF PENZANCE, TRIAL BY JURY (both T.V. movies, 1982). *ON THE WAY I LOST IT* (autobiography); W.H. Allen: London, 1976; pb.

TREVOR HOWARD

For nearly 40 years Trevor Howard has been one of Britain's best-loved and distinguished film actors, graduating from a gentlemanly leading man of the 1940s to a forceful character player during the 1960s. The son of Arthur Joseph Howard, a Lloyd's of London under-writer, and his wife, Mabel, he was born at Cliftonville, Kent, on 29 September 1916. When still an infant, his parents took him to Ceylon until he was 5 and in 1921 his father's shipping interests took them to the USA, then to Canada, where he attended school at Brantford, Ontario. Returning to G.B., he completed his education at Clifton College, Bristol, and young Howard excelled at most sports, including cricket, and hoped to play for his country at one time. However, he decided to become an actor and won a production Scholarship to RADA in 1933, making his professional début in 1934 at the Gate Theatre. During the 1930s he became a popular British stage actor, playing in the West End (including 'French Without Tears' for 2 years) and the Memorial Theatre, Stratford-on-Avon. During the war he served in the Armed Forces from 1940-43 and was one of the brave men parachuted into Nazi-occupied Norway to destroy 'heavy water' installations. On 8.9.44 he wed actress Helen Cherry, after playing opposite her in 'A Soldier For Christmas' at the Arts Theatre, London that year. Trevor Howard had come to the screen as the Naval Officer in THE WAY AHEAD (43) and after THE WAY TO THE STARS (45) his performance in BRIEF ENCOUNTER (46) made him a star. In 1947 he also made I SEE A DARK STRANGER and GREEN FOR DANGER, played with the Old Vic Company in 'Taming of the Shrew', but since then his stage appearances have been few and he has concentrated on movies, many of which have included THE THIRD MAN (49); ODETTE (50); THE CLOUDED YELLOW (51); THE HEART OF THE MATTER (53); THE COCKLESHELL HEROES (55); RUN FOR THE SUN (56); THE KEY (58); THE ROOTS OF HEAVEN (59); SONS AND LOVERS (60, Oscar nom.); MUTINY ON THE BOUNTY (62, as Capt. Bligh); VON RYAN'S EXPRESS (65); MORITURI (65); THE LONG DUEL (67); THE CHARGE OF THE LIGHT BRIGADE (68, as Lord Cardigan); RYAN'S DAUGHTER (70), THE NIGHT VISITOR (71); LUDWIG (72); 11 HARROWHOUSE (74) and CONDUCT UNBECOMING (75). For his service in the war Mr Howard was awarded the Military Cross (also taking part in the invasion of Sicily). His most recent films include STEVIE (78); SHILLINGBURY BLOWERS (79); THE SEA WOLVES (80); WINDWALKER (80); LIGHT YEARS AWAY (81); THE MISSIONARY (83) and he has been seen on T.V. in 'Sir Henry At Rawlinson End' (79), 'No Country For Old Men' (81, as Jonathon Swift) and 'Sherlock Holmes' the sign of Four' (83).

ROCK HUDSON

Between his welcome big-screen comeback in THE MIRROR CRACK'D and his early days as a popular young 195C star groomed by Universal, Rock Hudson has ventured successfully into sophisticated screen comedy roles as well a turning to the stage and a successful T.V. series. The son of Roy Scherer, an automobile mechanic, and his wif Katherine, he was born Roy Scherer Jr. at Winnetka, Illinois on 17 November 1925, his grandparents on his father side being of Swiss-German extraction. Owing to troubles during the Depression, his father left home when Roy wa very young — and divorced when he was 8, and two years later his mother became Mrs Fitzgerald. He received h education at New Trier H.S. and was always interested in the movies. Called up for war service in the U.S. Navy, h trained at Glenview, Bremerton and San Francisco, serving at an air base near Leyte in the Philippines as a mechan' checking Corsairs and Hell Divers. After the war Roy returned to his home town and worked as a postman, vacuu cleaner salesman, intending to study drama at university, but he had insufficient qualifications, so he got a regular job a a truck driver. With his 6'4" build and rugged good looks, friends had always suggested he try the movies for work and colleague advised him to get some photographs taken and circulate them to casting directors. There was no positiv response for some time, until he was tipped off that the Selznick Studio (whom he had not circulated) were interviewir new artistes. Roy duly phoned for an appointment, saw the ace talent spotter Henry Willson, who, although realising th youngster needed much training, took him under his wing and groomed him, at his own expense with dramatic trainin etc., while Roy still worked as a truck driver. He came to the screen in 1948 in a small role in FIGHTER SQUADROI changing his name to Rock Hudson. On 15 August 1949 he signed a long-term contract with Universal-Internationa lasting many years. He played in eighteen pictures in supporting roles, including I WAS A SHOPLIFTER (50 WINCHESTER 73 (50), TOMAHAWK (51) and BEND OF THE RIVER (52) while training hard at the studi drama school (with fellow student Tony Curtis (qv)). Bigger roles came in SEMINOLE (53), SEA DEVILS (53 THE GOLDEN BLADE (53), TAZA, SON OF COCHISE (54) and his performance in THE MAGNIFICEN OBSESSION (54) made him a star. From 1957-65 he featured in the Top Ten poll of box-office stars. His many movie have included CAPT. LIGHTFOOT (55); NEVER SAY GOODBYE (56); GIANT (56, Oscar nom.); WRITTEI ON THE WIND (56); THE TARNISHED ANGELS (57); A FAREWELL TO ARMS (57); THIS EARTH I MINE (59); PILLOW TALK (59); COME SEPTEMBER (61); LOVER COME BACK (61); MAN'S FAVOURIT SPORT? (64); STRANGE BEDFELLOWS (64); BLINDFOLD (66); SECONDS (66); ICE STATION ZEBR. (68); and DARLING LILI (69). Mr Hudson wed Phyllis Gates on 9 November 1955 but they divorced in 1958. He ha appeared on T.V. on several occasions, including 'The Big Party' (1959), narrator of 'The Hollywood Musical' (fc Kraft Music Hall) and portrayed Commissioner Stewart McMillan in a long-running series 'McMillan and Wif (1971-77). In 1976 he came to London and had good reviews for his stage work in 'I Do, I Do' and that year toured th States in 'John Brown's Body'. His latest films include SHOWDOWN (73); EMBRYO (75); AVALANCHE (79 THE MIRROR CRACK'D (80); THE STAR MAKER (81, mini-ser.); 'The Devlin Connection' (81, series) an WORLD WAR III (as The President, mini-ser, 1982).

SEASON HUBLEY

B.   . T.V. includes 'Loose Change', 'She Lives' (74, T.V. movie), 'All I Could See From Where I Stood', occasionally in 'Kung Fu' (74/75) series as Margit McLean and 'Family' (76/77) as Salina Magee; md. Kurt Russell (qv), 1 son Boston (born 1980); movies: LOLLY MADONNA XXX (73), CATCH MY SOUL (as Desdemona, 74), HARDCORE LIFE (78), ELVIS: THE MOVIE (as his wife, 78), ESCAPE FROM NEW YORK (80), VICE SQUAD (81).

GARETH HUNT

B. London 7.2.43. Ed. Singlegate School for Boys; 6 years Merchant Navy, butcher, baker, vacuum cleaner salesman, road labourer, then Webber-Douglas Drama Academy on £8-a-week grant; rep: Ipswich, Bristol, Coventry, Royal Court, others; md. 1. Carole (hairdresser) (div.), 1 son Gareth Jr.; R.S. Co., Nat. Theatre; popular on T.V. as footman in 'Upstairs, Downstairs' (74/74) and Gambit in 'New Avengers' series (76); films: LICENSED TO LOVE & KILL (78), HOUSE ON GARIBALDI STREET (78), WORLD IS FULL OF MARRIED MEN (79); stage: West End: 'Alpha Beta' (78), 'Death Trap' (79); md. 2. Annette Walter-Lax (Swedish model), 1980, 1 son Oliver (born 1980); recent T.V.: 'The Business of Murder' (81), 'That Beryl Marston...!' (81, series), 'Cuffy' (83, ser.); stage 1982: 'Season's Greetings', film: FUNNY MONEY (guest).

GAYLE HUNNICUTT

B. Fort Worth, Texas 6.2.43. Father a retired Colonel, head of Mounted Cavalry; ed. UCLA (studying literature and drama, gaining Hons. Degree); appearing in play 'The Hotel Babel Will Not Surrender', spotted by T.V. talent scout and appeared in episode of 'Beverley Hillbillies'; came to screen in WILD ANGELS (66); Gayle was also model; starred in NEW FACE IN HELL (67), MARLOWE (69), EYE OF THE CAST (69), FRAGMENT OF FEAR (70); md. 1. David Hemmings (qv) 1968, 1 son Nolan (born 1970) (div. 1974); of Spanish/English descent, Gayle has worked a great deal in GB, esp. T.V. and stage, T.V.: 'The Ambassadors', 'Fall of Eagles', 'Affairs of the Heart', 'Martian Chronicles', 'Dylan'; stage: 'Twelfth Night', 'The Tempest' (Oxford), 'A Woman of No Importance' (Chichester), as 'Peter Pan' (West End 1979); md. 2. Mr Simon Jenkins, ex-Editor, London 'Evening Standard' on 1.9.78; many other films including SCORPIO (72), THE SELLOUT (76), ONCE IN PARIS (78), A MAN CALLED INTREPID (78, T.V. movie), ONE TAKE TWO (79) and FANTOMAS (79); recent stage: 'The Philadelphia Story' (81, Oxford Playhouse); T.V.: 'The Darlingest Boy' (81, 'Ladykillers' series). Son, Edward Lloyd, born Feb., 1982; stage 1982: 'The Miss Firecracker Contest'.

JOHN HURT

'The Naked Civil Servant' (T.V.), MIDNIGHT EXPRESS and THE ELEPHANT MAN have been three works in which John Hurt has recently demonstrated his ability as an actor of tremendous versatility and as a result he is in great demand internationally for movies. He is the son of Rev. Arnould Herbert Hurt, formerly a brilliant mathematician, and his wife, Phyllis, and was born at Chesterfield, Derbyshire on 22 January 1940. John's brother went to Cambridge and became a monk (but has since renounced his vows). He attended school in Kent and The Lincoln School, Lincoln where he enjoyed sport, especially soccer and rugby, but from the age of 9, after playing a female role in a school play, he became keen on acting. He studied at the Grimsby School of Art, gaining a Nat. Diploma of Design, but then went on to study for the stage at R.A.D.A., his contemporaries there being Sarah Miles (qv), David Warner (qv) and Gemma Jones. In 1962 he made his professional stage début in 'The Infanticide in the House of Fred Ginger' at the Arts Theatre, London and also came to the screen as Phil in THE WILD AND THE WILLING. Further stage plays include 'Chips with Everything' (London 1962), 'Dwarfs' (London 1963, Variety Award—Most Promising Newcomer), 'Hamp' (Edinburgh Festival 1964, also Broadway début), 'Inadmissible Evidence' (1965, London) and played with the R.S.Co. in 1966. That year he continued his successful career as Richard Rich in A MAN FOR ALL SEASONS and he has since been seen in SINFUL DAVEY (69); BEFORE WINTER COMES (69); IN SEARCH OF GREGORY (69); 10 RILLINGTON PLACE (71, as Timothy Evans); THE PIED PIPER (72); FORBUSH AND THE PENGUINS (72); LITTLE MALCOLM AND HIS STRUGGLE AGAINST THE EUNUCHS (74, also stage); THE GHOUL (75); THE DISAPPEARANCE (77); SPECTRE (77); EAST OF ELEPHANT ROCK (77); WATERSHIP DOWN (77, voice only) and THE SHOUT (78). Mr Hurt was once married to actress Annette Robertson and his girlfriend for over 13 years has been former successful Vogue model Marie-Lise Volpeliere Pierrot. T.V. roles include in 'Playboy of the Western World', 'Nijinsky', 'I, Claudius' (as Caligula) and in 1975 he won acclaim for his performance as Quentin Crisp in 'The Naked Civil Servant' (BAFTA Award). Other movies: MIDNIGHT EXPRESS (77, BAFTA Award, BSA); Hollywood Golden Globe Award, BSA); ALIEN (78, Variety Club Award, BA); HEAVEN'S GATE (79); THE ELEPHANT MAN (79, Oscar nom.; BAFTA Award BA); NIGHT CROSSING (81); PARTNERS (82); THE PLAGUE DOGS (82, voice only); 'King Lear' (T.V., as The Fool), THE OSTERMAN WEEKEND and CHAMPIONS (as Jockey Bob Champion, all 1983).

WILLIAM HURT

B. Washington, 20.3.50. Ed. Tufts Univ. Boston, studying theology, but switched to acting: 3 years Julliard School; won awards on New York stage: member of off-Broadway Circle Rep. Co., winning Obie Award for 'My Life'; T.V. includes 'The Best of Families', 'Verna, USO Girl'; md. Mary Beth Hurt, actress (div.); has been seen on the big screen in ALTERED STATES (80); THE JANITOR (80); BODY HEAT (81); THE BIG CHILL (83); GORKY PARK (83).

OLIVIA HUSSEY

B. Buenos Aires, Argentina,   .51. Miss Hussey is part-English, part-Argentinian; came to U.K. aged 8, drama school at 10; studied ballet 5 years; 1st T.V. break in Charlie Drake series; motion-picture break 1968 in ROMEO & JULIET, discovered by Zeffirelli, remembering her from 'Jean Brodie' stage play, London 1966; md. 1. Dino Martin (son of Dean) 17.4.71, 1 son Alexander (div.); films: BATTLE OF VILLA FIORITA (65), CUP FEVER (65), ALL THE RIGHT NOISES (69), SUMMERTIME KILLER (72), LOST HORIZON (73), BLACK CHRISTMAS (75), CAT & THE CANARY (77), DEATH ON THE NILE (77), THE MAN WITH BOGART'S FACE (79), VIRUS (80); md. 2. Akira Fusei, a Japanese singer, in 1979; Olivia's T.V. includes her portrayal of the Madonna Virgin Mary in 'Jesus of Nazareth' (76) and a 2-part series, 'The Pirate'; 81 movie: TURKEY SHOOT; Rebecca in IVANHOE (T.V. movie, 1982).

JOHN HUSTON

B. Nevada, Missouri 5.8.06; father Walter Huston, distinguished stage/screen actor; John Huston commenced career as a boxer, later became short story writer, worked at Gaumont-British Pics.; early screenplay: MURDERS IN THE RUE MORGUE (32), worked at Warner's, Hollywood as writer: JEZEBEL (38), HIGH SIERRA (40), others; directed/wrote brilliant movies including MALTESE FALCON (41), TREASURE OF THE SIERRA MADRE (47, Oscar), KEY LARGO (48), ASPHALT JUNGLE (50), AFRICAN QUEEN (52), MOBY DICK (56); more recently acted in sev. pics. including THE CARDINAL (63), THE BIBLE (66, as Noah), CASINO ROYALE (66), JUDGE ROY BEAN (72), CHINATOWN (75); md. 1. E. Lesley 1937, 2. Evelyn Keyes, 1946, 3. Enrica Soma 1949 (1 son Walter 1950, 1 daughter Angelica 1951), 4. Ce Ce Shane 1972; recently directed HEAD ON (79), WISE BLOOD (80), VICTORY (81).
KING REBEL by W.F. Nolan; Sherbourne Press, USA, 1965;
JOHN HUSTON: A BIOGRAPHY: Axel Madsen; Robson Books: London, 1979;
AN OPEN BOOK (autobio.): MacMillan: London, 1981.

LAUREN HUTTON

B. Charleston, S. Carolina, USA, 17.11.43. Ed. Newcombe Coll.; Lauren was once the highest paid model in the world, gracing covers of numerous magazines, also a familiar face in 'Revlon' adverts; came to screen in PAPER LION (68), others include LITTLE FAUSS & BIG HALSEY (70), PIECES OF DREAMS (71), THE GAMBLER (74), GATOR (76), VIVA, KNIEVEL (77), WELCOME TO L.A. (77), AMERICAN GIGOLO (79), ZORRO—THE GAY BLADE (80), PATERNITY (81); T.V. includes Leslie Hawkewood in 'The Rhinemann Exchange' (77, Best Sellers), 'Someone's Watching Me' (78, T.V. movie); recent movies: STARFLIGHT ONE (82), THE CRADLE WILL FALL (T.V. movie, 1983).

TIMOTHY HUTTON

B. c. 1961. Parents—the late Jim Hutton (actor, who died of cancer June 1979) and his wife, Maryline; they divorced and Timothy has a sister, Heidi Tarquin, a year older; made his stage debut, appearing with his father, in stock co. production of 'Harvey'; after much T.V. work was selected by Robert Redford (qv) to play an important role in his first movie, ORDINARY PEOPLE (80), winning Tim a Hollywood Golden Globe Award and the Oscar as BSA; recent movies: TAPS (81); DANIEL (83).

WILFRED HYDE-WHITE

B. Bourton-on-the-Water, Glos., 12.5.03. Father William Edward White, former Canon of Gloucester; ed. Marlborough Coll., and studied stagecraft at RADA; stage début: Isle of Wight, 1922, in 'Tons of Money'; West End from 1925 and tours etc., becoming well-known for his portrayal of impeccable British types in films and on stage; md. 1. Blanche Hope Aitken 1927 (dec. 1948), 1 son Michael (born 1928); came to screen 1936 in REMBRANDT, scores of films including THE THIRD MAN (49), THE STORY OF GILBERT & SULLIVAN (54), SEE HOW THEY RUN (55), QUENTIN DURWARD (55), NORTH-WEST FRONTIER (59), CARRY ON NURSE (59), TWO-WAY STRETCH (61), MY FAIR LADY (64), YOU MUST BE JOKING (65), TEN LITTLE INDIANS (65), CHAMBER OF HORRORS (66), GAILY, GAILY (69); md. 2. Ethel Korenmann 1957, 1 son Alexander (born 1959), 1 daughter Juliet (born 1961); other stage includes work with Olivier's (qv) Co. in S'peare, Broadway in 'The Reluctant Debutante' (& London) 1955-56 — in recent years has worked in USA; CAT & THE CANARY, NO LONGER ALONE (both 77), BATTLESTAR GALACTICA (79), TARZAN THE APE MAN, THE LETTER (T.V. movie, both 1981), THE TOY (82), FANNY HILL (83); 'The Associates' (ser. 79/80).

JILL IRELAND

B. Hounslow, Middx. 24.4.36. Stage début aged 12 'Sleeping Beauty', Chiswick; London Palladium, cabaret, continental tours in ballet, fashion model, T.V. commercials; came to screen in solo dancing spot OH, ROSALINDA! (55); films: THE WOMAN FOR JOE (55), SIMON & LAURA (55), BIG MONEY (56), 3 MEN IN A BOAT (56); md. 1. David McCallum (qv) 1957, 3 sons: Paul (1958), Jason (1959), Valentine (1960), (div.); many other films including HELL DRIVERS (57), THE DESPERATE MAN (59), CARRY ON NURSE (59), GIRLS OF LATIN QUARTER (60), RAISING THE WIND (61), BATTLE AXE (62), VILLA RIDES (68), COLD SWEAT (70), THE MECHANIC (72), WILD HORSES (73), VALACHI PAPERS (73), BREAKHEART PASS (76), LOVE & BULLETS, CHARLIE (77); md. 2. Charles Bronson 1968 (qv), 1 daughter Zuleika (born 1971); Miss Ireland has appeared in the U.S. T.V. series 'Shane' (66) as Marian Starrett and guested on several occasions; DEATH WISH II (82); co-assoc. producer: THE EVIL THAT MEN DO (83).

JOHN IRELAND

B. Vancouver, British Columbia 30.1.14. As a youngster went to New York; entered show-biz 1935 as swimmer in water carnival; studied at Davenport Free Theatre; stock, Broadway début 1939 — 'Macbeth', 'The Moon is Down', 'Native Son'; md. 1. Elaine Sheldon 1940, 2 sons: John (born 1942), Peter (born 1945) (div. 1948); toured California in 'Taming of the Shrew'; came to screen in 1945 in A WALK IN THE SUN; md. 2. actress Joanne Dru 1949, (div. 1956); many movies including MY DARLING CLEMENTINE (46), ALL THE KING'S MEN (49, Oscar nom. BSA), THE SCARF (51), HURRICANE SMITH (52), THE GOOD DIE YOUNG (54), THE GUNFIGHT AT OK CORALL (57, as Johnny Ringo), PARTY GIRL (58), SPARTACUS (60), THE CEREMONY (64), FALL OF THE ROMAN EMPIRE (65), ARIZONA BUSHWACKERS (68), HOUSE OF 7 CORPSES (73), FAREWELL, MY LOVELY (74), SWISS CONSPIRACY (75), SHAPE OF THINGS TO COME (78), COURAGE OF KAVIK, WOLF DOG (79, T.V. movie); md. 3. Daphne Myrick 1962; T.V. series (GB 1960): 'The Cheaters'; recent movies: MARILYN: THE UNTOLD STORY (80, as John Huston); DAY OF THE ASSASSIN, INCUBUS (both 1981).

JEREMY IRONS

AMY IRVING

B. , c.1956. Miss Irving is the daughter of Jules Irving, one-time director of New York's Lincoln Centre Rep. Co. and now prod./dir. at Universal, and his wife, actress Priscilla Pointer (who appd. in CARRIE); Amy started acting aged 6 in her father's productions in San Francisco and studied acting in London; T.V. includes 'Once an Eagle' (76, Best-Sellers); movies: CARRIE (76), THE FURY (77), VOICES (79), HONEYSUCKLE ROSE (79), THE COMPETITION (80), YENTL, THE FAR PAVILIONS (both 1983).

BURL IVES

B. Hunt City, Illinois 14.6.09. Real name Burl Icle Ivanhoe Ives, one of 6 children; ed. Newton, Illinois, H.S. and State Teachers' Coll., Charleston, but dropped out of latter and toured USA, singing folk songs and ballads, many of which he had learned as a child from his grandmother back in the poor tenant farming country of the Illinois 'Bible Belt'; also itinerant worker/footballer; through late Will Geer got acting job and fame on Broadway in 'Boys From Syracuse' (1938); md. 1. Helen Ehrlich (prod. of his radio prog.) — their adopted son is now radio prod., Australia (div. 18.2.71); Broadway includes: 'Heavenly Express', 'This is the Army', 'Show Boat'; recordings include 'Big Rock Candy Mountain', 'The Bluetail Fly', 'The Foggy Dew'; came to screen 1946 in SMOKY; others: GREEN GRASS OF WYOMING, SIERRA, Big Daddy in CAT ON A HOT TIN ROOF (58, also stage 1955), THE BIG COUNTRY (58, Oscar BSA); md. 2. Dorothy Koster, 16.4.71, interior decorator/designer; T.V. series: 'O.K. Crackerby' (65), 'The Lawyers' (69/72); recent movies: BERMUDA DEPTHS (78), WHITE DOG, EARTHBOUND (both 1981).
WAYFARING STRANGER (autobio.); T.V. Boardman: London, 1952.

ANNE JACKSON

B. Allegheny, Pa. 3.9.26; ed. Brooklyn, New York; trained for stage at Neighborhood Playhouse, studying with Sanford Meisner, Herbert Berghof and Lee Strasberg (Actors' Studio); pro. début: Wilmington, Delaware in 'The Cherry Orchard', 1944; New York 1946 in same play, later joining American Rep. Co. 1946/47 for several productions, where she met and wed actor Eli Wallach (qv) in 1948; they have 2 daughters, Roberta (born 1955) and Katherine (born 1958) and a son, Peter (born 1951); Miss Jackson subsequently appd. regularly on the stage in stock, tours, Broadway and London, her few movies being SO YOUNG SO BAD (50), THE JOURNEY (58), TALL STORY (60), THE TIGER MAKES OUT (67), HOW TO SAVE A MARRIAGE (67), THE SECRET LIFE OF AN AMERICAN WIFE (68), THE ANGEL LEVINE (70), LOVERS AND OTHER STRANGERS (70), ZIG ZAG (70), DIRTY DINGUS MAGEE (70), NASTY HABITS (77), THE BELL-JAR (78), A PRIVATE BATTLE (80, T.V. movie), LEAVE 'EM LAUGHING (81, T.V. movie).

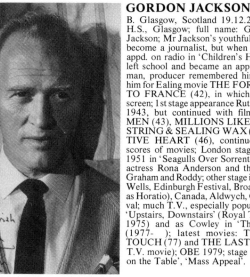

GORDON JACKSON

B. Glasgow, Scotland 19.12.23. Ed. Hillhe H.S., Glasgow; full name: Gordon Camer Jackson; Mr Jackson's youthful ambition was become a journalist, but when still a schoolb appd. on radio in 'Children's Hour' broadcas left school and became an apprentice draugh man, producer remembered him and suggest him for Ealing movie THE FOREMAN WEN TO FRANCE (42), in which he came to t screen; 1st stage appearance Rutherglen, Scotla 1943, but continued with film career: NIN MEN (43), MILLIONS LIKE US (43), PIN STRING & SEALING WAX (45), THE CA TIVE HEART (46), continued to appear scores of movies; London stage début Janua 1951 in 'Seagulls Over Sorrento', that year w actress Rona Anderson and they have 2 sor Graham and Roddy; other stage includes: Sadle Wells, Edinburgh Festival, Broadway ('Hamle as Horatio), Canada, Aldwych, Chichester Fes val; much T.V., especially popular as Hudson 'Upstairs, Downstairs' (Royal T.V. Soc. Awa 1975) and as Cowley in 'The Professiona (1977-); latest movies: THE MEDUS TOUCH (77) and THE LAST GIRAFFE (7 T.V. movie); OBE 1979; stage 1981/82: 'Car on the Table', 'Mass Appeal'.

B. Isle of Wight, 19.9.48. Father chartered accountant, director of Hawker-Siddeley; country born and bred, Jeremy early ambition was to become a vet; ed. Sherborne School, failed 'A' Levels, decided to become an actor after being school play 'The Critic' as Mr Puff; ASM at Marlowe Theatre, Canterbury, then trained at Bristol Old Vic Theat School for 2 years and at Bristol Old Vic Theatre for 3 further years; md. 1. actress Julie Hallam (div.); entered T. 1968; in London worked as domestic and street busker between jobs, later gaining role of John the Baptist in music show 'Godspell' for 2 years; T.V. work includes 'The Pallisers', 'Notorious Women', 'Love for Lydia', 'Voyse Inheritance'; md. 2. actress Sinead Cusack, 1 son Samuel (born 1978); stage includes 'Wild Oats', 'Rear Column' (bo 1978); movies: NIJINSKY (80); FRENCH LIEUTENANT'S WOMAN (81, Variety Club Award, BA MOONLIGHTING (82); BETRAYAL (82); other T.V.: 'All the World's a Stage' (1981), great success as Charl Ryder in 'Brideshead Revisited' (1981), 'The Captain's Doll' (1982, BBC film); THE WILD DUCK (83).

GLENDA JACKSON

ollowing varied experience in experimental and classical theatre, Glenda Jackson emerged in the 1970s as Britain's
remost leading lady, winning two Oscars and has alternated successfully her stage and motion-picture career. Born
lenda May Jackson at her grandmother's home in Birkenhead, Cheshire on 9 May 1936, she is the eldest daughter of
arry Jackson, a builder, and his wife, Joan, who was 26 years a 'daily' and 6 years a barmaid. Her parents' christened
r 'Glenda' after the actress Glenda Farrell and 'May' after her grandmother. Glenda's sisters are Gill, Lynne and
izabeth, and she attended Hoylake Church School, where she was stubborn but clever, loathed maths, but was an avid
ader and eventually won a place at West Kirby County Grammar School for Girls, gaining 'O' Levels in English
terature, Language and Geography, with the intention of becoming a librarian. She also took ballet tuition but became
o tall. Upon leaving school she worked for Boots the chemists which in the 1950s had a library service, but instead
und herself behind the medicine counter and loathed it. For a hobby she developed an interest in acting and dancing
erforming the latter at a YMCA theatre group) and Glenda was encouraged by a lady called Joan Banks, the wife of a
cal laundry owner, to consider the stage as a career. She took elocutions lessons in Liverpool and learned fencing,
plied to study at London's RADA and won a scholarship. Her stage début was in February 1957 in 'Separate Tables'
d 7 months later débuted in London at the Arts in 'All Kinds of Men'. Rep. followed at Dundee, Scotland and Crewe,
the latter she met her husband, Roy Hodges, then an actor, and they wed in 1958 (their son, Daniel, was born in 1969,
t the couple divorced on 26 January 1976 — Mr Hodges later became owner of an art gallery in London). Following
pearances as Alexandra in 'The Idiot' (1962) and as Siddie in 'Alfie', Miss Jackson joined the R.S.Co., appearing in
e experimental 'Theatre of Cruelty' season at LAMDA, 1964, the following year playing such roles as the Princess of
ance in 'Love's Labour's Lost', Ophelia in 'Hamlet' and Charlotte Corday in the 'Marat/Sade', which won her much
claim, repeating the role on Broadway, winning a 'Variety' and 'NY Critics' Award' and this production was filmed in
66. Other earlier films include BENEFIT OF THE DOUBT (67, RSCO. production); TELL ME LIES (68, Peter
ook production); NEGATIVES (68); but it was her performance as Gudrun Brangwen, the emancipated sculptress in
OMEN IN LOVE (69) that made her a star and won her first Hollywood Oscar in 1970. Since then she has most
ccessfully alternated stage work — 'Collaborators' (1973), 'The Maids' (1974) and tours of Britain, USA and
ustralia as 'Hedda Gabler' (75, also filmed), 'The White Devil' (1976, Old Vic), 'Stevie' (1978, stage & screen) and
ose' (1980) — with a busy film schedule — THE MUSIC LOVERS (70); THE BOYFRIEND (71, uncredited);
JNDAY, BLOODY SUNDAY (71, Oscar nom.); MARY, QUEEN OF SCOTS (71, as Queen Elizabeth I);
RIPLE ECHO (72); A TOUCH OF CLASS (72, Oscar winner); BEQUEST TO THE NATION (73, as Emma
amilton); THE MAIDS (74); THE TEMPTER (74); THE ROMANTIC ENGLISHWOMAN (75); HEDDA (75,
scar nom.); NASTY HABITS (76); THE INCREDIBLE SARAH (76, as Sarah Bernhardt); THE CLASS OF
ISS MacMICHAEL (77); LOST & FOUND (78); HOUSE CALLS (78); HOPSCOTCH (79) and HEALTH
9). Among her many T.V. roles, Miss Jackson won acclaim and an American 'Emmy' award in 1972 for her
rformance as 'Elizabeth R' in the BBC T.V. series of that title. She is part-owner, with Robert Enders, of a production
mpany, Bowden Films. A recipient of the C.B.E. in 1978, Miss Jackson's latest work includes 'Summit Conference'
2, stage) and the movies THE PATRICIA NEAL STORY (title role, T.V. movie, 1981); GIRO CITY (82, T.V.
ovie) and RETURN OF THE SOLDIER (82).
cordings include: *GLENDA JACKSON AS STEVIE SMITH* (CBS-70165 — film soundtrack);
GLENDA JACKSON READS STEVIE SMITH (Argo (1978) ZSW608)

KATE JACKSON

B. Birmingham, Alabama 29.10.49(?). Ed. Univ.
of Mississippi; Birmingham Southern Univ.; Kate
had youthful ambition to become tennis player,
but turned to acting after drama course at univ.;
appd. in summer stock, went to New York and
studied at Am. Acad. of D.A. (plays include
'Night Must Fall', 'Constant Wife'), then became
a model and guide at NBC, eventually landing 1st
T.V. role in series 'Dark Shadows' as Daphne
Harridge (also movie NIGHT OF DARK
SHADOWS (71); other T.V. series: Jill Danko
in 'The Rookies' (1972-76), Sabrina Duncan in
'Charlie's Angels' (from 1976); md. actor Andrew
Stevens (son of Stella Stevens (qv)) 1978; T.V.
movies include: KILLER BEES, JENNY STORM
HOMICIDE, DEATH AT LOVE HOUSE;
movies: LIMBO (72), THUNDER & LIGHT-
NING (77), DIRTY TRICKS (79), MAKING
LOVE (82). Md: 2. 'a New York businessman'.

DEREK JACOBI

B. East London 22.10.38. Ed. Leyton County
H.S.; scholarship to St. John's College, Cam-
bridge; leading roles with Nat. Youth Theatre and
ADC/Marlowe Soc. at Cambridge; pro. debut
September 1960 with Birmingham Repertory in
'One Way Pendulum', since then Mr Jacobi has
become a distinguished stage actor with the
National Theatre (at Old Vic) from 1963 and in
plays at Chichester Festival, Broadway, Green-
wich, Prospect Theatre Co. (European/Middle
East tours), Guildford, etc.; won acclaim on T.V.
in 'I, Claudius' (76, title role. BBC); movies:
OTHELLO (65, stage version), DAY OF THE
JACKAL (72), ODESSA FILE (73), JOSEPH
ANDREWS (76), THE MEDUSA TOUCH
(77), HUMAN FACTOR (79); recent stage: as
'Hamlet' (Old Vic, tour Australia, also BBC T.V.
79/80); films: THE MAN WHO WENT UP IN
SMOKE, ENIGMA (both 81), THE HUNCH-
BACK OF NOTRE DAME (T.V. movie, 1982),
INSIDE THE THIRD REICH (82, mini-ser., as
Hitler); stage 1982: Prospero in 'The Tempest'.

CLIFTON JAMES – see page 124

MICHAEL JAYSTON

B. Nottingham 29.10.36. Ed. Becket School,
Nottingham; early jobs include selling, buying
and wages clerk—Nottingham Fish Market and
trainee accountant National Coal Board; Guild-
hall School of Music & Drama; rep. Salisbury,
Bristol, Royal S'peare Co., National Theatre etc.;
T.V. from 1964 and success as Lincoln Dowling
in series 'The Power Game'; md. 1. Lynn Farleigh
(1.6.65-21.9.70); films: A MIDSUMMER
NIGHT'S DREAM (68), CROMWELL (70, as
Henry Ireton), as Tzar Nicholas in NICHOLAS
& ALEXANDRA (72), FOLLOW ME (72),
ALICE'S ADVENTURES IN WONDER-
LAND (72), A BEQUEST TO THE NATION
(73, as Capt. Hardy), TALES THAT WITNESS
MADNESS (73), THE HOMECOMING (73),
CRAZE (73), THE INTERNECINE PROJECT
(74), DOMINIQUE (77), ZULU DAWN (78);
md. 2. Ann; recent T.V.: 'Tinker, Tailor, Soldier,
Spy' (79); stage: London: 'Private Lives' (80),
'Sound of Music' (81, as Capt. Von Trapp); son
Richard, born July 1981.

CHARD JAECKEL

ong Beach, Long Island, New York 10.10.26.
l name Richard Hanley Jaeckel; a lightweight
er, he graduated from Hollywood H.S. in
3, took a job in the mailroom at 20th Century
 Studios, and was chosen for a role in the
vie GUADALCANAL DIARY (43); fol-
ing WING & A PRAYER (44) Richard spent
years in the Merchant Navy; his many movies
lude JUNGLE PATROL (48), SANDS OF
O JIMA (49), THE GUNFIGHTER (50),
E SEA HORNET (51), COME BACK,
TLE SHEBA (52), THE BIG LEAGUER
), APACHE AMBUSH (55), ATTACK!
), 3.10 TO YUMA (57), GALLANT HOURS
), 4 FOR TEXAS (63), DEVIL'S BRIGADE
, CHISUM (70), DROWNING POOL (75);
sted many times on T.V. and had series
ontier Circus' (61/62 as Tony Gentry), 'Ban-
' (72/73 as Lt. Pete McNeil), 'Firehouse' (74,
lank Myers); recent movies: 78: THE DARK,
EEDTRAP; T.V. movie 80: THE REWARD
ot) and 1981: THE CALIFORNIA DOLLS.

LIONEL JEFFRIES

B. Forest Hill, London .26(?). Ed. RADA, where he studied for the stage; came to the screen as extra/uncredited in STAGE FRIGHT (50), and since 1952 Mr Jeffries has been seen in scores of movies, including WINDFALL (54), THE COLDITZ STORY (55), BHOWANI JUNCTION (55), LUST FOR LIFE (56), REVENGE OF FRANKENSTEIN (57), BABY & THE BATTLESHIP (57), THE NUN'S STORY (59), THE TWO-WAY STRETCH (60), THE TRIALS OF OSCAR WILDE (60), THE NOTORIOUS LANDLADY (61), THE SPY WITH THE COLD NOSE (67), CHITTY, CHITTY, BANG BANG (68), EYEWITNESS (69), WHO SLEW AUNTI ROO? (72), THE PRISONER OF ZENDA (78); talented director of THE RAILWAY CHILDREN (70), BAXTER (72), THE AMAZING MR BLUNDEN (73), WATER BABIES, WOMBLING FREE (78); recent T.V. as actor: 'Father Charlie' (82), 'Tom, Dick & Harriet' (82, both ser.).

BEN JOHNSON

B. Pawhuska, Oklahoma 8.10.22. Ben was working for $1-a-day on his father's ranch in Oklahoma, when millionaire producer Howard Hughes called, searching for horses for his movie THE OUTLAW (43) — Ben was signed by Hughes as wrangler for the picture; continued to work at Hughes's studio and became stuntman/double, graduating to small roles in John Ford movies; his many movies, mostly western, include MIGHTY JOE YOUNG (49), RED RIVER (48), THREE GODFATHERS (48), SHE WORE A YELLOW RIBBON (49), SHANE (53), REBEL IN TOWN (56), THE TIN STAR (57), WARLOCK (59), ONE-EYED JACKS (61), CHEYENNE AUTUMN (64), EL DORADO (67), WILL PENNY (67), THE WILD BUNCH (69), CHISUM (70), THE TRAIN ROBBERS (73), BITE THE BULLET (75); md. Carol Lynn 1940; Oscar, 1971, BSA: THE LAST PICTURE SHOW; others inclu. HUSTLE, BREAKHEART PASS (both 76), THE SWARM (77), THE HUNTER (79), TERROR TRAIN, SOGGY BOTTOM, USA (both 80), RUCKUS, TEX (both 81), SHADOW RIDERS (T.V. movie, 1982), CHAMPIONS (83).

RICHARD JOHNSON

B. Upminster, Essex 30.7.27. Father ran the 200 year-old family paint business; trained for the stage at RADA; début 1944 at Manchester, then played small roles with Gielgud's rep. season of S'peare; rep. Perth 1945; 1945-48 in Royal Navy; Perth 1948-49; tours; walk-on roles in movies CALLING BULLDOG DRUMMOND (50), CAPT. HORATIO HORNBLOWER, R.N. (50), offered Ealing contract, but concentrated on stage career, becoming well-known in the 1950s, especially for S'pearean roles (R.S. Co. 1957-62), including Romeo and Pericles (also Moscow tour 1955); md. 1. Sheila Sweet (div.), 2 children; acted on Broadway several times; many movies include NEVER SO FEW (59), CAIRO (63), THE HAUNTING (63), 80,000 SUSPECTS (63), THE PUMPKIN EATER (63), THE AMOROUS ADVENTURES OF MOLL FLANDERS (65 — md. 2. co-star Kim Novak (qv) 15.3.65, but div. 26.5.66) OPERATION CROSSBOW (65, as Duncan Sandys), KHARTOUM (66), DEADLIER THAN THE MALE (66, as Bulldog Drummond), LADY HAMILTON (68, as Lord Nelson), SOME GIRLS DO (69), JULIUS CAESAR (70, as Cassius), HENNESSY (75, also story), ACES HIGH (76), THE COMEBACK, FOUR FEATHERS (both 77), ZOMBIE II, BIGGEST BANK ROBBERY (T.V. movie, both 79), MONSTER CLUB (81), HAYWIRE (T.V. movie, 82); 1 son Nicholas (mother Francoise Pascal); Md: 3. Marie-Louise Norlund, 1982; much T.V.; Dec, 1982: Chairman/Chief Exec.: 'United British Artists'.

FREDDIE JONES

B. Stoke-on-Trent, Staffs. 12.9.27. Father a potter; ed. Grammar School, Longton; Mr Jones started as a laboratory assistant, but a drama course at Tamworth in 1955 and a scholarship to the Rose Bruford Coll. of Speech & Drama sent him on an acting career; rep. Royal S'peare Co., West End, Broadway; he is a well-known face on T.V. and films; md. actress Jennifer Hesslewood, 3 sons: Toby, Rupert and Casper; T.V. includes 'Treasure Island', 'The Caesars' (1969, Best Actor, Monte Carlo Festival), 'Germinal', 'Sweeney Todd', 'Nana', 'Pennies from Heaven', 'The Ghosts of Motley Hall', 'Bull Week'; movies: DEADFALL (67), FAR FROM THE MADDING CROWD (67), THE BLISS OF MRS BLOSSOM (68), OTLEY (69), THE MAN WHO HAUNTED HIMSELF (70), CARRY ON DOCTOR (70), FRANKENSTEIN MUST BE DESTROYED (70), GOODBYE GEMINI (70), ANTHONY & CLEOPATRA (72), SITTING TARGET (72), THE SATANIC RITES OF DRACULA (73), JUGGERNAUT (74), ZULU DAWN (79), THE ELEPHANT MAN (79), MURDER IS EASY (T.V. movie, 1981), FIREFOX, CAPTAIN STIRRICK (T.V. movie, both 1982), KRULL, AND THE SHIP SAILS ON (both 1983).

ARTE JOHNSON

B.   . First role on Broadway in chorus of 'Gentlemen Prefer Blondes' (49); during lean spells Mr Johnson was clothes salesman; in 1955 he appeared in 'The Shoestring Revue 1955' and broke into T.V. in a series, 'It's Always Jan' as Stanley Shreiber and further T.V. work includes Bascomb Bleacher Jr. in 'Sally' (58), Seaman Shatz in 'Hennesey' (59/62), guest in 'General Electric True' (62), and Cpl. Lefkowitz in 'Don't Call Me Charlie' (62/63); films include MIRACLE IN THE RAIN (56), THE SUBTERRANEANS (60), THE THIRD DAY (65), THE PRESIDENT'S ANALYST (67), CHARGE OF THE MODEL T'S (77), LOVE AT FIRST BITE (78, as Renfield), WE'RE ALL CRAZY NOW (79); came to fame as regular in the 'Rowan & Martin Laugh-in' as the German soldier with catch-phrase expression 'Verrry Interesting!' (1968-71); recent T.V.: guest—'Fantasy Island'; 'Condominium...When the Hurrican Struck' (81, T.V. movie).

LYNN-HOLLY JOHNSON

B. Glenview, Chicago, Illinois 13.12.58. Lynn-Holly commenced her show-biz career aged 4, appearing in T.V. commercials for 'McDonald's', 'Burger King', 'Coca Cola', 'Kellogg's', 'Sears' and modelling sessions for 'Esquire', 'Life' and 'McCall's' mags.; she has an elder brother, Gregg, and sister, Kimberlee, and started ice-skating from the age of 4, attending Niles North H.S., Skokie, later moving to L.A., attending H.S. there; aged 10 she appd. to excellent notices in play 'The Miracle Worker' as Helen Keller at the Ivanhoe Theatre, Chicago and in 1974, as an amateur ice figure skater she won National Novice Free Skating Silver Medal, but later a fall fractured her left leg, took 7 months to heal, and in 1977 she turned professional as principal performer with the Ice Capades Show and entered T.V. in a pilot movie 'Mulligan's Stew', billed as Lynn-Holly in a small role. Since then she has starred as Lexie in ICE CASTLES (78), THE WATCHER IN THE WOODS (79) and in the Bond movie FOR YOUR EYES ONLY (81) as Bibi, an Olympic skater.

DEAN JONES

B. Morgan Co., Alabama 25.1.36. Ed. Ashburn Coll., Wilmore, Kentucky; U.S. Navy service; in 1954 was spotted by producer Arthur Freed while working as a night-club blues singer and M.C., signed to acting/recording contract, coming to the screen uncredited in GABY (55); Mr Jones gradually worked his way up to lead roles, very popular as Disney leading man; many movies include TEA & SYMPATHY (56), JAILHOUSE ROCK (58), TORPEDO RUN (58), NEVER SO FEW (59), UNDER THE YUM YUM TREE (64), TWO ON A GUILLOTINE (64), THAT DARN CAT (65), THE UGLY DUCKLING (66), ANY WEDNESDAY (66), MONKEYS GO HOME (67), BLACKBEARD'S GHOST (67), THE LOVE BUG (69), MILLION $ DUCK (71), SNOWBALL EXPRESS (73), MR SUPERINVINCIBLE (76);   Mr Jones appeared on Broadway in 'There Was a Little Girl' and 'Under the Yum Yum Tree' (1960); two T.V. series in which he appeared regularly were as 'Ensign O'Toole (1962-64) and as Linc McCray in 'The Chicago Teddy Bears' (71); in 1970 he appd. on B'way in 'Company'; HERBIE GOES TO MONTE CARLO (77), BORN AGAIN (78); Md: Lory Patrick, 1 son Michael, 2 daughters: Carol, Deanna; T.V. ser. 1982: 'Herbie, the Love Bug.'

JAMES EARL JONES

B. Arkabutla, Mississippi 17.1.31. Ed. Univ. of Michigan (B.A.); Mr Jones was interested in a medical career at H.S., but switched to drama, eventually studying for the stage at the American Theatre Wing and with Lee Strasberg and Tad Danielewsky; he became a distinguished stage actor after making his début in 1949 in Univ. production of 'Deep are the Roots' and work in this medium includes Michigan Summer Rep. 1955-59 ('Caine Mutiny', 'Tender Trap', title role 'Othello', etc.), New York début 1957 in 'Wedding in Japan', played with distinction in S'peare: Oberon in 'A Midsummer Night's Dream', Caliban in 'The Tempest', etc.; md. Julienne Marie, actress; movies: DR STRANGELOVE (63), THE COMEDIANS (67), THE END OF THE ROAD (68), THE GREAT WHITE HOPE (71, also stage—Tony award 1969), THE STING (73), CLAUDINE (74), THE BINGO LONG TRAVELLING ALL STARS (76), A PIECE OF THE ACTION (77), RED TIDE (80), BUSHIDO BLADE (80), CONAN (81); voice of 'Darth Vader' ('Star Wars'); much T.V. from 1952: 'Guiding Light' (series 1952), 'Jesus of Nazareth' (76), 'Roots—Next Generation' (as Alex Hailey, 1979); N.Y. stage 1982: as 'Othello'.

SAM JONES

B. West Palm Beach, Florida, . . .; from a non-showbusiness family, before heading for California, worked at 20 jobs, including restaurant manager, health club instructor, truck driver and semi-pro footballer; when in L.A. set himself '6 months to get somewhere' — Sam got small role in stage play and studied drama; discovered in a student showcase evening and signed up by an agent; T.V. roles: 'Co-Ed Fever' (pilot) and a stuntman in 'Stunts Unlimited' led to movie role in 10 (79) as bridegroom; following a T.V. appearance in 'The Dating Game' (78) signed up for first starring role in FLASH GORDON (79).

TERRY JONES

B. Colwyn Bay, N. Wales 1.2.42. Mr Jones entered the entertainment industry in 1965 and has become well-known as a member of the 'Monty Python' team on T.V. and the movies; T.V.: 'Do Not Adjust Your Set', 'Monty Python's Flying Circus', etc.; writer/director/performer; movies: AND NOW FOR SOMETHING COMPLETELY DIFFERENT (71), MONTY PYTHON & THE HOLY GRAIL (76, co-dir.), JABBERWOCKY (76), Brian's mum in LIFE OF BRIAN (79); he entered show-biz while appearing in revue and cabaret at Oxford, later wrote comedy scripts for T.V.; acted/directed MONTY PYTHON'S MEANING OF LIFE (82).

TOMMY LEE JONES

B. San Saba, Texas, 15.9.46. Part-Indian, grandmother having been a Comanche; father an oil rigger; ed. Elementary School, Midland, Texas, St. Mark's School of Texas (appeared in 1st play 'Under Milk Wood'); oil field worker; studied at Harvard, excelling at football and gaining degree in English; married, 2 children; New York stage includes 'A Patriot For Me', 'Four on a Garden'; T.V. includes 'One Life to Live', 'Baretta', 'Barnaby Jones', CHARLIE'S ANGELS (76, T.V. movie — pilot); SMASH-UP ON INTERSTATE 5 (76, T.V. movie); THE AMAZING HOWARD HUGHES (77, T.V. movie, title role); Mr Jones's movies: LOVE STORY (71, bit); JACKSON COUNTY JAIL (76); THE EYES OF LAURA MARS, ROLLING THUNDER, THE BETSY (all 77); COAL MINER'S DAUGHTER (79); BACK ROADS (81); EXECUTIONER'S SONG (82); SAVAGE ISLANDS (83).

LOUIS JOURDAN

B. Marseilles, France, 19.6.21(?). Real name Louis Gendre; in 1939 studying at René Simon's dramatic school in Paris, was discovered by a film talent scout and came to the screen in LE CORSAIR, but the war stopped production, and during German occupation Nazis allowed him to appear in non-political films (FIRST APPOINTMENT, L'ARLESIENNE (41), LA BELLE AVENTURE (42), etc.), but Louis refused pro-Nazi films and subsequently joined Resistance, helped publish/distribute newspaper for underground; in 1945 went to Hollywood, wed 1946 Berthe Frederique (their son, Louis Henry, born 1951); Mr Jourdan's many movies Hollywood/Europe include THE PARADINE CASE (48), LETTERS FROM AN UNKNOWN WOMAN (48), MADAME BOVARY (49), BIRD OF PARADISE (50), THE HAPPY TIME (52), DECAMERON NIGHTS (53), THREE COINS IN THE FOUNTAIN (54), THE SWAN (56), JULIE (56), GIGI (58), THE BEST OF EVERYTHING (59), CAN-CAN (60), THE COUNT OF MONTE CRISTO (61), THE V.I.P.'S (62), MADE IN PARIS (65), A FLEA IN HER EAR (68), TO COMMIT A MURDER (70); Broadway includes 'The Immoralist' (54), 'Tonight in Samarkand' (55); T.V. includes series, USA, 1955: 'Paris Precinct' as Insp. Beaumont, lead as 'Dracula' (77, GB); recent movies: SILVER BEARS (77), FRENCH ATLANTIC AFFAIR (T.V. movie, 79), DOUBLE DEAL (81), OCTOPUSSY (83); host: 'Romance' (T.V. 82).

MADELINE KAHN

B. Boston, Mass. 29.9.42. Madeleine's mother was once a singer, father a dress manufacturer; as a child raised in New York and had natural musical ability; she attended Hofstra Univ., studied speech therapy, considered being an opera singer but too much study; she did sing, however, at a New York beer garden, while studying; chose acting career and did plays, cabaret, satirical reviews, musicals ('Two by Two', 'La Bohème', 'Showboat', 'Candide'); T.V.—'Comedy Tonight' (70) series and movies: WHAT'S UP, DOC? (72), BLAZING SADDLES (72), PAPER MOON (73, Oscar nom. BSA), YOUNG FRANKENSTEIN (74), AT LAST LONG LOVE (74), ADVENTURES OF SHERLOCK HOLMES' SMARTER BROTHER (75), WON TON TON (76), CHEAP DETECTIVE, HIGH ANXIETY (both 77), MUPPET MOVIE, HAPPY BIRTHDAY, GEMINI, SIMON (all 79), WHOLLY MOSES (80), HISTORY OF WORLD, PT.1 (81), SLAPSTICK (82), YELLOWBEARD (83).

SHIRLEY JONES

B. Smithtown, Pennsylvania 31.3.34. An only child, father a brewer, they encouraged her to take singing lessons from Ken Welch (in Pittsburgh), appd. there with Light Opera Co. in 'Lady in the Dark', 'Call Me Madam' and became 'Miss Pittsburgh 1952'; went to New York, through singing teacher, met an agent, who in turn sent her to casting director for tour of 'Oklahoma', winning 7 year contract, but played small roles on Broadway in 'South Pacific', 'Me & Juliet', lead in latter on tour; tested and won movie lead as Laurey in OKLAHOMA (55), then CAROUSEL (56); md. 1. Jack Cassidy in Boston 6.8.56, 3 sons: Shaun (b. 1959), Patrick (b. 1962), Ryan (b. 1966), div. in 1975 and Mr Cassidy later died; she appd. in T.V. series 'The Partridge Family' (70-74) with step-son David Cassidy; other movies include APRIL LOVE (57), PEPE (60), ELMER GANTRY (60, Oscar BSA), MUSIC MAN (62), BEDTIME STORY (64), SECRET OF MY SUCCESS (65), THE HAPPY ENDING (70), BEYOND THE POSEIDON ADVENTURE (79); many T.V. movies include: SILENT NIGHT, HOLY NIGHT (69), WINNER TAKES ALL (75), AN EVENING IN BYZANTIUM (78); md. 2. actor/manager Marty Ingels, Nov '77; TANK (83).

RICHARD JORDAN

B. New York City 19.7.38. Mr Jordan comes from a wealthy and socially prominent family and after attending Harvard Univ., he embarked on a stage career; played on Broadway with distinction in 'Take Her, She's Mine' (61), 'A Patriot For Me' (69) and is a Shakespearean actor of note, including 'Romeo & Juliet' (61), 'The Tempest' (62), 'Troilus & Cressida' (65); md. actress Kathleen Widdoes, 1 daughter Nina (b. c.1965) (div.); movies include (supporting roles, graduating to stardom) LAWMAN (70), VALDEZ IS COMING (71), THE FRIENDS OF EDDIE COYLE (73), THE YAKUZA (75), KAMOURASKA (75), LOGAN'S RUN (76), ROOSTER COGBURN (76), INTERIORS (78), OLD BOYFRIENDS (79), RAISE THE TITANIC (79); Mr Jordan's T.V. work includes the series 'Captains & Kings', (76, as Joseph Armagh), LES MISERABLES (78, T.V. movie), THE BIGGEST BANK ROBBERY (79, T.V. movie), THE FRENCH ATLANTIC AFFAIR (79, T.V. movie), THE BUNKER (81, T.V. movie as Albert Speer).

CURT JURGENS

B. Munich, Germany 12.12.15(?). Full name Curt Gustaf Andre Gottlieb Jurgens; parents: father a German travelling salesman, mother a French teacher of the Russian Royal Family, their son 'conceived at the Imperial Russian Court at St. Petersburg'; leading man on German stage before War, in films from 1939; won acting awards for European films — DEVIL'S GENERAL (55, Cannes), LES HEROS SONT FATIGUES (56, Venice) and after AN EYE FOR AN EYE (56), AND WOMAN WAS CREATED (57) he went to Hollywood for ENEMY BELOW (57) and has since appeared regularly in international pictures: ME AND THE COLONEL (57), THE INN OF THE 6TH HAPPINESS (58), THE BLUE ANGEL (59), I AIM AT THE STARS (59, as Werner von Braun), FERRY TO HONG KONG (60), TAMANGO (60), LORD JIM (64), THE THREEPENNY OPERA (65), DAS LIEBES-KARUSSEL (65), ASSASSINATION BUREAU (68), THE BATTLE OF NERETVA (70), NICHOLAS AND ALEXANDRA (71), VAULT OF HORROR (73), SOFT BED, HARD BATTLES (74), THE SPY WHO LOVED ME (77), JUST A GIGOLO (78), FLYING DRAGON (78), BREAKTHROUGH (78), TEHERAN (80); Broadway includes 'The Great Indoors' (1966); Mr Jurgens has been divorced on 4 occasions, the last being Simone Bicheron; his fifth wife, Margie, is Austrian; recent TV: The General in 'Smiley's People' (BBC-1982). *Mr Jurgens died of heart failure, Vienna, 18.6.82.*

WILLIAM KATT

B. Los Angeles, California 16.2.51. His parents are well-known American screen artistes, Bill Williams (real name Katt) and Barbara Hale (known internationally for her role as Della Street in the 'Perry Mason' series); their son studied at California's Orange Coast College (majoring in piano and guitar), taking a drama course; acted with the South Coast Repertory Theatre, later concentrating in productions at the Abmanson & Mark Taper Theatres in Los Angeles; his movie appearances have included THE LATE LIZ (71), CARRIE (76), FIRST LOVE (77), BIG WEDNESDAY (78) and BUTCH & SUNDANCE — THE EARLY YEARS (78); Md: Debbie, 1 son, Clayton; stage 1982: 'The Rainmaker'.

STACY KEACH

B. Savannah, Georgia 2.6.41. Father a drama tutor; first role in school production as Rip Van Winkle; father brought to Universal Studios in early 40s to coach Maria Montez, family moved to California; Stacy saw Olivier (qv) movie HAMLET in 1949 and wanted to become actor; ed. Univ. of Calif. and Yale, working in all areas of drama, 1 year at LAMDA, London; taught drama at Yale, appd. in stock, off-Broadway, became well-known on Broadway in such productions as 'Hamlet' (64), 'The Country Wife' (65), 'Mac-Bird' (67), 'The Nigger Lovers' (67), 'Henry IV' (68), 'King Lear' (68), 'Indians' (69), 'Peer Gynt' (69); md. 1.   ; 2. Marilyn Akin, Dec. 1974; many movies include (billed in early films as Stacy Keach Jr.): HEART IS A LONELY HUNTER (68), TRAVELLING EXECU-TIONER(70), DOC(71), NEW CENTURIONS (72), LIFE & TIMES OF JUDGE ROY BEAN (72), GRAVY TRAIN (74), LUTHER (75), DYNASTY(76), THE SQUEEZE(76), GRAY LADY DOWN (77), UP IN SMOKE (78), THE LONG RIDERS (79); Mr Keach has won numerous stage awards; T.V.: Carlson in 'Get Smart' (66-67), Lt. Ben Logan in 'Caribe' (75) and Barabbas in 'Jesus of Nazareth' (1976); has also directed on T.V.; recent movies: A RUMOUR OF WAR, THE 9TH CONFIGURATION, ROAD GAMES (all 80), BUTTERFLY, NICE DREAMS (both 81), THAT CHAMPIONSHIP SEASON (82).

DIANE KEEN

B. London 29.7.46. Ed. Kenya and privately; Miss Keen spent 19 years of her early life in Kenya, where her father was a surveyor; after completing a repertory season at Nairobi, she came to Great Britain, mother advising her to take a secretarial course — she also worked as a night club disc jockey and demonstrated Dutch (Edam) cheese; first notable role on T.V. in 'The Cuckoo Waltz' and she has worked in other series such as 'The Fall of the Eagles', 'Robin Hood' (as Maid Marion), 'Rings on Their Fingers', 'The Feathered Serpent'; md. actor Paul Greenwood (div.), 1 daughter Melissa; films include SWEENEY! (75), THE SHILLINGBURY BLOWERS (79, T.V. movie) and SILVER DREAM RACER (79); Md: 2. TV producer Neil Zeiger, 9.10.82; recent TV: 'Shillingbury Tales' (81), 'Foxy Lady' (82).

ANDREW KEIR

B. Shotts, Lanarkshire, Scotland 3.4.26. Father a coalminer; Mr Keir left school at 14 to work at pithead; appd. in amateur dramatics, later joining Glasgow Citizens' Theatre and Aberdeen Theatre; has played in films since 1949, early titles include THE LADY CRAVED EXCITEMENT (50), THE BRAVE DON'T CRY (52), THE MAG-GIE (54), HEART OF A CHILD (57); md. Julie Wallace, 5 children; he is a familiar face on T.V., appearing in early series 'Ivanhoe', 'The 4 Just Men' and more recently 'Adam Smith' (71/72) and 'The Outsiders' (77); scores of films include PIRATES OF BLOOD RIVER (60), CLEOPATRA (63), LORD JIM (65), THE FALL OF THE ROMAN EMPIRE (65), DRACULA, PRINCE OF DARKNESS (65), THE VIKING QUEEN(67), QUATERMASS AND THE PIT (67), ATTACK ON THE IRON COAST (68), THE LAST GRENADE (69), THE ROYAL HUNT OF THE SUN(69), ZEPPELIN(70), BLOOD OF THE MUMMY'S TOMB (71) and more recently 39 STEPS (78), MEETINGS WITH REMARKABLE MEN (78), LION OF THE DESERT; T.V. 82: 'The World Cup: A Captain's Tale'.

BRIAN KEITH

B. Bayonne, New Jersey 14.11.21. Son of Robert Keith (Brian's real name), a well-known stage actor, he was born while father was touring in 'Three Wise Fools', and made film début only 3 years old in 'The Pied Piper of Malone'; from 1942-45 he served in the U.S. Marines; in 1946 appeared in play 'Hay Day', then spent 12 months in radio & T.V., understudied various roles in 'Mr Roberts' which toured (in cast was father, later took over his role) and with same play appd. on Broadway in role of Mannion; 'Darkness at Noon' (1951) followed, then summer stock at Cape Cod and a return to Broadway in 'Out West of 8th' (1951); md. 1. Frances Helm 1948 (div. 1954), 2. Judy Landon 1954, 5 children: Michael (1955, died 1963), Barbara (1961), Elizabeth (1962), Rory (1963), Mimi (1964), (div.); Mr Keith accepted Columbia contract in 1952 and has been in scores of movies including ARROW-HEAD(52), VIOLENT MEN(54), 5 AGAINST THE HOUSE (55), RUN OF THE ARROW (57), PARENT TRAP (61), THOSE CALLO-WAYS(65), NEVADA SMITH(66), McKEN-ZIE BREAK (71), THE WIND & THE LION (76, as Theodore Roosevelt); T.V.: guest: 'Ford Theatre', 'Studio '57'; series: 'The Crusader' (56), 'Family Affair' (66-71), 'The Little People' (72-74), 'Archer' (75); Md: 3. Victoria Young, 9.1.70, 1 son Robert (70), 1 daughter Maria ('71); SHARKEY'S MACHINE (81), CHARLIE CHAN & THE CURSE OF THE DRAGON QUEEN (81), WORLD WAR III (82, mini-ser.).

DIANE KEATON

B. Los Angeles, Calif. 5.1.46. Diane's family are Methodists, she has a younger brother, Randy, and 2 younger sisters, Dorrie and Robin; father is a civil engineer, mother's maiden name is Keaton (real name Diane Hall); raised in Santa Ana, she attended college there and became interested in theatre. Following summer stock she went to New York, played with the Neighbourhood Playhouse and made her Broadway début 1968 as the lead in 'Hair', then acted in 'Play It Again Sam' with Woody Allen in 1969 (later in film version, 1972); she came to the screen in LOVERS AND OTHER STRANGERS (70) and has been seen in THE GODFATHER (71), SLEEPER (74), LOVE AND DEATH(75), THE GODFATHER: PART II (75), I WILL, I WILL, FOR NOW (76), HARRY AND WALTER GO TO NEW YORK (76), ANNIE HALL (77, Hollywood Golden Globe Award—joint Best Actress, Academy Award, Best Actress, 1977), LOOKING FOR MR GOODBAR (77), MANHATTAN (78), INTERIORS (79), REDS (81, Oscar nom., BSA), SHOOT THE MOON (82).

GEOFFREY KEEN

B. London 21.8.18. Father Malcolm Keen, distinguished actor (1887-1970); ed. Bristol Grammar School studying with the Bristol Old Vic Theatre School where he made stage début in 1932 in his teens in 'The School for Scandal'; gained Lever-hulme S'ship to study at RADA in 1935, gaining the Bancroft Gold Medal in 1936; Mr Keen became distinguished actor on stage in the 30s and 40s, especially in S'peare, serving with the Army in 1940 and 4 years in 'Stars in Battledress'; he came to the screen in 1948 in THE FALLEN IDOL and has been solid support in over 100 movies; md. 1. actress Hazel Terry (div.), 2. Doris Groves, actress — 1 daughter Mary; a very well-known and popular face on T.V., Mr Keen's work here includes 'Mogul', 'The Troubleshooters' and guested many times — 'Crown Court', 'Church-ill & The Generals' (79), 'Cribb' (81); recent films: LICENSED TO LOVE AND KILL(78), MOONRAKER (79), RISE & FALL OF IDI AMIN (79).

HARVEY KEITEL

B. Brooklyn, New York,   .   .47. Mr Keitel left school and joined the Marine Corps; in 1967 he returned to New York and studied at New York Univ. where he met the now well-known film director Martin Scorcese who gave him the lead in a collegiate movie, WHO'S THAT KNOCKING AT MY DOOR? (69); he went on to study at the Actors' Studio with Lee Strasberg and Frank Corsaro, appeared in summer stock and little theatre productions before turning to T.V. and movies, the latter include MEAN STREETS (73), THE VIRGINIA HILL STORY (74, T.V. movie), ALICE DOESN'T LIVE HERE ANY-MORE (74), THAT'S THE WAY OF THE WORLD(75), MOTHER JUGS AND SPEED (76), WELCOME TO L.A. (76), BUFFALO BILL & THE INDIANS (76), TAXI DRIVER (76), THE DUELLISTS (76), FINGERS (77), EAGLE'S WING (77), BLUE COLLAR (78), SATURN 3 (79), BAD TIMING (79), DEATH WATCH (79), THE BORDER (80); Broadway includes 'Up to Thursday' (65): recent screen: EXPOSED (82), COPKILLER (83).

PENELOPE KEITH

B. Sutton, Surrey 2.4.   . Real name Penelope Hatfield; ed. Annecy Convent, Seaford, Sussex and at Bayeux; studied for the stage at the Webber-Douglas School, London, making pro. début at Chesterfield Rep. in 1959 in 'The Tunnel of Love'; further rep.: Lincoln and Manchester, joined Royal S'peare Co. 1963, London début 1964 with that Co. in 'Wars of the Roses' trilogy; further London plays include 'Ballad of the False Barman' (66), 'Mr Kilt & The Great I Am' (70), 'Suddenly At Home' (71) and 'The Norman Con-quests' (74); became well-known on T.V. as actress/comedienne in series 'Kate' (71/72) and especially as Margot Leadbetter in 'The Good Life' (BBC, BAFTA Award 1977) and as Audrey fforbes-Hamilton in 'To the Manor Born' (79/80, BBC T.V.); md. Mr Rodney Timson, a policeman (couple met Chichester Festival, June 1977) on 6 Feb. 1978; films: TAKE A GIRL LIKE YOU (69), EVERY HOME SHOULD HAVE ONE (69), PENNY GOLD (73), GHOST STORY (75, T.V. movie); many awards; other stage: 'Donkey's Years' (76), 'The Millionairess' (78/79), 'Moving' (81), 'Captain Brassbound's Conversion', 'Hobson's Choice' (82); film 1981: PRIEST OF LOVE; T.V. 1982: 'On Approval'.

GENE KELLY

One of the truly great delights the cinema has brought to us is surely the sight of Gene Kelly engaged in one of his many exuberant and skilfully choreographed dance routines of the 40s and 50s. Now in his sixtieth year, he is still very active, recently returning to dance on the screen in XANADU (80). He was born Eugene Curran Kelly in Pittsburgh, Pennsylvania on 23 August 1912, the third of five children born to James and Harriet Kelly. At school he liked sport more than dancing and at Pennsylvania State College studied journalism, but during the Depression he was forced to leave and earn a living by teaching gymnastics at Camp Porter, a YMCA camp near Pittsburgh. However, he entered amateur dancing competitions with his brother Fred as a duo specialising in tap-dancing on roller skates and worked as bricklayer, cement mixer and drug store attendant to help finance his tuition at the University of Pittsburgh, firstly studying economics, switching to law and graduating with a B.A. Degree in 1933. But his talent for dance made him return to help organise the family dancing school in his home town, later opening a second Gene Kelly School of Dance at Johnstown, Pennsylvania. With his brother he continued to perform in local clubs and children's theatre. He went to New York in 1937 to secure a dance teaching job, was unsuccessful, but the following year returned and got a chorus job in 'Leave It To Me!'. His talent began to impress producers and within 4 years he was an M-G-M star! He acted/danced in the show 'One For The Money' (39), choreographed 3 shows at Westport, Conn., spent 22 weeks in 'The Time Of Your Life' (1940), was dance director in 1941 of Billy Rose's famous 'Diamond Horseshow Revue', and it was his role in 'Pal Joey' on Broadway in 1940 that made him a star. He wed dancer Betty Blair on 22 September 1941 (their daughter, Kerry, was born in 1943), movie mogul David Selznick put him under contract, but he eventually came to the screen opposite Judy Garland (who had pushed for him after seeing him on Broadway) at M-G-M in FOR ME AND MY GAL (42). Among his best films (*co-directed) were COVER GIRL (44); ANCHORS AWEIGH (43, Oscar nom., B.A.); (1945-47 in U.S. Navy); THE PIRATE (48); THE THREE MUSKETEERS (48, as D'Artagnan); ON THE TOWN (49); AN AMERICAN IN PARIS (51, Kelly earning a Honorary Oscar 'in appreciation of his versatility as an actor, singer, director and dancer, and especially for his brilliant achievements in the art of choreography on film'); SINGIN' IN THE RAIN (52*); BRIGADOON (54); INVITATION TO THE DANCE (also directed, 56); INHERIT THE WIND (60) and THE YOUNG GIRLS OF ROCHEFORT (67). He divorced his first wife in 1957 and married Jeanne Coyne, his assistant choreographer since 1949, in 1960. Their son, Timothy, was born on 3 March 1962, but his second wife died in 1973. His T.V. work includes a series as Father Charles O'Mally in 'Going My Way' (1963) and host of 'The Funny side' (1971). He directed, amongst others, the mammoth HELLO DOLLY (69) and recently appeared in VIVA KNIEVEL (77) and XANADU (80).
GENE KELLY by Clive Hirschhorn; W.H. Allen: London, 1974;
THE FILMS OF GENE KELLY: SONG AND DANCE MAN by Tony Thomas; Citadel: Secaucus, USA, 1974;

MARTHE KELLER

B. Basle, Switzerland, . .45. Father a 'horse-racing Swiss farmer'; Marthe took ballet lessons from age 8, then had skiing injury; studied privately with Basle State Theatre for 1 year, 3 years with Munich's Stanislavsky School, modelling in evenings, sometimes for 'Vogue', in mornings studied sociology and philosophy at Munich Univ., appd. occasionally on T.V.; stage début at Heidelberg, but got disillusioned, then auditioned and won roles for Schiller Theatre, Berlin, in classical roles 1 year; went to Paris, appd. in film DEVIL BY THE TAIL, directed by Philippe de Broca (the father of her child, Alexandre), stayed for 1968 student revolt, appd. in 2 French T.V. series 'Arsene Lupin' and 'Le Demoiselle D'Avignon' and won stage award for play 'A Day in the Death of Joe Egg'; (had bit part, aged 16, in movie FUNERAL IN BERLIN) after films LES CAPRICES DE MARIE, DOWN THE ANCIENT STAIRS and AND NOW MY LOVE'; Hollywood beckoned and she has appd. in MARATHON MAN (75), BLACK SUNDAY (76), BOBBY DEERFIELD (77), FEDORA (77), THE FORMULA (80), THE AMATEUR (82), WAGNER (83).

BARBARA KELLERMANN

B. Manchester, ... Father senior lecturer in physics at Leeds Univ., mother, senior adviser of modern languages to Yorkshire Education Authority; Barbara, who also has a brother and sister, has appd. on T.V. on many occasions including 'General Hospital', '1990', 'Crown Court', 'The Professionals', 'Glittering Prizes', 'Quatermass', 'Ladykillers', 'Hammer House of Horror', she speaks French and German fluently, her films include SATAN'S SLAVE, THE SEA WOLVES (80, opp. Roger Moore (qv)) and the MONSTER CLUB (81); md. actor Robin Scobey. LIVING APART TOGETHER (83); T.V. 83: 'Number 10'.

JEREMY KEMP

B. nr. Chesterfield, Derbyshire 3.2.35. Real name Edmund Walker; ed. Abbottsholme, Staffs. and Central School of Speech & Drama (1955-58); Nat. Service: Gordon Highlanders; stage début: Felixstowe 1957; London début: June 1958, Royal Court; much stage includes 2 seasons Old Vic (played Malcolm in 'Macbeth'), Nottingham Playhouse, West End: 'Celebration', 'Incident at Vichy', 'Spoiled', 'The Caretaker'; much T.V. includes 'Z Cars' (regular, early 60s), frequent guest appearances; many films include CLEOPATRA (63, uncredited), DR TERROR'S HOUSE OF HORRORS (64), OPERATION CROSSBOW (64), THE BLUE MAX (65), ASSIGNMENT K (67), A TWIST OF SAND (67), THE STRANGE AFFAIR (67), DARLING LILI (70), SALTZBURG CONNECTION (72), THE BELLSTONE FOX (73), THE 7% SOLUTION (75), A BRIDGE TOO FAR (76), LEOPARD IN THE SNOW (77), CARAVANS (77), EAST OF ELEPHANT ROCK (77), PRISONER OF ZENDA (78), RETURN OF THE SOLDIER (83); recent T.V.: 'The Winter's Tale' (81), 'Unity' (81), Cornwall in 'King Lear' (83).

SALLY KELLERMAN

B. Long Beach, California 2.6.38(?). Parents: John and Edith Kellerman; ed. Hollywood H.S.; studied acting at New York's Actors' Studio and with Jeff Corey in Hollywood; early T.V.: episodes of 'Outer Limits', 'Mannix', 'It Takes a Thief'; came to screen in THE THIRD DAY (65) and has been seen in THE BOSTON STRANGLER (68), THE APRIL FOOLS (69), *M.A.S.H. (70), BREWSTER McCLOUD (70), LAST OF THE RED HOT LOVERS (72), THE LOST HORIZON (72), SLITHER (73), RAFFERTY & THE GOLD DANCE (75), THE BIG BUS (76), WELCOME TO L.A. (76), A LITTLE ROMANCE (79), THE SERIAL (79), HEAD ON (79), LOVING COUPLES (79), FOXES (80); md. Rick Edelstein 1970 (div. 1971); *Oscar nom. BSA; U.S. mini-series:'Centennial' (78).

DEFORREST KELLEY

B. Atlanta, Georgia, . .20. Mr Kelley decided at 17 that he wanted to be in show business — he sang with dance bands and ventured into acting, writing and producing plays; early films include FEAR IN THE NIGHT (47), DUKE OF CHICAGO (50), HOUSE OF BAMBOO (55), ILLEGAL (56), THE GUNFIGHT AT OK CORRAL (57, as Morgan Earp), WARLOCK (59) and JOHNNY RENO (66); md. Caroline; became a household name with his performance as Dr Leonard McCoy ('Bones'), Chief Medical Officer in the U.S. T.V. series 'Star Trek' (66-69); also voice for animated version of series and repeated his role in STAR TREK — THE MOTION-PICTURE (78), STAR TREK: VENGEANCE OF KHAN (82).

ARTHUR KENNEDY

B. Worcester, Mass. 17.2.14. Father, Dr J.T. Kennedy, a dentist; ed. Carnegie Institute of Technology, studying engineering, but turned to the stage, toured in S'peare, New York début in mid-1930s in 'Merrily We Roll Along', also played 'unidentified' small roles in 30s films; md. Mary Cheffey, actress 1940, 2 children; Mr Kennedy became distinguished stage and movie actor, scoring on Broadway in 'Life and Death of an American' (39), 'An International Incident' (40), 'All My Sons' (47) and 'Death of a Salesman' (49/50, Tony Award), others; first big screen role in CITY OF CONQUEST (40), gaining Warner Bros. contract, 'discovered on Broadway for screen by James Cagney', many roles in such pics. as THEY DIED WITH THEIR BOOTS ON (41), DEVOTION (46), THE WINDOW (49), CHAMPION (49, Oscar nom.), RANCHO NOTORIOUS (54), THE MAN FROM LARAMIE (55), PEYTON PLACE (57), A SUMMER PLACE (59), ELMER GANTRY (60), LAWRENCE OF ARABIA (62), NEVADA SMITH (65), ANZIO (68), MY OLD MAN'S PLACE (71), T.V. includes: host/narrator 'FDR' (65), MOVIE MURDERER (70, T.V. movie), NAKIA (74, and series as Sheriff Sam Jericho); recent films: THE SENTINEL (76), BORN AGAIN (78), COVERT ACTION (78).

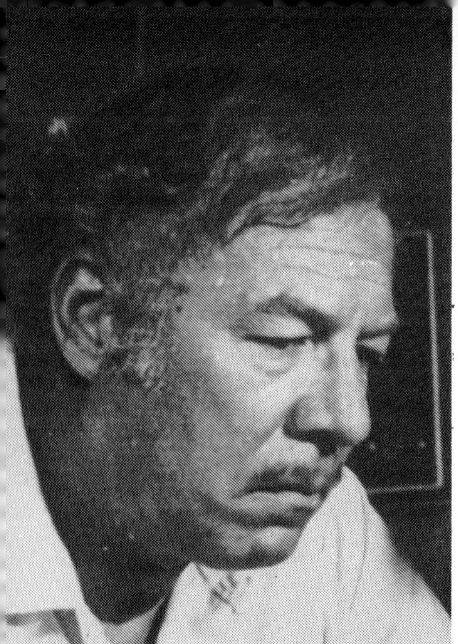

GEORGE KENNEDY

Turning to movies after a successful career in the U.S. Army, George Kennedy comes from a theatrical family, his father, George Snr., was a pianist, composer and orchestra leader at New York's Proctor Theatre, and his mother, Helen Meade, was a ballerina with the Ballet Classique. He was born when his parents were appearing in vaudeville, at New York City, on 25 February 1926(?), and he made his stage début in 'Bringing Up Father' aged 2, but when he was 4 his father died, and his mother worked as a waitress and shop assistant. At the age of 7 George was hosting his own children's show on radio, later becoming Long Island's youngest D.J., but his mother (who was remarried — to a railway detective) discouraged a show-biz career. So at the age of 17 he joined the U.S. Army and served for 15 years, earning 2 bronze stars and 4 rows of combat and service medals. Not ignoring show-biz activities, he worked in Forces radio and T.V., producing and directing shows, and as technical adviser of the 'Bilko' series (appearing in a few episodes). Discharged from service after a back injury, he sought further work on T.V., appearing in episodes of 'Sugarfoot', 'Cheyenne', coming to the screen in THE LITTLE SHEPHERD OF KINGDOM COME (60). He had wed actress Norma Jean 'Revel' Wurman, having 2 children, Karianne and Christopher George — the couple divorced in 1978. Starting in movies as a hefty villain, but graduating to more sympathetic roles, his over 50 movies include LONELY ARE THE BRAVE (62); CHARADE (63); SHENANDOAH (65); MIRAGE (65); FLIGHT OF THE PHOENIX (65); THE DIRTY DOZEN (67); COOL HAND LUKE (67, Oscar BSA); BANDOLERO! (68), AIRPORT (69); CHICAGO, CHICAGO (70); LOST HORIZON (72) and EARTHQUAKE (74). T.V. includes series 'Sarge' as Father Samuel Patrick Cavanagh (71/72) and 'The Blue Knight' as Wm. A. 'Bumper' Morgan (75). Mr Kennedy has remarried and his wife, Joan, has 2 daughters from a previous marriage, Shannon and Shauna. His more recent screen work has been DEATH ON THE NILE (77); THE DOUBLE McGUFFIN (78); MEAN DOG BLUES (78); STEEL (78); BRASS TARGET (78, as Gen. Patton); AIRPORT 80—CONCORDE (79); DEATH SHIP (79); HOT WIRE (80); VIRUS (80); MODERN ROMANCE (81); SEARCH & DESTROY (81); STRIKING BACK (81); CARNAUBA (81); JUST BEFORE DAWN (82) and A RARE BREED (83).

PERSIS KHAMBATTA

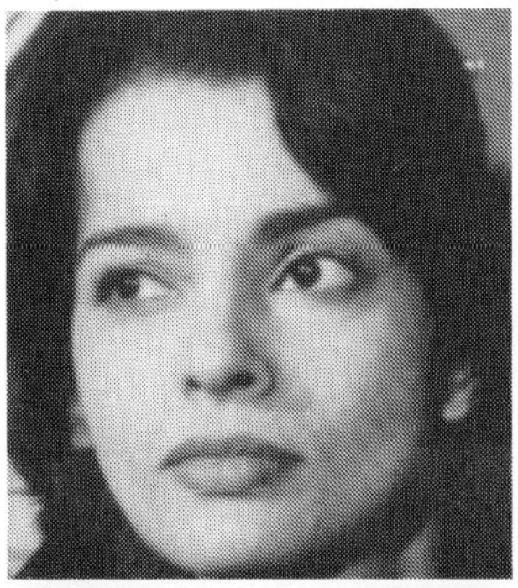

B. Bombay, India, . .50. A former Miss India, Miss Khambatta won a 'Best Actress Award' there in films and came to Europe and appeared in such movies as THE WILBY CONSPIRACY (75) and CONDUCT UNBECOMING (75); her work has since included the T.V. movie 'The Man With The Power' (79), played the role of Ilia in STAR TREK—THE MOTION PICTURE (79) and more recently NIGHT HAWKS (81), MEGAFORCE (82).

MARGOT KIDDER

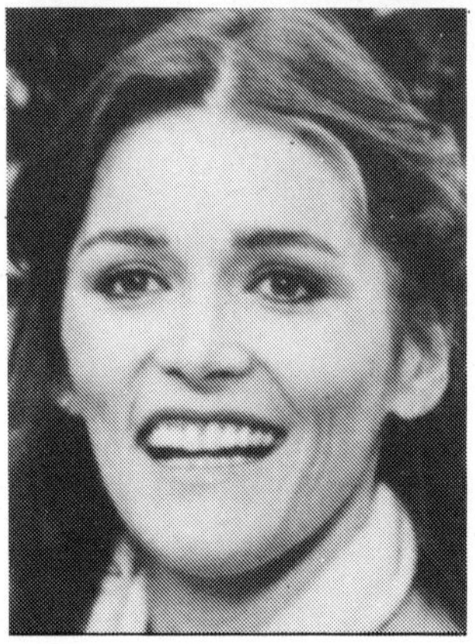

B. Yellowknife, Canada 17.10.48. Miss Kidder grew up among the arid mining towns of Quebec, constantly on the move, and she went to 12 schools in 11 years, also attending the University of British Colombia; md. 1. ——— (div.), 1 daughter Maggie; directed with Women's Directing Workshop (sponsored by A.F.I.) and her films as actress include GAILY, GAILY (70), SUDDENLY SINGLE (71, T.V. movie), THE BOUNTY MAN (72, T.V. movie), SISTERS (73), THE GRAVY TRAIN (aka THE DION BROTHERS, 74), 'Such Dust As Dreams Are Made Of' (74, pilot for 'Harry-O' series), HONKY TONK (74, T.V. movie), Lois Lane in SUPERMAN (77) and SUPERMAN II (81), THE AMITYVILLE HORROR (78), WILLIE & PHIL (79), HEARTACHES (81), SOME KIND OF HERO (81); md. 2. writer Tom McGuane, 1974 (div. 1977); stage 1982: 'Bus Stop'; recent films: SHOOT THE SUN DOWN (82), TRENCHCOAT (82), SUPERMAN III (83), LOUISIANA(83); Md:3.Philippe de Broca, 1983.

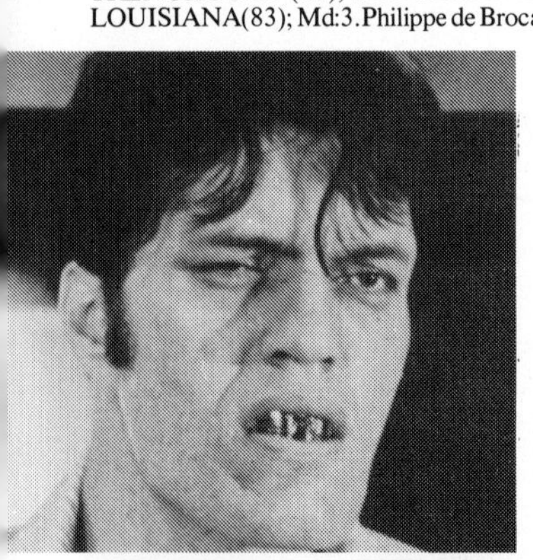

RICHARD KIEL

B. Detroit, . . . Mr Kiel, who was 7′2″ tall by the time he was 17, is a former bouncer in a California night spot and while selling Steinway grand pianos and Hammond Organs, decided on an acting career; early film: title role of EEGAH! (62); his work has since included the series and 'pilot' film 'Barbary Coast' (75), appearances in the Burt Reynolds picture THE MEAN MACHINE (74) and Gene Wilder's SILVER STREAK (76) and became well-known as 'Jaws' in the 2 Bond movies THE SPY WHO LOVED ME (77) and MOONRAKER (79); md. 1. ? (div.). 2. Diane, 3 sons: Richard George, Bennett, Christopher; Mr Kiel has business interests in real estate; other movies: FORCE TEN FROM NAVARONE (78), SO FINE (81), HYSTERICAL (82).

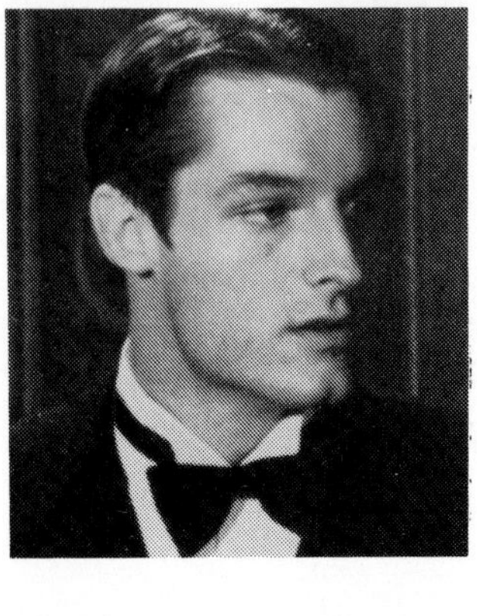

PERRY KING

B. Alliance, Ohio, . . . Ed. Yale Univ.; studied for the stage under Mr John Houseman (qv) at the Juillard School; Mr King came to the screen in THE POSSESSION OF JOEL DELANEY (72) and his work includes SLAUGHTERHOUSE-FIVE (72), THE LORDS OF FLATBUSH (74), THE WILD PARTY (74), MANDINGO (75), FOSTER AND LAURIE (75, T.V. movie), LIPSTICK (76), 2 U.S. T.V. 'Best Sellers': CAPTAINS & KINGS (76) and ASPEN (77), 'Rich Man, Poor Man' (Mini-series, 76), THE CHOIRBOYS (77), ANDY WARHOL'S BAD (77), A DIFFERENT STORY (78), THE CRACKER FACTORY, LOVE'S SAVAGE FURY (both T.V. movies, 1979), STRIKING BACK (81), 'The Quest' (T.V. ser. 1982), CLASS OF 1984, THE KILLING HOUR (both 1983).

BEN KINGSLEY

– see page see page 124

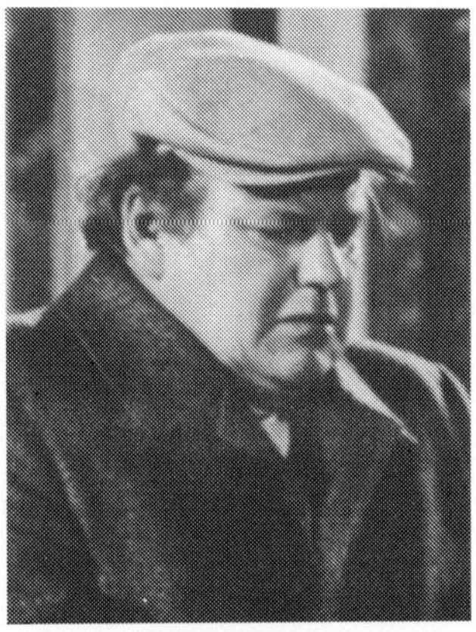

ROY KINNEAR

B. Wigan, Lancs. 8.1.34. Ed. George Heriot's School, Edinburgh & RADA; stage début: Newquay 1955 as Albert in 'The Young at Heart'; London début: Theatre Royal, Stratford E. 1959 in 'Make Me An Offer'; became well-known character-comedian in British movies and T.V.; work in latter includes 'That Was The Week That Was', 'Inside George Webley' and recently 'Cowboys' and Sidney Pratt in 'The Incredible Mr Tanner' (81); md. actress Carmel Cryan, 2 daughters Kirsty, Karina and 1 son Rory; screen début: 1962 in SPARROWS CAN'T SING (62, also stage), many films include, most recently, THE LONDON AFFAIR (78), HIGH RISE DONKEY (79), HAMMETT (80), HAWK THE SLAYER (80); stage includes Oxford Playhouse, London Palladium, R.S.C., L. Angeles & Nat. Theatre; recent T.V.: 'Agatha Christie Hour' (82); movies: HAMMETT (82), THE BOYS IN BLUE (83).

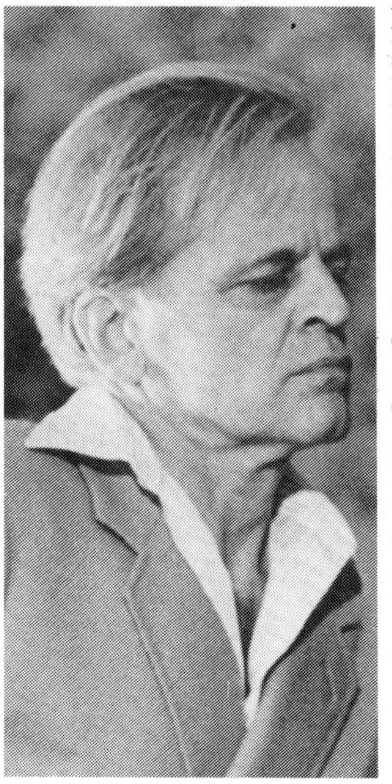

KLAUS KINSKI

B. Poland(?), . .27(?). Real name Nikolaus Nakszynski; Mr Kinski comes from a poor background, his father was an unsuccessful opera singer; at 16 served in the German army, imprisoned by British, returned to Germany after war; in late forties performed in German theatre, becoming well-known for his one-man shows and recitals in which he 'harangued' huge audiences; since early 50s has appeared in over 150 European films, these include LUDWIG II (54), A TIME TO LOVE AND A TIME TO DIE (58), CHILDREN, MOTHER & A GENERAL (58), TRAITOR'S GATE (64), DOCTOR ZHIVAGO (65), THAT MAN IN ISTABUL (66), FOR A FEW DOLLARS MORE (67), CIRCUS OF FEAR (67), A BULLET FOR A GENERAL (68), SONS OF SATAN (69), AGUIRRE, WRATH OF GOD (72), THE BLOODY HANDS OF THE LAW (73), OPERATION THUNDERBOLT (76), ZOO ZERO (78), NOSFERATU: THE VAMPIRE (78), WOYZECK (79), LOVE & MONEY (79), SCHIZOID (80), VENOM (80), BUDDY, BUDDY (81); md. 1. (?) Ruth ———, 1 daughter: actress Nastassia Kinski, who stars in TESS (80) and CAT PEOPLE (81); md. 2. Minhoi, a Vietnamese, 1 son; CHINA DOLL, FRUITS OF PASSION (both 81), ANDROID, THE SOLDIER (both 82).

Autobiography: *CREVER POUR VIVRE* (To Die of Living).

NASTASSIA KINSKI

– see page 12

JACK KLUGMAN

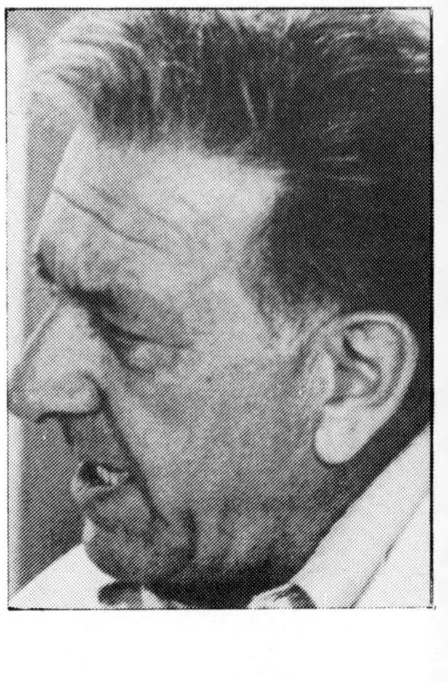

B. Philadelphia, Pa. 27.4.22. Ed. S. Philadelphia H.S., Carnegie Technical Coll. and studied for the stage at American Theatre Wing; Mr Klugman is a well-known stage actor, making his New York début in 1949 in 'Stevedore', between engagements working as postman/house painter; he played Dowdy opp. Henry Fonda (qv) in the 50/51 tour of 'Mister Roberts'; other stage includes 'Golden Boy' (Broadway début 1952), 'Gypsy' (59) and 'The Odd Couple' (66, as Oscar Madison, also T.V. series, 1970-75 (Emmy Awards 1971 & 73), U.S. tour and London stage); md. actress Brett Somers 1956 (sep.), 2 sons David (b. 1959), Adam (b. 1962); screen début: TIMETABLE (56), others: 12 ANGRY MEN (57), DAYS OF WINE AND ROSES (62), GOODBYE COLUMBUS (69), TWO-MINUTE WARNING (76), but perhaps best-known for T.V. series, including 'Harris Against the World' (64) and currently as Dr 'Quincy' (1977-).

HIRLEY KNIGHT

Goessel, Kansas 5.7.37. Ed. Phillips & Wichita niv.; while at latter starred in 32 college plays, d a weekly disc-jockey show at college and sang th a local dance band. Miss Knight later won a holarship to U.C.L.A., subsequently joining e Pasadena Community Playhouse and moving o T.V.; md. 1. writer/producer Gene Persson 59, 1 daughter Heavenly; since coming to the reen in 1959 in FIVE GATES TO HELL, her ovies have included ICE PALACE (60), THE ARK AT THE TOP OF THE STAIRS (60, scar nom., BSA), THE COUCH (62), SWEET RD OF YOUTH (62, Oscar nom., BSA), LIGHT FROM ASHIYA (63), THE GROUP), THE DUTCHMAN (67), PETULIA (68), HE RAIN PEOPLE (69), SECRETS (71), JGGERNAUT (74), FRIENDLY PERSUA-ON (75, T.V. movie); stage includes: 'Katherine the Day' (64), 'Kennedy's Children' (75); cent movies: BEYOND THE POSEIDON DVENTURE (79), PLAYING FOR TIME 0, T.V. movie), ENDLESS LOVE (81), THE ENDER, PRISONERS (both 1982).

ON KNOTTS

Morgantown, W. Virginia 21.7.24. Mr Knotts d early ambition to become ventriloquist, but at . Virginia Univ. majored in speech, interested teaching career; U.S. Army: at anti-aircraft hool, Fort Bliss, Tex., but after 6 months toured show 'Stars & Gripes' till war ended, returned school; md. Kay Metz, 1 daughter Karen, 1 son ommy; embarked on show-biz career: went to ew York, Army friend got him in show; then 5½ ears in radio show 'Bobby Benson of the B Bar B iders'; early T.V.: serials 'Tomorrow' (50s) as ilbur, 'Howdy Doody' (50s) as Tim Tremble; age show 'No Time For Sergeants' (55), began riting own comedy material, appd. on 'Steve llen Shows' from 1954 with success, consoli-ated it with role of Barney Fife in 'The Andy riffith Show' (60-68); movies include: WAKE E UP WHEN IT'S OVER (60), INCREDIBLE E LIMPET (62), RELUCTANT ASTRO-AUT (67), THE LOVE GOD (69), THE PPLE DUMPLING GANG (75), HERBIE OES TO MONTE CARLO (77), THE RIVATE EYES (81); Md: 2. Loralee; series 982; 'Three's Company'.

ALEXANDER KNOX

B. Strathroy, Ontario, Canada 16.1.07. Ed. Univ. of Western Ontario; Mr Knox made his stage debut at the Peabody Playhouse, Boston, Mass. 1929 in 'Dear Brutus'; came to London the following year debuting in 'Smoky Cell' and became well-known Shakespearean actor and scored in play 'The King of Nowhere' (38); md. Doris Nolan; came to the screen in GAUNT STRANGER (38), and has been a familiar face in scores of movies, gaining an Oscar nom. for his work as President WILSON (44); films include: THE SEA WOLF (40), THIS ABOVE ALL (42), OVER TWENTY-ONE (45), SISTER KENNY (46), THE SLEEPING TIGER (53), THE NIGHT MY NUMBER CAME UP (55), REACH FOR THE SKY (56), OPERATION AMSTERDAM (59), THE DAMNED (61), IN THE COOL OF THE DAY (63), KHAR-TOUM (66) and SHALAKO (68); he is also a playwright: 'Old Master' (39), 'Red on White' (63), 'The Closing Door' (64) and novelist: 'Bride of Quietness', 'Night of the Bear' and several detective novels; recent movies: MEETING AT POTSDAM (76, T.V. movie), HOLOCAUST 2000 (77); T.V.: 'Churchill & The Generals', 'Suez' (79); GORKY PARK (83).

DAVID KOSSOFF

B. London 24.11.19. Mr Kossoff is the youngest of three children of a poor Russian-Jewish tailor; ed. Elementary School and Northern Polytechnic; Mr Kossoff began work as a qualified technical draughtsman and during the war did backroom work on jet-aeroplane design; he had also joined London's Unity Theatre in 1942 and 1945 became professional, joining BBC Rep. Co.; 1st stage success as Russian Colonel in 'Love of 4 Colonels'; many films include: THE GOOD BEGINNING (53, debut), THE YOUNG LOVERS (55, BFA Aw.), A KID FOR TWO FARTHINGS (55), 1984 (55), THE IRON PETTICOAT (56), THE JOURNEY (59), FREUD (62), RING OF SPIES (64); md. Jennie Jenkins, 2 sons Paul (dec.), Simon; Mr Kossoff is well-known in Britain and abroad for his one-man stage shows and he is fondly remembered for his T.V. roles in 'The Bespoke Overcoat', 'The Outsider', 'The Larkins', 'Kossoff & Company' and for his reading of Bible stories; he was once one of Britain's top furniture designers; recent movie: THE LONDON CONNECTION (78).

YAPHET KOTTO

B. Harlem, New York City 15.11.37. Mr Kotto has much stage experience, including stock produc-tions of 'Raisin' in the Sun', 'Othello', off Broadway in 'Blood Knot', 'Black Monday', 'A Good Place to Raise a Boy', 'In White America' and played on Broadway in such plays as 'The Great Western Union' (65), 'The Zulu & The Zayda' (65) and 'The Great White Hope' (69); his films include NOTHING BUT A MAN (65), THE THOMAS CROWN AFFAIR (68), THE LIBERATION OF L.B. JONES (70), NIGHT CHASE (70, T.V. movie), ACROSS 110TH STREET (72), LIVE & LET DIE (72), TRUCK TURNER (74), SHARK'S TREASURE (74), REPORT TO THE COMMISSIONER (75), FRIDAY FOSTER (75), DRUM (76), RAID ON EN-TEBBE (77, as Pres. Amin), ALIEN, BLUE COLLAR (both 78), BRUBAKER (79), DEATH VENGEANCE, STAR CHAMBER (both 1982).

ALICE KRIGE

B. 'in Kalahari Desert', . .c.1955; early ambition to be dancer, switched to acting, but at Grahams-town Univ., S. Africa gained B.A. as clinical psychologist; 3 yrs. London Central Sch. Speech & Drama; stage includes 'Forever Yours', 'Arms & The Man' (latter S.W.E.T. Award 1981 'Most Promising Newcomer'); movies: CHARIOTS OF FIRE (81); A TALE OF TWO CITIES (T.V. movie, 1981); GHOST STORY (81); stage 1982: 'The Tempest' (R.S.Co.)

SYLVIA KRISTEL

B. Amsterdam(?), . .52; has sister, Marianne, ed. convent; Sylvia's first job in her parents' restaurant and hotel in Utrecht, Holland; then she became a secretary, nurse, door-to-door salesgirl; advised to become a model, she was accepted, eventually won 'Miss T.V. Europe' contest as 'Multilingual mistress-of-ceremonies' and came to the screen in BECAUSE OF THE CATS (72, directed by Hugo Claus, a Belgian, the couple have a son, Arthur, born in February 1975), made 2 more films in Holland and won fame in EMMANUELLE (74); Sylvia's other films inc-lude JULIA (75), BEHIND THE IRON MASK (76), GOODBYE, EMMANUELLE (77), MYSTERIES (78), THE FIFTH MUSKETEER (78), 4 TIGERS IN LIPSTICK. THE NUDE BOMB (both 79). AIRPORT '80 — THE CON-CORDE, PRIVATE LESSONS (81), LADY CHATTERLEY'S LOVER (82), MATA HARI (83); Md: Alan Turner, June 1982.

KRIS KRISTOFFERSON

B. Brownsville, Texas 22.6.37. 1 brother, 1 sister, father an army General who later became a commercial pilot; ed. Pomona Coll., a brilliant student, Kris won scholarship to Oxford, England, and after U.S. Army service, in which he taught English Literature at West Point, he turned to song writing and singing, becoming well-known with such hits as 'Help Me Make It Through The Night' and 'Me & Bobby McGee'; md. 1. Fran Beir 1961, 1 daughter Tracy, 1 son Kris Jr. (born 1962 & 69), (div. 1970); films: THE LAST MOVIE (71), CISCO PIKE (72), PAT GAR-RETT & BILLY THE KID (73), BRING ME THE HEAD OF ALFREDO GARCIA (74), BLUME IN LOVE (74), ALICE DOESN'T LIVE HERE ANYMORE (75), VIGILANTE FORCE (76), THE SAILOR WHO FELL FROM GRACE WITH THE SEA (76), CON-VOY (77), SEMI-TOUGH (77), FREEDOM ROAD (78), HEAVEN'S GATE (79), ROLL OVER (80); md. 2. singer Rita Coolidge 1973, 1 daughter Casey (b. 1974) (div. June 1980). *KRIS KRISTOFFERSON* by Beth Kalet; Quick Fox: N.Y., 1979.

BURT KWOUK

B. Manchester 18.7.30. Mr Kwouk was born in England when parents were there on business, father well-to-do Shanghai businessman in real estate/banking/textiles; Ed: Manchester, Univ. in USA (holds BA degree), aged 12-16 in Jesuit missionary school, Shanghai; came to G.B. in 1954, worked as £5-a-week dishwasher at Joe Lyons, porter at Westminster Hospital mortuary, other jobs, eventually advised to try acting, came to screen in WINDOM'S WAY (57), recently well-known as 'Cato' in PINK PANTHER films, many others include INN OF THE 6TH HAP-PINESS (58), THE WAR LOVER (62), 55 DAYS AT PEKING (63), GOLDFINGER (64), A SHOT IN THE DARK (64), YOU ONLY LIVE TWICE (66), SHOES OF THE FISHERMAN (68), MOST DANGEROUS MAN IN THE WORLD (69), DEEP END (71), MADAME SIN (71), RETURN OF THE PINK PANTHER (75), ROLLERBALL (75), THE PINK PANTHER STRIKES AGAIN (76), THE LAST REMAKE OF BEAU GESTE (76), REVENGE OF THE PINK PANTHER (78), THE FIENDISH PLOT OF FU MAN-CHU (80), TRAIL OF THE PINK PANTHER (82); recent T.V.: 'Keep It In The Family' (79), 'Shoestring' (80), Capt. Yamauchi in 'Tenko' (81), 'The Magnificent One' (82).

HARDY KRUGER

Having managed to avoid 'wicked German' roles which so often befall to German actors in British and America movies, Hardy Kruger has made an international success in a wide variety of film parts. The son of an electric engineer, he was born in Berlin on 12 April 1928 and as a youngster made his film début in a propaganda film YOUNG EAGLES. As a teenaged German soldier he was captured on three occasions by the Americans, but on each occasion escaped back to Hamburg. After the war he considered an engineering career, but from 1945-1956 he worked on the German stage, including the Hamburg State Theatre, graduating from walk-ons, such as the hunting boy in 'The Taming of the Shrew' to leading roles. Mr Kruger also worked in German radio and made 24 films. But it was in 1957 that he came to Britain to play THE ONE THAT GOT AWAY, portraying Franz Von Werra, the only German P.O.W. make a successful escape from this country. Since then he has worked steadily in international films, including BACHELOR OF HEARTS (58); REST IS SILENCE (59, German film of Hamlet); SUNDAYS AND CYBEL (60, France — many films in that country): TAXI TO TOBRUK (61); HATARI! (62); FLIGHT OF THE PHOENIX (65); played on Broadway 1965 in 'Postmark Zero', THE DEFECTOR (66); THE RED TENT (69 SECRET OF SANTA VITTORIA (69); NIGHT HAIR CHILD (71); DEATH OF A STRANGER (72); PAPE TIGER (75); BARRY LYNDON (75); A BRIDGE TOO FAR (76); HORIZONS (77, also directed); THE WIL GEESE (77). Divorced from his first wife, German actress Renate (one daughter), he wed Francesca Marazzi, a Swiss on 12 December 1965. Mr Kruger won a Best Actor award at Cannes in 1975 for his role in POTATO FRITZ, he had had his own short stories published in Germany as well as a novel, 'The Upside Down Tree', in 1977. His business interests in Africa include the supplying of animals to zoos all over the world. Latest movies are BLUE FIN (81), Australia, MAN WITH THE DEADLY LENS in the States, and SOCIETY LIMITED (both 1982).

SAM KYDD

B. Belfast, N. Ireland 15.2.15. Father Regular Army Officer; ed. Dunstable Grammar School; md. Pinkie Barnes (ex-international table tennis champ.), 1 son actor Jonathan Kydd; commenced acting during war when P.O.W. in Polish camp for 5 years, appropriately coming to the screen in THE CAPTIVE HEART (45), since then a very familiar face on the films and T.V.; scores of movies, often cameos, include THE SMALL BACK ROOM (48), SCOTT OF THE ANTARCTIC (48), TREASURE ISLAND (50), THE CRUEL SEA (53), THE RAINBOW JACKET (54), RAISING A RIOT (55), THE QUATERMASS EXPERIMENT (55), REACH FOR THE SKY (56), I'M ALRIGHT, JACK (59), FOLLOW THAT HORSE (60), THE TREASURE OF MONTE CRISTO (61), ISLAND OF TERROR (66); many T.V. programmes include: 'Pickwick Papers' (as Sam Weller), 'Mess Mates', 'Crane', 'Orlando', 'Sally Ann', 'The Shillingbury Blowers'; recent movies: HIGH RISE DONKEY (79) and Sam Turner in YESTERDAY'S HERO (80); recent TV: Frankie Baldwin in 'Coronation Street' (81/82). *FOR YOU THE WAR IS OVER* (wartime experiences) by S.K.; Bachman & Turner: London, 1973. *Mr Kydd died in London on 31.3.82.*

ALAN LAKE

B.   ,   .   .   . The actor/husband of actress Diana Dors (qv) (they have a son, Jason), Mr Lake has appeared on T.V. in such series as 'Crown Court', 'Blake's Seven', 'Rumpole's Return'; on the big screen in such pics. as CHARLIE BUBBLES (68); THE PLAYBIRDS (78); DAVID GALAXY AFFAIR (79); YESTERDAY'S HERO (79); stage 1981: 'On the Spot'.

DIANE LANE

B.   ,   .   .   . Diane's parents, who are divorced, are Colleen Farrington and Burt Lane, a drama tutor; she started acting aged 6, appearing in Greek classics 'Electra', 'The Trojan Women', 'Medea', touring Europe; aged 14 on Broadway in musical 'Runaways' as young prostitute, seen by director George Roy Hill and cast in his movie A LITTLE ROMANCE (79) and has also been in CATTLE ANNIE & LITTLE BRITCHES, TOUCHED BY LOVE (both 79), RUMBLE FISH (82), STREETS OF FIRE (83).

CHERYL LADD

B. Huron, S. Dakota 12.7.51. Real name Cheryl Jean Stoppelmoor; Cheryl's father is an engineer with the Chicago Northwestern Railroad Co.; she has 2 younger brothers, Brian and Seth, and an older sister, Mary Ann; as youngster studied voice/dancing, aspiring to music career — as teenager joined S. Dakota singing group 'The Music Shop', and toured; eventually signed contract with Capitol Records — 1st album/single 'Think It Over' (rel. Sept. '78); arrived L.A. late 1970, her voice used in cartoon series 'Josie & The Pussycats'; over 100 T.V. commercials; bits in T.V. shows 'Switch', 'Ironside', 'Police Woman' etc.; md. 1. David Ladd 1973, 1 daughter Jordan Elizabeth; Cheryl's T.V. break came 1977 replacing Farrah Fawcett (qv) in 'Charlie's Angels' as Kris Munroe (1977-81); other work: MARRIAGE OF A YOUNG STOCKBROKER (71); SATAN'S SCHOOL FOR GIRLS (T.V. movie, 73), WHEN SHE WAS BAD (T.V. movie, 81); frequent T.V. guest; Md: 2. Brian Russell, songwriter; NOW & FOREVER (82), KENTUCKY WOMAN (T.V. movie, 1982), THE GRACE KELLY STORY (T.V. movie, 1983).

FERNANDO LAMAS

B. Buenos Aires, Argentina 9.1.(15/20(?)). Orphaned aged 4, Fernando travelled extensively with grandparents, educated Argentina, Spain, Italy; wanted to be actor in teens, appd. Latin Amer. stage/radio and 'over 24 European/Latin Amer. movies', including HISTORIA DE UNA MALA MUJER (45); md. 1. Pearla Mux (Argentine actress) 1940 (div.), 2. Lydia Babachi, Uraguayan heiress, 1946, 1 daughter Alexandra (b. 1947); MGM contract 1950; movies include RICH, YOUNG AND PRETTY (51), LAW AND THE LADY (51), THE MERRY WIDOW (52, as Prince Danilo), JIVARO (54), ROSE MARIE (54), THE GIRL RUSH (55); md. 3. actress Arlene Dahl 1954, 1 son Lorenzo (b. 1958, now actor), (div. 1960), 4. ex-swimming star Esther Williams 1969; Mr Lamas now directs T.V. (including 'Mannix', 'Starsky & Hutch', 'The Rookies'), acted in 100 RIFLES (69), MURDER ON FLIGHT 502 (75, T.V. movie), THE CHEAP DETECTIVE (78); acclaim, Broadway, 1956, in 'Happy Hunting'. *Mr Lamas died in L.A., 10.10.82.*

BURT LANCASTER

No doubt that Burt Lancaster, now in his sixty-eighth year, and having recently won acclaim for his work in a character role in ATLANTIC CITY, can look back on his film career with pride, having spent some years as a screen action-man combined with top rank performances of the 1950s, culminating in an Oscar and involvement in several of his own productions. He was born Burton Stephen Lancaster at E. Harlem, a poor district of New York City on 2 November 1913, the youngest of 4 children born to James Lancaster, a Post Office supervisor, and his wife, the latter's father being Irish. Young Burt attended Public School No.83 and DeWitt High School; he was a bright student, excelled at al games, was an avid reader of library books, sang in the church choir and had also acted in his first play 'Three Pills in the Bottle'. His road to filmdom was a long one and Lancaster worked in several professions along the way — at 16 he entered New York University on an athletic scholarship, teaching basketball at a Settlement House, and while there was trained with boyhood pal Nick Cravat in a trapeze act, later débuting with Kay Bros. Circus in Petersburg, Virginia billed as 'Lang & Cravat'. he was 5 years in circuses, 2 years in vaudeville and fairs as an acrobat, and had a short-lived marriage in 1935/36 to June Ernst. He then worked as a floor-walker in a New York lingerie department, then men's outfitting salesman (doing cartwheels to relieve boredom), was engaged by a refrigeration concern, servicing packing plants, repairing broken cooling systems etc. Called up for military service while hoping for a job with CBS, he was a singing waiter in New Jersey taverns before joining the 5th Army, serving in N. Africa, Italy and Austria, where he was attached to Special Services organising troop entertainments. It was while in Montecatini, Italy, that he met his second wife, Norma Anderson, the widow of an army flyer (they wed in 1946, had 5 children — William (1947), James (1949) Susan (1951), Joanna (1954), Sighle (1956) — they were divorced in 1969). Upon discharge in 1946, he returned to New York, and by sheer chance he was seen by a stage producer in a lift and wearing his uniform at the time, Burt was considered ideal for the role of the tough sergeant in a play, 'The Sound of Hunting'. It ran for only a few performances but his work was seen by Warners producer Hal Wallis and the ex-acrobat was on his way to Hollywood and his first movie, THE KILLERS (46), made him a star. His best films have included BRUTE FORCE (47); THE FLAME AND THE ARROW (50); THE CRIMSON PIRATE (52); COME BACK, LITTLE SHEBA (52); FROM HERE TO ETERNITY (53, Oscar nom.); VERA CRUZ (54); TRAPEZE (56); GUNFIGHT AT O.K. CORRAL (57, as Wyatt Earp); ELMER GANTRY (60, Oscar winner); BIRDMAN OF ALCATRAZ (62, Oscar nom.); THE TRAIN (64); SEVEN DAYS IN MAY (64); THE PROFESSIONALS (66); THE SWIMMER (67) and 1900 (76). Returning to the Stage in 'Knickerbocker Holiday' in 1972, his most recent movies are GO TELL THE SPARTANS (77); ZULU DAWN (78); CATTLE ANNIE & LITTLE BRITCHES (79); THE SKIN (80); ATLANTIC CITY (81, BAFTA Aw.; Oscar nom., BA); LOCAL HERO and THE OSTERMAN WEEKEND (both 1983). *BURT LANCASTER* by Jerry Vermilye; Falcon Enterprises: N.Y., 1971.

MARTIN LANDAU

., Brooklyn, New York . .31(?). Mr Landau worked as a cartoonist and staff artist for the 'Daily News' following his graduation from college, but switched to drama studying with the Actors' Studio for 3 years; he has appd. in stage plays 'Middle of the Night', 'Uncle Vanya', 'Stalag 17', 'Wedding Breakfast', 'First Love', 'The Goat Song' and came to screen in 1959 in NORTH-BY-NORTHWEST; md. actress Barbara Bain, who acted opp. him in T.V. series 'Space 1999' ('75/76) when he played Commander John Koenig; other series: 'Mission-Impossible' (66-69) as Rollin Hand; movies include PORK CHOP HILL (59), THE GAZEBO (60), CLEOPATRA (63), HALLELUJAH TRAIL (65), NEVADA SMITH (65), THEY CALL ME MR TIBBS (70), METEOR (78), THE ROCKET (79), EASTER SUNDAY (81), THE RETURN (81), ALONE IN THE DARK (82).

FRANK LANGELLA

B. Bayonne, New Jersey 1.1.40; Mr Langella first appeared on stage aged 11 in school pageant at Bayonne as an 83 year old Abraham Lincoln; his professional debut was in L.A. in 'The White Devil' (also Broadway 1965), then as 'Dracula' (directed by Arthur Penn); he soon won acclaim in New York for his roles in 'Seascape' (Tony award 1975), 'The Old Glory' (joint 'Obie' award 1965) and opp. Miss Anne Bancroft (qv) in 'A Cry of Players' (68), as a young Shakespeare; other stage: 'The Immoralist' (63), 'Benito Cereno' (64), 'The Exhaustion of Our Son's Love' (65), 'Yerma' (66); his motion picture work includes THE 12 CHAIRS (70, Yugoslavia), DIARY OF A MAD HOUSEWIFE (71), THE DEADLY TRAP (72), THE WRATH OF GOD (72), title role DRACULA (79), THOSE EYES, THOSE LIPS (79), THE SPHINX (80); md. Ruth, in November 1977, a non-actress; T.V. movie 1974: THE MARK OF ZORRO; video/stage: 'Sherlock Holmes' (81).

PIPER LAURIE

B. Detroit, Michigan, 22.1.32. Real name Rosetta Jacobs; father of Russian extraction, mother of Polish parentage; ed. Detroit, and L.A. High School; at latter, awarded 7 year contract by Universal-International, coming to the screen in LOUISA (49) and was seen in THE MILKMAN (50), co-starred in THE PRINCE WHO WAS A THIEF (51), NO ROOM FOR THE GROOM (52), THE SON OF ALI BABA (51), MISSISSIPPI GAMBLER (55), THE GOLDEN BLADE (55), AIN'T MISBEHAVIN' (55) and others before going to New York to study, appd. there on stage in 'Rosemary' (60), 'The Alligators' (60), her screen performance in THE HUSTLER (61), won an Oscar nom. and the following year Piper wed critic/journalist Mr Joseph Morgenstern, and their daughter, Anna Grace, was born in 1971; she acted on stage in 1965 in 'The Glass Menagerie' and made a successful screen comeback in 1976 in CARRIE, gaining a BSA Oscar nom. and she has more recently been seen in IN THE MATTER OF KAREN ANN QUINLAN (77, T.V. movie), RUBY (77), THE BOSS'S SON, RAINBOW (both T.V. movies, 1978), TIM (81).

JOHN PHILLIP LAW

– see page 124

MARC LAWRENCE

B. Bronx, N.Y., . .10; Ed: N.Y. City Coll., Princetown P'house, Eva Le Gallienne Rep.; diverse career: G & S operas. Broadway, London, T.V. and film director/writer; Marc made his name in gangster roles on big screen — over 120 movies, inclu. WHITE WOMAN (33, and Columbia contract); TALL, DARK & HANDSOME (41); ASPHALT JUNGLE (50); NIGHTMARE IN THE SUN (64, wrote/directed); KREMLIN LETTER (71); FOUL PLAY, GOIN' COCONUTS, HOT STUFF (all 1978); SUPER FUZZ (81).

LEIGH LAWSON

B. Warwickshire 21.7.45. Ed. Technical Coll., Mountview Theatre School (supporting himself by selling posters, joss sticks, beads and 'hippy' bells from a stall in Petticoat Lane) and completed dramatic studies at RADA, receiving the Nannan-Clark prize from Peggy Ashcroft; stage includes Belgrade Theatre, Coventry; came to the screen in 1972 in BROTHER SUN, SISTER MOON, other movies include GHOST STORY (74), PERCY'S PROGRESS (74), LOVE AMONG THE RUINS (75, T.V. movie), GOLDEN RENDEZVOUS (77), THE DEVIL'S ADVOCATE (77); son Jason ('Ace') born August 1976 — mother actress Miss Hayley Mills (qv); Mr Lawson portrays Alec D'Urbeville in the acclaimed TESS, filmed in France in 1978; recent stage: 'The Second Mrs Tanqueray' (81); T.V.: 'The Captain's Doll' (82); movies: MURDER IS EASY (T.V. movie), TRISTAN & ISOLDE (both 1981), SWORD OF THE VALIANT (83).

JESSICA LANGE

B. Minnesota, . .50. Ed. Univ. of Minnesota; Jessica, who has a sister, Anne, studied mime for 2 years in Paris, then joined a Manhattan theatre group; she also worked as a waitress in a Greenwich Village pub to supplement her earnings from modelling in T.V. commercials; she came to fame as Dwan in a remake of KING KONG (76); md. Paco Grandi, a Spanish photographer (div.); Jessica has a daughter, Alexandra, born in 1981, the father being Russian ballet star Mikhail Baryshnikov; recent movies: ALL THAT JAZZ (79), HOW TO BEAT THE HIGH COST OF LIVING (79), THE POSTMAN ALWAYS RINGS TWICE (81); studied with Sandra Secat of Actors' Studio; FRANCIS (82, as actress Frances Farmer, Oscar nom. BA & BSA), TOOTSIE (82, winner Oscar BSA; N.Y. Film Critics' Aw., BSA).

ROBERT LANSING

B. San Diego, Calif. 5.6.29. Real name Robert Howell Brown; had directed school plays since 15; U.S. Army 1946, 2 years in Osaka, Japan, worked for Armed Forces Radio Service; on discharge went to Indiana to work in radio as announcer, then to New York, studying briefly at American Theatre Wing; first movie job: stand-in/double for Dick Haymes in film ST. BENNY THE DIP (51); stage includes tour 'Stalag 17', in 'Richard III' (53, with Jose Ferrer(qv)); live T.V. in New York; came to screen 1959 in THE 4-D MAN (59), other movies include THE PUSHER (60), A GATHERING OF EAGLES (62), UNDER THE YUM YUM TREE (63), NAMU—THE KILLER WHALE (66), AN EYE FOR AN EYE (67), THE GRISSOM GANG (72), WILD IN THE SKY (72), BITTER SWEET LOVE (76), EMPIRE OF THE ANTS (77), ACAPULCO GOLD (78), S.H.E. (79); Mr Lansing is very well-known on television in the States, his series including '87th Precinct' (61/62, as Det. Steve Carella), '12 O'Clock High' (64/66, as Brig. Gen. Frank Savage) and 'The Man Who Never Was' (66/67, as Peter Murphy/Mark Wainwright); his T.V. movies have included: 'Killer By Night' (72), 'The Astronaut' (72), 'Crime Club' (75), 'Widow' (76), 'The Deadly Triangle' (77); recent movie: ISLAND CLAWS (80); stage: 'Little Foxes' (81); Md: Anne Cecille Pivar.

ANGELA LANSBURY

B. London 16.10.25. Miss Lansbury's father, who died when she was 9, was a lumber merchant, and her mother was actress Moyna MacGill. Her grandfather, George Lansbury, was a socialist leader. She attended S. Hampstead H.S. for Girls from 1934-39, then studied with the Webber-Douglas Drama School for a year, before being evacuated during the war to the USA with her younger twin brothers, Bruce and Edgar, finishing her drama training in New York at the Feagin School of Drama & Radio. Miss Lansbury then went for a brief spell to Montreal, performing as a singer/imitator of Beatrice Lillie, then met up with her mother in Los Angeles, the two of them engaged as saleswomen in Bullock's dept. store, Angela working in cosmetics. Through an actor acquaintance she won a screen test and contract at MGM, coming to the screen in GASLIGHT (44), as a Cockney serving girl, earning an Oscar nom. as supporting actress, and she had a short-lived marriage to actor Richard Cromwell (45/46). Her second husband is an Irishman, Peter Shaw, now a retired film executive, whom she wed in 1949. They had two children, Anthony in 1952 and Deirdre in 1953. Miss Lansbury's films of the 40s/50s include NATIONAL VELVET (44), PICTURE OF DORIAN GRAY (45, Oscar nom. BSA), TILL THE CLOUDS ROLL BY (47), STATE OF THE UNION (48), SAMSON AND DELILAH (49), KIND LADY (51), REMAINS TO BE SEEN (53), THE PURPLE MASK (55) and THE COURT JESTER (56). In 1957 she embarked on a highly successful U.S. stage career with 'Hotel Paradiso' (New York), followed by 'A Taste of Honey' (60) and a huge success as Mame Dennis in 'Mame' (66), winning a Tony award and touring in this production; similar success came in 'Dear World' (69) and as Rose in 'Gypsy' (73 and 74, London and USA) and repeated awards. She played Gertrude in 'Hamlet' at the National Theatre, opening the Lyttleton in March 1976. Her other motion picture appearances have included THE MANCHURIAN CANDIDATE (62, Oscar nom. BSA), THE GREATEST STORY EVER TOLD (65), MOLL FLANDERS (65), DEAR HEART (65), MISTER BUDDWING (67), SOMETHING FOR EVERYONE (70), BEDKNOBS & BROOMSTICKS (71), DEATH ON THE NILE (77), THE LADY VANISHES (78), THE MIRROR CRACK'D (81), PIRATES OF PENZANCE (T.V. movie, 1982), SWEENEY TODD (T.V. movie, 1982), LITTLE GLORIA, HAPPY AT LAST (T.V. movie, 1982).

GEORGE LAZENBY

B. Goulburn, nr. Sydney, Australia, . .39(?). Father a greenkeeper at local bowls club; Mr Lazenby left school at 15, first worked at a saw mill, then as an apprentice motor mechanic, and a car salesman in several Australian cities; in April 1964 he bought a one-way ticket to England, lived in Earl's Court, sold cars in N. London, progressing to selling luxury limousines in Park Lane; while there a photographer suggested he took up male modelling, this he did and he soon became one of Britain's highest paid models; on T.V. he was 'Big Fry' in the chocolate commercial and others; seen by producer Albert R. Broccoli in Kurt's barber shop, Mayfair, Mr Lazenby was cast as James Bond in the 1969 movie ON HER MAJESTY'S SECRET SERVICE, which became a top money-maker in 1970; other movies: INTERNATIONAL SOLDIER (70), THE MAN FROM HONG KONG (75), KENTUCKY FRIED MOVIE (77), DEATH DIMENSION (77), SAINT JACK (79); md. Christine Townson, U.S. newspaper heiress (c. 1973), 3 children; T.V. includes Play for Today: 'The Operation' (73, BBC) and U.S. T.V. movies: 'Cover Girls' (77) and 'An Evening in Byzantium' (78).

CLORIS LEACHMAN

B. Des Moines, Iowa 30.4.26. Father: lumber manager, mother: actress Claiborne Cary; Northwestern Univ.; Miss Leachman appd. several stage productions: 'Sundown Beach' (4 'As You Like It' (50), 'A Story For a Sund Evening' (50) and 'Lo & Behold!' (51), on rad and is perhaps best-known in the States for h T.V. roles and series from 1949 ('Hold It, Pleas include: 'Charlie Wild, Private Detective' (51, Effie Perrine), 'The Bob & Ray Show' (52), an 'The Mary Tyler Moore Show' (70-75) as Phyl Lindstrom; as this character getting her own seri 'Phyllis' in 1975, plus scores of other appearance including many T.V. movies — 'A Brand Ne Life' (73), winning her an Emmy; md. produce director George Englund 1953, 5 children: Ada (1953), Bryan (1954), George (1956), Morga (1962), Diana (1966), (div. 1979); many movi include: KISS ME DEADLY (54), THE CHA MAN REPORT (62), BUTCH CASSIDY THE SUNDANCE KID (69), THE STEAGL (71), THE LAST PICTURE SHOW (71, Be Supporting Actress Oscar), HILL'S ANGEL (78), HIGH ANXIETY (78), S.O.S. TITAN (79), NORTH AVENUE IRREGULARS (79 YESTERDAY (80, guest), HISTORY OF TH WORLD, PART I (81).

JEAN-PIERRE LEAUD

B. Paris, France, . .44. Mother, an actress; father, an assistant film director; Truffaut advertised for boy to appear in his 1st feature (THE 400 BLOWS (59)), Jean-Pierre answered and became a star; played in TESTAMENT OF ORPHEUS (60); LOVE AT 20 (61); worked as assistant on LA PEAU DOUCE (64), MATA HARI — AGENT H-21 (65); assistant director of ALPHAVILLE (65); PIERROT LE FOU (65); returned to the screen as actor in MASCULIN-FEMININ (66) and has been seen in such pictures, mainly in France, as MADE IN USA (66); LA CHINOISE (67); WEEKEND (67); STOLEN KISSES (68); GAI SAVOIR (68); PIGSTY (69); DOMICILE CONJUGAL (70); UNE AVENTURE DE BILLY THE KID (70); LAST TANGO IN PARIS (72); Jean-Pierre made his stage début in the summer of 1967 at the Avignon Festival; LOVE ON THE RUN (79).

BERNARD LEE

B. London 10.1.08. Ed. Liverpool Collegiate School; stage début Oxford Music Hall, aged 6, in sketch 'The Double Event'; upon leaving school became fruit salesman in Southampton, but left to study at RADA; 1926 toured in 'White Cargo', subsequently becoming well-known stage actor in rep., West End, tours, making his screen début as early as 1935 in THE RIVER HOUSE MYSTERY; md. 1. Gladys Merredew (who died tragically in fire in the 1970s); Mr Lee served in the army 1940-45; scores of movies include THE TERROR (37), THE FALLEN IDOL (48), THE THIRD MAN (49), THE GIFT HORSE (52), FATHER BROWN (54), THE PURPLE PLAIN (55), BATTLE OF THE RIVER PLATE (56), DUNKIRK (58), THE ANGRY SILENCE (59), RING OF SPIES (63), THE SPY WHO CAME IN FROM THE COLD (65), DULCIMA (71); he is fondly remembered as 'M' in all the Bond films (except FOR YOUR EYES ONLY); md. 2. T.V. director's assistant Ursula McHale in 1975; recent T.V.: 'Saint Joan' (79), 'Dangerous Davies: Last Detective' (80, T.V. movie). *Mr Lee died of cancer, in London, on 17.1.81.*

CHRISTOPHER LEE

Christopher Lee was a small part-player for ten years before being catapulted to fame in the guise of some of Hammer' most formidable 'monsters' in the late 50s and early 60s and has since then worked many times in Europe and in th 1970s based his career in Hollywood. Born Christopher Frank Carandini Lee in Belgravia, London on 27 May 1922, he is the son of Geoffrey Trollope Lee (a soldier who was awarded the Croix de Guerre at the Somme battle, 1916) and hi wife, Contessa Estelle Marie Carandini (the Carandinis being one of the 6th oldest families in Italy). They divorce when he was six and Christopher was educated at Wellington College, excelling at languages. His first job was in the City of London, but at the outbreak of war he joined the R.A.F. serving in S. Africa, Rhodesia, later transferred to Intelligence. Upon demob. he decided on an acting career, but was soon dissuaded because of his height — 6'4" — 'You'll make the leading man look small', casting directors told him. But he persevered, and, through a cousin, manage to get his film breaks in CORRIDOR OF MIRRORS (47, his début), HAMLET (48, one line) and SCOTT OF THE ANTARCTIC (48), 'groomed' by the Rank 'Charm School' and getting repertory experience with the Overture Players, Worthing. In the early 50s he continued to play supporting roles in a wide range of film subjects (MOULIN ROUGE (53), DARK AVENGER (54), ALIAS JOHN PRESTON (56)) and do stunt-work and dubbing (thos languages again). 1956 proved to be the turning point in his career — he played the Frankenstein 'creature' in CURSE OF FRANKENSTEIN, displaying a skilful gift for mime, and the dissolute Marquis St. Evremonde in A TALE OF TWO CITIES (57). Hammer films, who had made the Frankenstein re-make, signed him up for the title role o DRACULA (HORROR OF ..., 58) and since then he has been chiefly associated with macabre roles including THE MUMMY (59); THE HOUND OF THE BASKERVILLES (59); THE TWO FACES OF DR JEKYLL (60); TASTE OF FEAR (61); PIRATES OF BLOOD RIVER (62); THE GORGON (64); FACE OF FU MANCHU (65); DRACULA, PRINCE OF DARKNESS (65) and RASPUTIN THE MAD MONK (65). He has played in over 100 movies and on 17.3.61 he wed Birgit (Gitte) Kroencke (the daughter of the director of Tuborg Breweries, Copenhagen). They have a daughter, Christina. His recent movies: RETURN TO WITCH MOUNTAIN (78); 1941 (79); BLOOD BEACH (79); RALLY, THE SALAMANDER (both 1980); AN EYE FOR AN EYE, DANCE — STEIGLER & STEIGLER, A DESPERATE CASE (both 1981); RETURN OF CAPT. INVINCIBLE, GOLIATH AWAITS (mini-ser.), CHARLES & DIANA: A ROYAL LOVE STORY (as Prince Philip, T.V. movie, all 1982); HOUSE OF THE LONG SHADOWS and THE FAR PAVILIONS (both 1983). *TALL, DARK AND GRUESOME* (autobio.); W.H. Allen: London, 1977; p/b: 1978.

RON LEIBMAN

B. New York City, 11.10.37. Ed. Ohio Wesleyan Univ.; trained at Actors' Studio, New York, making professional stage début in 'A View From the Bridge' in summer stock; T.V. work includes role as Martin 'Kaz' Kazinsky in 'Kaz' series (1978/79); movies include WHERE'S POPPA? (70); THE HOT ROCK (72); SLAUGHTERHOUSE FIVE (72); THE SUPER COPS (73); YOUR THREE MINUTES ARE UP (74); THE ART OF CRIME (75, T.V. movie); WON TON TON (76); A QUESTION OF GUILT (78, T.V. movie); NORMA RAE (79); ZORRO, THE GAY BLADE (81); ROMANTIC COMEDY (82).

PAUL LE MAT

B. N. Jersey, . . . Moved to California when 5; ed: San Diego City Coll., Chapman Coll., Cyprus Coll.; at Newport H.S. began acting; aged 21 went to N.Y., did stock and studied with Milton Katselas, the Herbert Bergoff Studio, Actors' Studio, American Conservatory Theatre in San Francisco and toured the South in 'Tobacco Road'; Paul served in Vietnam and the Philippines, was a promising award-winning amateur boxer, but gave up the sport after coming to screen in 1973 in AMERICAN GRAFFITI; other film work: FIREHOUSE (73, T.V. movie); ANNABELLE LEE (73, short); ALOHA, BOBBY & ROSE (75); CITIZEN'S BAND (77); MORE AMERICAN GRAFFITI (79); MELVIN & HOWARD (81); STRANGE INVADERS, DEATH VALLEY, JIMMY THE KID (all 82); Md: Suzanne.

JANET LEIGH

B. Merced, California 6.7.27. Real name Jeanette Helen Morrison; father in insurance/real estate; ed. Stockton, Calif., and Coll. of the Pacific, as a music major; aged 15 eloped with John K. Carlyle and wed 1942, but marriage annulled after 4 months; md. 2. Stanley Reames, whom she met at coll., wed 5.10.46, but div. 1948; Janet's mother worked at Sugar Bowl Ski Lodge, Soda Springs, had photo of her daughter on reception desk; actress Norma Shearer sent pic. to MGM, Janet was screentested, trained, and came to screen in ROMANCE OF ROSY RIDGE (47); many movies include THAT FORSYTHE WOMAN (49), SCARAMOUCHE (52), HOUDINI (53, with Tony Curtis, whom she wed in 1951 — they had 2 daughters, Kelly Lee (b. 1956) and Jamie Lee Curtis (qv, b. 1958) — they div. 1963), PRINCE VALIANT (54), TOUCH OF EVIL (58), PSYCHO (60, Oscar nom, BSA), WIVES & LOVERS (63), HARPER (66); many T.V. roles/T.V. movies; md. 4. stockbroker Bob Brant, 15.9.62; recent movies: NIGHT OF THE LEPUS (74), BOARDWALK (78), THE FOG (80); Janet also works for charity, SHARE (Share Happiness & Reap Endlessly); THE FALL GUY (T.V. movie; 'Tales of the Unexpected' (T.V., both 1981).

JOHN LE MESURIER

B. Bedford 5.4.12. Brought up in Bury St. Edmunds & London, and studied for the stage at Fay Compton's Drama School; entered show business in the 1930s, working in all mediums — rep., panto, variety, cabaret, West End; served in army during WWII; early movies: OLD MOTHER RILEY'S NEW VENTURE (47), DEATH IN THE HAND (48); md. 1. the late Hattie Jacques (div.), 2 sons Robin, Kim; Mr LeMesurier became a popular supporting player in scores of British movies of the 50s including BEAUTIFUL STRANGER (54), PRIVATE'S PROGRESS (55), I'M ALRIGHT, JACK (59), SCHOOL FOR SCOUNDRELS (60), THE REBEL (61), PUNCH & JUDY MAN (62), PINK PANTHER (62), MASQUERADE (64), THE WRONG BOX (66), MAGIC CHRISTIAN (69), etc.; he is also well-known on T.V.: 'Dad's Army' series, especially, as Wilson, from 1969-77, also the movie of 1971, and that year won a T.V. actor award for 'The Traitor'; md. 2. Joan Malin; recent movies: JABBERWOCKY (77), WHAT'S UP, NURSE! (77), SPACEMAN & KING ARTHUR (78), TOO MANY CHEFS (78), FIENDISH PLOT OF FU MANCHU (80). Recent T.V.: 'Brideshead Revisited' (81); 'A Married Man', 'Just Desserts' (series, both 1982).

JACK LEMMON

Recently emerging as a splendid character actor (THE CHINA SYNDROME), Jack Lemmon has for the past 25 years been one of America's most popular screen actor/comedians, winning 2 Oscars, some of his best work being with director Billy Wilder, with whom he is re-united in the recent BUDDY, BUDDY (81). He was born John Uhler Lemmon (Jr.) on 8 February, 1925 at Boston, Massachusetts, the son of a former actor who had become a well-to-do businessman. Educated at Rivers Country Day, Philips Andover and Harvard University (graduated with science degree), he acted at all three and at the latter was elected President of the 'Hasty Pudding Club' for his work in staging annual shows. During WWII he was a commissioned officer with rank of Ensign on the aircraft carrier U.S.S. Lake Champlain. Upon demob. he went to New York and appeared on radio in several 'soap operas' (Lemmon had, in fact, made his stage début aged 4 with his father in 'Gold in Them Thar Hills') and in the early 50s about 500 T.V. appearances, including 'That Wonderful Guy' (1950), 'The Couple Next Door' (1951/52), 'The Ad-libbers' (1951) and 'Heaven For Betsy' (1952/53), all in which his first wife, Cynthia Stone, appeared. They wed in 1950, and their son, Christopher (born 1954), is now an accomplished musician. In television he also produced, and found time to act in stock in the New England States. Jack made his Broadway début in 'Room Service' (1953) and on the strength of this a Columbia contract followed, making his motion-picture début in IT SHOULD HAPPEN TO YOU (54). He has turned his attention since then mainly to movies, the best of which include PHFFFT (54); MISTER ROBERTS (55, Oscar, BSA); COWBOYS (57); BELL, BOOK AND CANDLE (58); SOME LIKE IT HOT (59, Oscar nom.); THE APARTMENT (60, Oscar nom.); DAYS OF WINE AND ROSES (62, Oscar no.); IRMA LA DOUCE (63); HOW TO MURDER YOUR WIFE (65); THE GREAT RACE (65); THE ODD COUPLE (68); KOTCH (71, directed only); SAVE THE TIGER (73, Oscar winner); THE FRONT PAGE (74); THE ENTERTAINER (75) and AIRPORT 77. Mr Lemmon divorced in 1956 and wed Felicia Farr in 1962. Their daughter, Courtenay, was born in 1966. He returned to Broadway to play in 'Face of a Hero' (1960), 'Idiot's Delight' (1970, L.A.), 'Tribute' (1979, Denver and L.A., filmed in 1980, receiving an Oscar nom., but winning Canadian Genie Award 'Best Foreign Actor'). Jack's work in CHINA SYNDROME (79) gained him an Oscar nom. and Best Actor awards from the British Academy and Cannes Film Festival. Partnered by Gordon Carroll, Jalem is his own film production company and he has recently won more accolades for his work in MISSING (1982, BA Aw.; Cannes; Oscar & BAFTA noms., BA).

LEMMON by Don Widener; W.H. Allen: London, 1977.

KAY LENZ

B.   , 4.3.53. Kay's father was a disc-jockey who owned film co. making T.V. commercials; her T.V. movies include THE WEEKEND NUN ('72), LISA, BRIGHT & DARK (73), A SUMMER WITHOUT BOYS (73), THE UNDERGROUND MAN (74), UNWED FATHER ('74), THE F.B.I. STORY: THE F.B.I. VERSUS ALVIN KARPIS, PUBLIC ENEMY NO.1 ('74), JOURNEY FROM DARKNESS (75), Kate Jordache in RICH MAN, POOR MAN ('76, mini-series), THE GIRL IN THE PARK ('79), THE INITIATION OF SARAH (78), SANCTUARY OF FEAR (79); md. David Cassidy 4.4.77; films: BREEZY (73), WHITE-LINE FEVER (75), GREAT SCOUT & CAT-HOUSE THURSDAY (76), THE PASSAGE ('78), PRISONERS OF THE LOST UNIVERSE ('83); is div. from Mr Cassidy.

VALERIE LEON

B. London 12.11.45; Miss Leon appd. in rep., and played in several movies including several 'Carry On...' pics., QUEEN KONG (76), SPY WHO LOVED ME (76), WILD GEESE (77), REVENGE OF THE PINK PANTHER (78) and many times on T.V., particularly well-known for her 'Hai Karate' commercial; she is wed to BBC producer Mr Michael Mills and they have a young son, Leon; T.V. 1982: 'Strangers'.

JOHN LEYTON

B. Frinton-on-Sea, Essex 17.2.40(?). Mr Leyton began his career as a pop singer in the early 60s, combined with acting on T.V. in 'Biggles' series and after appearing in 'Harper's—West One' started his motion picture career: THE GREAT ESCAPE (63), EVERY DAY'S A HOLIDAY (64), GUNS AT BATASI (65), VON RYAN'S EXPRESS (65), THE IDOL (65), KRAKATOA, EAST OF JAVA (68); md. Diane Pearson, 2 children; T.V. series, USA: 'Jericho' (66/67); in mid-60s John ventured into business, buying property in California and G.B., and becoming restauranteur; more recent acting in SCHIZO (76) and DANGEROUS DAVIES: THE LAST DETECTIVE (80, T.V. movie).

FIONA LEWIS

B. Westcliff-on-Sea, Essex 28.9.46. Miss Lewis's many films include TELL ME WHOM TO KILL (66), THE FEARLESS VAMPIRE KILLERS (67), WHERE'S JACK (69), JOANNA (69), A DAY ON THE BEACH (69), OTLEY (69), VILLAIN (72), DRACULA (73, T.V. movie), LISZTOMANIA (75), DRUM (76), from 1977 she has worked in the USA: THE FURY (77), TINTOREA (77), WANDA NEVADA (78), STUNTS (79), DEAD KIDS (81).

JENNIE LINDEN

B. Worthing, Sussex 8.12.40. Ed. West Preston Manor, Sussex; trained at Central School of Speech & Drama and appd. on stage in 'Never Too Late', 'Thark', coming to screen in 1964 in Hammer's NIGHTMARE, other movies: DR WHO & THE DALEKS (66), WOMEN IN LOVE (69), A SEVERED HEAD (70), HEDDA (75), VALENTINO (76); Jennie has staged her own show of verse, prose and song, 'I Say, I Play' and appeared on T.V. on many occasions, recently in 'Lillie' (78), 'Charlie Muffin' (79, T.V. movie), 'Jessie' (80) and 'House on the Hill' (episode: 'Mistress of the House', 1981); stage 1979: 'Born in the Gardens'; she is wed to antique dealer Christopher Mann and they have a son, Rupert. Stage 1983: 'This Thing Called Love'; T.V.: 'The Home Front', 'Pepys'.

VIVECA LINDFORS – *see page 124*

DESMOND LLEWELYN

Mr Llewelyn is well-known internationally for his role as 'Q' in the James Bond films since FROM RUSSIA WITH LOVE (63) and can be seen in the latest epic, FOR YOUR EYES ONLY. He has appeared on the West End stage, including 'The Spider's Web' (57) and other movies include CHITTY CHITTY BANG BANG (68) and THE GOLDEN LADY (78). His home is on the East Sussex coast, near Bexhill. Mr Llewelyn returns as 'Q' in OCTOPUSSY (83).

SUE LLOYD

B. Aldeburgh, Suffolk 7.8.39. Before turning to the screen Sue had been a model and danced with the Sadler's Wells Ballet; in 1965 made hit film THE IPCRESS FILE and co-starred in series 'The Baron'; other films include: WHERE'S JACK (68), ATTACK ON THE IRON COAST (68), CORRUPTION (68), PERCY (71), INNOCENT BYSTANDERS (72), PENNY GOLD (73), SPANISH FLY (75), NO.1 OF THE SECRET SERVICE (77), THE STUD (78), THE BITCH (79); recent T.V.: 'Crossroads', as Barbara Hunter.

GARY LOCKWOOD

B. Van Nuys, Calif. 21.2.37. Real name John Gary Yusolfsky; 'grew up on father's onion farm in Calif.'; ed. U.C.L.A., excelling at football; commenced film career as stuntman, later Tony Perkins (qv) stand-in; appd. on Broadway in 'There Was a Little Girl' (60), discovered for screen by Joshua Logan, acting debut in TALL STORY (60); md. Stefanie Powers (div.); many movies include: SPLENDOUR IN THE GRASS (61), WILD IN THE COUNTRY (61), THE MAGIC SWORD (62), IT HAPPENED AT THE WORLD'S FAIR (63), FIRECREEK (67), 2001—A SPACE ODYSSEY (68), THEY CAME TO ROB LAS VEGAS (69), THE MODEL SHOP (70), EARTH II (70, T.V. movie), STAND UP & BE COUNTED (72), MANHUNTER (74, T.V. movie); Mr Lockwood played in two T.V. series: as Eric Jason in 'Follow the Sun' (61/62) and as Lt. William Rice in 'The Lieutenant' (63/64); recent work: BAD GEORGE ROAD (77), GHOST OF FLIGHT 401 (78, T.V. movie), INCREDIBLE JOURNEY OF DR MEG LAUREL (79, T.V. movie).

HERBERT LOM

B. Prague, Czechoslovakia 11.9.17. Real name: Herbert Charles Angelo Kuchacevich ze Schluderpacheru; ed. Prague Univ.; stage training: London Embassy, Old Vic, Sadler's Wells; was on stage in Prague and there made a number of movies, 1st British movie: MEIN KAMPF (40); WWII; with BBC European section (radio); appeared successfully on British stage, esp. as King of Siam in 'King & I' in 50s; well-known in movies, has been based in Britain for many years, pics. include THE DARK TOWER (43), THE SEVENTH VEIL (46), DUAL ALIBI (47), STATE SECRET (50), THE RINGER (52), THE LADYKILLERS (55), HELL DRIVERS (57), NORTH WEST FRONTIER (59), MYSTERIOUS ISLAND (61, as Capt. Nemo), EL CID (61), THE PHANTOM OF THE OPERA (62, title role), A SHOT IN THE DARK (64), GAMBIT (66), THE RETURN OF THE PINK PANTHER (74), MAN WITH BOGART'S FACE (79), HOPSCOTCH (79), PETER & PAUL (mini-ser., as Barnabus); also writer; Md: Dina Scheu (div.), 2 sons: Nicky & Alec; T.V. ser., 1962: 'The Human Jungle'; in THE YOUNG MR PITT (41), WAR & PEACE (56), he played Napoleon; recent movies: TRAIL OF THE PINK PANTHER (82), MEMED (83).

VIRNA LISI

B. Ancona, Italy 11.8.38. Real name Virna Li Pieralisi; studied at a technical and busines college in Rome, but turned to the screen aft being spotted by director Francesco Masel within a week Virna was in her 1st movie; m Franco Pesci, Italian industrialist, 1 son Corrad (wed in 1960); films: THE BLACK TULIP (63 EVA (63), HOW TO MURDER YOUR WIF (65), CASANOVA 70 (65), SIGNORE E SIC NORI (65), ASSAULT ON A QUEEN (66 NOT WITH MY WIFE YOU DON'T (66 THE GIRL AND THE GENERAL (67 ARABELLA (68), THE 25TH HOUR (68 BETTER A WIDOW (68), THE BIRDS, TH BEES & THE ITALIANS (68), THE GIR WHO WOULDN'T SAY NO (69), TH CHRISTMAS TREE (69), SECRET O SANTA VITTORIA (69), UN BEAU MON STRE (70), THE STATUE (71), THE SE\ PENT (72), BLUEBEARD (72), WHITE FAN\ (74), BEYOND EVIL (77), LA CICALA (80 MR RIGHT (80), VENETIAN LIES (81).

TONY LO BIANCO – *see page 124*

SONDRA LOCKE

B. Shelbyville, Tennessee, .47. In her first film, THE HEART IS A LONELY HUNTER, in 1968, Sondra gained an Oscar nomination as Best Supporting Actress, and her other films have included THE LOVEMAKERS, RUN, SHADOW, RUN, A REFLECTION OF FEAR, THE SECOND COMING OF SUZANNE, WILLARD (71); she is married to artist/sculptor Gordon Anderson, and has made her Los Angeles debut as a night club singer; she reached the bigtime in movies, playing opposite Clint Eastwood (qv) in THE OUTLAW—JOSEY WALES (76), THE GAUNTLET (77), EVERY WHICH WAY BUT LOOSE (78), BRONCO BILLY (80) and ANY WHICH WAY YOU CAN (80).

GINA LOLLOBRIGIDA

B. Subiaco (50 miles S.E. of Rome), Italy 4.7.2\ One of 4 daughters, Gina's father was furnitu\ manufacturer and real estate owner, but durin\ allied invasion of Italy business destroyed an\ family fled north; while in teens studied at Rome\ Academy of Fine Arts sculpture and painting f\ 3 years, also studying voice and won Miss Rom\ competition and runner-up, Miss Italy; discovere\ in street by director Mario Costa, hesitated abou\ film career, eventually accepted and made a h\ with first movie LOVE OF A CLOWN (47); m\ 1, Dr Drago Milko Skofic, a Yugoslav Physicia\ at Merminillo 1949, 1 son: Andrea Milko (\ 28.7.57), (div.); many films include FANFA\ LA TULIPE (51), BELLES DE NUIT (52 BREAD, LOVE & DREAMS (53), BEA\ THE DEVIL (54), LE GRAND JEU (54 TRAPEZE (56), THE HUNCHBACK O NOTRE DAME (57), SOLOMON & SHEB\ (59), COME SEPTEMBER (61), WOMA\ OF STRAW (64), STRANGE BEDFELLOW\ (65), BAMBOLE (65), HOTEL PARADIS\ (66), BUONA SERA, MRS CAMPBELL (68 STUNTMAN (69), BAD MAN'S RIVER (71 KING, QUEEN, KNAVE (72); md. 2. Georg\ Kaufman 1969; Gina's nickname 'La Lollo' is shortening of her real family name; she has wo\ acclaim for her work as a stills photographer.

MICHAEL LONSDALE

B. Paris, France 24.5.31. Michael's father English, his mother French; soon after his birt\ family went to G.B., so he grew up speakir\ French and English fluently; early 1939 fami\ moved to Morocco, stayed there during WWI\ he became avid filmgoer, appd. on 'Children\ Hour' on Radio Morocco; returned to Paris 194\ spent much time painting, then enrolled at dram\ classes for 3 years with Tania Balachova, makir\ French stage debut in 'The Country Girl' in Pari\ becoming distinguished actor; film debut 1956\ 'It Happened in Aden', he has filmed mainly\ France including CHUT!; STAVISKY; ALOIS\ LA TRAQUE; EDEN PALACE; L'IMPR\ CATEUR; LE PASSAGER; INDIA SON\ LE TELEPHONE ROSE; L'ADIEU NU; L\ FEMME GAUCHERIE; he is perhaps bes\ known internationally as the Police Chief huntir\ the assassin in DAY OF THE JACKAL (7\ and as Hugo Drax in MOONRAKER (79\ recent movies: ENIGMA (81), THE BUNKE\ (81, T.V. movie, as Martin Bormann); T.V. 198\ 'Smiley's People'.

SOPHIA LOREN

Oscar-winning Sophia Loren, one of the last remaining great glamour stars of the screen, is the daughter of Romilda ?illani and Ricardo Scicolone and she was born in Rome (another source gives Pozzuoli) on 20 September 1934. It was ? Pozzuoli, in the Gulf of Naples, that she spent her childhood, at 16 winning beauty contest 'Princess of the Naples ?ea'. She then went to Rome with her mother and worked as a photo model, appeared as an extra in the movie QUO ?ADIS? (made in that city in 1950) and, working under the name of Sofia Lazzaro, she appeared in 'fumetti' mags ?presented dramatic stories in pictures) and in 1953, at a party, she met producer Carlo Ponti who became her mentor, ?ophia coming to the screen in TRATTA DELLE BIANCHE. Two years later she had become one of Italy's biggest ?lamour stars and her movies included AIDA (53); SIGN OF VENUS (53); TEMPI NOSTRI (54); ATTILA THE ?UN (54); WOMAN OF THE RIVER (55) and LUCKY TO BE A WOMAN (56). She wed Ponti by proxy in 1957, ?eir sons Carlo and Edouardo were born in 1968 and 1973. In 1957 she went to Hollywood and made such pictures as ?RIDE AND THE PASSION (57); BOY ON A DOLPHIN (57); DESIRÉ UNDER THE ELMS (58); ?OUSEBOAT (58); HELLER IN PINK TIGHTS (60) and A BREATH OF SCANDAL (61). Better roles in ?urope came in TWO WOMEN (61, winning Oscar, Best Actress, also BFA); EL CID (61); YESTERDAY, ?ODAY AND TOMORROW (63); MARRIAGE—ITALIAN STYLE (64, Oscar nom.) and OPERATION ?ROSSBOW (65). Sophia has continued to work internationally during the last 15 years and her many movies have ?cluded JUSITH (65); ARABESQUE (66); LADY L (66); A COUNTESS FROM HONG KONG (66); MORE ?HAN A MIRACLE (69); CINDERELLA—ITALIAN STYLE (70); MAN OF LA MANCHA (72); BRIEF ?NCOUNTER (74, T.V. movie); THE VOYAGE (75); A SPECIAL DAY (77); THE CASSANDRA ?ROSSING (77); BRASS TARGET (78); FIREPOWER (78); BLOODFEUD (79) and recently she essayed the ?les of herself and her mother in a T.V. movie, SOPHIA LOREN: HER OWN STORY (80). 81: GET RITA.
?OPHIA by Donald Zec; W.H. Allen: London, 1975.
?HE FILMS OF SOPHIA LOREN by Tony Crawley; LSP Books: Godalming, 1974; p/b;
?OPHIA: LIVING AND LOVING by Sophia Loren (with A.E. Hotcher); Michael Joseph: London, 1979; p/b;
?OREVER SOPHIA by Alan Levy; Robert Hale: London, 1980;

JACK LORD

B. New York City 30.12.30(?). Real name: John Joseph Ryan; ed. Fort Trumbull Acad., Newcondon, Conn. & New York Univ., graduating with Bach. of Science Degree & Honours in fine arts (Jack later organised his own art school in Greenwich Village, some of his paintings exhibited at Metropolitan Museum of Art); played Varsity football for 3 years & threw javelin in track; third mate in Merchant Navy, became involved in training films and decided to study at Neighbourhood Playhouse for 2 years, his first important stage role in off Broadway tour 'Flame Out' (53), then Broadway in 'Travelling Lady' (54) and replaced Ben Gazzara (qv) in 'Cat on a Hot Tin Roof' (55); md. Marie de Narde, fashion designer, his 2nd marriage; movies include CRY MURDER (51), COURT MARTIAL OF BILLY MITCHELL (55), THE VAGABOND KING (56), GOD'S LITTLE ACRE (58), MAN OF THE WEST (58), DR NO (62), COUNTERFEIT KILLING (68); well-known on T.V. in series 'Stoney Burke' (62/63) and esp. as Steve McGarrett in 'Hawaii Five-O' from 1968, directing several episodes.

JOANNA LUMLEY

B. Srinagar, India 1.5.46. Father: Major James Lumley, formerly of the 2/6 Gurkhas; ed: Micheldene Primary School, Army School—Kuala Lumpur, Prep School—Rolvenden, St. Mary's Anglican Convent, Hastings; Joanna has 8 'O' Levels, 'A' Level French; she worked as a shop assistant in craft/furniture shop, went to RADA briefly, but turned to modelling, which she did successfully, appearing in Queen mag. etc.; movies include SOME GIRLS DO (68), O.H.M.S.S. (69), BREAKING OF BUMBO (70), GAMES THAT LOVERS PLAY (70), SATANIC RITES OF DRACULA (72), DON'T JUST LIE THERE, SAY SOMETHING (73, also stage, with B. Rix); son, James, born when Joanna was 20; md. actor/scriptwriter Jeremy Lloyd May 1970 (annulled 11.2.71); film 1980: LADY CHATTERLEY vs. FANNY HILL; T.V. ser.: 'New Avengers' (77/78), 'Sapphire & Steel' (79-81); recent film: TRAIL OF THE PINK PANTHER (82); stage: 'Noël & Gertie' (83).

CHERIE LUNGHI

B. , . . . Central School of Speech & Drama 1969-73; rep.: Newcastle, Nottingham, fringe; R.S.Co.; West End includes 'Teeth 'n' Smiles', 'Uncle Vanya' (1982); much T.V. includes 'Edward & Mrs. Simpson', 'Playhouse Preview' (82); EXCALIBUR (81); OLIVER TWIST, PRAYING MANTIS (both T.V. movies, 82); N.T. player.

SIMON MacCORKINDALE

B. Isle of Ely 12.2.52. Scottish parents, father Group Capt. in R.A.F., Simon spent some years in Germany, where father was stationed; while at drama school appd. in 'Dark Lady of the Sonnets'; pro. career commenced at Coventry Rep., appearing in 'Journey's End', 'The Front Page', 'Getting On' etc.; his T.V. appearances have included 'I, Claudius', 'Within These Walls', 'Life of Shakespeare' and 'Romance'; his films have included a small role in JUGGERNAUT (74) and starring roles in DEATH ON THE NILE (77), THE RIDDLE OF THE SANDS (78), CABO BLANCO (79); md. actress/singer Fiona Fullerton (qv —div.); recent T.V. includes 'Quatermass' (78), 'The Dukes of Hazard' (79), 'Hammer House of Horror' (80) and U.S. mini-series 'The Mannions of America' (81); movie 81: SWORD & THE SORCERER; 82: FALCON'S GOLD; 83: JAWS 3-D.

ARTHUR LOWE

B. Hayfield, Derbyshire 22.9.15. An only child, Arthur's father was a Manchester-based London & N.E. railways official, organising the transportation of theatre/circus co.'s; in 1931 left school and worked for £2.50 a week as store keeper for Brown Bros., pushing hand cart around; then joined the army as trooper with Duke of Lancs's Own Yeomanry, when war broke out went to Egypt, attaining rank of Sergeant-Major, later becoming involved in Forces entertainment; in 1945 took a RADA course, made his rep. debut Nov. 1945 at Hulme Rep., Manchester in 'Bedtime Story', where he met his wife, Joan Cooper: they wed in 1948, their son, Stephen (b. 1953) is in yachting business; Arthur became well-known stage actor — West End includes 'Call Me Madam' (52), 'Pajama Game' (55), worked in films from 1948 (debut: LONDON BELONGS TO ME) and appd. in T.V. from 1951, becoming household name with his portrayal of Mr Swindley in 'Coronation Street' (from 1961) and more recently as Capt. Mainwaring in 'Dad's Army' (from 1969 BBC T.V., feature film 1971, stage 1975); recent T.V. series:'Bless Me, Father' (81), 'A. J. Wentworth, B.A.', 'Wagner' (both '82): movie '78: SWEET WILLIAM; stage '81: 'Hobson's Choice'. *Mr Lowe died, following a stroke, on 15.4.82.*

CAROL LYNLEY

B. New York City 13.2.41(?). Real name Carol Lee Jones; father Cyril (Irish), mother Frances (American); Carol took dancing lessons aged 7, appd. on amateur T.V. programme as dancer, producer suggested she try modelling, became successful from age 10; 1st pro. T.V. role in 'Danger', then turned to stage, touring in 'Anniversary Waltz', aged 15 Broadway debut: 'The Potting Shed', became a star of Broadway in 'Blue Denim' (58), repeating role in movie, BLUE JEANS (59); had come to the screen in LIGHT IN THE FOREST (58); md. Mike Selsman, publicist (div.), daughter Jill Victoria, b. 3.3.62; her many movies have included RETURN TO PEYTON PLACE (61), THE LAST SUNSET (62), THE STRIPPER (63), THE CARDINAL (63), as HARLOW (65), BUNNY LAKE IS MISSING (65), THE SHUTTERED ROOM (68), NORWOOD (69), POSEIDON ADVENTURE (72) and her many T.V. movies include: COTTER (72), THE ELEVATOR (74), FLOOD (76): Carol played Sylvia Cartwright in the T.V. series 'The Immortal' (70/71); more recent movies: CAT AND THE CANARY (77), BAD GEORGIA ROAD (78), SHAPE OF THINGS TO COME (78); VIGILANTE (82).

ALI MacGRAW

B. Pund Ridge, New York 1.4.38. Real name Alice MacGraw; ed. Wellesley College, studying art, history and dramatics; md. 1. Robin Hoen 1961 (div. 1962); Miss MacGraw left a successful career as a fashion model after Paramount Pictures' executives saw her on the covers of a number of top mags, coming to the screen uncredited in A LOVELY WAY TO DIE (68); md. 2. producer Robert Evans, son Joshua born 16.1.71. (div. 1973); her movies include GOODBYE COLUMBUS (69), LOVE STORY (71, Oscar nom.), THE GETAWAY (72), CONVOY (77), PLAYERS (78), JUST TELL ME WHAT YOU WANT (80) and the T.V. series 'Winds of War' (83).

71

SHIRLEY MacLAINE

From Broadway chorus to film stardom in a number of weeks, Shirley MacLaine, recently seen in BEING THERE, has emerged as a most skilful American movie actress in roles often combining comedy with a tinge of pathos. The daughter of Ira O. Beatty, who was in real estate (and formerly a band-leader), and his wife Kathryn, a former stage actress and drama coach, she was born Shirley MacLaine Beatty (younger brother, Warren (qv), came later) on 24 April 1934 at Richmond, Virginia. At the age of three she was taking ballet lessons and a year later she danced at the famous Mosque recitals at Richmond. Receiving her education at Washington and Lee High School, Arlington, it was while still at the latter that she managed to get work in New York in the chorus of 'Oklahoma' (1950) and, later, 'Kiss Me Kate'. Cutting short her studies, she returned to the big City and 'demonstrated refrigerators around which she danced and pranced', did occasional T.V. bits and, later, modelled, danced with the National Symphony Orchestra in Washington, then landed her first good role in New York in chorus of 'Me & Juliet', and, in 'The Pajama Game' (1954), at short notice, she stepped in to replace an injured Carol Haney. Her performance was seen by Hal Wallis and she was immediately given a leading role in Hitchcock's THE TROUBLE WITH HARRY (55). Shirley had wed Steve Parker on 17 September 1954, their daughter Stephanie Sachikol ('Sachi' — in 1979 she was working as a stewardess with Australia's Quantas Airline) came the following year. Her many motion-pictures have included ARTISTS AND MODELS (56); AROUND THE WORLD IN 80 DAYS (56); SOME CAME RUNNING* (58); ASK ANY GIRL (59); CAN-CAN (60); THE APARTMENT* (60); LOUDEST WHISPER (62); IRMA LA DOUCE* (63); JOHN GOLDFARB, PLEASE COME HOME (64); GAMBIT (66); SWEET CHARITY (68); THE BLISS OF MRS BLOSSOM (68); 2 MULES FOR SISTER SARA (69); DESPERATE CHARACTERS (71); THE POSSESSION OF JOEL DELANEY (72); THE TURNING POINT (77)*; LOVING COUPLES (79) and BEING THERE (80). Her many T.V. appearances include a special — 'Shirley MacLaine At The Lido' (79), a documentary 'The Other Half of the Sky: A China Memoir' and her series, 'Shirley's World' (1971/72) as Shirley Logan. Recent work includes a T.V. show, 'Illusions' (82), the movie TERMS OF ENDEARMENT (83) and her cabaret show in October, 1982, in London, was described by one critic as 'a performance exhilarating in it's tireless virtuosity'. (*denotes Oscar nom.).
DON'T FALL OFF THE MOUNTAIN by S.M.; W.W. Norton & Co. Inc.: USA, 1970; p/b.
YOU CAN GET THERE FROM HERE by S.M.; The Bodley Head: London, 1975; p/b—Corgi;
OUT ON A LIMB by S.M.; Elm Tree Books: London, 1983.

PATRICK MacNEE

B. London 6.2.22. Patrick 'claims Robin Hood as ancestor' — his mother a member of the Hastings family, Earls of Huntingdon and grandfather Sir Daniel MacNee was Pres. of the Royal Academy; is a cousin of David Niven (qv); ed. Summerfields Prep. School, Banbury, Oxfordshire and Eton Coll., where he appeared in plays, including role of Queen Victoria; s'ship to drama school: Webber Douglas Acad., making rep. debut at Bradford, later Letchworth Garden City rep.; WWII: Naval Commander of a motor torpedo boat patrolling North Sea area; had come to screen in 1942 in LIFE & DEATH OF COLONEL BLIMP; md. 1. actress Barbara Douglas (div.); during 1950s Mr MacNee appd. in West End as Laurie in 'Little Women', toured the States with the Old Vic in 'A Midsummer Night's Dream' in 1954 and his movies included THE ELUSIVE PIMPERNEL (51), FLESH & BLOOD (52), 3 CASES OF MURDER (55), BATTLE OF THE RIVER PLATE (56) and LES GIRLS (58); md. 2. actress Catherine Woodville (div.); he has a son, Rupert, from his 1st marriage. and daughter Jennie, from 2nd; in the 1960s he worked a lot in T.V., including the organising of interviews for T.V. series 'Valiant Years', including Mountbatten and Monty, but from 1961 commenced his famous role as John Steed in 'The Avengers'; he has acted on stage in Australia, appd. many times on T.V. in the States and Canada, and in U.S. has business interests including land near Palm Springs and 120 acres in the desert; recent movies: SEA WOLVES, STROKE OF LUCK (both 1980), THE HOWLING, HOT TOUCH, THE CREATURE WASN'T NICE (all 1981), YOUNG DOCTORS IN LOVE (82), FOR THE TERM OF HIS NATURAL LIFE (mini-ser., 1983).

DAVID McCALLUM

B. Glasgow, Scotland 19.9.33. Son of leading violinist, David McCallum, his mother was a concert cellist; parents suggested their son studied playing the oboe, but, aged 14, young David sought a job in theatre as electrician's assistant — he was also property master with Glyndebourne Opera Co.; during his Nat. Serv., he served 10 months in Ghana as a lieutenant, and was involved in producing plays; studied at RADA from 1949-51, made screen début in teens in movie PRELUDE TO FAME (50) and in early 50s appeared in such reps as Frinton, Essex and at Oxford; movies include THE SECRET PLACE (56), HELL DRIVERS (57), ROBBERY UNDER ARMS (57), VIOLENT PLAYGROUND (57), A NIGHT TO REMEMBER (58), THE LONG, SHORT & THE TALL (61), JUNGLE STREET (61), FREUD (62), BILLY BUDD (62), GREAT ESCAPE (63), GREATEST STORY EVER TOLD (64), AROUND THE WORLD UNDER THE SEA (66), SOL MADRID (68), MOSQUITO SQUADRON (69), THE RAVINE (70), HAUDER'S MEMORY (70, T.V. movie), SHE WAITS (72, T.V. movie), FRANKENSTEIN: THE TRUE STORY (73, T.V. movie), DOGS (76), WATCHER IN THE WOODS (79); md. 1. actress Jill Ireland (qv), May 1957, sons: Paul (b. 1958), Jason (b. 1959), Valentine (b. 1960), (div.), 2. model Katherine Carpenter 1967; David is a very popular actor on T.V., has guested on many occasions and starred as Ilya Kuryakin in 'Man From U.N.C.L.E.' (64-68), 'Colditz' (72, BBC), Dr Daniel Westin in 'The Invisible Man' (75/76) and recently 'Sapphire & Steel'; recent movies: CRITICAL LIST, THE PERSONALS (both 1982).

KEVIN McCARTHY

B. Seattle, Washington 15.2.15(?). Ed. Minn. Univ., intended a diplomatic career, studied English Lit., making his Broadway debut in 1938 in 'Abe Lincoln in Illinois'; Mr McCarthy became a well-known New York actor, including roles in 'Joan of Lorraine' (46), 'Death of a Salesman' (49, also motion picture in 1951, gaining Kevin Oscar nom., BSA), 'The Sea Gull' (54), 'The Three Sisters' (64), many others; movies include STRANGER ON HORSEBACK (55), INVASION OF THE BODY SNATCHERS (56), THE MISFITS (61), THE BEST MAN (64), BIG HAND FOR A LITTLE LADY (66), KANSAS CITY BOMBER (72), BUFFALO BILL & THE INDIANS (76); his 1969 T.V. series was 'The Survivors', in which he played Philip Hastings, T.V. movies include A GREAT AMERICAN TRAGEDY (72) and EXOMAN (77), PIRANHA (78), THE HOWLING (81), THE TWILIGHT ZONE (82); T.V. series 1981: 'Flamingo Road'.

DOUG McCLURE

B. Glendale, California 11.5.35(?). Ed. U.C.L.A. a star football player, also excelling at swimmin and basketball; claims to be 'discovered whil surf-bathing, for T.V.' — first pro. job 'taking sudsy shower in soap commercial'; md. 1. Fay Brash (div.) 1957, 1 child; 2. Barbara Luna 196 (div.); many films include THE UNFORGIVEN (59), SHENANDOAH (65), KING'S PIRATE (67), AT THE EARTH'S CORE (76), MON STER (80); md. 3. Helen Crane 1967 (div.), 4 Diane 1973; Mr McClure is very popular on T.V and has made several series, including 'Overlan Trail' (60), as 'Flip' Flippen, 'Checkmate' (60 62), as Jed Sills, 'The Virginian' (62-71) a: 'Trampas', 'Search' (72/73) as C.R. Grover 'Barbary Coast' (75/76) as Cash Canover, an his many T.V. movies include BIRDMEN (71) 'The Rhinemann Exchange' (77); also an accom plished photographer; recent movies: THE CA FROM OUTER SPACE (78), CHARLIE CHAN & THE CURSE OF THE DRAGON QUEEN (81), EVIL UNDER THE SUN (82) CLASS OF 1982 (82).

MALCOLM McDOWELL

Malcolm McDowell, one of Britain's foremost younger stars to emerge in the late 1960s, has recently moved to America, where his career is now making headway. He was born Malcolm Taylor in Leeds, Yorkshire, on 13 June 1944, the son of a publican. He was educated in Kent, at Cannock College, where he appeared in school plays to 'get rid of his shyness and inhibitions', tackling the Bard and other classics. Working briefly at his father's pub in Liverpool, where the family had moved, as a wine waiter, Malcolm took a course in engineering and later became a sales representative for a U.S. coffee company, based in Yorkshire, but at the weekends he studied at a drama school in Liverpool, above Crane's, the big music store. He was later accepted at L.A.M.D.A., in London, becoming an associate of the academy, and made his repertory debut in 1964 at Shanklin, Isle of Wight and later appeared at Torquay for a season before being accepted with the Royal Shakespeare Co. at Aldwych and Stratford as a spear carrier. An agent got him a role in a T.V. play, 'Iron Johnny' and in 1968 he appeared at the Royal Court Theatre as Sebastian in 'Twelfth Night', where he met the director, Mr Lindsay Anderson, who was to prove influential to his career. Anderson cast him as Mick Travis, the public schoolboy rebel, in his production of IF . . (68, Malcolm had come to the screen in 1965 in a deleted role in POOR COW) and since then his film career has never looked back: he has appeared in THE RAGING MOON (69); FIGURES IN A LANDSCAPE (70); CLOCKWORK ORANGE (71); O! LUCKY MAN (73); ROYAL FLASH (75); VOYAGE OF THE DAMNED (76); ACES HIGH (76); CALIGULA (77); THE PASSAGE (78) and TIME AFTER TIME (78). He wed Margot Dullea, ex-wife of actor Keir Dullea (qv), on 21 April 1975, but the couple divorced in 1980 and in November of that year Malcolm wed actress Mary Steenburgen. Their daughter Lilly Amanda was born on 22 January 1981. His wife has played in such movies as GOIN' SOUTH (78) and MELVIN & HOWARD (80). The actor played on Broadway in 1980 in 'Look Back in Anger' and his most recent movies are CAT PEOPLE, BRITANNIA HOSPITAL (both 1981); BLUE THUNDER and FLIP OUT (both 1982).

ALEC McCOWEN

B. Tunbridge Wells, Kent 26.5.25. Full name Alexander Duncan McCowen; father a shopkeeper; ed. Skinner's School, Tunbridge Wells, and studied for the stage at RADA, making his pro. début in 'Paddy The Next Best Thing' at Macclesfield in 1942, followed by more rep., and in 1945 played in India and Burma with E.N.S.A. in 'Love In A Mist'; Mr McCowen subsequently became one of Britain's most accomplished stage actors, appearing in the West End, on Broadway and with The Old Vic Co., The R.S. Co., including U.S.S.R. tour, winning awards, esp. for his roles in 'Hadrian VII' (67/68), 'The Philanthropist' ('70) and 'The Misanthrope' (73); occasional movies include TIME WITHOUT PITY (57), IN THE COOL OF THE DAY (63), THE WITCHES (66), MASTER OF THE ISLANDS ('70), FRENZY (72), TRAVELS WITH MY AUNT (72), STEVIE (78), HANOVER STREET (78), NEVER SAY NEVER AGAIN (83); recent stage: one-man presentation, 'St. Mark's Gospel' (81), 'Portage to San Cristobal of A.H.' (82); TV: 'Henry V' (79), 'all For Love' (ser., 82). *DOUBLE BILL* (part-autobio); Elm Tree Books: London, 1980.

PETER McENERY

B. Walsall, Staffs., 21.2.40; studied for the stage at Brighton School of Speech & Drama at 16; during holidays got A.S.M. job at Palace Pier Theatre, Brighton at 30/- per week, left drama school, went to Court Players, Peterborough; u/study and played in 'Flowering Cherry', replacing Andrew Ray (qv., Haymarket, London 1958); appd. on T.V. and won success in play 'Look Homeward, Angel' (60); also toured in 'Five Finger Exercise'; Peter has been seen on the big screen in TUNES OF GLORY (60), VICTIM (61), THE MOONSPINNERS (64), THE FIGHTING PRICE OF DONEGAL (65), THE GAME IS OVER (66), I KILLED RASPUTIN (68), BETTER A WIDOW (68), NEGATIVES (69), ADVENTURES OF GERARD (70), ENTERTAINING MR SLOANE (70), CAT & THE CANARY (77), others; recent stage: Treves in 'Elephant Man' (80, Lyttleton Theatre); Brutus in 'Julius Caesar' (83); R.S.Co. player; recent T.V.: 'A Midsummer Night's Dream' (81), 'Pictures' (ser., 1983).

PATRICK McGOOHAN

B. New York City 19.3.28. Parents Irish, family moved from New York to Ireland when he was 7, later to Yorkshire, left school, worked for British Rope Co., Sheffield, then became bank manager of tiny sub-branch, then chicken farmer, but was later laid up on his back for 6 months; after several temporary office jobs, had interest in amateur acting, applied for job at Sheffield Rep., which he secured, stayed there for 4 years, beginning as stage manager, graduating to leading man — met and wed actress Joan Drummond (3 daughters: Catherine, Frances and Anne); Mr McGoohan appd. at other reps., including Bristol Old Vic, 'Q' and Embassy Theatres; won acclaim in 'Serious Charge' at Garrick Theatre, London 1955; that year moved into T.V., including 'The Vise', his many movies include PASSAGE HOME (55), ZARAK (57), HELL DRIVERS (57), NOR THE MOON BY NIGHT (58), ALL NIGHT LONG (62), THE QUARE FELLOW (62), DR SYN (63), ICE STATION ZEBRA (68), MARY, QUEEN OF SCOTS (72, as James Stuart); well-known on T.V. for his acting as John Drake in 'Danger Man' (series 60-61) and the cult series in 1967, as No.6 — 'The Prisoner'; recent series: 'Rafferty' (77); movies: SILVER STREAK (77), SCANNERS (79), THE HARD WAY (79, T.V. movie), FINDING KATIE (83); 'Jamaica Inn' (ser., 1983).

RODDY McDOWELL

B. Herne Hill, London 17.9.28. Ed. St. Joseph's Coll., Highgate, N. London; as a child Roddy showed signs of acting talent, his parents sent him to the Hanover Acad., London and he soon appeared in such movies as SCRUFFY (38, uncredited), MURDER IN THE FAMILY (38, credited) and as Ginger in JUST WILLIAM (39); during the early years of the War, Roddy, his mother and sister moved to the USA—to Hollywood, and he won the role of young Huw Morgan in John Ford's classic HOW GREEN WAS MY VALLEY (41, Oscar, Best Movie); he went on to appear in MAN HUNT (41), THE PIED PIPER (42), LASSIE COME HOME (43), THE WHITE CLIFFS OF DOVER (44), HOLIDAY IN MEXICO (46), and many others—after THE STEEL FIST (52) he was absent from screen until 1960; that year he won 'Tony' Award on Broadway as Supporting Actor in 'The Fighting Cock' and began to make headway on the big screen again in adult roles, becoming one of Hollywood's busiest actors, many movies include THE SUBTERRANEANS (60), CLEOPATRA (63), 5 CARD STUD (68), 3 'Ape' movies, plus portraying Galen in 'Planet of the Apes' T.V. series (74); other T.V.: Dr Jonathan Willoway in 'Fantastic Journey' (77) and Bobby Ballard in DEATH RACE (73), SATAN'S TRIANGLE (75), ROOTS, DISASTER IN THE SKY (both 1977), WILD & WOOLLY (78), THE REBELS (mini-ser., 79).

DARREN McGAVIN

B. San Joaquin Valley, California (/or Spokane, Washington(?)), 7.5.22. Ed. Coll. of Pacific, appearing in 'Lady Windermere's Fan', studied at Neighborhood Playhouse 1948, played on Broadway 1949 in 'Cock-a-Doodle Do', same year replaced Cameron Michell (qv) in 'Death of a Salesman'; Darren has done much Broadway and in 50s studied with Actors's Studio, came to the screen in QUEEN FOR A DAY (51), and became a star of T.V.: Casey in 'Crime Reporter' (51/52), Mike Hammer in 'Mike Hammer, Detective' (58) and Grey Holden in 'Riverboat' (59-61); success on Broadway 1954 in 'The Rainmaker'; has also directed on T.V.: many movies include BEAU JAMES (57), DELICATE DELINQUENT (57), BULLET FOR A BADMAN (64), MISSION MARS (69); over 10 T.V. movies, inclu. 'Ike: The War Years' (79); recent films: HANGAR 18 (80), WAIKIKI (T.V. movie, 1980), CHRISTMAS STORY (83).

IAN McKELLEN

B. Burnley, Lancashire 25.5.35. Ed. Wigan Grammar School, Bolton School and St. Catherine's College, Cambridge (B.A.), where he embarked on his successful stage career, making his professional debut at Coventry in 1961; since then he has played in such companies as the Ipswich Rep. (62-63), the Nottingham Playhouse (63-64), made his West End debut 1964 in 'A Scent of Flowers', joined the National Theatre in 1965 and became one of Britain's most brilliant stage actors, distinguishing himself in roles at Chichester, on Broadway, at the Edinburgh Festival and for the Royal Shakespeare Company, amongst others; Mr McKellen has made few films and these have been ALFRED THE GREAT (69), THE PROMISE (69, also stage. London and Broadway) and a TOUCH OF LOVE (69); he has, however, appeared on T.V. on many occasions, including 'David Copperfield' (66) and televised his stage triumphs as 'Richard II' and 'Edward II'; also stage director; founder member: Actors' Co. (72); recent stage: 'Amadeus' ('Tony' Aw. 8.6.81); continental tour 'Acting Shakespeare' (82); recent films: PRIEST OF LOVE (82, as D.H. Lawrence), WALTER (T.V. movie, 82), SCARLET PIMPERNEL (T.V. movie, 82), THE KEEP (83).

VIRGINIA McKENNA

B. Regent's Park, London 7.6.31. Ed. Heron's Ghyll, Horsham and at Cape Town, S. Africa; father a well-known member of Christie's, the London auctioneers, and a cousin of Fay Compton; Virginia's mother was a pianist, lead a group called 'That Certain Trio'; although often affectionately called the 'English Rose', she has a mixture of Scots, Irish and French blood, only a little English; parents encouraged her to go on stage in school plays, she attended London's Central School of Speech & Drama, went into repertory at Dundee, Scotland for 6 months and was later spotted by a top agent and soon made a name for herself in the West End in 'A Penny For a Song' and as Perdita in 'The Winter's Tale' (both 51); the following year she came to the screen in FATHER'S DOING FINE (52) and her many films have included THE CRUEL SEA (52), SIMBA (54), A TOWN LIKE ALICE (55, BAFTA Aw.), BARRETT'S OF WIMPOLE STREET (56), SMALLEST SHOW ON EARTH (57), CARVE HER NAME WITH PRIDE (58), 2 LIVING ONE DEAD (62), BORN FREE (66, as Joy Adamson, Evening Standard Aw.), RING OF BRIGHT WATER (69), SWALLOWS AND AMAZONS (74), BEAUTY & THE BEAST (76), HOLOCAUST 2000 (77), THE DISAPPEARANCE (77); Miss McKenna has frequently returned to the stage, including Anna Leonowens in 'The King & I' (79/80), 'The Letter' (81), 'A Personal Affair' (82).
SOME OF MY FRIENDS HAVE TAILS by V. Mc.; Collins/Harvill: London, 1970; p/b.

LEO McKERN

B. Sydney, N.S.W., Australia 16.3.20. Real name Reginald McKern; Mr McKern began working as an engineer but as a result of an injury turned successfully to commercial art, but had experience as an amateur actor; joined Australian Army for WWII, having made his professional acting début in Sydney in 1944 in 'Uncle Harry'; came to Britain in Sept. 1946 and gradually built up his reputation as a character actor of note, performing with the Old Vic, The Shakespeare Memorial Theatre Co., including an Australian tour; came to the big screen in 1955 in ALL FOR MARY and has been seen in dozens of movies, including X—THE UNKNOWN (56), A TALE OF 2 CITIES (57), YESTERDAY'S ENEMY (59), JAZZBOAT (60), THE DAY THE EARTH CAUGHT FIRE (61), THE INSPECTOR (62), THE HORSE WITHOUT A HEAD (63), HELP! (65), A MAN FOR ALL SEASONS (66, as Thomas Cromwell, also London/Broadway stage), DECLINE AND FALL (68), SHOES OF THE FISHERMAN (68), RYAN'S DAUGHTER (71), THE ADVENTURES OF SHERLOCK HOLMES' SMARTER BROTHER (76), THE OMEN (76), THE OMEN: PART II (78, uncredited), THE BLUE LAGOON (79), THE FRENCH LIEUTENANT'S WOMAN (81); much T.V., including 'Rumpole of the Bailey' (ser.), 'Reilly' (83), 'King Lear' (83, as Gloucester); stage 1982: 'The Housekeeper'.

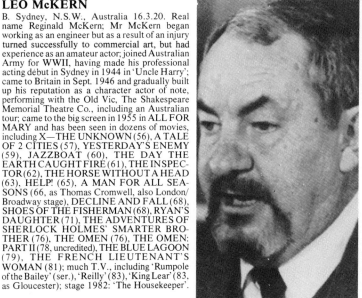

KRISTY McNICHOL

B. Los Angeles, California 11.9.62. Miss McNichol is a former child actress, popular on television in the United States in the series 'Apple's Way', as Patricia Apple (74/75), and as Letitia 'Buddy' Lawrence in 'Family' (76); her other T.V. work has included guest spots in Dick Clark's Live Wednesday' and 'People' (both 78); her T.V. movies include THE LOVE BOAT II (77), LIKE MOM, LIKE ME (78), SUMMER OF MY GERMAN SOLDIER (78) and she is now making headway in motion pictures, having been seen in THE END (77, small role), LITTLE DARLINGS (79), THE NIGHT THE LIGHTS WENT OUT IN GEORGIA (80), ONLY WHEN I LAUGH (80), WHITE DOG (81), THE PIRATE MOVIE (82).

IAN McSHANE

B. Blackburn, Lancashire 29.9.42. Ed. Stretfor Grammar School, Lancs.; father Harry McShane former Manchester Utd. footballer; Ian traine for the stage at RADA and went straight int movie THE WILD & THE WILLING (62); me 1. actress Suzan Farmer (div.), 2. Ruth Post, son and 1 daughter (div.); he is equally popular o T.V. and in the movies, latter have included SK WEST & CROOKED (65), THE PROMISE (67), THE BATTLE OF BRITAIN (68), SIT TING TARGET (72), LAST OF SHEIL (73), RANSOM (74), ROOTS (77, mini-series JESUS OF NAZARETH (77, T.V. movie, Judas), THE SEWERS OF GOLD (78), TH FIFTH MUSKETEER (78), YESTERDAY HERO (79), THE LETTER (T.V. movie, 1981 EXPOSED (82), as Prince Rainier in TH GRACE KELLY STORY (T.V. movie, 1983 Md: 3. actress Gwen Humble; much T.V. incl 'Wuthering Heights', 'Disraeli' (77); recent stag U.S.A., 'Betrayal' (82).

PATRICK MAGEE

B. Armagh, N. Ireland, . .24. Mr Magee the son of a farmer; upon leaving school eventually did stage work in Ireland with Ane McMaster's Co. and came to London, making name for himself in Beckett's play 'Krapp's La Tape' at the Royal Court Theatre; he becam well-known on the stage as a character acto playing with distinction with the Royal Shake peare Co., the Old Vic and also on Broadway, h work in 'Marat Sade' winning a 'Tony' Award 1966 (also filmed); he has frequently appeared movies, including THE CRIMINAL (60), TH SERVANT (63), ZULU (64), MASQUE O THE RED DEATH (64), THE SKULL (65 ANZIO (68), BIRTHDAY PARTY (68), TH FIEND (71), CLOCKWORK ORANGE (71 ASYLUM (72), BARRY LYNDON (76), TELE FON (77), ROUGHCUT (79), MONSTE CLUB (81); recent T.V.: Gen. Wavell in 'Churchill The Generals' (79), 'The Flipside of Domin Hide' (80).
Mr Magee died in London on August 15, 198.

LEE MAJORS

B. Wyandotte, a suburb of Detroit, Michiga 23.3.40. Real name Harvey Lee Yeary; Lee parents died when he was young and he wa adopted by an aunt and uncle; at school h became a star athlete and later turned down a offer from St. Louis Cardinals in final year at F Kentucky State Coll. to pursue an acting caree James Dean had been Lee's boyhood screen id and he went to see his agent, Dick Clayton; latte took him on his books, in the meantime Le worked as playground supervisor for L.A. Rec reation & Parks Dept., N. Hollywood Park an studied with Estelle Harmon, MGM drama coac for 6 months; 1st role as Heath Barkley in 'Th Big Valley' T.V. series (65-69); movies: WIL PENNY (67), LIBERATION OF L.B. JONE (70), KILLERFISH (78), THE NORSEMA (78), STEEL (78), AGENCY (79), LAS CHASE (79); well-known on T.V.: Roy Tate i 'Men From Shiloh' (70/71), Jess Brandon i 'Owen Marshall' (71-74) and Steve Austin th 'Six Million Dollar Man' (74-78); md. Farra Fawcett (qv) 28.7.73 (div.); has son, Lee Jr., fror 1st marriage to Kathy Robinson (58-65); Lee ha played in many T.V. movies, recently JUST LITTLE INCONVENIENCE (77) and HIGI NOON PART II: RETURN OF WILL KAN (80); hit T.V. ser. 1982/83: 'The Fall Guy', a Colt Seavers;
FARRAH & LEE by Connie Berman; p/back– Tempo Books: New York 1977.

KARL MALDEN

B. Gary, Indiana 22.3.14. Real name Mladen Sekulovich(?); Karl started acting during the tough depression of the 1930s; he worked as a steelworker for 2½ years in his home town, but a job in a theatre erecting sets made him choose a stage career; for 15 years was distinguished Broadway player, including 'Golden Boy' (38), 'Key Largo' (39) 'Truckline Cafe' (46), 'All My Sons' (47), 'A Streetcar Named Desire' (47); md: Mona Graham, 2 daughters: Mila (b. 1948), Carla (b. 1953); Mr Malden came to the screen in 1940 in THEY KNEW WHAT THEY WANTED, concentrated on movie career from early 50s, many include WINGED VICTORY (44), 13 RUE MADELEINE (46), BOOMERANG (47), THE GUNFIGHTER (50), WHERE THE SIDEWALK ENDS (50), A STREETCAR NAMED DESIRE (51, Oscar BSA), ON THE WATERFRONT (54, Oscar nom. BSA), BABY DOLL (56), directed TIME LIMIT (57), POLYANNA (60), ONE-EYED JACKS (61), GYPSY (62), DEAD RINGER (64), THE SILENCERS (66), HOTEL (67), BILLION DOLLAR BRAIN (67), PATTON: LUST FOR GLORY (69), WILD ROVERS (71); T.V. series, 1972-77, portrayed Lt. Mike Stone in 'The Streets of San Francisco'; films: 77: METEOR and 'Captain's Courageous' (T.V. movie); 80: WORD OF HONOUR (T.V. movie).

DOROTHY MALONE

B. Chicago, Ill., 30.1.25. Real name Dorothy Maloney; ed. Ursuline Convent & Highland Park H.S., Dallas; Hockaday Jun. Coll.; Southern Methodist Univ.; college prod. of 'Starbound' brought Dorothy film offer, but she declined; later went to Hollywood, studied dancing/diction for 1 year and seen by talent scout in amateur play, 'Ladies Unmasked', came to the screen in FAL-CON & THE CO-EDS (43); made dozens of movies, including BIG SLEEP (46), NIGHT & DAY (48), YOUNG AT HEART (54), won Oscar, BSA, for WRITTEN ON THE WIND (56), WARLOCK (59); md. actor Jacques Bergerac 1959 (div. 1964), 2 daughters: Mimi (b. 1960), Diane (b. 1961), 2. banker Robert Tomarkin (1969, but annulled that year); Miss Malone became a household name as Constance MacKenzie in T.V. series 'Peyton Place' (1964-8); she has made many T.V. movies; 1979 films: DAY TIME ENDED, WINTER KILLS; md. 3. Charles H. Bell in 1971.

JANET MARGOLIN – see page 124

ALFRED MARKS

B. Holborn, London 28.1.21. Ed. Bell Lane School, London, leaving at 14; parents both milliners; Mr Marks first appd. on stage as amateur, aged 14, as soprano in Boys' Brigade; WWII served in RAF in Middle East/Italy; pro. stage début 1946 at Kilburn Empire in variety, then 2 years resident comedian Windmill Theatre, becoming well known on stage, in variety, on T.V. in many series and the movies; md. actress Paddie O'Neil in 1952, 1 daughter Danielle Elizabeth, 1 son Gareth John; films include PENNY POINTS TO PARADISE (51), JOHNNY, YOU'RE WANTED (56), DESERT MICE (59), THERE WAS A CROOKED MAN (60), FRIGHTENED CITY (61), WEEKEND WITH LULU (62), SCREAM & SCREAM AGAIN (69), OUR MISS FRED (72), VALENTINO (77); well-known on radio; T.V. 1979: 'Ghosts of Motley Hall'; awarded O.B.E. 1976; T.V. 1981: host 'Theatre Quiz'; recent movies: COX & BOX, YEOMAN OF THE GUARD (T.V. movies, 1982), FANNY HILL (83).

JOHN MARLEY

B.   ,   .   . Mr Marley has played in several New York productions including 'Johnny Doodle' (1942), 'Sing Me No Lullaby' (1954), 'Compulsion' (1957); much T.V. includes 'Three Steps to Heaven' (1953/54), Sam Crown in 'Hawk' series 1966); many movies including MY SIX CON-VICTS (52); THE JOE LOUIS STORY (53); THE SQUARE JUNGLE (56); TIMETABLE 56); I WANT TO LIVE! (58); AMERICA! AMERICA! (65); CAT BALLOU (66); FACES 68); LOVE STORY (70, Oscar nom. BSA); A MAN CALLED SLEDGE (70); GODFATHER 72); W.C. FIELDS & ME (76); THE GREATEST (77); THE CAR (77); HOOPER 78); PRIVATE FILES OF J. EDGAR HOOVER 78); IT LIVES AGAIN (78); TRIBUTE (80); WORD OF HONOUR (T.V. movie, 1980); MOTHER LODE, THE AMATEUR (both 2); UTILITIES (83).

JEAN MARSH

B. Stoke Newington, London,   .   .38. Mother was in domestic service, later becoming dresser to actress Hy Hazell; trained for the stage at Central School of Speech & Drama; she has played supporting roles in many movies, including CLEOPATRA (63), THE LIMBO LINE (68), FRENZY (71), JANE EYRE (71) and THE EAGLE HAS LANDED (76); much T.V. has included the series 'The Informer' (66) and especially the series 'Upstairs, Downstairs', in which she played the maid, Rose, the story for the show being her own idea, running from 1972-76; Miss Marsh played on Broadway in the play 'Habeas Corpus' in 1975 and 'Who's Life Is It, Anyway' in 1979; U.S. T.V. 1975 hostess of 'International Animation Festival'; stage 1982: 'On the Rocks'; T.V. ser. 1982: '9 to 5'; recent films: THE CHANGELING (77). GOLIATH AWAITS (mini-ser., 1982).

E. G. MARSHALL

B. Owatonna, Minn. 18.6.10. Ed. Charleton Coll., University of Minnesota; father Norwegian; started in radio in 1932, stage début with Oxford Players 1933, involved in the Federal Theatre project of the 30s, became very well-known actor on Broadway and U.S. stage; md. 1. Helen Wolf 1939, 1 daughter Jill, 1 son Degen, (div. 1953), 2. Judith ———, 3 children; came to screen 1945 in THE HOUSE ON 92ND STREET, others include CALL NORTHSIDE 777 (48), PUSH-OVER (55), CAINE MUTINY (55), 12 ANGRY MEN (57), TOWN WITHOUT PITY (61), THE CHASE (66), THE BRIDGE AT RE-MAGEN (69), THE PURSUIT OF HAPPINESS (71), SUPERMAN II (80), many T.V. movies; he is very well-known on T.V., appearing in productions since 1947, including the series 'The Defenders' (61-65, 'Emmy Aw.' 1963) as Lawrence Preston, 'The Bold Ones' (69/70), 'Saigon' (82), as Henri Denault in 'Falcon Crest' (82/83); recent films: THE PHOENIX (T.V. movie), CREEPSHOW (both 1982).

STEVE MARTIN – see page 124

PAMELA SUE MARTIN

B.   ; one of the more prominent young actresses on the U.S. motion picture scene today, Pamela began her career as a teenage model and came to the screen, while still a High School student, in Columbia's TO FIND A MAN (72). Her movies have since included THE POSEIDON ADVENTURE (72), THE GIRLS OF HUNT-ING HOUSE (73, T.V. movie), BUSTER & BILLIE (74), OUR TIME (74), THE GUN & THE PULPIT (74, T.V. movie), the series—playing title role—'Nancy Drew Mysteries' (77/78), OF HUMAN FEELINGS (78, T.V. movie) and recently, in THE LADY IN RED (79), she portrays Polly Franklin, the farm girl turned hooker who unwittingly betrays gangster John Dillinger; in T.V. ser., 'Dynasty' (81-   ), she portrays Fallon Carrington.

LEE MARVIN

Lee Marvin, immensely popular internationally for his tough screen portrayals, emerged from solid supporting roles as a bad guy of the 1950s, to a major star from 1964 onwards. The son of a New York advertising executive, he was born in that city on 19 February 1924. He is a descendent of the first Chief Justice of the State of Connecticut, and also of Ross G. Martin, who was an assistant to Admiral Peary on Polar expeditions. Attending 11 different schools, several of which he was expelled from, he first worked as a runner for a Wall Street firm at 16½ dollars a week, but an injury to his hand on a fishing trip cost him his job. Lee then enlisted in the U.S. Marines for war service, but was severely wounded in the South Pacific and was unable to walk for a year. During recuperation he got interested in acting and upon discharge in 1945 he joined a theatre group and earned his living as a plumber's mate. However, aided by the G.I. Bill of Rights, he studied more extensively with the U.S. Theatre Wing and toured with a New England stock company, making his debut in the role of Texas in 'Roadside' in 1947. He moved into T.V. a year later and off-Broadway in 1949 in 'Uniform of Flesh' and 'The 19th Hole of Europe'. 1951 marked his Broadway début in 'Billy Budd', his first movie, walking-on in YOU'RE IN THE NAVY NOW and also tours of stage productions 'A Streetcar Named Desire' and 'The Hasty Heart'. That year he wed Betty Edeling and they had 4 children—Christopher (1952), Courtney (1954), Cynthia 1956) and Claudia (1958), but the couple ended their marriage in 1967. By the end of the 1950s Lee had made his mark in supporting roles in important movies — including THE BIG HEAT (53); THE WILD ONE (54); THE CAINE MUTINY (54); BAD DAY AT BLACK ROCK (54); PETE KELLY'S BLUES (55); THE RACK (56); ATTACK 56), gained a wide audience on T.V. in such shows as 'Doctors of Pawnee Hill', 'Easygoing Man', and especially as Lt. Frank Ballinger in 177 episodes of 'M Squad' (1957-60). In the 60s he made THE COMMANCHEROS (61); THE MAN WHO SHOT LIBERTY VALANCE (62); DONOVAN'S REEF (63) and Don Siegel's THE KILLERS (64) made him a star. After a fine performance in SHIP OF FOOLS (65), his work in CAT BALLOU (65) brought him an Academy Award. In this movie he gave a hilarious portrayal of Kid Shelleen, a famous drunken gunman, and also played the dual role of his evil brother, Tim Strawn. Following his success in this western spoof he starred in such pictures as DIRTY DOZEN, THE PROFESSIONALS, POINT BLANK (all 1967); HELL IN THE PACIFIC 58); PAINT YOUR WAGON (69, his recording of 'Wandrin' Star' in this musical went to the top of the hit parade); MONTE WALSH (70; THE ICEMAN COMETH (73); SHOUT AT THE DEVIL (76); AVALANCHE EXPRESS (78); DEATH HUNT (81) and GORKY PARK (83). He is divorced from his second wife, Pamela Freeley, whom he wed in 1970.
MARVIN: THE STORY OF LEE MARVIN by Donald Zec; New English Library: London, 1979; N.E.L. p/b. 1981.

JAMES MASON

James Mason always can be relied upon to bring a touch of quality to many a motion-picture — he has remained one o
Britain's most popular film actors since he first came to the screen in the mid-'30s. Born John Neville Mason i
Huddersfield, Yorkshire on 15 May 1909, he is the son of John Mason, and his wife Mabel, attending Marlboroug
College and Peterhouse College, Cambridge, where he graduated with an M.A. degree. He soon gave up a career as a
architect (he holds a B.A. degree in Architecture) to pursue a living as an actor, having played several roles in universit
productions. He 'answered an advertisement for a leading man' in a touring production of 'Rasputin the Rascal Monk
and made his professional début in that production at the Hippodrome, Aldershot in 1931. Following more repertory
including Croydon, his London début in 'Gallows Glorious (1933), and seasons with the Old Vic (1933/34) an
Dublin's Gate Theatre (1934/35), Mason came to the screen in 1935 in LATE EXTRA. During the next 8 years h
played on Broadway, wed Pamela Kellino in 1940 (a daughter, Portland, was born in 1948, a son, Morgan, th
following year) and made 19 films, including I MET A MURDERER (39, part-screenplay); HATTER'S CASTL
(42); THUNDER ROCK (43) and THE MAN IN GREY (43) which made him a star. Further movies, THI
SEVENTH VEIL (46); THE WICKED LADY (46) and THE ODD MAN OUT (46) consolidated his success — h
won the Daily Mail Award as 'Most Popular British Male Star for 1946 and 1947'. America beckoned, and afte
'Bathsheba' on Broadway (1947), he went to Hollywood and made many movies. These included MADAMI
BOVARY (49); PANDORA AND THE FLYING DUTCHMAN (51); THE DESERT FOX (51, as Rommel)
FIVE FINGERS (52); THE PRISONER OF ZENDA (52); JULIUS CAESAR (53, as Brutus); 20,00(
LEAGUES UNDER THE SEA (54, as Capt. Nemo); A STAR IS BORN (54, Oscar nom.); NORTH-BY
NORTHWEST (59); JOURNEY TO THE CENTRE OF THE EARTH (59). In the 1950s he also played on
Broadway in 'Measure For Measure' and 'Oedipus Rex' (both 1954) and during 1954/55 was host of T.V.'s 'Lux Videc
Theatre'. Divorcing Miss Kellino in 1964, he wed Clarissa Kaye on 13.8.71. Other movies have included LOLITA (62)
FALL OF THE ROMAN EMPIRE (64); PUMPKIN EATER (64); THE BLUE MAX (66) and more recently
'Jesus of Nazareth' (77, T.V. movie, as Joseph of Arimathea); HEAVEN CAN WAIT (77); BOYS FROM BRAZIL
(77); THE PASSAGE (78); WATER BABIES (78); SHERLOCK HOLMES— MURDER BY DECREE (78, a
Dr Watson); BLOODLINE (79); NORTH SEA HIJACK (79); DANGEROUS SUMMER (82); IVANHOE (82.
T.V. movie); EVIL UNDER THE SUN (82); THE VERDICT (82, Oscar nom., BSA) and YELLOWBEARD (83).
JAMES MASON: AN AUTHORISED BIOGRAPHY by Jno.P. Monaghan; (papercover) World Film Publications
London 1947.
THE FILMS OF JAMES MASON by Clive Hirschhorn; L.S.P. Books: Godalming, England, 1975.
BEFORE I FORGET by James Mason (autobio.); Hamish Hamilton: London, 1981. Sphere p/b: 1982.

MARSHA MASON

B. St. Louis, Missouri 3.4.43. Ed. Webster Coll.,
Miss Mason went to New York to continue
dramatic studies and embarked on her theatrical
career, appearing off-Broadway in such works as
'The Deer Park' (1967), 'Happy Birthday, Wanda
June' (70) and on Broadway in 'Cactus Flower';
T.V. included Judith Cole in 'Love of Life'; md.
Neil Simon 1973; movies: BLUME IN LOVE
(72), CINDERELLA LIBERTY (73, Oscar
nom., B.A.), AUDREY ROSE (77), THE
GOODBYE GIRL (77, Oscar nom., B.A. &
joint-holder Hollywood Golden Globe Aw., B.A.),
THE CHEAP DETECTIVE (77), PROMISES
IN THE DARK (79), CHAPTER TWO (79,
(Oscar nom., BA), ONLY WHEN I LAUGH
(81, Oscar nom., BA), LOIS GIBBS & THE
LOVE CANEL (T.V. movie), MAX DUGAN
RETURNS (both 1982): stage also includes
work with American Conservatory Theatre, San
Francisco.

MARCELLO MASTROIANNI

B. Fontana Liri, Italy 28.9.24. Formerly a draughtsman in Rome from 1940-43, Marcello trained
with the University of Rome Theatre Co., and
played with distinction on the Italian stage in such
productions as 'Streetcar Named Desire' and
'Angelica'; md. Flora Gabriella in 1950 — 1
daughter, Barbara (c. 1953); movies include: bit
part in I MISERABILI (47), winning acclaim in
SUNDAY IN AUGUST (49), GIRLS OF THE
SPANISH STEPS (51), THE BIGAMIST (55),
WHITE NIGHTS (57), I SOLITI IGNOTI
(58), LA DOLCA VITA (59), LA NOTTE (61),
DIVORCE—ITALIAN STYLE (62), 8½ (63),
THE ORGANISER (65), THE STRANGER
(67), DIAMONDS FOR BREAKFAST (68),
LEO THE LAST (69), DRAMA DELLA
GELOSIA (70, Best Actor, Cannes 1970),
WHAT? (72), BLOWOUT (73); he is one of
Italy's most popular actors — more recent films:
A SPECIAL DAY (77, Oscar nom., B.A.),
WIFEMISTRESS (78), DIVINE NYMPH (79),
BLOOD FEUD (79), TERRAZZA (79), THE
SKIN (80); 1 daughter Chiara (mother: Catherine
Deneuve (qv)); recent films: GET RITA, CITY
OF WOMEN (both 81), BEYOND THE DOOR
(82), GABRIELA (83).

WALTER MATTHAU

With his magnificently gloomy looks, ideally suited to wry comedy roles — one of which earned him an Oscar, Walter Matthau
is now one of the big names in American movies, following a successful career on the stage. He was born in New York City on 1
October 1920(?), the son of milton Matusschanskayasky(?), who apparently, and wisely, shortened his name to Matthau.
Young Matthau first appeared on the stage aged 4 in a religious play at a New York settlement house, read Shakespeare when 7,
and played Polonius in 'Hamlet' aged 14. Upon leaving school he had numerous jobs — file clerk, boxing instructor, basketball
coach, radio operator, factory worker and studied journalism. During the last war he served with distinction in the U.S. Air
Force, earning 6 battle stars and upon his discharge embarked on his theatrical career, studying with Raiken Ben-Ari and also
with Erwin Piscator at the Dramatic Workshop of New School for Social Research, making his professional début at the Erie
County Playhouse in July 1946. In the late 40s and 1950s he steadily earned a reputation as a stage actor in such productions as
'Season in the Sun' (1951), 'One Bright Day' (1952), 'Glass Menagerie' (1952, tour), 'A Certain Joy' (1953) and 450
performances of 'Will Success Spoil Rock Hunter?' (1955/56). He had wed Grace Johnson in 1948, a marriage which lasted
10 years — they had a son, David, in 1949, and a daughter, Jennifer, in 1950. He came to the screen in 1955 in THE

KENTUCKIAN and other early films included THE INDIAN FIGHTER (55),   A FACE IN THE CROWD (57) and
KING CREOLE (58). In 1958 he won the New York Drama Critics' Award for 'Once More With Feeling' and the following
year wed Carol Marcus Saroyan. Their son, Charles, was born in 1960 and that year he directed a movie, GANGSTER
STORY. In 1961 he had his own T.V. series, as Lex Rogers in 'Tallahassee 7000', and started to concentrate on his film career
with such movies as LONELY ARE THE BRAVE (62); ISLAND OF LOVE (63); CHARADE (63); FAIL SAFE (64);
MIRAGE (65); THE FORTUNE COOKIE (66, Oscar, BSA); THE ODD COUPLE (68, also Broadway stage: his role as
Oscar Madison winning New York Critics' and 'Tony' awards, 1965); SECRET LIFE OF AN AMERICAN WIFE (68);
CANDY (68); HELLO DOLLY! (69, as Vandergelder); PLAZA SUITE (71); KOTCH (71, Oscar nom., BA); CHARLEY
VARRICK (73); EARTHQUAKE (74); THE FRONT PAGE (75); THE SUNSHINE BOYS (75); CASEY'S
SHADOW (77); HOUSE CALLS (77); CALIFORNIA SUITE (78); LITTLE MISS MARKER (79); HOPSCOTCH
(79); THE FIRST MONDAY IN OCTOBER (81); BUDDY, BUDDY (81); I OUGHT TO BE IN PICTURES
(82) and THE SURVIVORS (83).

BILL MAYNARD

. Farnham, Surrey 8.10.28. Real name Frederick Williams; ed. Kibworth Beauchamps Grammar School; when youngster family moved to Leicester; monologues aged 8 at working men's clubs; delivered newspapers for guitar/dancing lessons; at 15 played football for Kettering Town & Leic. ity, but had knee injury; performed in working men's clubs, worked as coalman, commercial traveller, salesman; season: Butlin's, Skegness; toured Germany in 'Piccadilly Hayride'; big break: Windmill Theatre; 50s: T.V., including 'Great Scott, It's Maynard'; 60s: rep. actor, coming to screen in TILL DEATH US DO PART (68), others: STEPTOE & SON RIDE AGAIN (74), CONFESSIONS OF A POP PERFORMER(75), ROBIN & MARIAN (76); much T.V. includes 'Coronation Street', 'Oh, No, It's Selwyn Frogitt', 'Dangerous Davies—The Last Detective' (80, T.V. movie); md. Muriel, 1 daughter, Jane, 1 son, Martin; THE PLAGUE DOGS (82, voice).
THE YO-YO MAN (autobio.); Golden Eagle: London, 1975.

MICHAEL MEDWIN

B. London 18.7.23. Ed. Dorset and Switzerland (Institut Fischer); as youngster studied at Italia Conti Stage School making debut as sea witch in 'Where the Rainbow Ends' (40), coming to the screen in THE ROOT OF ALL EVIL(46); well-known face on T.V. and the films, is also writer and more recently *film producer, founding Memorial Enterprises with Albert Finney (qv) in 1965; many movies include BOYS IN BROWN (49), TOP SECRET (52), MALTA STORY (53), ABOVE US THE WAVES(55), DOCTOR AT SEA (55), A HILL IN KOREA (56), CARRY ON NURSE (59), NIGHT MUST FALL (64), CHARLIE BUBBLES* (67), IF* (68), SPRING AND PORT WINE*(69), GUMSHOE* (71), ALPHA BETA* (73), O LUCKY MAN (73), LAW & DISORDER* (73); much T.V. including his series 'The Army Game' (59), 'The Love of Mike' (60), 'Three Live Wires' (61) and more recently, regular in 'Shoestring', the hit BBC T.V. series (79-); he has co-produced many West End plays and acted with the National Theatre; acted in THE SEA WOLVES (80), THE JIGSAW MAN (83); co-produced MEMOIRS OF A SURVIVOR (81).

KEITH MICHELL

B. Adelaide, S. Australia 1.12.28; ed. Pt. Pirie H.S., Adelaide Univ. Teachers' College, School of Arts & Crafts; father a furniture manufacturer; began career as an art teacher, while painting actor he was advised to try radio work; acted with Australian Broadcasting Corp., when L. Olivier toured that country Michell was auditioned and came to G.B., studying with Old Vic School for 2 years; joined Young Vic 1950 and subsequently became outstanding stage actor, particularly in S'pearean roles with the Shakespeare Memorial Theatre and the Old Vic; tours, West End musicals ('Irma La Douce', etc.); md. actress Miss Jeanette Sterke, Oct. 1957, 1 son Paul and 1 daughter Helena; came to the screen in 1957 in TRUE AS A TURTLE (57), others include DANGEROUS EXILE (57), GYPSY & THE GENTLEMAN (58), ALL NIGHT LONG (62), 7 SEAS TO CALAIS (62), PRUDENCE & THE PILL (68), THE EXECUTIONER(70), MOMENTS (73), THE STORY OF JACOB & JOSEPH (74, T.V. movie); well-known on T.V. for his award-winning portrayal in 'The Six Wives of Henry VIII' (69); has directed on the stage; recent theatre: 'On the 20th Century' (80), 'On the Rocks', 'The Tempest' (Australia, both 1982); T.V. movies, 82: RUDDIGORE, THE GONDOLIERS.

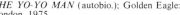

BETTE MIDLER

B. Honolulu,   . . . Father a house painter, mother named her 'Bette' after Bette Davis; spent one year at Honolulu University, considered diplomatic career; packed pineapples in Honolulu; film extra in HAWAII (66), used earnings to travel to New York, singing in coffee bars; got chorus job on Broadway, eventually lead to role of Tevye's oldest grand-daughter, Tzeitel, in show 'Fiddler on the Roof'; guested on 'Johnny Carson Show', made 2 records: 'Bette Midler' and 'The Divine Miss M'; broke attendance records for Broadway revues, 1973 and 75; 1975 won 'Tony' Award for Broadway show 'Clams on the Half Shell'; 1976 did a bawdy T.V. Special, 1977 did another version for NBC 'Ol' Red Hair Is Back'; movies: THE DIVINE MR J, THE ROSE (79, Oscar nom., B.A.), STRIKE & HYDE (80), DIVINE MADNESS (80, composite of 3 shows at Pasadena Civic Auditorium), JINXED (81).
A VIEW FROM A BROAD by BM; Angus & Robertson; London, 1980.
BETTE MIDLER by Rob Baker; Fawcett Publications Inc., USA, 1975; p/b: Coronet, GB, 1980.

LOIS MAXWELL

B. Kitchener, Ontario, Canada 14.2.27; when 1 week old family moved to Toronto; as youngster appd. as prof. dancer, coached in dramatics, studied Canadian Royal Acad. of Music; aged 14 broadcasting on radio; 1 year at RADA; rep., tours; came to screen in CORRIDOR OF MIRRORS (48) and after making many films in the 50s, a few in Hollywood (THAT HAGEN GIRL, THE CRIME DOCTOR'S DIARY, THE DARK PAST, DECISION OF CHRISTOPHER BLAKE), Lois became well-known as Miss Moneypenny in the James Bond films from 1962 (DR NO); has had her own column in 'The Toronto Sun' newspaper; other work: LOLITA (62), THE HAUNTING (63), OPERATION KID BROTHER (67), OCTOPUSSY (83); Md: Peter Marriott, 1957 (dec. 1973), 1 son, Christian, 1 daughter, Melinda; Lois has business manufacturing crowd-control barriers.

RALPH MEEKER

B. Minneapolis, Minnesota, 21.11.20. Real name Ralph Rathgeber; ed. Northwestern Univ. 1938-42, appeared in plays; pro. debut in 'The Doughgirls' (43); WWII: U.S. Navy, Mediterranean area; became star of Broadway ('Mister Roberts' (1948), 'A Streetcar Named Desire' (1949, replacing Brando (qv), also tour), 'Picnic' (1953), others; md. actress Salome Jens, 1964 (div.); many films including TERESA (51, debut); SOMEBODY LOVES ME (52); THE NAKED SPUR (53); KISS ME DEADLY (56, as Mike Hammer); PATHS OF GLORY (58); ADA (61); SOMETHING WILD (61); WALL OF NOISE (63); THE DIRTY DOZEN (67); THE GENTLE GIANT (67); THE ST. VALENTINE'S DAY MASSACRE (67, as Bugs Moran); THE DETECTIVE (68); THE DEVIL'S EIGHT (69); I WALK THE LINE (70); THE ANDERSON TAPES (71); WINTER KILLS (79); WITHOUT WARNING (80); several T.V. movies.

BURGESS MEREDITH

B. Cleveland, Ohio 16.11.08. Parents: Dr and Mrs William George Meredith, Burgess the youngest of 3 children; ed. Amherst Coll. (M.A.), Cathedral Choir School, New York and Hoosac School; 4 years a boy soprano at a New York cathedral; left college and worked on a newspaper, sold haberdashery at Macy's, was a Wall Street runner, a clerk and also manned a steamship to S. America before deciding to be an actor, spending 3 years with Civic Rep. Co., New York, from 1931, becoming one of America's foremost stage actors and directors; Maxwell Anderson wrote role of Mio in 'Winterset' esp. for him and he came to the screen in the film version in 1936; many movies include IDIOT'S DELIGHT (39), OF MICE AND MEN(39), SECOND CHORUS (40), THE STORY OF G.I. JOE (45, as revered columnist Ernie Pyle), Mr Meredith served in WWII with U.S. Air Corps 1942-45; ON OUR MERRY WAY (48), MINE OWN EXECUTIONER (48), ADVISE AND CONSENT (62), MADAME X (66), BATMAN (66, and T.V. series, as 'The Penguin'), THERE WAS A CROOKED MAN (70); md. 1. Helen Derby (1932-35), 2. Margaret Perry (1936-38), 3. Miss Paulette Goddard(1943-48), 4. Kaja Sundsten, 1 son Jonathan, 1 daughter Tala Beth; many T.V. movies including TAIL GUNNER JOE (77, Emmy award); won numerous stage awards, also served as Vice President of Actors' Equity; recent movies: *DAY OF THE LOCUST (75), ROCKY (76), MAGIC (78), LAST CHANCE (79), WHEN TIME RAN OUT (80), TRUE CONFESSIONS, DISASTER IN THE SKY (T.V. movie, both 81), ANSWERS (T.V. movie, 1 segment, 82). (*Oscar nom., BSA).

TOSHIRO MIFUNE

B. Tsingtao, China 1.4.20. Mr Mifune's parents were Japanese, the family later returned to their country and he spent five years in the army; on leave in Tokyo, he was discovered for the screen by a director, joining the Toho Studio in 1946, becoming a favourite of director Kurosawa; his many films include DRUNKEN ANGEL (48), THE STRAY DOG (49), RASHOMON (50), THE SEVEN SAMURAI (54), I LIVE IN FEAR (55), THE LOWER DEPTHS (57), THE THRONE OF BLOOD (58), YOJIMBO (61), GRAND PRIX (66), REDBEARD (68), HELL IN THE PACIFIC (69), RED SUN (71), PAPER TIGER (75), MIDWAY (76), WINTER KILLS (79), 1941 (79), INCHON! (79), THE BUSHIDO BLADE (80), THE EQUALS (81); his son, Shiro, had a role in PAPER TIGER; Mr Mifune directed one film, THE LEGACY OF THE FIVE HUNDRED THOUSAND (63) and he is Japan's No.1 star; a Japanese T.V. series in which he produced and starred was entitled 'Chuchingura'; others in which he acted only include 'Shogun' (80, USA) and 'The 47 Samurai Story' (81, Japan).

SARAH MILES

B. Ingatestone, Essex 31.12.42. Father John Miles, a steel mill designer; Sarah's brother, Christopher, film director; ed. Roedean, nr. Brighton (from 9-12) and other schools; RADA aged 15, rep. at Worthing (including 'Saint Joan'); appd. in plays 'Dazzling Prospect' ('slaughtered by press, but Sarah got good notices') and discovered in 'The Moon is Blue', selected from 63 girls for movie début in TERM OF TRIAL (62); many others include THE SERVANT (63), THE CEREMONY(64), I WAS HAPPY HERE (65), BLOW-UP (66), RYAN'S DAUGHTER (70, Oscar nom., BA—md: writer Robert Bolt 1967, div. Oct. 1975, 1 son Thomas), LADY CAROLINE LAMB (72), THE HIRELING (73), THE MAN WHO LOVED CAT DANCING (73), GREAT EXPECTATIONS (75), DYNASTY (76, T.V. movie), THE SAILOR WHO FELL FROM GRACE FROM THE SEA (76), THE BIG SLEEP (77); much stage includes productions at Royal Court, National Theatre, Chichester (Sussex), West End and USA (Los Angeles, title role 1974, 'Saint Joan'); recently: 'Macbeth' (1982); movies: VENOM (82), WALTER (T.V. movie, 1982).

VERA MILES

B. Boise City, Oklahoma, 23.8.30(?). Real name Vera Ralston; ed. public schools, Pratt & Wichita, Kansas; 1948: beauty contest winner; md. 1. Robert Miles, 1949-54, 1 daughter Deborah (born 1950), 1 daughter Kelly (born 1952). 2. Gordon Scott, 1954-59, 1 son Michael; Miss Miles played in T.V. shows and came to screen in 1952 in FOR MEN ONLY, her many movies since then have included THE CHARGE AT FEATHER RIVER(53); WICHITA (55); THE WRONG MAN (57); BEAU JAMES (59); PSYCHO(60); BACK STREET (61); A TIGER WALKS (64); GENTLE GIANT (67); HELL-FIGHTERS(68); ONE LITTLE INDIAN (73); JUDGE HORTON & THE SCOTTSBORO BOYS (76, T.V. movie); TWILIGHT'S LAST GLEAMING (77); md. 3. Keith Larsen, 1960 (div.), 1 son Erik; 4. Bob Jones, 1973; T.V. includes 'The Law-breakers', 'Gentle Ben' and regular: 'Stump the Stars' (69); recent work: ROUGHNECKS (80, T.V. 'Best Sellers'); BRAINWAVES (82); PSY-CHO II (83); HELEN & THE TEACHER (T.V. movie, 1983).

RAY MILLAND

First coming to the screen in 1929, Ray Milland has had a very successful career, graduating from handsome British/Hollywood leading man of the 1930s, to Oscar-winning character player and also turned in some competent movies as director in which he also starred. He was born Reginald Alfred John Truscott-Jones at Cymla, near Neath, in Wales on 3 January 1908, and educated at Gnoll Hall School, Radyr School (in the Taff Valley) and King's College, Cardiff. When still a youngster his parents separated and he spent his school holidays for six years on an aunt's farm, where he became a proficient horseman and it was this skill, upon leaving school, which gained him service with the Household Cavalry for four years. He became acquainted with film actress Estelle Brody, who advised him to contact her should he ever be interested in film work. This he later did, upon leaving the Guards. He got himself an agent, and his first film job, passing the audition with an amazing feat of marksmanship, on THE INFORMER (the British 1929 version). Simultaneously, he got a leading role in THE FLYING SCOTSMAN and changed his name to Raymond Milland (derived from 'Mill land' — nostalgia for his youth). He toured for 5 weeks in the play 'The Woman in Room 13' and had to cancel a contract with Andre Charlot when M-G-M, impressed by his work in FLYING SCOTSMAN, sent him to Hollywood and he made his début there in BACHELOR FATHER (31). That year he wed showgirl Muriel Webster. They had a son, Daniel David, born in 1940, who died tragically in L.A. on 24.3.81. Their daughter, Victoria Francesca, was born in 1941. Mr Milland played supporting roles until 1936 when he co-starred in THE JUNGLE PRINCESS. Of over 100 films his best-remembered are BEAU GESTE (39); FRENCH WITHOUT TEARS (39); ARISE MY LOVE (41); THE MAJOR AND THE MINOR (42); REAP THE WILD WIND (42); THE UNINVITED(44); MINISTRY OF FEAR (44); KITTY (45); THE BIG CLOCK (48); ALIAS NICK BEAL (49); THE THIEF (52); DIAL M FOR MURDER (54); THE MAN WITH THE X-RAY EYES (63); LOVE STORY (70). He has appeared on many occasions on American television, including the series 'The Ray Milland Show' (1954/55) as Prof. Ray McNutly and as Roy Markham in 'Markham' (1959/60). In 1958 he hosted 'Trails West'. Mr Milland won an Academy Award in 1945 in THE LOST WEEKEND, portraying a chronic alcoholic. His most recent pictures have been BATTLESTAR GALACTICA (78); GAMES FOR VULTURES (79); THE ATTIC (79); CAVE IN! (79) and BLACKOUT (81).
WIDE-EYED IN BABYLON (autobiography); The Bodley Head: London, 1976.

SPIKE MILLIGAN

B. Ahmadnagar, India 16.4.18. Real name Terence Alan Milligan; father a soldier; ed. Poona, St. Paul's H.S., Rangoon, Brownhill Boys' School, Catford, London Polytechnic; stage début aged 8, nativity play, Poona; came to Britain 1933; singer/trumpeter 1936-39, later guitarist; WWII involved in troop shows, pro. début 1945 in Naples; 1949 radio début 'Opportunity Knocks'; md. June (div.), 2 daughters Laura, Sile, 1 son Sean; became well-known on radio, esp. for 'Goon shows' and numerous T.V. comedies; many films include THE CASE OF THE MUK-KINESE BATTLE HORN (56), WATCH YOUR STERN (60), INVASION QUARTET (61), POSTMAN'S KNOCK (62), MAGIC CHRISTIAN (69), ADOLF HITLER—MY PART IN HIS DOWNFALL (72), THREE MUSKETEERS (73), LAST REMAKE OF BEAU GESTE (77), PRISONER OF ZENDA (78); md. 2. Patricia Ridgway ('Paddy'), former actress/singer ('Sound of Music') who died 8.2.81, they have a daughter, Jane; recent T.V.: 'There's a Lot of It About' (ser. 82); YELLOWBEARD (83).
ADOLF HITLER—MY PART IN HIS DOWN-FALL (wartime experiences) by SM; Michael Joseph: London, 1971; p/b: Penguin, 1972.

HAYLEY MILLS

B. London 18.4.46. Father Sir John Mills (qv) mother Mary Hayley Bell, authoress; ed. Elmhurst School, Camberley, Surrey; came to the screen 1959 in TIGER BAY with great success, opp. her father; went to Hollywood, appd. in POLLYANNA (60, winning Special Oscar) THE PARENT TRAP (61), then alternated work in U.K. and U.S.A.: WHISTLE DOWN THE WIND (60), SUMMER MAGIC (62), IN SEARCH OF THE CASTAWAYS (63), THE CHALK GARDEN (64), THE MOONSPIN-NERS (65), TROUBLE WITH ANGELS (66) THE FAMILY WAY (66), PRETTY POLLY (67), TWISTED NERVE (68), ENDLESS NIGHT (72), DEADLY STRANGERS (75) THE KINGFISHER CAPER(75), DIAMOND HUNTERS (77); md. Roy Boulting, film producer, June 1971, 1 son Crispian (div. 16.9.77); she has other son, Jason (b. Aug. 1976), father being actor Leigh Lawson (qv); Hayley Mills made her stage début in 1969, as Peter Pan, in London, and has made several appearances since; stage 1982: 'Talley's Folly'; T.V. ser. 1981: 'Flame Trees of Thika'; Oscar for 'the most outstanding juvenile performance during 1960'.

JULIET MILLS

B. London 21.11.41. Father Sir John Mills (qv); came to screen 11 weeks old in IN WHICH WE SERVE (42); other child roles in OCTOBER MAN (47), SO WELL REMEMBERED (47), HISTORY OF MR POLLY (49); ed. Elmhurst Ballet School, Camberley, Surrey; md. 1. singer/songwriter Russell Alquist, 1 son Sean, md 15.4.64. (div.); stage début: London 1955 as Alice in 'Alice Through the Looking Glass', has since played in successful productions, G.B. and U.S.A.; md. 2. Michael Miklenda, a Czech building tycoon (div.); many other movies include NO, MY DARLING DAUGHTER (61), TWICE ROUND THE DAFFODILS (62), NURSE ON WHEELS (63), CARRY ON JACK (64), THE RARE BREED (66), AVAN-TI! (72), BARNABY & ME (77); many U.S. T.V. movies including 'The Cracker Factory' (79); popular on T.V. as Phoebe Figalilly in 'Nanny & the Professor' (70/71); Md: 3. actor Maxwell Caulfield; movie 1981: LE GUEPIOT.

YVETTE MIMIEUX

B. Los Angeles, California 8.1.42(?). Father a Frenchman, Rene A. Mimieux, appd. in several early Gable pictures; mother Mexican, Carmen Montemayor; ed. Vine Street School, Le Conte Junior High, L.A., Los Ninos Heroes de Chapultepec, Mexico City, Hollywood H.S. (majoring in Science/Art); played with theatre group 'Theatre Events', eventually won contract to MGM; many movies include RICH, YOUNG & DEADLY (60), THE TIME MACHINE (60), THE LIGHT IN THE PIAZZA (62), DIAMOND HEAD (63), THE REWARD (65), THE MERCEN-ARIES (66), SKYJACKED (71), AVANTI! (72), JACKSON COUNTY JAIL (76), THE BLACK HOLE (79), MYSTIQUE (80); md. 1. Evan Engber (div.), 2. Stanley Donen, famous director; she starred as Vanessa Smith in the 1970 T.V. ser. 'The Most Deadly Game'; T.V. movies inclu. BLACK NOON (71), SNOWBEAST (77), HOUND OF HELL, DISASTER ON THE COASTLINER (both 79), FORBIDDEN LOVE (82); movies: BRAINWASH (82), NIGHT PARTNERS (83).

JOHN MILLS

A movie actor since 1932, Sir John Mills has had one of the most successful screen careers, alternating portrayals of sincere leading men with sterling work as a character player, which was deservedly recognised in 1970 with an Oscar. The son of Lewis Mills, and his wife, Edith, he was born on 22 February 1908 at North Elmham, Suffolk. His father was headmaster of Watts Naval Training School, but his son showed no sign of following in his footsteps. Young John, upon leaving school, worked for three years in the family corn business, but he always wanted to go on the stage. He ventured to London, practically penniless, got no stage work, but he was employed as a travelling salesman for lavatory paper, working in Brixton, Streatham and Guildford. This, at least, paid for dancing lessons and he made his professional debut in the chorus of 'The Five O'Clock Girl' at the London Hippodrome in March, 1929. He then joined a theatrical company called 'The Quaints' who toured the Far East with several plays, including 'Journey's End', portraying Raleigh. He had impressed Noel Coward with his work, and, back in London, he appeared in such Coward productions as 'London Wall' and 'Cavalcade', both in 1931. During the 1930s he became well-known on the London stage, later in this decade playing at the Old Vic, and he scored a personal triumph as George in 'Of Mice and Men' (1939). Mills had come to the screen in 1932 in THE MIDSHIPMAID with Jessie Matthews and several of his 30s films included THOSE WERE THE DAYS (34), CHARING CROSS ROAD (35), TUDOR ROSE (36) and GOODBYE MR CHIPS (39). He had wed actress Aileen Raymond, but this marriage ended in divorce (when his ex-wife re-married she had a son who is actor Ian Ogilvy). His second marriage, in January 1941, was more successful. He wed actress/writer Mary Hayley Bell and they have 2 daughters, Juliet and Hayley (qv), who have had very successful careers as actresses, and son Jonathan works in the States. In the 1940s Mr Mills made headway in films such as COTTAGE TO LET (41); IN WHICH WE SERVE (42), being released from Army service; WATERLOO ROAD (44); WAY TO THE STARS (45); GREAT EXPECTATIONS (46); THE OCTOBER MAN (47), as SCOTT OF THE ANTARCTIC (48) and THE HISTORY OF MR POLLY (49). He was one of the Top British Moneymaking Stars in 1945, '46, '47, '49, '50 and '54. He received the C.B.E. in 1960 and was knighted in 1976. He has appeared on T.V. in the U.S. and U.K. in such series as 'Dundee & The Culhane' (67, USA), 'The Zoo Gang' (75, UK), 'Quatermass' (78, UK) and 'Young at Heart' (81, UK). Other movies (he has made over 100) include HOBSON'S CHOICE (53); TOWN ON TRIAL (57); TIGER BAY (59); TUNES OF GLORY (60); SWISS FAMILY ROBINSON (61); directed SKY WEST AND CROOKED (65) and he received an Oscar in 1970 for his work in RYAN'S DAUGHTER as Best Supporting Actor. More recently: THE BIG SLEEP (77); THE 39 STEPS (78); GANDHI (82); SAHARA (83), a T.V. series; 'Little Lord Fauntleroy' (81) and the acclaimed musical stage version of 'Goodbye, Mr Chips' (Chichester, 1982).

UP IN THE CLOUDS, GENTLEMEN, PLEASE (autobio.); Weidenfeld & Nicolson: London, 1980.

LIZA MINNELLI

Following in the footsteps of her talented parents, the late, great Judy Garland and film director Vincente Minnelli, Liza was born in Los Angeles on the 12th of March, 1946. Following a cameo, as a child, in her mother's film, IN THE GOOD OLD SUMMERTIME (49), she studied at Scarsdale High School, N.Y., in the early 60s at the University of Paris de la Sorbonne, and drama with Uta Hagen and Herbert Berghof. Her first stage appearance was with her mother at the Palace Theatre, N.Y., when she was 14. Subsequent stage work includes 'Take Me Along' (62); 'Diary of Anne Frank' (63); 'Flora, the Red Menace' (65, 'Tony' Award) and highly successful U.S., European tours in revue and cabaret, winning numerous awards including 'Female Star of the Year' (Las Vegas) 1972 & 1974. Her marriages have been to Australian rock singer Peter Allen (1967-72); on 16.9.77 she wed Jack Haley Jr., but divorced in 1978, and on December 4, 1979 she wed Broadway producer Mark Gero. Her movies include: CHARLIE BUBBLES (67); POOKIE (69, Oscar nom., BA); TELL ME THAT YOU LOVE ME, JUNIE MOON (70); CABARET (72, Oscar, BA); LUCKY LADY (75); SILENT MOVIE, A MATTER OF TIME (both 1976); NEW YORK, NEW YORK (77); ARTHUR (80).

LIZA by James Robert Parish (with Jack Arno); W. H. Allen: London, 1975.

HELEN MIRREN

B. Chiswick, W. London, . .46. Real name Elena Mirrenova; father Russian, a retired civil servant; brought up in Southend-on-Sea; at convent won acting prizes — 'quite wanted to be Bardot or someone'; joined National Youth Theatre and later played with the Old Vic in 1965, at Manchester 1967 and joined R.S. Co. later that year (Diana in 'All's Well That End's Well', Cressida in 'Troilus and Cressida', other roles); films: AGE OF CONSENT (69), A MIDSUMMER NIGHT'S DREAM (69), SAVAGE MESSIAH (72), O LUCKY MAN (73), CALIGULA (77), HUSSY (79), S.O.S. TITANIC (79), THE LONG GOOD FRIDAY (79), THE FIENDISH PLOT OF DR FU MANCHU (80); T.V. 1982: 'After the Party'; recently acclaimed stage actress: 'The Duchess of Malfi' (80/81), 'A Midsummer Night's Dream' (81), 'Anthony & Cleopatra' (82).

CAMERON MITCHELL
– see page 125

JAMES MITCHUM

B. Los Angeles, California 8.5.41. Father Robert Mitchum, actor (qv): excellent athlete at Univ. H.S., L.A., then went to Hollywood Professional School, later joining Barter Stock Co., Virginia; came to screen in THUNDER ROAD (58), starring his father; 'wrote/performed song which entered hit parade'; md. Wendy Wagner; many films including THE BEAT GENERATION (59), GIRLS' TOWN (59), THE LAST TIME I SAW ARCHIE (61), THE VICTORS (63), YOUNG GUNS OF TEXAS (63), RIDE THE WILD SURF (64), IN HARM'S WAY (65), AMBUSH BAY (66), THE TRAMPLERS (66), THE MONEY TRAP (66), MOONRUNNERS (75), TRACKDOWN (76), THE DAY TIME ENDED (79); brother Chris is also an actor and played in movie THE LAST HARD MEN (75); Jim also breeds and races quarter horses; recent movie: BLACKOUT (81).

WARREN MITCHELL
– see page 125

ROBERT MITCHUM

Robert Mitchum, since becoming a big name in the movies in 1945, has remained a highly popular American actor in a great number of roles, whose lazy style underestimates the versatile actor he undoubtedly is. The son of James Mitchum, a railroad worker, and his wife, Anne, he was born in Bridgeport, Connecticut, on 6 August 1917. Mitchum Sr. died when his son was only 18 months old and his wife later re-married and went into the newspaper business. Young 'Mitch' already had a taste of show-biz when, at the age of 8, he partnered his older sister, Julie, in a song-and-dance act. He later attended Duke University, Durham, N. Carolina, and, before entering movies, he did a variety of jobs, starting in Florida, where he later took a cargo boat to S. America. He returned north, wed in 1940 Dorothy Spence, and worked in a Lockheed factory, operating a drop-hammer for nearly two years. Their two sons, Jim and Chris, were born on 8 May 1941 and 16 October 1943 respectively. Sister Julie had become an actress with the Longbeach Theatre Guild, and, upon going backstage, young Mitchum found he liked the atmosphere, and decided to become an actor. He appeared in such productions as 'Rebound', 'Remember the Day' and 'The Petrified Forest'. Impressed by his physical presence, his sister's agent suggested he try the movies for work. His first job, in 1943, was replacing an actor who had been killed on a 'Hopalong Cassidy' western, and, billed as Bob Mitchum, he appeared in supporting roles in nine of these films. He worked steadily, and sixteen pictures later, following such productions as THE DANCING MASTERS (43, with Laurel & Hardy) and 30 SECOND OVER TOKYO (44), he was cast as Lieutenant Walker in THE STORY OF G.I. JOE, a war picture, and this won him a Best Supporting Actor Oscar nomination and consolidated his success in movies. Of over seventy films since his best have included such titles as PURSUED (47); OUT OF THE PAST (47); CROSSFIRE (47); THE BIG STEAL (49); MACAO (52); ANGEL FACE (53); NIGHT OF THE HUNTER (55); HEAVEN KNOWS, MR ALISON (57); THUNDER ROAD (58); HOME FROM THE HILL (60); THE SUNDOWNERS (60); THE LONGEST DAY (62); MR MOSES (65); ANZIO (68); YOUNG BILLY YOUNG (69); RYAN'S DAUGHTER (70); FAREWELL MY LOVELY (as Philip Marlowe, 75) and THE LAST TYCOON (76). His daughter, Petrine, was born on 3 March 1952. Mitchum has remained continually loyal to the movies over the years and restricted his T.V. appearances. In 1983, however, he has filmed a hit series, 'Winds of War'. Recent movies: BREAKTHROUGH (78); AGENCY (79); NIGHT KILL (80) and THAT CHAMPIONSHIP SEASON (82).

THE ROBERT MITCHUM STORY by Mike Tomkies; W.H. Allen: London, 1972; Star p/b.
ROBERT MITCHUM ON THE SCREEN by Alvin H. Marill; A.S. Barnes & Co.: N.Y., 1978.

RICARDO MONTALBAN

B. Mexico City 25.11.20. Ed. Fairfax H.S., California, appd. in plays, studied drama at L.A. High School; singer, appd. with Tallulah Bankhead on Broadway in 'Her Cardboard Lover'; later returned to Mexico when mother was ill; 1941-45 appd. in Mexican films, including LOS NOSOTROS, won Mexican Oscar in 1945; md. Georgiana Young (sister of Loretta) 1944, 2 sons Mark (b. 1947) and Victor, 2 daughters Laura (b. 1949), Anita (b. 1952); many T.V. appearances include series, 1976: 'McNaughton's Daughter' as Charles Quintero; Hollywood contract 1947, many pics. include FIESTA (47), THE KISSING BANDIT (49), BORDER INCIDENT (49), BATTLEGROUND (50), ACROSS THE WIDE MISSOURI (51), SOMBRERO (53), A LIFE IN THE BALANCE (55), SAYONARA (57), ADVENTURES OF A YOUNG MAN (62), LOVE IS A BALL (63), CHEYENNE AUTUMN (64), SWEET CHARITY (69), TRAIN ROBBERS (72), STAR TREK II: WRATH OF KHAN (82); many T.V. movies inclu. DESPERATE MISSION (71), MARK OF ZORRO (74); autobio: *REFLECTIONS: A LIFE IN TWO WORLDS.*

YVES MONTAND

B. Venice (another source: Monsumano, Italy?) 13.10.21. Real name Yvo Livi; his poor family fled from Mussolini's rule in 1923 and they made their home in Marseilles, France; aged 11 delivery boy, later worked in sister's business as hairdresser's apprentice, then in a metal factory as a truck loader, and waiter at a dockside bar; he got a singing act together, in the style of Chevalier, performed in cafés and music-halls in Marseilles, Bordeaux and Toulouse; 1940 to Paris, 1944 appd. at Paris A.B.C. music-hall; discovered and given first break by Edith Piaf, gave him advice and came to screen 1945 with her in ETOILE SANS LUMIERE; became star of French cinema, later internationally, films include LES PORTES DE LA NUIT (46), SOUVENIRS PERDUS (50), WAGES OF FEAR (53), NAPOLEON (54), LET'S MAKE LOVE (60), IS PARIS BURNING? (65), ON A CLEAR DAY YOU CAN SEE FOREVER (70), VINCENT, FRANCOIS, PAUL ET LES AUTRES (74); md. Simone Signoret 1951; popular in one-man show and night club act, has played on Broadway and in 1982 had U.S. cabaret tour.

DUDLEY MOORE

Dudley Moore has gained international recognition with two recent box-office hits, 10 and ARTHUR. British-born (Dagenham, Essex) on April 19, 1935, he attended Dagenham County High School, the Guildhall School of Music a Magdalen College, Oxford (gaining B.A. degrees). His gift as a musician began early: a pianist from the age of 8, viol at 12 and organ at 17. Graduating from Oxford, he toured the U.S. with the Vic Lewis Band, composed incidental mus at London's Royal Court Theatre, and played with the Johnny Dankworth Orchestra before great success in the rev 'Beyond the Fringe' (Edinburgh, London and Broadway, 1960-61-62); revue, T.V., movie success with Peter Coc (qv); movies: THE WRONG BOX (66); 30 IS A DANGEROUS AGE, CYNTHIA (67); MONTE CARLO O BUST, BEDAZZLED (both 1968); THE BEDSITTING ROOM (69); ALICE'S ADVENTURES IN WONDEI LAND (72); HOUND OF THE BASKERVILLES, FOUL PLAY (both 1977); Md: 1. Model/actress Suzy Kenda (1968-?); 2. Actress Tuesday Weld (1974-1979), 1 son Patrick; recent movies: 10, WHOLLY MOSES! (both 1979 ARTHUR (81, Oscar nom., BA; Golden Globe Aw. BA); SIX WEEKS, LOVESICK, DEREK & CLIVE (video ROMANTIC COMEDY (all 1982); Dudley was voted 'Film Star of the Year 1982' by USA's National Association Theatre Owners; UNFAITHFULLY YOURS (83).

RON MOODY

B. Tottenham, N. London 8.1.24. Real name Ronald Moodnick; graduated from London School of Economics with B.Sc. degree; formerly Research Graduate in Sociology and accountant; stage debut London 1952, in revue 'Intimacy at Eight', becoming well-known on stage in revue, cabaret, musicals (including Fagin in 'Oliver!', London/USA), Shakespeare and pantomime; came to the screen in supporting roles in 1953 and his many appearances include MAKE MINE MINK (59), SUMMER HOLIDAY (63), MURDER MOST FOUL (64), EVERY DAY'S A HOLIDAY (64), THE SANDWICH MAN (65), OLIVER! (68, scoring great success as Fagin, winner: Hollywood Golden Globe, Moscow Film Festival, Variety Club of G.B. awards, Best Actor), DAVID COPPERFIELD (69), THE 12 CHAIRS (70), FLIGHT OF THE DOVES (71), DOGPOUND SHUFFLE (74), LEGEND OF THE WEREWOLF (75), DOMINIQUE (77), SPACEMAN AND KING ARTHUR (78), MAN WITH THE DEADLY LENS (82); a novelist, he has written musicals and directed on the stage: T.V. 81: 'Into the Labyrinth'.

MARY TYLER MOORE

B. Brooklyn, New York 29.12.36. Father California gas co. executive; family moved to L.A. when Mary was 10; at 17 she began her career as a professional dancer, including spot as 'Happy Hotpoint, the dancing elf' in Hotpoint T.V. commercials, and in chorus lines of variety shows; md. 1. Richard Meeker (1960-62); early T.V.: Bachelor Father' (series 1957-62), voice only in 'Richard Diamond, Private Detective' (59), sev. other series; great success 1961-66 as Laura Petrie in 'The Dick Van Dyke Show', winning 2 Emmy awards; movies: X-15 (61), THOROUGHLY MODERN MILLIE (67), WHAT'S SO BAD ABOUT FEELING GOOD? (68), DON'T JUST STAND THERE (68), CHANGE OF HABIT (69), RUN A CROOKED MILE (69, T.V. movie), FIRST YOU CRY (78, T.V. movie); son Richard from 1st marriage (died October 1980); md. 2. Grant Tinker, T.V. executive; Mary acclaimed 1980 for her work in ORDINARY PEOPLE, gaining BA Oscar nom.; has her own production co., 'MTM Company'; SIX WEEKS (82).

ROGER MOORE

For over twenty years handsome and debonair Roger Moore has remained a top international movie star personalit working his way up gradually from humble film extra to highly paid film star of the 70s and 80s. The only child of Georg A. Moore, a policeman, and his wife, Lily, he was born in Stockwell, S. London, on 14 October 1928 and educated a Hackford Road Elementary School, Battersea Grammar and Dr Challoner's Grammar (Amersham, Bucks) School Art was his best subject and his first job upon leaving school was as tracer/filler in for a Soho cartoon film company. H then got work on CAESAR & CLEOPATRA (44) as an extra, a director advised him to try for an acting career and h spent three terms at R.A.D.A. where he met his first wife, Doorn van Steyn. From 1945-52 he worked in rep. Cambridge, did more film extra work (PICCADILLY INCIDENT, TROTTIE TRUE, PERFECT STRANGERS did National Service in the army (emerging as captain), walk-on parts in West End (MISTER ROBERTS understudied (THE LITTLE HUT), organised and worked as a male model (toothpaste, knitting patterns, etc.) and wa T.V. studio stage manager. The turning point in his career came in the early '50s when, now romantically linked wit singer Dorothy Squires, Moore accompanied her to the United States and found himself in demand for T.V. plays. The wed on 6 July 1953. A Broadway play, 'A Pin to See the Peepshow', in which he appeared, closed after one night. H had done enough work, however, to attract the attention of M-G-M, and following a stage tour in England, returned t the States and to Hollywood, appearing in THE LAST TIME I SAW PARIS (54); INTERRUPTED MELOD' (55); THE KING'S THIEF (55) and he starred opposite Lana Turner in DIANE (55). Returning to G.B., he played i 'Family Tree' at Worthing and was signed up to play 'Ivanhoe' (1957) in 39 T.V. episodes. Warner Bros. beckoned i Hollywood and he made the movies THE MIRACLE (59), THE SINS OF RACHEL CADE (60) and th prophetically titled GOLD OF THE 7 SAINTS (61). He also made the series 'The Alaskans', as Silky Harris, an 'Maverick', appearing as Beau. Back in Europe he filmed RAPE OF THE SABINES (61) and NO MAN'S LANE (61), on which he met his third wife, Luisa Mattioli, although the couple could not marry until 11 April 1969. They hav three children — Deborah (born 1963), Geoffrey (born 1966) and Christian (born 1973). From 1961-68 he playe Simon Templar in 'The Saint' T.V. series, a role which suited him perfectly and was shown in over 80 countries Following further movies, CROSSPLOT (68) and THE MAN WHO HAUNTED HIMSELF (69) and a series, 'Th Persuaders', Moore took over the role of James Bond in LIVE AND LET DIE (73) and has since played this part i MAN WITH THE GOLDEN GUN (74), THE SPY WHO LOVED ME (76), MOONRAKER (79) and FOl YOUR EYES ONLY (81). Non-Bond films have been THAT LUCKY TOUCH (74); STREET PEOPLE (76 SHERLOCK HOLMES IN N.Y. (76, T.V. movie); SICILIAN CROSS (77); WILD GEESE (77); ESCAPE TC ATHENA (78); NORTH SEA HI-JACK (79); THE SEA WOLVES (79); SUNDAY LOVERS (80); THE CANNONBALL RUN (81) and he returns as 007 in OCTOPUSSY (83). The actor and his family have homes i Gstaad, Switzerland, on the Riviera at St. Paul de Vence, and Beverly Hills in California.
ROGER MOORE AS JAMES BOND 007 (account of his filming LIVE AND LET DIE); p/back; Pan: London, 1973
ROGER MOORE by Paul Donovan; W.H. Allen: London, 1983.

KENNETH MORE

Kenneth More, remembered with affection for his 1970s movies in which he impeccably portrayed the determined and jovial Englishman, has emerged as a splendid character actor more recently on the stage and especially on T.V. More was born in Gerrards Cross, Bucks, on 20 September 1914, and educated at Worthing and Jersey, where his father, Bertie More, was general manager of Jersey Eastern Railways. Upon leaving school he worked briefly for an engineering firm at Shrewsbury. Following an even briefer stay in Canada, from which he was deported, he eventually got a job at London's Windmill Theatre working backstage, graduating to acting in various sketches. This whetted his appetite for an acting career and after 2 years at the Windmill he worked at Newcastle and Wolverhampton and toured in 'To Have and To Hold'. He wed actress Beryl Johnstone in 1940 and then served during the war with distinction in the navy, mainly with H.M.S. Aurora. His daughter, Susan Jane, was born in 1941. Following the war years, his acting career began to take shape — he appeared in the West End in 'And No Birds Sing' (1946); 'Power Without Glory' (1947) and 'Peace In Our Time' (1948) and his early films include SCOTT OF THE ANTARCTIC (48); MAN ON THE RUN (49); MORNING DEPARTURE (50); CHANCE OF A LIFETIME (50); NO HIGHWAY (51) and APPOINTMENT WITH VENUS (51). In the early 50s he wed for a second time, to Mabel Edith Barkby, and they had a daughter, Sarah Elizabeth. In 1952 he had a stage success as Freddie Page in 'The Deep Blue Sea' and a year later his performance as Ambrose Claverhouse in the now classic GENEVIEVE gained him deserved recognition as Britain's most popular film actor. He consolidated this success with such movies as DOCTOR IN THE HOUSE (54, B.F.A. Award, B.A.); THE DEEP BLUE SEA (55); REACH FOR THE SKY (56, as Douglas Bader); THE ADMIRABLE CRICHTON (57); A NIGHT TO REMEMBER (58); NORTHWEST FRONTIER (59) and SINK THE BISMARK! (60). In SOME PEOPLE (62) and THE COMEDY MAN (63) he appeared with Angela Douglas. The couple wed on 17 March 1968. In 1967 he played with distinction in the classic BBC serial 'The Forsyte Saga', portraying young Jolyon. Another series was 'Father Brown' and Mr More's latest films are LEOPARD IN THE SNOW (77), THE SPACEMAN & KING ARTHUR (78) and A TALE OF TWO CITIES (80). For several years he has suffered from Parkinson's disease. *Mr More died at his Fulham, W. London home, on July 13, 1982.*
HAPPY GO LUCKY (autobio.); Robert Hale Ltd: London, 1959; p/b;
MORE OR LESS (autobio.); Hodder & Stoughton; London, 1978;

JEANNE MOREAU

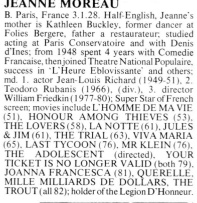

B. Paris, France 3.1.28. Half-English, Jeanne's mother is Kathleen Buckley, former dancer at Folies Bergere, father a restaurateur; studied acting at Paris Conservatoire and with Denis d'Ines; from 1948 spent 4 years with Comedie Francaise, then joined Theatre National Populaire, success in 'L'Heure Eblovissante' and others; md. 1. actor Jean-Louis Richard (1949-51), 2. Teodoro Rubanis (1966), (div.), 3. director William Friedkin (1977-80); Super Star of French screen; movies include L'HOMME DE MA VIE (51), HONOUR AMONG THIEVES (53), THE LOVERS (58), LA NOTTE (61), JULES & JIM (61), THE TRIAL (63), VIVA MARIA (65), LAST TYCOON (76), MR KLEIN (76), THE ADOLESCENT (directed), YOUR TICKET IS NO LONGER VALID (both 79), JOANNA FRANCESCA (81) QUERELLE, MILLE MILLIARDS DE DOLLARS, THE TROUT (all 82); holder of the Legion D'Honneur.

RITA MORENO

B. Humacao, Puerto Rico 11.12.31. Real name Rosita Dolores Alverio; as child went to New York with parents; aged 5 danced at Greenwich Village night club — at 15 in Broadway show 'Skydrift' (45); sang with rhythm band; dubbed U.S. films for Spanish-speaking territories; radio, T.V., club work, discovered for screen by MGM scout; debut PAGAN LOVE SONG (50); many movies include TOAST OF NEW ORLEANS (50), VAGABOND KING (55), KING AND I (56, as Tuptim), THE DEERSLAYER (57), WEST SIDE STORY (61, Oscar, as Anita, BSA), SUMMER & SMOKE (61), MARLOWE (69), CARNAL KNOWLEDGE (71), THE RITZ (76, also stage), HAPPY BIRTHDAY, GEMINI (79), THE 4 SEASONS (80); md. Leonard Gordon, a cardiologist, 1965, 1 child Fernanda (b. 1966); T.V. ser., 1982: '9 to 5', as Violet.

HENRY MORGAN

Detroit, Michigan 10.4.15. Real name Harry ratsburg; Mr Morgan appeared on stage in such oductions as 'Gentle People' and 'Thunder ock'; is a well-known face on T.V. and the films, tter include THE OX-BOW INCIDENT (43), IGH NOON (52), NOT AS A STRANGER 5), INHERIT THE WIND (60), THE BARE-OOT EXECUTIVE (71), APPLE DUMP-ING GANG (75), THE SHOOTIST (76), AT FROM OUTER SPACE (78); T.V. series: December Bride', 'Pete & Gladys' (60-62), Kentucky Jones' (64/65), Officer Bill Gannon in Dragnet' (67-70), 'The D.A.' (71/72) and as ol. Potter in 'M*A*S*H*' (75-).

ROBERT MORLEY

B. Semley, Wiltshire 26.5.08. Ed. Wellington College and in France, Germany and Italy; father Major in the Guards; originally intended for diplomatic career, but studied for the stage at RADA; 1st stage appearance Margate, May 1928, in 'Dr Syn'; subsequently became popular and distinguished stage and screen character actor; theatre including Sir Frank Benson's S'peare Co., 'Richard of Bordeaux', 'Oscar Wilde', Henry Higgins in 'Pygmalion' (Old Vic & New York), West End, tours—Australia/New Zealand, etc.; md. Joan Buckmaster 1940, 1 son Sheridan (b. 1941), 1 daughter Annabel (b. 1944); many movies include MARIE ANTOINETTE (38, as Louis XVI, Oscar nom. BSA), MAJOR BARBARA (40), YOUNG MISTER PITT (42), OUTCAST OF THE ISLANDS (51), THE STORY OF GILBERT & SULLIVAN (53, as Gilbert), THE AFRICAN QUEEN (53), as OSCAR WILDE (60), THE YOUNG ONES (61), MURDER AT THE GALLOP (63), THE ALPHABET MURDERS (65), GENGHIS KHAN (65), HOTEL PARADISO (66), SIN-FUL DAVEY (69), WHEN EIGHT BELLS TOLL (71), THEATRE OF BLOOD (73), THE BLUE BIRD (76), TOO MANY CHEFS (78), THE HUMAN FACTOR (79), LOOP-HOLE (81); as writer his plays include 'Short Story' (35), 'Edward, My Son' (co-wrote 1947); received C.B.E. 1957; recent T.V.: host, 'Lady-killers' (80/81), 'The Old Man at the Zoo' (83); film 1983: HIGH ROAD TO CHINA.
RESPONSIBLE GENTLEMAN (with Sewell Stokes); Heinemann: London, 1966; *ROBERT MORLEY: LARGER THAN LIFE* by Margaret Morley; Robson Books: London, 1979; p/b: Coronet, 1980.

MICHAEL MORIARTY

B. Detroit, Michigan 5.4.41. Ed. Dartmouth College; trained for stage at L.A.M.D.A., London; Mr Moriarty is a distinguished stage actor in the U.S.A., making New York debut in 1963; roles include 'Richard III' (74) and won a 'Tony' award 1974 for 'Find Your Way Home'; several movies include HICKEY & BOGGS (72), BANG THE DRUM SLOWLY (73), THE GLASS MENA-GERIE (73, T.V. movie), A SUMMER WITH-OUT BOYS (73, T.V. movie), SHOOT IT BLACK, SHOOT IT BLUE (74), THE LAST DETAIL (74), REPORT TO THE COM-MISSIONER (75), HOLOCAUST (78, T.V. movie, 'Emmy' Aw. BA), WHO'LL STOP THE RAIN? (78), WINDS OF KITTY HAWK (78, T.V. movie, as Wilbur Wright), Q: THE WINGED SERPENT (82), THE SOUND OF MURDER (T.V. movie, 1982).

VIC MORROW

B. The Bronx, New York 14.2.32. Ed. Florida Southern college (changing the course from law to drama), Mexico City College and Paul Mann's New York Actors' Workshop; in 1949 he served in the U.S. Navy; Mr Morrow has since become involved with producing plays 'off-Broadway' and on T.V., as well as acting; md. Barbara, 1957, 2 daughters: Carrie and Jennifer; he came to the screen as Artie West in the acclaimed film BLACKBOARD JUNGLE (55) and his movies have since included TRIBUTE TO A BADMAN (56), MEN IN WAR (57), GOD'S LITTLE ACRE (58), KING CREOLE (58), CIMARRON (60), PORTRAIT OF A MOBSTER (61), SLEDGE (directed only, 69), A STEP OUT OF LINE (71, T.V. movie), THE POLICE STORY (73, T.V. movie), DIRTY MARY, CRAZY LARRY (74), THE TAKE (74), DEATH STALK (75, T.V. movie), CAPTAINS AND KINGS (76, T.V. movie), BAD NEWS BEARS (76), TREASURE OF MATECUMBE (76), ROOTS (77, T.V. movie), MESSAGE FROM SPACE (78); he directed a short film, LAST YEAR AT MALIBU, and his screen version of his off-Broadway production of 1958, DEATH-WATCH, also collaborating on screenplay and co-producing; he appeared as Sergeant Chip Saunders in the T.V. series, 'Combat' (1962-67) and guested in such series as 'Charlie's Angels' and 'Paris'; recent movies: THE EVICTORS (79), MONSTER (80).
Mr Morrow died tragically in a helicopter accident, July 23, 1982.

BARRY MORSE

B. London 10.6.19. Trained at RADA; stage début: People's Palace, Mile End; 1937-41, over 200 rep. roles; many films include THE GOOSE STEPS OUT (42), WHEN WE ARE MARRIED (42), THIS MAN IS MINE (46), LATE AT NIGHT (46), MRS FITZHERBERT (47), DAUGHTER OF DARKNESS (48); Mr Morse then moved to Canada and directed/acted on T.V., occasionally working in the States, esp. as Lieut. Philip Gerard in 'The Fugitive' T.V. series (1963-67); other movies include KINGS OF THE SUN (64), JUSTINE (68), RUNNING SCARED (71), ASYLUM (72), TRUMAN AT POTSDAM (75), WELCOME TO BLOOD CITY (77), COUP D'ETAT (77), THE SHAPE OF THINGS TO COME (78), THE CHANGE-LING (78), KLONDIKE FEVER (79), CRIES IN THE NIGHT (79), THE HOUNDS OF NOTRE DAME (81); recent T.V.: 'Whoops Apocalypse' (82, ser.), 'The Rothko Conspiracy' (83).

HELEN MORSE

B. Wembley, Middx. . . . Has lived mainly in Australia; stage début aged 5: 'Rumpelstiltskin'; trained at National Institute of Dramatic Art, Sydney, graduating 1965; became one of Australia's most successful stage actresses, work includes 'A Taste of Honey' (Independent Theatre), 'School For Scandal' (Old Tote Theatre); T.V. includes 'Twelfth Night', 'Intersection', 'You Can't See Around Corners'; 1981 series: 'A Town Like Alice' (as Jean Paget), 1982 series: 'Silent Reach'; md. Australian producer/director Sandy Harbutt; movies include CADDIE (77); AGATHA (78); FAR EAST (82); 1983 tour, Australia, 'Duet For One'.

PATRICK MOWER

B. Oxford (Pontypridd?) 12.9.40. Ed. Oxford Grammar School; formerly apprentice engineering draughtsman, but decided to study at RADA and become actor — left drama school in Jan. 1963 and appd. on stage in such productions as 'Alfie' (Mermaid Theatre), musical—'House of Cards' (Phoenix Theatre), 'John Gabriel Borkman' (Duchess Theatre) and 'Edward II' (Birmingham 1966); Mr Mower's T.V. appearances have included 'Front Page Story', 'The Avengers', 'Callan' and his own series 'Special Branch' and 'Target'; he has guested on T.V. on many occasions; md. Audrey Latimer, 1 son Sam, 1 daughter Claudia; his motion pictures have included THE DEVIL RIDES OUT (67), THE SMASHING BIRD I USED TO KNOW (68), DOCTORS WEAR SCARLET (69), CRY OF THE BANSHEE (69), BLACK BEAUTY (70), PERCY (70), CATCH ME A SPY (71), ONE AWAY (76), CARRY ON ENGLAND (76), THE DEVIL'S ADVOCATE (77); stage 1979: 'Night & Day' (Phoenix Theatre, London) and T.V.: 'The Flockton Flyer'; 81: 'Bergerac'.

ARTHUR MULLARD

B. Islington, London 19.9.10. Ed. Elementary School; butcher's boy, Regimental Policeman, pro. boxer for 3 years (suffered concussion); md. Flo (dec.), 2 sons, 1 daughter; 'totter' (collected lumber, resold it in market); WWII: ammunition loader, joined Royal Artillery, trained for anti-aircraft, as a sergeant drilled troops and was boxing/PT instructor, thought it was all an act and decided to become actor on demob!; from 1945 for 9 years worked as film extra: 1st job as S.S. man in Ealing film (Arthur can be glimpsed in MAN IN THE WHITE SUIT (50) and LAVEN-DER HILL MOB (51)), later stand-in/stunt double for Archie Duncan, did a few stage jobs; in 1955 commenced T.V. roles, well-known for his burly Cockney characters, hundreds of appearances with top comedians; films include LONELINESS OF LONG-DISTANCE RUNNER(61), POST-MAN'S KNOCK (61), WRONG ARM OF THE LAW (62), MORGAN (65), LOCK UP YOUR DAUGHTERS (68), VAULT OF HOR-ROR (73), ADVENTURES OF A PLUMMER'S MATE (77); T.V. series: 'Yus, My Dear', 'Romany Jones', 'Whizzkids Guide' (81). 'OH, YUS, IT'S ARTHUR MULLARD' by A.M.; p/back: Everest, London, 1977.

CAROLINE MUNRO

B.   ,   . . . Ed. Convent at Rottingdean, nr. Brighton; her mother sent her to modelling school and she appeared in various mags., a spread of her photos in the U.S. edition of 'Vogue' was seen by a Hollywood film executive and she played her first role in A TALENT FOR LOVING (68), having been one of the girls in CASINO ROYALE a year earlier; her other movies have included WHERE'S JACK? (68), THE ABOMI-NABLE DR PHIBES (71), DR PHIBES RIDES AGAIN (72), DRACULA A.D. 1972, THE GOLDEN VOYAGE OF SINBAD (72), CAP-TAIN KRONOS: VAMPIRE HUNTER (74), AT THE EARTH'S CORE (76), Naomi in THE SPY WHO LOVED ME (77) and STAR-CRASH (Italy, 1977); Caroline has, since 1968, been featured on Lamb's Navy Rum calendar; she is wed to Mr Judd Hamilton, the American singer/record producer and she has 2 step-children, Judd Jr. and Tami; in 1979 she filmed MANIAC in the U.S.A.; THE LAST HORROR PICTURE (81).

BRIAN MURPHY

B. Ventnor, Isle of Wight 25.9.33. Mr Murph always wanted to be an actor and after Nationa Service in the R.A.F., he trained at RADA ar joined the famed Theatre Workshop Company i London's East End, coming to the screen in one their productions, SPARRER'S CAN'T SINC in 1962; his other films have included SAI FERRY ANN (65), JUST LIKE A WOMA (65), THE DEVILS (71), THE BOYFRIEN (72); md. Carole, 2 sons: Trevor, Kevin; becam well-known for his roles in the two T.V. serie 'Man About the House' and especially as Georg in 'George and Mildred', a feature film of whic was made in 1980; recent T.V.: 'The Incredibl Mr Tanner' (81), 'L For Lester' (82-83); stage 'The Soldier's Fortune' (81), 'On Your Way Riley' (82, as Arthur Lucan); T.V. movie 1982 IT'S YOUR MOVE.

MICHAEL MURPHY

B. Hollywood, California   .   .49. Raised in Arizona; Mr Murphy has been seen in the fol-lowing films: THE ARRANGEMENT (70), COUNT YORGA, VAMPIRE (70), M*A*S*H (70), BREWSTER McCLOUD (70), McCABE AND MRS MILLER (71), WHAT'S UP, DOC? (71), THE THIEF WHO CAME TO DINNER (72), THE CROOKED HEARTS (72, T.V. movie), THE AUTOBIOGRAPHY OF MISS JANE PITTMAN (74, T.V. movie), I LOVE YOU, GOODBYE (74, T.V. movie), PHASE IV (74), NASHVILLE (75), THE FRONT (76), AN UNMARRIED WOMAN (77), THE CLASS OF MISS MacMICHAEL (77), NEVER TRUST AN HONEST THIEF (79), MAN-HATTAN (79), DEAD KIDS (80), THE YEAR OF LIVING DANGEROUSLY (82).

DON MURRAY

B. Los Angeles, California 31.7.29. Real name Donald Patrick Murray; father Dennis Murray, dance director; mother Ethel Cook, former Zieg-feld girl; aged 9 months, moved to New York with parents; ed. Long Island, Cleveland and Texas, moving as parents toured the country; attended American Acad., New York and made stage début in summer stock, eventually reaching Broad-way in 'The Insect Comedy' (48) and following his work in 'Rose Tattoo' (51) and 'The Skin of Our Teeth' (55) came to the screen in BUS STOP (56); md. actress Hope Lange in April 1956, 1 son Christopher, 1 daughter Patricia (div.); his many films include BACHELOR PARTY (57), A HATFUL OF RAIN (57), SHAKE HANDS WITH THE DEVIL (58), THE HOODLUM PRIEST (61), ADVISE & CONSENT (62), BABY, THE RAIN MUST FALL (65), SWEET LOVE, BITTER (67), THE BORGIA STICK (67, T.V. movie), THE VIKING QUEEN (67), CROSS & THE SWITCHBLADE (70), CON-QUEST OF THE PLANET OF THE APES (72), HAPPY BIRTHDAY, WANDA JUNE (72), DEADLY HERO (76), many T.V. movies; Earl Corey in series 'The Outcasts' (68/69); md. 2. Betty Johnson, 1962; recent movie: ENDLESS LOVE (81); regular 'Knots Landing' T.V. series (80/81).

PATRICIA NEAL

Born Packard, Kentucky, 20.1.26. Real name Patsy Louise Neal; ed. Northwestern University, studying drama; appeared in summerstock, went to New York in 1943, worked as doctor's assistant, cashier, model, jewellery store clerk before winning fame on Broadway in 'Another Part of the Forest', winning 3 drama awards; went to Hollywood, appeared in many pictures including JOHN LOVES MARY (49, début); THE HASTY HEART (GB, 50); THE FOUNTAINHEAD (49); BRIGHT LEAF (50); WEEKEND WITH FATHER (51); DAY THE EARTH STOOD STILL (51); STRANGER FROM VENUS (52); but had more success on stage including 'The Children's Hour' (1952), 'A Room Full of Roses' (1955), and 'The Miracle Worker' (1959); married Mr Roald Dahl, 2 July 1953; children: Olivia (died Nov. 1962), Theo, Tessa (now an actress), Lucille, Ophelia; in 1965 Patricia suffered 3 strokes and survived brain surgery; other movies include: A FACE IN THE CROWD (57); BREAKFAST AT TIFFANY'S (61); HUD (63, Oscar BSA); IN HARM'S WAY (64); THE SUBJECT WAS ROSES (68, Oscar nom.); WIDOW'S NEST (77); THE PASSAGE (78); GHOST STORY (81); sev. T.V.movies; div.5.7.83. *PAT & ROALD* by Barry Farrell; Hutchinson: London, 1970.

HILDEGARD NEIL

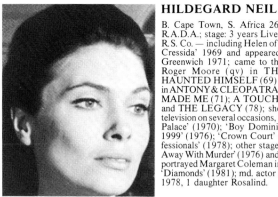

B. Cape Town, S. Africa 26.5.39. Trained at R.A.D.A.; stage: 3 years Liverpool 'Everyman', R.S. Co. — including Helen of Troy in 'Troilus & Cressida' 1969 and appeared in 'Macbeth' at Greenwich 1971; came to the screen opposite Roger Moore (qv) in THE MAN WHO HAUNTED HIMSELF (69) and has been seen in ANTONY & CLEOPATRA (71); ENGLAND MADE ME (71); A TOUCH OF CLASS (72) and THE LEGACY (78); she has appeared on television on several occasions, including 'Imperial Palace' (1970); 'Boy Dominic' (1974); 'Space 1999' (1976); 'Crown Court' (1978); 'The Professionals' (1978); other stage includes 'Getting Away With Murder' (1976) and Miss Neil recently portrayed Margaret Coleman in the A.T.V. series 'Diamonds' (1981); md. actor Brian Blessed (qv) 1978, 1 daughter Rosalind.

KATE NELLIGAN

. London, Ontario 16.3.51. Ed. St. Martin's Catholic School, London, Ontario, York Univ., Toronto; mother (dec.) primary school teacher, father park-keeper; Miss Melligan had wanted to act since age of 16 when she appeared as Gertrude in 'Hamlet' in school play; 3 years at Central School of Speech & Drama; professional début Bristol Little Theatre, 1972, in 'Barefoot in the Park', then played several roles with Bristol Old Vic 1972/73; London début March 1974, as Jenny in 'Knuckle' (comedy); National Theatre 1975 in 'Heartbreak House'; she is very well-known on British T.V. in such plays as 'Licking Hitler' (1977); 'Dreams of Leaving' (1980); as Therese Raquin' (1980) and the series 'Forgive Our Foolish Ways' (80); she has played with the Royal S'peare Co. and her films are THE COUNT OF MONTE CRISTO (74); THE ROMANTIC ENGLISHWOMAN (75); Miss Lucy in DRACULA (79); MIDNIGHT MATINEE (80); VICTIMS (T.V. movie), EYE OF THE NEEDLE (both 1981); WITHOUT A TRACE (82); stage 1982: 'Plenty'.

FRANCO NERO

B. Parma, Italy 23.11.41. Real name Franco Sparanero; Mr Nero has 1 brother, 3 sisters; attended school in his home town, played in operatic choruses as a child singer; gained degree in Business Studies at university in Italy, went into the army and spent all his free time organising shows for the troops; aged 22 left for Rome to take up acting career, graduating to stage roles, documentaries and made 11 Italian feature films; international roles: Abel in THE BIBLE (65) and after THE TRAMPLERS (66) made Hollywood debut with success as Lancelot in CAMELOT (67, co-starring Vanessa Redgrave, they have son, Carlo Gabriel, born 1969); THE DAY OF THE OWL (68); A QUIET PLACE IN THE COUNTRY (68); TRISTANA (70); THE BATTLE OF NERETVA (70); THE VIRGIN & THE GYPSY (70); POPE JOAN (72); THE MONK (72); 21 HOURS TO MUNICH (72, T.V. movie); WHITE FANG (74); FORCE TEN FROM NAVARONE (77); THE PIRATE (78, T.V. movie); THE MAN WITH BOGART'S FACE (79); UN DRAMMA BORGHESE (79); THE SALAMANDER (80); Mr Nero produced 2 feature films in 1970: DROPOUT and THE VACATION; T.V. movie 1975: LEGEND OF VALENTINO; recent films: ENTER THE NINJA (81); MEXICO IN FLAMES, QUERELLE, GROG, WAGNER, 10 DAYS THAT SHOOK THE WORLD (all 1982).

BARRY NEWMAN

B. Boston, Mass., 26.3.38. Mr Newman has an Austrian father and a Swedish mother, emigrating to USA in the 1920s; ed. Brandeis Univ., gaining a degree in anthropology; an early ambition was to be a jazz musician as he plays the saxophone and clarinet; following a stint in the U.S. Army he left Columbia Univ. to become an actor; after appearing on stage he came to the screen in THE LAWYER (69) and has been seen in VANISHING POINT (71), FEAR IS THE KEY (72), THE SALZBURG CONNECTION (72) and NIGHT GAMES (74, T.V. movie), then playing in the T.V. series 'Petrocelli' as Tony Petrocelli from 1974-76; he was also in the long-running series as John Barnes, 'The Edge of Night'; in more recent years he has completed SEX AND THE MARRIED WOMAN (77, T.V. movie); CITY OF FIRE (78); AMY (80) and SHADOW EFFECTS (pilot and series in 81, Australia).

NANETTE NEWMAN

B. Northampton, ... Miss Newman comes from a theatrical family, her father being a cabaret artiste; she trained at the Italia Conti School and R.A.D.A. and has appeared many times on T.V. and in movies, esp. those directed by her husband, director/writer/producer Bryan Forbes (qv); early T.V. includes 'The Golden Days', 'The Wedding Veil' and movies PERSONAL AFFAIR (53); HOUSE OF MYSTERY (58); THE REBEL (61); PIT OF DARKNESS (61); THE L-SHAPED ROOM (62*); SEANCE ON A WET AFTERNOON (64*); she has 2 daughters, Sarah Kate Amanda, who is now a journalist, and Emma Katy, studying ballet; recent T.V. work includes 'Jessie' (80, BBC*) and the series 'Stay With Me Till Morning' (81); further movies (* denotes directed by her husband) include THE WRONG BOX (66*); THE WHISPERERS (66*); DEADFALL (67*); MADWOMAN OF CHAILLOT (68*); CAPT. NEMO & THE UNDERWATER CITY (69); THE RAGING MOON (70*); THE LOVE BAN (72); MAN AT THE TOP (73); THE STEPFORD WIVES (74*); INTERNATIONAL VELVET (77*); Miss Newman has authored several children's story books, including 'The Pig That Never Was' (1979) and stars in her own T.V. series. 'Let There Be Love' (82/83).

OLIVIA NEWTON-JOHN

B. Cambridge 28.9.48. Real name Olivia John; father Welsh, Prof. of German Lit., became head of King's Coll., Camb.; Olivia has a brother who is a doctor, and a sister, an actress-singer; aged 5 she went to Australia where father had teaching appointment in Melbourne; aged 12 won Hayley Mills look-alike competition; aged 14 formed quartet Sol Four, later sang solo in coffee house, advised to enter T.V. contest and won £100 and trip to U.K., but chose to finish schooling in Australia; at 16 came to G.B. with mother (who is German born and the daughter of Nobel Prize-winning physicist Max Born); appd. in clubs, on T.V. and became success in the States, then internationally; movies: TOOMORROW (68); FUNNY THINGS HAPPEN DOWN UNDER (short, Australia); GREASE (77); XANADU (79); O.B.E. 1979; numerous awards including 41 Gold and Platinum records from U.S., Japan and G.B.; own co.: 'Olivia Newton-John Enterprises'.

PAUL NICHOLAS

B. London 3.12.45. Father Oscar Beuselinck; Mr Nicholas was for a while a pianist with 'Screaming Lord Sutch' and was pop singer named 'Oscar' and toured Europe; London stage break as one of the original stars of the musical 'Hair' (68/69); appeared in movies CANNABIS (69, France); BLIND TERROR (71); WHAT BECAME OF JACK & JILL? (72) and back on stage as Jesus in 'Jesus Christ Superstar' (72/73) and 'Grease' (74); md. Susan (div.), 3 children; other movies include STARDUST (74); TOMMY (74); LISZTOMANIA (75); SERGEANT PEPPER'S LONELY HEARTS CLUB BAND (77); THE WORLD IS FULL OF MARRIED MEN (79); YESTERDAY'S HERO (79); ALICE (79); he is a well-known recording artist of LPs and singles, has appeared on T.V. on many occasions including 'A Little Rococo' (81). 'Doubting Thomas' (83); recent stage: 'Cats' (82); movies: NUTCRACKER (82); INVITATION TO THE WEDDING (83).

PAUL NEWMAN

Since his screen début in the mid-1950s, Paul Newman has remained one of the top American screen actors and in th 1960s consolidated his career by appearing in some of the best films and also emerged as a talented director. The son o Arthur Newman, who owned a successful sporting goods concern with his wife, Theresa, Paul was born at Clevelan Heights, Cleveland, Ohio, on 26 January 1925. As a youngster he appeared in plays and attended Cleveland's Malver Grammar and Shaker Heights High Schools, progressing to Kenyon College on an athlete's scholarship where h excelled at football, basketball and swimming. He majored in Economics, but was called up for war service in the U.S Navy, spending 3 years in the Pacific riding torpedo planes as a radioman. Returning to College, he got seriousl interested in drama, appeared in 10 plays and did a season of summer stock at Williams Bay, Wisconsin in 1949. Hi father died and Paul managed the family business for 18 months, handed it over to his older brother and enrolled at Yal drama school. In December 1947 he had wed actress Jacqueline Witte and son, Scott, was born in 1950 (who die tragically, aged 28), daughters Susan and Stephanie in 1951 and 1952. After Yale Newman headed for New York, go roles in T.V. ('The Web', 'Danger'), understudied Ralph Meeker in 'Picnic' but later won acclaim on Broadway in thi play as Alan Seymour in 1953. This led to his screen début in THE SILVER CHALICE (54), but he was disappointe with the movie and returned to New York for good work in 'The Desperate Hours' (55) and on T.V., includin 'Appointment With Danger', 'Playwrights '55' and 'Producer's Showcase'. He returned to Hollywood and embarke on his highly successful movie career with THE RACK (56); SOMEBODY UP THERE LIKES ME (56, as Rock Graziano); THE LONG HOT SUMMER (58); THE LEFT-HANDED GUN (58, as William Bonney); CAT ON HOT TIN ROOF (58, Oscar nom.); THE YOUNG PHILADELPHIANS (59); THE HUSTLER (61, Oscar nom.) SWEET BIRD OF YOUTH (62); HUD (63, Oscar nom.); THE PRIZE (63); THE OUTRAGE (64); HARPEI (66); HOMBRE (67); COOL HAND LUKE (67, Oscar nom.); WINNING (69); BUTCH CASSIDY & THE SUNDANCE KID (69); W.U.S.A. (70); SOMETIMES A GREAT NOTION (71, and directed); JUDGE ROY BEAN (72); THE STING (73); THE TOWERING INFERNO (74); BUFFALO BILL & THE INDIANS (76 and SLAP SHOT (77). Mr Newman has returned to Broadway to play in 'Sweet Bird of Youth' (1959), 'Baby Want Kiss' (1964) and in 1969 he formed First Artists Production Co. (with Sidney Poitier, Steve McQueen and Barbr Streisand). Divorcing his first wife in 1956, two years later he wed the talented Oscar-winning actress Joann Woodward (qv) and they have appeared together in several movies. His direction of her in RACHEL, RACHEL (69 won him a New York Critics' Circle award. The couple have three daughters, Elinor (born 1959), Melissa (1961) an Claire (1965). Daughter Susan Kendall Newman from his first marriage acted in movies A WEDDING (78), WANNA HOLD YOUR HAND (78) and co-produced Paul and Joanne's THE SHADOW BOX (80). Newman' hobby is motor-racing and he took part/narrated T.V. movie 'Once Upon a Wheel'. His most recent movies ar QUINTET (78); WHEN TIME RAN OUT (79); FORT APACHE, THE BRONX (81); ABSENCE OF MALICE (81, Oscar nom.); THE VERDICT (82, Oscar nom.) and HARRY & SON (83, star/director).

THE FILMS OF PAUL NEWMAN by Lawrence J. Quirk; Citadel: Secaucus, N.J., 1971. revised, 1981.
PAUL NEWMAN by Charles Hamblett; W.H. Allen: London, 1975.
PAUL NEWMAN—SUPERSTAR by Lionel Godfrey; Robert Hale: London, 1979.
PAUL NEWMAN: AN ILLUSTRATED BIOGRAPHY by J.C. Landry; Sidgwick & Jackson: London, 1983.

JACK NICHOLSON

Jack Nicholson has emerged as a Super Star of current American cinema in a variety of roles to suit his engaging screen personality, culminating with his Oscar-winning success in the 1975 movie, ONE FLEW OVER THE CUCKOO'S NEST. He was born at Neptune, New Jersey on 22 April 1937, the son of John Nicholson, a window dresser and sign-writer, and his wife, Ethel, who ran a beauty parlour. Jack's parents separated when he was young, his father leaving home. He was bright at school and did well at exams, but, accompanied by his elder sister, June, he went to California and got a £10-a-week job in the postroom at M-G-M. Producer Joe Pasternack was impressed by the young man's confidence and gave him a screen test which he apparently failed, but Nicholson managed to break into movies and for 10 years he worked in 'B' pictures, coming to the screen in CRY BABY KILLER in 1958. Other movies of this era include TEENAGE LOVERS (60); BROKEN LAND (62); THE RAVEN, THE TERROR (both 63) and BACK DOOR TO HELL (65). He wrote THUNDER ISLAND (63), THE TRIP (67), RIDE IN THE WHIRLWIND (66, also acted) and HEAD (68, co-wrote). The actor had wed former actress Sandra Knight in 1961 but the marriage lasted only 5 years, their daughter Jennifer being born in 1963. His breakthrough came in 1969 as the drunken young lawyer in EASY RIDER and his major films have included 5 EASY PIECES (69, Oscar nom.); CARNAL KNOWLEDGE (71); THE KING OF MARVIN GARDENS (72); THE PASSENGER, TOMMY, CHINATOWN (Oscar nom.), THE LAST DETAIL (all 74); THE FORTUNE (75); THE MISSOURI BREAKS (76); THE LAST TYCOON (77); GOIN' SOUTH (78, also directed); THE SHINING (80); THE BORDER (80); POSTMAN ALWAYS RINGS TWICE (81); REDS (81, BAFTA Aw., BSA; Oscar nom., BSA) and TERMS OF ENDEARMENT (83). For his performance in ONE FLEW OVER THE CUCKOO'S NEST, Jack Nicholson won the 1975 Academy Award.

JACK NICHOLSON by Derek Sylvester; Proteus: London & N.Y., 1982.

LESLIE NIELSEN

B. Regina, Saskatchewan, 11.2.26(?); preparing for an engineering course, landed job instead as radio announcer/disc jockey; studied at Toronto Acad. of Dramatic Arts and at Neighbourhood Playhouse, New York; radio, repertory, New York stage ('Seagulls Over Sorento' 1952) and T.V.; md. Monica, 2 daughters; many movies including VAGABOND KING (55); FORBID-DEN PLANET (56); OPPOSITE SEX (57); TAMMY & THE BACHELOR (57); HARLOW (65); BEAU GESTE (66); DAYTON'S DEVILS (68); TRIAL RUN (69, T.V. movie); THE POSEIDON ADVENTURE (72); SNATCHED (73, T.V. movie); THE LETTERS (73, T.V. movie); LITTLE MO (78, T.V. movie); CITY OF FIRE (78); AIRPLANE! (79); PROM NIGHT (79); CAVE IN! (79); much T.V. includes the series, as Lieu. Price Adams in 'The New Breed' (1961/62), John Bracken in 'Bracken's World' (1969-71), Sam Danforth in 'The Bold Ones' (72) and in 1982 in 'Police Squad!'; over 15 T.V. movies; recent big screen: THE CREATURE WASN'T NICE (81), MAN WITH THE DEADLY LENS (82).

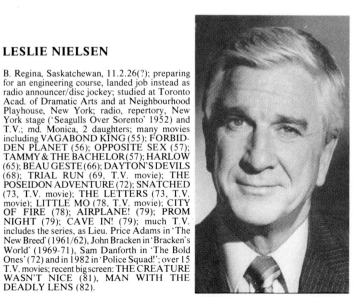

LEONARD NIMOY

B. Boston, Mass., 26.3.31. Professional début aged 9 in 'Hansel & Gretel' in home town; ed. Boston College, studying English and Drama, Antioch College and the Pasadena Playhouse; stage includes 'Three Musketeers' (1950), 'Dr Faustus' (1950), 'Streetcar Named Desire' (1955), 'Cat on a Hot Tin Roof' (1959) and Mr Nimoy has played leads in such musicals as 'Fiddler on the Roof', 'Oliver!', 'Camelot' and 'King & I'; md. Sandi Zober 21.2.54, 1 daughter Julie (born 21.3.55), 1 son Adam (born 9.8.56); many movies include QUEEN FOR A DAY (50); THE BALCONY (63); CATLOW (72); INVASION OF THE BODYSNATCHERS (77); well-known on T.V. as Mr Spock in 'Star Trek' (1966-69) and as Paris in 'Mission Impossible' (1967-71); he has made records and had books on photography and poetry published; A WOMAN CALLED GOLDA (82, T.V. movie), as Lord Achmed in 'Marco Polo' (1982, mini-series), STAR TREK II THE WRATH OF KHAN (82).

I AM NOT SPOCK by L.N.; paperback: Ballan-tine: New York, 1977.

DAVID NIVEN

An actor of considerable appeal, Oscar-winning David Niven had an adventurous life before working his way up from Hollywood film extra to British leading man of the 1930s. The son of William Niven (who was killed at Gallipoli in 1915) and his wife, Henriette, he was born in Kirriemuir, Angus, in Scotland on 1 March 1910 and educated near Worthing, at Heatherdown, near Ascot (being expelled), at Southsea (for 'difficult' boys), Penn Street in Bucks and Stowe Public School. Young David was the first of three Stowe boys to gain commissions in the Regular Army, graduating from Sandhurst. Serving with the Highland Light Infantry mainly in Malta, he got restless, worked as an extra in an Allan Jeayes film, and resigned his commission. With the help of an ex-Major of Grenadier Guards, he sailed to Canada, went to New York, worked as a waiter at cocktail parties, was a liquor salesman, and helped form the American Pony Express Racing Association, but this venture collapsed in Atlantic City. Deciding to try the movies, he sailed for California, via Cuba and Panama, became acquainted with Loretta Young and her sisters and tried to get film extra work but had no work permit. Through further influential film people he got his permit via Mexico, registered as Anglo-Saxon type No. 2008 and promptly worked in his first Hollywood film as an extra — as a Mexican. Eventually, with the help of director Edmund Goulding, he landed a contract with Sam Goldwyn, coming to the screen officially with one line in WITHOUT REGRET (35). He gradually got better roles and emerged as a very popular star, particularly during the 1940s. Appearing in over 80 movies, his best include THANK YOU, JEEVES (36, as Wooster); CHARGE OF THE LIGHT BRIGADE (36); DODSWORTH (36); THE PRISONER OF ZENDA (37); THE DAWN PATROL (38); BACHELOR MOTHER (39); RAFFLES (40); WWII: British Army, rank of Colonel; THE WAY AHEAD (44); A MATTER OF LIFE & DEATH (46); THE BISHOP'S WIFE (47); SOLDIERS THREE (51); THE MOON IS BLUE (53); CARRINGTON V.C. (55); AROUND THE WORLD IN 80 DAYS (56); THE LITTLE HUT (57); SEPARATE TABLES (58, Oscar, B.A.); GUNS OF NAVARONE (61); THE PINK PANTHER (64) and PAPER TIGER (75). In 1940 Mr Niven wed Primula Rollo, who died tragically in 1946 — they had 2 sons, David Jr. (now a producer) in 1942, and Jamie, in 1945. His second wife is Hjordis Tersmeden — they wed in 1948 and have 2 daughters, Kristina and Fiona. He has appeared many times on T.V., in 1951 formed a company, 4 Star, was host of 'The David Niven Show' in 1959, appeared in 'The Rogues' (64/65) and his 1971 autobiography became a best-seller. More recent films are MURDER BY DEATH (76); DEATH ON THE NILE (77); CANDLESHOE (77); ESCAPE FROM ATHENA (78); A MAN CALLED INTREPID (78, T.V. movie); ROUGHCUT (79); THE SEA WOLVES (80) and MENAGE A TROIS (82). He was deservedly given a special 'New Evening Standard Film Award for his contribution to the cinema' in 1980.
THE MOON'S A BALLOON by D.N. (autobio.); Hamish Hamilton: London, 1971; p/b.
BRING ON THE EMPTY HORSES by D.N.; Hamish Hamilton: London, 1975.
THE FILMS OF DAVID NIVEN by Gerard Garrett; L.S.P. Books: Godalming, 1976.
GO SLOWLY, COME BACK QUICKLY (novel) by D.N.; Hamish Hamilton: London, 1981.

Mr Niven passed away at his Chateau d'Oex, Switzerland home, on Friday, July 29, 1983.

NICK NOLTE

B. Omaha, Nebraska, . . 41. Father irrigation project engineer; youthful ambition: to be footballer; attended 5 colleges in 4 years; in early '60s drifted into L.A. and various jobs, including steel construction; advised by Bryan O'Byrne, acting coach, to study acting, which Nick did, for several months; repertory: Phoenix, Denver, Minneapolis, Chicago; in L.A. he won acclaim in play 'The Last Pad' (by Wm. Inge), produced by ex-convict; his screen work has included WINTER KILL, THE CALIFORNIA KID, DEATH SENTENCE (74, all T.V. movies); THE RUNAWAY BARGE (75, T.V. movie); RETURN TO MACON COUNTY (75) and recognition in mini-series RICH MAN, POOR MAN (76); md. Sharon Haddad, on 10.5.78, in Las Vegas; other movies: THE DEEP (77); DOG SOLDIERS (77); NORTH DALLAS FORTY (79); HEARTBEAT (79); CANNERY ROW (81); 48 HOURS (82); UNDER FIRE (83).

CHUCK NORRIS

B. ———, . . . While in Air Force in Korea taught karate; returned home to Torrance, a Los Angeles suburb, and won karate world middle-weight championship in 1968; held title until he retired, undefeated, in 1974; ran karate school; choreographed karate fight between himself and late Bruce Lee in RETURN OF THE DRAGON (72); Steve McQueen, a student of his at karate school, advised Chuck to try acting; studied with Lee Strasberg and Zina Provendie; movies: BREAKER! BREAKER! (77); GOOD GUYS WEAR BLACK (78); A FORCE OF ONE (79); THE OCTAGON (80); AN EYE FOR AN EYE, SLAUGHTER IN SAN FRANCISCO, SILENT RAGE (all 1981); LONE WOLF McQUADE (83).

KIM NOVAK

Making a welcome comeback in the recent hit Agatha Christie film, THE MIRROR CRACK'D, is Kim Novak, former pin-up star of the 1950s, the era when she made her best movies. She was born Marilyn Novak in Chicago, Illinois on 13 February 1933, the daughter of Joseph Novak, a former history teacher who then worked for the Chicago-Milwaukee railroad, and his wife, Blanche. A shy and withdrawn girl, Kim's mother urged her to join the local 'Far Teens Club' to lose her inhibitions. At the age of 11 she embarked on a modelling career, but she disliked it and attended school at Chicago, Farragut High School and Wright Junior College, where she majored in drama, appearing in one play 'Our Town' (one source of reference states she, aged 12, 'appeared in a teenage radio series'). Young Kim worked in temporary jobs such as the groomer of horses, ran an elevator, dental nurse and worked in a Xmas card factory, and, as 'Miss Deep Freeze', demonstrated fridges. Later selected with 3 other girls, she toured N.Y., Georgia, Texas and California as a model for a washing machine company and following this she went with her mother and a friend to Los Angeles, enrolled at the Caroline Leonetti Modelling Agency and landed a walk-on part and her first movie appearance in THE FRENCH LINE (53). Choreographer Billy Daniel got her to see an agent, Louis Shurr, and she eventually landed a Columbia Pictures contract. Since then she has made such movies as PUSHOVER (54); PHFFFT (54); THE MAN WITH THE GOLDEN ARM (55); PICNIC (55); THE EDDY DUCHIN STORY (55); JEANNE EAGELS (57); PAL JOEY (57); VERTIGO (58); BELL, ROCK & CANDLE (58); MIDDLE OF THE NIGHT (59); PEPE (60); STRANGERS WHEN WE MEET (60); THE NOTORIOUS LANDLADY (62); BOYS' NIGHT OUT (62); OF HUMAN BONDAGE (64); KISS ME, STUPID (64); THE AMOROUS ADVENTURES OF MOLL FLANDERS (65); THE LEGEND OF LYLAH CLARE (68); THE GREAT BANK ROBBERY (69); TALES THAT WITNESS MADNESS (73); THE THIRD GIRL FROM THE LEFT (73, T.V. movie); SATAN'S TRIANGLE (75, T.V. movie); WHITE BUFFALO (77); JUST A GIGOLO (78) and THE MIRROR CRACK'D (81). Kim wed actor Richard Johnson (qv), her MOLL FLANDERS costar, on 15 March 1965, but they divorced 26 may 1966. She is now wed, since 1976, to veterinary surgeon Robert Mallory, and with her husband devotes most of her time to the care of animals.
KIM NOVAK ON CAMERA by Larry Kena; Tantivy Press: London, 1981.

SIMON OAKLAND

B. New York City, . . . Professional violinist; during WWII 3½ years in armed forces; studied with American Theatre Wing and made 1st Broadway appearance in 'Skipper Next to God' (1948); much other stage includes Moss Hart's 'Light Up The Sky' (1948), 'Caesar & Cleopatra' (1949), 'Harvey' (1950), 'Men in White' (1955), 'The Great Sebastians' (1956), 'Five Evenings' (1963) and 'Angela' (1969); Mr Oakland is a very familiar face in movies,' these include THE BROTHERS KARAMAZOV (58); I WANT TO LIVE (58); RISE & FALL OF LEGS DIAMOND (60); PSYCHO (60); WEST SIDE STORY (61); FOLLOW THAT DREAM (62); THE RAIDERS (63); WALL OF NOISE (63); THE SATAN BUG (65); SAND PEBBLES (67); BULLITT (68); THE CABLE CAR MURDER (71, T.V. movie); CHATO'S LAND (72); EMPEROR OF THE NORTH (73); T.V. series have been as Insp. Spooner in 'Toma' (1973/74); Tony Vincenzo in 'The Night Stalker' (1974/75) and Gen. Moore in 'Baa Baa Black Sheep' (1976-78); T.V. movie 78: AN EVENING IN BYZANTIUM; *died 5.9.83, near Palm Springs.*

HAZEL O'CONNOR

B. ———, 10.5.56, Coventry. Left school in 1971, studied art 1 year; street theatre, Paris; taught English and did dancing, hostessing and modelling in Japan, 9 months; in 1974 went to Beirut, then West Africa, retd. to U.K. via Sahara Desert; sang with group in Germany, wrote own material; 1978 contract with Albion records; played Kate in BREAKING GLASS (80) and wrote 13 songs — 'Variety Club of G.B. Award 1980, BA; T.V. ser. 1982: 'Jangles'.
HAZEL O'CONNOR — UNCOVERED PLUS by H. O'C.; Proteus: London, 1981 p/b.

JACK O'HALLORAN

B. ———, . . . Mr O'Halloran at one time ranked fifth in the boxing world, with 76 fights, including bouts with George Foreman and Ken Norton, before a rare pituitary disorder forced him to retire; he had also played professional football with Philadelphia Eagles; came to the screen in FAREWELL, MY LOVELY (74) and has been seen in KING KONG (76), MARCH OR DIE (77), THE BALTIMORE BULLET (80) and especially as 'Non' in the two SUPERMAN movies, in 1976 and 1981.

WARREN OATES

B. Depoy, Kentucky, 5.7.28. Ed. High School, Louisville, then served in the U.S. Marine Corps; entered Louisville Univ. and took active part in dramatics and then studied drama in New York; worked as hat-check at '21 Club' and tested gags for 'Beat the Clock' on T.V.; New York stage includes 'The Wisteria Tress' (1955); since 1958 Mr Oates has worked steadily in T.V. including occasionally in series 'Wanted: Dead or Alive' (1958-61) and as Wes Paineter in 'Stoney Burke' (1962/63), and in movies, starting as solid support, emerging in 70s as star, including UP PERISCOPE (58, uncredited); PRIVATE PROPERTY (60); GUNS IN THE AFTERNOON (62); THE ROUNDERS (64); MAJOR DUNDEE (64); THE WILD BUNCH (69); THERE WAS A CROOKED MAN (70); TOM SAWYER (73), as DILLINGER (73); THE WHITE DAWN (74); RACE WITH THE DEVIL (75); DRUM (76); TRUE GRIT (78, T.V. movie, as Cogburn); CLAYTON & CATHERINE (78); BRINK'S JOB (79); 1941 (79); THE BORDER (80); STRIPES (81) and Cyrus in EAST OF EDEN (81 T.V. Movie); film '82: SLEEPING DOGS. *Mr Oates died of heart attack, L.A., 5.4.82.*

IAN OGILVY

B. Woking, Surrey, 30.9.43. Ian wanted to be an actor from age of 10; ed: Eton; of Scottish descent father (dec.) former actor, Cambridge classic scholar, head of advertising agency, mother former actress Eileen Raymond (wed to John Mills (qv) in her teens); at 18 A.S.M. at Royal Court Theatre, then R.A.D.A. (while there formed group with Nicky Henson (qv)); rep.: Colchester Canterbury, Northampton; much T.V.; films REVENGE OF THE BLOOD BEAST (66); STRANGER IN THE HOUSE, THE SORCERERS, DAY THE FISH CAME OUT (all 67); WITCHFINDER GENERAL (68); WUTHERING HEIGHTS (70); WATERLOO (70); FENGRIFFIN (72); NO SEX, PLEASE WE'RE BRITISH (73); FROM BEYOND THE GRAVE (73); AND NOW THE SCREAMING STARTS (73); T.V. includes 'Upstairs, Downstairs', 'Candide', 'I, Claudius' and well-known as Simon Templar in 'Return of the Saint' (77/78) Richard in 'Tom, Dick & Harriett' (82/83); Md Diane (she has 1 daughter from previous marriage) 1 son Titus; recent stage: 'Stage Struck' (80) 'Design For Living' (82).

LAURENCE OLIVIER

One of the most distinguished actors of our time, Lord Olivier, a professional actor since 1925 (and in movies for over 50 years), has perhaps performed his best work on the stage, but still presented us with many outstanding movies and performances, in particular his Shakespearean classics. The son of the Rev. Gerard Kerr Olivier and his wife, Agnes, he was born in Dorking, Surrey, on 22 May 1907, educated at St. Edward's School, Oxford, and made his first stage appearance at Stratford-on-Avon in April, 1922, in a special boys' performance of 'Taming of the Shrew'. Deciding on a theatrical career, he studied with Elsie Fogarty and later from 1926-28 played with the Birmingham Rep. and eventually gained London success in such plays as 'Journey's End' and 'Beau Geste' and thus began his highly acclaimed international stage career. Laurence Olivier had come to the screen in 1930 in a 38-minute movie, TOO MANY CROOKS, with Dorothy Boyd. That year he had wed the actress, Jill Esmond, their son Simon being born in 1936. Alternating with his successful stage career, he continued to make movies such as WESTWARD PASSAGE (31); CONQUEST OF THE AIR (35); AS YOU LIKE IT (36); DIVORCE OF LADY X (38); WUTHERING HEIGHTS (39*); PRIDE AND PREJUDICE (40); REBECCA (40*); LADY HAMILTON (41, as Lord Nelson, opp. Vivien Leigh, to whom he was wed from 1940-61); THE DEMI-PARADISE (43); WWII: served in Fleet Air Arm; HENRY V (44*); HAMLET (48, Academy Award); THE BEGGAR'S OPERA (52); RICHARD III (56*); THE DEVIL'S DISCIPLE (59); SPARTACUS (60); THE ENTERTAINER (60); TERM OF TRIAL (62); OTHELLO (65*); SLEUTH (72*); MARATHON MAN (76*); JESUS OF NAZARETH (T.V., mini-ser.), THE BETSY, BOYS FROM BRAZIL (both 1977); A LITTLE ROMANCE, INCHON! (both 1979); THE JAZZ SINGER (80); JIGSAW MAN (83) and THE SAGA OF H.M.S. BOUNTY (84). His third marriage, to actress Joan Plowright (qv), has produced 3 children — son Richard (born 1963) and daughters Tamsin (1964) and Julie-Kate (1966). Numerous honours include a Knighthood (1947), a Peerage (1970), Special Oscars in 1946 (for HENRY V) and 1979, and in January, 1983, he received the C.B. DeMille Award 'for outstanding contributions in the entertainment field'. Recent T.V.: 'Brideshead Revisited' (82, T.V. mini-ser., Emmy Aw.); 'The Voyage Around My Father' (82) and acclaim as 'King Lear' (83). (*Denotes Oscar nom.).
THE OLIVIERS by Felix Barker; Hamish Hamilton: London, 1953.
LAURENCE OLIVIER by John Cottrell; Weidenfeld & Nicolson: London, 1976.
LAURENCE OLIVIER: THEATRE AND CINEMA by Robert L. Daniels; Tantivy: London, 1981.
OLIVIER: THE LIFE OF LAURENCE OLIVIER by Thomas Kiernan; Sidgwick & Jackson: London, 1981.
CONFESSIONS OF AN ACTOR (autobio.); Weidenfeld & Nicolson: London, 1982.

JAMES OLSON

B. Evanston, Illinois, 8.10.30. Aged 10 portrayed Hans Brinker in 'The Silver Skates' at Evanston's Children's Theatre; school plays, awarded scholarship to Northwestern Univ., appeared in many productions; 1952-54: U.S. Army Military Police, Albuquerque; became well-known New York stage actor, studied with Actors' Studio; James is a Shakespearean actor and has also played on London stage; movies: THE SHARKFIGHTERS (56); THE STRANGE ONE (57); RACHEL, RACHEL (69); THE ANDROMEDA STRAIN (70); MOON ZERO TWO (70); WILD ROVERS (71); PAPER MAN (71, T.V. movie); INCIDENT ON A DARK STREET (71, T.V. movie); MANHUNTER (74, T.V. movie); A TREE GROWS IN BROOKLYN (74, T.V. movie); THE SEX SYMBOL (74, T.V. movie); THE FAMILY NOBODY WANTED (75, T.V. movie); LAW & ORDER (76, T.V. movie); THE SPELL (77, T.V. movie); THE THREE SISTERS (77); CAVE-IN! (79); MOVIOLA: GARBO & GILBERT (80, T.V. movie); RAGTIME (81); AMITYVILLE II: THE POSSESSION (82).

KATE O'MARA

B. Leicester 10.8.39. Md. actress Hazel Bainbridge; ed. privately; teacher (speech therapist at Sussex girls' school), studied for stage at Aida Foster School; stage debut 1963 at Newcastle and has performed many roles in the theatre including Welsh Theatre Co., Leatherhead, West End, Bristol, Guildford productions; md. director/actor Jeremy Young (div. 27.10.76), 1 son Dickon; Kate began in movies 1955 as child actress, films include THE LIMBO LINE, CORRUPTION, GREAT CATHERINE (all 68); THE DESPERADOS (69); THE VAMPIRE LOVERS (70); THE HORROR OF FRANKENSTEIN (70); THE TAMARIND SEED (74); FEELINGS (77); Miss O'Mara is particularly well-known on T.V. and has appeared in scores of series, including 'Triangle' (1981) and as Jane Maxwell in 'The Brothers'; T.V. movie 1978 as Salome in THE NATIVITY; recent stage: 'Much Ado About Nothing' (81), 'Taming of the Shrew' (82); T.V. ser. 'Triangle' (82).

RYAN O'NEAL

Ryan O'Neal, due to his great success in the movie LOVE STORY in 1970, has emerged as one of the most popular of the younger American male stars, following great success on T.V. in the 1960s. He is the son of Charles O'Neill, a writer, and his wife, Patricia, a former actress, and was born in Los Angeles on 20 April 1941. As a youngster he toured the world with his parents and when in Munich, West Germany, he attended the U.S. Army School. A series for T.V. was due to be filmed in the area and young Ryan got an interview with the producer (although previously turned down) and was employed on the show, 'Tales of the Vikings', as stuntman and played small roles. Back in the States he was a regular in the series 'Empire' as Tal Garrett in 1962/63, which starred Richard Egan and he guested on such shows as 'The Untouchables' and 'My Three Sons'. His marriage in 1963, to actress Joanna Moore, produced two daughters, Tatum (qv), in 1963, and Griffin, in 1964, the latter having appeared in the movies NICKLEODEON (76) and THE ESCAPE ARTIST (80). 1964 brought the turning point in O'Neal's career when he was cast as Rodney Harrington in the phenomenally successful T.V. series, 'Peyton Place' which ran from 1964-69, the actor appearing in 501 episodes. He then switched to the big screen and made such movies as THE BIG BOUNCE (69); LOVE STORY (70, Oscar nom., B.A.); GAMES (70); THE WILD ROVERS (71); LOVE HATE, LOVE (71, T.V. movie); WHAT'S UP, DOC? (72); PAPER MOON (73); THE THIEF WHO CAME TO DINNER (73); BARRY LYNDON (75); NICKLEODEON (76) and as Gen. Gavin in A BRIDGE TOO FAR (76). His first marriage ended in 1966 and the following year wed Leigh Taylor-Young, who appeared in 'Peyton Place'. They had a son, Patrick, in 1967, but divorced in 1969. In 1979 Ryan produced a documentary, 'The Contender', about boxer Hedgemon Lewis. As an actor his most recent movies are THE DRIVER (77); OLIVER'S STORY (78); THE MAIN EVENT (79); GREEN ICE (80); SO FINE (81); PARTNERS (82) and IRRECONCILABLE DIFFERENCES (83).

PATRICK O'NEAL

B. Ocala, Florida, . . 27. Gregory Peck's stand-in when filming THE YEARLING (46) in Florida; ed. Univ. of Florida; played with Neighbourhood Playhouse and in stock; T.V. from 1951: Broadway 1953: 'Oh Men! Oh Women!'; came to screen 1954 in THE MAD MAGICIAN and BLACK SHIELD OF FALWORTH, but retd. to T.V.: Karl Manning in 'Portia Faces Life' (1954/55), Dick Starrett in 'Dick and The Duchess' (1957/58), Dr Coffe in 'Diagnosis: Unknown' (60) and others; stage 1961: 'Night of the Iguana'; over 30 movies/T.V. movies, including THE CARDINAL (63); KING RAT (65); ALVAREZ KELLY (66); CASTLE KEEP (69); WAY WE WERE (73); DEATH HOUSE (81).

TATUM O'NEAL

B. Los Angeles 5.11.63. Parents: Ryan O'Neal (qv) and Joanna Moore, actress (div. when Tatum was 3, brought up mainly by father); name 'Tatum' comes from a southern grandmother on her mother's side of the family; father encouraged her to play Addie Pray in movie PAPER MOON, role winning her Oscar 1973 as Best Supporting Actress, youngest artiste ever to win this award; other motion-pictures are BAD NEWS BEARS (76); NICKLEODEON (76); INTERNATIONAL VELVET (77); CIRCLE OF TWO (79); LITTLE DARLINGS (79); CAPTURED (81); PRISONERS (82).

JENNIFER O'NEILL

. Rio de Janeiro 20.2.48. The daughter of a bank president, Oscar O'Neill, Jennifer became a model 'in order to buy a horse'; by the age of sixteen she had appeared on the cover of such magazines as 'Vogue' and 'Seventeen' and soon became one of the exclusive Top 5 models in U.S.; md. 1. Deed Rossiter, 1966, 1 daughter Aimee (born 1967), div. 1972; 2. Joseph Koster, 1973-74; 3. Nick DeNoia, theatre director, 1975-6; appd. at the Neighbourhood Playhouse and broke into movies: RIO LOBO (70); SUMMER OF '42 (71); SUCH GOOD FRIENDS (71); THE CAREY TREATMENT (72); GLASS HOUSES (72); LADY ICE (73); THE REINCARNATION OF PETER PROUD (75); WHIFFS (75); CARAVANS (77); STEEL (78); LOVE'S SAVAGE FURY (79, T.V. movie); CLOUD DANCER (79); A FORCE OF ONE (79); SCANNERS (79); md. 4. Jeff Barry, songwriter, 1978.

RICHARD O'SULLIVAN

B. Chiswick, W. London, 7.5.44. Educated at the Corona Stage School, Richard made his film debut as a child actor in THE STRANGER'S HAND (54) opposite Trevor Howard (qv) and Richard Basehart (qv); several films for the Children's Film Foundation throughout the 1950s; other movies include DANGEROUS EXILE (57); A STORY OF DAVID (60); THE YOUNG ONES (61); MIDDLE OF NOWHERE (61); SUMMER HOLIDAY (63); CLEOPATRA (63); WONDERFUL LIFE (64); THE HAUNTED HOUSE OF HORROR (70); he has appeared on stage in such productions as 'The Government Inspector', 'Boeing-Boeing' and the Palladium pantomime 'Cinderella'; he is equally well-known on T.V. for such series as 'Doctor in Charge', 'Father, Dear Father' (and 1973 film), 'Man About The House' (and 1975 film), 'Robin's Nest' and the title role in 'Dick Turpin'; he is divorced from model Diana Terry.

PETER O'TOOLE

A larger-than-life character, Peter O'Toole is continually in demand for movies with many fine performances to his credit, recently receiving much acclaim for his work as the director in STUNTMAN. He has remained a top star for twenty years, following much good work in the theatre. He was born Seamus Peter O'Toole in Connemara, Co. Galway, Ireland, on 2 August 1932, the son of Patrick Joseph O'Toole, a bookmaker, and his wife, Constance. He received his education in Ireland, Gainsborough and Leeds, Yorkshire, where he was raised. Young Peter's ambition, upon leaving school, was to become a journalist and he spent five years in the photographic department of the 'Yorkshire Evening News' and dabbled in amateur theatricals, making his first stage appearance at the Civic Theatre, Leeds, in 1949. Following National Service in the Royal Navy, as a seaman and decoder on a submarine, he won a scholarship to study at R.A.D.A. and in September 1955 he joined the Bristol Old Vic company, making his début as a cabman in 'The Matchmaker'. He spent over three years at Bristol, playing 73 roles, including the Duke of Cornwall in 'King Lear', Bullock in 'The Recruiting Officer', Lodovico in 'Othello', Alfred Doolittle in 'Pygmalion', Jimmy Porter in 'Look Back In Anger', John Tanner in 'Man and Superman' and the title role in 'Hamlet'. With the same company he had made his London stage début in 'Major Barbara' as Peter Shirley, at the Old Vic in July 1956. While touring in 1958 in the play 'The Holiday' he met the actress Sian Phillips (qv) and the couple wed in Dublin in December 1959, their daughters, Kate and Pat, being born in 1960 and 1963. O'Toole had come to the screen in 1959 in KIDNAPPED and that year, with producer Jules Buck, he formed Keep Films, the partnership having produced some of the actor's best films. The turning point in his career came when, after winning a Best Actor of the Year Award for his performance in 'The Long and the Short and the Tall', as Private Bamforth, on the London stage, he joined the Shakespeare Memorial Theatre Company at Stratford-on-Avon for its 1960 season. He played such roles as Petruchio in 'The Taming of the Shrew' and Shylock in 'The Merchant of Venice', the latter role he also essayed in New York. Following movies such as THE DAY THEY ROBBED THE BANK OF ENGLAND and SAVAGE INNOCENTS (both 1960), O'Toole won the much-coveted role of T.E. Lawrence in David Lean's spectacular LAWRENCE OF ARABIA, and the picture won an Oscar for best film of 1962, the actor receiving an actor nomination. He played 'Hamlet' in the National Theatre Company's inaugural production in October 1963 at the Old Vic and the following year, playing opposite Richard Burton in the film version of BECKET, both actors received Oscar nominations. Alternating his already successful stage career, he made such pictures as LORD JIM (65); WHAT'S NEW, PUSSYCAT? (65); HOW TO STEAL A MILLION (66); THE BIBLE (66); NIGHT OF THE GENERALS (67); GREAT CATHERINE (68); THE LION IN WINTER (68, Oscar nom.); GOODBYE, MR CHIPS (69, Oscar nom.); COUNTRY DANCE (70); MURPHY'S WAR (70); UNDER MILK WOOD (70); THE RULING CLASS (72, Oscar nom.); THE MAN OF LA MANCHA (72); ROSEBUD (75); MAN FRIDAY (75); FOXTROT (75); ROGUE MALE (76, T.V. movie, G.B.). In 1976 he appeared at the Dublin Festival, playing three parts in 'Dead-Eyed Dicks'. On 14 August 1979 his marriage to Sian Phillips ended in divorce. In 1980 a production of 'Macbeth', in which he took the title role, was staged at the Old Vic and received much publicity. In more recent years his movies have included Gore Vidal's CALIGULA (77); COUP D'ETAT (77); ZULU DAWN (78); STRUMPET CITY (78); MASADA (79, T.V. mini-ser.); THE STUNTMAN (80, Oscar nom., BA; Am. Nat. Soc. of Film Critics Aw., BA); SVENGALI (82, T.V. movie); MY FAVOURITE YEAR (82, Oscar nom., BA) and SUPERGIRL (84). 'Man & Superman' (82) proved to be a successful return to the London stage for the actor.
PETER O'TOOLE by Michael Freedland; W.H. Allen: London, 1983.
PETER O'TOOLE by Nicholas Wapshott; New English Library: London, 1983.

AL PACINO

With comparatively few movies to his credit, Al Pacino has emerged as an important acting talent in the States with suc[h] movies as SERPICO, BOBBY DEERFIELD and AND JUSTICE FOR ALL, recognised on several occasions by th[e] Academy. Born of a Sicilian family in Manhattan on 25 April 1940, he was raised in the Bronx by his mother. H[e] showed talent for acting at school and later attended the High School of Performing Arts taking a variety of jobs t[o] bolster the family income, including theatre usher, building superintendent, and messenger. Studying acting wit[h] Charlie Laughton, he made his professional stage début in 'The Seagull' and after further study with Herbert Berghof an[d] the Actor's Studio, with Lee Strasberg, he played in hundreds of stage productions, including those staged by the Theatr[e] Co. of Boston. In New York Mr Pacino won an 'Obie' award for his role in 'The Indian Wants the Bronx' (1968) an[d] 'Tony' awards for 'Does a Tiger wear a Necktie? (1969) and 'The Basic Training of Pablo Hummel' (1972). He ha[d] come to the screen in a 1969 movie, ME NATALIE, and after PANIC IN NEEDLE PARK (71) he won a Bes[t] Supporting Actor nomination from the Academy for his role in THE GODFATHER (72). After playing 'Richard II[I]' in Boston, he returned to the screen in SCARECROW (73), and SERPICO (73) won him a further Oscar nominatio[n]. He won the award in 1974 as Best Supporting Actor for his role in THE GODFATHER, PART II, and since then h[e] has played in DOG DAY AFTERNOON (75, Oscar nom., B.A.); BOBBY DEERFIELD (77); AND JUSTIC[E] FOR ALL (79, Oscar nom., B.A.); CRUISING (79) and AUTHOR! AUTHOR! (82).

NICOLA PAGETT

B. Cairo, Egypt, 15.6.45. Father oil company executive; ed. Japan and 5 years in Sussex boarding schools; R.A.D.A., stage debut: Worthing 1964; became distinguished stage actress, playing with Old Vic, in West End, etc.; md. actor/writer Graham Swannell 1977, 1 daughter Eve (born April 1979); much T.V. includes 'Anna Karenina' (1977); movies: VIKING QUEEN (67) ANNE OF THE 1000 DAYS (69); THERE'S A GIRL IN MY SOUP (70); OPERATION DAYBREAK (74); OLIVER'S STORY (78); PRIVATES ON PARADE (83); recent T.V.: 'Redundant! or the Wife's Revenge' (83).

MICHAEL PALIN

B. Sheffield, 5.5.43. Ed. Shrewsbury School and Brazenose Coll., Oxford; well-known on T.V. and the movies for his 'Monty Python' series; as writer/actor worked on 'Do Not Adjust Your Set' (1967-69), 'Complete and Utter History of Britain' (1969) and more recently 'Monty Python's Flying Circus' and 'Ripping Yarns'; md. Helen, 1 daughter Rachel, 2 sons Thomas, William; films: AND NOW FOR SOMETHING COMPLETELY DIFFERENT (71), MONTY PYTHON AND THE HOLY GRAIL (74), THE LIFE OF BRIAN (79), MONTY PYTHON'S MEANING OF LIFE (82), THE MISSIONARY (83).

LILLI PALMER

B. Posen, Austria (Germany?), 24.5.14. Father surgeon; real name Lillychen Peiser; ed. High School, Berlin (spent holidays in Kent, learning English); mother former actress; at 10 wanted to be actress, later studied at Ilka Gruning School, Berlin; stage from 1932: Darmstadt, Frankfurt; 1933: cabaret, act with sister in Paris; came to G.B. 1934. appd. in several films including CRIME UNLIMITED (34); FIRST OFFENCE (35) and W. End stage; md: Rex Harrison (qv) 1943, 1 son Carey (1944), div. 1958; 2. Carlos Thompson, actor/author 1958; international movies include THUNDER ROCK (42); THE RAKE'S PROGRESS (45); MY GIRL TISA (47); BODY & SOUL (48); THE FOUR-POSTER (52); CONSPIRACY OF HEARTS (60); NIGHT HAIR CHILD (71); BOYS FROM BRAZIL (78); SOCIETY LIMITED (82); T.V. inclu. 'Lilli Palmer Show' (53/54), 'Imaginary Friends' (83); also novelist. *CHANGE LOBSTERS & DANCE* (autobio.); W.H. Allen: London, 1976.

BARBARA PARKINS

B. Vancouver, Canada, 22.5.45. Went to Hollywood with mother to attend convention of dancing teachers when 16, took dancing jobs there and studied drama at Desilu Workshop; small roles in films (10,000 EYES (61)) and T.V. ('Wagon Train' etc.), becoming household name in 425 episodes of 'Peyton Place' (1964-69) as Betty Anderson; since then many films and T.V. movies, including VALLEY OF THE DOLLS (68); THE KREMLIN LETTER (69); MEPHISTO WALTZ (70); PUPPET ON A CHAIN (71); THE HOUSE UNDER THE TREES (73); ASYLUM (73); SNATCHED (73, T.V. movie); CHRISTINA (74); CAPTAINS & KINGS (76, T.V. movie); SHOUT AT THE DEVIL (76); TESTIMONY OF 2 MEN (77, T.V. movie); THE CRITICAL LIST (78, T.V. movie); BEAR ISLAND (79); BREAKFAST IN PARIS (81), 'Manions of America' (1981, mini-series).

DOLLY PARTON

B. Sevier, Tennessee, 19.1.46. 1 of 12 children; father a farmer/construction worker; ed. Mountain View, Caton's Chapel School, Sevier Co. H.S.; as child sang/wrote songs; at 10 appeared on radio; 1st record: 'Puppy Love', aged 13; big break 1967 on 'Porter Wagoner T.C. & Road Show'; T.V. show 1976 'Dolly'; Dolly became biggest female artist on U.S. Country Circuit; movies: NINE TO FIVE (80); THE BEST LITTLE WHORE-HOUSE IN TEXAS (82). *DOLLY* by Alanna Nash; p/b: Panther/Granada: London, 1979.

JACK PALANCE

B. Lattimer, Pennsylvania 18.2.20(?). Born into coal mining family; real name Walter Jac[k] Palahnuik; attended Univ. of N. Carolina, be[-] coming star athlete and boxer; worked as coa[l] miner, cook, radio repairman, salesman, lifeguar[d] and pro. boxer, then called up for WWII servic[e] as bomber pilot — plane shot down in flames an[d] Palance survived, needed extensive plastic surger[y] to burns on face; did not deter him from bein[g] actor — at Stanford Univ. Drama Club played i[n] 'The Seagull' (1948); in New York roles in 'Th[e] Big Two' (1947), 'A Temporary Island' (1948[)] 'The Silver Tassle' (1949), turning point cam[e] when he took over lead in 'A Streetcar Name[d] Desire', after understudying Anthony Quinn an[d] Marlon Brando role; md. actress Virginia Bake[r] actress 1949, 2 daughters: Holly (1950), Brook[e] (1951); 1 son: Cody (1955), div.; became forcefu[l] movie actor, many films include PANIC IN TH[E] STREETS (50); HALLS OF MONTEZUM[A] (50); SUDDEN FEAR (52, Oscar nom, BSA[)] SHANE (52, Oscar nom., BSA); ARROWHEA[D] (53); SIGN OF THE PAGAN (54); THE BI[G] KNIFE (55); ATTACK! (56); THE MAN IN[-] SIDE (58); 10 SECONDS TO HELL (59[)] BARABBAS (62); THE MONGOLS (62, an[d] other European 'epics'); ONCE A THIEF (65[)] THE PROFESSIONALS (66); CHE (69, a[s] Fidel Castro); THE HORSEMAN (72); OKLA[-] HOMA CRUDE (73); DRACULA (73, T.V[.] movie); SHAPE OF THINGS TO COME (78[)] HAWK THE SLAYER (80); ANGEL[S] BRIGADE (81); ALONE IN THE DAR[K] (82); PORTRAIT OF A HIT MAN (83); T.V[.] series: Johnny Slate in 'The Greatest Show o[n] Earth' (64/65) and Lt. Alex Bronkov in 'Bronk['] (75/76).

IRENE PAPAS

B. Nr. Corinth, Greece, 9.3.26. Real name Irene Lelekos; attended drama school from age 12; at 16 sang and danced in variety shows; grad. from Royal Drama School, Athens, played on Greek stage ('The Idiot', 'Journey's End', 'Merchant of Venice', etc.); md: Alkis Papas (1947-51); 2. Jose Kohn (1957, annulled); came to screen in Greek films (LOST ANGELS (51), DEAD CITY, etc.); then contract to Lux Films, Italy and THEODORA (54); WHIRLPOOL (54); UN-FAITHFUL WOMEN (54); ATTILA (54); eventually active internationally: POWER AND THE PRIZE (55); TRIBUTE TO A BADMAN (56); GUNS OF NAVARONE (61); ELECTRA (62); BEYOND THE MOUNTAINS (66); THE BROTHERHOOD (68); Z (68); A DREAM OF KINGS (69); ANNE OF THE 1000 DAYS (70, as Queen Katherine); THE TROJAN WOMEN (71); MOSES (75); IPHIGENIA (76); THE MESSAGE (77); BLOODLINE (79); LION OF THE DESERT (81); IN THE SHADOW OF THE GREAT OAK TREE (mini-ser., 1983).

MICHAEL PARKS

B. Corona, California, . . 38. Ed. Sacramento High School; through talent scout landed many T.V. roles, coming to the screen in 1964 in WILD SEED; 1969/70 T.V. series: Jim Bronson in 'Then Came Bronson'; many movies including BUS RILEY'S BACK IN TOWN (65); Adam in THE BIBLE (65); THE IDOL (66); THE HAPPENING (67); STRANGER ON THE RUN (67, T.V. movie); THE YOUNG LAW-YERS (69, T.V. movie); CAN ELLEN BE SAVED? (74, T.V. movie); THE STORY OF PRETTY BOY FLOYD (74, T.V. movie); THE LAST HARD MEN (76); MURDER AT THE WORLD SERIES (77, T.V. movie); SIDE-WINDER ONE (77); PRIVATE FILES OF J. EDGAR HOOVER (78, as Robert F. Kennedy); NIGHT CRIES (78, T.V. movie); BREAK-THROUGH (78); THE EVICTORS (79); NORTH SEA HIJACK (79); FAST FRIENDS (79, T.V. movie); HARD COUNTRY (80); REWARD (T.V. movie, 1980).

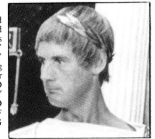

GREGORY PECK

From his very first movie in 1943, likeable and reliable Gregory Peck has remained a top star, selecting roles in some he movies, climaxed by winning an Academy award in 1962. The son of Gregory Peck Snr., a druggist, and his wife, ernice, he was born at La Jolla, California on 5 April 1916. He was educated at San Diego College and the University California, studying medicine with the intention of becoming a doctor, but after taking part in theatrical productions ose a stage career. His first taste of show-biz was as a barker at the World's Fair in 1939. Following a job as a radio ity guide, young Peck won a 2 year scholarship to the Playhouse School of Dramatics and worked in stock at the Barter heatre, Virginia. He then played in such productions as 'The Doctor's Dilemma' (with Katherine Cornell, 1941) and New York in 'The Morning Star' (1942), 'The Willow and I' (1942) and 'Sons and Soldiers (1943). The actor was able to take part in active war service owing to a spinal injury from college — but there was a shortage of leading men r movies, and he now alternated roles in major productions with top studios. His first picture was DAYS OF GLORY, 1943. Subsequently he has played in over 50 top pictures and these have included splendid work in THE KEYS OF HE KINGDOM (44*); THE VALLEY OF DECISION (44); SPELLBOUND (45*); THE YEARLING (46*); UEL IN THE SUN (46); GENTLEMAN'S AGREEMENT (47*); YELLOW SKY (48); 12 O'CLOCK HIGH 9*); THE GUNFIGHTER (50); DAVID AND BATHSHEBA (51); as CAPT. HORATIO HORNBLOWER 1); THE SNOWS OF KILIMANJARO (52); ROMAN HOLIDAY (53); THE MILLION POUND NOTE (54); HE MAN IN THE GREY FLANNEL SUIT (56); MOBY DICK (56, as Ahab); THE BIG COUNTRY (58); ORK CHOP HILL (59); ON THE BEACH (59); THE GUNS OF NAVARONE (61); CAPE FEAR (61); EHOLD A PALE HORSE (64); MIRAGE (65); ARABESQUE (66); THE STALKING MOON (68); AROONED (69); I WALK THE LINE (70); SHOOTOUT (71); BILLY TWO HATS (73); THE OMEN (76); MacARTHUR (77); THE BOYS FROM BRAZIL (77) and THE SEA WOLVES (79). Mr Peck's first wife was reta Rice Konen, a hairdresser, whom he wed in 1942. Their sons Stephen, Jonathan and Carey were born in 1944, 6 and '49 respectively. Jonathan died tragically in 1975. This marriage ended in 1954 and the following year he wed rmer 'France-Soir' reporter Veronique Passani. The couple have a son, Anthony, born in 1956 and a daughter, ecelia, in 1958. In 1947 and 1952 he was voted one of the Ten best money-making stars by the Motion-Picture erald, and for his performance as Atticus Finch, a small-town Alabama lawyer in the movie TO KILL A OCKINGBIRD, he received an Academy Award as Best Actor of 1962. He co-produced THE BIG COUNTRY 8) and was solely responsible for production of THE TRIAL OF THE CATSONVILLE NINE and THE DOVE 4). Mr Peck has more recently been involved as an actor on T.V. in 'Dodsworth' (1981) and 'The Blue and The Gray', mini-series (82), as Abraham Lincoln, and 'The Scarlet & the Black' (83, T.V. movie). (*Denotes Oscar nom.). *REGORY PECK—A BIOGRAPHY* by Michael Freedland; W.H. Allen: London, 1980; p/b; Coronet: 1981.

USAN PENHALIGON

St. Ives, Cornwall, . . 50. Father a Shell ecutive; trained for stage in Sussex and rep. cludes Worthing, appearing as Juliet in 'Romeo d Juliet' (1971); md. 1. actor Nicholas Loukes ec.); she has played on T.V. on many occasions, cluding 'Play For Today', 'Country Matters' d esp. 'Bouquet of Barbed Wire' (1975); her ms have included UNDER MILK WOOD 1); NO SEX, PLEASE, WE'RE BRITISH 3); THE LAND THAT TIME FORGOT 5); NASTY HABITS (76); LEOPARD IN HE SNOW (76); SOLDIER OF ORANGE 7); THE UNCANNY (77); PATRICK (78); d. 2. documentary director David Munro, 1978, son Truan; other T.V.: 'Dracula' (1977), 'Fear-ss Frank' (1978), 'The Racing Game' (79), ries 1981: 'A Fine Romance'; 'Tales of the nexpected' (82), 'Heather Ann' (83).

ANTHONY PERKINS

B. New York City 14.4.32. Father Osgood Perkins, distinguished Broadway actor. Anthony attended The Garden School, New York, Browne and Nichols School, Cambridge, Rollins Coll., Florida and studied for 2 years at Columbia Univ., New York. While still at college, and during a vacation, he hitchhiked to Hollywood and managed to get a screen-test with M-G-M and came to the screen in 1953 in THE ACTRESS. He returned to his studies, did summer stock and replaced John Kerr on Broadway as Tom Lee in 'Tea and Sympathy' in June 1954 for over a year. T.V. work followed, including 'The World Out There' ('Windows'—anthology) and his next film role, as the son in FRIENDLY PERSUASION, gained him a Supporting Actor Oscar nom., in 1956. He returned to the theatre for a long run in 'Look Homeward, Angel' from November 1957. Since then his movies have included THE LONELY MAN, FEAR STRIKES OUT, THE TIN STAR (all 57); THIS ANGRY AGE, THE MATCH-MAKER, GREEN MANSIONS (all 58); ON THE BEACH (59); TALL STORY (60); PSY-CHO (60); GOODBYE AGAIN (61); PHAEDRA (62); THE TRIAL (62); TWO ARE GUILTY, THE FOOL KILLER (65); IS PARIS BURNING? (66); THE CHAMPAGNE MURDERS (68); PRETTY POISON (68); WUSA (70); HOW AWFUL ABOUT ALLAN (70, T.V. movie); CATCH 22 (70); 10 DAYS WONDER (71); PLAY IT AS IT LAYS (72); JUDGE ROY BEAN (72); MURDER ON THE ORIENT EXPRESS (74); MAHOGANY (75); LES MISERABLES (78); THE BLACK HOLE (79); REMEMBER MY NAME (79); WINTER KILLS (79); NORTH SEA HIJACK (79). In the late 1950s Mr Perkins made several records as a vocalist and 'A Fool in Love' made the charts. In 1973 he wed Barenthia Berenson and their sons, Osgood and Elvis, were born in 1974 and 1976 respectively. In more recent years the actor has returned to the stage and also directed with distinction. He co-wrote screenplay on LAST OF SHEILA (73). Acting recently in TWICE A WOMAN (80); PSYCHO II (83); FOR THE TERM OF HIS NATURAL LIFE (mini-ser., 1983).

GEORGE PEPPARD

B. Detroit, Michigan, 1.10.33. The son of Geo. Peppard Snr., a contractor, and his wife — opera-singer Vernelle Rohrer, Peppard Jr. received his education at Dearborn High School where he studied engineering. This was followed by 19 months in the U.S. Marine Corps, joining when he was 17. He then returned to his studies, attending Purdue University, gaining a B.A. Degree in Fine Arts. After several jobs, including building contractor, fencing instructor, bank teller, taxi driver and motor cycle mechanic, he finally chose an acting career and joined the Pittsburgh Playhouse in 1949, also working part-time as a disc-jockey. He wed Helen Davies in 1954, son Bradford and daughter Julie being born in 1955 and 1956 respectively. The actor played in New York in such works as 'The Beautiful Changes', 'Girls of Summer' (both 1956), came to the screen in 1957 in THE STRANGE ONE and played with success back on Broadway in 'The Pleasure of His Company' a year later. Of over 36 movies his work has included HOME FROM THE HILL (60); BREAKFAST AT TIFFANY'S (61); HOW THE WEST WAS WON (62); THE VICTORS (63); THE CARPETBAGGERS (64); THE THIRD DAY (65); THE BLUE MAX (65); ROUGH NIGHT IN JERICHO (66); TOBRUK! (67); NEW FACE IN HELL (68); HOUSE OF CARDS (68); CANNON FOR CORDOBA (70); THE BRAVOS (72, T.V. movie); NEWMAN'S LAW (74, T.V. movie); ONE OF OUR OWN (75, T.V. movie); SURVIVAL RUN (76); THE LONG ESCAPE (77); DAMNATION ALLEY (77); CRISIS IN MID-AIR (78, T.V. movie); FROM HELL TO VICTORY (78); FIVE DAYS FROM HOME (78); YOUR TICKET IS NO LONGER VALID (79); BATTLE BEYOND THE STARS (80). Mr Peppard divorced his first wife in 1965 and the following year, on April 18, wed actress Elizabeth Ashley (qv), their son Christopher being born in 1968. T.V. work includes the series 'Banacec' (1972-74) and 'Doctors' Hospital', as Dr Jake Goodwin (1975/76). On 30 January 1975 he married Sheri Boucher; RACE FOR THE YANKEE ZEPHYR (82); TARGET EAGLE (82).

VALERIE PERRINE

B. Galveston, Texas, 3.9.44; Father U.S. Army Lieu.-Col., mother former dancer in Geo. White Scandals; spent her early years travelling world with her parents, first school a convent in Yokohama; studied ballet, tap, acrobatic and graduated from High School in Scotsdale, Arizona; for a while lead a 'hippie' existance in Paris, later performed as a show-girl in 'Lido de Paris' in Las Vegas and invited by director Geo. Roy Hill to play in movie SLAUGHTERHOUSE FIVE (72); has been seen in THE COUPLE TAKES A WIFE (72, T.V. movie); THE LAST AMERICAN HERO (73); W.C. FIELDS AND ME (75); LENNY (74, New York Film Critics' Award; Oscar nom.); MR BILLION (77); Eve in SUPERMAN (77); ZIEGFELD: THE MAN AND HIS WOMEN (78, T.V. movie); THE MAGICIAN OF LUBLIN (78); ELECTRIC HORSEMAN (79); AGENCY (79); CAN'T STOP THE MUSIC (79); THE BORDER (80). SUPERMAN II (81).

JOANNA PETTET – see page 125   BERNADETTE PETERS – see page 125

MICHELLE PHILLIPS

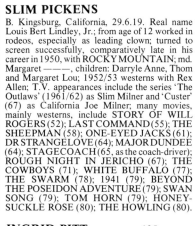

B. Long Beach, N. Jersey, 4.6.44. Real name Holly Michelle Gillian; Michelle lived in L.A. until she was 5, when her mother died; she then moved to Mexico with her father and sister; at 17 she was a very successful model and then joined group 'New Journeymen', touring college and nightclub circuit; in 1960s also member of group 'Mamas & Papas'; md. 1. folk-singer John Phillips, 1 daughter Chynna (div. 1970); 2. actor/director Dennis Hopper ('md. for 8 days only'); movies include THE LAST MOVIE (71); DILLINGER (73); DEATH SQUAD (74, T.V. movie); CALIFORNIA KID (74, T.V. movie); VALENTINO (76); ASPEN (77, mini-series); THE USER (78, T.V. movie); SIDNEY SHELDON'S BLOODLINE (79); THE MAN WITH BOGART'S FACE (79); SAVAGE HARVEST (81); MOONLIGHT (T.V. movie, 1982); Md 3. B'casting exec. Bob Burch, 1978 (div. 1980).

MARIE-FRANCE PISIER
– see page 125

SLIM PICKENS

B. Kingsburg, California, 29.6.19. Real name Louis Bert Lindley, Jr.; from age of 12 worked in rodeos, especially as leading clown; turned to screen successfully, comparatively late in his career in 1950, with ROCKY MOUNTAIN; md. Margaret ———, children: Darryle Anne, Thom and Margaret Lou; 1952/53 westerns with Rex Allen; T.V. appearances include the series 'The Outlaws' (1961/62) as Slim Milner and 'Custer' (67) as California Joe Milner; many movies, mainly westerns, include STORY OF WILL ROGERS (52); LAST COMMAND (55); THE SHEEPMAN (58); ONE-EYED JACKS (61); DR STRANGELOVE (64); MAJOR DUNDEE (64); STAGECOACH (65, as the coach-driver); ROUGH NIGHT IN JERICHO (67); THE COWBOYS (71); WHITE BUFFALO (77); THE SWARM (78); 1941 (79); BEYOND THE POSEIDON ADVENTURE (79); SWAN SONG (79); TOM HORN (79); HONEYSUCKLE ROSE (80); THE HOWLING (80).

INGRID PITT – see page 125

DONALD PLEASENCE

B. Worksop, Notts., 5.10.21. Father a Lincolnshire stationmaster; at 7 Donald was winning medals for recitations; ed. Ecclesfield Grammar School; joined Jersey Rep. 1939, as actor/A.S.M., début in 'Wuthering Heights', London début 1942 in 'Twelfth Night'; WWII: registered as a conscientious objector and worked as lumberjack in Lake District, but got disillusioned and joined R.A.F. He flew 60 missions, was shot down over France and spent 1944-46 in P.O.W. camp; retd. to the stage and became one of Britain's most distinguished theatre/movie/T.V. players, often in eccentric roles; stage triumphs: as the foul tramp, Davies, in 'The Caretaker' (1960/61), 'Poor Bitos' (1964) and 'The Man in the Glass Booth' (1967/68—'Variety Award—Actor of the Year' 1968), (these plays London and New York); md. 1. actress Miriam Raymond, 2 daughters Angela, Jean (div.); 2. actress/singer Josephine Crombie, 2 daughters Lucy, Polly; Mr Pleasance came to the screen in 1954 in THE BEACHCOMBER and has since made over 50 films, these include MANUELA (57); FLESH & THE FIELDS (59, as body-snatcher Wm. Hare); STORY OF DAVID (62); as DR CRIPPEN (63); THE CARETAKER (63); GREAT ESCAPE (63); FANTASTIC VOYAGE (65); CUL-DE-SAC (65); OUTBACK (71); BLACK WINDMILL (74); COUP D'ETAT (77); DRACULA (79); ESCAPE FROM NEW YORK (80); writes children's books about 'Scouse the Mouse'; md. 3. Israeli bass-guitarist of 'The Mother Truckers', Meira Shore, 1 daughter Miranda; West End stage 1980: 'Reflections'; recent movies: HALLOWEEN II (81); WITNESS FOR THE PROSECUTION (T.V. movie), RACE FOR THE YANKEE ZEPHYR, ALONE IN THE DARK (all 1982).

JOAN PLOWRIGHT

B. Brigg, Lancs., 28.10.29. Father a newspaper editor; ed. Scunthorpe Grammar School and Old Vic Theatre School; distinguished stage career commenced 1951 at Croydon; md. 1. actor Roger Gage (div.); 2. Laurence Olivier (qv) 1961, 1 son Richard (1961); 2 daughters Tamsin (1964), Julie Kate (1966); few film appearances include MOBY DICK (56); TIME WITHOUT PITY (56); THE ENTERTAINER (60, also stage); THE THREE SISTERS (70, as Masha Prosorov); EQUUS (77); BRITANNIA HOSPITAL (81); BRIMSTONE & TREACLE (82); T.V. 1982: 'Wagner' (mini-series), Edith in 'All For Love' (series); awarded CBE 1970; stage 1982: 'Cavell'.

SIAN PHILLIPS

B. Bettws, Carmarthenshire, Wales, 14.5.34. BBC sound radio, Cardiff, from the age of 11; Pontardawe Grammar School and the Univ Wales (Hons. degree in English and Philosoph much Welsh T.V. (fluent Welsh) as announc actress during teens, including opening preser of TWW; studied at R.A.D.A., then embarkec distinguished stage career, including R.S. Co., End, etc., recently: Pal Joey' (1980/81); md (?—'in student days'); 2. actor Peter O'Toole (1959-79, 2 daughters Pat & Kate; few movies BECKET (64); YOUNG CASSIDY (6 LAUGHTER IN THE DARK (69); GOODB MR CHIPS (69); MURPHY'S WAR (70) a UNDER MILK WOOD (72); Miss Phillips v elected to the Hon. Order of Druids for service Welsh Drama; md. 3. actor Robin Sachs, 19 recent T.V.: Clementine in 'Churchill—T Wilderness Years' (81); stage 82: 'Dear Liai

RONALD PICKUP

B. Chester 7.6.41. Ed. King's School, Chester and Leeds University; trained for stage at R.A.D.A.; Mr Pickup's stage career began in 1964 at Leicester and he has since played with distinction at the National Theatre, Royal Court, the Old Vic in a wide range of parts, especially the S'pearean classics, including Malcolm in 'Macbeth' (1972) and as 'Richard II' (1972); md. Lans Traverse; came to the screen in THE THREE SISTERS (70) and has been seen in DAY OF THE JACKAL (72); MAHLER (74); JOSEPH ANDREWS (76); ZULU DAWN (78); THE 39 STEPS (78); NIJINSKY (79, as Stravinsky); IVANHOE (82, T.V. movie); he is very well-known on T.V. and work in this medium includes Lord Randolph Churchill in 'Jennie' (75); recent stage: 'Hobson's Choice' (81), 'Uncle Vanya' (82); T.V.: THE LETTER (T.V. movie, 1981), 'Verdi' (ser., Italy, 82).

SUZANNE PLESHETTE

B. New York City, 31.1.37. Father film exhibit mother dancer; ed. Syracuse Univ.; New Yc stage; screen début: GEISHA BOY (58); md. actor Troy Donahue (md. & div. 1964), Thomas Joseph Gallagher, 1968; Suzanne h played in many movies including LOVERS MUST LEARN (62); 40 POUND OF TROUBLE, THE BIRDS (both 1963); DISTANT TRUMPET, FATE IS TH HUNTER, YOUNGBLOOD HAWKE (i 1964); A RAGE TO LIVE (65); NEVAD SMITH (66); ADVENTURES OF BULLWH GRIFFIN (67); BLACKBEARD'S GHOS THE POWER (both 1968); SUPPORT YOU LOCAL GUNFIGHTER (71); THE SHAGG D.A. (76); HOT STUFF (79); many T.V. movie T.V. ser., inclu. 'Bob Newhart Show' (72-78 THE STARMAKER (mini-ser., 1981).

CHRISTOPHER PLUMMER

B. Toronto, Ontario, Canada, 13.12.27. (or 29 Ed. public and private schools in Canada, nurs early ambitions to become concert pianist, turned to school plays and acting, '...at last feeli I was doing something useful and exciting'; e barked on his successful stage career in 1950 Ottawa, becoming a powerful force in the classi theatre, especially Shakespearean productions USA, Canada and G.B., winning several awar including 'Evening Standard Award' for 'Beck (1961); md. actress Tammy Grimes (1956-60) daughter Amanda (born 1957); 2. Patricia Lew journalist (1962-68); Mr Plummer came to screen in STAGE STRUCK (58) and has be seen since in WIND ACROSS THE EVE GLADES (58); FALL OF THE ROMA EMPIRE (64); INSIDE DAISY CLOVER (6 SOUND OF MUSIC (66); NIGHT OF TH GENERALS (66, as Rommel); TRIPLE CRO (67); OEDIPUS THE KING (68); NOBOI RUNS FOREVER (68); LOCK UP YOU DAUGHTERS (69); BATTLE OF BRITA (69); ROYAL HUNT OF THE SUN (7(WATERLOO (70, as Duke of Wellingtor THE PYX (72); RETURN OF THE PIN PANTHER (74); SPIRAL STAIRCASE (7 CONDUCT UNBECOMING (75); THE MA WHO WOULD BE KING (76, as Kiplin ACES HIGH (76); ASSASSINATION A SARAJEVO (76); THE MONEYCHANGE (77, T.V. movie, Emmy Award); THE DI APPEARANCE (77); JESUS OF NAZARET (77, T.V. movie, as Herod Antipas); INTE NATIONAL VELVET (77); THE SILEN PARTNER (77); STARCRASH (77); HA OVER STREET (78); SHERLOCK HOLME —MURDER BY DECREE (78, as S.H.); HIG POINT (79); SOMEWHERE IN TIME (7 Md: 3. actress Elaine Taylor, 1970; stage 198 'Othello' (N.Y.); recent movies: DESPERA VOYAGE, WHEN THE CIRCUS CAME T TOWN (both T.V. movies), THE JANITOR (i 1980); THE SHADOW BOX (T.V. mov 1981); LITTLE GLORIA, HAPPY AT LAS (mini-ser.), THE AMATEUR (both 1982); TH SCARLET & THE BLACK (T.V. movi DREAMSCAPE (both 1983).

IDNEY POITIER

car-winning Sidney Poitier has had the distinction of being the most successful black actor ever to appear in movies, career spanning over thirty years. He is the son of Reginald Poitier, who was a farmer, and his wife, Evelyn, and he s born in Miami, Florida on 20 February 1927 (or 1924). He was raised in Nassau, British West Indies, attended the vernor's High School and upon leaving worked at several jobs, including drug store clerk, parking lot attendant, nstruction worker, ditch digger, trucker, longshoreman and trained as a physiotherapist in a medical hospital before ning the U.S. Army aged 18. Upon discharge he chose a stage career, but owing to his thick West Indian accent failed audition at the U.S. Negro Theatre but took a job backstage as a janitor in return for acting lessons with Paul Mann d Lloyd Richards, leading to bit parts. Due to producer James Light he landed his first bit part on Broadway and in 46 played in 'Lysistrata' and, later, 'Freight' (49). Poitier had come to the screen in three short army films, one of ich was FROM WHENCE COMETH HELP (49). In the 1950s his movie career picked up and he has played in ch movies as NO WAY OUT (50); RED BALL (52); CRY, THE BELOVED COUNTRY (52); GO, MAN, GO!); THE BLACKBOARD JUNGLE (55); GOODBYE, MY LADY (56); SOMETHING OF VALUE (57); GE OF THE CITY (58); DEFIANT ONES (58, Oscar nom.); PORGY & BESS (59); VIRGIN ISLAND (60); RIS BLUES (62); PRESSURE POINT (62); THE LONG SHIPS (64); BEDFORD INCIDENT (64); THE ENDER THREAD (65); A PATCH OF BLUE (65); DUEL AT DIABLO (66); TO SIR WITH LOVE (66); UESS WHO'S COMING TO DINNER (67); IN THE HEAT OF THE NIGHT (67); FOR LOVE OF IVY (68); IE LOST MAN (69); THEY CALL ME MR TIBBS (70); THE ORGANISATION (71); BROTHER JOHN); BUCK AND THE PREACHER (72*); A WARM DECEMBER (73*); UPTOWN SATURDAY NIGHT 4*); THE WILBY CONSPIRACY (75); LET'S DO IT AGAIN (76*); A PIECE OF THE ACTION (77*). His t wife was dancer Juanita Hardy, in 1950, and they had three daughters, Beverly (born 1951), Pamela (1952) and erry (1953). He is now wed, since 1976, to actress Joanna Shimkus and they have two children. Through film Mr Poitier s done much to represent the honourable American negro and in 1963 he won an Oscar for his performance in LIES OF THE FIELD. In 1980 he directed (*) STIR CRAZY, in 1982, HANKY PANKY.
IE LONG JOURNEY by Caroline H. Ewers; Signet paperback, USA, 1969; reprinted 1974.
IE CINEMA OF SIDNEY POITIER by Lester J. Keyser and Andre H. Ruszkowski; A.S. Barnes & Co. Inc.: w York, 1980.
IIS LIFE (autobiography); Hodder & Stoughton: London, 1980; p/back: Coronet, 1981.

ICHAEL J. POLLARD

———, . . 39. Mr Pollard appeared on adway in such plays as 'Comes a Day' (1958), Loss of Roses' (1959), 'Our Town' (1959), the enile lead in 'Bye Bye Birdie' (60) and as rvin in 'Enter Laughing' (1963); on T.V. de an impression in the early 60s in 'The man Comedy', a Du Pont Show 'Show of the nth', and took the role of Jerome Krebs in 'The any Loves of Dobie Gillis' (series 1960); vies include HEMINGWAY'S ADVEN- RES OF A YOUNG MAN (62); THE RIPPER (63); SUMMER MAGIC (63); IE WILD ANGELS (66); CAPRICE (66); IE SMUGGLERS (68, T.V. movie); HANNI- AL BROOKS (68); LITTLE FAUSS & BIG ALSY (70); DIRTY LITTLE BILLY (72, as ly the Kid); SUNDAY IN THE COUNTRY); BETWEEN THE LINES (77); as 'C.W. oss' in BONNIE & CLYDE (67) he received a st Supporting Actor Oscar nom.

ERIC PORTER

B. London 8.4.28. Ed. Elementary School, Carshalton, Surrey and Wimbledon Technical College; Mr Porter made his 1st stage appearance at Cambridge in 1945 in a Shakespearean production and subsequently became one of Britain's most distinguished stage actors, esp. in works by the latter playwright, at Bristol/London Old Vic and the R.S. Co., etc.; several films include THE PUMPKIN EATER (64); HEROES OF TELE-MARK (65); LOST CONTINENT (68); HANDS OF THE RIPPER (71); HITLER: THE LAST 10 DAYS (72); THE BELSTONE FOX (73); CALLAN (74); HENNESSY (75); THE 39 STEPS (78); LITTLE LORD FAUNT-LEROY (80); admired by millions for his work as Soames Forsyte in BBC's 'The Forsyte Saga' series, on T.V. in 1967; recent T.V.: 'The Sin Bin' (81), as Neville Chamberlain in 'Churchill: the Wilderness Years' (81); 'The Jewel in the Crown' (83).

ROBERT POWELL

B. Salford, nr. Manchester, 1.6.44. From the age of 6 always interested in acting; ed. Manchester Grammar School (concentrating on Latin, Greek and Ancient History) and Manchester Univ. (reading law, but switched to drama); stage début with Stoke-on-Trent Rep., other reps. include role of 'Hamlet' at Leeds; R.S. Co., etc.; much T.V. from late 1960s, including success as Toby Wren in 'Doomwatch'; md. former dancer with 'Pan's People', Barbara Lord, 1977, 1 son Barnaby (born 25.11.77), 1 daughter Katherine (born 14.8.79); films: ROBBERY (67); THE ITALIAN JOB (69); SECRETS (70); RUNNING SCARED (71); THE ASPHYX (71); ASY-LUM (72); MAHLER (74); TOMMY (74); BEYOND GOOD & EVIL (77); THE 4 FEATHERS (77); THE 39 STEPS (78); JANE AUSTIN IN MANHATTAN (79); HARLE-QUIN (79, Best Actor, Paris Film Festival (1980); THE SURVIVORS (80); JANE AUSTIN IN MANHATTAN (81); HUNCHBACK OF NOTRE DAME (T.V. movie), IMPERATIVE (both 82); THE JIGSAW MAN (83); recent stage: 'Terra Nova', 'Private Dick' (both 82); T.V.: as 'Jesus of Nazareth' (mini-ser., 1977), Higgins in 'Pygmalion' (81).

STEPHANIE POWERS

B. Hollywood, L.A., California, 2.11.42; real name Stephania Federkiewicz; ed. Hollywood H.S.; a dancer, Stephanie got small role in WEST SIDE STORY film, school commitments made her withdraw from movie, but her screen-test lead to subsequent film roles in TAMMY, TELL ME TRUE (61); GRIP OF FEAR (61); THE IN-TERNS (62); McLINTOCK! (63); LOVE HAS MANY FACES (65); FANATIC (64); STAGE-COACH (66); WARNING SHOT (67); THE BOATNIKS (70); HERBIE RIDES AGAIN (73); MANHUNTER (74, T.V. movie); SKY HEIST (75, T.V. movie); NOWHERE TO RUN (78, T.V. movie); several others; md. actor Gary Lockwood (div.); Stephanie speaks Polish, Spanish, French, Italian and Russian fluently, she has adopted son, Silvano Rampucci (when she was 18); T.V. series: April Dancer in 'Girl From U.N.C.L.E.' (1966/67), Toni Danton in 'The Feather and the Father Gang' (1977), Sally Whalen in 'Washington: Behind Closed Doors' (1977) and Jennifer Hart in 'Hart to Hart' (1979-). Director of the 'Holden Wildlife Foundation'.

AULA PRENTISS

San Antonio, Texas, 4.3.39. Of Sicilian extrac- n; real name Paula Ragusa; ed. St. Ann's and mar H.S., Houston, at 16 entered Randolph acon Women's Coll., Virginia as pre-med. dent; at 18 won scholarship, voted 'Most autiful Girl on Campus', did summer acting urse, then North-Western Univ.; summer stock: gle's Mere, Pa; voted 'Best Actress' at Univ., ned B.A. degree in Drama; seen and contract M-G-M, early movies include WHERE THE YS ARE (60); BACHELOR IN PARADISE); MAN'S FAVOURITE SPORT? (63); IN RM'S WAY (65); CATCH 22 (70), etc.; V. series: 'He & She' (1967/68) as Paula llister, opp. husband Richard Benjamin (qv); . 26.10.60, in New York, 1 son Ross Thomas rn 1974); Broadway includes Rosalind in 'As u Like It' (63); other films: MOVE (70); RN TO WIN (71); LAST OF THE RED T LOVERS (72); THE COUPLE TAKES WIFE (72, T.V. movie); CRAZY JOE (73); IE PARALLAX VIEW (74); STEPFORD IVES (75); BLACK MARBLE (79); BUDDY, JDDY, SATURDAY THE 14TH (both 1981); CKING IT IN (82).

ROBERT PRESTON

B. Newton Highlands, Mass., U.S.A., 8.6.18(?). Real name Robert Preston Meservey; ed. Lincoln H.S., L.A.; family moved to L.A. when Robert was 2; acted on stage from early teens: Patia Power Co.; 2 years with Pasadena Playhouse, where he was discovered, awarded Paramount movie contract, coming to screen in KING OF ALCATRAZ (38); md. Catherine Feltus (actress Catherine Craig), 1940; early movies include BEAU GESTE (39); NORTHWEST MOUNTED POLICE (40); THIS GUN FOR HIRE (42); WILD HARVEST (47); THE LADY GAM-BLES (49); CLOUDBURST (52); Robert became a Broadway star in 1950s and '60s, work included 'The Male Animal' (1952), 'The Tender Trap' (1954), Harold Hill in 'The Music Man' (1957-60 — Tony Award and New York Drama Critics Award, BA — filmed 1962), 'I Do, I Do' (1966 & 1968, ditto awards); more recent pics.: JUNIOR BONNER (72); CHILD'S PLAY (72); MAME (73); MY FATHER'S HOUSE (75, T.V. movie); SEMI TOUGH (77); THE CHIS-HOLMS (79, mini-series); S.O.B. (80); VICTOR/VICTORIA (82, Oscar nom., BSA); COLD READING (82, T.V. movie). WWII: U.S. Air Force.

VINCENT PRICE

Although he has been America's foremost film actor in the macabre genre since the early 1950s, and more especially the Roger Corman-directed series of the 1960s, Vincent Price had been making movies since 1938 and has also do extensive stage work. The son of Vincent and Marguerite Price, he was born in St. Louis, Missouri, on 27 May 19. After attending the St. Louis Country Day School, he went to Yale University and dabbled in G. & S. operettas. He th worked briefly as a schoolmaster at Riverdale Country School, New York, but came to England and studied at University of London for a degree in History and also Art at the Courtauld Institute. Switching to the stage, he play Charles Murdock and the Judge in 'Chicago' at the Gate Theatre in March 1935, and at the same theatre scored as Prince Consort in 'Victoria Regina'. Returning to the States, he appeared in this same production for 1½ yea December 1935-June 1937, and, following much stage work, made his screen début in SERVICE DELUXE in 19. that year he also wed actress Edith Barrett and their son, Barrett, was born the following year. The couple divorce 1948. His many film appearances include ELIZABETH & ESSEX (39, as Raleigh); TOWER OF LONDON (40, Clarence); HUDSON'S BAY (40, as Charles II); THE SONG OF BERNARDETTE (43); KEYS OF TI KINGDOM (44); DRAGONWYCK (46); THE THREE MUSKETEERS (49); HIS KIND OF WOMAN (5 HOUSE OF WAX (53); THE MAD MAGICIAN (54); THE TEN COMMANDMENTS (56); THE STORY (MANKIND (57); THE FLY (58); THE BAT (59); THE HOUSE ON HAUNTED HILL (60); THE FALL (THE HOUSE OF USHER (61); THE PIT AND THE PENDULUM (61); TALES OF TERROR (62); TI RAVEN (63); THE TOMB OF LIGEIA (64); CITY UNDER THE SEA (65); THE OBLONG BOX (69); TI ABOMINABLE DR PHIBES (71); THEATRE OF BLOOD (73); MADHOUSE (74) and THE MONSTI CLUB (81). In 1949 he wed Mary Grant and their daughter, Mary, was born in 1962. This marriage ended in 197 Mr Price is an Art expert, and, is a member of the Fine Arts Commission for the White House. He has guested American television on numerous occasions, from being the host of 'Pantomime Quiz' from 1950-52, as 'Egghead' 'Batman' series (1965/66), as Prof. Multiple in 'Voyage to the Bottom of the Sea' (1960s) to the mini-series 'Ti Express' (79) opposite his third wife, actress Coral Browne (qv), whom he wed in 1974. Recently, in 1981, he toured States in a one-man show as Oscar Wilde and he returned to the screen in RUDDIGORE (82, T.V. movie) a HOUSE OF THE LONG SHADOWS (83).   *I LIKE WHAT I KNOW* (autobio.); 1959, US

VICTORIA PRINCIPAL

B. Tokyo, Japan, 3.1.45. Father U.S. Air Force Officer, travelled with family when youngster; ed. Dade Junior Coll., Florida as pre-med. student, had bad car accident and while in hospital decided to become actress; recovered, modelled in New York, further studies in London and 3 years with Royal Ballet School; in Hollywood, came to the screen in THE LIFE AND TIMES OF JUDGE ROY BEAN (72) and has been seen in THE NAKED APE (73), EARTHQUAKE (74); LAST HOURS BEFORE MORNING (75, T.V. movie); VIGILANTE FORCE (76); left acting for a time in 1975 to become agent; I WILL, I WILL... FOR NOW (76); FANTASY ISLAND (77, T.V. movie — pilot); THE NIGHT THEY TOOK MISS BEAUTIFUL (77, T.V. movie); md. actor Christopher Skinner (sep.); from 1978 Victoria has played the role of Pamela Barnes Ewing in the phenomenally successful T.V. ser., 'Dallas'; NOT JUST ANOTHER AFFAIR (T.V. movie, 1981).

DAVID PROWSE

B. Bristol 1.7.35. 6'8" tall and with a 50" chest, Dave was British Heavyweightlifting Champion in 1962/63/64; he came to the screen as the Frankenstein Monster in CASINO ROYALE (66) and has been seen in THE HORROR OF FRANKENSTEIN (70); A CLOCKWORK ORANGE (71); CARRY ON HENRY (71); VAMPIRE CIRCUS (72); FRANKENSTEIN AND THE MONSTER FROM HELL (73); GULLIVER'S TRAVELS (75); JABBER-WOCKY (76); THE PEOPLE THAT TIME FORGOT (77); md. Norma, 2 sons Steven, James, 1 daughter Rachel; he has appeared on T.V. occasionally, including 'Morecambe & Wise Show', 'Arthur' and especially as the Green Cross Code Man in commercials promoting road safety; Keep Fit consultant to several organisations, including Harrod's, runs own gym; Darth Vader in the fantastically successful STAR WARS (76) and EMPIRE STRIKES BACK (79); books: 'Fitness For Fun', 'Play Safe With The Stars'; T.V. 1981: Stanley in 'The Rose Medallion'; returns as Darth Vader in RETURN OF THE JEDI (83).

RICHARD PRYOR

B. Peoria, Illinois, 1.12.40. Father a construction worker; from age of 7 Richard had 1st taste of show-biz, playing drums; brought up in 'rough red-light district', attended integrated school, went into U.S. Army but forced to leave owing to racism; returned home, married, 1 son, Richard, born 1962; pro. début as comic in club at Peoria; went on road with female impersonators; later scored as T.V. comic ('Johnny Carson Show', 'On Broadway Tonight' (1964/65)); also wrote scripts for Lily Tomlin and Flip Wilson; md. 2. Maxine, 1967, 2 daughters Elizabeth (1967), Rain (1970) (div.); movies: BUSY BODY (67); WILD IN THE STREETS (68); THE YOUNG LAWYERS (69, T.V. movie); THE PHYNX (70); BLAZING SADDLES (71, co-scripted); LADY SINGS THE BLUES (72); WATTSTAX (73); UPTOWN SATURDAY NIGHT (74); SILVER STREAK (77); GREASED LIGHT-NING (77); WHICH WAY IS UP? (77); THE WIZ (78); CALIFORNIA SUITE (78); IN GOD WE TRUST (79); FAMILY DREAM (79); STIR CRAZY, WHOLLY MOSES! (both 80); SOME KIND OF A HERO, BUSTIN' LOOSE (both 81); RICHARD PRYOR LIVE ON SUNSET STRIP, DYNAMITE CHICKEN, THE TOY (all 82); SUPERMAN III (83); own T.V. show (77); Md: 3. Deborah McGuire (77), 1 daughter Renee.

JONATHAN PRYCE

B.   , N. Wales, . . ; studied Art for years, then won scholarship to RADA; 18 mon with Liverpool Everyman Co., becoming one Britain's most talented young stage actors (C Vic, National, Royal Court, etc.), winning seve awards; much T.V. includes series 'Roger Does Live Here Anymore' (1981); movies: VOYAG OF THE DAMNED (76); THE DAY CHRIS DIED (79, T.V. movie); PETER & PAUL (7 BREAKING GLASS (79, Evening Standa Award); LOOPHOLE (81); MURDER IS EAS (81, T.V. movie); SOMETHING WICKE THIS WAY COMES (82); THE PLOUGH MAN'S LUNCH (83); recent stage: 'Talley Folly' (82); T.V.: 'Praying Mantis' (82).

RANDY QUAID

B. ———, . . 53. Discovered by Peter Bogdanovich in production at the Drama Dept. of Univ. of Houston and came to screen in LAST PICTURE SHOW (71); others: WHAT'S UP DOC? (72); PAPER MOON (73); LOLLY-MADONNA XXX (73); LAST DETAIL (73, Oscar nom., B.S.A.); THE APPRENTICESHIP OF DUD-DY KRAVITZ (74); BREAKOUT (75); BOUND FOR GLORY (76); THE MISSOURI BREAKS (76); MIDNIGHT EXPRESS (77); THE CHOIRBOYS (77); LAST RIDE OF THE DALTON GANG (78, T.V. movie); THE LONG RIDERS (79); HEART BEEPS (81); his brother Dennis is also successful actor, stars recently in Jaws 3-D and DREAMSCAPE (83).

ANTHONY QUAYLE

B. Ainsdale, Lancashire, 7.9.13. After receivi his education at Rugby School, Mr Quayle train for the stage at R.A.D.A.; he made his first sta appearance at the Q Theatre in December 19. in 'Robin Hood' and he later became one Britain's most distinguished Shakespearean acto — for several years from 1948 he was actor/direc with the Shakespeare Memorial Theatre a toured the Commonwealth in productions; md. Hermione Hannen (div.), 2. actress Dorot Hyson, 2 daughters, 1 son; Mr Quayle's occasior movies include HAMLET (48); SARABAN FOR DEAD LOVERS (48); OH ROSALIND (55); BATTLE OF THE RIVER PLATE (5(THE WRONG MAN (57); NO TIME FC TEARS (57); WOMAN IN A DRESSIN GOWN (57); ICE COLD IN ALEX (5 SERIOUS CHARGE (59); TARZAN'S GREA ADVENTURE (59); GUNS OF NAVARONE (61); LAWRENC OF ARABIA (62); H.M.S. DEFIANT (6 FALL OF THE ROMAN EMPIRE (64); EAS OF SUDAN (64); OPERATION CROSSBO (64); A STUDY IN TERROR (65); BEFOR WINTER COMES (69); DESTINY OF A SF (69, T.V. movie); ANNE OF THE 1000 DA (70, as Cardinal Wolsey); JARRETT (73, T. movie); QBVII (74, T.V. movie); THE TAM. RIND SEED (74); THE EAGLE HAS LANDE (76); HOLOCAUST 2000 (77); SHERLOC HOLMES — MURDER BY DECREE (78 other stagework includes acting/directing in We End and Broadway; he was created a C.B.E. 1952 and has appeared on T.V. in such series 'Strange Report' (1969, as Adam Strange), Aaron in 'Moses' (1976), in 'Masada' (197 mini-series), 'Tales of the Unexpected' (198 and 'Manions of America' (1981, mini-series stage 1981: 'Dandy Dick' (acting/directing 1982: tour/West End: 'Hobson's Choice' a 'Coat of Varnish'.

ANTHONY QUINN

Solid and bear-like Anthony Quinn, the winner of two Oscars, had found the road to motion-picture stardom a long one, before his deserved success from the 1950s. He is the son of Frank Quinn, an Irishman, and his wife, Manuella, who was Mexican, and he was born in Chihuahua, Mexico, on 21 April 1915. His parents became separated during the Pancho Villa (for whom his father served) Revolution and young Anthony was taken by his mother first to El Paso and then to Los Angeles. During these tough times he studied at Los Angeles Junior and Polytechnic High Schools. His parents had meanwhile been re-united and his father worked as a cameraman at a place known as the Old Selig Zoo, but he died in a car accident when his son was twelve. Throughout his youth Anthony had numerous jobs, including shoe-shine boy, newspaper salesman, butcher's assistant, taxi driver, water boy and cement mixer, window cleaner, boxer and the cutter of women's dresses in a factory. He'd also learned to play saxophone and organised an orchestra. At 17 he had an operation on his tongue to cure a speech defect and took elocution lessons. This lead to an interest in an acting career and at 19 he appeared in his first play, 'Clean Beds', with Mae West. One of his first screen roles was in THE PLAINSMAN, in 1936, as a Cheyenne Indian, speaking jibberish. The picture was a C.B. DeMille production and a year later he wed the producer's adopted daughter, Katherine, on 2 October 1937. They had 5 children: Christopher (who drowned in 1941), Christina (born 1.12.41), Katherine (11.11.42), Duncan (3.8.45) and Valentina (26.12.52). They divorced in 1965. Nearly 100 movie appearances include UNION PACIFIC (39); THEY DIED WITH THEIR BOOTS ON (41, as Crazy Horse); BUFFALO BILL (44); CHINA SKY (45); TYCOON (48); VIVA ZAPATA (52, Oscar, BSA); RIDE VAQUERO! (53); LA STRADA (54); LUST FOR LIFE (56, as Gauguin, Oscar, BSA); as THE HUNCHBACK OF NOTRE DAME (56); BLACK ORCHID (58); WARLOCK (59); THE BUCCANEER (59, directed only); SAVAGE INNOCENTS (60); LAWRENCE OF ARABIA (62); BARABBAS (62); THE VISIT (63); ZORBA THE GREEK (64, Oscar nom., B.A.); THE HAPPENING (67), THE SHOES OF THE FISHERMAN (68); A WALK IN THE SPRING RAIN (69); THE MESSAGE (76); JESUS OF NAZARETH (77, T.V. movie, as Caiaphas); THE GREEK TYCOON (77) and THE PASSAGE (78). 1947 marked his New York stage début, in 'The Gentleman From Athens' and other work includes Henry II in 'Becket' (1960). His second marriage, to Yolanda Addolori, has produced three children, Francesco, Daniele and Lorenzo. During WWII he served in the U.S. Armed Forces. T.V. work includes the role of Thomas Alcala in 'The Man and The City' and host/narrator of '10 Who Dare' (77). Recent movies: THE SALAMANDER (80); HIGH RISK, LION OF THE DESERT, THE CON ARTISTS (all 81) and REGINA (82).
THE ORIGINAL SIN (autobio.); W.H. Allen: London, 1973; paperback: Star, 1974.
THE FILMS OF ANTHONY QUINN by Alvin H. Marill; Citadel: Secaucus, N.J., 1976.

DIANA QUICK

B. Bexley, 23.11.46; Father a doctor (dec.); 2 brothers, 1 sister; ed. Oxford Univ. — Diana was first woman president of Oxford Univ. Dram. Soc. (played in 'The Crucible', etc.); BA Degree — Lit.; stage: National Youth Theatre, Red Ladder (Left-wing theatre co-op.), National Theatre, R.S. Co. etc.; md. ? (div.); much T.V. includes acclaimed 'Brideshead Revisited' (1981); movies: NICHOLAS & ALEXANDRA (71); A PRIVATE ENTERPRISE (73); THE DUELLISTS (77); THE BIG SLEEP (78); THE ODD JOB (78); other stage includes 'Billy', 'Mindkill' (1982); recent T.V.: 'The Woman in White' (1982).

KATHLEEN QUINLAN

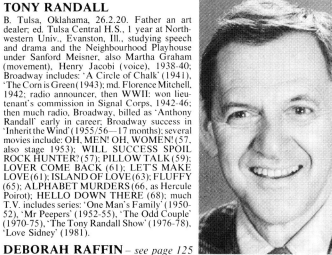

B. ———, . . . Kathleen is a former gymnast who intended to become a gym teacher, but chose to concentrate on acting and moved to L.A.; she stood in for actress Trish Van Devere, doing a highboard jump in ONE IS A LONELY NUMBER; while still attending High School at Mill Valley, nr. San Francisco, she played a small role in AMERICAN GRAFFITI (74); then played in such T.V. series as 'Kojak', 'Police Woman' and 'The Waltons' and movies have since included CAN ELLEN BE SAVED? (74, T.V. movie); WHERE HAVE ALL THE PEOPLE GONE (74, T.V. movie); THE MISSING ARE DEADLY (75, T.V. movie); LUCAS TANNER (75, T.V. movie); THE ABDUCTION OF SAINT ANNE (75, T.V. movie); THE TURNING POINT OF JIM MALLOY (75, T.V. movie); LITTLE LADIES OF THE NIGHT (77, T.V. movie); AIRPORT 77 (77); LIFEGUARD (77); I NEVER PROMISED YOU A ROSE GARDEN (78); THE PROMISE (78); THE RUNNER STUMBLES (79); SUNDAY LOVERS (80); RIDERS ON THE STORM (81); HANKY PANKY, TWILIGHT ZONE, RESTLESS (all 82); THE LAST WINTER (83).

TONY RANDALL

B. Tulsa, Oklahoma, 26.2.20. Father an art dealer; ed. Tulsa Central H.S., 1 year at Northwestern Univ., Evanston, Ill., studying speech and drama and the Neighbourhood Playhouse under Sanford Meisner, also Martha Graham (movement), Henry Jacobi (voice), 1938-40; Broadway includes: 'A Circle of Chalk' (1941), 'The Corn is Green (1943); md. Florence Mitchell, 1942; radio announcer, then WWII: won lieutenant's commission in Signal Corps, 1942-46; then much radio, Broadway, billed as 'Anthony Randall' early in career; Broadway success in 'Inherit the Wind' (1955/56—17 months); several movies include: OH, MEN! OH, WOMEN! (57, also stage 1953); WILL SUCCESS SPOIL ROCK HUNTER? (57); PILLOW TALK (59); LOVER COME BACK (61); LET'S MAKE LOVE (61); ISLAND OF LOVE (63); FLUFFY (65); ALPHABET MURDERS (66, as Hercule Poirot); HELLO DOWN THERE (68); much T.V. includes series: 'One Man's Family' (1950-52), 'Mr Peepers' (1952-55), 'The Odd Couple' (1970-75), 'The Tony Randall Show' (1976-78), 'Love Sidney' (1981).

DEBORAH RAFFIN – see page 125

CRISTINA RAINES – see page 125

DENIS QUILLEY

B. London, 26.12.27. Ed. Bancroft's School, Woodford Green, Essex; pro. stage début 1945 as actor/ASM with Birmingham Rep.; Nat. Service; md. Stella Chapman; London stage début in 1950 in 'The Lady's Not For Burning', became distinguished actor in a wide range of roles from Shakespearean drama ('Macbeth'), revue ('Airs on a Shoestring') and musical comedy ('Grab Me a Gondola'); Denis has played in few movies, namely LIFE AT THE TOP (70); ANNE OF THE 1000 DAYS (70); THE BLACK WINDMILL (74); MURDER ON THE ORIENT EXPRESS (74); EVIL UNDER THE SUN (82); PRIVATES ON PARADE, ORPHEUS IN THE UNDERWORLD (T.V. movie), MEMED (all 1983); has 2 daughters, 1 son; stage 1980: 'Sweeney Todd'; recent T.V.: 'Number 10' (as Gladstone, 83).

CHARLOTTE RAMPLING

B. Sturmer, Cambs., 5.2.46. Father Colonel Godfrey Rampling, prof. soldier (also former Olympic medal-winning sprinter); her childhood spent in variety of NATO postings with parents; ed. Jeanne d'Arc School, Fontainbleu; St. Hilda's School, Bushey, Herts; Harrow Technical College; at latter did secretarial course, then idled around Spain for a while'; temp. secretary in London, discovered by photographer and became fashion model; first movie: ROTTEN TO THE CORE (64); T.V.; other movies include GEORGY GIRL (66); LONG DUEL (67); THREE (68); THE DAMNED (69); VANISHING POINT (71); ASYLUM (72); CORKY (72); HENRY VIII & HIS SIX WIVES (73, as Anne Boleyn); NIGHT PORTER (74); FAREWELL, MY LOVELY (75); ORCA (76); FOXTROT (76); PURPLE TAXI (78); STARDUST MEMORIES (80); md. 1. Bryan Southcombe, 17.2.72, 1 son Barnaby (div. 1978); 2. pop composer Jean-Michel Jarre (son of Maurice Jarre) 7.10.78, 1 son David. THE VERDICT (82).

ANDREW RAY

B. Southgate, London, 31.5.39. Father actor/comedian, late Ted Ray; brother Robin is authority/presenter of classical music, T.V./radio; discovered while accompanying father to radio show, Andrew got role on show 'Hi Gang!' instead of brother, aged 11 selected for star role in movie THE MUDLARK (50), becoming popular child actor in British films: THE YELLOW BALLOON (52); ESCAPE BY NIGHT (54); A PRIZE OF GOLD (55); ESCAPADE (55); WOMAN IN A DRESSING GOWN (57); YOUNG & THE GUILTY (58); THE HORSE'S MOUTH (58); SERIOUS CHARGE (59); md. Susan, children: Madeleine, Mark; Mr Ray has acted in the U.S.A.; British stage includes 'Ring For Cathy' (56) and created role of George VI in 'Crown Matrimonial' (1973), also in T.V. series: 'Edward and Mrs Simpson' (1978); other movies include TWICE ROUND THE DAFFODILS (62); THE SYSTEM (64); ROUGHCUT (79); recent T.V.: 'Atom Spies' (79), 'Bognor' (81), 'Death of an Expert Witness' (83); movie: MISSION PHANTOM (82).

ROBERT REDFORD

Superstar Robert Redford has consolidated his success in the late 1960s by appearing in some of the most important American pictures of the next decade and in 1981 his first movie as a director, ORDINARY PEOPLE, gained him an Oscar. He is the son of Charles Robert Redford, and his wife, the former Martha Hart, and he was Santa Monica, California, born on 18 August 1937. Robert Jr.'s mother died when he was young and his father worked his way up, after the war, from being a milkman to gaining a top job with Standard Oil. He was educated at Van Nuys High School, California, and the University of Colorado, leaving the latter in 1956. Redford recalls he can't remember much of that year although he was sacked as a carpenter, shop assistant and oil field worker. Saving some money he went to Europe, painted pictures in Paris and Florence for 13 months, selling his work as he went. In 1958, returning to the USA, he studied art at the Pratt Institute, but via the American Academy of Dramatic Art he changed careers and studied drama. That year he also wed Lola Van Wangemen. The couple have four children: daughters Shauna and Amy, and sons James and Scott. He managed to gain walk-on roles on Broadway in 'Tall Story', 'The Highest Tree' (both 1959) and 'Little Moon of Alban' (1960) and starred in 'Sunday in New York' in 1961. Next year he made his first movie, WAR HUNT (62), but returned to Broadway and success in 'Barefoot in the Park', in 1963. From then on he has concentrated on such movies as SITUATION HOPELESS, BUT NOT SERIOUS (65); INSIDE DAISY CLOVER (65); THE CHASE (66); THIS PROPERTY IS CONDEMNED (67); BAREFOOT IN THE PARK (67); BUTCH CASSIDY AND THE SUNDANCE KID (69); TELL THEM WILLIE BOY IS HERE (69); DOWNHILL RACER (69, also produced); LITTLE FAUSS AND BIG HALSY (71); THE CANDIDATE (72); THE HOT ROCK (72); JEREMIAH JOHNSON (72); THE WAY WE WERE (73); THE STING (73, Oscar nom., B.A.); THE GREAT GATSBY (74); THE GREAT WALDO PEPPER (75); THREE DAYS OF THE CONDOR (75); ALL THE PRESIDENT'S MEN (76); A BRIDGE TOO FAR (77); ELECTRIC HORSEMAN (79) and BRUBAKER (79). As director of ORDINARY PEOPLE (80) in addition to receiving an Oscar, Mr Redford also won a Golden Globe Award.
THE FILMS OF ROBERT REDFORD by James Spada; Citadel: Secaucus, N.J., 1977.
ROBERT REDFORD by David Downing; W.H. Allen: London, 1982.

CORIN REDGRAVE

B. London 16.7.39. Son of Sir Michael Redgrave and Rachel (Kempson), distinguished thespians; ed. Westminster and King's College, Cambridge; Mr Redgrave appd. in plays at University and made his professional début in London in 'A Midsummer Night's Dream' (1962); much stage work has included the New York stage, West End and R.S. Co.; md. Deidre Hamilton-Hill (div.); has son, mother-actress Kika Markham; movies: THE DEADLY AFFAIR (66); A MAN FOR ALL SEASONS (66); THE MAGUS (68); THE CHARGE OF THE LIGHT BRIGADE (68); OH! WHAT A LOVELY WAR (69); DAVID COPPERFIELD (69); WHEN EIGHT BELLS TOLL (69); VON RICHTHOFEN AND BROWN (71); in more recent years he has acted on stage in such plays as 'The Case of David Anderson, Q.C.' (Hammersmith, London, 1981); EUREKA (82).

LYNN REDGRAVE

B. London 8.3.43. Daughter of Sir Michael Redgrave, sister of Vanessa (qv) and Corin (qv); ed. Queen's Gate School, London; Lynn studied at the Central School of Speech and Drama, made her stage début in London in 1962, subsequently appearing with the National Theatre, and, from 1967, on the American stage; md. John Clark, her manager, 1967, children: Benjamin (1968), Kelly (1970), Annabel (1981); movies: TOM JONES (63); THE GIRL WITH GREEN EYES (64); GEORGY GIRL (66, Oscar nom.); DEADLY AFFAIR (66); SMASHING TIME (67); VIRGIN SOLDIERS (69); BLOOD KIN (69); KILLER FROM YUMA (71); EVERY LITTLE CROOK & NANNY (72); EVERYTHING YOU ALWAYS WANTED TO KNOW ABOUT SEX (73); TURN OF THE SCREW (74, T.V. movie); NATIONAL HEALTH (74); DON'T TURN THE OTHER CHEEK (75); THE HAPPY HOOKER (75); THE BIG BUS (76); SOONER OR LATER (79, T.V. movie); SUNDAY LOVERS (80); SEDUCTION OF MISS LEONA (81, T.V. movie); COLD READING (82, T.V. movie); T.V. ser., 1981: 'House Calls'.

CHRISTOPHER REEVE

B. Princeton, N. Jersey, 25.9.52. Parents (now divorced): father professor, novelist, translator, mother newspaper reporter; stepfather a stockbroker; Christopher grew up in Princeton, N. Jersey, with his brother, Benjamin, and while still in High School, worked in professional rep., touring in 'The Irregular Verb to Love' with Celeste Holm. He then entered Cornell Univ., graduating with a B.A. Degree, and had toured Britain preparing a paper on our repertory system, worked as 'dogsbody' at the Old Vic in 1972 and advised on U.S. accents for 'The Front Page' play; worked at Comedie Francaise, France, 1976: Broadway/tour of 'A Matter of Gravity', also daytime T.V. series in 'Love of Life'; small screen role GRAY LADY DOWN (77), followed by stardom as SUPERMAN (78); 1 son Matthew (born 21.12.79), mother British model Gae Exton; other movies: SOMEWHERE IN TIME (79); SUPERMAN II (81); DEATH TRAP (81); Broadway 1981: 'Fifth of July'; 82: MONSIGNORE (Italy); 83: SUPERMAN III.

BERYL REID

B. Hereford 17.6.20. Ed. Lady Barne House School, Withington H.S., Levenshulme H.S., Manchester; since making her stage début in a concert party in Bridlington, 1936, Miss Reid became a well-known comedienne on radio (especially as Monica in 'Educating Archie'), West End, revue, play 'The Killing of Sister George' (1965, Broadway 1966 and 'Emmy' Award 1967 — film version 1969); pantomime and Old Vic; md. Bill Worsley (div.), 2. Derek Franklin; films: BELLES OF ST. TRINIAN'S (54); EXTRA DAY (56); TWO-WAY STRETCH (60); DOCK BRIEF (62); STAR! (68); INSP. CLOUSEAU (68); ENTERTAINING MR SLOANE (70); THE BEAST IN THE CELLAR (71); DR PHIBES RIDES AGAIN (72); PSYCHOMANIA (72); FATHER, DEAR FATHER (73); NO SEX, PLEASE, WE'RE BRITISH (73); JOSEPH ANDREWS (76); YELLOWBEARD (83); has had her own T.V./radio ser.; recent T.V.: 'Irish R.M.' (83); 'Smiley's People' (82: BAFTA Aw.)

VANESSA REDGRAVE

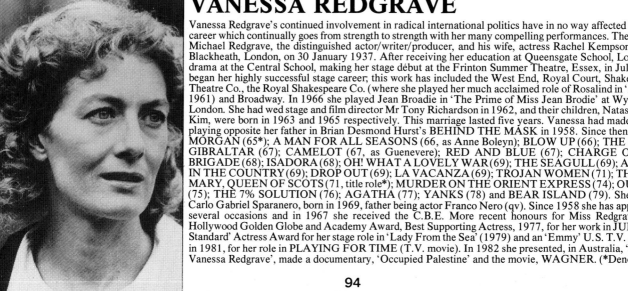

Vanessa Redgrave's continued involvement in radical international politics have in no way affected her film and stage career which continually goes from strength to strength with her many compelling performances. The eldest child of Sir Michael Redgrave, the distinguished actor/writer/producer, and his wife, actress Rachel Kempson, she was born in Blackheath, London, on 30 January 1937. After receiving her education at Queensgate School, London, she studied drama at the Central School, making her stage début at the Frinton Summer Theatre, Essex, in July 1957. And thus began her highly successful stage career; this work has included the West End, Royal Court, Shakespeare Memorial Theatre Co., the Royal Shakespeare Co. (where she played her much acclaimed role of Rosalind in 'As You Like It' in 1961) and Broadway. In 1966 she played Jean Broadie in 'The Prime of Miss Jean Brodie' at Wyndham's Theatre, London. She had wed stage and film director Mr Tony Richardson in 1962, and their children, Natasha Jane and Joely Kim, were born in 1963 and 1965 respectively. This marriage lasted five years. Vanessa had made her screen début playing opposite her father in Brian Desmond Hurst's BEHIND THE MASK in 1958. Since then she has played in MORGAN (65*); A MAN FOR ALL SEASONS (66, as Anne Boleyn); BLOW UP (66); THE SAILOR FROM GIBRALTAR (67); CAMELOT (67, as Guenevere); RED AND BLUE (67); CHARGE OF THE LIGHT BRIGADE (68); ISADORA (68); OH! WHAT A LOVELY WAR (69); THE SEAGULL (69); A QUIET PLACE IN THE COUNTRY (69); DROP OUT (69); LA VACANZA (69); TROJAN WOMEN (71); THE DEVILS (71); MARY, QUEEN OF SCOTS (71, title role*); MURDER ON THE ORIENT EXPRESS (74); OUT OF SEASON (75); THE 7% SOLUTION (76); AGATHA (77); YANKS (78) and BEAR ISLAND (79). She has another son, Carlo Gabriel Sparanero, born in 1969, father being actor Franco Nero (qv). Since 1958 she has appeared on T.V. on several occasions and in 1967 she received the C.B.E. More recent honours for Miss Redgrave have been the Hollywood Golden Globe and Academy Award, Best Supporting Actress, 1977, for her work in JULIA, the 'Evening Standard' Actress Award for her stage role in 'Lady From the Sea' (1979) and an 'Emmy' U.S. T.V. Award, presented in 1981, for her role in PLAYING FOR TIME (T.V. movie). In 1982 she presented, in Australia, 'An Evening With Vanessa Redgrave', made a documentary, 'Occupied Palestine' and the movie, WAGNER. (*Denotes Oscar nom.).

OLIVER REED

In the 1960s it took Oliver Reed under ten years to graduate from humble film extra to one of Britain's biggest international stars. He is the son of Peter Reed, a racing correspondent, and his wife, Marcia, who later divorced, and he was born in Wimbledon, South London, on 13 February 1938. His uncle was film director Sir Carol Reed, his grandfather Sir Herbert Beerbohm Tree, the distinguished actor-manager. Young Oliver attended 13 schools, including Hoe Place, Woking, Wimbledon Preparatory School, Neville House, Eastbourne, Ewell Castle, Surrey, excelling at boxing and athletics, coming 3rd in the All England Cross Country at St. George's College. An early job, during school holidays, was as an exhibition fighter in a boxing booth on Mitcham Green. After leaving school he lived with his grandmother in Wimbledon, trying to get acting work while working at a succession of jobs, including one month in a Soho Club as a bouncer, a clerk with Carter's Tested Seeds at Raynes Park and operating theatre orderly at St. Helier Hospital, Carshalton. Following two years National Service in the Medical Corps in Hong Kong he became a film extra, his first jobs being in HELLO LONDON, THE SQUARE PEG and THE CAPTAIN'S TABLE, in 1958. Managing to bluff a BBC producer at an audition, he landed the role of the Duke of Gloucester in a serial 'The Golden Spur', which lead to further T.V. and bit parts in movies such as BEAT GIRL (59); ANGRY SILENCE (60); LEAGUE OF GENTLEMEN (60); THE 2 FACES OF DR. JEKYLL (60); BULLDOG BREED (61); NO LOVE FOR JOHNNIE (61); HIS AND HERS (61) and THE REBEL (61). Many of his early movies were for Hammer Films and he starred in CURSE OF THE WEREWOLF (62) and had good roles in THE DAMNED (62); THE SCARLET BLADE (63); THE PARTY'S OVER (63) and PARANOIAC (64). He wed Irish model Katherine Byrne in 1960 and their son, Mark, was born in 1962. 1964 proved to be a good year for him — he starred on T.V. as composer Debussy and in Michael Winner's film THE SYSTEM. Since then he's been in constant demand for the movies and in recent years filmed internationally. His best films have included THE TRAP (65); THE SHUTTERED ROOM (66); THE JOKERS (67); I'LL NEVER FORGET WHAT'S 'IS NAME (67); OLIVER! (68, as Bill Sikes); ASSASSINATION BUREAU (68); HANNIBAL BROOKS (69); WOMEN IN LOVE (69); LADY IN THE CAR (71); THE HUNTING PARTY (72); THE DEVILS (72); SITTING TARGET (72); THE THREE/FOUR MUSKETEERS (73 & 74, as Athos); TEN LITTLE INDIANS (74); ROYAL FLASH (75); TOMMY (75); BURNT OFFERINGS (76); GT. SCOUT AND CATHOUSE THURSDAY (76); PRINCE AND THE PAUPER ('76); TOMORROW NEVER COMES (77); THE BIG SLEEP (77); CLASS OF MISS MacMICHAEL (77); THE BROOD (78); A TOUCH OF THE SUN (79); LION OF THE DESERT (79); CONDORMAN (80); DR HECKYL & MR HYPE (80); VENOM (82); DEATH BITE (82); STING II (83); SPASMS (83) and FANNY HILL (83). He has a daughter, Sarah (born 1970), the mother being Jackie Daryl.
REED ALL ABOUT ME (autobio.); W.H. Allen: London, 1979; Coronet paperback, 1981.

LEE REMICK

Attractive and talented American actress Lee Remick has for over twenty years remained at the top of her profession by her shrewd selection of varied and interesting roles. Born in Quincy, Massachusetts, on 14 December 1937 (or 1935) and the daughter of Frank E. Remick, a department store owner, and his wife, formerly successful New York actress Patricia Remick, Lee went to school at Thaylerland College, an institute of learning run by a Miss Hewitt, took drama lessons and studied ballet at the Swoba School of Dance (New York). Soon after graduating from Barnard College, she appeared on Broadway in December 1953 as Lois in 'Be Your Age', which flopped. Another play, 'Top Man' had the same fate. However, she went into summer stock, appearing in 'Oklahoma!', 'Annie Get Your Gun' and 'Showboat' and toured in 'Paint Your Wagon' (in the song and dance lead), opposite Art Carney (qv) in 'The 7 Year Itch' and Rudy Vallee in 'Jenny Kisses Me'. She then moved successfully into television ('Studio 1', etc.), wed T.V. director Bill Colleran in 1957 (children: son Matthew (1961) and daughter Katherine Lee (born 28.1.62)) and that year was discovered on T.V. by Elia Kazan, coming to the big screen in A FACE IN THE CROWD. She has since played in THE LONG HOT SUMMER (58); THESE 1000 HILLS (59); WILD RIVER (60); SANCTUARY (61); GRIP OF FEAR (62); DAYS OF WINE AND ROSES (62, Oscar nom.); THE RUNNING MAN (63); THE WHEELER DEALERS (63); BABY, THE RAIN MUST FALL (65); HALLELUJAH TRAIL (65); NO WAY TO TREAT A LADY (67); THE DETECTIVE (68); HARD CONTRACT (68); LOOT (70); A SEVERED HEAD (70); AND NO ONE COULD SAVE HER (73, T.V. movie); BLUE KNIGHT (73, T.V. movie); QBVII (74, T.V. movie); HUSTLING (75, T.V. movie); A GIRL NAMED SOONER (75, T.V. movie); HENNESSY (75); THE OMEN (76); MEDUSA TOUCH (77); TELEFON (77); BREAKING UP (78, T.V. movie); WHEELS (78, mini-series); TORN BETWEEN TWO LOVERS (78, T.V. movie); THE EUROPEANS (79); TRIBUTE (80) and THE COMPETITION (80). Divorced in 1968, she wed William R. Gowens in 1970. She has returned to New York for such plays as 'Anyone Can Whistle' (64) and 'Wait Until Dark' (66). Lee is also remembered on T.V. in the British series, 'Jennie' (74), as Lady Randolph Churchill, and in the mini-series 'Ike: The War Years' (79), as Kay Summersby. Her most recent film roles include Leslie Crosbie in a T.V. movie version of THE LETTER (81), and the actress Margaret Sullavan in another T.V. movie, HAYWIRE (82).

CLIVE REVILL

B. Wellington, New Zealand, 18.4.30. Ed. Rongotai College and Victoria Univ., Wellington; Mr Revill began his career as an accountant, but turned to the stage at Auckland in 1950, coming to Britain and studying at the Old Vic School 1950-52; stage followed in New York, Ipswich Repertory (3 years) and success with Shakespeare Memorial Theatre, West End, Broadway (including Fagin in 'Oliver!'); md: Valerie Nelson; many films include REACH FOR THE SKY (56); MODESTY BLAISE (66); KALEIDOSCOPE (66); A FINE MADNESS (66); FATHOM (67); NOBODY RUNS FOREVER (68); SHOES OF THE FISHERMAN (68); AVANTI (72); BLACK WINDMILL (74); THE GREAT HOUDINIS (76, T.V. movie); MATILDA (77); 'Centennial' (78, mini-series); CHARLIE MUFFIN (79, T.V. movie); MOVIOLA: 'The Scarlet O'Hara War' (80, T.V. movie, as Chas. Chaplin); EMPIRE STRIKES BACK (80, voice of Emperor); ZORRO — THE GAY BLADE (81); G & S Operas: THE MIKADO, THE SORCERER (T.V. movies, 1982).

FERNANDO REY

B. La Coruna, Spain, .. 17(?). Mr Rey, whose real name is Fernando Arambillet, has appeared in many international pictures, including THE RUNNING MAN (63); THE CEREMONY (64); RETURN OF THE 7 (66); VILLA RIDES! (68); GUNS OF THE MAGNIFICENT 7 (69); CANDIDATE FOR A KILLING (69); THE ADVENTURERS (70); LIGHT AT THE EDGE OF THE WORLD (71); THE FRENCH CONNECTION (72); DISCREET CHARM OF THE BOURGEOISIE (72); WHITE FANG (74); FRENCH CONNECTION II (75); SEVEN BEAUTIES (76); JESUS OF NAZARETH (77, mini-series); THE WOMAN WITH RED BOOTS (77); THE MURRI AFFAIR (77); THAT OBSCURE OBJECT OF DESIRE (77); QUINTET (78); CABOBLANCO (79); THE CUENCA CRIME (80); L'INGORGO, ILLUSTRIOUS CORPSES (both 1981); MONSIGNORE (82); 'Confessions of Felix Krull' (series, 1982).

BURT REYNOLDS

Graduating steadily via several T.V. roles to one of America's most virile action Superstars of the 1970s and 80s, Burt Reynolds is the son of a former Chief of Police at Palm Beach, Florida. Burt's grandmother was a full-blooded Cherokee Indian who married a forestry teacher on her reservation where his father was born. He married an Italian girl from Georgia and their son was born on 11 February 1935 (several sources give Palm Beach as his birth place, other Waycross, or Atlanta, Georgia). He attended Florida State College, excelling at football and hoped to make it a career but an unfortunate car accident forced him to change his mind and he chose acting, studying drama at Palm Beach Junior College, and having a success in 'Outward Bound'. He went to New York and his first role of importance was in 'Mister Roberts', with Chuck Heston (qv) in 1956. His rugged good looks were soon in demand for television and he played supporting roles in such shows as 'M Squad', and as Ben Frazer was a regular member of the cast of 'Riverboat (1959/60); in 1961 he returned to the New York stage for 'Look, We've Come Through', and made his big screen debut in ARMOURED COMMAND and ANGEL BABY. T.V. beckoned again and he had a long spell in 'Gunsmoke' from 1962-65 as Quint Asper, an Indian blacksmith, and this led in 1966 to his own series, as the tough detective, John 'Hawk'. On 28 June 1963 he had wed British actress Judy Carne, later to win fame in the 'Laugh-in' series, but it was a short-lived marriage, ending in 1965. Following movies OPERATION CIA (65); NAVAJO JOE (67); SHARK (68); 100 RIFLES (69); SAM WHISKEY (69); IMPASSE (69) and SKULLDUGGERY (69), he made a further T.V. series, as 'Dan August' (1970/71) but has since then concentrated on such motion-pictures as HUNTERS ARE FOR KILLING (70, T.V. movie); RUN, SIMON, RUN (70, T.V. movie); EVERYTHING YOU WANTED TO KNOW ABOUT SEX (72); FUZZ (72); DELIVERANCE (72); SHAMUS (73); THE MAN WHO LOVED CAT DANCING (73); THE LONGEST YARD (74); WHITE LIGHTNING (74); W.W. AND THE DIXIE DANCE KINGS (75); AT LAST LONG LOVE (75); HUSTLE (76); NICKLEODEON (76); LUCKY LADY (76); GATOR (76, also directed); SMOKEY AND THE BANDIT (77); THE END (77, also directed); SEMI-TOUGH (77); HOOPER (78); STARTING OVER (78); ROUGH CUT (79); SMOKEY AND THE BANDIT II (80); THE CANNONBALL RUN (80); PATERNITY (80); SHARKEY'S MACHINE (81); BEST LITTLE WHOREHOUSE IN TEXAS (82); JUST FRIENDS (82); STAND ON IT (82) and THE MAN WHO LOVED WOMEN (83).
BURT REYNOLDS: PORTRAIT OF A SUPERSTAR by Dianna Whitby; Grosset & Dunlap: New York, 1979.
BURT REYNOLDS by Bernhardt J. Hurwood; Quick Fox: London/New York, 1979, Large p/back.
THE FILMS OF BURT REYNOLDS by Nancy Streebeck; Citadel: Secaucus, N.J., 1982.
BURT REYNOLDS by Sylvia Safran Resnick; W.H. Allen: London, 1983.

RALPH RICHARDSON

Basically a man of the British theatre, Sir Ralph Richardson has always been a popular dominating film personality working regularly in this medium since 1933. He was born in Cheltenham, Gloucestershire, on 19 December 1902, the son of Arthur Richardson and his wife, Lydia. After studying art, his father's profession, he decided to become an actor and in 1918 he joined Frank R. Growcott's St. Nicholas Players in Brighton, not as an actor, but painted scenery, and was property man, general mechanic and stage electrician. In 1921 he moved to Lowestoft and made his professional stage début in 'Merchant of Venice'. It was the start of a very distinguished stage career for Mr Richardson — he toured for four years, joined the Birmingham Rep., played in the West End and in 1930 joined the Old Vic Company where he subsequently became one of Britain's most respected actors of the classical theatre. He had wed Muriel Hewitt in 1924 but she died in 1942. Richardson had made his first movie in 1933, titled THE GHOUL, which starred Boris Karloff. His other 1930s films were FRIDAY THE THIRTEENTH (33); THE RETURN OF BULLDOG DRUMMOND (34, as Hugh Drummond); JAVA HEAD (34); KING OF PARIS (34); BULLDOG JACK (35); THINGS TO COME (36); THE MAN WHO COULD WORK MIRACLES (36); THUNDER IN THE CITY (37); SOUTH RIDING (38); THE DIVORCE OF LADY X (38); THE CITADEL (38); Q PLANES (39); THE FOUR FEATHERS (39); THE LION HAS WINGS (39); ON THE NIGHT OF THE FIRE (39). On the outbreak of war he joined the Fleet Air Arm and retired, with the rank of Lieutenant Commander, in 1944 to re-establish the Old Vic Co with Laurence Olivier (qv). That year he also wed Meriel Forbes, and their son, Charles, was born in 1945. Continuing with his stage work internationally, he continued to make such films as THE DAY WILL DAWN (42); THE SILVER FLEET (43); SCHOOL FOR SECRETS (46); ANNA KARENINA (48); THE FALLEN IDOL (48); THE HEIRESS (49, Oscar nom., B.S.A., as Dr Sloper); AN OUTCAST OF THE ISLANDS (51); HOME AT SEVEN (52, also directed); THE SOUND BARRIER (52); THE HOLLY & THE IVY (53); RICHARD III (56); SMILEY (57); THE PASSIONATE STRANGER (57); OUR MAN IN HAVANA (59); OSCAR WILDE (60); EXODUS (61); THE 300 SPARTANS (62); WOMAN OF STRAW (64); DOCTOR ZHIVAGO (66); THE WRONG BOX (66); KHARTOUM (67, as Gladstone); OH! WHAT A LOVELY WAR (69); THE MIDAS RUN (69); THE BEDSITTING ROOM (69); THE BATTLE OF BRITAIN (69); THE LOOKING GLASS WAR (69); DAVID COPPERFIELD (70, T.V. movie, as Mr Micawber); EAGLE IN A CAGE (71); WHO SLEW AUNTIE ROO? (71); TALES FROM THE CRYPT (71); LADY CAROLINE LAMB (72); ALICE'S ADVENTURES IN WONDERLAND (72); A DOLL'S HOUSE (73); O LUCKY MAN (73); FRANKENSTEIN: THE TRUE STORY (73, T.V. movie); ROLLERBALL (75); JESUS OF NAZARETH (77, T.V. movie); MAN IN THE IRON MASK (77, T.V. movie); WATERSHIP DOWN (77, voice); DEATH ON THE NILE (78); TIME BANDITS (82); DRAGONSLAYER (82); WITNESS FOR THE PROSECUTION (82, T.V. movie); WAGNER (83); INVITATION TO THE WEDDING (83); GREYSTOKE — THE LEGEND OF TARZAN, LORD OF THE APES (83) and GIVE MY REGARDS TO BROAD STREET (83). Knighted in 1947, his recent stage work includes 'Early Days' (80/81, also T.V. play, 1982) and in 1981 he was honoured by the S.W.E.T. and 'The Standard' with a '60 Years in the Theatre' Special Award. *Sir Ralph died in London, on 10.10.83.*
RALPH RICHARDSON by Harold Hobson; Rockliff: London, 1958.
RALPH RICHARDSON: AN ACTOR'S LIFE by Garry O'Connor; Hodder & Stoughton: London, 1982.
RALPH RICHARDSON: A TRIBUTE by Robert Tanitch; Evans Brothers: London, 1982.

DIANA RIGG

B. Doncaster, Yorkshire, 20.7.38. Father in Indian Civil Service, Diana spending early years in Jodhpur; ed. Prep School, Bucks., and Fulneck Girls School, Leeds; aged 13 in school play as Goldilocks; studied for the stage at R.A.D.A., modelled for 4 months in stores; rep.: ASM at Chesterfield and following York Rep. joined Royal Shakespeare Co., Stratford in 1959, remaining there to attain great success with the same company in London and touring productions (especially as Helena in 'A Midsummer Night's Dream'); in 1966/67 fabulous success on T.V. as Emma Peel in 'The Avengers', being voted actress of the year in 16 countries; few movies: A MIDSUMMER NIGHT'S DREAM (68); ASSASSINATION BUREAU (68); Tracy in ON HER MAJESTY'S SECRET SERVICE (69); JULIUS CAESAR (70); THE HOSPITAL (71); THEATRE OF BLOOD (73); A LITTLE NIGHT MUSIC (76); GREAT MUPPET CAPER! (81); EVIL UNDER THE SUN (82); md. 1. Menachem Gueffen, Israeli artist (July 1973—3.9.76); daughter Rachel Atlanta born 30.5.77; U.S.T.V. ser: 'Diana' (73/74); recent stage: 'Heartbreak House' (83); T.V.: 'King Lear' (83); WITNESS FOR THE PROSECUTION (82, T.V. movie); *NO STONE UNTURNED* (humorous collection of fellow-artistes' stage reviews, compiled by D.R.); Elm Tree: London, 1982.

JASON ROBARDS JR.

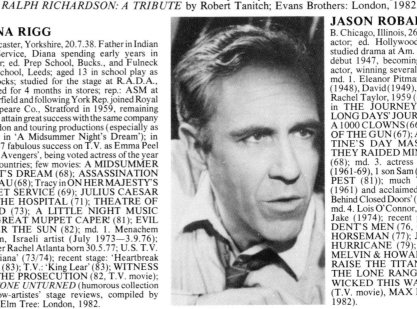

B. Chicago, Illinois, 26.7.22. Father stage/screen actor; ed. Hollywood H.S.; WWII in Navy, studied drama at Am. Acad. D.A., making stage début 1947, becoming distinguished Broadway actor, winning several awards; T.V. from 1948, md. 1. Eleanor Pitman, 1946-58, 2 sons: Jason (1948), David (1949), 1 daughter Sara (1947); 2. Rachel Taylor, 1959 (div.); came to screen 1958 in THE JOURNEY, several in 60s include LONG DAYS' JOURNEY INTO NIGHT (62); A 1000 CLOWNS (66); Doc Holliday in HOUR OF THE GUN (67); Al Capone in ST. VALENTINE'S DAY MASSACRE (67); NIGHT THEY RAIDED MINSKY'S (68); ISADORA (68); md. 3. actress Miss Lauren Bacall (qv 1961-69), 1 son Sam (1962, screen début: TEMPEST (81)); much T.V. includes 'Acapulco (1961) and acclaimed mini-series 'Washington Behind Closed Doors' (1977) as Richard Monkton; md. 4. Lois O'Connor, children: Shannon (1972), Jake (1974); recent pics: ALL THE PRESIDENT'S MEN (76, Oscar, BSA); COMES A HORSEMAN (77); JULIA (77, Oscar, BSA); HURRICANE (79); CABO BLANCO (79); MELVIN & HOWARD (79, Oscar nom., BA); RAISE THE TITANIC (79); LEGEND OF THE LONE RANGER (81); SOMETHING WICKED THIS WAY COMES, HAYWIRE (T.V. movie), MAX DUGAN RETURNS (all 1982).

RACHEL ROBERTS

B. Llanelli, Wales, 20.9.27. Father a minister; ed. Univ. of Wales (B.A.); trained for the stage at R.A.D.A., previously working briefly as a nurse, cook and circus programme seller; stage career began 1951, with Shakespeare Mem. Theatre, Stratford, later winning acclaim and awards for her many performances (at Old Vic, Bristol, West End, Royal Court, musical as 'Maggie May', etc., later U.S. stage); md. 1. actor Alan Dobie (div.); over 25 movies including VALLEY OF SONG (52, début); WEAK & THE WICKED (54); OUR MAN IN HAVANA (59); SATURDAY NIGHT & SUNDAY MORNING (60, BFA, Best Actress); THIS SPORTING LIFE (63, BFA—Best Actress, Oscar nom.); A FLEA IN HER EAR (68, opp. Rex Harrison (qv), whom she married (1962-71)); WILD ROVERS (71); O LUCKY MAN (73); BELSTONE FOX (73); MURDER ON THE ORIENT EXPRESS (74); PICNIC AT HANGING ROCK (75); A CIRCLE OF CHILDREN (77, T.V. movie); YANKS (78, BFA, BSA); FOUL PLAY (78); THE HOSTAGE TOWER, WHEN A STRANGER CALLS (80); CHARLIE CHAN AND THE CURSE OF THE DRAGON QUEEN (81).
Miss Roberts passed away, Los Angeles, 27.11.80.

TONY ROBERTS

B. New York City, 22.10.39; Ed. Northwestern Univ.; stage includes 1962: 'Something About a Soldier', 'Take Her, She's Mine', 1964: 'The Last Analysis', 1965: Paul Bratter in 'Barefoot in the Park', 1970: toured in 'Promises, Promises'; till 1972 known as 'Anthony' Roberts; films: THE $1,000,000 DUCK (71); STAR-SPANGLED GIRL (72); PLAY IT AGAIN, SAM (72, also stage); SERPICO (74); TAKING OF PELHAM ONE, TWO, THREE (74); THE LINDBERG KIDNAPPING CASE (76, T.V. movie); THE SAVAGE (77); ROSETTI & RYAN: MEN WHO LOVED WOMEN (77, T.V. movie); ANNIE HALL (77); GIRLS IN THE OFFICE (79, T.V. movie); A QUESTION OF HONOUR (81, T.V. movie); A MIDSUMMER NIGHT'S SEX COMEDY (82).

TANYA ROBERTS

B. Bronx, New York, 15.10. . In teens appeared on stage in New York and Canada; at 17 in T.V. commercials, little theatre/off Broadway productions, studying with Uta Hagen, Alice Spivak, Alice Hermes and Lee Strasberg; md. Barry Roberts, writer; to Hollywood summer 1977; small roles in T.V. movies 'Pleasure Cove' and 'Zuma Beach' (78), several movies and 2-hour 'Vegas' epis. before chosen to play Julie Rogers in 'Charlie's Angels' (1981); THE BEASTMASTER (82).

CLIFF ROBERTSON

B. La Jolla, Calif., 9.9.25. Full name: Clifford Parker Robertson III; ed. Antioch College; early ambitions: pilot and sailor, but appeared in school plays; studied Actors' Studio; worked as 'private bodyguard/detective'; in 'Mister Roberts', Chicago and tour; early 1950s: several T.V. appearances including series as Ranger 'Rod Brown of the Rocket Rangers' (1953/54); New York stage: 'Late Love' (53); 'The Wisteria Trees' (55) — wife of Joshua Logan (producer) saw him, and husband cast Cliff in movie PICNIC (55); md. Cynthia Stone 1957, 1 daughter Stephanie (1959) (div.); 2. Dina Merrill 21.12.66, 1 daughter Heather; approx. 40 motion-pictures including AUTUMN LEAVES (56); NAKED & THE DEAD (58); THE INTERNS (62); PT 109 (62, as J.F. Kennedy); SUNDAY IN N.Y. (64); THE BEST MAN (64); UP FROM THE BEACH (65); CHARLY (68, Oscar B.A.); J.W. COOP (72, also wrote/dir.); OBSESSION (76); MIDWAY (76); SHOOT (76); RETURN TO EARTH (76, T.V. movie); DOMINIQUE (77); OVERBOARD (78, T.V. movie); THE PILOT (81, also directed); other T.V. includes Action Playhouse: 'Verdict for Truth' (1971) and 'Washington: Behind Closed Doors' (1977, miniser.); BRAINSTORM, STAR 80, CLASS (all 1982); also play/script-writer, owner/flyer of vintage aircraft.

FLORA ROBSON

B. South Shields, Durham, 28.3.02. Ed. Palmer's Green H.S. and trained R.A.D.A., winning Bronze Medal, 1921, stage début that year, London in 'Will Shakespeare', but in 1925 left profession to work as welfare worker in factory at Welwyn; resumed career 1929, becoming one of Britain's most respected stage actresses, created CBE in 1952, and Dame of B. Empire, 1960; movies include DANCE PRETTY LADY! (31); as the Empress Elizabeth in CATHERINE THE GREAT (34); Queen Elizabeth I in FIRE OVER ENGLAND (36); WUTHERING HEIGHTS (39); SARATOGA TRUNK (46, Oscar nom., USA); CAESAR & CLEOPATRA (46, as Ftateeta) and recently DOMINIQUE (77); LES MISERABLES (78, T.V. movie); A MAN CALLED INTREPID (78, T.V. movie); A TALE OF TWO CITIES (80); Dame Flora holds Hon. Litt.D.—Durham, Wales, London, Oxford; CLASH OF THE TITANS (81).
FLORA ROBSON by Janet Dunbar; Harrap: London, 1960; FLORA: An Appreciation of the Life & Work of Dame Flora Robson by Kenneth Barrow; Heinemann: London, 1981.

CESAR ROMERO

B. New York City, 15.2.07. Father Ceasar Julius Romero, Cuban sugar trader; grandfather was revolutionary and poet; ed. Collegiate and Riverdale Country Schools, studied dramatics; Cesar was a bank messenger, but switched to a dancing career, appeared on Broadway in 'Lady Do!' (1927), show closed but he later gained fame as speciality dancer with Elizabeth Higgins; straight actor in plays such as 'Strictly Dishonourable' (1930), 'Dinner at Eight' (1932); came to screen 1933 in THE SHADOW LAUGHS (33), becoming debonair Hollywood star of 1930s and '40s in such pics as THE THIN MAN (34); CLIVE OF INDIA (35); THE DEVIL IS A WOMAN (35); RETURN OF THE CISCO KID (39, title role and several sequels); THE GAY CABALLERO (40); TALL, DARK AND HANDSOME (41); ORCHESTRA WIVES (42); CONEY ISLAND (43); WWII service: U.S. Coast Guard; CAPTAIN FROM CASTILE (47); ONCE A THIEF (50); VERA CRUZ (54); VILLA! (58); OCEAN'S 11 (60); DONOVAN'S REEF (63); CROOKS AND CORONETS (68); MIDAS RUN (69); opened L.A. restaurant 1972: 'Cappucino'; much T.V. includes 'Batman' (series 1965/66 as 'The Joker'), 'Cesar's World' (1968); more recent movies: THE SPECTRE OF EDGAR ALLEN POE (74); STRONGEST MAN IN THE WORLD (75); guest 1982: 'Matt Houston' (T.V.).

ANTON RODGERS

B. Wisbech, Cambs., 10.1.33. Ed. Westminster City School and the Italia Conti Stage School; early stage début, aged 14, in 'Carmen' at Covent Garden, London, followed by tours 'Great Expectations' as Pip, and as 'The Winslow Boy'; following further rep., trained at LAMDA; became well-known in British theatre as distinguished actor in wide range of productions, and notable stage director; md. Morna (Head of Drama, Richmond Coll.); 1 daughter Thalia, 1 son Adam; few motion-pictures include ROTTEN TO THE CORE (64); THE MAN WHO HAUNTED HIMSELF (69); SCROOGE (70); THE DAY OF THE JACKAL (72); and EAST OF ELEPHANT ROCK (77); a familiar face on television, Mr Rodgers has played in such programmes as 'The Organisation', 'Zodiac', 'Rumpole of the Bailey' and in 1978 in 'Lilly'; stage credits in more recent years include Australian tour National Theatre in 'Front Page' (1974), directed 'Death of a Salesman' (1975, Oxford); London: 'Gaslight' (1976, Criterion) and 'Songbook' (1979, Globe); recent T.V.: 'Preview' (82), 'Pictures' (83); stage: 'Windy City' (82/83).

MICKEY ROONEY

B. Brooklyn, New York, 23.9.20(?). Real name Joe Yule, Jr.; ed. Studio Schools, Dayton Heights & Vine St. Grammar Schools; stage debut aged 11 months in act with parents; 1st movie, aged 5, NOT TO BE TRUSTED, then, as Mickey McGuire, a series of short comedies; at 12, returned to stage, but in 1935 given M-G-M contract, very popular in 'Andy Hardy' films, musicals, headed popularity polls, U.S.A. in 1939, 40 and 41 and special Academy Award in 1938; WWII, entertained more than 2 million GI's in 'Jeep Shows'; Marriages: 1. actress Ava Gardner (1942-43); 2. Betty Jane Rase (1944-?), 2 sons Mickey (1944), Timothy (1947); 3. actress Martha Vickers (1949-51), 1 son Teddy (born ?); 4. Elaine Mahnken (1952-59); 5. Barbara Thomason (1959—widowed 1966), 2 daughters Kelly (1959), Kerry (1960), 1 son Kyle (1961); 6. Margaret Lane (1966-67); 7. Carolyn Hockett (1969-73); 8. country/western singer Janice Chamberlain (1978); Mickey's most recent movies: DOMINO KILLINGS (77); PETE'S DRAGON (77); THE BLACK STALLION (79, Oscar nom., BSA); MAGIC OF LASSIE (78); ARABIAN ADVENTURE (78); BLACK STALLION RETURNS (81), LEAVE 'EM LAUGHING (81, T.V. movie); 'Sugar Babies' (B'way, 79); 'Bill' (82, Golden Globe Aw.); Honorary Oscar, 1982.
I.E.: AN AUTOBIOGRAPHY by M.R.; G.P. Putnam & Sons: New York, 1965.

DIANA ROSS

B. Detroit, Michigan, 26.3.45(?). Father minister; while at school Diana formed group, 'The Primettes' with friends Florence Ballard, Mary Wilson and Barbara Martin; in 1960 auditioned for Motown Record Corp., and became session singers for Motown acts; upon leaving school renamed 'The Supremes' and toured with Motor Town Revue; first disc 1962 and 1st big hit, 1964, 'Where Did Our Love Go?'; appeared in movie, BEACH BALL, in 1965, and sang on soundtrack of THE HAPPENING (66); 'The Supremes' had 15 consecutive hit records and once have five consecutive records in No.1 spot in charts; Diana split with group in 1969, singing in clubs and on T.V. ('An Evening With Diana', etc.); md. Bob Silberstein, 20.1.71 (div. 1977), 3 daughters: Rhonda Suzanne (1971), Tracey Joy (1972), Chudney (1975); Billie Holliday in LADY SINGS THE BLUES (72, Oscar nom., B.A.); MAHOGONY (75); Dorothy in THE WIZ (77). *SUPREME LADY* by Connie Berman, 1978; *DIANA ROSS* by Geoff Brown; Sidgwick & Jackson: London, 1981.

LEONARD ROSSITER

B. Liverpool 24.10.26. Ed. Liverpool Collegiate School: he couldn't afford to go to univ., so he worked in an insurance office for 6 years; commenced career on stage as ASM, Preston Rep., 1954, following other reps., built up a steady reputation as character actor, including work on Broadway and won Variety Club B.A. Award (1969) in 'Resistible Rise of Arturo Ui'; supporting roles in numerous movies including A KIND OF LOVING (62); THIS SPORTING LIFE (63); BILLY LIAR (63); WRONG BOX (66); DEADLIER THAN THE MALE (66); KING RAT (66); HOTEL PARADISO (66); DEVIL'S OWN (66); DEADFALL (67); THE WHISPERERS (67); 2001: A SPACE ODYSSEY (68); OLIVER! (68, as Mr Sowerberry); OTLEY (69); LUTHER (75); BARRY LYNDON (75); PINK PANTHER STRIKES AGAIN (77); VOYAGE OF THE DAMNED (77); md. 1. Josephine Tewson (div.); 2. Gillian Raine, 1 daughter Camilla; recent outstanding T.V. success in 'Fall & Rise of Reginald Perrin' (1975-77), 'Rising Damp' (1976-78, and movie 1980) series, 'Cinzano' ads; film 82: BRITANNIA HOSPITAL; stage 82: 'Rules of the Game'. *THE LOWEST FORM OF WIT* by L.R.; Michael Joseph: London, 1981.

GENA ROWLANDS

B. Cambria, Wisconsin, 19.6.36. Real name Virginia Cathryn Rowlands; father Wisconsin State Senator; ed. Univ. of Wisconsin and Am.A.D.A. (met and md. actor/director John Cassavetes (qv), 1954); early T.V. at this time was the role of Powell, an assistant in 'Top Secret USA' (1954); Gena understudied and later played the Girl in 'Seven Year Itch' and in 1956 she attained success for 18 months in 'Middle of the Night' in New York, leading to movie début in THE HIGH COST OF LOVING (58); other movies: LONELY ARE THE BRAVE (62); THE SPIRAL ROAD (62); A CHILD IS WAITING (62*); TONY ROME (67); FACES (68*); THE HAPPY ENDING (69); MINNIE & MOSKOWITZ (71*); A WOMAN UNDER THE INFLUENCE (74*, Oscar nom., BA); TWO-MINUTE WARNING (76); A QUESTION OF LOVE (78, T.V. movie); THE BRINK'S JOB (78); STRANGERS: THE STORY OF A MOTHER & DAUGHTER (79, T.V. movie) and GLORIA (80*, Oscar nom., BA) (* directed by husband); children: Alexandra (born 1965), Nicholas (1967) and Zoe (70); frequent T.V. guest and series: '87th Precinct' T.V. ser.: Teddy Carella in '87th Precinct' (61/62), Adrienne Van Leyden in 'Peyton Place' (67); movie 1981: TEMPEST.

KURT RUSSELL

B. Springfield, Mass., 17.3.51. Father Bing Russell, former baseball player-turned-actor who played Elvis's father in ELVIS: THE MOVIE; Kurt broke into movies in the early 60s as a child actor: IT HAPPENED AT THE WORLD'S FAIR (63); subsequently appeared in many Disney movies; T.V. series 1963/64: 'The Travels of Jaimie McPheeters' (title role); other films include FOLLOW ME, BOYS! (66); THE ONE & ONLY, GENUINE, ORIGINAL FAMILY BAND (68); THE HORSE IN THE GRAY FLANNEL SUIT (68); THE BAREFOOT EXECUTIVE (71); NOW YOU SEE HIM, NOW YOU DON'T (72); CHARLEY & THE ANGEL (73); SUPERDAD (74); THE DEADLY TOWER (75, T.V. movie); STRONGEST MAN IN THE WORLD (75); SEARCH FOR THE GODS (75, T.V. movie); md. actress Season Hubley (qv), 1 son Boston (born 1980); he played Elvis in 'Elvis: The Movie' (79); other pictures: USED CARS (79); ESCAPE FROM NEW YORK (80); FOX & THE HOUND (81, voice only); THE THING (82); other T.V.: Love Story: 'Beginner's Luck' (74) and Bo Larsen in 'The New Land' (74, ser.); movie 1983: SILKWOOD.

KATHERINE ROSS

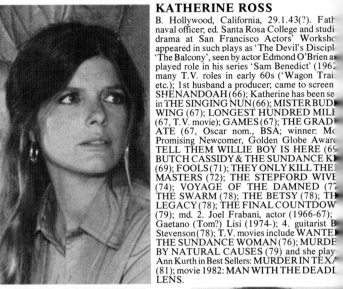

B. Hollywood, California, 29.1.43(?). Fath... naval officer; ed. Santa Rosa College and studi... drama at San Francisco Actors' Worksho... appeared in such plays as 'The Devil's Discipl... 'The Balcony', seen by actor Edmond O'Brien a... played role in his series 'Sam Benedict' (1962... many T.V. roles in early 60s ('Wagon Trai... etc.); 1st husband a producer; came to screen... SHENANDOAH (66); Katherine has been se... in THE SINGING NUN (66); MISTER BUD... WING (67); LONGEST HUNDRED MILE... (67, T.V. movie); GAMES (67); THE GRAD... ATE (67, Oscar nom., BSA; winner: M... Promising Newcomer, Golden Globe Awar... TELL THEM WILLIE BOY IS HERE (69... BUTCH CASSIDY & THE SUNDANCE K... (69); FOOLS (71); THEY ONLY KILL THE... MASTERS (72); THE STEPFORD WIVE... (74); VOYAGE OF THE DAMNED (7... THE SWARM (78); THE BETSY (78); TH... LEGACY (78); THE FINAL COUNTDOW... (79); md. 2. Joel Frabani, actor (1966-67); Gaetano (Tom?) Lisi (1974-); 4. guitarist B... Stevenson (78); T.V. movies include WANTE... THE SUNDANCE WOMAN (76); MURDE... BY NATURAL CAUSES (79) and she play... Ann Kurth in Best Sellers: MURDER IN TEXA... (81); movie 1982: MAN WITH THE DEADL... LENS.

RICHARD ROUNDTREE

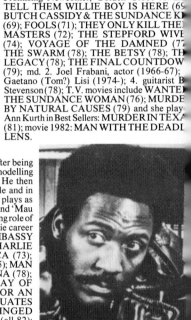

B. New Rochelle, New York, 7.9.42. After being educated at S. Illinois, Richard took up modelling for the Ebony Magazine Fashion Fair. He then joined the Workshop of Negro Ensemble and in the late 60s played in New York in such plays as 'Kongi's Harvest', 'Man, Better, Man' and 'Mau Mau Room'; his performance in the leading role of 'The Great White Hope' lead to his movie career and he has played in SHAFT (71); EMBASSY (72); SHAFT'S BIG SCORE (72); CHARLIE ONE-EYE (72); SHAFT IN AFRICA (73); EARTHQUAKE (74); DIAMONDS (75); MAN FRIDAY (75); ESCAPE TO ATHENA (78); GAMES FOR VULTURES (79); DAY OF THE ASSASSINS (80); AN EYE FOR AN EYE, INCHON! (both 81); THE GRADUATES OF MALIBU HIGH, Q: THE WINGED SERPENT, ONE DOWN, 2 TO GO (all 82); PORTRAIT OF A HIT MAN (83); T.V. movie 73: FIREHOUSE; T.V. ser., 74: as 'Shaft'; miniser. 77: ROOTS.

JENNY RUNACRE

B. Cape Town, S. Africa, 18.8.43. Miss Runac... appeared in rep. in the north of England, London in such productions as 'Highwayman' the Round House, 'Bitter Tears of Petra v... Kant' in Hampstead, and work with the Op... Space, King's Head, Basement and Bush Theatr... — she was also in the original cast of 'O Calcutt... following her big screen début in HUSBAND... (70), she won the 'Evening News Best Scre... Newcomer' award for THE FINAL PRO... RAMME, in 1973; other motion-pictu... appearances have been in THE MACKINTOS... MAN (74); CANTERBURY TALES (74, se... ment: 'The Miller's Tale), THE PASSENGE... (75); THE DUELLISTS (76); JOSEPH ANI... REWS (76); JUBILEE (77); THE LAD... VANISHES (78); HUSSY (79) and ALTE... NATIVE MISS WORLD (80); Jenny, who al... works as a professional journalist has been se... on T.V. in such series as 'The New Avenger... 'The Sweeney' and 'Brideshead Revisited' (198...

BARBARA RUSH

B. Denver, Colorado, 4.1.28(?). Stage débu... aged 10, Loberto Theatre, Santa Barbara... 'Golden Ball'; ed. U.C.L.A., award for role... 'Little Foxes' — won scholarship to Pasader... Playhouse; spotted in production of 'Anthony... Cleopatra', coming to screen in THE FIRS... LEGION (51); md. 1. actor Jeffrey Hunt... (dec.), 1950-54(55?), 1 son Christopher (1952... 2. Warren Cowan, 1 daughter Lynn (born 31.7.63... Barbara's T.V. includes Lizzie Hogan in 'Sain... & Sinners' (1962/63), Margot Brighton in 'Ne... Dick Van Dyke Show' (1973/74); md. 3. Jam... Gruzalski; movies include WHEN WORLD... COLLIDE (51); TAZA, SON OF COCHIS... (54); KISS OF FIRE (55); THE BRAMBL... BUSH (60); COME BLOW YOUR HOR... (63); ROBIN & THE 7 HOODS (64); HOMBR... (67); SUPERDAD (74); DEATH CAR O... THE FREEWAY (79, T.V. movie); CAN... STOP THE MUSIC (80); 'Flamingo Roa... (1981, series).

THERESA RUSSELL

B. San Diego, . .57. Theresa attended Burbar... H.S., where she acted and at 16 went to New Yor... to study with Lee Strasberg for 2 years; she cam... to the screen in THE LAST TYCOON (76... returned to study for 1 year at Actors' Studi... screen work has since included STRAIGH... TIME (77); as Maureen Dean in the mini-seri... BLIND AMBITION (79); BAD TIMING (79... EUREKA (82).

EVA MARIE SAINT

, Newark, New Jersey, 4.7.24. Ed. Bowling Green State Univ., Ohio (B.A. Degree); md. Jeffrey Heyden, 1951, 1 son Darrell (1955), 1 daughter Laurette (1958); much T.V.; Broadway — 'The Trip to Bountiful' (1953); movies include IN THE WATERFRONT (54, Oscar BSA); RAINTREE COUNTY (57); A HATFUL OF RAIN (57); NORTH-BY-NORTHWEST (59); EXODUS (60); LOVING (69); THE MACAHANS (76, T.V. movie); A CHRISTMAS TO REMEMBER (78, T.V. movie); CURSE OF KING TUT'S TOMB (80, T.V. movie); JANE DOE (83, T.V. movie).

DOMINIQUE SANDA

., Paris, France, . . 48. Real name Dominique Varaigne; educated by nuns at the St. Vincent school in Paris, Dominique later began a course in interior design at the Beaux-Arts, but skipped classes to work as a photographic model. When director Robert Bresson saw her photograph in 'Vogue' magazine he cast her in UNE FEMME DOUCE, in 1970; she has since been seen internationally in such productions as FIRST LOVE (70); THE CONFORMIST (70); THE GARDEN OF THE FINZI-CONTINIS (70); WITHOUT APPARENT MOTIVE (72); IMPOSSIBLE OBJECT (73); STEPPENWOLF (74); THE MACKINTOSH MAN (74); CONVERSATION PIECE (75); DAMNATION ALLEY (78); BEYOND EVIL (77); REMEMBER MY NAME (78); UTOPIA (78); CABOBLANCO (79); VOYAGE EN DOUCE (81).

CHRIS SARANDON – see page 126

MICHAEL SARRAZIN

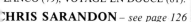

B. Quebec City, Canada, 22.5.40. Real name Jacques Michel Andre Sarrazin; parents French-Canadians, father an attorney; Michael started acting at Loyola Junior College in Montreal, including production of 'The Winslow Boy'; attended Canadian Drama Studio; aged 17 became professional actor with leads in 4 historical documentaries for National Film Board of Canada, his performance in play for Canadian Broadcasting T.V., Toronto, in 1965, won him 4-year Universal contract; 1st U.S. T.V. role in 'The Virginian' epis.; movies include GUNFIGHT IN ABILENE (66); THE FLIM FLAN MAN (67); DOOMSDAY FLIGHT (66, T.V. movie); JOURNEY TO SHILOH (68); THE SWEET RIDE (68); A MAN CALLED GANNON (69); EYE OF THE CAT (69); THEY SHOOT HORSES, DON'T THEY (69); IN SEARCH OF GREGORY (70); THE PURSUIT OF HAPPINESS (71); BELIEVE IN ME (71); SOMETIMES A GREAT NOTION (71); THE GROUNDSTAR CONSPIRACY (72); FRANKENSTEIN: THE TRUE STORY (73, T.V. movie, as Creature); FOR PETE'S SAKE (75); REINCARNATION OF PETER PROUD (75); GUMBALL RALLY (76); LOVES & TIMES OF SCARAMOUCHE (76); CARAVANS (78); Best Sellers: BEULAH LAND (80, T.V. movie); THE SEDUCTION, DEATH VENGEANCE (both 1982).

SUSAN ST. JAMES

B. Los Angeles, California 17(?).8.46. Real name Susan Miller; when young family moved to Rockford, Ill.; ed: Sacred Heart Academy for Girls; Susan had ambitions to become singer when in Paris, but had trouble with vocal chords; turned to modelling, 1963, in New York and Europe; discovered by Universal and given contract; movies: FAME IS THE NAME OF THE GAME (66, T.V. movie); WHERE ANGELS GO . . . TROUBLE FOLLOWS (68); NEW FACE IN HELL (PJ) (68); WHAT'S SO BAD ABOUT FEELING GOOD?; (68); MAGIC CARPET (72, T.V. movie); OUTLAW BLUES (76); SCOTT FREE (76, T.V. movie); LOVE AT FIRST BITE (78); DESPERATE WOMEN (78, T.V. movie); NIGHT CRIES (78, T.V. movie); HOW TO BEAT THE HIGH COST OF LIVING (79); THE GIRLS IN THE OFFICE (79, T.V. movie); md. 1. writer Richard Neubert (1967-68); 2. make-up man Tommy Lucas (1971—div.), 1 daughter Sunshine (born 1972), 1 son Harmony (1973); Susan is well-known on T.V., appearing in such series as; 'It Takes a Thief' (1968) as Chuck Brown, 'The Name of the Game' (1968-71—winning her an Emmy Award 1969) as Peggy Maxwell and 'McMillan and Wife' (1971-76) as Sandy McMillan; recent movies: CARBON COPY (80); DON'T CRY, IT'S ONLY THUNDER (82); md. 3. Dick Ebergol.

SUSAN SARANDON

B. New York City 4.10.46. Following her education at Catholic Univ., Susan ventured to New York in the hope of an acting career; became a model with the Ford Model Agency, coming to the screen eventually in 1970, in JOE; md. actor Chris Sarandon (qv) (div.); T.V. series: Patrice Kahlam in 'A World Apart' (70/71); motion-pictures include THE FRONT PAGE (74); LOVIN' MOLLY (74); F. SCOTT FITZGERALD & 'THE LAST OF THE BELLES' (74, T.V. movie); THE GREAT WALDO PEPPER (75); THE ROCKY HORROR PICTURE SHOW (75); DRAGONFLY (76); THE OTHER SIDE OF MIDNIGHT (77); CHECKERED FLAG OR CRASH (77); THE GREAT SMOKEY ROAD-BLOCK (78); PRETTY BABY (78); KING OF THE GYPSIES (79); LOVING COUPLES (79); ATLANTIC CITY (Canadian 'Genie' Aw., Oscar nom., BA), TEMPEST (both 81); THE HUNGER (82); THE BUDDY SYSTEM (83); stage 82: 'Extremities'.

JOHN SAVAGE

B. ———, . . . Mr Savage trained at the Am.A.D.A. and in Manhattan organised Children's Theatre Group which performed in Public Housing; he has since played in many plays in New York; he won a Drama Circle Award for his performance in 'One Flew Over The Cuckoo's Nest', staged in Chicago and Los Angeles; other plays in which he has performed include 'Sensations', 'Fiddler on the Roof', 'Ari', 'Siamese Connections', 'The Hostage' and 'American Buffalo'; he played Jim Malloy in a short-lived series, 'Gibbsville', in 1976 and his motion-pictures appearances include BAD COMPANY (72); STEELYARD BLUES (73); ALL THE KIND STRANGERS (74, T.V. movie); THE TURNING POINT OF JIM MALLOY (75, T.V. movie); THE DEERHUNTER (78); HAIR (78); THE ONION FIELD (79); INSIDE MOVES (80); CATTLE ANNIE & LITTLE BRITCHES (81); COMING OUT OF THE ICE, THE AMATEUR, THE KILLING KIND (all 1982); 'Laverne & Shirley' (T.V. ser., 1982).

TELLY SAVALAS

Prior to his international success from 1973 in the T.V. series 'Kojak', Telly Savalas was already a respected character player in dozens of movies after varied work in broadcasting and television. He was born Aristotle (after the Greek philosopher) Savalas on 21 January 1924 at Garden City, New York, the son of Nicholas Savalas, an import/export tobacco salesman, and his wife, Christina. There were three other sons (including George, who also became an actor) and one daughter. Young Telly attended Holy Cross School, Connecticut at the age of 5, but when the Depression came in the early 30s, his father's business suffered and he helped him build up a successful bakery concern in New York City. Wounded in WWII while in the National Guard, he was invalided out, attended Columbia University, studying psychology with the aim to become a psychologist. While there he wed a fellow graduate, Catherine, and their daughter, Christine, was born. After University he worked at the Information Dept. of the Dept. of State (known as the Voice of America), becoming a senior director of news and special events. Becoming interested in theatre, he ran a stock company in Connecticut for three years and later administered the Garden City Little Theatre. His first acting job was on T.V. in the Armstrong Circle Theatre: 'Bring Home a Baby', as a Greek judge, in 1959. David Susskind discovered him and gave him the lead role as gangster Lucky Luciano in a T.V. episode of 'The Witness' (59). In 1960 Savalas entered his second marriage, to Marilyn Gardner, and daughters Penelope and Candace were born in 1962 and 1963 respectively. In 1961 he played 'Mr Carver' in a short-lived series, 'Acapulco', and began his highly successful movie career in MAD DOG COLL and THE YOUNG SAVAGES. The latter starred Burt Lancaster (qv) and the established Superstar saw that Telly had an important role in BIRDMAN OF ALCATRAZ, winning him an Academy Award nomination as Best Supporting Actor of 1962. He has since played in over 40 movies, including CAPE FEAR (63); GENGHIS KHAN (65); THE GREATEST STORY EVER TOLD (65, as Pontius Pilate); BATTLE OF THE BULGE (65); BEAU GESTE (66, as the evil sergeant); THE DIRTY DOZEN (67); THE SCALPHUNTERS (67) and O.H.M.S.S. (69, as Blofeld). Divorced from his second wife, he has a son, Nicholas, mother being Sally Adams. As Theo 'Kojak', the show premiered on U.S. T.V. on 24 October 1973. Recent movies include DIAMOND MERCENARIES (76); CAPRICORN ONE (77); ESCAPE TO ATHENA (78); BEYOND THE POSEIDON ADVENTURE (79); FRENCH ATLANTIC AFFAIR (79, T.V. movie); FAKE OUT (81); HELLINGER'S LAW (81, T.V. movie) and BEYOND REASON (82, also wrote/directed).
TELLY SAVALAS by Marsha Daly; Sphere Books: London, 1975; p/b.

JOHN SAXON

B. New York City 5.8.35. Real name Carmen Orrico; father Italian dockworker; John attended New Utrecht H.S. where he appeared in several plays; walking in a New York street he was advised by a photographer to take up photographic modelling; this he did and his photos were seen by Hollywood agent Henry Wilson; he took small roles on T.V., studied acting at Carnegie Hall under Betty Cashman and eventually signed a Universal Intn'l contract, coming to the screen in 1955 in RUNNING WILD; he has since played in many movies, guested on T.V. on several occasions, recently one of Hollywood's busiest actors; played Dr Ted Stuart in series 'The New Doctors' (1969-72); movies include ROCK, PRETTY BABY (57); RESTLESS YEARS (58); RELUCTANT DEBUTANTE (59); THE PLUNDERERS (60); WAR HUNT (62); THE CARDINAL (63); WINCHESTER 73 (67, T.V. movie); ISTANBUL EXPRESS (68, T.V. movie); DEATH OF A GUNSLINGER (69); THE INTRUDERS (70, T.V. movie); SNATCHED (73, T.V. movie); LINDA (73, T.V. movie); CAN ELLEN BE SAVED? (74, T.V. movie); BLACK CHRISTMAS (75); SWISS CONSPIRACY (75); RAID ON ENTEBBE (77, T.V. movie); STRANGE SHADOWS IN AN EMPTY ROOM (77, T.V. movie); MOONSHINE COUNTY EXPRESS (77); THE BEES (78); MITCHELL (78); ZIEGFELD: THE MAN & HIS WOMEN (78, T.V. movie); SPECIAL COP IN ACTION (78); FAST COMPANY (78); BEYOND EVIL (79); BLOOD BEACH (79); THE ELECTRIC HORSEMAN (79); BATTLE BEYOND THE STARS (79); THE GLOVE (80); MAN WITH THE DEADLY LENS (82); PRISONERS OF THE LOST UNIVERSE (83); T.V. 82: 'Dallas'.

CATHERINE SCHELL

B. Budapest, Hungary, .. 46. Real name Catherine Von Schell; parents: Baron and Baroness Von Schell; family escaped Russian-occupied Hungary in 1949; for seven years they lived in the United States, in 1958 moving to Munich, where Catherine completed her education, coming to the screen, aged 18, in LANA, QUEEN OF THE AMAZONS; since 1969 has based her career in England, commencing with one of the Bond girls in ON HER MAJESTY'S SECRET SERVICE; other movies include MOON ZERO TWO (69); MADAME SIN (71); CALLAN (74); THE BLACK WINDMILL (74); RETURN OF THE PINK PANTHER (74); THE PINK PANTHER STRIKES AGAIN (76); PRISONER OF ZENDA (78); md. actor William Marlowe (div. May 1977); many T.V. plays have included 'Napoleon & Love' (1974), 'Looking For Clancy' (1975), 'Space 1999' (1976, series), 'Dr Who' (1979), 'Thriller: Look Back in Darkness' (1980), Paula Brandt in 'The Spoils of War' (1981, ser.); 'Island of Adventure', 'Strangers' (both 82); ON THE THIRD DAY (83).

ARNOLD SCHWARZENEGGER
– see page 126

MARIA SCHNEIDER

B. Paris, 27.3.52. Father Daniel Gelin, French stage/screen actor; mother a Rumanian; left school at 15 to play a dancer in 'Superposition', running for 3 months at Theatre 347 in Paris, 1968; lead to walk-on screen roles in MADLY (71); CARI GENITORI (with Helmut Berger); THE OLD MAID (with Annie Girardot); her first speaking role was in Vadim's HELLO and she has since been seen in LAST TANGO IN PARIS (72); THE PASSENGER (74); LA DEROBADE (80); MAMA DRACULA (80); HATE (81); CERCASI GESU (82), others.

PAUL SCOFIELD

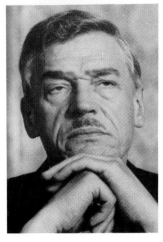

B. Hurstpierpoint, Sussex, 21.1.22. Father a headmaster; ed. Varndean School for Boys, Brighton, Sussex, making stage debut in that town at the Theatre Royal, while still a boy in 'The Only Way' (36); studied at London Mask Theatre School; became one of Britain's foremost stage actors, making few movies; md: actress Joy Parker 1944, 1 daughter Sarah, 1 son Martin; received the CBE in 1956; films: Philip of Spain in THAT LADY (55); CARVE HER NAME WITH PRIDE (57); THE TRAIN (64); A MAN FOR ALL SEASONS (66, as Sir Thomas More, Oscar BA, also stage: London (1960) and New York (1961)); TELL ME LIES (68); KING LEAR (69); BARTLEBY (70); SCORPIO (72); A DELICATE BALANCE (74); numerous stage awards and Honours; T.V. 1981: 'The Potting Shed', 'If Winter Comes'.
PAUL SCOFIELD by J.C. Trewin; Rockliff: London, 1956.

ROY SCHEIDER

B. Orange, N. Jersey, 10.11.35. Ed. Franklin a⟨nd⟩ Marshall College, Pa.; intended to go to la⟨w⟩ school, but as a teenager won two There⟨sa⟩ Helburn Acting Awards at college before servi⟨ng⟩ with U.S. Air Force; worked as waiter befo⟨re⟩ getting first stage/T.V. roles; billed early in care⟨er⟩ as 'Roy R. Scheider'; 1st major stage role Mercutio in 'Romeo and Juliet' (1961) at Ne⟨w⟩ York S'peare Fest.; played with Lincoln Cent⟨re⟩ Rep. Co., etc., stage includes 'Duchess of Mal⟨fi⟩ (1962), 'Stephen D' (1966), 'The Nuns' (196⟨9⟩ many others; md. Cynthia (a film editor), daughter Maxmilia (1964); came to the scre⟨en⟩ 1964 in CURSE OF THE LIVING CORPS⟨E⟩ supporting roles to Superstardom in 70s; STA⟨R⟩ (68); PAPER LION (68); STILETTO (6⟨9⟩ LOVING (70); PUZZLE OF A DOWNFAL⟨L⟩ CHILD (70); KLUTE (71); FRENCH CO⟨N⟩ NECTION (71, Oscar nom., BSA); ASSIGN⟨⟩ MENT: MUNICH (72, T.V. movie); PLO⟨T⟩ (73); THE OUTSIDE MAN (73); THE SEVE⟨N⟩ UPS (73); THE INHERITOR (73); SHEIL⟨A⟩ LEVINE IS DEAD AND LIVING IN NE⟨W⟩ YORK (75); MARATHON MAN (76); JAW⟨S⟩ (76); SORCERER (77); JAWS II (78); TH⟨E⟩ LAST EMBRACE (78); ALL THAT JAZ⟨Z⟩ (79, Oscar nom., BSA); STILL OF THE NIGH⟨T⟩ BLUE THUNDER (both 1982); on Broadwa⟨y⟩ 1979, won Drama League Award for 'Betraya⟨l⟩

MAXIMILIAN SCHELL

B. Vienna, Austria, 8.12.30. Of Swiss-Austrian parentage, father a writer, mother an actress; sister Maria, brother Karl also thespians; family moved to Switzerland during war; at 11 Maximilian wrote/produced school play, 'William Tell'; ed. Zurich and later Munich Univ., studying languages, theatrical science, also music (an accomplished pianist, has appeared in concert with Mr Leonard Bernstein); during studies was drama critic and sports reporter on Swiss paper; acted on stage from 1952 in Basle, Essen, Bonn, Berlin, etc., coming to screen in Germany in KINDER, MUTTER UND EIN GENERAL (55); 1st American film: THE YOUNG LIONS (58); that year played in New York in 'Interlock'; April 1959 played on U.S. T.V. German lawyer in JUDGEMENT AT NUREMBERG, when filmed 1961 won B.A. Oscar, also New York Film Critics' and Golden Globe Awards; international films include FIVE FINGER EXERCISE (62); THE CONDEMNED OF ALTONA (63); TOPKAPI (64); RETURN FROM THE ASHES (65); THE DEADLY AFFAIR (66); BEYOND THE MOUNTAINS (68); COUNTERPOINT (67); KRAKATOA (68); FIRST LOVE (69, also co-wrote, directed); ODESSA FILE (73); MAN IN THE GLASS BOOTH (75, Oscar nom., B.A.); ST. IVES (76); END OF THE GAME (directed, co-prod.); A BRIDGE TOO FAR (76); CROSS OF IRON (77); JULIA (77, Oscar nom., BSA); THE DAY THAT SHOOK THE WORLD (77); AVALANCHE EXPRESS (78); I LOVE YOU, I LOVE YOU NOT (78); PLAYERS (79); THE BLACK HOLE (79); TALES OF THE VIENNA WOODS (79, dir./prod./co-wrote only); THE CHOSEN (80); PHANTOM OF THE OPERA (82).

ROMY SCHNEIDER

B. Vienna, Austria, 23.9.38. Daughter of German stage actor Wolf Albach-Retty and screen actress Magda Schneider, Romy (Rose Marie) came to the screen in her mother's film WENN DER WEISSE FLIEDER WIEDER BLÜHT (53); within next 6 years made nearly 20 German movies (FEUERWERK (54); DER LETZTEMANN (55); MONPTI (57), etc.) and well-known 'SISSI' series; STORY OF VICKIE (58) shown in U.S.A., offered Disney contract, but she declined; BOCCACCIO 70 (62) made her intn'l star; md. 1. producer Harry Mayer-Haubenstok 15.7.66; 1 son David (born 3.12.66, but died tragically in Paris 6.7.81) (div.); 2. Daniel Biasini 1975; many movies include THE TRIAL, THE VICTORS, THE CARDINAL (all 1963); WHAT'S NEW, PUSSYCAT? (65); TRIPLE CROSS (66); BLOOMFIELD (71); LUDWIG (72); THAT MOST IMPORTANT THING: LOVE (77); MADO (77); A WOMAN AT HER WINDOW (78); BLOODLINE (79); A SIMPLE STORY (80); LA BANQUIERE (80). THE CAREFREE PASSER-BY (82). *Miss Schneider died of a heart attack, Paris, May 29, 1982.*

RICKY SCHRODER

B. Staten Island, New York, .. 70. Ricky is the so⟨n⟩ of Diane Schroder, his father being a telephon⟨e⟩ manager; he has an elder sister, Dawn, who is ⟨a⟩ model/actress; he began his show-biz career as ⟨a⟩ 4-month-old baby in T.V. commercials and i⟨n⟩ 1978 he won acclaim, after being selected b⟨y⟩ director Franco Zeffirelli, playing the Jacki⟨e⟩ Cooper role in a remake of THE CHAMP; he ha⟨s⟩ since been seen in THE LAST FLIGHT O⟨F⟩ NOAH'S ARK, THE EARTHLING (both 79⟨)⟩ LITTLE LORD FAUNTLEROY (80); SOME⟨⟩ THING SO SO RIGHT (82, T.V. movie); se⟨r.⟩ 1982/83: 'Silver Spoons'.

GEORGE C. SCOTT

The publicity gained by George C. Scott for his refusal to accept recognition by the Academy has perhaps overshadowed his undoubted talent as a stage and screen actor over the years. George Campbell Scott, the son of a former miner, was born in Wise, Virginia, on 18 October 1927. His mother died when he was very young and he moved with his father to Michigan and Detroit and after leaving school spent four years in the Marine Corps. He then attended the University of Missouri, studying journalism, but switched to English and Drama, intent on an acting career. He gained experience in various stock companies and by 1957 he had played 150 roles and had been wed twice, to actress Carolyn Hughes and singer/actress Patricia Reed. In 1957 he played on the New York stage for the first time and soon became well-known, especially for Shakespearean roles, including 'Richard III', and on television, such as 'U.S. Steel Hour: Trap For A Stranger' and 'Sunday Showcase: People Kill People Sometimes'. Mr Scott was soon in demand for big screen roles, débuting in THE HANGING TREE (58) and his next two roles, in ANATOMY OR A MURDER (59) and in THE HUSTLER (61), gained him Oscar nominations as Best Supporting Actor. He continued to act and also direct on the stage but by the late 1960s movies occupied most of his time. He had also wed, in 1960, actress Colleen Dewhurst. They had two sons, Alexander (in 1961) and Campbell (1962), divorced in 1965, re-married in 1967, but divorced again in 1972. His other movies have included LIST OF ADRIAN MESSENGER (63); DR STRANGELOVE (63); YELLOW ROLLS-ROYCE (64); THE BIBLE (65, as Abraham); NOT WITH MY WIFE, YOU DON'T (67); THE FLIM-FLAN MAN (67); PETULA (68); THEY MIGHT BE GIANTS (71); THE HOSPITAL (71, Oscar nom., B.A.); JANE EYRE (71, as Rochester); THE LAST RUN (72); THE NEW CENTURIANS (72); RAGE (73, and directed); DAY OF THE DOLPHIN (73); OKLAHOMA CRUDE (73); THE SAVAGE IS LOOSE (74, and directed); BANKSHOT (75); THE HINDENBURG (75); FEAR ON TRIAL (75, T.V. movie); BEAUTY & THE BEAST (76, T.V. movie); ISLANDS IN THE STREAM (77); HARDCORE (78); PRINCE & THE PAUPER (78); MOVIE, MOVIE (78); THE CHANGELING (79); THE FORMULA (80) and TAPS (81). He portrayed Neil Brock in 26 episodes of 'East Side, West Side', a T.V. series in 1963, and on 14 September 1972 he wed actress Trish Van Devere (qv), who has played in several of his pictures. Although he refused to accept it, he won an Oscar in 1970 for his magnificent performance as General George S. Patton Jr. in PATTON: LUST FOR GLORY. Recently: OLIVER TWIST (T.V.) and Broadway acclaim in 'Present Laughter' (both 1982, also directing latter).

GEORGE SEGAL

For nearly twenty years George Segal has been one of America's most amiable film actors, in the last decade giving highly polished performances with emphasis on comedy. The son of George Segal Sr., and his wife, Fanny, he was born in New York City on 13 February 1934. An avid filmgoer as a youngster, he attended school at Great Neck, Long Island, and Haverford College, near Philadelphia, where he dabbled in a magic act and created 'Bruno Lynch and His Imperial Jazz Band' when still a student, going on to Columbia University, gaining a B.A. Degree. Following service in the U.S. Army he chose a stage career, went to New York, and while hoping for his first breaks worked as a janitor, ticket taker, soft drink salesman and stage door-keeper at an off-Broadway theatre. He managed to understudy at the Circle in the Square Theatre and appeared in a night club singing act, billed as 'George Segal and Patricia Collins Singing Their Little Hearts Out'. He worked in several off-Broadway theatre groups and his initial stage début was in 'Don Juan' at Downtown Theatre, in 1956. That year he reached Broadway in 'The Iceman Cometh' and in 1959 he played in 'Our Town' and 'Anthony & Cleopatra'. He also got good notices for his ad lib performance in the spontaneous revue 'The Premise' and played a killer in an episode of the T.V. series 'The Naked City'. Producer Lawrence Turman brought him to the big screen in THE YOUNG DOCTORS (61) and since then, apart from New York productions such as 'Rattle of a Simple Man' (63) and 'The Knack' (64), he has concentrated on movies, such as THE LONGEST DAY (62); ACT ONE (63); THE NEW INTERNS (64); INVITATION TO A GUNFIGHTER (64); SHIP OF FOOLS (65); LOST COMMAND (65); a great success in KING RAT (65); THE QUILLER MEMORANDUM (66); WHO'S AFRAID OF VIRGINIA WOOLF? (66, Oscar nom. BSA); ST. VALENTINE'S DAY MASSACRE (67); NO WAY TO TREAT A LADY (68); BYE, BYE BRAVERMAN (68); SOUTHERN STAR (69); THE GIRL WHO COULDN'T SAY NO (69); BRIDGE AT REMAGEN (70); LOVING (70); OWL & THE PUSSYCAT (70); WHERE'S POPPA? (70); BORN TO WIN (71, also co-produced); THE HOT ROCK (72); BLUME IN LOVE ('73); A TOUCH OF CLASS (73); TERMINAL MAN (74); CALIFORNIA SPLIT (74); DUCHESS AND THE DIRTWATER FOX (75); THE BLACK BIRD (75, as Sam Spade, Jr.); RUSSIAN ROULETTE (76); FUN WITH DICK AND JANE (76); ROLLERCOASTER (77); TOO MANY CHEFS (78); LOST AND FOUND (78); THE LAST MARRIED COUPLE IN AMERICA (79); CARBON COPY (81) and THE COLD ROOM (83). Mr Segal wed Marion Sobol in 1956 and they have 2 daughters, Elizabeth and Patricia, born in 1957 and 1958 respectively.

DAVID SELBY

B. Morganstown, W. Virginia, . . . Father a carpenter; after attending W. Virginia Univ. Mr Selby appeared in stock and was also assistant instructor in Literature at S. Illinois Univ.; New York stage: 'Devil's Disciple', etc.; T.V. series 'Dark Shadows', as Quentin Collins; Roger Castle in 'Washington: Behind Closed Doors' (1977); films include NIGHT OF DARK SHADOWS (71); UP THE SANDBOX (72); SUPER COPS (73); TELETHON (77, T.V. movie); NIGHT RIDER (79); RAISE THE TITANIC (79); RICH AND FAMOUS (81); md. 10.8.63 Claudeis 'Chip' Newman, 3 children: Todd, Brooke, Amanda; T.V. ser.: Dick Channing in 'Falcon Crest' (82).

GEORGE SEWELL

B. 31.8.24. Formerly a member of Joan Little-wood's Theatre Workshop — he played in 'Oh! What a Lovely War!' in East London, West End and Broadway (1963-64), and is a familiar face in such films as SPARROWS CAN'T SING (63); ROBBERY (67); CARTER (71); OPERATION DAYBREAK (74) and especially on T.V. in 'Paul Temple' (70); Col. Alec Freeman in 'U.F.O.' (71); 'Special Branch' (1972), and, more recently, 'Tinker, Tailor, Soldier, Spy' (1979), 'Rat Trap' (1979), 'West End Tales' (1981), 'If You Go Down in the Woods Today' (1981. T.V. movie); 'Callan: Wet Job' (81); 'Andy Robson' (83); recent stage: 'Who Killed William Hickey?', Iago in 'Othello' (both 82).

CAROLYN SEYMOUR

B. Buckinghamshire 6.11.47. Miss Seymour came to the screen in 1970 in UNMAN, WITTERING & ZIGO; on T.V. she has been seen in such productions as 'Take Three Girls', 'Who Killed Santa Claus?' and 'Hazell'; also U.S. stage (1976); other movies include GUMSHOE (71); STEP-TOE & SON (72); THE RULING CLASS (72); YELLOW DOG (73); THE ASSIGNMENT ('76); THE ODD JOB (78); THE BITCH (79); ZORRO THE GAY BLADE (80).

TOM SELLECK – *see page 126*

JANE SEYMOUR

Miss Seymour, whose real name is Joyce Penelope Wilma Frankenberg, is the daughter of a Harley Street obstetrician gynaecologist, and her mother runs a diplomatic supply company. She was born in Hillingdon, Middx. on 15 February 1951, and has 2 sisters, Sally and Anne. She attended Wimbledon High School until 13, when she joined Arts Educational School, studying ballet, dancing with the Russian Kirov Co., but sustained a knee injury and turned to acting. In 1969 she came to the screen in OH! WHAT A LOVELY WAR, wed Michael Attenborough (div.) and starred in THE ONLY WAY. Stage includes 'Hamlet' and 'The Net'; T.V.: 'The Strauss Family' (as Caroline), 'The Onedin Line'. Jane's earlier movies have been YOUNG WINSTON (71); BEST PAIR OF LEGS IN THE BUSINESS (71); LIVE & LET DIE (73, as Solitaire); FRANKENSTEIN: THE TRUE STORY (73, T.V. movie). Following a British T.V. role in 'Our Mutual Friend' (1975), she has worked mainly in the U.S.A.: CAPTAINS & KINGS (76, T.V. mini-series, Emmy nom.); SEVENTH AVENUE (77, T.V. movie); BENNY & BARNEY: LAS VEGAS UNDERCOVER (77, T.V. movie); SINBAD AND THE EYE OF THE TIGER (77); KILLER ON BOARD (77, T.V. movie); THE 4 FEATHERS (78); THE AWAKENING LAND (78, T.V. movie); LOVE'S DARK RIDE (78, T.V. movie); BATTLESTAR GALACTICA (78); DALLAS COWBOYS' CHEERLEADERS (79, T.V. movie); SOMEWHERE IN TIME (79). Jane wed management consultant Geoff Planer on 20 August 1977, but this marriage ended in divorce. In 1981 she had excellent notices on Broadway in 'Amadeus' and wed David Flynn. Their daughter, Katherine Jane, was born 7.1.82. Recently: THE SCARLET PIMPERNEL (82, T.V. movie); 'Jamaica Inn' (ser., 1983); PHANTOM OF THE OPERA (82, Hungary).

OMAR SHARIF

A popular movie actor since gaining recognition internationally after his performance in LAWRENCE OF ARABIA in 1962, handsome Omar Sharif was born in Alexandria, Egypt, on 10 April 1932, the son (real name: Maechel Shalhoub) of Joseph Shalhoub, a wealthy lumber merchant, and his wife, Claire. When Omar was 4 the family moved to Cairo and he attended Victoria College (the equivalent of an English university) where, at the age of 14, he directed and played in a production of 'Hamlet' and was President of the College Dramatic Society. He also studied for a while in France and worked in his father's business, but was determined to become an actor. Poised to come to London to study at R.A.D.A., he successfully auditioned for a role in an Egyptian movie, THE BLAZING SUN, in 1955, and promptly wed, on 5 February, the film's leading lady and a top Egyptian actress, Faten Hamama. Their son, Tarek Omar, was born on 21 March 1957. Subsequently Sharif went on to play in 25 Middle East productions and 2 in France. His work in GOHA, made in Tunisia in 1959 was seen by Mr Sam Spiegel, which resulted in the actor securing an important role in LAWRENCE OF ARABIA, as Sherif Ali Ibn el Kharish, resulting in an Oscar nomination as Best Supporting Actor. Since then his international films have included FALL OF THE ROMAN EMPIRE (63), BEHOLD A PALE HORSE (63); THE YELLOW ROLLS-ROYCE (63); MARCO THE MAGNIFICENT (65); as GENGHIS KHAN (65); as DOCTOR ZHIVAGO (66); DANGER GROWS WILD (66); NIGHT OF THE GENERALS (66); MORE THAN A MIRACLE (68); MAYERLING (68); McKENNA'S GOLD (68); FUNNY GIRL (68); THE APPOINTMENT (69); CHE! (69, as Che Guevera); THE LAST VALLEY (70); THE HORSEMEN (71); LE CASSE (71); L'ILE (71); THE BURGLARS (71); THE TAMARIND SEED (73); THE MYSTERIOUS ISLAND OF CAPT. VENUS (74); ACE UP MY SLEEVE (75); FUNNY LADY (75); CRIME & PASSION (75); JUGGERNAUT (75); THE RIGHT TO LOVE (77); ASHANTI (78); BLOODLINE (79); S.H.E. (79); GREEN ICE (80); BALTIMORE BULLET (80); OH, HEAVENLY DOG (81). Mr Sharif's main interest, apart from acting, is tournament bridge, and he is generally acknowledged to be one the world's best players, competing in many competitions. In 1977 he wed Sohair Ramzi, in 1981 he made a mini-series, 'Pleasure Palace', and in 1982 starred/narrated 'Return to Eden', a semi-documentary. In 1983 he played on stage in England, at Chichester, in 'The Sleeping Prince' and in the movie, THE FAR PAVILIONS.
THE ETERNAL MALE by Omar Sharif; W.H. Allen: London, 1977; p/b: Star, 1978.

DELPHINE SEYRIG

B. Beirut, . . 32. Delphine played on New York stage in 'Le Jardin des Delices' (1969); her brother, Francis, wrote score for movie MARIE SOLEIL; acting internationally, her movies include: PULL MY DAISY (58, short); LAST YEAR IN MARIENBAD (61); MURIEL (64); LA MUSICA (66); ACCIDENT (67); STOLEN KISSES (68); MR FREEDOM (68); THE MILKY WAY (69); DAUGHTERS OF DARKNESS (70); DONKEY SKIN (71); DISCREET CHARM OF THE BOURGEOISE (72); A DOLL'S HOUSE (73); DAY OF THE JACKAL (73); BLACK WINDMILL (74); ALOUISE (75); CARO MICHELE (77); FACES OF LOVE (78); London stage 1981: 'Bitter Tears of Petra Von Kant'; BBC play 1981: 'Man of Destiny'; I SENT A LETTER TO MY LOVE (81).

WILLIAM SHATNER

B. Montreal, Canada, 22.3.31. Ed. McGill Univ., Montreal (B.A.); Mr Shatner first appeared on stage in Children's Theatre as Tom Sawyer; in summer stock he was assistant business manager, but finally chose an acting career; for 3 years played in rep., joining Stratford, Ontario, S'peare Co. in 1954 and became one of his country's leading Shakespearean players; success on Broadway in 'World of Suzie Wong' (1958 and 508 performances); md. actress Gloria Rand, 2 daughters Lesley, Lisabeth; he is best known on T.V. for his series: 'For the People' (65) as David Koster, 'Star Trek' (1967-69) as Capt. James Kirk and 'Barbary Coast' (75) as Jeff Cable; md. 2. Marcy Lafferty, T.V. production assistant, 1976; movies: BROTHERS KARAMAZOV (58); JUDGEMENT AT NUREMBERG (61); EXPLOSIVE GENERATION (61); THE INTRUDER (61); THE OUTRAGE (64); SOLE SURVIVOR (70, T.V. movie); VANISHED (71, T.V. movie); A PATTERN OF MORALITY (71, T.V. movie); THE PEOPLE (72, T.V. movie); HOUND OF THE BASKERVILLES (72, T.V. movie); INCIDENT ON A DARK STREET, GO ASK ALICE, THE HORROR AT 37,000 FEET, PIONEER WOMAN (all 73, T.V. movies); BIG BAD MAMA (74); INDICT & CONVICT (74, T.V. movie); PRAY FOR THE WILDCATS (74, T.V. movie); DEAD OF NIGHT (75); DEVIL'S RAIN (75); PERILOUS VOYAGE (76, T.V. movie); A WHALE OF A TALE (77); TESTIMONY OF 2 MEN (77, mini-series); KINGDOM OF THE SPIDERS (77); THE BASTARD, CRASH, LITTLE WOMEN (all 78, T.V. movies); LAND OF NO RETURN (78); STAR TREK: THE MOTION PICTURE (79); DISASTER ON THE COAST-LINER (79, T.V. movie); KIDNAPPING OF THE PRESIDENT (80); STAR TREK II: THE VENGEANCE OF KHAN (82); T.V. ser. 82/83: as 'T.J. Hooker'.

MARTIN SHAW

B. Birmingham, 21.1.45. Ed. Gt. Barr Comprehensive, Birmingham; sales clerk; LAMDA, rep. (including Britsol Old Vic) and then into T.V., which included 'Travelling Light', 'Doctor At Large', 'Helen—A Woman of Today', many others; md. actress Jill Allen, January 1969, 2 sons Luke, Joseph; support in movies MACBETH (71); SINBAD'S GOLDEN VOYAGE (73); OPERATION DAYBREAK (74); Martin gained T.V. Superstardom from 1977 as Doyle in 'The Professionals' hit series; other T.V.: 'Cream In My Coffee' (1981) and stage: 'They're Playing Our Song' (81); Md: 2. Maggie Mansfield, 1982; recent T.V.: 'East Lynne' (82); movie: HOUND OF THE BASKERVILLES (83).

RAY SHARKEY

B. New York, circa 1953 — 'On the day I was born Marlon Brando and Elia Kazan were shooting 'On the Waterfront' across the street from the hospital'; career details: 'I'd like to keep my private life private'; Mr Sharkey graduated from small roles to stardom: STUNTS (77); PARADISE ALLEY (78); WHO'LL STOP THE RAIN? (78); HOT TOMORROWS (78); WILLIE & PHIL (79); THE IDOL MAKER (80); LOVE AND MONEY (81); SOME KIND OF HERO (81); REGINA (82).

MARTIN SHEEN

B. Dayton, Ohio, 3.8.40. Real name Ramon Estevez; mother Irish, father Spanish; 1 of 10 children, Martin, when a child, won talent contest reading the Bible; New York stage from 1959, distinguishing himself in many plays, including 'Calvary' (1960), 'The Subject Was Roses' (64, over 1 year) and in S'peare; md. Janet, 4 children: T.V. includes Jack Davis in serial 'As the World Turns', 'Love Story: Mirabelle's Summer' (1973); THE INCIDENT (67); THE SUBJECT WAS ROSES (68); THEN CAME BRONSON (69, T.V. movie); CATCH 22 (70); NO DRUMS, NO BUGLES (71); GOODBYE, RAGGEDY ANN, MONGO'S BACK IN TOWN (both 71, T.V. movie); WELCOME HOME, JOHNNY BRISTOL, THAT CERTAIN SUMMER, PURSUIT (all 72, T.V. movies); CRIME CLUB, LETTERS FROM THREE LOVERS, CATHOLICS, MESSAGE TO MY DAUGHTER (all 73, T.V. movies); THE MISSILES OF OCTOBER (as Sen. Robert Kennedy), CALIFORNIA KID, THE EXECUTION OF PRIVATE SLOVIK (Emmy nom., B.A.), THE STORY OF PRETTY BOY FLOYD (all 74, T.V. movies); BADLANDS (74); THE LAST SURVIVORS, SWEET HOSTAGE (both 75, T.V. movies); THE LEGEND OF EARL DURAND (75); THE LITTLE GIRL WHO LIVES DOWN THE LANE (77); EAGLE'S WING (77); CASSANDRA CROSSING (77); APOCALYPSE NOW (77); THE FINAL COUNTDOWN (79); BLIND AMBITION (79, mini-series); LOOPHOLE (80); GHANDI, ENIGMA, MAN, WOMAN & CHILD, IN THE CUSTODY OF STRANGERS (T.V. movie, all 1982); THAT CHAMPIONSHIP SEASON (83); 'Kennedy' (T.V., 1983).

CYBILL SHEPHERD

B. Memphis, Tennessee, 18.2.50. Sybill attended Hunter and New York University, but was 'too inhibited' to participate in any plays; upon leaving college she became a beauty queen and model and worked in T.V. commercials; director Peter Bogdanovich saw her on the cover of a fashion magazine in a supermarket in Van Nuys, California, and said 'Find Me That Girl — she's the one I want for THE LAST PICTURE SHOW'; she duly came to the screen in that production in 1972 and has since been seen in HEARTBREAK KID (72); DAISY MILLER (73); AT LAST LONG LOVE (75); SPECIAL DELIVERY (76); TAXI DRIVER (76); SILVER BEARS (78); A GUIDE FOR THE MARRIED WOMAN (78, T.V. movie); THE LADY VANISHES (78); EARTH-RIGHT (80); THE RETURN (81); she wed Memphis Mercedes dealer David Ford in 1978, and their daughter, Clementine, was born the following year. They divorced in October, 1982: Miss Shepherd toured U.S.A. in stock, 1982.

VLADEK SHEYBAL

B. Krzemieniec, S.E. Poland, . . 33(?). Father painter/art historian; during WWII took part in 1944 Warsaw uprising, smuggled Molotov Cocktails through German lines; caught, sent to concentration camp in N. Germany; survived and returned home, studied at drama school, became leading actor with Polish National Theatre; won acting award for movie KANAL (57), allowed him to study theatre Paris/London; md. actress Irene Eichlerovna (div.); 1958 to London and Oxford Univ.; directed opera, moved to BBC in early 60s, directing 'Pagliacci' and others; 1st English acting role in 'Birth of a Private Man'; stage includes 'Mahler', 'Salome'; many movies include FROM RUSSIA WITH LOVE (63); B'LLION DOLLAR BRAIN (67); WOMEN IN LOVE (69); LEO THE LAST (70); THE LAST VALLEY (70); THE BOYFRIEND (71); PUPPET ON A CHAIN (72); INNOCENT BYSTANDERS (72); SCORPIO (72); S.P.Y.S. (74); QBVII (74, T.V. movie); THE WIND & THE LION (75); THE SELLOUT (75); Mr Sheybal has appeared on T.V. on many occasions ('Strange Report' (69), 'Strauss' (69) etc.), had a play performed on BBC Radio 4 and wrote/co-produced a movie, 'All About a Prima Ballerina'; more recent movies: THE LADY VANISHES (78); THE APPLE (79); AVALANCHE EXPRESS (79); FUNNY MONEY (82); MEMED (83); recent T.V.: 'Shōgun' (80), 'Smiley's People' (82).

BROOKE SHIELDS

B. New York City, 31.5.65. Miss Shields' parents (now divorced) are Frank (a Helena Rubenstein executive) and Terri Shields (a former actress, now her daughter's manager) and she has two half-sisters and a step-sister. At the age of 11 months she was discovered by photographer Francesco Scavullo and made her modelling début in 'Ivory Snow' soap ads and she later became America's top child model, including jobs as the 'Breck' girl in commercials and in Richard Avenon's Colgate ad. for 3 years. She was in the Playboy Press Book, 'Sugar and Spice' in 1975 and Brooke came to the big screen in ALICE, SWEET ALICE in 1978. Other movies: THE PRINCE OF CENTRAL PARK (77, T.V. movie); KING OF THE GYPSIES (78); PRETTY BABY (78); TILT (79); JUST YOU AND ME, KID (79); WANDA NEVADA (79); THE BLUE LAGOON (79); ENDLESS LOVE (81); SAHARA (83).

TALIA SHIRE

B. Lake Success, New York, . . 47. Sister of Francis Ford Coppola, director/producer/writer; when young toured USA with father, who arranged Broadway musicals; 2 years at Yale School of Drama, then stage in L.A.; md. composer David Shire, 1970, 1 son Matthew (1975) (div. 1979); billed in early movies as Talia Coppola; pictures include THE DUNWICH HORROR (71); THE CHRISTIAN LICORICE STORE (71); THE GODFATHER (72); THE OUTSIDE MAN (73); THE GODFATHER: PART II (74, Oscar nom. BSA); FOSTER & LAURIE (75, T.V. movie); ROCKY (76, Oscar nom., BA); RICH MAN, POOR MAN (76, mini-series); KILL ME IF YOU CAN (77, T.V. movie); DADDY, I DON'T LIKE IT LIKE THIS (78, T.V. movie); ROCKY III (82); Md: 2. lawyer/movie producer Jack Schwartzman.

HENRY SILVA

B. Brooklyn, New York, . . 28. Parents Puerto Rican—brought up in East Side of Manhattan; appeared in plays at school; studied acting for 2 years, also worked as delivery boy, stevedore, soda hustler, bank clerk; appeared in group theatre, co-financed/staged 8 plays at Salisbury, N. Hampshire; studied Actors' Studio; given T.V. role early 50s by director Del Mann; also Broadway: 'Camino Real' (1953) and following 'Viva Zapata', success as 'Mother' in 'A Hatful of Rain' (1955), later in movie (57); many films include CROWDED PARADISE (56); THE TALL T (57); THE BRAVADOS (58); LAW & JAKE WADE (58); GREEN MANSIONS (59); OCEAN'S 11 (60); SERGEANTS 3 (62); THE MANCHURIAN CANDIDATE (62); JOHNNY COOL (63); THE PLAINSMAN (66); 5 SAVAGE MEN (70); THE KIDNAP OF MARY LOU (75); SHOOT (76); CONTRACT ON CHERRY STREET (77, T.V. movie); LOVE & BULLETS (77); BUCK ROGERS IN THE 20TH CENTURY (78); THIRST (79); VIRUS (80); DAY OF THE ASSASSINS (80); SHARKEY'S MACHINE (81); TRAPPED (81); MAN WITH THE DEADLY LENS (82); MEGAFORCE (82); CHAINED HEAT (83).

JEAN SIMMONS

B. Crouch Hill, London, 31.1.29. Ed. Orange Hill School for Girls, Edgware; outbreak of WWII evacuated to Somerset, but returned to study at Aida Foster School of Dancing; in 1943 won film role, without even a screen test, in GIVE US THE MOON; lead in short, SPORTS DAY (45), then supporting roles, stardom and Hollywood; THE WAY TO THE STARS, MEET SEXTON BLAKE (both 45); CAESAR & CLEOPATRA (46); GREAT EXPECTATIONS (46, as young Estella); BLACK NARCISSUS (47); HAMLET (48, as Ophelia, Oscar nom. BSA); BLUE LAGOON (48); SO LONG AT THE FAIR (50); others; md. 1. Stewart Granger (qv) 20.12.50, 1 daughter Tracy (born 10.9.56) (div. 1960); Miss Simmons' other pics. include ANGEL FACE (52); ANDROCLES & THE LION (53); YOUNG BESS (53); THE ROBE (53); THE ACTRESS (53); THE EGYPTIAN (54); GUYS & DOLLS (56); UNTIL THEY SAIL (57); THE BIG COUNTRY (58); ELMER GANTRY (60, directed by her 2nd husband, Richard Brooks, whom she wed 1.11.60 (1 daughter Kate (born 1961)); SPARTACUS (60); THE GRASS IS GREENER (61); LIFE AT THE TOP (65); MISTER BUDDWING (66); ROUGH NIGHT IN JERICHO (67); DIVORCE AMERICAN STYLE (67); HEIDI (68, T.V. movie); THE HAPPY ENDING (69, Oscar nom. BA); SAY HELLO TO YESTERDAY (71); DOMINIQUE (77); THE DAIN CURSE (78, T.V. movie); BEGGARMAN THIEF (79, T.V. movie); GOLDEN GATE (81, T.V. movie); VALLEY OF THE DOLLS (mini-ser., 1981); THE THORN BIRDS (mini-ser., 1982); stage 74/75: 'A Little Night Music'.

O. J. SIMPSON

B. San Francisco 9.7.47. Full name Orenthal James Simpson; ed. U.C.L.A.; md. ——— (when he was 19 — lasted 11 years); Mr Simpson is a former American football star, who earned one million dollars a year; he has been seen in such productions as THE KLANSMAN, TOWERING INFERNO (both 74); KILLER FORCE (75); ROOTS (T.V., mini-series); A KILLING AFFAIR (T.V.); CASSANDRA CROSSING (all 77); CAPRICORN ONE (78); GOLDIE & THE BOXER (T.V.); DETOUR (T.V.); FIRE-POWER (all 79).

JOAN SIMS

B. Laindon, Essex, 9.5.30. Ed. St. John's School, Billericay, Essex and County H.S., Brentwood, Essex; R.A.D.A. and stage début 1950 at Chorlton-cum-Hardy, became well-known, especially in revue in London; T.V. from 1952; came to screen in 1953 in COL. MARCH INVESTIGATES; best-loved by filmgoers for her many appearances in the CARRY ON... movies, from 1959 in CARRY ON NURSE; many others include DOCTOR IN THE HOUSE (54); DRY ROT (56); THE NAKED TRUTH (58); TWICE ROUND THE DAFFODILS (62); FOLLOW THAT CAMEL (67); DOCTOR IN TROUBLE (70); ONE OF OUR DINOSAURS IS MISSING (75); CARRY ON EMMANUELLE (78); recent T.V.: voice of Belle Elmore in 'Ladykillers' (1981); and series 'Born and Bred' (1982) as Molly Peglar.

TOM SKERRITT

B. Detroit, Michigan, 25.8.35. Ed. Mackenzie H.S.; 4 years in U.S. Air Force, returned to Detroit and attended Wayne State University, appeared in college plays 'as a therapy for shyness'; also acted with Dearborn Players, followed by 2 years stock in Michigan and Ohio; then enrolled at UCLA in 1960 studying T.V. production, but continued to act and given 1st film role in WAR HUNT (62); while awaiting film/T.V. roles worked as door-to-door salesman, furniture, carpenter, bricklayer, women's shoe salesman; T.V. includes 'Cimarron Strip', 'Mannix', 'F.B.I.', 'The Fugitive', 'Gunsmoke' etc.; md. 1. ———, 3 sons, Andy, Aaron, Matthew (div.); films include THOSE CALLOWAYS (64); M*A*S*H (70); THE BIRDMEN (71, T.V. movie); WILD ROVERS (71); FUZZ (72); BIG BAD MAN, THIEVES LIKE US, RUN, RUN, JOE! (all 74); THE DEVIL'S RAIN (75); THE LAST DAY (75, T.V. movie); THE TURNING POINT (77); ICE CASTLES, UP IN SMOKE, ALIEN (all 78); MANEATERS ARE LOOSE! (78, T.V. movie); SILENCE OF THE NORTH (79); SAVAGE HARVEST (81); DANGEROUS SUMMER, DEATH VENGEANCE (both 1982); has also played in movies in Italy, has written play/movie scripts and directed on stage; Md: 2. Susan, 1 son, Colin; T.V. ser., 1983: 'Ryan's Four'.

CHARLES MARTIN SMITH

B. Los Angeles, 1955; Ed: Calif. State University; father animation artist Frank Smith; Mr Smith has been seen in such motion-pictures as THE CULPEPPER CATTLE CO. (72); FUZZ (72); THE SPIKES GANG (74); AMERICAN GRAFFITI (74); RAFFERTY & THE GOLD DUST TWINS (74); NO DEPOSIT, NO RETURN (76); THE BUDDY HOLLY STORY (77); MORE AMERICAN GRAFFITI (79); HERBIE GOES BANANAS (79); NEVER CRY WOLF (82).

JACLYN SMITH

B. Houston, Texas, 26.10.47. Real name Jacqueline Ann Smith; father a dentist; ed. Pershing Jun. High School, Houston, then to Lamar High School and was very interested in ballet; at Trinity Univ., San Antonio, Jaclyn studied drama/psychology, but left after 1 year; went to New York, appeared in ballet in Central Park and was discovered by model agent, which lead to T.V. commercials for Listerine, Diet-Rite, Camay, and she was the Wella Balsam and Breck Shampoo Girl; small role in THE ADVENTURERS (68); md. 1. actor Roger Davis, 1968 (div. 1975); 2. actor Dennis Cole (div.); T.V. includes 'McCloud', 'The Rookies', PROBE (72, T.V. movie); SWITCH (75, T.V. movie) and from 1977 great success as Kelly Garrett in 'Charlie's Angels' T.V. series; md. 3. British movie cameraman Tony Richmond in August 1981; other T.V.: ESCAPE FROM BOGEN COUNTY (77, T.V. movie); THE USERS (78, T.V. movie); NIGHT KILL (80); GENE TIERNEY STORY (80, T.V. movie, title role); JACQUELINE BOUVIER KENNEDY (81, T.V. movie, title role). 1 son, Gaston, born 1982; RAGE OF ANGELS (83, mini-ser.).

MAGGIE SMITH

One of Britain's foremost stage actresses, Maggie Smith was born in Ilford, Essex, on 28 December 1934, the daughter of Nathaniel Smith, a pathologist, and his wife, Margaret. She attended Oxford High School for Girls and later studied dramatics with the Oxford Playhouse, graduating from ASM. Following stage work in the Edinburgh Festival revue, 'New Faces of 1956' (and in New York) and the West End, she joined the Old Vic Co. in 1959. Recognition came with the 'Evening Standard' Award for her work in a double-bill, 'The Private Ear' and 'The Private Eye', in 1962 and a similar award for 'Mary, Mary', in 1963. Her earlier movies were NOWHERE TO GO (58); GO TO BLAZES (61); THE V.I.P.'s (63); THE PUMPKIN EATER (64); YOUNG CASSIDY (65) and the filmed performance of her stage interpretation of Desdemona in OTHELLO (65) brought her a B.S.A. Oscar nom. Her first husband was actor Robert Stephens (qv) in 1967, and sons Christopher and Toby were born in 1967 and 1969. Her other movies: THE HONEYPOT (67); HOT-MILLIONS (68); PRIME OF MISS JEAN BRODIE (69, Oscar nom. BA); O! WHAT A LOVELY WAR! (69); TRAVELS WITH MY AUNT (72, Oscar nom. BSA); LOVE, PAIN & THE WHOLE DAMN THING (73); MURDER BY DEATH (76); DEATH ON THE NILE (77); CALIFORNIA SUITE (78, Oscar, BSA); CLASH OF THE TITANS (79); QUARTET (80); WHOSE LITTLE GIRL ARE YOU? (82); recent stage: 'Virginia' (81, as Virginia Woolf); md. 2. author Beverley Cross (23.6.75). THE MISSIONARY (83).

CARRIE SNODGRESS

B. Park Ridge, Illinois, 27.10.46. Ed. Univ. of N. Illinois; real name Caroline Snodgress; appeared in such plays as 'All the Way Home', 'Oh! What a Lovely War', 'Caesar & Cleopatra' at Goodman Theatre, Chicago and was engaged for T.V. work; Carrie failed to get role of POOKIE in movie, but went to Hollywood, coming to screen in RABBIT, RUN (70); she has son, Zeke, born 1973, father being Neil Young; films include DIARY OF A MAD HOUSEWIFE (70, Oscar nom., BA); THE FURY (77); THE ATTIC (79) and T.V. movies THE FORTY-EIGHT HOUR MILE (68); THE WHOLE WORLD IS WATCHING, SILENT NIGHT, LONELY NIGHT (both 69); THE IMPATIENT HEART (71); LOVE'S DARK RIDE (78); FAST FRIENDS (79); HOMEWORK (82); HEAVEN (83).

ELKE SOMMER

B. Berlin 5.11.41. Real name Elke Schletz; father a minister, died when she was 14; Elke came to England in her teens, working as an au pair, and had ambition to enter the German Diplomatic service as an interpreter. However, later on, while in Italy, she was urged to enter a local dance contest near Pisa and became 'Miss Viareggio of 1959' — she was seen by an Italian producer and subsequently appeared in 17 movies in France, Italy, Germany and England, in the latter her first being DON'T BOTHER TO KNOCK (60) (1st German: THE DEATH SHIP (59); md. Joe Hyams, writer, 19.11.64., 3 step-children (sep.); Elke's other movies have included THE VICTORS (63); THE PRIZE (63); A SHOT IN THE DARK (64); FRONTIER HELLCAT (64); THE ART OF LOVE (65); THE OSCAR (66); THE VENETIAN AFFAIR (66); DEADLIER THAN THE MALE (66); THE CORRUPT ONES (67); WICKED DREAMS OF PAULA SCHULTZ (68); THE WRECKING CREW (69); ZEPPELIN (71); PERCY (71); BAD BLOOD (72); PROBE (72, T.V. movie); PERCY'S PROGRESS (74); TEN LITTLE INDIANS (74); CARRY ON BEHIND (76); THE SWISS CONSPIRACY (76); TOP OF THE HILL (78, T.V. movie); THE DOUBLE McGUFFIN (78); PRISONER OF ZENDA (78); FANTASTIC 7 (79); THE BIGGEST BANK ROBBERY (79, T.V. movie); T.V. pilot: 'Elke' (1972).

DAVID SOUL

B. Chicago, Illinois, 28.8.44(?). Real name David Solberg; David is the eldest of 5 children of Dr Richard Solberg, a Lutherian minister. Shortly before his 10th birthday, he was taken with the family to Germany where his father was required to work, relocating families after WWII. They later returned to the States, living in Mexico for 1 year, and eventually settled in Minnesota. He had by now wanted to become an actor, and also developed an interest in music. he sang in New York coffee bars as a folk-singer, adopting a gimmick of wearing a mask and being known as 'The Covered Singer'; md. 1. Karen Smith (1964-69), college sweetheart, 1 son Kristopher; he sang on T.V., including 25 appearances on the 'Merv Griffin Show', and when a producer discovered he was an actor he appeared in 52 episodes of 'Here Comes the Brides' (1968-70) as Joshua Bolt and subsequently met his 2nd wife in the series: Karen Carlson, married 1970-72 and had a son, Jon; he also played Ted Warrick in 'Owen Marshall' (1974) and guested on 'Ironside', 'Cannon', etc. before becoming a household name as Ken Hutchinson in the series 'Starsky and Hutch' from 1975; movies include JOHNNY GOT HIS GUN (71); MAGNUM FORCE (73); SPOT (74); THE STICK-UP (77); LITTLE LADIES OF THE NIGHT (77, T.V. movie); SWAN SONG (79, co-produced); RAGE (80, T.V. movie); SALEM'S LOT (80, miniseries) and THE MANIONS OF AMERICA (81, mini-series); WORLD WAR III (mini-ser., 81); in 1977, Mr Soul's first single, 'Don't Give Up On Us', went to the top of the record charts; Md: 3. Patricia, 1980.

SISSY SPACEK

B. Quitman, Texas, 25.12.50. Real name Mary Elizabeth Spacek; father local county agent for Dept. of Agriculture; at 17 Sissy went to New York and stayed with cousin, actor Rip Torn (qv) and his wife, Geraldine Page; returned home, her father died, and she returned to New York, her cousin suggested she took acting lessons; Actors' Studio and worked as model; worked on T.V. ('The Waltons', 'The Rookies', etc.) and came to the screen in PRIME CUT (72); md. production designer-turned film director Jack Fisk, 1974; other movies include THE GIRLS OF HUNTING HOUSE (73, T.V. movie); THE MIGRANTS (74, T.V. movie); BADLANDS (74); KATHERINE (75, T.V. movie); WELCOME TO L.A. (76); CARRIE (76, Oscar nom., B.A.); THREE WOMEN (77, New York Film Critics' Award); HEART BEAT (78); COAL MINER'S DAUGHTER (79, Awards: Oscar and Nat. Board of Review, BA (as country singer Loretta Lynn); RAGGEDY MAN (81); MISSING (82, Oscar nom., BA); daughter, Schuyler Elizabeth, born 1982.

CAMILLA SPARV

B. Stockholm, Sweden, .. 44(?); Camilla modelled in her home town and Paris before working in New York; refused several screen tests before Columbia made her an offer; md. 1. actor-turned-producer Robert Evans, 1964 (div.); movies include THE TROUBLE WITH ANGELS (66); DEAD HEAT ON A MERRY-GO-ROUND (66); MURDERER'S ROW (67); ASSIGNMENT K (67); MACKENNA'S GOLD (68); DOWNHILL RACER (69); THE ITALIAN JOB (69); md. 2. Herbert W. Hoover III (grandson of Hoover founder), 2 sons: Max (born April 1971) and Herbert IV; THE GREEK TYCOON (78); CABOBLANCO (79); VALLEY OF THE DOLLS (81, mini-ser.).

ROBERT STACK

No doubt Robert Stack can look back contentedly at a career, commencing as bright young star of the 1940s and 50s and graduating, in more recent years, to even more popularity as a television actor. He was born in Los Angeles on 13 January 1919, the family name being Modini — his uncle, Richard Bonelli, was the Metropolitan Opera baritone. From the age of 5 to 11 young Robert studied in Paris and was able to speak French before he mastered English. Later, back in the States, he attended the University of Southern California, excelled at sports — with his brother he won the International Outboard Motorboat Championship in Venice, played the saxophone and clarinet and won renown for polo playing. Deciding to be an actor he studied for 6 months, appeared in 'little theatre' productions, and eventually accepted (he had earlier turned down an offer) a screen role in Universal's FIRST LOVE (39), opposite young Deanna Durbin; he subsequently appeared in such productions as THE MORTAL STORM (40); A LITTLE BIT OF HEAVEN (40); NICE GIRL? (41); BADLANDS OF DAKOTA (41); TO BE OR NOT TO BE, EAGLE SQUADRON, MEN OF TEXAS (all 42); then service in U.S. Armed Forces, WWII; A DATE WITH JUDY, MISS TATLOCK'S MILLIONS, FIGHTER SQUADRON (all 48); MR MUSIC (50); MY OUTLAW BROTHER (51); BWANA DEVIL (52); WAR PAINT, CONQUEST OF COCHISE, SABRE JET (all 53); THE HIGH AND THE MIGHTY (54); THE IRON GLOVE (54); HOUSE OF BAMBOO (55); GOOD MORNING, MISS DOVE (55); GREAT DAY IN THE MORNING (56); WRITTEN ON THE WIND (56, Oscar nom., BSA); TARNISHED ANGELS (57); THE GIFT OF LOVE (58); JOHN PAUL JONES (59); THE LAST VOYAGE (60); THE CARETAKERS (63); IS PARIS BURNING? (66); THE CORRUPT ONES (67); ACTION MAN (68); THE STORY OF A WOMAN (70); THE STRANGE AND DEADLY OCCURRENCE, ADVENTURES OF THE QUEEN, MURDER ON FLIGHT 502 (75, all T.V. movies); MOST WANTED (76, T.V. movie); 1941 (79); AIRPLANE! (79). He had appeared on U.S. T.V. in the 50s in such programmes as 'All-Star Theatre' and 'Hollywood Opening Night' and during this decade wed Rosemarie Bowe, in 1956, with whom he had acted. They have a daughter, Elizabeth, born in 1957 and now pursuing an acting career, and son Charles, born in 1958. His T.V. series have been 'The Untouchables', a hard-hitting gangster saga, as Eliot Ness (1959-63 — he won an Emmy award, presented on 20 June 1960 as Best T.V. Actor) — a pilot movie, THE SCARFACE MOB, was released in 1958, as Dan Farrell in 'The Name of the Game' (1968-72), as Capt. Lincoln Evans in 'Most Wanted' (1976/77) and in 1981 he filmed 'Strike Force' for T.V.

SYLVESTER STALLONE

B. New York City 6.7.46. Parents Italian immigrants, father a hairdresser; after H.S. taught at American College of Switzerland, instructing children of career diplomats, young royalty, etc.; returned to USA in 1967, graduating from University of Miami in 1969; chose acting career, going to New York at one time 'broke, cold and sick, living in a bus terminal'; part-time job: usher at Walter Reade Theatres, wrote film scripts; md. Sacha 1970(?), 2 sons: Sage and Seth; bit parts in films: BANANAS (71); LORDS OF FLATBUSH (74, lead); FAREWELL, MY LOVELY; CAPONE; DEATH RACE 2000; PRISONER OF SECOND AVENUE (all 1975); Sylvester wrote screenplay for movie, ROCKY, insisted he play lead, and this he did in Oscar-winning film of 1976, gaining him acting nom.; subsequent movies as star: F.I.S.T. (78, co-wrote); PARADISE ALLEY (78, also directed); ROCKY II (79, also directed); NIGHT HAWKS (80); ESCAPE TO VICTORY (81); ROCKY III, FIRST BLOOD (both 1982).

LIONEL STANDER

B. New York City 11.1.08; studied to become certified accountant; worked on New York newspaper, then decided on stage career, appearing in New York from 1928; md. 1. Lucy Dietz, 1928-6, child: Mikele; in movies, starting in quickies, from 1935: THE SCOUNDREL; other features include MR DEEDS GOES TO TOWN (36); A STAR IS BORN (37); PROFESSOR BEWARE (38); many others; md. 2. Alice Twitchell (1938-2); 3. Vehanne Havens Monteagle (1945-50), 2 children: CALL NORTHSIDE 777 (48); UNFAITHFULLY YOURS (48); others, blacklisted by Hollywood, returned to New York stage, became a Wall Street broker', eventually lived in Rome, making many pictures in Italy; md. 4. Diana Radbec (1953-63), 1 daughter; 5. Maria Fenn (1963— div.), 1 daughter; 6. Stephanie Van Rennick, 1971, 1 daughter Jennifer (born 1971); recently back in U.S. movies, including TREASURE ISLAND (72, as Billy Bones); PULP (72); THE BLACK BIRD (75); THE CASSANDRA CROSSING (76); NEW YORK, NEW YORK (77); MATILDA (78); CYCLONE (78) and a regular, as Max, in the hit series, 'Hart to Hart' (79-), winning him Golden Globe Aw.

MAUREEN STAPLETON

B. Troy, New York, 21.6.25. Ed. Troy High School, studied for stage at Actors' Studio and with Herbert Berghof; 1st New York appearance, 1946; became well-known and award-winning stage actress (esp. in 'The Rose Tattoo' (1951)); md. 1. Max Allentuck (1949-59), 1 son Daniel 1950), 1 daughter Katherine (1954); 2. David Rayfiel (div.); films include THE LONELY HEARTS (58, Oscar nom., BSA); THE FUGITIVE KIND (60); A VIEW FROM THE BRIDGE (62); BYE-BYE BIRDIE (62); TRILOGY (69); PLAZA SUITE (70); AIRPORT (70); TELL ME WHERE IT HURTS (74, T.V. movie); QUEEN OF THE STARDUST BALLROOM (75, T.V. movie); CAT ON A HOT TIN ROOF (76, T.V. movie); THE GATHERING (77, T.V. movie); LOST & FOUND (78); INTERIORS (78); THE RUNNER STUMBLES (78); ON THE RIGHT TRACK, REDS (Oscar winner, BSA; joint BAFTA Aw.); THE FAN (all 81); LITTLE GLORIA, HAPPY AT LAST (82, mini-ser.); stage 81: 'Little Foxes'.

TERENCE STAMP

B. Stepney, E. London, 22.7.39. Father a Thames tug driver; ed. Council School, living in Poplar and Plaistow; aged 16, developed an interest in golf, having 18-20 handicap, joining Wanstead Club as assnt. professional; commercial artist, messenger boy in advertising; work as visualiser typographer brought him into contact with actors, chose theatrical career; 1 year at Webber-Douglas School; rep.: ASM at S. Moulton, Devon; Colchester, Canterbury, Windsor; took over role as Whittaker in 'Long, Short and the Tall' tour; West End: 'A Trip to the Castle', 'This Year, Next Year'; 1st film: TERM OF TRIAL (62); seen by Peter Ustinov in play 'Why the Chicken?', given title role in his acclaimed movie, BILLY BUDD (62); Mr Stamp's other pictures include THE COLLECTOR (65); MODESTY BLAISE (66); FAR FROM THE MADDING CROWD (67); POOR COW (67); BLUE (68); HISTOIRES EXTRAORDINAIRES (68); MIND OF MR SOAMES (69); THEOREM (69); SUPERMAN, MEETINGS WITH REMARKABLE MEN, THIEF OF BAGHDAD, TOGETHER (all 1978); THE DIVINE NYMPH (78); SUPERMAN II (81); DEATH IN THE VATICAN (82).

HARRY DEAN STANTON

B. Kentucky 14.7.26. Ed. LaFayette High School; WWII: U.S. Navy, seeing action in Okinawa; then 3 years at University of Kentucky, played in theatrical productions, including role of Doolittle in 'Pygmalion', chose acting career; enrolled at Pasadena Playhouse and drama school for 4 years, toured in several plays, settled in L.A. in 1958, coming to screen that year (as Dean Stanton) in THE PROUD REBEL; T.V. includes 'Gunsmoke', 'The Virginian' and subsequent films include PORK CHOP HILL (59); THE ADVENTURES OF HUCKLEBERRY FINN (60); COOL HAND LUKE (67); A TIME FOR KILLING (67); DAY OF THE EVIL GUN (68); THE MINI-SKIRT MOB (68); KELLY'S HEROES (70); TWO LANE BLACKTOP (billed as H.D. Stanton, 1971); then as Harry Dean Stanton: CISCO PIKE (72); PAT GARRETT & BILLY THE KID (73); WHERE THE LILLIES BLOOM (74); ZANDY'S BRIDE (74); THE GODFATHER: PART II (74); 92 IN THE SHADE (75); RANCHO DELUXE (75); FAREWELL, MY LOVELY (75); RAFFERTY & THE GOLD DUST TWINS (75); MISSOURI BREAKS (76); STRAIGHT TIME (78); ALIEN (78); RENALDO & CLARA (78); BLACK MARBLE (79); GIRLS OF THE ROAD (79, T.V. movie); WISE BLOOD (79); UFORIA (80); PRIVATE BENJAMIN (80); ESCAPE FROM NEW YORK (80); TOUGH ENOUGH (81); YOUNG DOCTORS IN LOVE (82).

GRAHAM STARK

B. Wallasey 20.1.22. A familiar face on T.V. and in the movies, often in cameos, work includes THE MILLIONAIRESS (61); WATCH IT, SAILOR (62); A SHOT IN THE DARK (64); ALFIE (66); FINDERS KEEPERS (66); SALT AND PEPPER (68); THE MAGIC CHRISTIAN (69); CARRY ON DOCTOR (70); produced/directed THE MAGNIFICENT SEVEN DEADLY SINS (72); PRINCE AND THE PAUPER (76); LET'S GET LAID (77); REVENGE OF THE PINK PANTHER (78); THE PRISONER OF ZENDA (78); THERE GOES THE BRIDE (79); SEA WOLVES (81); TRAIL OF THE PINK PANTHER (82); also photographer.

RINGO STARR

B. Dingle, Liverpool, 7.7.40. Real name Richard Starkey; parents (sep. when Ringo was 3) worked in bakery; joined 'The Beatles' 16.8.62 as drummer, 1st concert success in Hamburg, Germany; 1st intn'l hit 'Love Me Do' (62); md. 1. hairdresser Maureen Cox, 11.2.65, children: Zak (born 13.9.65), Jason (19.8.67), Lee (27.11.70), div. 1975; with 'Beatles' in films A HARD DAY'S NIGHT (64); HELP! (65); YELLOW SUBMARINE (67, cartoon: music only); LET IT BE (70, group disbanded that year); solo films include CANDY (68); THE MAGIC CHRISTIAN (69); 200 MOTELS (71); BLINDMAN (72); THAT'LL BE THE DAY (73); LITZOMANIA (75); THE LAST WALTZ (76); SEXTETTE (77); solo albums include 'Sentimental Journey' (70); 'Goodnight Vienna' (74); hit single: 'It Don't Come Easy' (71); md. 2. actress Barbara Bach, 27.4.81, his CAVEMAN (81) co-star; THE COOLER (82, short); GIVE MY REGARDS TO BROAD STREET (83).

MARY STEENBURGEN

B. Little Rock, Kansas(?), . .53; father freight train conductor; 'Since I was six I had wanted, and knew, I would be an actress'; at 20 went to New York, sold books at Doubleday's, Fifth Avenue, then waitress at 'Magic Pan'; acted with group 'The Cracked Tokens', seen by talent scout and eventually won role in GOIN' SOUTH (78); md. Malcolm McDowell (qv), 1980, 1 daughter Lilly Amanda (born 22.1.81); TIME AFTER TIME (80, with husband); Mary won an Oscar for her role in MELVIN & HOWARD (81, BSA); RAGTIME (81); CROSS CREEK (82, as author Marjorie Kinnan Rawlings); A MIDSUMMER NIGHT'S SEX COMEDY (82); ROMANTIC COMEDY (83).

ANTHONY STEEL

B. Chelsea, London, 21.5.20. Full name Anthony Maitland Steel; spent youth in India, where father was army officer; ed. private schools, S. Ireland & Cambridge; aged 18, joined Grenadier Guards, leaving in 1945 as Major; for a while 'broke up tramlines at Clapham Junction for £6-a-week; Worthing Repertory; film extra (SARABAND FOR DEAD LOVERS (48)) and small roles in such pics. as TROTTIE TRUE (49), BLUE LAMP (50) and eventual stardom in THE WOODEN HORSE (50); md. Swedish actress Anita Ekberg from 1956-1962; Mr Steel's many other films include THE MUDLARK (50); LAUGHTER IN PARADISE (51); THE MALTA STORY (52); ALBERT R.N. (53); THE MASTER OF BALLANTRAE (53); THE SEA SHALL NOT HAVE THEM (55); STORM OVER THE NILE (56); THE BLACK TENT (56); CHECKPOINT (56); A QUESTION OF ADULTERY (57); HARRY BLACK (58); HONEYMOON (60); THE SWITCH (63); HELL IS EMPTY (67); ANZIO (68); MASSACRE IN ROME (74); THE STORY OF O (76); HARDCORE (77); LET'S GET LAID (77); THE WORLD IS FULL OF MARRIED MEN (78); THE MIRROR CRACK'D (81, actor in film sequence); THE MONSTER CLUB (81); T.V. includes guest: 'The Professionals' (1977), 'Crossroads' (1978), 'Return of the Saint' (79), 2 episodes 'Tales of the Unexpected' (1980), 'Artemis 81' (81), 'Andy Robson' (83); stage: 'Conduct Unbecoming' (82, tour).

ROD STEIGER

Oscar-winning Rod Steiger, one of the finest American character actors in movies, was born on 14 April 1925 at West Hampton, New York, and attended school at Newark, New Jersey. Upon leaving school he worked as a leather cutter, ice loader and driver, and barker until America entered WWII and he served for four years from 1941 in the U.S. Navy. In 1946 he worked as a clerk for the Navy Department of Dependents and Beneficiaries and the following year was employed by an office machine company, joining their amateur dramatic society mainly 'to meet the girls'. He found he enjoyed acting and decided to venture to New York and study it seriously. He attended the New York Theatre Wing, the Dramatic Workshop and finally, under Elia Kazan, at the Actors' Studio, he embarked on his highly successful career. In New York he played in such productions as 'Stevedore' (1949), 'John Brown (1950), 'Enemy of the People' (1950/51), 'Night Music' (1951), 'Seagulls Over Sorrento' (1952), entered T.V. in such programmes as 'Sure as Fate', 'Kraft T.V. Theatre', 'Philco T.V. Playhouse', but it was his brilliant performance as 'Marty', shown on 24 May 1953, that won him acclaim. He had made his big-screen début in 1951 in a movie called TERESA, and in 1954, as Marlon Brando's brother in ON THE WATERFRONT, he received an Oscar nomination as Best Supporting Actor. In 1952 Steiger had wed Sally Gracie, but this lasted only two years. His movies have included THE BIG KNIFE, OKLAHOMA! (as Jud Fry), THE COURT-MARTIAL OF BILLY MITCHELL (all 55); THE UNHOLY WIFE, JUBAL, THE HARDER THEY FALL (all 56); RUN OF THE ARROW, ACROSS THE BRIDGE, BACK FROM ETERNITY (all 57); as AL CAPONE, CRY TERROR (both 58); on 19 September 1958 he wed actress Claire Bloom — they appeared in a stage play 'Rashomon' together, and their daughter, Anna Justine, was born in 1960. They divorced in 1969; SEVEN THIEVES (59); THE MARK (61); ON FRIDAY AT ELEVEN (61); THE LONGEST DAY (62); CONVICTS FOUR (62); TIME OF INDIFFERENCE (63); HANDS OVER THE CITY (63); THE PAWNBROKER (65, Oscar nom.); THE LOVED ONE (65); DOCTOR ZHIVAGO (65); THE GIRL AND THE GENERAL (66); IN THE HEAT OF THE NIGHT (67, Oscar, Best Actor); A MAN CALLED JOHN (68); NO WAY TO TREAT A LADY (68); THE SERGEANT (68); THE ILLUSTRATED MAN (69); THREE INTO TWO WON'T GO (69); WATERLOO (70, as Napoleon); A FISTFUL OF DYNAMITE (71); HAPPY BIRTHDAY WANDA JUNE (72); LOLLY MADONNA XXX (72); LUCKY LUCIANO (73); HENNESSY (74); LAST DAYS OF MUSSOLINI (74); W.C. FIELDS AND ME (76, title role); JESUS OF NAZARETH (77, T.V. series, as Pontius Pilate); LOVE & BULLETS, CHARLIE (77); F.I.S.T. (77); BREAKTHROUGH (78); THE AMITYVILLE HORROR (78); WOLF LAKE (79); LION OF THE DESERT (79, as Mussolini); THE LUCKY STAR (79); JACK LONDON'S KLONDIKE FEVER (80); THE CHOSEN (80) and CATTLE ANNIE & LITTLE BRITCHES (81).

ANDREW STEVENS – see page 126

ROBERT STEPHENS

B. Bristol, 14.7.31; ed. Bristol; md. 1. Tarn Bassett (div.); studied drama at Bradford Civic Theatre School, beginning career with Caryl Jenner Mobile Theatre Co. and became very distinguished stage actor (Royal Court, W. End, New York, Nat. Theatre, etc.) and director; md. 2. actress Maggie Smith (qv) 1967-75, 2 sons Christopher (born 1967) and Toby (1969); occasional films: CIRCLE OF DECEPTION (60); A TASTE OF HONEY, THE QUEEN'S GUARDS, PIRATES OF TORTUGA, A TASTE OF HONEY (all 1961); THE INSPECTOR (62); CLEOPATRA, THE LUNCH HOUR, SMALL WORLD OF SAMMY LEE (all 63); MORGAN (66); ROMEO & JULIET (68); PRIME OF MISS JEAN BRODIE (69); PRIVATE LIFE OF SHERLOCK HOLMES (69, title role); THE ASPHYX (72); TRAVELS WITH MY AUNT (73); LUTHER (73); QBVII (74, T.V. movie); THE DUELLISTS (77); LA NUIT TOUS LES CHATS SONT GRIS (77); THE SHOUT (78); HOLOCAUST (78, miniseries); recent T.V.: 'Eden End' (81); 'Year of the French', 'Studio' (both ser., 1983).

STELLA STEVENS

B. Hot Coffee, Mississippi, 1.10.38. Real name Estelle Eggleston; ed. Memphis H.S. College, joined drama group at latter, seen by Fox talent scout in production of 'Bus Stop', came to screen with small role in SAY ONE FOR ME (59); md. (at 15) Herman Stevens, 1 son Andrew (now actor) (div.); at 19 Stella modelled for 'Playboy'; many movies and T.V. films include L'IL ABNER (59); TOO LATE BLUES (61); COURTSHIP OF EDDIE'S FATHER (63); THE NUTTY PROFESSOR (63); SYNANON (65); THE SILENCERS (66); BALLAD OF CABLE HOGUE (70); THE POSEIDON ADVENTURE (72); ARNOLD (74); LAS VEGAS LADY (76); NICKLEODEON (76); KISS ME, KILL ME (76, T.V. movie); WANTED: THE SUNDANCE WOMAN (76, T.V. movie); THE NIGHT THEY TOOK MISS BEAUTIFUL (77, T.V. movie); CHARLIE COBB (77, T.V. movie); CRUISE INTO TERROR (78, T.V. movie); THE JORDAN CHANCE (78, T.V. movie); THE MANITOU (78); T.V. series 1981: 'Flamingo Road'.

JAMES STEWART

Characterised by his slow drawl and lanky walk, Oscar-winning James Stewart has, for over forty years, epitomised the honest American in some of the best movies ever made. The son of Alexander and Elizabeth Stewart, he was born James Maitland Stewart on 20 May 1908 at Vinegar Hill, Pennsylvania. His grandfather had founded the local hardware store and the youngster attended Mercersberg Academy, Pa., and later Princeton University, where he studied electrical engineering, politics, but later switched to architecture, gaining his Bachelor of Science Degree in 1932. He made the mistake of graduating during the depression, however, and architects were at a discount. At University he had enjoyed acting with the Princeton Triangle Club and was also an accordionist, so he seriously embarked on a theatrical career, making his professional début with the Falmouth Players, Cape Cod, Mass. in the summer of 1932 in 'Goodbye Again'. For the next three years he worked steadily in the theatre, including stage managing a production of 'Camille', and appearing in 'Carry Nation' (1932), 'Spring in Autumn' (1933), 'Yellow Jack' (1934) and 'Divided By Three' (1934). Hedda Hopper, the actress/columnist appeared in the last production and advised M-G-M of the young actor's talent and he subsequently made his screen début in THE MURDER MAN (35). The public were attracted to his amiable style and his best 30s movies included SEVENTH HEAVEN (37); VIVACIOUS LADY (38); YOU CAN'T TAKE IT WITH YOU (38); MR SMITH GOES TO WASHINGTON (39, Oscar nom.); DESTRY RIDES AGAIN (39); THE SHOP AROUND THE CORNER (39) and won an Oscar for his work as the magazine reporter in THE PHILADELPHIA STORY (40). During the War he served in the U.S. Air Force as a Lieu. Colonel, based in England and earned a D.F.C. He returned to movies in IT'S A WONDERFUL LIFE (46, Oscar nom.) and in 1947 returned successfully to the stage for 'Harvey' (repeated for the screen in 1950). In 1949 he wed Gloria Hatrich McLean, and their twins, Kelly and Judy, were born in 1951 — he was stepfather to Michael and Ronald, the latter tragically killed in Vietnam in June 1969. He continued his highly successful film career with such pictures as CALL NORTHSIDE 777 (47); ROPE (48); WINCHESTER 73 (50); BROKEN ARROW (50); NO HIGHWAY (51); THE GREATEST SHOW ON EARTH (51); THUNDER BAY (53); THE GLENN MILLER STORY (53, title role); REAR WINDOW (54); THE MAN FROM LARAMIE (55); THE SPIRIT OF ST. LOUIS (57, as Chas. Lindbergh); VERTIGO (58); ANATOMY OF A MURDER (59, Oscar nom.); THE F.B.I. STORY (59); MR HOBBS TAKES A VACATION (62); SHENANDOAH (65); CHEYENNE SOCIAL CLUB (70); DYNAMITE MAN FROM GLORY JAIL (71); THE SHOOTIST (76); AIRPORT 77, THE MAGIC OF LASSIE (78); THE BIG SLEEP (78). He was continually in the Top 10 of the Motion-Picture Herald Fame Poll in 1950, '52, '54, '57 and was No.1 Star in 1955. In the 1970s he moved into T.V. with 2 series, 'The Jimmy Stewart Show' (1971/72) and as Billy Jim Hawkins in 'Hawkins' (1973/74). He filmed THE GREEN HORIZON in Africa in 1980. 1980.

THE FILMS OF JAMES STEWART by Kenneth D. Jones; Castle Books: New York, 1970.

SUSAN STRASBERG

B. New York City 22.5.38. Parents: Paula and Lee Strasberg (drama teacher/founder Actors' Studio); 1953: 'Maya' (off-Broadway); 1954: 'Diary of Anne Frank' (New York stage) and T.V. series, as Emily Marriott in 'The Marriage'; other T.V./stage; Susan's many movies include PICNIC, THE COBWEB (both 1955); STAGESTRUCK (57); TASTE OF FEAR (61); DISORDER (64); THE BROTHERHOOD (68); THE TRIP (69); T.V. 1973/74: 'Toma', as Patty Toma; md. actor Christopher Jones, 1 daughter Jenny (div.); recent: ROLLERCOASTER (77); THE MANITOU (78); IN PRAISE OF OLDER WOMEN (78); BLOODY BIRTHDAY (80); DISASTER IN THE SKY (T.V. movie, 1981).

PETER STRAUSS

B. Croton-on-Hudson, New York City, 20.2.47; N. Western Univ., twice Best Actor Award, met son of Hollywood agent, lead to film HAIL HERO! (69); had appeared in stock Maine & Pennsylvania; md. 2. Shana Hoffman; screenwork includes SOLDIER BLUE (69); RICH MAN, POOR MAN (76, T.V. movie); THE LAST TYCOON (76); THE FORGOTTEN KENNEDY (77, T.V. movie, as Joe Kennedy); THE JERICHO MILE (79, T.V. movie, 'Emmy' Award); MASADA (79); ANGEL ON MY SHOULDER (80, T.V. movie); A WHALE FOR THE KILLING (81, T.V. movie); SPACE-HUNTER: ADVENTURES IN THE FORBIDDEN ZONE (83).

STING – *see page 126*

MERYL STREEP

Meryl Streep, whose real name is Mary Louise, was born at Basking Ridge, New Jersey, on 22.9.49. Her father is a pharmaceutical executive, mother a graphic artist. At school Meryl became swimming champion and was voted most popular student, winning a scholarship to Yale University, where she garnered a Fine Arts degree and was an acclaimed actress. After further success in New York she came to the big screen with a supporting role in JULIA (77) and her performance as the German girl, Inga, in the mini-series 'Holocaust' (78) won her a T.V. 'Emmy'. She married sculptor Don Gummer in late 1978 and they have a son, Henry, born the following year. Her other screen work has been in THE DEADLIEST SEASON (77, T.V. movie); THE DEER HUNTER (78); MANHATTAN (78) and as the wife in KRAMER VS. KRAMER she won an Academy Award as Best Supporting Actress of 1979. Further films are THE SEDUCTION OF JOE TYNAN (78); THE FRENCH LIEUTENANT'S WOMAN (81, Oscar nom.; winner: Golden Globe Aw., BAFTA Aw., BA); STILL OF THE NIGHT (82); SOPHIE'S CHOICE (82, Oscar winner, BA, also Golden Globe Aw., N.Y. Film Critics' Circle Aw.); SILKWOOD (83); T.V. 1982: 'Alice at the Palace'.

BARBRA STREISAND

Barbra Streisand emerged from the 1960s as one of the most fabulously successful and popular stage and screen personalities, winning an Oscar for her very first movie, and continued to be one of the world's leading international stars. She is the daughter of Emanuel Streisand and his wife, Diana, and was born in Brooklyn, New York, on 24 April 1942, attending Erasmus Hall High School and Yeshiva of Brooklyn. She had always wanted to act, and, having had part-time drama tuition, upon leaving college played a summer season in stock, concurrently working as switchboard girl and usherette. Winning a singing competition in Greenwich Village which lead to an engagement at a Village night spot, she became a popular cabaret artiste, appearing in New York, San Francisco, Las Vegas, Los Angeles and other cities. An Off-Broadway part in the revue 'Another Evening With Harry Stoones' in October 1961, lead to her big break on Broadway as Miss Marmelstein in 'I Can Get It For You Wholesale' in 1962, winning her a New York Critics' Award. Also in the cast was actor Elliott Gould (qv) and the couple wed on 13 September 1963, their son, Jason, being born 29 December 1966. Following 'Wholesale' Barbra was much in demand for T.V. and cabaret and in the summer of 1963 appeared at the Hollywood Bowl with Sammy Davis Jr. Back on Broadway in 1964 she appeared in the smash-hit, 'Funny Girl', as Fanny Brice, playing the role in London in 1966, gaining more awards, and in 1968, in the motion-picture version, she earned Best Actress, receiving an Academy Award. Since then her movies have been HELLO DOLLY (69); ON A CLEAR DAY YOU CAN SEE FOREVER (70); THE OWL AND THE PUSSYCAT (70); WHAT'S UP, DOC? (72); UP THE SANDBOX (72); THE WAY WE WERE (73, Oscar nom.); FOR PETE'S SAKE (74); FUNNY LADY (75); A STAR IS BORN (76); MAIN EVENT (79) and ALL NIGHT LONG (80). Barbra was divorced from Mr Gould in 1971. She won 'Granny Awards' in 1963, '64 and '65 in U.S.A. as Best Female Vocalist, and in 1965 she also won an 'Emmy' for her T.V. Special, 'My Name is Barbra'. In addition to starring in YENTL (83), she also co-scripts, produces and directs.

BARBRA — THE FIRST DECADE: THE FILMS & CAREER OF BARBRA STREISAND by James Spada; Citadel: Secaucus: N.J. (USA), 1974 (published in G.B., 1982, by W.H. Allen, as 'Streisand: the Woman and the Legend').

STREISAND by Rene Jordan; W.H. Allen: London, 1976.

BARBRA: AN ILLUSTRATED BIOGRAPHY by Frank Brady; Grosset & Dunlap: N.Y., 1979; Large p/b.

BARBRA: A BIOGRAPHY OF BARBRA STREISAND by Donald Zec and Anthony Fowler; New English Library: London, 1981. p/b: N.E.L., 1982.

STREISAND THROUGH THE LENS by Frank Teti & Karen Moline; Sidgwick & Jackson: London, 1983; Large p/b.

DON STROUD

B. Hawaii, . . 37. From a theatrical family, Don left school at 15 to become a Waikiki beach boy, also film and T.V. extra; to U.S. mainland, parking lot attendant, then manager and bouncer of 'Whisky-a-Go-Go', a Sunset Strip nightclub; recommended to Monique James, head of talent at Universal City and came to screen uncredited in BANNING (67); many films/T.V. movies since include COOGAN'S BLUFF (68); BALLAD OF JOSIE (68); MADIGAN (68); GAMES (68); JOURNEY TO SHILOH (68); WHAT'S SO BAD ABOUT FEELING GOOD? (68); SPLIT SECOND TO AN EPITAPH (68, T.V. movie); SOMETHING FOR A LONELY MAN (68, T.V. movie); A DREAM OF KINGS (69); EXPLOSION (70); BLOODY MAMA (70); ANGEL UNCHAINED (70); SCALAWAG (71); THE D.A.: CONSPIRACY TO KILL (71, T.V. movie); THE DEADLY DREAM (71, T.V. movie); JOE KIDD (72); THE DAUGHTERS OF JOSHUA CABE (72, T.V. movie); ROLLING MAN (72, T.V. movie); SLAUGHTER'S BIG RIP-OFF (73); SCALAWAG (73); THE ELEVATOR (74, T.V. movie); THE RETURN OF JOE FORRESTER (75, T.V. movie); DEATH WEEKEND (76); HIGH RISK (76, T.V. movie); SUDDEN DEATH (77); THE CHOIRBOYS (77); HOUSE BY THE LAKE (77); THE BUDDY HOLLY STORY (78); KATIE: PORTRAIT OF A CENTREFOLD (78, T.V. movie); THE AMITYVILLE HORROR (79); DEATH THREAT (80); THE NIGHT THE LIGHTS WENT OUT IN GEORGIA (80); T.V. series as Sgt. Varrick, 'Kate Loves a Mystery' (80); SEARCH AND DESTROY (81).

BARRY SULLIVAN

B. New York City 29.8.12. Real name Patrick Barry Sullivan; ed. New York and Temple Univ.; a would-be lawyer, Mr Sullivan worked as an usher in a theatre and a buyer for a department store before choosing an acting career; he played extensively on stage including New York: 'Brother Rat' (1936), 'The Land is Bright' (1941) and the classic 'Man Who Came to Dinner' before movie début in HIGH EXPLORER in 1942; also well-known on T.V. in the series 'The Man Called X' (1956) as Ken Thurston, 'Harbormaster' (1957) as Capt. David Scott, 'The Tall Man' (1960-62) as Sheriff Pat Garrett and as Jordan Braddock in 'The Immortal' (1970); md. actress Marie Brown; his many movies include LADY IN THE DARK (43); TWO YEARS BEFORE THE MAST (44); AND NOW TOMORROW (44); SUSPENSE (46); THE GREAT GATSBY (49); THE OUTRIDERS (50); THE BAD AND THE BEAUTIFUL (52); TEXAS LADY (55); FORTY GUNS (57); SEVEN WAYS FROM SUNDOWN (60); MY BLOOD RUNS COLD (64); SEE YOU IN HELL, DARLING (66); EARTHQUAKE (74); HURRICANE (74, T.V. movie); TAKE A HARD RIDE (75); THE HUMAN FACTOR (75); ONCE AN EAGLE (76, mini-series); OH, GOD! (77); THE BASTARD, THE IMMIGRANTS (78, both mini-series); CARAVANS (78); S.S. CASINO (79, T.V. movie); BACK STAIRS AT THE WHITE HOUSE (79, mini-series).

DONALD SUTHERLAND

With consistently good performances in a wide range of roles, including the acclaimed ORDINARY PEOPLE Donald Sutherland has remained a top international star for over a decade. He was born at St. John, New Brunswick Canada on 17 July 1934(?) and his father ran the local bus, gas and electricity company. When a youngster of 11, he wa confined to bed for a year with rheumatic fever, but three years later, following a school visit to a radio station, he becam Canada's youngest announcer and disc-jockey. He later enrolled at the University of Toronto to study engineering, bu good reviews following a production of 'The Tempest' in which he performed at the Hart House Theatre, made hir switch to English. Following small roles in summer stock in Canada he came to London and studied at L.A.M.D.A., bu resigned in mid-term following a dispute with a tutor. Five years of hard work in rep. followed, including stints wit companies at Perth, Carlisle, Brighton, Chesterfield, Sheffield, Hammersmith, Bromley, Windsor, Nottingham an Manchester. His West End début was in a play titled 'August For The People' (and some sources give WORLD TEN TIMES OVER (63) as his first movie), then 'Two For the Seesaw' and following 'Spoon River Anthology' at the Roya Court, he was offered and played 2 roles in an Italian movie, CASTLE OF THE LIVING DEAD. His first tw marriages ended in divorce. They were to Canadian actresses Lois Hardwick and Shirley Douglas (latter from 1966-71 they had twins, Kiefer and Rachel, in 1967). He has two other children, sons Roeg (born 1974) and Rossif (1978 mother being Francine Racette. His motion-pictures have included THE BEDFORD INCIDENT (64); DF TERROR'S HOUSE OF HORRORS (64); FANATIC (65); PROMISE HER ANYTHING (66, uncredited); THE DIRTY DOZEN (67); OEDIPUS THE KING (68); INTERLUDE (68); JOANNA (68); SUNSHINE PATRIOT (68, T.V. movie); THE SPLIT (68); KELLY'S HEROES (70); a great success in M*A*S*H (70); START THE REVOLUTION WITHOUT ME (70); ACT OF THE HEART (70); JOHNNY GOT HIS GUN (71); ALEX IN WONDERLAND (71); LITTLE MURDERS (71); KLUTE (71); STEELYARD BLUES (72); LADY ICE (73 DON'T LOOK NOW (73); ALIEN THUNDER (73); S*P*Y*S (74); DAY OF THE LOCUST (75); THE EAGLE HAS LANDED (76); Fellini's CASANOVA (76); BLOOD RELATIVES (77); KENTUCKY FRIEL MOVIE (77); THE DISAPPEARANCE (77); 1900 (77); INVASION OF THE BODYSNATCHERS (77); A MAN, A WOMAN, AND A BANK (78); NATIONAL LAMPOON'S ANIMAL HOUSE (78); THE FIRST TRAIN ROBBERY (78); SHERLOCK HOLMES—MURDER BY DECREE (78); BEAR ISLAND (79) NOTHING PERSONAL (79); ORDINARY PEOPLE (79); THE EYE OF THE NEEDLE (80); THRESHOLI (80); GAS (81); MAX DUGAN RETURNS (82) and CRACKERS (83).

DUDLEY SUTTON

B. East Molesey, Surrey, 6.4.33. A familiar face on T.V. and the big screen, Mr Sutton has acted extensively on stage (including New York in 'The Hostage' (1960) and 'Entertaining Mr Sloane' (1965) in England (including 'Curse of the Starving Class' (1977)); T.V. includes 'The Sweeney', Thriller: 'Cry Terror' (1975), 'A Celebration of Sean O'Casey' (1980); his many movies include: THE LEATHER BOYS (64); ROTTEN TO THE CORE (65); CROSSPLOT (69); ONE MORE TIME (70); THE WALKING STICK (70); THE DEVILS (71); MADAME SIN (71); GREAT EXPECTATIONS (74, T.V. movie); PAGANINI STRIKES AGAIN (74); THE PRINCE & THE PAUPER (76); Fellini's CASANOVA (76); THE BIG SLEEP (77); VALENTINO (77); THE LONDON CONNECTION (79); THE ISLAND (79); GEORGE AND MILDRED (80); T.V. series, 1981: 'Marmalade Atkins In Space'; 1982: 'Radio', 'Shine on, Harvey Moon', 'Smiley's People'.

JANET SUZMAN

B. Johannesburg, S. Africa, 9.2.39. Ed. Kings mead College and Witwatersrand Univ. (B.A degree, English and French); intending to becom a doctor, Janet played in college theatricals an decided to become an actress, coming to Englanc and studying at L.A.M.D.A.; progressing to the R.S. Co. in 1962, she became one of Britain' leading younger stage actresses (esp. in S'pear classics); md. Mr Trevor Nunn, stage director 1969, 1 son Joshua, born 11.11.80; a well-know face on T.V., her work includes 'St Joan' (1968) 'Macbeth' (1970), 'Hedda Gabler' (1972) an the series 'Clayhanger' (1975/76); her movies: A DAY IN THE DEATH OF JOE EGG (70) THE BLACK WINDMILL (74); VOYAGE OF THE DAMNED (76); THE HOUSE ON GARIBALDI STREET (78); NIJINSKY (79) THE PRIEST OF LOVE (80) and THE DRAUGHTSMAN'S CONTRACT (81); fo her interpretation of the Empress Alexandra in NICHOLAS & ALEXANDRA (71), she gaine an Oscar nom.; T.V. 1982: 'Six Feet of the Country: Praise'.

BO SVENSON

. Goteburg, Sweden, 13.2.41. Height 6'6"; went
 U.S.A. aged 17, studied at U.C.L.A.; spent six
 ears in the U.S. Marines, seeing action in
 uantánamo Bay during the missile crisis, also
 erving in Japan and Vietnam; in Japan first
 ppeared on stage, returned to U.S. worked at
 everal jobs, including stock/formula car racer,
 ootlegged moonshine' between Florida and
 eorgia, sold life insurance, lifeguard at Miami
 each 1964/65, underwater demolition as a diver,
 olunteered for Israeli 1967 war, before breaking
 to show-biz in 'South Pacific' at Miami; off-
 roadway in 'Pidgeons Don't Cry' lead to T.V.:
 The Bravos' (72, T.V. movie), as the Monster in
 Frankenstein' (73, T.V. movie) and as Big Swede
  series 'Here Comes the Brides' (1968-70);
 ovies include MAURIE (73); THE GREAT
 /ALDO PEPPER (75); PART TWO: WALK-
 NG TALL (75); TARGET RISK (75, T.V.
 ovie); SNOWBEAST (77, T.V. movie); FINAL
 HAPTER: WALKING TALL (77); NORTH
)ALLAS FORTY (79); GOLD OF THE
 MAZON WOMEN (79, T.V. movie); VIRUS
 0); BUTCHER, BAKER, NIGHTMARE
 1AKER (82); PORTRAIT OF A HIT MAN
 33).

ERIC SYKES

B. Oldham, Lancs, 4.5.23. Father worked at
cotton mill; ed. Ward Street Central School,
Oldham; left school at 14, worked at joiner's shop;
painter; greengrocer's assistant; office boy; store
keeper in cotton mill; 1941 joined R.A.F. and 1st
taste of show-biz in revue; after war Oldham Rep.,
then in 1948 commenced successful career as
radio script-writer ('Educating Archie', etc.); md.
Elizabeth Milbrandt, ex-nurse, 3 daughters:
Catherine, Susan, Julie; 1960 appeared in own
T.V. show, running 20 years; Eric's movies
include WATCH YOUR STERM (60); INVA-
SION QUARTET (61); VILLAGE OF
DAUGHTERS (62); KILL OR CURE (63);
HEAVEN'S ABOVE! (63); THE BARGEE
(63); ONE-WAY PENDULUM (64); ROTTEN
TO THE CORE (65); MAGNIFICENT MEN
IN THEIR FLYING MACHINES (65); THE
LIQUIDATOR (65); THE SPY WITH THE
COLD NOSE (67); SHALAKO (69); MONTE
CARLO OR BUST (69); RHUBARB (70, also
dir.); THEATRE OF BLOOD (73); GHOST
IN THE NOONDAY SUN (74); IF YOU GO
DOWN IN THE WOODS TODAY (81, T.V.
movie); IT'S YOUR MOVE (T.V. movie, 82);
BOYS IN BLUE (83); wr./dir.: THE PLANK
(67 & 79, T.V.); well-known intn'l stage tour: 'Big
Bad Mouse'.
ERIC SYKES OF SEBASTOPOL TERRACE
by E.S. (humorous stories); Michael Joseph:
London, 1981.

ELIZABETH TAYLOR

n many occasions her much-publicised private life has perhaps overshowed her screen career, but Liz Taylor's
eputation as a highly professional actress has never been questioned, and she has now been in the profession for forty
ears, and recognised by the Academy several times. She was born in North London on 27 February 1932, the daughter
f Francis Taylor, an art dealer, and his wife, Sara, both Americans. As a child Elizabeth attended Byron House School
nd had ballet lessons with the celebrated Vaccani, and she already displayed artistic talent. When war broke out in
urope, the Taylor family moved to California, staying with relatives in Pasadena, and the youngster was continually
dvised that she was ideal for movies and eventually came to the screen in THERE'S ONE BORN EVERY MINUTE
2), for Universal. Her father, then an air-raid warden, met producer Sam Marx, who secured Elizabeth for a role in
ASSIE COME HOME (43), and thus commenced her long association with M-G-M. NATIONAL VELVET (44)
ade her a star, and other work at this time included CYNTHIA (47); LITTLE WOMEN (49) and FATHER OF
HE BRIDE (50). Husband No.1 was Nicholas Conrad Hilton Jr. (wed 6.5.50, div. 29.1.51). She was then married to
ritish star, the late Michael Wilding, on 21.2.52, and they had 2 sons, Michael (born 6.1.53) and Christopher
7.2.55). They divorced in 1956 and the following year she wed producer Michael Todd, and their daughter Elizabeth
as born on 6 August 1957. Mr Todd was tragically killed in a plane crash in 1958. Miss Taylor made some fine movies
 the 50s and these included A PLACE IN THE SUN (51); IVANHOE (52); GIANT (56); RAINTREE
OUNTRY (57); CAT ON A HOT TIN ROOF (58, Oscar nom., BA) and SUDDENLY, LAST SUMMER (59,
scar nom., BA). her fourth husband was singer Eddie Fisher, in 1959, and the following year she won an Academy
ward as Gloria Wandrous in BUTTERFIELD 8. Her role of CLEOPATRA (1962/63) gained much publicity for
er and co-star Richard Burton (qv) and subsequently their movies together have included THE V.I.P.s (63); THE
ANDPIPER (65); WHO'S AFRAID OF VIRGINIA WOOLF? (66, Oscar, BA); THE TAMING OF THE
HREW (67, as Katharina) and BOOM (68). They wed first from 1964-74, divorced, re-married the following year,
ut this was short-lived and in 1976 she became Mrs John Warner, her husband being a U.S. lawyer/senator (sep.).
ther movies include ZEE AND CO (71); DIVORCE HIS/DIVORCE HERS (73, T.V. movie); A LITTLE
IIGHT MUSIC (76); THE BLUE BIRDS (76); THE MIRROR CRACK'D (80) and GENOCIDE (81, co-
arrator). She divorced Mr Warner 6.11.82. Recently she played on stage in 'The Little Foxes' (81/82, U.S.A. &
ondon) and 'Private Lives' (83, Boston & Broadway), the latter re-uniting her, yet again, with Richard Burton.
HIS IS LIZ TAYLOR by Alistair Revie; Consul Books: London, 1962, p/b; *ELIZABETH TAYLOR* by Ruth
Vaterbury; Robert Hale: London, 1964; p/b: Pan, 1966; *ELIZABETH—THE LIFE AND CAREER OF
LIZABETH TAYLOR* by Dick Sheppard; W.H. Allen: London, 1975; *FOR LOVE OF LIZ* by Joan Joseph; Manor
ooks: New York, 1976, p/b; *WHO'S AFRAID OF ELIZABETH TAYLOR?* by Brenda Maddox; Hart-Davis-
1acGibbon: London, 1977; *RICHARD AND ELIZABETH* by Lester David & Jhan Robbins; Arthur Barker:
ondon, 1977; *ELIZABETH TAYLOR: THE LAST STAR* by Kitty Kelly; Michael Joseph: London, 1981;
LIZABETH TAYLOR: HER LIFE, HER LOVES, HER FUTURE* by Ruth Waterbury (with Gene Arceri); p/b:
antam: N.Y., 1982; *ELIZABETH TAYLOR* by Tom Hutchinson; Galley Press: London, 1982.

OD TAYLOR

 Sydney, N.S.W., Australia, 1.11.29. Real
 ame Robert Taylor; ed. Fine Arts College;
 ommenced career as an artist, but turned to the
 age in Australia; movies in his native country:
 ONG JOHN SILVER, KING OF THE
 ORAL SEA (54), then to U.S. screen and T.V.:
 cludes TOP GUN (55); GIANT (56); RAIN-
 REE COUNTRY (57); SEPARATE TABLES
 8); ASK ANY GIRL (59); THE TIME
 ACHINE (60); md. 1. model Peggy Williams
 iv.); 2. New York model Mary Hilem, 3.6.63., 1
 ughter Felicia Roderica (div.); T.V. series:
 lenn Evans in 'Hong Kong' (1961), Hank
 ackett in 'Bearcats' (1971) and Evan Thorpe in
 he Oregon Trail' (77); many other films include
 EVEN SEAS TO CALAIS (62); THE BIRDS
 3); THE V.I.P.'s (63); 36 HOURS (64);
 OUNG CASSIDY (65); THE LIQUIDATOR
 5); HOTEL (67); CHUKA (67); THE MER-
 ENARIES (68); NOBODY RUNS FOREVER
 8); ZABRISKIE POINT (70); POWDERKEG
 1, T.V. movie); DEADLY TRACKERS (73);
 RADER HORN (73); A MATTER OF WIFE
 . OR DEATH (76, T.V. movie); HELL-
 IVER (78); PICTURE SHOW MAN (77);
 ELLINGER'S LAW (81, T.V. movie);
 ACQUELINE BOUVIER KENNEDY (81,
 V. movie); ON THE RUN (82).

JOHN TERRY

B. ———, . . 49. Mr Terry worked in Alaska,
made a 400 mile trip down the Yukon River on a
raft, living on fish and game; other work: diver for
sunken Spanish galleons, a game warden, ploughed
fields in Carolina; 1977 building cabins in Blue
Ridge Mountains, took part in musical production;
went to New York to get acting work, did odd jobs,
got role in movie THERE GOES THE BRIDE
(79); acting classes in New York, T.V. movie
HOT WIRE (79); then to G.B., stars in HAWK
THE SLAYER (80).

TERRY-THOMAS

B. Finchley, N. London, 14.7.11. Real name
Thomas Terry Hoar Stevens; ed. Ardingly, Sussex;
pro. dancer: Cricklewood Palais; tour mimicking
Richard Tauber, radio and WWII: 'Stars in
Battledress'; great success cabaret 'Piccadilly
Hayride', then T.V.; md. 1. dancer Ida Patlawsky
(1938-62); 2. Belinda Cunningham, 20.8.63, 2
sons Trumper, Cushion; much-loved debonair
British comic actor, many pictures include HEL-
TER SKELTER (49); PRIVATE'S PROGRESS
(56); NAKED TRUTH (58); I'M ALRIGHT,
JACK (59); HOW TO MURDER YOUR WIFE
(65); MONTE CARLO OR BUST (69);
HOUNDS OF THE BASKERVILLES (77);
LAST REMAKE OF BEAU GESTE (77);
THE HUMAN BRAIN (81).
FILLING THE GAP by T.T.; Max Parrish:
London, 1959.

JOHN THAW

B. Manchester 3.1.42. Father long-distance lorry driver; ed. Ducie Technical H.S., Manchester; John worked for 3 months as porter at fruit market; 2 months baker's apprentice; did youth club drama at Burnage, took elocution lessons, decided to be actor; R.A.D.A. (Vanbrugh Aw.); 60/61 prize-winning rep. season, Liverpool; West End, Royal Court, Edinburgh Fest., etc.; md. 1. Sally Alexander, 1 daughter Abigail (div.); 2. actress/producer Sheila Hancock, 1 daughter Joanna; films: LONELINESS OF THE LONG-DISTANCE RUNNER (62); FIVE TO ONE (63); BOFORS GUN (68); LAST GRENADE (70); SWEENEY! (76, and very popular as Regan in T.V. series (1975-78)); SWEENEY 2 (77); THE GRASS IS SINGING (81); other T.V. includes Sgt. Mann in 'Redcap' (65), Sir Francis Drake in 'Drake's Venture' (80), 'Where is Betty Buchus?' (82), 'Mitch' (ser., 1983).

RICHARD THOMAS

B. New York City 13.6.51. Parents pro. ballet dancers; aged 6, appeared in summer theatre with father; through school teacher got Broadway role for 1 year in 'Sunrise at Campobello'; Actors' Studio and Columbia Univ.; New York stage: 'Strange Interlude' (1963), 'Everything in the Garden' (1967), others; T.V.: Great Ghost Tales: 'Shredni Vashtar' (1961), Chris in 'A Time For Us' (1965/66) and T.V. drama 'The Homecoming', lead to series 'The Waltons' (1972-77) with great success as John-Boy ('Emmy' Award 1973); md. Alma Gonzales, 1975, 1 son Richard (born 1976) and triplets, born Hollywood 27.8.81: Barbara, Gwyneth & ?; Richard's movies include WINNING, LAST SUMMER (both 69); THE TODD KILLINGS (70); CACTUS IN THE SNOW, WHAT ARE WE GOING TO DO WITHOUT SKIPPER?, RED SKY IN THE MORNING (all 71); YOU'LL LIKE MY MOTHER (72); RED BADGE OF COURAGE (74, T.V. movie); THE SILENCE (75, T.V. movie); 9/30/55 (77); GETTING MARRIED (78, T.V. movie); ROOTS: NEXT GENERATIONS (79, mini-series); NO OTHER LOVE, ALL QUIET ON THE WESTERN FRONT (both 79, T.V. movies); BERLIN TUNNEL 21 (81, T.V. movie); also writer of books of poetry.

INGRID THULIN – *see page 126*

RICHARD TODD

B. Dublin, Eire, 11.6.19. Real name Richard Andrew Palethorpe-Todd; ed. Shrewsbury and privately; trained for stage at Italia Conti School, London; début: Regent's Park, 1936, in 'Twelfth Night'; founder member/performer Dundee Rep. Co., 1938; WWII: distinguished service with King's Own Yorkshire Light Infantry and the Parachute Regiment, 1939-46; retd. to Dundee, spotted by talent scout and came to the screen in FOR THEM THAT TRESPASS (48) and THE HASTY HEART (49) made him a star; md. 1. Catherine Grant-Bogle, 1949, 1 son and 1 daughter (div.); many films include STAGE FRIGHT (50); FLESH AND BLOOD (51); ROBIN HOOD (52, title role); SWORD & THE ROSE (53); ROB ROY (53, title role); THE DAM BUSTERS (55); D-DAY: THE 6TH JUNE (56); ST. JOAN (57, as Dunois); YANG-TSE INCIDENT (57); INTENT TO KILL (58); DANGER WITHIN (58); NEVER LET GO (60); LONG, THE SHORT, AND THE TALL (61); DON'T BOTHER TO KNOCK (61); THE HELLIONS (61); THE BOYS (62); THE VERY EDGE (63); DEATH DRUMS ALONG THE RIVER (63); COAST OF SKELETONS (64); OPERATION CROSS-BOW (65); BATTLE OF THE VILLA FIORITA (65); SUBTERFUGE (68); LAST OF THE LONG-HAIRED BOYS (69); DORIAN GRAY (70); ASYLUM (72); NO.1 OF THE SECRET SERVICE (77); THE BIG SLEEP (77); HOME BEFORE MIDNIGHT (78); in 1957 Mr Todd started to devote much of his time to a dairy farming venture; md. 2. former model Virginia Mailer, 1970, 2 sons; much stage work in recent years, forming Triumph Theatre Prods. in 1970, appearing in international tours etc.; tour 1981: 'Murder in Mind'; West End 1982/83: 'The Business of Murder'; HOUSE OF THE LONG SHADOWS (83).

ROY THINNES

B. Chicago 16.4.38. Acted when a teenager, entering profession after 6 months in U.S. Army; T.V. series: as Dr Phil Brewer 'General Hospital' (1963), as Ben Quick in 'The Long, Hot Summer' (1965/66), as David Vincent in 'The Invaders' (1967/68); md. 1. ———, child: Leslie (div.). 2. Lynn Loring, 1967, 1 son Chris (born 18.1.68); TOYS IN THE ATTIC (63); DOPPEL-GANGER (69); THE OTHER MAN (70, T.V. movie); BLACK NOON (71, T.V. movie); CHARLEY ONE-EYE (72); HORROR AT 37,000 FEET, THE NORLISS TAPES, SATAN'S SCHOOL FOR GIRLS, DEATH RACE (all 73 T.V. movies); AIRPORT 75, THE HINDENBERG, MAN HUNTER (76, T.V. movie); SECRETS (77, T.V. movie); RETURN OF MOD SQUAD (79, T.V. movie). SCRUPLES (81, T.V. movie); T.V. series 1982/83: Nick Hogan in 'Falcon Crest'.

LINDA THORSON

B. Toronto, Ontario, 18.6.47. Real name Linda Robinson; father had confectionery business; ed. Bishop Strachan School, Toronto; Linda, a juvenile ice-skating champion, came to England to study at R.A.D.A., gaining an honours diploma, and was also trained as a soprano, pianist and ballet dancer; she played with the Bristol Old Vic Co., and replaced Diana Rigg (qv) in 'The Avengers' T.V. series, as Tara King (1968/69); md. T.V. cameraman Barry Bergthorson (div. 1970); stage includes 'The Club' (1978); movies: VALENTINO (77); THE GREEK TYCOON (78); CURTAINS (81).

OLIVER TOBIAS

B. Switzerland 6.8.47. Father Robert Freita Swiss theatre director; m. Maria Becker, Germ actress; came to U.K. aged 8; ed. Sussex/Londo boarding schools; left school, toured contine including Switzerland, as guitarist with ro group; E.15 drama school; West End: 'Ha (1968) and tour; movies: ROMANCE OF HORSE THIEF (70); 'TIS A PITY SHE'S WHORE (72); THE GOD KING (74); TH STUD (78); ARABIAN ADVENTURE (78 THE BIGGEST BANK ROBBERY (79, T. movie); very popular on T.V., Oliver's wo includes 'Arthur of the Britons' (1972), 'Luke Kingdom', 'Smuggler' (1980) and guest star 'Dick Turpin's Greatest Adventure' (81); sta 1983: 'Pirates of Penzance'; movie: TH WICKED LADY: Md: Camilla Ravenshe 1982, 1 daughter, born 1983.

LILY TOMLIN

B. Detroit, Michigan, .9.39. Ed. Wayne State Coll., where she first invented characters for comedy sketches; aged 14 — clerk in store; comedienne on the cafe and night club circuit in N.Y., other jobs include office book-keeper, paying expense accounts; Lily's big break came on T.V. in 13 episodes of 'The Music Scene' (1969/79) as one of 'The Music Scene Troupe' and esp. as Ernestine, the switchboard operator in 'Rowan & Martin Laugh-In' (1970-73); other T.V. includes guest: 'Johnny Carson Show', 'Saturday Night Live', one-woman stage shows and Broadway revue, 'Appearing Nitely'; movies: NASHVILLE (75, Oscar nom. BSA); THE LATE SHOW (77); MOMENT BY MOMENT (78); IN-CREDIBLE SHRINKING WOMAN (80); NINE TO FIVE (80).

DAVID TOMLINSON

B. Henley-on-Thames 7.5.17. Ed. Tonbrid School; 1934: joined Grenadier Guards; 193 amateur dramatics; 1936-38: rep.: Folkeston Leeds, etc., West End: 1938 and tours; spotted l Anthony Asquith, director, came to screen QUIET WEDDING (41); WWII: RAF, 194 47; md. Audrey Freeman, 4 sons; popular, amiab 'typically British' roles in many movies, includi THE WAY TO THE STARS (45); MIRAND (48); THREE MEN IN A BOAT (55); MAR POPPINS (64); THE LOVE BUG (69); BEI KNOBS AND BROOMSTICKS (71); DOM NIQUE (78); WATER BABIES (78); WOM LING FREE (78); on the stage, Mr Tomlins has toured (including Africa) and also directe

TOPOL

B. Tel Aviv, Israel, 9.9.35; Full name Chaim Topol ('Topol' means 'tree', and 'Chaim', pronounced 'hyam', means 'life'); upon leaving school, Chaim joined the Israeli army in 1953, was discharged in 1956 and helped found the Municipal Theatre at Haifa, serving as leading actor; md. former actress, Galia, 2 daughters: Anat and Adi; his first movie in Israel was I LOVE MIKE, others include SALLAH (65, also produced) and CAST A GIANT SHADOW (65); discovered by stage producer Hal Prince, he won acclaim for his role as Teyve in the musical 'Fiddler on the Roof', staged on Broadway in 1967 and opened in London on 16.2.67, gaining him an award as 'Man of the Year' from London critics; other movies have included BEFORE WINTER COMES (69); A TALENT FOR LOVING (70); FIDDLER ON THE ROOF (71, Oscar nom. BA); THE PUBLIC EYE (72); GALILEO (74, title role); THE HOUSE ON GARIBALDI STREET (79); FLASH GORDON (79); FOR YOUR EYES ONLY (81); London stage 1983: 'Fiddler on the Roof.
TOPOL BY TOPOL: Weidenfeld & Nicholson: London, 1981.

RIP TORN

B. Temple, Texas, 6.2.31. Real name Elmore Torn Jr.; ed. Texas A & M Coll. and Univ. of Texas (Fine Arts Degree 1953); oilfield and pipeline roustabout; qualified architectural draughtsman; studied for stage with Lee Strasberg, Alice Hernes, Sanford Meisner; also dance at Martha Graham School; became award-winning stage actor in U.S., also directing; md. 1. Ann Wedgeworth, 1 daughter Danae (div.), 2. actress Genevieve Page, 1963, 1 daughter Angelica (born 1964), twins: Anthony, Jonathan (1965); many movies including BABY DOLL (56); CAT ON A HOT TIN ROOF (58, also stage); PORK CHOP HILL (59); KING OF KINGS (61, as Judas); CRITIC'S CHOICE (63); BEACH RED (67); MAIDSTONE (70); SLAUGHTER (72); CRAZY JOE (73); PAYDAY (73); THE MAN WHO FELL TO EARTH (76); BIRCH INTERVAL (76); NASTY HABITS (77); COMA (77); PRIVATE FILES OF J. EDGAR HOOVER (78); BLIND AMBITION (79, mini-series, as Richard M. Nixon); SOPHIA: HER OWN STORY (80, T.V. movie, as Carlo Ponti); A STRANGER IS WATCHING (81); JINXED (81); CROSS CREEK, MISUNDERSTOOD, SCARAB (all 1982).

JOHN TRAVOLTA

With comparatively few movies, John Travolta has emerged from the 1970s as one of the most popular of the younger American stars, with great success in SATURDAY NIGHT FEVER and GREASE, and developed into an actor of considerable appeal. Born in Englewood, New Jersey on 18 February 1954, he is the youngest child of Salvatore Travolta and his wife Helen. When he was born, John's father (the son of Italian immigrants) was a semi-professional footballer and co-owner with his brother of a tyre shop in Hillsdale, and his mother, of Irish stock, was an ex-actress and drama teacher, a director of a local and summer theatre before her family (she had 6 children) took up her time. John, from the age of 6, had dancing lessons from Fred Kelly, brother of Gene, who ran a dancing school, and at the age of 12, appeared in his first play, 'Who'll Save the Plowboy?'. His first professional role was in a dinner theatre club play in a small role, when 16, earning $50, and the following year he dropped out of High School, appeared in summer theatre, went to New York, and played off-Broadway in 'Rain', did T.V. commercials and eventually reached Broadway in 'Grease' (plus a 10-month tour) and 'Over Here On Broadway' for 10 months. He had a supporting role in the movie THE DEVIL'S RAIN (75) and won international fame as Vinnie Barbarino in the T.V. series 'Welcome Back, Kotter' from 1975-78. In 1976 he also played in a T.V. movie, THE BOY IN THE PLASTIC BUBBLE and had a small role in the thriller CARRIE. Movie stardom came in the disco movie SATURDAY NIGHT FEVER (77) and the film version of GREASE (78), in which John co-starred with Olivia Newton-John (qv). Since then he has completed MOMENT BY MOMENT (78); URBAN COWBOY (79); BLOW OUT (81) and Stallone's STAYING ALIVE (83). In 1982 he played on stage as a priest in 'Mass Appeal', at Snowmass Village, Colorado. His brother, Joey, has acted in such movies as SUNNYSIDE (79) and CRASHED CARS (80).
JOHN TRAVOLTA by Michael Reeves; Jove Books: New York, 1978, p/b.

FRANCOIS TRUFFAUT

B. Paris 6.2.32. At 14 office boy/messenger/ welder in factory; organised small ciné-clubs in Paris; journalist for 'Work & Culture'; Nat. Serv.—army 1951-53; film dept.: Min. of Agriculture; critic for magazine 'Cahiers du Cinéma'; assistant to Rossellini; Mr Truffaut began directing with 2 shorts: UNE VISITE (55) and LES MISTONS (58), his first feature being THE 400 BLOWS (59); his films have won numerous awards, and he has acted in L'ENFANT SAUVAGE (69), DAY FOR NIGHT (73, as the director, Oscar, Best Foreign Language Film), THE GREEN ROOM (78), all of which he directed; he played the French scientist in the 1977 international success, CLOSE ENCOUNTERS OF THE THIRD KIND.

TWIGGY

B. Twickenham, Middx., 19.9.49. Real name Lesley Hornby; father a carpenter; ed. Kilburn H.S. for Girls; hairdresser's assistant-cum-international fashion model girl of the Swinging 60s; came to screen as Polly in THE BOYFRIEND (71), has also been seen in W (73), THERE GOES THE BRIDE (79), THE BLUES BROTHERS (80), others; much T.V., stage, including pantomime, voted in 1977 'World's Loveliest Woman'; md. actor Michael Whitney 1977, 1 daughter Carly (born 1.12.78); T.V. 1981: Eliza in 'Pygmalion'; Broadway 1983: 'My One & Only'.
TWIGGY by Twiggy; Hart-Davis-MacGibbon: London, 1975; Mayflower p/b, 1976.

LIV ULLMANN

Of Norwegian parents, Liv Ullmann was born in Tokyo, Japan, on 16 December 1939. Liv (pronounced 'Leev', which means 'life') was raised in Canada, having left Japan during the war. Educated in Toronto and New York as a youngster she was a teenaged playwright — 'Invariably religious tragedies', she trained for the stage in London, at the Webber-Douglas Academy, making her film début in THE WAYWARD GIRL (59). Her marriage to psychiatrist Jappe Stang in 1960 ended in divorce five years later. She made a name for herself in a number of movies directed by Ingmar Bergman (from whom she has a daughter, Linn, born in 1965) her films include PERSONA (65); HOUR OF THE WOLF (67); THE SHAME (68); THE PASSION OF ANNA (69); THE NIGHT VISITOR (70); COLD SWEAT (70); THE DEVIL'S IMPOSTER (72); CRIES AND WHISPERS (72, BA, New York Film Critics); THE EMIGRANTS (72, Oscar nom. BA); hostess of 'Scenes From a Marriage' (Swedish T.V. series, 1973); FORTY CARATS (73); ZANDY'S BRIDE (74); THE ABDICATION (74, as Queen Christina); FACE TO FACE (76, Oscar nom. BA); LEONOR (77); A BRIDGE TOO FAR (77); THE SERPENT'S EGG (78); AUTUMN SONATA (78); RICHARD'S THINGS (80); LOVE (80, also directed her segment); as JENNY (82).
CHANGING by L.U.; Star Book/W.H. Allen: London, 1978, p/b (first published in Sweden in 1976); *WITHOUT MAKE-UP: LIV ULLMANN — A PHOTO BIOGRAPHY* — David E. Outerbridge; Wm. Morrow & Co. Inc: New York, 1979.

PETER USTINOV

A highly entertaining raconteur — his recent autobiography has been a best-seller, Peter Ustinov has contributed much to film over the years, as a masterly, award-winning character actor as well as being a talented writer and director. The son of Iona and Nadezhda Von Ustinov, he was born in Swiss Cottage, North London, on 16 April 1921, and educated at Westminster School, progressing to the London Theatre Studio at 16, studying with Michel St. Denis. His professional stage début was in 'The Wood Demon' as Waffles, in 1938, at the Barn Theatre, Shere, in Surrey. This marked the beginning of his highly successful stage career, especially as actor, writer and director of his own productions, and he first appeared in London, at the Players' Theatre Club, in 1939, in his own sketch, 'The Bishop of Limpopoland'. He was soon appearing in movies such as HULLO FAME, MEIN KAMPF (both 40); THE GOOSE STEPS OUT (41); ONE OF OUR AIRCRAFT IS MISSING, LET THE PEOPLE SING (both 42) and cowrote with Eric Ambler, THE WAY AHEAD (44). Ustinov served with the army during the war with the Royal Sussex Regiment from 1942-46 and, at 19, had wed Isolde Denham. Their daughter, Tamara, was born on 25 July 1945, but the couple divorced two years later. His stage career now flourishing, he appeared in occasional movies such as SCHOOL FOR SECRETS (46, wrote/directed); VICEVERSA (48, wrote/directed); PRIVATE ANGELO (49, also author, producer, director); ODETTE (50); HOTEL SAHARA, THE MAGIC BOX (cameo, both 51) and his performance as Nero in QUO VADIS? gained him an Oscar nom. as Best Supporting Actor of 1951. In 1953 his play 'The Love of Four Colonels' received the Donaldson Award as Best Play of the Broadway season written by a 'new author' and the following year he wed Suzanne Cloutier, and they had 2 children, Pavla (born 2.6.54) and Igor (30.4.56). Subsequent movies have included BEAU BRUMMELL (54, as George IV); THE EGYPTIAN (54); WE'RE NO ANGELS (55); LOLA MONTEZ (55); THE MAN WHO WAGGED HIS TAIL (57); THE SPIES (57); SPARTACUS (60, Oscar BSA); ROMANOFF AND JULIET (61, also directed/writer); BILLY BUDD (62, also directed/co-scripted); TOPKAPI (64, Oscar, BSA); LADY L (65, also wrote/directed); THE COMEDIANS (67); HOT MILLIONS (68); ONE OF OUR DINOSAURS IS MISSING (75); TREASURE OF MATECUMBE (76); LAST RE-MAKE OF BEAU GESTE (77); JESUS OF NAZARETH (mini-ser., 77, as Herod the Great); DEATH ON THE NILE (78) and PURPLE TAXI (78). Divorced from Miss Cloutier, his third wife is Helene du Lau d'Allemans, marrying in 1972. Mr Ustinov received the C.B.E. in the Queen's Birthday Honours in 1976, and his most recent work includes the movies CHARLIE CHAN & THE CURSE OF THE DRAGON QUEEN (81, title role); EVIL UNDER THE SUN (82, again as Poirot), MEMED THE HAWK (83, star/director/script), the opera 'The Marriage' (81, Milan, acted/produced), West End plays 'Overheard' (81, wrote), 'Beethoven's Tenth' (83, acted/wrote) and the T.V. play 'Imaginary Friends' (83, acted).
USTINOV IN FOCUS by Tony Thomas; p/b: Zwemmer/Barnes, 1971.
DEAR ME by Peter Ustinov (autobio.); Wm. Heinemann: London, 1977; p/b: Penguin, 1978.

BRENDA VACCARO

B. Brooklyn, New York, 18.11.39. Of Italian extraction; ed. Thos. Jefferson H.S. Dallas; trained at the Neighborhood Playhouse School of Theatre, making professional début 1961 at Margo Jones Theatre, Dallas; distinguished Broadway actress, winning 'Tony' awards; seen by Schlesinger on stage and cast in MIDNIGHT COWBOY movie, 1969; other pictures: WHERE IT'S AT (69); I LOVE MY WIFE (70); TRAVIS LOGAN, D.A. (71, T.V. movie); WHAT'S A NICE GIRL LIKE YOU...? (71, T.V. movie); SUMMERTREE (71); GOING HOME (71); SUNSHINE (73, T.V. movie); HONOR THY FATHER (73, T.V. movie); ONCE IS NOT ENOUGH (75, Oscar nom. BSA); THE BIG RIPOFF (75, T.V. movie); DEATH WEEKEND (76); THE MOONBEAM RIDER (76); AIRPORT 77, THE HOUSE BY THE LAKE (77); SANS JOE MILE (77); CAPRICORN ONE (78); O GOD, O GOD (80); CHANEL SOLITAIRE (80); THE FIRST DEADLY SIN (80); ZORRO, THE GAY BLADE (81); md. 1. Marty Fried (1965-70), 2. attorney W.S. Bishop (div. 1977); T.V. 'Emmy' award 1976 as Sara Yarnell in series 'Sara'; md. 3. photographer Charles Cannizzaro (1981); 'The Star Maker' (mini-ser., 1981); SUPERGIRL (84).

RAF VALLONE

B. Tropea, Calabria, Italy, 17.2.17. Raised in Turin; excelled at sport, aged 14 was earning 1,000 lira-a-month as an apprentice for Turin F.C.; Turin Univ., graduating with Doctorates of Law & Philosophy; journalist with Turin daily; advised by former critic Guiseppe de Santis to try acting and Raf came to the screen in BITTER RICE (49); Italian movies, then from 1961 international, including VENDETTA (49); PATH OF HOPE (51); IL CRISTO PROIBITO (51); ANNA (51); ROME—11 O'CLOCK (52); DAUGHTERS OF DESTINY (52); THE BEACH (53); PASSIONATE SUMMER (55); TERESA RAQUIN (58); TWO WOMEN (60); EL CID (61); A VIEW FROM THE BRIDGE (62); PHAEDRA (62); THE CARDINAL (63); THE SECRET INVASION (64); HARLOW (65); NEVADA SMITH (66); BEYOND THE MOUNTAINS (66); KISS THE GIRLS AND MAKE THEM DIE (67); THE DESPERATE ONES (67); THE ITALIAN JOB (69); THE KREMLIN LETTER (70); CANNON FOR CORDOBA (70); A GUNFIGHT (71); HONOUR THY FATHER (73, T.V. movie); CATHOLICS (73, T.V. movie); SUMMERTIME KILLER (73); ROSEBUD (75); THE HUMAN FACTOR (75); THE DEVIL'S ADVOCATE (77); THE OTHER SIDE OF MIDNIGHT (77); THE GREEK TYCOON (78); LION OF THE DESERT (79); RETURN TO MARSEILLES (80); T.V. 1982: 'I Remember Nelson'.

LEE VAN CLEEF

B. Somerville, New Jersey, 9.1.25. Of Dutch ancestry, father accountant, mother a singer; dropped out of H.S. to join U.S. Navy; farmhand; in Manhattan worked in factory, public accounting at night; assnt. manager, summer camp; amateur theatricals lead to professional début, touring in 'Mister Roberts' (1950), in L.A. spotted by Stanley Kramer, came to screen in HIGH NOON (52); md. Ruth Ann (div.), 2. Joan, a concert pianist, children: Alan, Deborah, Davis (div.); featured player, Hollywood, until catapulted to fame in 1965 in Spanish-made westerns; movies include UNTAMED FRONTIER (52); ARENA (53); THE DESPERADO (54); THE BIG COMBO (55); THE CONQUEROR (56); THE TIN STAR (57); THE BRAVADOS (58); RIDE LONESOME (59); HOW THE WEST WAS WON (63), etc.; md. 3. Barbara, concert pianist, 1974; FOR A FEW DOLLARS MORE (65, Spain); DEATH RIDES A HORSE (67); GOOD, THE BAD & THE UGLY (67); DAY OF ANGER (68); SABATA (69); BARQUERO (70); EL CONDOR (70); MAGNIFICENT 7 RIDE (72); THE GUN (73); BLOOD MONEY (74); TAKE A HARD RIDE (75); POWER TO KILL (75); GANGSTER STORY (76); VENDETTA (76); KID VENGEANCE (77); NOWHERE TO HIDE (77, T.V. movie); GOD'S GUN (78); THE HARD WAY (79, T.V. movie); ESCAPE FROM NEW YORK (80); THE OCTAGON (80).

TRISH VAN DEVERE

B. Englewood Cliffs, New Jersey, 9.3.45. Real name Patricia Dressel; ed. Ohio Wesleyan; after appearing in New York in such productions as 'Kicking the Castle Down' (1967) Miss Van DeVere appeared on T.V. in 'Search For Tomorrow' and as Meredith Lord Wolek in 'One Life to Live'; md. George C. Scott (qv) 14.9.72 movies include WHERE'S POPPA? (70); THE LAST RUN (71); ONE IS A LOVELY NUMBER (72); DAY OF THE DOLPHIN (73); THE SAVAGE IS LOOSE (74); STALK THE WILD CHILD (76, T.V. movie); BEAUTY AND THE BEAST (76, T.V. movie); SHARON PORTRAIT OF A MISTRESS (77, T.V. movie); MOVIE, MOVIE (78); THE HEARSE (79); THE CHANGELING (80); ALL GOD'S CHILDREN (80, T.V. movie).

ROBERT VAUGHN

A popular movie actor for over twenty years, Robert Vaughn has consolidated this success with equally good performances in important T.V. series, such as 'Washington: Behind Closed Doors', which brought him an Emmy award. Born Robert Francis Vaughn in New York City on 22 November 1932, he is the son of Gerald Vaughn, a prominent radio actor, and his wife, Marcella Frances Gaudel, an established Broadway actress. Raised in Minneapolis by his grandparents, Vaughn enrolled at Minnesota's School of Journalism, but became increasingly interested in their drama department and eventually played for them in such productions as 'Hamlet' (title role), 'Death Takes a Holiday' and 'Knickerbocker Holiday'. 1951 brought him a prize for his radio acting and he enrolled L.A. City College as a drama student, appearing in 'Mister Roberts' and during the summer vacation he worked as resident director and leading actor for a theatre company in Albuquerque, graduating from his studies with a B.A. Degree in 1956. After appearing in 'End As a Man' in Los Angeles, he won a movie contract, but this was short-lived, coming to the screen in such movies as HELL'S CROSSROADS, TEENAGE DELINQUENTS (both 57), TEENAGE CAVEMAN and UNWED MOTHER (58). He began guesting on T.V. ('Zorro', etc.), and after movies GOOD DAY FOR A HANGING (59) and THE YOUNG PHILADELPHIANS (59, for which he won a B.S.A. Oscar nom.) he played in the western hit, as one of THE MAGNIFICENT SEVEN (60). He spent a year 1963/64 in the T.V. series 'The Lieutenant', as Capt. Raymond Rambridge, but his big break, as far as getting a huge following was concerned, was in the slickly produced spy-spoof series, 'The Man From U.N.C.L.E.', as Napoleon Solo, running from 1964-68. Several movie spin-offs included TO TRAP A SPY (66), THE KARATE KILLERS (67) and HOW TO STEAL THE WORLD (68). Vaughn's other feature films have included THE BIG SHOW (61); THE CARETAKERS (63); THE VENETIAN AFFAIR (67); BULLITT (68); IF IT'S TUESDAY, IT MUST BE BELGIUM (69); THE BRIDGE AT REMAGEN (69); THE MIND OF MR SOAMES (69); JULIUS CAESAR (69, as Casca); THE STATUE (71); THE CLAY PIGEON (71); THE WOMAN HUNTER (72, T.V. movie); THE TOWERING INFERNO (74); KISS ME, KILL ME and CAPTAINS AND KINGS (76, T.V. movie and mini-series). He played Harry Rule in a 1971 T.V. series, 'The Protectors', wed actress Linda Staab in 1974 and portrayed such U.S. Presidents as Franklin D. Roosevelt in a stage play 'That Man, F.D.R.', Harry S. Truman in 'Portrait: The Man From Independence' and Woodrow Wilson in 'Backstairs At The White House', a T.V. movie and mini-series respectively. Other work has included movies BRASS TARGET (78); THE ISLANDER (78, T.V. movie); 'Centennial' (78, mini-series); NIGHTMARE AT PENDRAGON'S CASTLE (78); THE REBELS (79, mini-series); PANIC ON PAGE ONE (79, T.V. movie); VIRUS (80); HANGAR 18 (80); S.O.B. (80); THE ISLANDER (81, T.V. movie); QUESTION OF HONOUR (81, T.V. movie); SWEET DIRTY TONY (81); INSIDE THE THIRD REICH (82, mini-ser.); SILENT REACH (82, mini-ser.) and THE COURAGEOUS (83).

DICK VAN DYKE

B. West Plains, Missouri, 18.12.25; after H.S. went into U.S. army; advertising business, but went bankrupt; started night-club act 1947, having ppd. in Nat. service shows; md. actress Marjorie Willett, 1948, 3 sons: Christian (born 1950), Barry (1952), Stacey (1955), 1 daughter Carrie (1961); 6 years night-club comic; Broadway includes 'The Girls Against the Boys' (1959), Tony Award 1960 for 'Bye Bye Birdie'; very popular on U.S. T.V.: on panel: 'Nothing But the Truth' (56), host: 'Mother's Day' (1958/59), regular: 'The Chevy Showroom' (1958), host: Laugh Line' (1959), Rob Petrie in 158 episodes of 'Dick Van Dyke Show' (1961-66); movies: BYE BYE BIRDIE (63); MARY POPPINS (64); WHAT A WAY TO GO (64); THE ART OF LOVE (65); LIEU. ROBINSON CRUSOE (65); DIVORCE AMERICAN STYLE (67); FITZWILLY (67); CHITTY CHITTY BANG BANG (68); NEVER A DULL MOMENT (68); SOME KIND OF A NUT (70); THE COMIC (70); COLD TURKEY (71); THE MORNING AFTER (74, T.V. movie); THE RUNNER STUMBLES (78); other T.V.: regular: 'Carol Burnett Show' (1967), Dick Preston in 'The New Dick Van Dyke Show' (1971-74), host: 'Van Dyke & Co.' (1976).

PETER VAUGHAN

B. Wem, Shropshire, .24. Real name Peter Ohm; father a bank clerk; Wolverhampton Rep.; Army service; Birmingham Rep., West End etc.; md. 1. actress Billie Whitelaw (div.); 2. actress Lillias Walker, 1 son David; solid actor, very well-known on T.V. in several series: 'Deadline Midnight', 'The Gold Robbers', 'Oliver Twist', 'Citizen Smith', etc.; movies: SAPPHIRE (59); VILLAGE OF THE DAMNED (60); PUNCH & JUDY MAN (63); FANATIC (65); ROTTEN TO THE CORE (65); THE NAKED RUNNER (66); TWIST OF SAND (67); HAMMERHEAD (68); THE BOFORS GUN (68); ALFRED THE GREAT (69); STRAW DOGS (72); SAVAGE MESSIAH (72); 11 HARROW-HOUSE (74); VALENTINO (76); ZULU DAWN (78); PORRIDGE (79); TIME BANDITS (81); FRENCH LIEUTENANT'S WOMAN (81); THE MISSIONARY (83), others; T.V. inclu. 'Winston Churchill — The Wilderness Years' (81); 'Coming Out of the Ice', 'Jamaica Inn' (both 83).

LINO VENTURA

B. Parma, Italy, 14.7.19(?). Real name Lino Borrini; a former boxer, Mr Ventura is a star of French movies, progressing to more internationally-based projects of the 1970s; movies include TOUCHEZ PAS AU GRISBI (53); RAZZIA SUR LA CHNOUF (54); CRIME & PUNISHMENT (56); MARIE OCTOBRE (57); CLASSE TOUS RISQUES (59); THE WOMAN IN THE WINDOW (61); DIE DREIGROSCHENOPER (62); CROOKS IN CLOVER (63); LES AVENTURIERS (66); THE SICILIAN CLAN (70); FANTASIA CHEZ LES PLOUCS (70); VALACHI PAPERS (72); WILD HORSES (72); LA BONNE ANNÉE (73); THE SLAP (74); THE CAGE (74); MEDUSA TOUCH (78); THE FRENCH DETECTIVE (79); SUNDAY LOVERS (80, French segment); JIGSAW (80).

JOHN VERNON

B. Regina, Saskatchewan, Canada, 24.2.35 (32?); appeared extensively on Canadian and Broadway stage; md. former actress Nancy West, 3 children; many films include POINT BLANK (67); JUSTINE (69); TRIAL RUN (69, T.V. movie); TELL THEM WILLIE BOY IS HERE (69); TOPAZ (69); DIRTY HARRY (71); ONE MORE TRAIN TO ROB (71); FEAR IS THE KEY (72); COOL MILLION (72, T.V. movie); BLACK WINDMILL (74); BRANNIGAN (74); THE QUESTOR TAPES (74, T.V. movie); MOUSEY (74, T.V. movie); THE VIRGINIA HILL STORY (74, T.V. movie); SWISS FAMILY ROBINSON (75, T.V. movie); MATT HELM (75, T.V. movie); DRUM (76); OUTLAW JOSEY WALES (76); A SPECIAL DAY (77); GOLDEN RENDEZVOUS (77); NATIONAL LAMPOON'S ANIMAL HOUSE (78); HERBIE GOES BANANAS (79); THE SACKETTS (79, T.V. movie); CURTAINS (81); CHAINED HEAT (83); came to screen in Canada in NOBODY WAVED GOOD-BYE (64).

JAN-MICHAEL VINCENT

B. Denver, Colorado, 15.7.44. Grew up on family farm; ed. Venturay City College, majoring in Art; when living in Mexico was called up for U.S. Army service; after discharge he went to L.A. and was discovered by agent Dick Clayton who brought him to the screen in LOS BANDIDOS, made in Mexico; early movies: JOURNEY TO SHILOH (68); THE UNDEFEATED (69); billed as Michael Vincent; T.V.: Link Simmons in 'Danger Island' (69), Jeffrey Carlyle in 'The Survivors' (70); other movies: TRIBES (70, T.V. movie); THE SOLDIER WHO DECLARED PEACE (70, T.V. movie); GOING HOME (71); THE MECHANIC (72); SANDCASTLES (72, T.V. movie); THE CATCHER (72, T.V. movie); THE WORLD'S GREATEST ATHLETE (73); DELIVER US FROM EVIL (73, T.V. movie); BUSTER & BILLIE (74); BITE THE BULLET (74); WHITE LINE FEVER (75); SHADOW OF THE HAWK, BABY BLUE MARINE, VIGILANTE FORCE (all 76); DAMNATION ALLEY (77); BIG WEDNESDAY (78); HOOPER (78); DEFIANCE (79); THE HARD COUNTRY (80); THE RETURN (81); LAST PLANE OUT (82); THE WINDS OF WAR (mini-ser., 1983).

MONICA VITTI

B. Rome, .33. Miss Vitti studied at the Rome Academy of Drama and appeared on the Italian stage; her movies, mainly based in Italy, have included L'AVVENTURA (59); LA NOTTE (60); ECLIPSE (62); DRAGEES AU POIVRE (63); NUTTY, NAUGHTY CHATEAU (63); SWEET & SOUR (63); RED DESERT (64, Italian Film Critics Aw.. BA); HIGH INFIDELITY (65); MODESTY BLAISE (66); THE QUEENS (66); ON MY WAY TO THE CRUSADES I MET A GIRL WHO... (67); GIRL WITH A PISTOL (69); THE PACIFIST (71); MIDNIGHT PLEASURES (75); DUCK IN ORANGE SAUCE (75) and more recently THE OBERWALD MYSTERY (81) and CAMERA D'ALBERGO (81). JEALOUSY TANGO (81); I KNOW THAT YOU KNOW THAT I KNOW (82).

JON VOIGHT

Born in Yonkers, New York, 29.12.38, Jon Voight is the son of Elmer Voight, a golf pro. (dec.), and his wife, Barbara. He attended Archbishop Stepinac H.S. and Catholic Univ., graduating in 1960 with a B.A. in Fine Arts. Early stage appearances with the Neighborhood Playhouse and a company in Vermont were followed by a year's study with Josh Shelley and Sanford Meisner. New York appearances include 'O, Oysters' (1961), 'Sound of Music', 'A View From the Bridge' (1965) and 'That Summer, That Fall' (1967). He played Romeo at the San Diego Festival, appeared on T.V. in 'Cimarron Strip', 'Gunsmoke' and broke into movies in 1967 with OUT OF IT, HOUR OF THE GUN and FEARLESS FRANK. His first two marriages ended in divorce: actress Lauri Peters (1960-67) and Marcelline Bertrand (1971-76, 1 son and 1 daughter) . Other movies: MIDNIGHT COWBOY (69, Oscar nom. BA); CATCH 22 (70); THE REVOLUTIONARY (70); DELIVERANCE (72); ALL AMERICAN BOY (73); ODESSA FILE (74); CONRACK (74); MURDER ON THE BRIDGE (75); COMING HOME (Best Actor: Oscar; New York Film Critics'; Golden Globe, 1979); THE CHAMP (78); LOOKIN' TO GET OUT (80); TABLE FOR FIVE (83).

LINDSAY WAGNER

B. Los Angeles 22.6.49. Ed. N. Hollywood H.S., Portland H.S., University of Oregon; Lindsay appeared in school plays in Oregon; at 13 attended ballet school, but after 2 weeks decided to become actress; played lead in local production of 'This Property is Condemned'; went to L.A. 1968: worked as model and sang with rock group; 1st T.V. role in 'Marcus Welby' epis., others include 'Rockford Files', 'F.B.I.', 'Owen Marshall'; came to screen 1973 in TWO PEOPLE; others THE PAPER CHASE (73) and SECOND WIND (in Canada); md. 1. music publisher Allan Rider (1972-74); in 2 episodes of '$6M Man', Lindsay was such a success, given her own series as Jamie Somers, the 'Bionic Woman' (1976-78); md. 2. actor Michael Brandon (1976-78); other movies: INCREDIBLE JOURNEY OF DR MEG LAUREL (79); THE PASSION OF JENNIE LOGAN (79); HIGH RISK (80); NIGHT HAWKS (80); series 1980: 'Scruples'.

CHRISTOPHER WALKEN

B. Astoria, Long Island, New York, 31.3.43. Father a banker; ed. Hofstra Univ., studying dramatics, majoring in Eng. Lit.; early stage career 1959 (New York début in 'J.B.'), 1964 worked under name 'Ronald Walken'; worked for several years on Broadway as dancer, from 1965 as actor, including Philip of Spain in 'The Lion In Winter' (66, Clarence Derwent Award) and 'Rose Tattoo' (66, Theatre World Award); md. Georgianne; movies: THE ANDERSON TAPES (71, début); THE HAPPINESS CAGE (72); NEXT STOP, GREENWICH VILLAGE (76); ROSELAND (77); THE SENTINEL (77); ANNIE HALL (77); won acclaim as Nick in THE DEER HUNTER (78), winning Oscar as B.S.A., also New York Film Critics' Award; other stage: 'Lemon Sky' (1970), 'The Judgement' (1972), 'Enemies' (1972), 'Macbeth', 'Hamlet' (1974, title roles); recent movies: LAST EMBRACE (79); HEAVEN'S GATE (79); THE DOGS OF WAR (80); PENNIES FROM HEAVEN (81); BRAINSTORM (82); SHOOT THE SUN DOWN (83).

MAX WALL

B. Brixton, London, 12.3.08. Real name Maxwell George Lorimer; father well-known comedian Jack Lorimer; 1st stage appearance, aged 14, as Jack in 'Mother Goose'; became well-known in variety and musical theatre in Britain; films include ONE OF OUR DINOSAURS IS MISSING (76); JABBERWOCKY (77); HOUND OF THE BASKERVILLES (77); HANOVER STREET (78); md. 1. Marian Pola (div.), 2. beauty queen Jennifer Chimes (div.), 3. Christine Clements; stage 1981: 'Aspects of Max Wall' (Garrick Theatre), 'Waiting For Godot' (Roundhouse); guest 'Minder' (1982, T.V.), Tommy Tonsley in 'Born and Bred' (1982, T.V.). 'Father's Day' (83, T.V.)

DEE WALLACE

B.   ,   .   . ; 'has been working at her acting career since the age of four'; Md: actor Christopher Stone; Miss Wallace has played in numerous T.V. series, including 'Chips', 'Hart to Hart', 'Lou Grant' and 'Starsky & Hutch'; her movies include 10 (79); THE HOWLING (80); WAIT TILL YOUR MOTHER GETS HOME (T.V. movie) and the fabulously successful E.T. — THE EXTRA TERRESTRIAL (both 1982); JIMMY THE KID (82); CUJO (83).

MAX VON SYDOW

B. Lund, Sweden, 10.4.29. Real name Max Ca Adolph Von Sydow; stage début in Cathedra School of Lund production of 'The Nobel Prize'; years in Swedish Quartermaster Corps.; aged 1 studied at Royal Drama Theatre School, Swede then toured municipal theatres, becoming star Swedish stage and screen; 1954 recipient Sweden's Royal Foundation Cultural Award stage roles include 'Faust', which came to Londo in 1959; md. Keratin Olin, 2 sons Clas (bor 1952), Henrik (1953); screen début: MISS JULI (50); others include THE SEVENTH SEA (56); WILD STRAWBERRIES (57); TH FACE (58); SO CLOSE TO LIFE (58); THI VIRGIN SPRING (59); THROUGH A GLAS DARKLY (61); WINTER LIGHT (62); THI MISTRESS (62); THE GREATEST STOR EVER TOLD (65, as Jesus); THE REWAR (65); HAWAII (66); QUILLER MEMORAN DUM (66); HOUR OF THE WOLF (67); TH SHAME (68); KREMLIN LETTER (69); PASSION (70); THE TOUCH (71); THE EM GRANTS (72); EMBASSY (72); THE EXOR CIST (73); THE ULTIMATE WARRIOR (75 T.V. movie); 3 DAYS OF THE CONDOR (76 FOXTROT (76); VOYAGE OF TH DAMNED (76); EXORCIST II—THE HERE TIC (77); MARCH OR DIE (77); HURRICAN (78); BRASS TARGET (78); FLASH GORDO (79); SHE DANCES ALONE (80); ILLUS TRIOUS CORPSES, ESCAPE, VENETIAI LIES (all 81); CONAN THE BARBARIAN TARGET EAGLE (both 82); NEVER SA NEVER AGAIN, DREAMSCAPE (both 83

ROBERT WAGNER

Born in Detroit, Michigan, on 10 February 1930, Robert Wagner is the son of Robert Wagner Sr., who was successful in the steel business. He graduated from Santa Monica High School in 1947, having moved with the family to California at the age of 8, when he was already hooked on movies. Early studio biographies state Bob was caddying at Bel Air Country Club, and asked Clark Gable to help him get a movie break. This lead to his début, at M-G-M, in THE HAPPY YEARS (50) which starred Dean Stockwell. He then won a Fox contract, and, still in his early 20s, was soon playing leads. Pictures included HALL OF MONTEZUMA (50); LET'S MAKE IT LEGAL (51); TITANIC (53); as PRINCE VALIANT (54); BROKEN LANCE (54); WHITE FEATHER (55); THE TRUE STORY OF JESSE JAMES (57, title role); MARDI GRAS (58) and ALL THE FINE YOUNG CANNIBALS (60). He wed actress Natalie Wood (qv) on 28 December 1957 but they divorced in 1962, and actress Marion Marshall became his second wife on 21 July 1963. Their daughter Katherine was born in 1964. 1960s movies included THE WAR LOVER (62); THE CONDEMNED OF ALTONA (62); PINK PANTHER (64); HARPER (66); BANNING (67); THE BIGGEST BUNDLE OF THEM ALL (68); DON'T JUST LIE THERE (68) and he has moved successfully into T.V. with such series as 'It Takes a Thief' (1968/69), as Alexander Mundy, 'Colditz' (1973, BBC), 'Switch' (1975-78) as Pete Ryan and 'Hart to Hart' (1979). Divorcing Miss Marshall in 1971, he wed Natalie Wood for a second time on 16 July 1972, and their daughter, Courtney, was born in 1973. Miss Wood died tragically in a drowning accident on 29 November 1981. Mr Wagner's latest movies include CAT ON A HOT TIN ROOF (76, T.V. movie); MIDWAY (76); THE CRITICAL LIST (78, T.V. movie); PEARL (78, miniseries); THE CONCORDE—AIRPORT '79. From 1979, as Jonathan in 'Hart to Hart' (T.V. ser.).

ELI WALLACH

B. Brooklyn, New York, 7.12.15. Ed. Univ. Texas and College of the City of New York trained in N'hood P'house and became founde member Actors' Studio, 1947; md. actress Ann Jackson (qv) 1948, 1 son Peter, 2 daughter Roberta, Katherine; Mr Wallach is a distinguishe stage actor, coming to the screen in 1956 in BAB DOLL (BFA Aw.); his many films since includ SEVEN THIEVES (60); THE MAGNIFICEN SEVEN (60); THE MISFITS (61); THE VIC TORS (63); THE MOONSPINNERS (64 LORD JIM (65); GOOD, THE BAD & TH UGLY (67); ADVENTURES OF GERARI (70); ROMANCE OF A HORSETHIEF (71 CRAZY JOE (73); CINDERELLA LIBERT (73); INDICT & CONVICT (74, T.V. movie THE SENTINEL (77); SEVENTH AVENU (77, mini-series); THE DEEP (77); NAST HABITS (77); THE DOMINO KILLERS (77 GIRLFRIENDS (78); MOVIE, MOVIE (78 THE PIRATE (78, mini-series); WINTE KILLS (79); THE HUNTER (79); THE SALA MANDER (80); G.B. T.V. guest 'Tales of th Unexpected' (81); movie 1982: THE EXECU TIONER'S SONG.

SAM WANAMAKER

B. Chicago, Illinois, 14.6.19. Ed. Drake University; studied for the stage at the Goodman Theatre, Chicago; actor/director Chicago summer theatres 1936-39; then New York, WWII; U.S. Armed Forces 1943-46; scored in 'Joan of Lorraine' play (1946), came to screen in CLOAK & DAGGER (46), others: MY GIRL TISA (48); GIVE US THIS DAY (49); MR DENNING DRIVES NORTH (51); md. Charlotte Holland; since 1952 has based his successful career, mainly as stage actor/director, in Britain; also director on T.V.; 1977: founder/executive director Globe Playhouse Trust; other movies include THE CRIMINAL (60); TARAS BULBA (62); MAN IN THE MIDDLE (64); SPY WHO CAME IN FROM THE COLD (65); WARNING SHOT (67); directed CATLOW (72, and others); THE SELLOUT (77); DEATH ON THE NILE (78); BILLY JACK GOES TO WASHINGTON (78); THE COMPETITION, PRIVATE BENJAMIN (both 80); recently directed operas 'Aida' (with Pavarotti), 'Oedipus' (in U.S.A.).

SIMON WARD

B. Beckenham, S.E. London, 19.10.42. Ed. Alleyn's School, Dulwich; 1956 joined National Youth Theatre; trained at RADA; md. Alexandra Malcolm, 31.1.63, 3 daughters: Sophie, Claudia, Kitty; West End repertory, Broadway, Young Vic, Chichester Theatre, etc.; much T.V., films: FRANKENSTEIN MUST BE DESTROYED (70); I START COUNTING (71); QUEST FOR LOVE (71) and lead as YOUNG WINSTON (72); HITLER—THE LAST 10 DAYS (73); ALL CREATURES GREAT & SMALL (73); THREE MUSKETEERS (73); DRACULA (74, T.V. movie); ACES HIGH (75); CHILDREN OF RAGE (77); BATTLE FLAG (77); THE 4 FEATHERS (77); HOLOCAUST 2000 (77); DOMINIQUE (77); ZULU DAWN (78); LA SABINA (79); THE LAST GIRAFFE (79, T.V. movie); THE MONSTER CLUB (80); Broadway 1979: 'A Meeting By The River'; T.V. 1980: 'Rear Column'; 1981 series 'Diamonds'. Recent stage: 'Dial M For Murder' (82, tour), 'Heartbreak House' (83, tour/London).

JACK WARDEN

B. Newark, New Jersey, 18.9.20 (25?). Of Irish extraction; ed. Newark; Jack was a professional welterweight boxer under the name of Johnny Costello prior to WWII; began stage career with stock companies, 5 years with company at Dallas, Texas; became distinguished Broadway actor ('Golden Boy' (1952), 'A View From the Bridge' (1955), 'Man in the Glass Booth' (1969), others); md. actress Vanda Dupre, 1 son Christopher (born 1962); screen début: THE FROGMEN (51); much T.V. including series: Bobo in 'Norby' (1955), Matthew Gower in 'Asphalt Jungle' (1961), Mike Haines in 'N.Y.P.D.' (1967-69) and Maj. Simon Butcher in 'The Wackiest Ship in the Army' (1965/66); many movies include EDGE OF THE CITY (57); BACHELOR PARTY (57); 12 ANGRY MEN (57); MIRAGE (65); Oscar nom. as BSA for SHAMPOO (75); more recent movies are ALL THE PRESIDENT'S MEN (76); RAID ON ENTEBBE (77, T.V. movie); WHITE BUFFALO (77); DEATH ON THE NILE (78); HEAVEN CAN WAIT (78); DREAMER (78); AND JUSTICE FOR ALL (79); BEYOND THE POSEIDON ADVENTURE (79); BEING THERE (79); USED CARS (79); A PRIVATE BATTLE (80, T.V. movie); GREAT MUPPET CAPER (80); SO FINE, CARBON COPY, CHU CHU & THE PHILLY FLASH (all 1981); THE VERDICT (82); CRACKERS (83); HELEN & THE TEACHER (83, T.V. movie).

DAVID WARNER

B. Manchester 29.7.41. Ed. Feldon School, Leamington Spa; formerly a bookseller, Mr Warner studied at RADA, made his professional stage début in 1962 at the Royal Court, becoming one of Britain's best younger Shakespearean actors; md. 1. Harriett ——— (Scandinavian) (1968-75); many films include TOM JONES (63); MORGAN (65); DEADLY AFFAIR (66); WORK IS A FOUR-LETTER WORD (67); THE BOFORS GUN, THE FIXER, A MID-SUMMER NIGHT'S DREAM (as Lysander) (all 68); THE SEAGULL, MICHAEL KOHLHAAS (both 69); THE ENGAGEMENT, PERFECT FRIDAY, BALLAD OF CABLE HOGUE (all 70); TALES FROM THE CRYPT (72); STRAW DOGS (72, uncredited); A DOLL'S HOUSE, FROM BEYOND THE GRAVE (both 73); LITTLE MALCOLM, MR QUILP (both 74); THE OMEN (76); CROSS OF IRON, AGE OF INNOCENCE, PROVIDENCE, THE DISAPPEARANCE (all 77); SILVER BEARS, HOLOCAUST (mini-series); NIGHTWING, 39 STEPS, TIME AFTER TIME (all 1978); MASADA (Emmy Award, BSA); S.O.S. TITANIC (T.V. movie); THE CONCORDE—AIRPORT 79, THE ISLAND (all 79); TIME BANDITS (80); TRON, THE FRENCH LIEUTENANT'S WOMAN (both 81); THE MAN WITH 2 BRAINS (82); T.V. 82: 'Nancy Astor'; Md: 2. Sheilah, 1 daughter, Melissa (b. 81).

LESLEY ANN WARREN

B. Manhattan, New York, 16.8.46. Aged 6 started ballet training; ed. H.S. of Music & Art; also studied jazz technique with Stella Adler; senior year at H.S. studied at Actors' Studio; Broadway: aged 16: '110 In The Shade' (and tour), then T.V. special: 'Cinderella'; New York: 'A Sign of Affection', musical 'Drat the Cat'; md. (when 20) Jon Peters, 1 son Christopher; screen début 1967 in THE HAPPIEST MILLIONAIRE (67), then THE ONE & ONLY GENUINE ORIGINAL FAMILY BAND (68); much T.V.: SEVEN IN DARKNESS (69, T.V. movie); Dana Lambert in 'Mission—Impossible' (1970/71); LOVE, HATE, LOVE (71, T.V. movie); ASSIGNMENT: MUNICH, THE DAUGHTERS OF JOSHUA CABE (72, T.V. movies); THE LETTERS (73, T.V. movie); LEGEND OF VALENTINO (75, T.V. movie); '79 Park Avenue' (77, mini-series); BETRAYAL, 'Pearl' (78, T.V. movie & mini-series); PORTRAIT OF A STRIPPER (79, T.V. movie); 'Beulah Land' (80, mini-series); other movies: HARRY & WALTER GO TO NEW YORK (76); VICTOR/VICTORIA (82, Oscar nom., BSA); RACE TO THE YANKEE ZEPHYR (82); HEAVEN (83).

MONA WASHBOURNE

B. Birmingham, 27.11.03. Ed. Yardley Secondary School, Birmingham; stage début 1924 in concert party as pianist and soubrette, followed by repertory, becoming distinguished stage actress in London, also playing in America and touring India, etc.; md. Basil Dignam; occasional films: (early work uncredited) CHILD'S PLAY (54, lead); CAST A DARK SHADOW (55); GOOD COMPANIONS (57); BRIDES OF DRACULA (60); COUNT YOUR BLESSINGS (60); BILLY LIAR (63, also stage); NIGHT MUST FALL (64); MY FAIR LADY (64); ONE-WAY PENDULUM (64); THE COLLECTOR (65); THE THIRD DAY (65); IF... (68); MRS BROWN, YOU'VE GOT A LOVELY DAUGHTER (69); FRAGMENT OF FEAR (70); WHATEVER BECAME OF JACK & JILL? (72); O LUCKY MAN (73); MISTER QUILP (74); STEVIE (78); THE LONDON AFFAIR (78); recent T.V.: 'Brideshead Revisited' (1981), 'Pygmalion' (1981), 'Sleeping Beauty' (1982); the Queen Mother in CHARLES & DIANA — A ROYAL LOVE STORY (82, T.V. movie).

DENNIS WATERMAN

The son of Harry Waterman and his wife, Rose, Dennis was born in Clapham, S. London on 24 February 1948 and as a youngster attended the Corona Stage School. Aged 11 he made his first film, NIGHT TRAIN TO INVERNESS and played William in the T.V. series 'Just William'. In 1960 he played in the movie SNOWBALL and in May played at Stratford in 'The Winter's Tale'. The role of Neville Finch in the series 'Fair Exchange' took him to the States and that year, 1962, he played Winthrop Paroo in the West End musical, 'Music Man'. His brother, Peter, was one-time British & European welterweight boxing champion. Dennis played in various productions at the Royal Court and his many movies have included PIRATES OF BLOOD RIVER (61); UP THE JUNCTION (67); THE SMASHING BIRD I USED TO KNOW (69); MY LOVER, MY SON (70); I START COUNTING (70); MAN IN THE WILDERNESS (71); SCARS OF DRACULA (70); FRIGHT (71); ALICE'S ADVENTURES IN WONDERLAND (72); THE BELSTONE FOX (73) and in 1974 he gained great success as Sgt. George Carter in the series 'The Sweeney' bringing two film spin-offs, SWEENEY! (76) and SWEENEY 2 (77). His first marriage to Penny, a teacher, ended in divorce and his second wife is actress Patricia Maynard. They have 2 daughters Hannah (born 1975) and Julia (1979). He has also earned success as recording artiste, compositions include 'Love's Left Me Bleeding', 'Down With the Angels' and 'I Could Be So Good For You', the latter being the theme song of his hit series 'Minder', in which he portrayed Terry McCann (79/   ). He was divorced from Miss Maynard on 1.11.82. Recent T.V. has included 'The World Cup: A Captain's Tale' (82) and he has made headway on stage in 'Saratoga' (79), to excellent notices, and the musical version of 'Front Page Story', titled 'Windy City', in London, 1982/83.

SAM WATERSTON
B. Cambridge, Mass., 15.11.40. Ed. Groton School and Yale University; stage trained: Yale and the American Actors' Workshop and Actors' Studio; early stage début, aged 7, in 'Antigone'; in 1962 first played in New York in 'Oh Dad, Poor Dad...' and thus began his highly successful stage career in wide variety of roles including title role: 'Hamlet'; md. 1. Barbara Waterston (div.), 2. Lynn Woodruff; movies: PLASTIC DOME OF NORMA JEAN (65); THREE (69); A TIME FOR GIVING (69); SAVAGES (72); THE GLASS MENAGERIE (73, T.V. movie); A DELICATE BALANCE (73); THE GREAT GATSBY (74); REFLECTIONS OF MURDER (74, T.V. movie); RANCHO DE LUXE (75); JOURNEY INTO FEAR (75); SWEET REVENGE (77); EAGLE'S WING, SWEET WILLIAM, CAPRICORN ONE, INTERIORS (all 78); HOPSCOTCH (79); FRIENDLY FIRE (79, T.V. movie); HEAVEN'S GATE (79); Q.E.D. (82); T.V. series 1980: as 'Oppenheimer'.

JACK WATSON
B. London 15.5.21. In variety for 15 years, playing stooge to father, comedian Nosmo King; md. Betsy, 2 daughters: Penelope, Fiona; a well-known face on T.V., includes work in 'Coronation Street', 'Red Gauntlet', 'The Troubleshooters', 'Arthur of the Britons', and 'The Camerons'; many movies include CAPT. HORATIO HORNBLOWER (51, uncredited); KONGA (61); THIS SPORTING LIFE (63); MASTER SPY (63); THE IDOL (65); THE HILL (65); GRAND PRIX (66); TOBRUK (66); THE DEVIL'S BRIGADE (68); THE STRANGE AFFAIR (68); EVERY HOME SHOULD HAVE ONE (70); THE MACKENZIE BREAK (71); KIDNAPPED (72); THREE MUSKETEERS (74); JUGGERNAUT (74); 11 HARROWHOUSE (74); SCHIZO (76); THE PURPLE TAXI (76); WILD GEESE (78); SEA WOLVES (81); recent T.V.: 'Heather Ann', 'Tangier' (83).

DENNIS WEAVER
Born in Joplin, Missouri, on 4 June 1925, Dennis Weaver attended Joplin Junior College, served in the Naval Air Force and, in 1946, entered Oklahoma Univ., excelling at athletics (Decathlon Champ.) and appearing in amateur dramatics, graduated with a Degree in Fine Arts in 1948. He was on Broadway in 1951 in 'Out West of Eighth', and after 'Come Back, Little Sheba' he landed the role of Chester in the long-running series, 'Gunsmoke' (1955-64). Other T.V. includes 'Kentucky Jones' (1964/65), Tom Wedloe in 'Gentle Ben' (1967-69) and as Sam McCloud in 'McCloud' (1970-77), introduced as a T.V. movie, MCCLOUD: WHO KILLED MISS U.S.A.? (70). Mr Weaver wed Geraldine Stowell in 1945 and they have 3 sons, Richard (born 1948), Robert (1953) and Rustin (1959). Other T.V. and film work has included COLUMN SOUTH (53); THE NEBRASKAN (53); WAR ARROW (54); DANGEROUS MISSION (54); DRAGNET (54); TEN WANTED MEN (55); VALLEY OF FURY (55); SEVEN ANGRY MEN (55); STORM FEAR (56); TOUCH OF EVIL (58); THE GALLANT HOURS (60); WAY...WAY OUT (66); DUEL AT DIABLO (66); GENTLE GIANT (67); WHAT'S THE MATTER WITH HELEN? (71); THE FORGOTTEN MAN (71, T.V. movie); DUEL (71, T.V. movie); A MAN CALLED SLEDGE (71); ROLLING MAN (72, T.V. movie); FEMALE ARTILLERY, THE GREAT MAN'S WHISKERS, TERROR ON THE BEACH (all 73 T.V. movies); INTIMATE STRANGERS (77, T.V. movie); THE ISLANDER, A CRY FOR JUSTICE, ISHI: THE LAST OF HIS TRIBE (all 78, T.V. movies); 'Pearl' (1978, 3-part mini-series); THE ORDEAL OF PATTY HEARST (79, T.V. movie) and a further T.V. series in 1979, 'Stone'. His portrayal of Chester Goode in 'Gunsmoke' gained him an 'Emmy' award in 1960.

SIGOURNEY WEAVER
B. New York City, . .c49. Real name Susa Weaver. Father Sylvester 'Pat' Weaver, distin guished pioneer of U.S. T.V. and President o N.B.C. during 1950s, married former actres (RADA trained); ed. Chapin School, Manhattan Ethel Walker School, Conn., Stanford Univ. majoring in English; Yale Drama School; 1s stage job: u/study in 'The Constant Wife'; othe stage includes 'The Conquering Event', 'Gemini 'The Nature & Purpose of the Universe', 'Da Lusitania Songspiel' (also co-wrote), 'Beyon Therapy'; T.V. series: 'The Best of Families (1979); Sigourney (this name derived from character in 'The Great Gatsby' novel) came to the screen in ALIEN (78), which gained her large following, and has also been seen in THE JANITOR (81); THE YEAR OF LIVINC DANGEROUSLY (82); DEAL OF THE CENTURY (83).

ROBERT WEBBER
B. Santa Ana, Calif., 14.10.28. Ed: Belmon High, Van Nuys High, Oakland Technical H.S. Compton Jun. Coll.; WWII: U.S. Marine Corps Summer stock; became distinguished Broadwa actor ('A Loss of Roses', etc.); movies includ HIGHWAY 301 (51); 12 ANGRY MEN (57 THE NUN & THE SERGEANT (62); THE STRIPPER (63); HYSTERIA (64); THE SAND PIPER (64); THE THIRD DAY (65); NC TEARS FOR A KILLER (65); HARPER (66) THE HIRED KILLER (66); DEAD HEA ON A MERRY-GO-ROUND (66); THE SILENCERS (67); THE DIRTY DOZEN (67) DON'T MAKE WAVES (67); THE BIC BOUNCE (69); THE GREAT WHITE HOPI (70); THE MOVIE MURDERER, HAUSER' MEMORY (70, both T.V. movies); THIEF (71 T.V. movie); DOLLARS (72); HAWKINS OF MURDER, DOUBLE INDEMNITY (73, both T.V. movies); BRING ME THE HEAD OF ALFREDO GARCIA (74); MURDER OF MERCY (74, T.V. movie); DEATH STALK (75, T.V. movie); MIDWAY (76); REVENGE OF THE PINK PANTHER, THE CHOIR BOYS (both 77); CASEY'S SHADOW (78) '79 Park Avenue' (1979, mini-series); 10 (79) S.O.B. (80); TENSPEED AND BROWN SHOE (81); MAN WITH THE DEADLY LENS WHO DARES WINS, STARFLIGHT ONE (all 1982); ANSWERS (82, T.V. movie, I segment).

FRITZ WEAVER
B. Pittsburgh, Pa., 19.1.26; Ed: Univ. of Chicago (BA degree, 1952); stage debut Abingdon, Virginia, 1952, becoming distinguished actor of the U.S. stage, including leading Shakespearean roles; Md: Sylvia Short; films: FAIL SAFE (64); TO TRAP A SPY (66); THE BORGIA STICK (T.V. movie, 1967); THE MALTESE BIPPY (69); BERLIN AFFAIR (T.V. movie), A WALK IN THE SPRING RAIN (both 1970); THE SNOOP SISTERS (T.V. movie, 1972); HUNTER (T.V. movie); DAY OF THE DOLPHIN (both 1973); THE LEGEND OF LIZZIE BORDEN (T.V. movie, 1975); MARATHON MAN (76); CAPTAINS COURAGEOUS (T.V. movie), BLACK SUNDAY, DEMON SEED (all 1977); HOLOCAUST (mini-ser.), THE BIG FIX (both 1978); CREEPSHOW (82).

RAQUEL WELCH
Glamour girl Raquel, who gained success in the mid-1960s with the backing of one of the most intensive publicity campaigns ever, was born in Chicago on 5 September 1940, the daughter of Armand Tejada, a Bolivian engineer, and his wife, Josephine. The family moved to La Jolla when she was 2, ans she received her education at High School, gaining a dramatic scholarship to San Diego State College, but she found her studies interrupted by her first marriage, in 1959, to schoolmate James Welch, which produced two children, Damon, in 1960, and Tahnee, in 1962. At the age of 15 Raquel had won a La Jolla beauty competition and by the early 1960s she was working as a cocktail waitress, a model in Dallas, and in 1964 she broke into showbiz, earning $250-a-week as a glamorous billboard girl on the 'Hollywood Palace' T.V. show and had a walk-on part in the Elvis movie, ROUSTABOUT. Divorcing Welch in 1965, she played in DO NOT DISTURB and A HOUSE IS NOT A HOME, and, now managed by Patrick Curtis (becoming her husband in 1967), she appeared on the covers of 92 European and 16 America magazines in 1966 and had starring roles in A SWINGIN' SUMMER, FANTASTIC VOYAGE and ONE MILLION YEARS B.C. Since then she has played in such movies as SHOUT LOUDER . . . LOUDER, I DON'T UNDERSTAND (66); THE QUEENS (66); THE BIGGEST BUNDLE OF THEM ALL (67); THE OLDEST PROFESSION (67); FATHOM (67); BEDAZZLED (68); LADY IN CEMENT (68); BANDOLERO! (68); 100 RIFLES (69); MAGIC CHRISTIAN (69, guest); FLARE UP (70); MYRA BRECKINRIDGE (70); THE BELOVED (72); HANNIE CAULDER (72); FUZZ (72); KANSAS CITY BOMBER (73); THE LAST OF SHEILA (73); THE THREE MUSKETEERS (74); THE WILD PARTY (74); THE FOUR MUSKETEERS (74); MOTHER JUGGS AND SPEED (76); CROSSED SWORDS (77); EL ANIMAL (77); THE LEGEND OF WALKS FAR WOMAN (79, T.V. movie). Miss Welch divorced Curtis in 1971 and on 5 July 1980 she wed French screenplay writer André Weinfeld. In December 1981 she made her Broadway début in 'Woman of the Year' to much acclaim, replacing Lauren Bacall.
THE FOX GIRLS by J.R. Parish (part-bio.); Castle Books: New York, 1972.

TUESDAY WELD

B. New York 27.8.43. Real name Susan Ker Weld; by age of 2, she had modelled baby clothes; ed. Public School 135; moved with mother, sister, brother to Fort Lauderdale, Florida; aged 11 returned to New York, did modelling/T.V. work and in teens u/studied and played in 'Dark at the Top of the Stairs'; discovered by agent Dick Clayton, went West and did 'Matinee Theatre' on T.V.; came to screen in ROCK, ROCK, ROCK (56); Hollywood Professional School; RALLY ROUND THE FLAG, BOYS (58); T.V. series: 'The Many Loves of Dobie Gillis', as Thalia Menninger (1959/60); THE FIVE PENNIES (59); BECAUSE THEY'RE YOUNG, SEX KITTENS GO TO COLLEGE, HIGH TIME, PRIVATE LIVES OF ADAM & EVE (all 60); RETURN TO PEYTON PLACE (61); WILD IN THE COUNTRY (62); BACHELOR FLAT, SOLDIER IN THE RAIN (both 63); CIN-CINATTI KID, I'LL TAKE SWEDEN (both 65); md. 1. Claude Harz (1965-71), 1 daughter Natasha, 2. Dudley Moore (qv) (1975-div.), 1 son Patrick (1976); LORD LOVE-A-DUCK (66); PRETTY POISON, SHE LET HIM CON-TINUE (both 68); I WALK THE LINE (70); A SAFE PLACE (71); PLAY IT AS IT LAYS (73); REFLECTIONS OF MURDER (74, T.V. movie); F. SCOTT FITZGERALD IN HOLLY-WOOD (76, T.V. movie); LOOKING FOR MR GOODBAR (77, Oscar nom. BSA); DOG SOL-DIERS (78); A QUESTION OF GUILT (78, T.V. movie); THE SERIAL (79); VIOLENT STREETS (80); MOTHER & DAUGHTER (81, T.V. movie); AUTHOR! AUTHOR! (82) 'The Rainmaker' (82, stage).

OSKAR WERNER

B. Vienna, Austria, 13.11.22. Real name Oscar Joseph Bschliessmayer; drafted into German army during WWII, deserted before war's end; acted in rep., Burg Theatre, Vienna; many movies include EROICA (49); ANGEL WITH A TRUMPET (49); DECISION BEFORE DAWN (51); WONDER KID (51, G.B.); RUF AUS DEM AETHER (51); LOLA MONTES (55); SPIONAGE (55); THE LIFE OF MOZART (56); JULES & JIM (61); SHIP OF FOOLS (65); SPY WHO CAME IN FROM THE COLD (65); FAHRENHEIT 451 (66); INTERLUDE (68); SHOES OF THE FISHERMAN (68); md. 1. actress Elizabeth Kallina (1946-50), 1 daughter Eleonore, 2. Anna Power (adopted daughter of Ty Power); VOYAGE OF THE DAMNED (77).

JACK WESTON

B. Cleveland, Ohio, 21.8.15. Real name: Morris Weinstein; stage début 1934 in children's theatre, Cleveland, and studied with the American Theatre Wing, N.Y.; WWII: U.S. Army in Europe; Broadway début 1950 in play 'Season in the Sun', other stage includes 'Bells Are Ringing' (1956), 'Last of the Red Hot Lovers' (1971, and tour); T.V. from the early 1950s including series 'Rod Brown of the Rocket Rangers' (1953), 'My Sister Eileen' (1960/61), 'The Hathaways' (1961/62); films: STAGE STRUCK, I WANT TO LIVE! (both 58); IMITATION OF LIFE (59); PLEASE DON'T EAT THE DAISIES (60); ALL IN A NIGHT'S WORK; THE HONEYMOON MACHINE (both 61); IT'S ONLY MONEY (62); PALM SPRINGS WEEKEND (63); THE INCREDIBLE MR LIMPET (64); MIRAGE, THE CINCINNATI KID (both 65); FAME IS THE NAME OF THE GAME (66, T.V. movie); WAIT UNTIL DARK (67); THE COUNTER-FEIT KILLER, THE THOMAS CROWN AFFAIR, NOW YOU SEE IT, NOW YOU DON'T (all 68, T.V.); APRIL FOOLS, CACTUS FLOWER (both 69); A NEW LEAF (71); FUZZ (72); I LOVE A MYSTERY; MARCO; DELI-VER US FROM EVIL (all 73, T.V.); THE RITZ (also stage); GATOR (both 76); 79 PARK AVE-NUE (T.V.); CUBA (both 79); CAN'T STOP THE MUSIC (80); THE FOUR SEASONS (81); HIGH ROAD TO CHINA (82).

BILLIE WHITELAW

B. Coventry 6.6.32. Father an electrician; ed. wartime evacuee in Liverpool; aged 11 on BBC Children's Hour and N. Region radio; aged 17, rep. début Leeds; became distinguished T.V./stage actress, many awards; md. 1. actor Peter Vaughan (qv), 1 son Matthew, (div.), 2. Robert Muller; movies: THE FAKE (53); MAKE MINE MINK (59); BOBBIKINS (59); HELL IS A CITY (60); THE FLESH AND THE FIENDS (60); NO LOVE FOR JOHNNIE (61); MR TOPAZE (61); PAYROLL (61); THE COMEDY MAN (63); TWISTED NERVE (68); CHARLIE BUBBLES (68, BFA); THE ADDING MACHINE (69); LEO AND THE LAST (70); GUMSHOE (71); EAGLE IN A CAGE (71); FRENZY (72); NIGHTWATCH (73); THE OMEN (76); LEOPARD IN THE SNOW (77); WATER BABIES (78); AN UNSUITABLE JOB FOR A WOMAN (82); DARK CRYSTAL (voice), SLAYGROUND (both 83); T.V. ser: 'Jamaica Inn' (83).

ORSON WELLES

B. Kenosha, Wisconsin, 6.5.15. Parents: Richard Head Welles, inventor and Beatrice Welles, concert pianist/political suffragette; Ed. Todd School, Woodstock, Illinois; md. 1. Virginia Nicholson (1934-40), 1 son Christopher (born 1938); radio/stage actor, co-founder with John Houseman (qv) of the famous Mercury Theatre/ Players in 1937; in 1938 caused stir in U.S. with 'Wars of the Worlds' radio broadcast; 1941: famous film CITIZEN KANE (acted, directed, co-wrote, Oscar nom. all three, winner 3rd); acted in many films, including JOURNEY INTO FEAR (42); JANE EYRE (43, as Rochester); FOLLOW THE BOYS (44); TOMORROW IS FOREVER (44); THE STRANGER (45, and dir.); LADY FROM SHANGHAI (47, and dir., md. 2. co-star Rita Hayworth 1943-47, 1 daughter Rebecca (1944); MACBETH (48, and dir.); THE THIRD MAN (49); OTHELLO (51, and dir.); TOUCH OF EVIL (58, and dir.); THE TRIAL (62, and dir.); A MAN FOR ALL SEASONS (66, as Cardinal Wolsey); TREASURE ISLAND (72, as L.J. Silver); md. 3. Paola Mari (1955), 1 daughter Beatrice (1956); much work on Broad-way, T.V., etc.; Special Oscar 1977 'for superlative artistry and versatility in the creation of motion-pictures'; F FOR FAKE (74, acted/directed/ script); NEVER TRUST AN HONEST THIEF (79, Canada); biographies include THE FABU-LOUS ORSON WELLES by Peter Noble: Hutchinson: London, 1956; WELLES by Joseph McBride; Secker & Warburg: London 1972.

TIMOTHY WEST

B. Bradford, Yorkshire, 20.10.34. Father Lock-wood West, actor; ed. John Lyon School, Harrow and others; Regent St. Polytechnic; acted Shakes-peare in pubs with 'The Taverners'; office furniture salesman; recording engineer with E.M.I.; stage manager: Wimbledon, Salisbury and other reps.; Mr West became distinguished stage actor/director; well-known on T.V.; md. 1. dancer Jacqueline Boyer (div.), 1 daughter Juliet; few films include DEADLY AFFAIR (66); TWISTED NERVE (68); LOOKING GLASS WAR (69); NICHO-LAS & ALEXANDRA (71); SOFT BEDS, HARD BATTLES, HITLER: THE LAST 10 DAYS, DAY OF THE JACKAL (all 73); OPERATION DAYBREAK (74); HEDDA (76); DEVIL'S ADVOCATE, AGATHA (both 77); 39 STEPS (78); md. 2. Prunella Scales, 2 sons: Sam, Joe; 1980: artistic director, Old Vic; 1981 stage includes Shylock in 'Merchant of Venice'; OLIVER TWIST (82, T.V. movie); 'Brass' (83, T.V. ser.).

CAROL WHITE

B. 1.4.44. Named by father 'after Carole Lom-bard'; aged 9, in hairdressers, advised to go to stage school; 6 years at Corona Stage School; movies include CIRCUS OF FRIENDS (56); CARRY ON TEACHER (59); NEVER LET GO (60); SLAVE GIRLS (66); POOR COW (66); I'LL NEVER FORGET WHAT'S 'IS NAME (67); THE FIXER (68); md. 1. Michael King (div. 1971); 2 sons Sean, Stephen, 2. Stuart Lerner (div. 1976), 3. composer Michael Arnold, 25.11.77; DULCIMA (71); MADE (72); THE SQUEEZE (77), NUTCRACKER (82).

SHEILA WHITE

B. Highgate, N. London, 18.10.50. Corona Stage School; pantomime, West End 'Oliver', 'Dames at Sea' (also Paris); movies include HERE WE GO ROUND THE MULBERRY BUSH (66); THE GHOST GOES GEAR (66); OLIVER! (68); MRS BROWN, YOU'VE GOT A LOVELY DAUGHTER (69); CONFESSIONS OF A WINDOW CLEANER (74); C.O.A. POP PERFORMER (75); C.O.A. DRIVING IN-STRUCTOR (76); SPACEMAN & KING ARTHUR (78); SILVER DREAM RACER (79); stage 1981: Mary Pickford in 'The Biograph Girl'; T.V. 1982 series: Dixie in 'Don't Rock the Boat'.

LEONARD WHITING

B. London, . .50. Ed. Camden; aged 12, Leonard was in recording studio with pop group, seen by agent and got him role of Artful Dodger in stage show, 'Oliver!'; films include LEGEND OF YOUNG DICK TURPIN (65); Romeo in ROMEO & JULIET (68); ROYAL HUNT OF THE SUN (69); YOUNG CASANOVA (70); SAY HELLO TO YESTERDAY (70); FRAN-KENSTEIN: THE TRUE STORY (73, T.V. movie, title role); RACHEL'S MAN (74); md. model Cathee Dahman, 1 daughter Beth; recently he has returned to stage internationally (1979 tour 'These Foolish Things') and he is also a writer.

STUART WHITMAN

B. San Francisco, 1.2.29. Attended 26 different schools, excelled at football; Army Engineers June 1945-Sept. 1948, good boxer (uncle boxing ref.); 2 years drama study at L.A. City Coll. and Ben Bard's Training School; appeared in Chekhov and Stage Society productions; 1951: screen début in WHEN WORLD'S COLLIDE and DAY THE EARTH STOOD STILL; md. 1. Patricia LaLonde (1952-66), 3 sons: Anthony, Michael, Scott, 1 daughter Linda; 2. Caroline Bubois(?) 1966; in 1950s worked on bull-dozer levelling hillsides between acting jobs; T.V. series in 1967/68 as Marshall Jim Crown in 'Cimarron Strip'; many movies include RHAPSODY (54); CHINA DOLLS (58); TEN NORTH FREDE-RICK (58); THE SOUND & THE FURY (59); THE STORY OF RUTH (60); THE MARK (61, Oscar nom., BA); MURDER INC. (61); THE COMANCHEROS (62); SHOCK TREATMENT (64); RIO CONCHOS (64); SANDS OF THE KALAHARI (65); THE INVINCIBLE SIX (68); REVENGE (71, T.V. movie); WOMAN HUNTER (72, T.V. movie); CAT CREATURE (73, T.V. movie); CRAZY MAMA (75); LAS VEGAS LADY (76); RUBY, WHITE BUFFALO, EATEN ALIVE, THE THOROUGHBREDS, STRANGE SHADOWS IN AN EMPTY ROOM (all 77); GUYANA—CRIME OF THE CENTURY, MONSTER CLUB (both 80); GREED, BUTTERFLY (both 81); Best Sellers: CONDOMINIUM—WHEN THE HURRICAN STRUCK (81, T.V. movie); guest: 'Tales of the Unexpected' (1981, G.B. T.V.); SWEET DIRTY TONY, DEMONOID (both 1981).

RICHARD WIDMARK

B. Sunrise, Minnesota, 26.12.14. Father a sales-man; ed. Princeton H.S., Ill., Lake Forest Univ., where he was brilliant student, grad. in 1936 in speech & political science; 1936-38: professor of Speech & Dramatics at that Univ.; 1938: New York radio, stock and Broadway actor from 1943; perforated ear-drum prevented war service; md. Jean Hazelwood, 1942, 1 daughter Anne; Broad-way included 'Kiss and Tell', 'Get Away, Old Man' (1943), 'Trio' (1944), 'Kiss Them For Me', 'Dunnigan's Daughter' (1945); T.V. series 1972 as Sgt. Dan 'Madigan'; over 60 movies, these include KISS OF DEATH (47, début, and Oscar nom. BSA); YELLOW SKY (49); NIGHT & THE CITY, PANIC IN THE STREETS (both 50); RED SKIES OF MONTANA (52); PICK-UP ON SOUTH STREET (53); BROKEN LANCE (54); BACKLASH, THE LAST WAGON (both 56); LAW & JAKE WADE (58); WARLOCK (59); THE ALAMO (60, as Jim Bowie); CHEYENNE AUTUMN (64); THE BEDFORD INCIDENT (65); ALVAREZ KELLY (66); THE WAY WEST (67); MADI-GAN (68); DEATH OF A GUNFIGHTER (69); MOONSHINE WAR (70); VANISHED (71, T.V. movie); WHEN THE LEGENDS DIE (72); BROCK'S LAST CASE (73, T.V. movie); MURDER ON THE ORIENT EX-PRESS (74); THE LAST DAY (75, T.V. movie); TO THE DEVIL...A DAUGHTER (76); ROLLERCOASTER, THE SELL OUT, COMA, TWILIGHT'S LAST GLEAMING (all 77); THE SWARM, THE DOMINO KILLINGS (both 78); BEAR ISLAND (79); MR HORN (79, T.V. movie); ALL GOD'S CHILDREN (80, T.V. movie); HANKY PANKY, WHO DARES WINS (both 82).

GENE WILDER

One of the most popular American actor/comedians to emerge from movies in the 1970s, due mainly to his teaming with Mel Brooks (qv), Gene Wilder has also ventured into directing his own projects. The son of a prosperous manufacturer of miniature beer and whisky bottles, he was born Gerald Silberman in Milwaukee, Wisconsin on 11 June 1934. When he was 6 his mother had a serious illness which left her an invalid and Gene entertained her with carefully controlled routines and by the age of 15 he was presenting his own dramatisations of famous plays. Graduating from the University of Iowa in 1955, he came to Britain, entered the Bristol Old Vic School, excelling at fencing, returned to the USA and studied at the Actors' Studio with Lee Strasberg, while working as a chauffeur and fencing coach. In 1961 he was off-Broadway in 'Roots' and on Broadway in 'The Complaisant Lover' and started to make a name for himself in such other productions as 'One Flew Over the Cuckoo's Nest' (1963, BSA nom., New York Film Critics'), 'Dynamite Tonight', 'The White House' (both 1964) and 'Luv' (1965). In 1967 Gene wed Mary Joan Schultz (they have an adopted daughter, Katherine) and made his film début in a supporting role in BONNIE AND CLYDE. He had acted on Broadway in 'Mother Courage and Her Children' with Anne Bancroft (qv) in 1963 and her husband, Mel Brooks, cast him in his movie, THE PRODUCERS (68), gaining the actor an Oscar nomination. Since then Mr Wilder has played in such pictures as START THE REVOLUTION WITHOUT ME (69); QUACKSER FORTUNE HAS A COUSIN IN THE BRONX (70); WILLY WONKA AND THE CHOCOLATE FACTORY (71); EVERYTHING YOU ALWAYS WANTED TO KNOW ABOUT SEX (72); THE LITTLE PRINCE (73); RHINOCEROS (73); THURSDAY'S GAME (74, T.V. movie); BLAZING SADDLES (74); YOUNG FRANKENSTEIN (74); ADVENTURES OF SHERLOCK HOLMES' SMARTER BROTHER (76, and s/play, directed); SILVER STREAK (77); THE WORLD'S GREATEST LOVER (77, and s/play, directed); THE FRISCO KID (78); STIR CRAZY (80); SUNDAY LOVERS (80, part-directed) and HANKY PANKY (82).

TOYAH WILLCOX

B. Birmingham, . .c.59. Ed. girls' public school; trained at the Old Rep. Theatre School, Birming-ham; T.V. includes 'Look, Hear & Listen', Second City Firsts: 'Glitter' (1976), 'Quatermass', 'Shoe-string', THE CORN IS GREEN (78, T.V. movie); Christmas 1977, formed own band called 'Toyah' — LPs include 'The Blue Meaning', 'Toyah, Toyah, Toyah'; came to screen as Pun-kette, Mad, in JUBILEE (77), then Monkey, the mod chick, in QUADROPHENIA (79), then THE TEMPEST (80); stage 1980: 'Sugar and Spice'; T.V. 1981: 'Little Girls Don't', 'Tales of the Unexpected'; LP 1981: 'Anthem'; single: 'Thunder in the Mountains'; 'Tanzi' (83, stage); *TOYAH* by Mike West; Omnibus: London, 82; Large p/b.

KENNETH WILLIAMS

B. London 22.2.26. Ed. Lyulph Stanley School and Bolt Court, London; before National Service in India he was a lithographic draughtsman; in India, 1946, appd. on stage with Combined Entertainment Services; repertory début May 1948 at Newquay, Cornwall; rep., then West End 1952, in 'Peter Pan'; became a very well-known actor/comedian of theatre, radio, T.V. and the movies, characterised by his distinctive voice; also in revue and directed play, 1981, 'Entertaining Mr Sloane'; came to the screen in 1952 with supporting roles in TRENT'S LAST CASE and THE BEGGAR'S OPERA; others: RAISING THE WIND (61); TWICE ROUND THE DAFFODILS (62); DON'T LOSE YOUR HEAD (67); FOLLOW THAT CAMEL (68); HOUND OF THE BASKERVILLES (77) and since 1958, commencing with CARRY ON SERGEANT, he has played in over 25 'CARRY ON...' comedies, most recently CARRY ON EMMANUELLE (78); stage roles include the Dauphin in 'Saint Joan' (1954/55), revue 'One Over the Eight' (1961), Truscott in 'Loot' (1965) and Henry in 'My Fat Friend' (1972). *ACID DROPS* by K.W. (humorous compilation); J.M. Dent & Sons: London, 1980; p/b: Coronet, 1981; *BACK DROPS: Pages From a Private Diary* by K.W.; J.M. Dent & Sons: London, 1983.

BILLY DEE WILLIAMS

B. New York City 6.4.37. Mr Williams com-menced his acting career at the age of seven, on Broadway in a musical, 'Firebrand of Florence'; he trained for the stage with the Harlem Actors' Workshop (with Paul Mann and Sidney Poitier) and won a scholarship to the Nat. Acad. of Fine Arts & Design, winning the Hallgarten Award for painting (a skill pursued seriously today); he came to the screen in 1959 in THE LAST ANGRY MAN and appd. on Broadway in such productions as 'The Cool World' (1960), 'A Taste of Honey' (61), 'The Blue Boy in Black' (63), 'The Firebugs' (68), 'Slow Dance on the Killing Ground' (70), in L.A. in 'Trial of Abraham Lincoln' and played Martin Luther King in 'I Have a Dream'; over the years he has won 3 'Image' awards as Best Actor; movies include THE OUT-OF-TOWNERS (70); CARTER'S ARMY (70, T.V. movie); BRIAN'S SONG (71, T.V. movie, as football great Gale Sayers, 'Emmy' nom.); LADY SINGS THE BLUES (72); HIT! (73); MAHOGANY (75); T.V. series 'Another World'; THE BINGO LONG TRAVELLING ALL STARS & MO-TOR KINGS (76); SCOTT JOPLIN (78, title role); CHRISTMAS LILIES OF THE FIELD (79, T.V. movie); NIGHT HAWKS (80) and Lando Calrissian in EMPIRE STRIKES BACK (81); named 'Star of the Year' by the Virgin Islands Film Assoc.; RETURN OF THE JEDI (83).

ROBIN WILLIAMS

B. Edinburgh, Scotland, 21.7.51. When he was 1 family moved to U.S.; ed. Claremont Men's College, California, studied acting at Coll. of Marin, Calif., then to New York Juilliard School; did club work in San Francisco, then L.A. at 'The Comedy Store', 'Ice House' and others, T.V. début in 'Laugh-in'; came to screen in THE LAST LAUGH; md. Valerie Velardi, 1978; T.V. guest: 'American Tonight', 'The Alan Hamel Show' and Mork in 'Mork & Mindy' (1978-); stars as Popeye in POPEYE (80); THE WORLD ACCORDING TO GARP (82); THE SUR-VIVORS (83); 1 son, Zachary, born April, 1983.

CINDY WILLIAMS – see page 126

118

SIMON WILLIAMS

B. Windsor 16.6.46. Father Hugh Williams (actor/playwright); ed. Harrow; 6'4" tall; at 16 began in rep. at Worthing, then Birmingham, Guildford, West End; md. actress Belinda Carroll, October 1968 (sep. 1980), 1 son Tamlyn, 1 daughter Amy; popular T.V. actor esp. as James Bellamy in 'Upstairs, Downstairs', 'Agony', others; Simon has also directed on stage and played in such movies as THE TOUCHABLES (68); BLOOD ON SATAN'S CLAW (71); INCREDIBLE SARAH (76); NO LONGER ALONE (77, as Wm. Douglas-Home); JABBER-WOCKY (77); THE ODD JOB (78); PRI-SONER OF ZENDA (78); FIENDISH PLOT OF FU MANCHU (79); T.V. 1981: 'Kinvig'; stage 81: 'Deathtrap'; directed 'Underground' (83, stage).

NICOL WILLIAMSON

B. Hamilton, Scotland, 14.9.38. (Details of early career unavailable.) Mr Williamson began stage career with the Dundee Rep. for 2 years 1960/61 and in 1961 he first appeared on the London stage and became an actor of distinction in Britain and America in many classical plays (including title role, 'Hamlet') gaining several awards; films: SIX-SIDED TRIANGLE (63, 30-min. short); THE BOFORS GUN (68); INADMISSIBLE EVIDENCE (68, also stage 64/65); HAMLET (69, title role); LAUGHTER IN THE DARK (69); THE RECKONING (70); THE JERU-SALEM FILE (71); THE WILBY CONSPIRACY (74); ROBIN & MARIAN (74, as Little John); THE SEVEN PERCENT SOLUTION (75); THE GOODBYE GIRL (77, cameo); 'The Word' (78, mini-series); THE CHEAP DETEC-TIVE (78); THE HUMAN FACTOR (79); VENOM (80); EXCALIBUR (80, as Merlin); I'M DANCING AS FAST AS I CAN (81); he has also directed on the stage and acted on T.V.; 1981 saw him back on Broadway in 'Inadmissible Evidence'.

PAUL WINFIELD

B. Los Angeles, . .40. Ed. U.C.L.A.; Mr Win-field portrayed Paul Cameron in the T.V. series 'Julia' (1968-70) and has appeared in such movies as THE LOST MAN (69); RPM (70); BRO-THER JOHN (71); SOUNDER (72, Oscar nom., BA); THE HORROR AT 37,000 FEET (73, T.V. movie); GORDON'S WAR (73); CONRACK, HUCKLEBERRY FINN (both 74); IT'S GOOD TO BE ALIVE (74, T.V. movie); HUSTLE (75); DAMNATION ALLEY, THE GREATEST, TWILIGHT'S LAST GLEAMING, A HERO AINT NOTHIN' BUT A SANDWICH (all 77); GREEN EYES (77, T.V. movie); KING (78, mini-series, as Martin Luther King Jr., Emmy nom., BA); BACK-STAIRS AT THE WHITE HOUSE, ROOTS: THE NEXT GENERATIONS (79, both mini-ser.); CARBON COPY (80); WHITE DOG (81); ON THE RUN, STAR TREK II: WRATH OF KHAN (both 1982).

HENRY WINKLER

B. New York 30.10.45. Ed. Emerson Coll.; family ran timber business; graduated from Yale University with M.A. Degree, acted with Yale Rep. Co. and played in New York on radio and on stage, including 'The Bacchae' (1969); 'Don Juan', 'Three Philip Roth Stories', 'Cops and Horrors', 'Story Theatre Repertory' (all 1970); 30 T.V. commercials and guest spots in T.V. programmes before success in series 'Happy Days' from 1974 as Arthur 'Fonzie' Fonzarelli, King of Cool; md. Stacey Weitzman May 1978, 1 step-son Jed, 1 daughter Zoe Emily (born 1980); movies: CRAZY JOE (74); THE LORDS OF FLATBUSH (74); KATHERINE (75, T.V. movie); HEROES (77); THE ONE & ONLY (78); NIGHT SHIFT (82); in Dec., 1982, Mr Winkler was recipient of 'Louella Parsons Award' for 'projecting the best image of Hollywood through his personal and professional life'.

RAY WINSTONE

B. Hackney, London, . . . Aged 16-18 London Boxing Federation champion; boxed for England, versus Wales when 18, reaching semi-finals, but broke hand; out of 58 fights as Junior lost only 8, as Senior lost none; in plays at school, at 17 enrolled at Corona Stage School for 2½ years; T.V. includes roles in 'Sweeney', 'Plays For Britain', 'Sunshine Over Brixton', 'Scum' and series, 1979, 'Fox'; stage includes 'Not Quite Jerusalem' (July 1980); movies: THAT SUM-MER (78); SCUM, QUADROPHENIA (both 79); HERO (82, short).

TREAT WILLIAMS

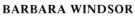

B. Rowayton, Connecticut, . .52. Ed. Kent School for Boys; Franklin & Marshall Coll., Pennsylvania; chose acting career at college, appd. in summer theatre with Fulton Rep. Co., Lancaster, Pa., in S'peare, musicals, contem-porary drama; recommended to New York agent after spotted in coll. prod. of 'Twelfth Night'; Broadway: u/study & leading role of Danny Zuko in 'Grease' (74, and tour), 'Over Here'; movies: DEADLY HERO, THE RITZ, EAGLE HAS LANDED (all 76); Berger in HAIR (78); 1941, WHY SHOULD I LIE?, PURSUIT (all 80); much acclaim as Danny Ciello in PRINCE OF THE CITY (81); ONCE UPON A TIME IN AMERICA (82); Md: actress Lisa Eichhorn.

BARBARA WINDSOR

B. Whitechapel, London, 6.8.37. Real name Barbara Anne Deeks; ed. Our Lady's Convent, Stamford Hill, London and Aida Foster Stage School, making her stage début as an Aida Foster Babe in 'Sleeping Beauty' in 1950, becoming well-known, especially in movies, for her por-trayals of blonde extrovert Cockney characters; stage includes 2 years in musical 'Love From Judy' (1952/53) and as Rosie in 'Fings Aint What They Used To Be' (1959/60); much T.V., came to big screen in BELLES OF ST. TRINIANS (54, uncredited); others: LOST (56, uncredited); TOO HOT TO HANDLE (60); SPARROWS CAN'T SING (63); CROOKS IN CLOISTERS (63); A STUDY IN TERROR (65); CHITTY CHITTY BANG BANG (68); THE BOY FRIEND (71) and, of course, affec-tionately remembered for roles in numerous CARRY ON... films including CARRY ON SPYING (64); CARRY ON CAMPING (69); CARRY ON GIRLS (73); md. Ronald Knight; stage tour 1979 as 'Calamity Jane'.

JONATHAN WINTERS

B. Dayton, Ohio, 11.11.25; full-name: Jonathan Harshman Winters; commercial artist; D.J. at Dayton and Columbus stations; night club come-dian, becoming U.S. T.V. star in 1950s: 'And Here's the Show' (55); 'NBC Comedy Hour' (56); 'Jonathan Winters Show' (56/57); 'Andy Williams Show' (1965-67, 1970/71); 'The Wacky World of Jonathan Winters' (72), others; Md: Eileen Ann Schauder, 1948, 1 son 'Jay' (1950), 1 daughter Lucinda (1956); movies: IT'S A MAD, MAD, MAD WORLD (63); THE LOVED ONE (65); PENELOPE, THE RUSSIANS ARE COMING, THE RUSSIANS ARE COMING (both 1966); OH, DAD, POOR DAD, MAMA'S HUNG YOU IN THE CLOSET & I'M FEELING SO SAD (67); NOW YOU SEE IT, NOW YOU DON'T (T.V. movie), 8 ON THE LAM (both 1968); VIVA MAX! (69); THE FISH THAT SAVED PITTSBURGH (79); HUNGRY i REUNION (81); U.S. T.V. 1982: Mearth in 'Mork & Mindy'; autobio: THE IRON CLOWN.

SHELLEY WINTERS

Born Shirley Schrift on 18 August 1922, Shelley Winters was educated at St. Louis and Brooklyn, New York, and as a youngster made her stage debut in Jamaica, Long Island, New York in 1930 in 'Waiting for Lefty'. Upon leaving school, she was a model, a salesgirl at Woolworth's, and worked in various gown shops in the Garment Centre, in her spare time appearing in amateur plays ('Pins & Needles', etc.). Studying acting at the Drama Workshop of New School for Social Research, she made her New York stage debut in 'Night Before Christmas' in 1941, having pre-viously u/studied. Her marriage to Mack P. Mayer, a textile salesman at this time, ended in divorce in 1948. She soon landed a Columbia movie contract, coming to the screen in WHAT A WOMAN!, subsequently appearing in over 90 pictures so far in her career. These include SAILOR'S HOLIDAY (44); A DOUBLE LIFE, RED RIVER (both 48); A PLACE IN THE SUN (51, Oscar nom., BSA); PLAYGIRL, EXECUTIVE SUITE (both 54); I AM A CAMERA, NIGHT OF THE HUNTER (both 55); THE DIARY OF ANNE FRANK (59, Oscar winner, BSA); LOLITA, THE CHAP-MAN REPORT (both 62); THE BALCONY (63); A HOUSE IS NOT A HOME (64); A PATCH OF BLUE (65, Oscar winner, BSA); ALFIE (66); THE SCALPHUNTERS (68); BLOODY MAMA (70); REVENGE (71, T.V. movie); POSEIDON ADVENTURE (72, Oscar nom., BSA); DIAMONDS (75); PETE'S DRAGON (77); THE INITIATION OF SARAH (78, T.V. movie); THE MAGICIAN OF LUBLIN, KING OF THE GYPSIES (both 78); ELVIS—THE MOVIE (as El's mum); GIRL IN THE WEB, RED NECK COUNTY (all 79); THE FRENCH ATLANTIC AFFAIR (79, T.V. movie); S.O.B. (80); her two other marriages were to actors Vittorio Gassman (1952-54, 1 daughter Vittoria) and Anthony Franciosa (57-60); member, Actors' Studio; stage: 'The Gingerbread Lady' (82); 1983 movies: FANNY HILL, MY DARLING SHIKSA. SHELLEY — also known as Shirley by S.W.; Granada Publ.: St. Albans, 81; p/b: 1982.

JOSEPH WISEMAN

Born Montreal, Canada, 15 May 1918; educated Montreal and New York City; Mr Wiseman made his professiona stage début in New York in 1936 and first appeared on Broadway in 'Abe Lincoln in Illinois' in 1938; he became one o America's most distinguished stage actors in classical roles, both on Broadway and in stock, occasionally working i T.V. and the movies. Married: 1. Nell Kinard (div.), 1 son, 1 daughter, 2. Pearl Lang. Movies: WITH THESE HANDS (50, documentary); DETECTIVE STORY (51, also stage 1949); VIVA ZAPATA!, LES MISERABLES (both 1952); CHAMP FOR A DAY (53); THE SILVER CHALICE (54); THE PRODIGAL (55); THREE BRAVE MEN, THE GARMENT JUNGLE (both 57); THE UNFORGIVEN (60); THE HAPPY THIEVES, a DR NO (both 62); THE OUTSIDER (67, T.V. movie); BYE, BYE BRAVERMAN, THE COUNTERFEI KILLER, THE NIGHT THEY RAIDED MINSKY'S (all 68); STILETTO (70); THE MASK OF SHEBA (70 T.V. movie); LAWMAN (70); THE VALACHI PAPERS (72); PURSUIT (72, T.V. movie); MEN OF THE DRAGON (74, T.V. movie); THE APPRENTICESHIP OF DUDDY KRAVITZ (74); QBVII (74, T.V. movie) JOURNEY INTO FEAR (75); HOMAGE TO CHAGALL (77, co-narrator); MURDER AT THE WORLD'S SERIES (77, T.V. movie); THE BETSY, JAGUAR LIVES (both 78); BUCK ROGERS IN THE 25TH CENTURY (79) and MASADA (79, mini-ser.).

NATALIE WOOD

Natalie Wood's real name is Natasha Gurdin and she was born in San Francisco on 20 July 1938, her parents being Russian. Her father, Nicholis, was a former set and stage designer and specialist in film props, and her mother, Maria, a ballet dancer. At the age of 4, she was chosen from among the townspeople of Santa Rosa for a small role in the movie, THE HAPPY LAND. Irving Pichel, the director, remembered the talented youngster and put her in TOMORROW IS FOREVER three years later. Now a child star, Natalie attended schools on the various studio lots and her early movies included MIRACLE ON 34TH STREET (47, winning box-office Blue Ribbon award); THE GHOST AND MRS MUIR (47); DRIFTWOOD (47); THE GREEN PROMISE (49); OUR VERY OWN (50); winning Child Star of the Year Awards in 1947 and 1949. In the 50s she broke into T.V., including 'All Star Theatre', Ann Morrison in 'Pride of the Family' series (1953/54), 'Playhouse '54' and 'Heidi' (1955). Movies included DEAR BRAT (51); THE STAR (53); SILVER CHALICE (55); REBEL WITHOUT A CAUSE (55, Oscar nom., BSA); THE SEARCHERS (56) and CASH McCALL (59). She wed actor Robert Wagner (qv) on 28.12.57, but they divorced in 1962. Her second husband was British producer Richard Gregson. They wed in May 1969, divorced three years later, and on 16.7.72 she re-married Mr Wagner. She has a daughter, Natasha, from her second marriage and another, Courtney, was born to the Wagners in 1974. Her many other movies included SPLENDOUR IN THE GRASS (61, Oscar nom., BA); WEST SIDE STORY (62, as Maria); GYPSY (62); LOVE WITH A PROPER STRANGER (63, Oscar nom., BA); INSIDE DAISY CLOVER (65); THIS PROPERTY IS CONDEMNED (66); BOB AND CAROL AND TED AND ALICE (69); THE AFFAIR (73, T.V. movie); FROM HERE TO ETERNITY (79, mini-series); METEOR (79); LAST MARRIED COUPLE IN AMERICA (79); MEMORY OF EVA RYKER (80, T.V. movie). *MISS WOOD DIED TRAGICALLY IN A DROWNING ACCIDENT NEAR SANTA CATALINA ISLAND, OFF CALIF. COAST, 29.11.81.* Her last movie, BRAINSTORM (81).

EDWARD WOODWARD

B. Croydon, Surrey, 1.6.30. Ed. State schools and Kingston Commercial College; worked in the office of a sanitary engineer, but later won s'ship to study at R.A.D.A.; pro. début at Farnham Rep., Surrey, December 1946; other reps: Perth, Oxford, Guildford; 1951: toured India/Ceylon in S'peare, Shaw, met and later wed actress Venetia Barrett, 2 sons Tim, Peter (both actors), 1 daughter Sarah (sep.); after varied stage work became well-known West End actor (esp. Percy in 'Rattle of a Simple Man', S. Africa, London, New York, 1961/62/63) and acclaimed/award-winning T.V. actor for his 'Callan' role, from 1967; came to screen in WHERE THERE'S A WILL (54, also stage); others: FILE OF THE GOLDEN GOOSE (68); SITTING TARGET, YOUNG WINSTON (both 72); THE WICKER MAN (73); CALLAN (74); STAND UP, VIRGIN SOLDIERS (76); acclaim in BREAKER MORANT (79, Australia); stage 1979: 'The Beggar's Opera'; Mr Woodward is a recording artiste, winning Gold Disc in Australia, 1975; received O.B.E. 1978 honours; short film 1981: HUNTED; T.V. 1981 includes 'Blunt Instrument', 'Callan—Wet Job', Sir Samuel Hoare in 'Winston Churchill: The Wilderness Years'; THE APPOINTMENT (81). WHO DARES WINS (82); COMEBACK, CHAMPIONS (both 1983).

KEENAN WYNN

B. New York City 27.7.16. Real name Francis Xavier Aloysius Keenan Wynn; ed. St. John's Milit. Acad.; grandson of Frank Keenan, stage and silent screen actor; son of Ed Wynn, famous clown of stage, screen and radio; played on stage, radio; md. 1. Eve Abbott, 1938, 2 sons: Edmund (born 1941) and Tracy Keenan Wynn (now script-writer) (1945) (div. 1946); Mr Wynn played on Broadway in '10 Minute Alibi', 'The Stag at Bay', 'The Little Inn' (all 1935) and in stock at Skowhegan; came to screen in NORTHWEST RANGERS (42); has played in over 80 pictures including ANNIE GET YOUR GUN (50); KISS ME, KATE (53); THE ABSENT-MINDED PROFESSOR (61); DR STRANGE-LOVE (64); STAGECOACH (68); FINIAN'S RAINBOW (68); LOVING (69); HIT LADY (74, T.V. movie); THE DEVIL'S RAIN, NASH-VILLE (both 75); ORCA, COACH, LASER-BLAST (all 77); THE BASTARD (75, mini-series); THE DARK, PIRANHA (both 78); THE CLONUS HORROR, SUNBURN (both 79); THE GLOVE (80); md. 2. Betty Butler, 1949 (div. 1953), 3. Sharley Hudson, 1954, 2 daughters: Hilda (born 1955), Edwynna (1960); has played on T.V. on many occasions, including 'Broadway' (55); host of 'The Westerners', Kodiak in the series 'The Troubleshooters' (1959/60) and frequent guest star; 1982 films: A PIANO FOR MRS CIMINO (T.V. movie), BEST FRIENDS, HYSTERICAL. *ED WYNN'S SON* by K.W. (as told to James Brough); Doubleday: N.Y., 1959.

JOANNE WOODWARD

A talented movie actress with an Oscar early in her film career, Joanne Woodward has also worked successfully with her actor/husband Paul Newman, their work nearly bringing her a second Academy Award. The daughter of Wade Woodward, a publisher, and his wife, Elinor, she was born Joanne Gignilliat Woodward in Thomasville, Georgia, on 27 February 1930, being brought up in Greenville, South Carolina. After attending the High School, she went to the University of Louisiana in Baton Rouge, studying drama, and later enrolled at the Neighbourhood Playhouse, New York, where she attracted the attention of agents. Joanne understudied Janice Rule and Kim Stanley in the Broadway play, 'Picnic', in 1953, where she first met her future husband, Paul Newman. In New York she played in 'Lovers' and had already made headway in T.V. and appeared in such programmes as 'Kraft T.V. Theatre', 'The Web: Welcome Home' (1954), 'Ponds Theatre' (1955), 'Alcoa Hour' and 'Star Tonight' (1955/56), coming to the big screen in COUNT THREE AND PRAY (55) and A KISS BEFORE DYING (56). Gaining a contract with 20th Century Fox, she won an Academy Award for her performance in THE THREE FACES OF EVE, in 1957, and the following year she wed Mr Newman. The couple have three daughters, Elinor (born 1959), Melissa (1960) and Claire (1965). She has since appeared in such movies as NO DOWN PAYMENT (57); THE LONG, HOT SUMMER, RALLY 'ROUND THE FLAG, BOYS (both 58); THE SOUND AND THE FURY, THE FUGITIVE KIND (both 59); FROM THE TERRACE (60); PARIS BLUES (61); THE STRIPPER, A NEW KIND OF LOVE (both 63); SIGNPOST TO MURDER (64); BIG DEAL AT DODGE CITY, A FINE MADNESS (both 66); THE JEST OF GOD, RACHEL, RACHEL (68, Oscar nom., B.A. director: Paul Newman); WINNING (69); W.U.S.A. (70); THEY MIGHT BE GIANTS (71); THE EFFECT OF GAMMA RAYS ON MAN-IN-THE-MOON MARIGOLDS (72, director: Paul Newman); SUMMER WISHES, WINTER DREAMS (73, Oscar nom., B.A.); THE DROWNING POOL (75); SYBIL (76, T.V. movie); THE END (77); COME BACK, LITTLE SHEBA (77, T.V. movie); SEE HOW SHE RUNS, A CHRISTMAS TO REMEMBER (78, both T.V. movies); THE SHADOW BOX (80, T.V. movie, director: Paul Newman) and HARRY & SON (83, dir./co-star: Paul Newman). Biographies: see PAUL NEWMAN.

MICHAEL YORK

After success in several British movies, handsome Michael York has worked internationally in a wide range of roles. He was born in Fulmer, Bucks, on 27 March 1942, and has always shown an interest in acting. Still in his teens, he played in productions for the Bromley Little Theatre Company, a semi-professional group. At Oxford University he appeared in plays with the Dramatic Society and graduated with a Bachelor of Arts Degree in Literature. He joined Michael Croft's National Youth Theatre, toured Europe and also did a season with the Dundee Repertory in Scotland, before playing with the famous National Theatre in many notable productions, including 'Much Ado About Nothing', in 1965, director Franco Zeffirelli. This director remembered Michael and cast him in his first screen role, as Lucentio in THE TAMING OF THE SHREW. That year, 1966, he also played in a short film, RED AND BLUE. Following ACCIDENT, SMASHING TIME (both 67) and ROMEO AND JULIET (68, as Tybault) he starred in THE STRANGE AFFAIR (68). In 1968 he also wed Patricia McCallum, an American, whom he had met while filming SMASHING TIME. His other movie appearances have been in THE GURU (68); ALFRED THE GREAT, JUSTINE (both 69); SOMETHING FOR EVERYONE, BLACK FLOWERS FOR THE BRIDE (both 70); ZEPPELIN, LA POUDRE, D'ESCAMPETTE (both 71); CABARET, ENGLAND MADE ME, LOST HORIZON (all 72); THE THREE MUSKETEERS (73, as D'Artagnan); MURDER ON THE ORIENT EXPRESS, GREAT EXPECTATIONS (as Pip) (both 74); CONDUCT UNBECOMING, THE FOUR MUSKETEERS (both 75); 7 NIGHTS IN JAPAN, LOGAN'S RUN (both 76); FEDORA (as himself), THE ISLAND OF DR MOREAU, THE LAST RE-MAKE OF BEAU GESTE (all 77); JESUS OF NAZARETH (as John the Baptist; mini-series, 77); THE RIDDLE OF THE SANDS (78); A MAN CALLED INTREPID (79, T.V. movie); THE FINAL ASSIGNMENT (80); VENDREDI (81); THE WHITE LIONS, FOR THOSE I LOVED (both 1982). Michael has acted extensively on T.V. and in 1980 he played on Broadway in 'Bent'.

SUSANNAH YORK

Miss York was born Susannah Yolande Fletcher in London on 1 January 1941. Raised mainly in Scotland, she was educated at Troon and later, Northampton. Her first stage appearance was in an amateur production of 'The Crucible' at Croydon. After studying at R.A.D.A. for 2 years she appeared in rep. at Worthing, made her T.V. début in 'The Rebel and The Soldier', and appeared in pantomime at Derby before Ronald Neame brought her to the big screen in TUNES OF GLORY (60). As one of Britain's promising young actresses she has subsequently played in such pictures as THERE WAS A CROOKED MAN (60); GREENGAGE SUMMER (61); FREUD (62); TOM JONES (63); SEVENTH DAWN (64); SCENE NUN, TAKE ONE (short, 64); SANDS OF THE KALAHARI (65); KALEIDOSCOPE, A MAN FOR ALL SEASONS (as Margaret More), A GAME CALLED SCRUGGS (all 66); SEBASTIAN (67); DUFFY (68); LOCK UP YOUR DAUGHTERS!, THE KILLING OF SISTER GEORGE, O! WHAT A LOVELY WAR, BATTLE OF BRITAIN, THEY SHOOT HORSES, DON'T THEY (Oscar nom., BSA, all 69); COUNTRY DANCE, JANE EYRE (title role) (both 70); HAPPY BIRTHDAY, WANDA JUNE (71); ZEE AND CO, IMAGES (72); GOLD (73); THE MAIDS (74); THAT LUCKY TOUCH, CONDUCT UNBECOMING (both 75); SKY RIDERS (76); THE SILENT PARTNER (77); SUPERMAN, MEMORIES, THE SHOUT (all 78); GOLDEN GATE MURDERS (79, T.V. movie); FALLING IN LOVE (also co-scripted); THE AWAKENING (both 79); ALICE (80); SUPERMAN II, LONG SHOT, LOOPHOLE (all 81) and YELLOWBEARD (83). She is divorced from actor Michael Wells, whom she married in 1960. Their daughter, Sacha, was born in May, 1972, their son, Orlando, in 1973. T.V. appearances in more recent years include 'Prince Regent' (79, as Mrs Fitzherbert); 'Second Chance' (80, ser.); 'We'll Meet Again' (82, ser.) and 'Macho' (83). In 1982 she was back on the London stage as 'Hedda Gabler'.

ANTHONY ZERBE

B. Lakewood Village, California, 20.5. . Mr Zerbe is a distinguished stage actor, including work with the Stratford S'peare Festival, the Old Globe S'peare Fest., the L.A. Mark Taper Forum and in New York in 'The Cave Dwellers' (1961), 'Macbeth', 'The Moon Besieged' (both 1962), 'The Devils' (1963) and 'Trial of the Catonsville Nine' (70); md. Arnette, an artist, 1 son Jared, 1 daughter Jenny; guest in many T.V. shows and regular as Lt. K. C. Trench in 'Harry O' (1975/76); movies: COOL HAND LUKE, WILL PENNY (67); THE LIBERATION OF L.B. JONES (69); THEY CALL ME MR TIBBS, COTTON COMES TO HARLEM (both 70); THE O-MEGA MAN (71); THE PRIEST KILLER (71, T.V. movie); HOUND OF THE BASKER-VILLES (72, T.V. movie); PAPILLON, THE LAUGHING POLICEMAN (both 73); SNATCHED, SHE LIVES (73, both T.V. movies); THE PARALLAX VIEW (74); THE HEALERS (74, T.V. movie); FAREWELL, MY LOVELY (75); ONCE AN EAGLE (76, mini-series); ROOSTER COGBURN (76); DOG SOLDIERS, TURNING POINT (both 77); IN THE GLITTER PALACE (77, T.V. movie); ATTACK OF THE PHANTOMS (78); THE CHISHOLMS, CENTENNIAL (both 79 mini-series); FIRST DEADLY SIN (80); A QUES-TION OF HONOUR (81, T.V. movie); SOGGY BOTTOM, U.S.A. (82); B'way 1981: 'The Little Foxes'.

BURT YOUNG

B. ———, . . ; took a variety of jobs before studying at the Actors' Studio, New York; roles in off-Broadway plays lead to Hollywood; played in such T.V. series as 'Baretta', 'M*A*S*H'; Mr Young is also writer; big screen work includes THE GANG THAT COULDN'T SHOOT STRAIGHT (71); CINDERELLA LIBERTY (73); THE GAMBLER, CHINATOWN (both 1974); THE KILLER ELITE (75); ROCKY (76); THE CHOIRBOYS, TWILIGHT'S LAST GLEAMING (both 77); CONVOY (78); also screenplay/actor: UNCLE JOE SHANNON (78); actor: THE CALIFORNIA DOLLS (81); LOOKING TO GET OUT (81); BLOOD BEACH (81); AMITYVILLE II: THE POS-SESSION (82); ALBY'S SPECIAL (83).

ADDENDA

ROBERT BLAKE

B. Nutley, New Jersey, 18.9.34; real name Michael James Vijencio Gubitosi. Parents Italian. Career started aged 2½ with family in song & dance act called 'The Hillbillies'; regular in 'Our Gang' film comedies and child actor in features ANDY HARDY'S DOUBLE LIFE (43); THE HORN BLOWS AT MIDNIGHT (45); and TREASURE OF THE SIERRA MADRE (47). In Republic series 'Red Ryder' as Little Beaver. Also worked as film stuntman, for a while ran drama school and was in the Richard Boone rep. co. (also his T.V. prog. 1963). Was in U.S. services for 2 yrs. Movies include: REVOLT IN THE BIG HOUSE (58); BATTLE FLAME (59); THE PURPLE GANG (60); THE GREATEST STORY EVER TOLD (65); IN COLD BLOOD (67); TELL THEM WILLIE BOY IS HERE (69); CORKY (72); ELECTRA GLIDE IN BLUE (73). Md. Sondra Kerry, actress 1964 (div.), 1 son Noah b. 1965, 1 daughter Delinah b. 1966. Popular T.V. series 1975: 'Baretta'; more recent movies: BUSTING (75); SECONDHAND HEARTS (78) COAST TO COAST, THE BIG TRADE (T.V. movie, both 1980).

JUDY DAVIS

B. Perth, W. Australia, . .55; Ed: Convent; left home at 17, sang with band touring Taiwan and Japan; at 18 returned to Australia; studied Nat. Institute of Dramatic Art, Sydney, appd. in HIGH ROLLING (77) while student; rep.; night club singer; movies: MY BRILLIANT CAREER '80, BA: BAFTA, Australian Acad. Aw.); WINTER OF OUR DREAMS, HEATWAVE, WOODWINK (all 1981); A WOMAN CALLED GOLDA (82, T.V. movie); stage '82: 'Insignificance', as Marilyn Monroe.

BRUCE DAVISON

B. Philadelphia, ... Ed. Penn. State, N.Y. University. When studying at the Lincoln Centre Repertory was chosen to play in movie LAST SUMMER in 1969, and has been seen also in THE STRAWBERRY STATEMENT (69); WILLARD (70); BEEN DOWN SO LONG IT LOOKS LIKE UP TO ME (71); THE JERUSALEM FILE (72); ULZANA'S RAID (72); MAME (73); THE AFFAIR (73, T.V. movie); MOTHER, JUGS AND SPEED (76); SHORT EYES (77); FRENCH QUARTER (78); BRASS TARGET (78); DEADMAN'S CURVE (as popstar Dean Torrence, 78); HIGH RISK (80); TEXAS LEGEND (80). Mr Davison has appeared on Broadway and guested on T.V. including 'Owen Marshall: Counsellor at Law' (from which our still is taken) and MIND OVER MURDER (T.V. movie, 1980); recent movie: KISS MY GRITS (82).

EILEEN BRENNAN

B. Los Angeles, ; mother silent screen actress Jean Manahan; Ed: Georgetown Univ., Am.A.D.A.; success off Broadway in 'Little Mary Sunshine' (59), later playing in 'The Student Gypsy', 'The King & I' (both 1963), 'Hello Dolly!' (64), etc. on B'way; much TV includes such series as a regular on 'Rowan & Martin Laugh-in' (68), 'A New Kind of Family' (79), as Felicia Winters in '13 Queen's Boulevard' (79) and Capt. Doreen Lewis in 'Private Benjamin' (1981/2, winner of Golden Globe Aw., B.A. - Comedy or Musical); Miss Brennan's movies: DIVORCE - AMERICAN STYLE (67); LAST PICTURE SHOW (71); PLAYMATES (1972, T.V. movie); THE STING, SCARECROW (all 1973); THE BLUE KNIGHT (mini-ser.), DAISY MILLER (74); MY FATHER'S HOUSE, THE NIGHT THAT PANICKED AMERICA (both T.V. movies); AT LAST LONG LOVE, HUSTLE (all 1975); MURDER BY DEATH (76); THE DEATH OF RICHIE (1977, T.V. movie); BLACK BEAUTY (mini-ser.); THE CHEAP DETECTIVE, FM, THE GREAT SMOKEY ROADBLOCK (all 1978); WHEN THE CIRCUS CAME TO TOWN (T.V. movie); PRIVATE BENJAMIN (both 80); ANSWERS (1 segment, (1982 T.V. movie); THE FUNNY FARM (83).

JULIE HAGERTY

B. Cincinatti, Ohio, . . ; at 15 Julie was discovered at High School by N.Y. model agent Eileen Ford and modelled for 4 years. When her brother, Michael (she has another brother, Kim), formed his own theatre company, she played in 'Mutual Benefit Life' for only 3 weeks, but she gained an agent. While rehearsing another play the co-directors of AIRPLANE! (80) screen-tested her and gave her the role of Elaine Dickinson in their movie. Julie has subsequently been seen in A MIDSUMMER NIGHT'S SEX COMEDY (82) and AIRPLANE II: THE SEQUEL (82).

JESSICA HARPER

B. Chicago, Illinois, . .49. Upon leaving Sarah Lawrence College, Miss Harper joined the Broadway cast of the musical, 'Hair', utilising her talents as a singer and dancer. She came to the screen in 1971 in TAKING OFF and has been seen in PHANTOM OF THE PARADISE (74); LOVE AND DEATH, INSERTS (both 1975); SUSPIRIA (77); THE EVICTORS (79) and on TV in such mini-series as LITTLE WOMEN (as Jo March), STUDS LONIGAN, THE INNOCENT AND THE DAMNED (all 1979); her more recent movies have been STARDUST MEMORIES (80); SHOCK TREATMENT, MY FAVOURITE YEAR (both 1981); PENNIES FROM HEAVEN (82).

VALERIE HARPER

B. Suffern, N.Y., 22.8.40; Miss Harper started as a dancer in stage shows at the Radio City Music Hall and made her acting debut in summer stock in Connecticut; early Broadway plays included 'Take Me Along' (59); 'Wildcat'; 'Subways Are For Sleeping' (61); 'Story Theatre' (70); md: actor/writer Dick Schaal, 1964 (div. 1978); great success in 'The Mary Tyler Moore Show' (T.V.), winning 3 'Emmy' Awards in 1970/71, 71/72 & 72/73, in her role as Rhonda Morgenstern she was given her own series, 'Rhoda', from 1974 - 78, winning another 'Emmy', 1974/75; movies: THURSDAY'S GAME (71, but released as T.V. movie, 1974); FREEBIE & THE BEAN (74); NIGHT TERROR (1977, T.V. movie); CHAPTER TWO (79); THE LAST MARRIED COUPLE IN AMERICA (80); THE SHADOW BOX (1980, T.V. movie); FARRELL FOR THE PEOPLE (1982, T.V. movie).

RUTGER HAUER

B. Breukelen, Holland, . .44; at the age of 15 Mr Hauer joined the Dutch Merchant Marine; he later became a distinguished and acclaimed Dutch stage performer, playing in such Dutch movies as KEETJE TIPPLE, MAX HAVELAAR (77); SPETTERS (cameo) and a great success in Paul Verhoeven's SOLDIER OF ORANGE (79); his international films have included THE WILBY CONSPIRACY (75); NIGHTHAWKS (80); CHANEL SOLITAIRE (81); EUREKA, BLADE RUNNER (both 1982); Albert Speer in T.V. mini-series INSIDE THE THIRD REICH (82); THE OSTERMAN WEEKEND, A BREED APART (both 1983).

CLIFTON JAMES

B. N.Y. City, 29.5.21 (22?); WWII: 5 years in Pacific as infantryman; Ed: Univ. of Oregon (degree), Actors' Studio; md: Laura, 6 children; much stage inclu. S'peare and hit 'American Buffalo'; films: ON THE WATERFRONT (54); THE STRANGE ONE (57); EXPERIMENT IN TERROR, DAVID & LISA (both 1962); BLACK LIKE ME (64); THE HAPPENING, WILL PENNY, COOL HAND LUKE, CARNIVAL OF THIEVES (all 1967); THE REIVERS (69); TICK, TICK, TICK (70); THE NEW CENTURIONS (72); THE LAST DETAIL, LIVE & LET DIE (both 1973); MAN WITH THE GOLDEN GUN, THE BANK SHOT (both 1974); RANCHO DELUXE (75); SILVER STREAK (76); BAD NEWS BEARS IN BREAKING TRAINING (77; CABOB-LANCO (79); SUPERMAN II (81); T.V. inclu. Lt. Quint in series 'City of Angels' (76); 'Texas' (series 1982).

BEN KINGSLEY

B.   ; Real name Krishna Bhanji; fath an Indian doctor who had a general practice Manchester; mother a former fashion model; E Manchester Grammar School, intended to becom a doctor, but in 1962, aged 19, at Stratford sa 'Richard III' and decided to become an acto joining an amateur group in Salford; applied f RADA, but failed; 1st prof. job touring school then seasons at Stoke and Chichester; md: 1. (div.); 2. Alison Sutcliffe, 1 son, Edmund (b. '82 joined R.S.C. 1964 and subsequently distinguishe himself in Shakespearean roles including 'Hamle Mr Kingsley's other work includes a one-ma stage performance, 'Kean', TV in 'Merry Wive of Windsor' and movies, progressing with bit ro in FEAR IS THE KEY (73), to stardom BETRAYAL (82) and his magnificent performanc as GANDHI (82, B.A. Aw. America's Nation Board of Review; L.A. Film Critics; Golde Globe; N.Y. Film Critics; BAFTA Aw. & 198 Oscar); T.V. 1983: 'Kean'.

NASTASSIA KINSKI

B. Berlin,   .61 (60?); real name Nastassja Naksznski; father Klaus Kinski, famous actor (qv); mother Ruth; Nastassia's parents separated when she was three; she received much of her education in Rome, Munich and Caracas and in her early teens she studied English in the USA, and Drama at the Actors' Studio under Lee Strasberg; she came to the screen in Germany, in Wim Wenders' WRONG MOVEMENTS (75) and has been seen in TO THE DEVIL . . . A DAUGHTER (76); STAY AS YOU ARE (77); PASSION FLOWER HOTEL (78); a great success in TESS (1980, winning her a Golden Globe Award); ONE FROM THE HEART, CAT PEOPLE, EXPOSED, FOR YOUR LOVE ONLY (all 1982); SPRING SYMPHONY, UNFAITHFULLY YOURS, LA LUNE DANS LE CANIVEAU (all 1983).

JOHN PHILLIP LAW

B. Los Angeles, 3.9.37; father a deputy sheriff, mother an actress, John grew up in H'wood: a film extra at 8, first screen role in THE MAN WITH 30 SONS (50); considered engineering career, but enrolled at Univ. of Hawaii to study law, switched to drama and trained at the NY Lincoln Centre Rep. and with Elia Kazan; B'way inclu. 'Tartuffe' (65); first movie breaks in Italian (*) films; movies: SMOG*(62); HIGH INFI-DELITY*, 3 NIGHTS OF LOVE (segment: 'The Hospital Friar')* (both (1965); THE RUSSIANS ARE COMING, THE RUSSIANS ARE COMING (66); HURRY SUNDOWN (67); BARBARELLA*, DEATH RIDES A HORSE*, DIABOLIK*, SKIDOO, THE SERGEANT (all 1968); CERTAINLY, CERTAINLY, IN FACT . . . PROBABLY*, MASTER OF THE ISLANDS (both 1970); THE RED BARON (as Von Richtofen), THE LAST MOVIE, THE LOVE MACHINE (all 1971); THE GOLDEN VOYAGE OF SINBAD (73); OPEN SEASON (74); THE SPIRAL STAIRCASE (75); THE CASSANDRA CROSSING (76); HOOPER (78); THE BEST PLACE TO BE (1979, T.V. movie); TARZAN: THE APE MAN (81); TIN MAN (83).

VIVECA LINDFORS

B. Uppsala, Sweden, 29.12.20; father army officer (publisher?), and, when young, Viveca travelled extensively, gaining fluency in English, German and French; trained at Royal Dramatic Theatre Sch., Stockholm, 1937-40; Swedish stage; Md. 1. Folke Rogard (1941-49), 1 daughter Lena (1942), 1 son Jan (1943); Swedish movie 1940: SNUR-RIGA FAMILJEN (40), others; after work in Italy went to H'wood 1946, early movies there inclu. ADVENTURES OF DON JUAN (49); DARK CITY (50); JOURNEY INTO LIGHT (51); RUN FOR COVER (55); Md: 2. director Don Siegel (1949-53), 1 son (1950), now actor Kristoffer Tabori; Miss Lindfors became well-known on U.S. stage from 1950s; Md: 3. George Tabori, writer (1954-72); more recent movies: THE WAY WE WERE (73); WELCOME TO L.A. (76); A QUESTION OF GUILT (T.V. movie); A WEDDING, GIRL FRIENDS (all 1978); LINUS (Sweden), NATURAL ENE-MIES, VOICES (all 1979); THE HAND, MARILYN: THE UNTOLD STORY (both 1981); CREEPSHOW (82).

TONY LO BIANCO

B.   ,   ; has played on New York stage, inclu. 'Yanks 3, Detroit O' (Obie Award); 'The Office'; 'The Rose Tattoo', 'Royal Hunt of the Sun'; T.V. inclu. Tony Calbrese in 'Police Story' (1973-77); movies: HONEYMOON KILLERS (70); FRENCH CONNECTION (71); MR INSIDE/MR OUTSIDE (T.V movie), THE SEVEN UPS (both 1973); STORY OF JACOB & JOSEPH (1974, T.V. movie); JESUS OF NAZARETH (mini-ser.), GOLDENROD (T.V. movie), DEMON (all 1977); F.I.S.T., BLOODBROTHERS, THE LAST TENANT (T.V. movie, all 1978); A LAST CRY FOR HELP, CHAMPIONS: A LOVE STORY (both T.V. movies), VALENTINE (all 1979); SEPARATE WAYS (81); THE DOORMAN (83, directed).

JANET MARGOLIN

B. N.Y. City, 25.7.43; Ed: Walden Sch. & N.Y. High Sch. for Performing Arts; B'way success 1961: 'Daughter of Silence' and film debut 1962: DAVID & LISA; others: BUS RILEY'S BACK IN TOWN, GREATEST STORY EVER TOLD (as Mary of Bethany), MORITURI (all 1965); THE EAVESDROPPER, NEVADA SMITH (both 1966); ENTER LAUGHING (67); BUENA SERA, MRS CAMBELL (68); TAKE THE MONEY & RUN (69); THE LAST CHILD (T.V. movie, 1971); FAMILY FLIGHT (T.V. movie, 1972); YOUR THREE MINUTES ARE UP (73); PRAY FOR THE WILDCATS, PLANET EARTH (both T.V. movies, 1974); LANIGAN'S RABBI (T.V movie, 1976); MURDER IN PEYTON PLACE, SHARON: PORTRAIT OF A MISTRESS (both T.V. movies, 1977); ANNIE HALL (77); LAST EMBRACE (79); THE TRIANGLE FACTORY FIRE SCANDAL (T.V. movie, 1979); THE PLUT-ONIUM INCIDENT (T.V. movie 1980).

STEVE MARTIN

B. Waco, Texas,   .46; Ed: Long Beach State Coll. majoring in philosophy, switched to U.C.L.A., studying theatre; got club act (including magic) together, playing such clubs as the Prison of Socrates, Balboa Island, and he later graduated to T.V. spots, such as a regular in 'Andy Williams Presents Ray Stevens' (70); 'The Ken Berry 'Wow' Show' (72); 'The Sonny & Cher Comedy Hour' (1972/3); 'The Smothers Brothers Comedy Hour' (75, 'Emmy' nom., as writer); 'Johnny Cash Show' (76) and his own series as Navin in 'The Jerk'; Mr Martin has also played in such movies as SERGEANT PEPPER'S LONELY HEARTS CLUB BAND (78); THE MUPPET MOVIE (guest). THE JERK (both 1979); PENNIES FROM HEAVEN (81); DEAD MEN DON'T WEAR PLAID (also co-scripted), THE MAN WITH TWO BRAINS (both 1982); THE LONELY GUY (83).

AMERON MITCHELL

, Dallastown, Pennsylvania 4.11.18. Real name ameron Mizell; trained at New York Theatre chool, appearing with New York Theatre Guild)38-40; radio announcer and sportscaster before ining U.S. Armed Forces as bombardier 1942- 4; had played with the Lunts in 'Taming of the hrew' (40); came to the screen in THEY WERE XPENDABLE (45); won acclaim on Broadway 'Death of a Salesman' (49, movie—52); md. 1. Johanna Mendel 1942, 3 sons (div.), 2. ———, 1 aughter Carmelia, 1 son Freddie; his many films nclude LOVE ME OR LEAVE ME (54), AROUSEL (56, as Jigger), MONKEY ON IY BACK (57), HOMBRE (67), BUCK & HE PREACHER (71), VIVA KNIEVEL! '7), SLAVERS (78); many T.V. movies and ell-known as Buck Cannon in 'High Chapparral' .967-71) and as Jeremiah Worth in 'Swiss amily Robinson' (75/76); recent movies: ILENT SCREAM (80), TEXAS LIGHTNING 11), THE DEMON (81), THE SECOND IILE (81), GUNS & THE FURY (82).

WARREN MITCHELL

B. London, .26; trained for the stage at RADA, making his stage debut at Finsbury Park Open Air Theatre 1950; during 1950s appd. in such stage productions as 'Can-Can' (54) and 'The Threepenny Opera' (56); md. Constance Wake; in the 1960s appd. in many films and became especially well-known on T.V. as Alf Garnett in 'Till Death Us Do Part' (68/69); many films include TOMMY THE TOREADOR (60), POSTMAN'S KNOCK (62), THE SMALL WORLD OF SAMMY LEE (63), INTELLI-GENCE MEN (64), HELP! (65), ARRIVER-DERCI, BABY! (66), THE ASSASSINATION BUREAU (68), TILL DEATH US DO PART (69), ALL THE WAY UP (70), INNOCENT BYSTANDERS (71), THE GARNETT SAGA (72), STAND UP, VIRGIN SOLDIERS (77), MEETINGS WITH REMARKABLE MEN (77); recent stage: won acclaim at National Theatre in 'Death of a Salesman' (79), winning 'Evening Standard Award'; recent T.V. series 1981: 'Till Death . . .', 'The Caretaker'; stage 82/83: 'Ducking Out'; films: NORMAN LOVES ROSE (82, BSA Aw., Australian Film Awards); THE PLAGUE DOGS (82, voice).

BERNADETTE PETERS

. Jamaica (Queens?), N.Y., 28.2.48; real name ernadette Lazzara; T.V. from age 5: 'Horn & Hardart Children's Hour'; 'Juvenile Jury'; 'Name hat Tune'; stage debut N.Y. City Centre in 'The Most Happy Fella'; at 13, 8 months in 'Gypsy' Dur; Miss Peters became Broadway star; other tage includes 'The Penny Friend'; 'Johnny No rump'; 'Curley McDimple'; 'George M!'; (also V version); 'Dames at Sea'; 'La Strada'; 'On the own'; 'Mack and Mabel'; other T.V. includes uest on 'Carol Burnett Show'; Charlotte Drake series 'All's Fair' (1976/77); THE ISLANDER 1978, T.V. movie); Bernadette has a sister, Donna, and a brother, Joseph; movies: ACE ELI AND RODGER OF THE SKIES (73); THE LONGEST YARD (74); W.C.FIELDS & ME, ILENT MOVIE (both 1976); THE JERK 79); PENNIES FROM HEAVEN (Golden Globe Aw., B.A.), TULIPS, HEARTBEEPS all 1981); ANNIE (82).

JOANNA PETTET

B. London, 16.11.44; Joanna, although born in England, grew up in Canada, and trained at the Neighborhood Playhouse, New York. Her first break on Broadway came in 'Take Her, She's Mine' (1961), and after 'The Chinese Prime Minister' and 'Poor Richard' (both 1964) on the stage she came to the screen in 1965 in THE GROUP. Her Movies since then have included NIGHT OF THE GENERALS (66); ROBBERY, CASINO ROYALE (both 1967); THE BEST HOUSE IN LONDON, BLUE (both 1968); THE DELPHI BUREAU, FOOTSTEPS, THE WEEKEND NUN (all T.V. movies, 1972); PIONEER WOMAN (T.V. movie 1973); A CRY IN THE WILDERNESS (T.V. movie), TENDER FLESH (both 1974); THE DESPE-RATE MILES (T.V. movie, 1975); CAPTAINS & THE KINGS (mini-ser.), THE DARK SIDE OF INNOCENCE (T.V. movie, both 1976); SEX AND THE MARRIED WOMAN (T.V. movie 1977); THE EVIL (78); THE RETURN OF FRANK CANNON (T.V. movie, 1980); DOUBLE EXPOSURE (82).

MARIE-FRANCE PISIER

. Vietnam, 10.5.44 (49?). Father (divorced) a iplomat; ed. Univ. of Paris (degrees in Law & 'olitical Science); aged 16 auditioned for Truffaut qv) and won role in AMOUR A VINGT ANS 61); Marie has played in 33 movies, gaining the Cesar (the French Oscar) for COUSIN-COUSINE 76); recent movies: THE OTHER SIDE OF MIDNIGHT (77); CELINE & JULIE GO BOATING (78); SCRUPLES (79, mini-series); BAROCCO (80); THE HOT TOUCH (81).

INGRID PITT

B. Berlin(?), . . . Escaped internment camp in Poland, went to W. Berlin, later defected to E. Berlin, acting with Berliner Ensemble; disliked regime, fled to U.S.; 1 daughter Stephanie (father: U.S. Army officer); fought for Indians' rights; acted on Spanish stage; entered movies as stuntgirl; movies: WHERE EAGLES DARE (69); VAM-PIRE LOVERS (70); HOUSE THAT DRIPPED BLOOD (71); COUNTESS DRACULA (71); NOBODY ORDERED LOVE (71); WICKER MAN (72); THE WOLF (75); WHO DARES WINS (82); wed to an Englishman, Ingrid is also a writer, has acted on stage/T.V.

DEBORAH RAFFIN

B. Los Angeles, 13.3.53; daughter of retired actress Trudy Marshall; Ed: Valley Coll.; Miss Raffin was a fashion model before becoming an actress, her screen debut being in FORTY CARATS 73), and she was discovered by Ted Witzer; Md: her manager Michael Viner; her movies include THE DOVE (74); ONCE IS NOT ENOUGH 75); NIGHTMARE IN BADHAM COUNTRY T.V. movie, 1976); THE SENTINEL, DEMON, MANIAC (all 1977); SKI LIFT TO DEATH HOW TO PICK UP GIRLS! (T.V. movies, 1979); WILLA, MIND OVER MURDER (both T.V. movies, 1979); THE LAST CONVERTIBLE mini-ser.), TOUCHED BY LOVE (both 1980); Gloria Munday in a short-lived series 'Foul Play' 81); HONEYMOON HOTEL, HAYWIRE both T.V. movies), DANCE OF THE DWARFS all 1982).

CRISTINA RAINES

B. Manilla, Philippines, 28.2. ; 'Tina', as she prefers to be called, is of Colombian and English ancestry. When 7, her father, an overseas executive with Proctor & Gamble, was transferred to Venezuela, and she spent some time of her childhood there. Later, at Coral Gables High School, Florida, she took acting classes, but intended to become a vet, taking up modelling to pay her way through college. A would-be modelling job landed her a successful screen test and Tina made her debut in HEX, in 1973, that year also appearing in THE STONE KILLER and SUN-SHINE (T.V. movie). She has since played in the mini-series LOOSE CHANGE, CENTENNIAL (both 1978), 'Flamingo Road' and on the big screen in NASHVILLE, RUSSIAN ROULETTE (both 1975); THE SENTINEL (77); THE 10TH MONTH (unreleased); THE DUELLISTS (both 1978); THE CHILD STEALER (T.V. movie, 1979); SILVER DREAM RACER (80); REAL LIFE (83).

CHRIS SARANDON

B. Beckley, W. Virginia, 24.7.42. Ed. Univ. of West Virginia and Catholic Univ.; Mr Sarandon played in summer stock, a production going to New York; in that city he played in 'Stephen D' (1966) and 'The Rothschilds', amongst others; md. actress Susan Sarandon (div.); he has played in such movies as THURSDAY'S GAME (74, T.V. movie); THE FRONT PAGE (74); DOG DAY AFTERNOON (75, for which he received an Academy Award nom. as Best Supporting Actor); LIPSTICK (76); THE SENTINEL (77); YOU CAN'T GO HOME AGAIN (79, T.V. movie); CUBA (79); BROKEN PROMISE (81, T.V. movie); he portrayed Jesus in a Fox T.V. film, 'The Day Christ Died', in 1979.

ARNOLD SCHWARZENEGGER

B. Austria, . .47; father a former military officer turned police chief; Arnold spent his early years in the tiny Austrian village of Thal; star of school football team, at 15 started weight training; at 18, absent-without-leave from Austrian Army, he won Junior Mr Europe contest; in the next few years he won 5 'Mr Universe' and 7 'Mr Olympia' titles; graduated from Univ. of Winsconsin with B.A. degrees in Business Administration and Economics; a self-made millionaire, he has interests in real-estate, a mail order business and has written three body-building instruction manuals; since coming to the screen in 1975 in Bob Rafelson's STAY HUNGRY, he has been seen in such pictures as PUMPING IRON (77); CACTUS JACK (78); THE JAYNE MANSFIELD STORY (T.V. movie, 1980); CONAN THE BARBARIAN (81).

TOM SELLECK

B. Detroit, 29.1.45; father was vice-president of a property company, family moved to California when Tom was 4; at University of Southern California took business course, but trained for a sports career with University of Southern California Trojans; became a top male model and did T.V. commercials, especially for male Cologne for Revlon; Mr Selleck studied at the now defunct 20th Century Fox talent school and made his screen debut in U.S. Air Force Training film; Md: actress Jacqulyn (sep.), 1 step-son, Kevin; supporting roles in movies inclu. MIDWAY (76); COMA (78); T.V. series include 'The Young & the Restless', 'The Concrete Cowboys' (81) and 'Magnum' (81); voted 'Male Star of the Year' by H'wood Women's Press Club, 1982; recent movies: SHADOW RIDERS (T.V. movie), THE DAY-BREAKERS (both 1982); HIGH ROAD TO CHINA (83).

ANDREW STEVENS

B. Memphis, Tennessee, .6.55; parents: actres Stella Stevens, Memphis electrician Herma Stevens (divorced); during school years brough up mainly by grand-parents; developed interest a a drummer, but at school turned to acting an local community theatre work — won State actin competition, Nashville; 1st T.V. role in epis. c 'Adam 12'; at Immaculate Heart College appd. i 'Candide', 'Rimers of Eldridge' and T.V. i 'Apple's Way' (74) epis.; movies and T.V.: THI LAST SURVIVORS, WEREWOLF OF WOOD STOCK (both T.V. movies), SHAMPOO (al 1975); DEPORTEE (short); ONCE AN EAGLE THE OREGON TRAIL (both T.V. movies MASSACRE AT CENTRAL HIGH, VIGIL ANTE FORCE, LAS VEGAS LADY (all 1976 SECRETS (T.V. movie), DAY OF THI ANIMALS (both 1977); THE BASTARD (mini ser.), THE BOYS IN COMPANY C, THI FURY (all 1978); THE REBELS (mini-ser. WOMEN AT WEST POINT (T.V. movie, bot 1979); DEATH HUNT (81); FORBIDDEI LOVE (T.V. movie, 1982); 10 TO MIDNIGH (83).

STING

B. Wallasend, Northumberland, 2.10.51; real name: Gordon Sumner; father, engineer, later dairy worker; mother, hairdresser; Ed: St. Cuthbert's Grammar Sch.; formerly a primary and secondary school teacher, in 1976, as an unknown, he signed a contract with Virgin Music, becoming well-known as lead singer of group, 'The Police', adopting name of 'Sting', because he wore a black and white jumper and looked like a bumble-bee; films: QUADROPHENIA (79); RADIO ON (80); BRIMSTONE & TREACLE (82); Md: Frances Tomelty, May 1976, 1 son, Joe (born 1979). *THE POLICE RELEASED:* Big O Publishing: London, 1980; *THE POLICE: A VISUAL DOCUMENTARY* by Miles; Omnibus Press: London, 1981.

INGRID THULIN

B. Solleftea, Sweden, 27.1.29; stage debut at 15; trained Royal Drama Theatre, Stockholm; Swedish rep. also directed; Md: Harry Schein; well-known on Swedish screen from 1955; many movies inclu. FOREIGN INTRIGUE (55); WILD STRAWBERRIES (57); THE FACE, BRINK OF LIFE (both 1958, latter winner BA Aw., Cannes Film Festival); THE 4 HORSEMEN OF THE APOCALYPSE, WINTER LIGHT (both 1962); THE SILENCE (63); RETURN FROM THE ASHES (65); LA GUERRE EST FINI, NIGHT GAMES (both 1966); HOUR OF THE WOLF (68); THE DAMNED, THE RITE (both 1969); CRIES & WHISPERS (72); MOSES: THE LAWGIVER (mini-ser., 1975); CASSANDRA CROSSING (76); SALON KITTY (77); ONE ON ONE (79); also film director/B'way actress.

RACHEL WARD

B. , . .58; eldest daughter of journalist Peter Ward and niece of the Earl of Dudley; Ed: boarding schools; brought up near village of Chipping Norton, Oxfordshire; at 16 went to Paris, studying art for 1 year; returned to London, attended Byam Shaw Art School, but later became very successful model, appearing in 'Harpers & Queen', 'Vogue', and, in the U.S.A., in 'Town & Country', 'Cosmopolitan', 'Time' and commercials both sides of the Atlantic.; for 10 months Rachel studied acting with Stella Adler and Robert Modica, making her movie debut in Ken Hughes' TERROR EYES, and the unreleased THREE BLIND MICE; she has played in the more recent NIGHT SCHOOL (81); SHARKY'S MACHINE (81); DEAD MEN DON'T WEAR PLAID (82); THORN BIRDS (82, mini-ser.); Md: actor Bryan Brown, on 9.4.83, at Chipping Norton, England.

CINDY WILLIAMS

B. Van Nuys, California, 22.8.47; Ed: L.A. City College; appd. in High School & College plays; played in several U.S. T.V. series in the early 1970s, including 'Barefoot in the Park', 'Nanny & the Professor' and as a regular in 'The Funny Side' (71); movies: GAS-S-S-S (70, debut); CHRISTIAN LICORICE STORE, DRIVE, HE SAID (both 1971); BEWARE! THE BLOB, TRAVELS WITH MY AUNT (both 1972); AMERICAN GRAFFITI, THE KILLING KIND (both 1973); THE MIGRANTS (T.V. Movie), THE CONVERSATION (both 1974); MR RICCO (75); THE FIRST NUDIE MUSICAL (76); SUDDENLY, LOVE (T.V. movie, 1978); THE CREATURE WASN'T NICE (81); Md: singer Bill Hudson; from 1976 Cindy has been popular on U.S. T.V. as Shirley Feeney in 'Laverne & Shirley', directing several episodes; THE KILLING KIND (82).

ACKNOWLEDGEMENTS

The following reference books and magazines, worthy additions to any film historian's bookshelf, were consulted for *WHO'S WHO ON THE SCREEN:*

A.T.V. SHOW BOOK; Purnell, c. 1957 – c. 1968; *ACADEMY AWARDS ILLUSTRATED* by Robert Osborne; Ernest E. Schworck: La Habra, U.S.A., 1966; *THE AMERICAN MUSICAL* by Tom Vallance; Zwemmer/Barnes, 1970; *BRITISH FILM & T.V. WHO'S WHO* (serialised); Picturegoer Magazine, 1953; *BRITISH FILM CATALOGUE 1895-1970*; Editor: Denis Gifford; David & Charles, 1973; *BROADS* by Ian & Elisabeth Cameron; Movie Magazine Ltd., 1969; *THE COMPLETE DIRECTORY TO PRIME TIME NETWORK T.V. SHOWS 1946 — PRESENT* by Tim Brooks & Earl Marsh; Ballantine Books: N.Y., 1981; *THE FILM BUFF'S CHECKLIST OF MOTION-PICTURES (1912-1979)*; Editor: D. Richard Baer; Hollywood Film Archive, 1979; *THE FILMGOER'S COMPANION*; Editor: Leslie Halliwell; MacGibbon & Kee Ltd., 1965 and subsequent volumes; F. Maurice Speed's *FILM REVIEW ANNUAL* (1944-current): W.H. Allen; *THE FILM SHOW ANNUAL*; c. 1958-1960; Printed by L.T.A. Robinson Ltd.; *THE HEAVIES* by Ian & Elisabeth Cameron; Movie Magazine Ltd., 1967; *HOLLYWOOD TODAY* by Pat Billings & Allen Eyles; Zwemmer/Barnes, 1971; *INTERNATIONAL MOTION-PICTURE ALMANAC* (1929-present); Editor: Richard Gertner; Quigley Publishing Co. Inc. (N.Y./London); *MOVIE GREATS* by Paul Michael; Garland Books, U.S.A. 1969; *MOVIES-MADE-FOR-TELEVISION* by Alvin H. Marill; U.S.A., 1980; *PICTUREGOER'S WHO'S WHO & ENCYCLOPAEDIA*; Odhams Press, 1933; various issues of *PICTURE SHOWS WHO'S WHO* magazine 1932, 1938, 1949 and 1956 (book); Amalgamated Press; *SCREEN INTERNATIONAL* newspaper; Editor: Peter Noble; King Publications Ltd. (current); *SCREEN INTERNATIONAL FILM & T.V. YEARBOOK* (1945-current, formerly *BRITISH FILM YEARBOOK*); Editor: Peter Noble; King Publications; John Willis' *SCREEN WORLD ANNUAL* (1949-current), U.S.A.; *STARS OF THE SCREEN 1934*; Compiler/Editor: J.S. Ross; Herbert Joseph; *STAR STATS* by Kenneth S. Marx; Price/Stern/Sloan Publishers Inc., L.A., 1979; *T.V. ANNUAL*; Odhams Press; circa 1952-1960; *T.V. TIMES' EXTRA WHO'S WHO ON T.V.*; I.T.V. Publications Ltd., 1970; *THE WESTERN: AN ILLUSTRATED GUIDE* by Allen Eyles; Zwemmer/Barnes, 1967; *WHO'S WHO*; Adam & Charles Black, 1966; *WHO'S WHO IN HOLLYWOOD* by David Ragan; Arlington House: N.Y., 1979; *WHO'S WHO IN HOLLYWOOD* (magazine); (1960s) Dell Publishing, N.Y.; *WHO'S WHO IN SHOW BIZ.*; Purnell & Sons Ltd., 1963 and 1964; *WHO'S WHO IN T.V.* by Richard Heller; Dell Publishing Co. Inc., N.Y., 1967; *WHO'S WHO IN THE THEATRE*; Editor: Ian Herbert; Pitman Publishing Ltd., 1977; *WINCHESTER'S SCREEN ENCYCLOPAEDIA*; Editor: Clarence Winchester; Winchester Publications Ltd., 1948.
(All London Publishers, except where stated).

WHO'S WHO ON THE SCREEN could never have been produced without the co-operation of many individuals in the motion-picture industry. I should like to take this opportunity of expressing sincere gratitude to the following press and publicity officers, personal managers and theatrical agents and motion-picture and television companies, who were kind enough to supply relevant information, and, in particular, photographic material:

A.B.C. Press Relations (New York); A.T.V. Network Limited; American International Pictures Export Corporation; Susan Angel Associates Limited; Anglia T.V. Limited; Associated Film Distribution; Avco Embassy Pictures; Barber Dann Films Limited; Barber Rose; Bruce Birmelin; Bordeaux International Films Limited; Brent Walker Film Distributors Limited; British Lion Films Limited; Gary Bryan; C.C.A. Personal Management; Peter Charlesworth Limited; Chatto & Linnit Limited; Cinegate Limited; Cinema International Corporation; Cinerama Releasing (U.K.) Limited; CIP Filmproduktions GmbH; Columbia-E.M.I.-Warners Distributors; Crouch Associates and Caroline Dawson; Larry Dalzell Associates Limited; Danjaq, S.A.; Dennis Davidson Associates Limited; Enterprise Pictures Limited; Brian Doyle of Eon Productions Limited; Essanay Limited; David Farrell; Kate Feast Management; Fraser & Dunlop Limited; Geoff Freeman; G.T.O. Films; Gala Film Distributors Limited; Gamma III Distribution Company; Harry Gillard; Joan Riley of Granada Television; Norman Gryspeerdt; Keith Hamshere; Handmade Films; Wally Heim; Hemdale International Films Limited; Hope & Lyne; I.T.C. Film Distributors; Leading Artists; Derek Leathers; Paddy Leitch; Lion's Gate Films; London Screen Distributors; London Weekend Television; Lorimar Productions; M.C.A. T.V.; M-G-M Inc.; Caroline Renton of M-L-R Limited; Jette Bonnevie of Married Men Productions; A1 Mitchell Associates; N.B.C. (Burbank & N.Y.); Namara Films; New World Pictures; Odhams Press Limited; Brian O'Dowd; Jerry Ohlinger's Movie Material Inc.; Orion Pictures; Wendy Taylor of P.I.C. Publicity Limited; Paramount Pictures; Bob Penn; The Press Association; The Rank Organisation; John Redway & Associates Limited; Stella Richards Personal Management; Paul Ronald; Ron Samuels Enterprises; Anna Scher Theatre Management Limited; Scotia-Barber Distributors; Brian McLaurin of Scottish T.V. Limited; Neville Shulman; Brett Garwood of Spelling-Goldberg Productions; Richard Stone; Target International Pictures Limited; Tina Halvorsen of Thames Television; Tigon Film Distributors Limited; Topix; Twentieth-Century Fox; Philip Day of United Artists Corporation Limited; United Press International; Universal City Studios Incorporated; Viacom; Walt Disney Productions; George Courtney Ward; Warner Brothers Incorporated; David White Associates; Yorkshire Television and special thanks to the Information Department of The British Film Institute, London. Artistes Mark Burns, Peter Bowles, Fiona Fullerton, Georgina Hale, Spike Milligan, David Prowse and Sam Wanamaker I should like to thank for contacting me personally regarding their entries.

JOHN WALTER SKINNER.

Oh! What a Lovely War (69)

Born in Surbiton, Surrey, John Walter Skinner was educated at private schools in Horsham and Worthing. Filmstruck from his early teens, 'learning all there was to know about film from Hammer and screen epics!', he worked in a department store for three years before entering the film industry in 1968 as a soldier in *OH! WHAT A LOVELY WAR*. He subsequently spent eighteen months in London playing walk-on roles in numerous film and television productions, although, he hastens to add, his only speaking role was saying 'I'm sorry, Sir' in an episode of *'The Expert'!* He then did seasons of repertory in South Wales and Sidmouth, Devon, and from 1972-1980 edited and published the quarterly magazine for film'buffs, *'International Film Collector'*, which was well-received, and continued acting with leading roles for Worthing Theatre Guild in such productions as *'Camelot', 'Salad Days'* and *'The Dancing Years'*. He also filmed a 16mm colour documentary film of his home town, *"Twixt Sea and Downs'*, and, more recently, played in Brighton in the revue, *'Ivor and Noël'*. With *WHO'S WHO ON THE SCREEN* John proudly continues his family's association with publishing — his great-grandfather, Walter Robert Skinner, was founder of *'The Mining Manual'* (now *'The Financial Times Mining International Year Book'*).

COVER PHOTOGRAPHS

Front cover, left to right: Roger Moore in *FOR YOUR EYES ONLY* (1981, U.A.); Jane Fonda, Lily Tomlin, Dolly Parton in *NINE TO FIVE* (1980, Fox); *E.T. THE EXTRA-TERRESTRIAL* (1982, Universal); Meryl Streep, Jeremy Irons in *THE FRENCH LIEUTENANT'S WOMAN* (1981, U.A.); Clint Eastwood in *PAINT YOUR WAGON* (1969, Paramount); Harrison Ford in *THE RAIDERS OF THE LOST ARK* (1981, Paramount); Jill Clayburgh, Gene Wilder, Richard Pryor in *SILVER STREAK* (1977, Fox); Sean Connery in *DIAMONDS ARE FOREVER* (1971, U.A.) and James Coburn, Sophia Loren in *FIREPOWER* (1979, I.T.C.).

Back cover: Elliott Gould, Michael Caine, James Caan in *HARRY & WALTER GO TO NEW YORK* (1976, Columbia); Glenda Jackson, Walter Matthau in *HOPSCOTCH* (1980, Avco-Embassy); Louise Fletcher, Madeline Kahn, Marsha Mason, Peter Falk in *THE CHEAP DETECTIVE* (1978, Columbia); Christopher Reeve, Jane Seymour in *SOMEWHERE IN TIME* (1980, Universal) and Robert Powell, Karen Dotrice in *THE THIRTY-NINE STEPS* (1978, Rank).